"STONER IS THE PUREST EXAMPLE OF THE HARD-BOILED PI IN PRINT TODAY. AS HE HONORABLY PURSUES HIS CASE, HE'S CONFRONTED BY A FOUL WORLD IN WHICH GREED RULES, LOVE IS A WEAPON, AND FAMILIES ARE CONDUITS BY WHICH THE SINS OF ONE GENERATION ARE VISITED ON THE NEXT. VALIN IS AS GOOD AS ANYONE WORKING THE MYSTERY FIELD TODAY."   —*Booklist*

Jonathan Valin

SECOND CHANCE

"THE BEST OF ALL WRITERS WHO HAVE APPEARED IN THE PAST DECADE. . . . Valin is a writer first, and secondly, a detective story writer—he goes on his nerve and his genuine feeling for both people and language—and that puts him in the very small class of people who transcend the noble ghosts of Chandler and Hammett."

—Peter Straub

"MR. VALIN'S TOUGH GUY STYLE [IS] A CAREFUL COMPOSITION OF SORDID SIGHTS, FLINTY DIALOGUE AND UNSPARING CHARACTERIZATIONS."
—*The New York Times Book Review*

"VALIN'S STRENGTHS: CRISP NARRATION, PERFECT-PITCH DIALOGUE, QUICK-STROKED DESCRIPTIONS, MEMORABLE SUPPORTING CHARACTERS, AND A HERO-NARRATOR WITH A DISTINCTIVE VOICE AND OUTLOOK." —*The Washington Post*

SECOND CHANCE

Jonathan Valin

A Dell Book

Published by
Dell Publishing
a division of
Bantam Doubleday Dell Publishing Group, Inc.
666 Fifth Avenue
New York, New York 10103

ISBN: 0-440-21222-7

Reprinted by arrangement with Delacorte Press

Printed in the United States of America

Published simultaneously in Canada

May 1992

10 9 8 7 6 5 4 3 2 1

RAD

*To Katherine, as always,
and to Dominick, at last*

1

Two roads diverged in a wood, and I . . . I took the one to the right, which put me back on Camargo Pike, heading south.

I'd been driving through Indian Hill for better than ten minutes, trying to find a little side street called Woodbine Lane. The woman who'd phoned me early that snowy Sunday morning had said to watch for an antiques shop on the left-hand side of Camargo. An antiques shop—like a gas station in the sticks. With the snow blowing and the tires skating along the frozen blacktop I'd had trouble staying on the road, much less finding her antiques shop.

It would have helped if the side streets had been clearly marked, but the only signs in that rich, Byzantine neighborhood were planted along the main drag. Everything else was private property—unnamed access roads that ran screaming off into the woods the moment they spotted you, tar drives that turned their backs behind gateposts or rested their elbows on hedgerows and glared through the brambles as you drove by. Nothing as mundane as a name on a mailbox. Not that I could have seen a mailbox in the snow. It had started falling as soon as I left the office. By the time I got to Indian Hill, it was as thick as smoke from a grease fire.

After emerging from the woods onto Camargo for the third time, I swallowed my pride and went looking for an open gas station or convenience store with a phone booth—and got absurdly lucky. Six miles down the pike, almost at the corporation limit, I spotted a gabled building that looked like a converted residence. If there was a sign saying

"Antiques" in one of its windows, the snow had covered it up. But there was a parking lot in front and an access road to its left.

I took a chance and turned left onto the unmarked road. A half-mile farther on an estate house squatted in a grove of pine trees—English-style country home, all mullioned windows and snow-dappled slate, big-eyed and brindled as a cow. I pulled up in a drive to the right of the house, parked the rusty Pinto beside a new Mercedes with a physician's plate, and sat there for a moment, listening to the wind howl and wondering whether I had the right address or whether the folks inside were already on the phone to the Indian Hill cops. The lady who'd called that morning had said her name was Pearson, Louise Pearson. She hadn't mentioned that she or her husband was a doctor.

As I sat there brooding, a tall woman in a dark blue Icelandic sweater and khaki slacks stepped out the front door of the house. She peered at me for a moment through the blowing snow, hugging her arms to her breasts against the cold. I got out of the car and waved at her.

"Mrs. Pearson?" I shouted.

She said something that was swallowed by the wind, but I could tell from her expression that I'd lucked on to the right spot. I hustled across the snowy yard, through the door, and inside.

The woman smiled knowingly as she closed the door behind me. "You had trouble finding us, didn't you?"

"A little trouble."

"You don't have to be polite about it," she said with an abrupt laugh that made me smile too. "Everyone has trouble finding us. In this weather it must have been murder." She held out her hand. "I'm Louise Pearson."

"Harry Stoner," I said, shaking with her.

I had realized that she was tall, but up close Louise Pearson's size and build were startling. She was a statuesque woman in her late thirties—big-breasted, big-hipped, with short curly brown hair and a tan, sportive, square-jawed face, a little wrinkled by the sun around the eyes and at the corners of the mouth but strikingly attractive in a no-nonsense way.

"Come into the living room and warm up, Mr. Stoner."

I followed her down a hall into a large, fussy living room. The walls were covered in pale grey watered silk, the moldings painted a deeper grey. The furniture was cozy English—chintz couches, Queen Anne tables and sideboards. On the far wall a wingback chair sat in front of an open fireplace. Louise Pearson patted the back of the chair as if she'd put it there especially for me.

"Sit," she said.

I sat.

"Can I get you something to drink? Coffee or brandy maybe?"

"Coffee would be good."

There was a silver service set on a sideboard behind her. She walked over to it and poured coffee into a blue china cup. "I'm really sorry to call you out on a miserable day like this," she said over her shoulder, "but we've got this . . . situation. At least Phil thinks it's a situation." She turned back to me, the steaming coffee cup in her hand. "Maybe he's right."

She said it dubiously, as if that wasn't often the case.

"Phil is?"

"My husband," she said, handing me the cup. "He should be back any minute—he had an emergency at his office."

"He's a physician?"

"A psychiatrist."

Louise Pearson walked over to the fireplace and leaned up against the mantel. Behind her in a far corner of the room a large tinseled Christmas tree flickered like a loose bulb.

"Drink," Louise Pearson said in her peremptory way.

I drank.

The woman was altogether too ripe and sturdy for lace and chintz. I wondered if she'd inherited the house from someone else, if she'd stepped into that cozy room from a more robust kind of life—a life among men. That was the way she talked, as if she was used to handling men, parrying them, fending them off. It amused me to speculate about her in that way—it was a sure sign that I found her attractive.

Between the fire and the coffee I slowly warmed up. I started to smell things again: the fresh cut pine of the Christmas tree, the cedar logs on the fire, the coffee. And something else. Something sweet and sensual that I didn't place until the woman came closer to me, and I realized it was her scent.

"I don't mean to sound cynical about Phil," Louise Pearson said, drawing a chair up across from mine. "It's just that most psychiatrists tend to read portents into normal behavior, even their own behavior. Believe me, it can be grueling to have your inner life constantly analyzed and second-guessed like a parlor game. I know Kirsten, my stepdaughter, feels that way." She turned her head to look at the fire, and her hair caught the light and turned reddish gold. "Kirsten's the reason we called you."

"She has a problem?"

The woman smiled sadly. "The world is Kirsten's problem," she said. And then, as if she didn't like the melodramatic sound of that, she added: "She was badly wounded by life with her mother—her real mother, Phil's first wife. Those childhood years left Kirsty . . . well, they've made her an emotional cripple. She and her brother, alike. Phil's tried his best to make it up to both of the kids—to give them a fresh chance. So have I. But even loving parents can't erase the past or control the future. I'm not at all sure it's a good idea to try—or to hire someone else to."

I said, "You don't think I'm needed, do you?"

The woman shrugged noncommittally. "I don't know if you are or not, Mr. Stoner. I don't know if Kirsty can use anyone's help. Without trying to minimize her neuroses, which can be pretty damn disabling, I tend to think that the more time she spends on her own the better. I'm sure Phil will have a different view of it, but that's the way I feel."

As if on cue, a tall handsome man with black hair and beard stepped into the room. There was half-melted snow in his hair and on the shoulders of his overcoat.

"*Is* that the way you feel?" he said to the woman.

Louise Pearson stiffened in the chair. "You could have announced yourself, Phil."

"And spoiled your spiel?" He laughed, brushing the snow out of his hair and beard as he walked over to the fireplace. "I love to hear you talk psychology, Lou. You know that. It turns me on."

Smiling expansively, he came up and extended a hand. I shook with him. Like his wife, Pearson made a tall, imposing figure, although he looked older than she did up close, and worse for wear. His tan skin was heavily lined and deeply grooved at the cheeks. His eyes were a brilliant blue, nervously, almost shockingly alert. For a second I found it difficult to hold his stare. It was as if he was looking for something I didn't have.

"Phil Pearson," he said.

"Harry Stoner."

"Good," he said, dropping my hand. He clapped his own hands together loudly and said, "Good," again.

"I guess you'll want to take over now, Phil," Louise Pearson said, rising from the chair. "That's the way it usually works, isn't it?"

For a split second the man looked crestfallen, as if he was losing his audience in the middle of a speech. "You don't have to leave, Lou."

"Oh, I think I do."

She smiled at me warmly. "It was a pleasure meeting you, Mr. Stoner. I'm sure we'll talk again."

She walked out of the room, leaving her husband staring blankly after her. The woman's exit effected an immediate change in Pearson's manner. He stopped smiling. He stopped talking, too. In fact he didn't say another word until he'd unbuttoned his topcoat, draped it on the sideboard, and poured himself a cup of coffee from the silver server.

"Not everyone shares my sense of humor," he said in a subdued voice. "I can be abrasive at times."

I didn't say anything. I didn't feel like coddling a grown man. He looked chastened by my silence, as if I'd boxed his ear. Then he looked resentful. I started to get the feeling that this wasn't a grown man, after all.

Pearson sat down across from me and took a sip of coffee while he collected himself. "Living with a psychiatrist can be tough," he said after a time. "My wife's had her fill of me recently. Of me and my kids. You know what they say about psychiatrists' kids, don't you? Like ministers' kids." He smiled pastily. "Has Lou told you about Kirsten?"

"She said that you were having a problem with her. She didn't tell me what that problem was."

"Of course, she wouldn't," he said quickly. "The kids are *my* responsibility, after all. I think we can agree on that."

He glanced quickly at the door, as if he was hoping Louise was listening in as he had been listening to her. In spite of the friction between them, the man seemed lost without his wife.

"Has Kirsten run away, Dr. Pearson?" I said, trying to put him back on course.

He sighed. "Not exactly. I'm really not sure what's happened to her, if anything."

"Then why call me?"

"Why call you?" he echoed. "I'm worried, that's why. My daughter has serious emotional problems, as Lou may have told you. They were severe enough to put Kirsten in a hospital this past summer. She returned to school this fall, to the University of Chicago. But I'm not sure she was ready to be on her own again."

"You have reason to think she's not doing well?"

"There have been signs," he said vaguely.

"What kind of signs?"

The man shifted uneasily in his chair. "At the moment, I'm concerned that she hasn't come home for the holidays."

"Concerned enough to hire a detective?"

"Yes."

"Couldn't Kirsten have gone to visit a friend over the break, Dr. Pearson? Kids often do that."

"I talked to her myself on Wednesday of last week, and she said she was planning to fly home Thursday afternoon. Since then I've been in touch with her roommate, her therapist, the airlines, and several university officials—not one of them knows where she's gone. Not one."

"Your daughter's problems," I said delicately, "are they . . . are you worried that she may have become depressed?"

He nodded. "Yes."

"Have you contacted the police in Chicago?"

"I haven't been able to bring myself to . . ." His voice dropped to a whisper. "No, I haven't called the police."

A peal of feminine laughter rang out somewhere in the house. It made Phil Pearson start in his chair. He glanced toward the hall almost desperately, as if he longed to be near his wife again—to make it up with her.

"I may be overreacting," he said, looking quickly back at me, looking to see if I'd caught his mind wandering. "Still I'd feel better if you could find Kirsten."

"I can try," I told him.

"Good," he said, rubbing his hands together nervously. "Good."

2

After finishing with the Pearsons I went to my apartment on Ohio Avenue, packed an overnight bag, called the airport, and booked a seat on Delta for two p.m. I would gain an hour on the flight, so I figured on arriving at O'Hare about the same time that I'd left Cincinnati. Pearson had promised to call Kirsten's roommate, a girl named Marnee Thompson, to let her know I'd be coming. He said he'd contact the university too, although I didn't expect him to find anyone home on a Sunday afternoon during Christmas break. Before I left his house, he gave me duplicate keys to Kirsten's apartment in case the roommate was out.

In spite of the Brent Spence traffic and the inevitable slowdown at the cut of the Ft. Mitchell hill, I managed to get to the Delta terminal by one-thirty. The snow had stopped falling by then, and the temperature had risen enough to turn the roadside ice to slush. I'd been worried that the bad weather might delay the flight, but the attendant at the Delta booth said the only delay would be on the Chicago end—at O'Hare.

With a half hour to kill I walked down to one of the boarding area bars and ordered up the usual round of artillery. It was a short flight, so I settled on two double Scotches, straight up. If they didn't kill the preflight jitters, I promised myself a third shot on the plane.

"You said *two* doubles?" the bartender asked.

"I don't like airplanes," I told him. "I don't understand them. And I don't want to discuss it."

He served up the booze and left me alone.

Pearson had given me a photograph of his daughter, a

high school snap. I dug it out of my coat pocket and took a look at it between swallows of Scotch. Kirsten was a studious-looking, half-pretty girl with dark brown hair and her father's blue piercing eyes. If I'd known more about her, if Pearson had been more forthcoming about her "problems," past and present, I might have been able to make something specific of the vaguely hostile, vaguely damaged look of those eyes. But Phil Pearson had kept his daughter's history to himself—at least enough of it to make it next to impossible for me to personalize her. The girl in the photo could have been anyone's troubled daughter. Given the fact that I hadn't liked the man, I decided it was better that way.

The flight to Chicago was mercifully short. We arrived at O'Hare about forty minutes after we took off and were backed up on the ground for another forty minutes. I didn't understand the guy sitting next to me, who kept complaining about the long wait on the runway.

"We're on the ground!" I finally said to him. "What the hell's the matter with you?"

It was two-thirty central time when I got out of the terminal and caught a cab to Hyde Park. It had been snowing heavily in Chicago, and the traffic on the Eisenhower was bumper-to-bumper all the way to the Dan Ryan. By the time we got to the 51st Street exit it was a quarter of four.

I said to the cabbie, "It took longer to get from O'Hare to the south side than it did to fly from Cincinnati to Chicago."

"What are you going to do," he said philosophically. "It's Christmas, and this ain't Cincinnati."

Kirsten Pearson's apartment was on 54th Street near Blackstone. The building was a three-story brownstone tenement, the third in a dismal block of brownstones. The

stained facades of the tenements, the dirty snow, the bare
bent maples planted in the sidewalk boxes, reflected the
raw grey of the winter sky. A few months of that kind of
weather would have left me feeling just as raw.

The outer door of the Pearson girl's apartment house
opened onto a tiled vestibule. The framed-glass inner door
was locked, but I could see through it into a wainscoted
lobby with a dark wood staircase leading to the upper floors.
The vestibule smelled like dust and heat and cat piss. I
could have used one of the keys that Pearson had given me,
but I didn't want to startle anyone. So I pressed an intercom
button on the side wall.

A girl answered in a sharp, distracted voice. "Yes? Who is
it?"

"My name's Harry Stoner. I'm working for Phil Pearson,
Kirsten Pearson's father."

"I know who you are," the girl said ominously.

A moment wont by then a buzzer went off, unlocking the
door. I stepped into the dark foyer. A red-haired girl with a
pale, starved, willfully unhappy-looking face appeared at
the head of the stairs. She held a book in one hand and a
pair of tortoiseshell glasses in the other. It was obvious that
she was annoyed by the interruption.

"Marnee Thompson?" I said to her.

She nodded. "You're the detective?"

"I'm the detective."

Marnee Thompson studied me for a moment, bouncing
the glasses in her hand. "Kirsten isn't here, you know. I told
Phil that last week."

"Have any idea where she's gone?"

"No. I'm not in charge of her."

"No one said you were."

"Tell it to Phil," the girl said bitterly. "You realize this is

ridiculous, don't you? And borderline illegal? Kirsty's almost twenty years old. I mean, why do they have to send
detectives after her? It's humiliating."

"Her father's worried."

"Her father's an asshole. Everyone else knows it. Now
you do, too."

"Miss Thompson, I'm just trying to do a job. If you'll let
me come up and look around, I can be out of your hair in a
few minutes."

The girl glanced behind her, toward an open door at the
top of the staircase. "All right," she said, turning back to me.
"But make it quick."

I started up the stairs.

The apartment was spare, functional, serious as all
hell. Board-and-brick bookshelves stuffed with books and
weighted down on top with more books, an easel-desk with
a gooseneck lamp clamped to it, a stool in front of the desk,
a Camus poster on one wall, a Vermeer print on another, a
Goodwill chair with claw legs and a silk throw over it, a gas
hearth with a droopy asparagus fern in the fireplace, a tatty
rug. No other furnishings. Through an archway I could see a
bedroom, with a mattress lying on the floor and a mirror full
of grey winter sky propped against the inner wall.

The bare utility of the place was like an advertisement for
Marnee Thompson, for her own seriousness and respectable student poverty. But Kirsten Pearson had lived there,
too. And I couldn't help wondering where she had fit in.
There was no second desk in the front room, and when I
thumbed through several of the books on top of the book-
shelf they all had Marnee Thompson's bookplate in them.

"Her room was at the end of the hall," the girl said, as if
she'd read my mind. "She preferred it that way."

"Preferred what?" I said, putting down a green-and-black paperback copy of *Dubliners*.

"The privacy."

Marnee Thompson walked over to the armchair and sat down. The girl had a style of her own—that early in life—a blunt self-assertiveness that was snotty but impressive, too. If Kirsten Pearson had identity problems, I figured this one'd probably been good for her.

"How long have you and Kirsten lived here?"

"Since September." She put on her tortoiseshell glasses, tilted her head, and studied me with pale blue eyes. "She could have lived anywhere, you know. Phil has plenty of money."

She said it like a boast, as if she were telling me that, instead of Phil's money, Kirsten had chosen her.

"Where did you two meet?" I said, sitting down on the desk stool across from her.

"We were in several classes together, last year. We hit it off so well we decided to set up this place during the summer, but . . . Kirsty couldn't move in until the fall."

"Kirsten had some trouble last year, didn't she?"

The girl didn't say anything.

"She had to leave school?"

"She was taken out of school, yes," Marnee Thompson said.

"By her father?"

She nodded.

I studied her grave young face, softly shaded by the fading window light. Her pale hollow cheeks, her high brow, her blue lashless eyes, reminded me of the Vermeer on the living room wall—a woman counting pearls. "If Kirsten's having trouble again, I might be able to help."

"How? By taking her away again?"

"I've been hired to find her, Marnee. *Not* to bring her home."

The girl gave me a wary look.

"Think about it." I got up from the stool and walked down the hall to Kirsten's bedroom.

3

The door at the end of the hall was closed but unlocked. Kirsten, or someone who had lived there before her, had tacked a little handwritten warning to it: NO SECOND CHANCES. I went in anyway.

It was life on a different block in Kirsten's room. Dirty clothes hung from the open drawers of an oak dresser and dribbled out the door of a closet. Books, stacked like old newspapers, climbed in crazy towers four feet up each wall. Typed papers, dozens of them, were scattered thickly across the top of a desk, on the desk chair, and the floor. A portable TV with a brassiere dangling from its antenna sat on a stool across from an unmade bed. An ashtray full of cigarette butts, Winstons, was lying on the pillow of the bed. A *Soap Opera Digest* nestled in the blankets at its feet. A urinous smell of mildewed paper, cigarette smoke, and unwashed flesh hung heavily in the air.

After the strict order of Marnee Thompson's life, the rank clutter of Kirsten Pearson's bedroom startled me. I knew it was just a messy college kid's messy room, but it still startled me—the way a crime scene can get to you. I had the unmistakable feeling that violence had occurred there.

I did my job anyway, going through the closet first, sifting the soiled clothes on the floor, searching the pockets of the blouses and jeans left on the hangers. I didn't find anything but loose change and wadded-up tissues.

I tried the top drawer of the desk next and found an address book in the rubble of pencil stubs, coins, paper clips, and linty ballpoint pens. None of the names meant anything to me, except for Phil Pearson's. I found what

looked like a manuscript in the side drawer, boxed and
sealed with tape. Someone had written "We have to talk
about this!" on top of the box and underlined the words
twice to show he meant it. I put the box aside with the
address book.

There were some postcards under the manuscript—a
dozen of them from a dozen different midwestern towns.
Yellow Springs. Madison. Antioch. Columbus. College
towns. The postcards were the sort of things that motels
give away, along with letterhead stationery and embossed
pencils. Each one pictured a mundane motel facade with
the words "Greetings From" printed in a corner. Each one
was signed "Ethan." Whoever Ethan was, he had moved
around over the past year. The oldest card, from The Green
Gables Motel in Forest Park, Missouri, was postmarked November 16, 1988. The latest, November 5, 1989, from The
Bluegrass Motel in Ft. Thomas, Kentucky.

I put the postcards with the manuscript and the address
book and moved on to the dresser. A vanity mirror and a
glass dish were sitting on top of it. The dish had held
makeup judging from the traces of face powder on the
glass, but I couldn't find a makeup kit in the drawer. I did
come across an empty birth control pill dispenser, however,
stashed among some underwear.

I also found an old photograph of Papa Pearson,
facedown in the panties. Or half a photo. The picture had
been torn lengthwise, indicating that someone else had
been photographed along with Pearson—someone Kirsten
apparently hadn't liked.

I left the photo where I'd found it and took the postcards,
address book, and manuscript with me back into the living
room. Marnee Thompson was still sitting silently in the
Goodwill chair. When she saw the booty I was carrying, she
looked dismayed.

"You can't have that," she said, leaping to her feet. "That's Kirsty's."

"I don't want to take it, Marnee. I want to talk about it."

I put the stuff on Marnee's desk and sat on the stool. The girl sat back down slowly on the chair. It was almost dark outside, and the gooseneck lamp, lighting the desktop and Kirsten's belongings, was the main light in the room. Marnee Thompson stared forlornly at the little pile of spotlighted things—her friend's things.

"When's the last time you saw Kirsten, Marnee?"

"Thursday morning. She was packing the car, getting ready to leave. I had a conference to go to. When I got back that afternoon, the car was gone. I assumed she went to the airport."

"What kind of car does she drive?"

"A yellow VW Bug. I don't know what year it is, but it's pretty beat up."

"Did Kirsten plan to see anyone before leaving for home?"

"She might have mentioned stopping at a friend's."

"What friend?"

The girl balked. "Look, I don't know what to say. I don't want anything bad to happen to Kirsty. But I don't want to feed her dad's obsessions, either. If you knew what he's done to her, what he's put her through . . ."

"Why don't you tell me about it?"

Marnee Thompson bit her lower lip so hard it turned white. She'd started to look younger, less cocksure of herself. More like a nineteen-year-old girl who was worried about a friend and didn't know what to do about it.

I smiled reassuringly. "I just want to find Kirsty, Marnee. If she's okay, I go home and make my report to her dad."

"And if she isn't okay?"

"Then we can talk about what to do—you and me and Kirsten."

"You're not going to . . . de-program her or something?"

I laughed. "Somebody'd have to re-program me, first."

The girl half smiled. I had the feeling that that was all she ever permitted herself—half a smile—like it was a kind of dieting.

"We could get some coffee, maybe," Marnee Thompson allowed.

"Okay," I told her.

The coffee shop was on 54th Street and Lake, a little storefront with an icy awning over its window. It was a student hangout, warm, trendy, and virtually empty on a Sunday night. We sat at a wooden table with a big bowl of unshelled peanuts in its center. The hardwood floors were covered with peanut shells that crackled underfoot. Peanuts seemed to be the theme.

I said, "I wouldn't want the job of sweeping up in here."

Marnee Thompson gave me her Weight Watchers grin. "They don't sweep up. They harvest."

I laughed. "Are you from Chicago?"

She shook her head, no. "Cleveland, Ohio. I came here because I didn't want to go east."

The way she said it, "east" sounded like the place where the rich snobs congregated.

"Chicago's a serious school," she said, unbuttoning her topcoat. "And, believe me, I'm serious about my education."

I believed her.

"What's your major?"

"English Lit," she said. She stored her mittens carefully

in the pockets of her coat. "Kirsty's an English major, too, but she's a writer not a scholar."

"What does she write?"

"Poetry. Several of her pieces have been published in small magazines. *TriQuarterly. Antioch Review.* Last spring, one of her poems was almost accepted by *The New Yorker.* Kirsty's very talented—the most talented person I know."

I was surprised and impressed by Kirsten Pearson's achievements. I was also impressed by the pleasure that Marnee Thompson took in her friend's success. In my day students weren't quite so gracious about each other's accomplishments. "The manuscript I found in Kirsten's room," I said, "is poetry?"

Marnee shook her head, no. "Kirsty's been working on a novel. She completed the first draft right before the break. I haven't seen it yet."

"Someone must have read it. It had a message written on it in big letters."

"That's from Dr. Heldman," the girl said. "He's Kirsty's adviser."

"Maybe I should talk to him?"

"It couldn't hurt. He lives in Hyde Park. His address is in Kirsty's book."

Marnee Thompson toyed with the bowl of peanuts, while I sipped coffee.

"If I talk to you about her," she said, without looking up, "it's because I'm worried. I don't want to do Phil any favors. And I don't want to get Kirsty in trouble. But I *am* worried."

"Why?"

Marnee Thompson cracked open a peanut between her thumb and forefinger. "I think she started to see Jay again a few weeks ago."

"Is Jay the friend she said she was going to visit before leaving on Thursday?"

Marnee nodded. "He's the one who caused all the trouble last year. Jay Stein. He's an adjunct instructor in the department. He and Kirsty . . . they had an affair last spring." She dropped the cracked peanut shell back in the bowl and looked up at me nervously. "Nobody's supposed to know that. I don't even think Phil knows it. If he did, he'd probably kill the son of a bitch."

"This guy, Stein, teaches at the university?"

"Creative writing," Marnee said with a forced laugh. "He's just a thirty-year-old swinging dick—one of those perpetual grad fellows who hang out in English departments instead of singles' bars. If Kirsty hadn't been so damn naive, it wouldn't have happened. Jay hits on everybody in the world, but Kirsty didn't understand that. She thought he was someone special, and he took advantage of her. Christ, she didn't know anything about sex."

She knew now, judging from what I'd found in her bureau drawer.

"What happened this spring?" I asked.

"What always happens with a guy like Jay," Marnee said sarcastically. "She got attached to him and he dropped her. He stopped seeing her. He wouldn't take her calls. Kirsty was so emotionally vulnerable anyway . . . Jay just pushed her over the edge."

"She had a breakdown?"

"That's what Phil called it. She did get pretty violent for a while, but I think she would have been all right if he'd given her a chance to recover on her own. She was under medication and seeing a therapist at the university clinic. But that wasn't good enough for Phil. He came storming up here like God Almighty and just . . . took her away. She didn't have a choice. He just did it to her."

Marnee Thompson gave me an incredulous, accusatory look, as if that was what men always did to women.

"If she was suicidal . . ."

"You don't understand," Marnee said angrily. "It goes way beyond paternalism with him or concern for her health. It's sick the way he spies on her and interrogates her and runs her life. He acts like he owns her soul."

Some kid at a nearby table laughed loudly, and Marnee scowled at him as if she thought he was laughing at her.

"Drink some coffee," I said to the girl.

"Don't patronize me!" she snapped.

"Don't drink, then," I said. "You're a hard person to be nice to, Marnee."

"I don't want to be made nice to. Christ, you're just doing a job." She dropped her head. "And I'm helping."

"You're helping Kirsty."

"I hope so," she whispered.

4

Marnee Thompson didn't have anything more to say to me at the restaurant. She was feeling guilty, and she wasn't trying to disguise it. But then she loved Kirsten and despised Papa Phil. Her hatred of the man was so intense that it made me wonder if she'd told the whole truth about the past summer. It was possible that Marnee had taken it upon herself to phone Phil Pearson when Kirsten became distraught over her failed love affair. It would have been the natural thing to do under the circumstances. If so, she'd unwittingly put her friend in a mental ward—and that would have made anyone vengeful. Her anger toward Pearson had that kind of feel to it—the feel of betrayal.

It occurred to me that, even if I was only half right, Marnee Thompson had to be more worried about Kirsty than she'd let on or she wouldn't have said anything at all.

I didn't force the issue. As it was, she'd given me enough to get started. More than enough.

So we finished our coffee in silence, then walked in silence through the bitter cold to the apartment house. Upstairs, I found Kirsten's address book and looked up Jay Stein and Professor Heldman. Stein lived at 8550 Kenwood, apartment 917. Arthur Heldman lived on 56th and Blackstone.

While I was waiting for a cab, I thumbed through the postcards I'd found in Kirsty's desk. There were no messages on any of them—just the name Ethan. Marnee Thompson watched me from the living room chair.

"They're from her brother," she said, breaking the long silence between us.

"He seems to travel around a good deal."

"I think that's all he does. He's sort of a Gypsy. Kirsty's the only person in the family he talks to. In fact he called the other night to talk. Kirsty says he's got a terrible grudge against Phil."

"How come?"

"I don't know. Maybe Phil put him in a mental ward, too."

"It's an odd family," I said, putting the stack of cards back down on the desk.

"It's a tragic family," she said solemnly.

"Fathers get panicky and do stupid things, Marnee. It happens."

"That's not what I meant." She shook her head, instead of completing the thought.

A car honked outside, making the girl jump.

"That's the cab," I said.

As I put on my coat and hat, Marnee stood up and came over to me.

"I haven't been much help, have I?" she said, biting her lip.

"Enough."

"If she isn't with Jay . . ."

"I'll find her, Marnee."

It was past six when the cab dropped me in front of Jay Stein's apartment building on Kenwood. It was a modern high rise set on pylons sunk into a concrete plaza. The ground floor was all glassed-in lobby, with a bank of brass mailboxes and elevators in its center. A border of potted ferns and chrome-and-plastic benches ran around the edges like selvage.

The outer door was unlocked, but the inner door leading

to the lobby had an intercom system. I found Stein's name and pressed the button. Through the plate-glass window I could see the cab heading down the icy block. If Stein wasn't home I was in for a long walk back to Kirsty's apartment.

But I was lucky because Jay Stein buzzed me through. He must have been expecting someone because he didn't bother to ask who I was. If I was really lucky, he might have been expecting Kirsten Pearson.

I asked myself what I was going to do if the girl was there —or showed up—and decided to see how she reacted to me before doing anything. I had no legal right to interfere in her life, although, after what Marnee told me, I knew that I wasn't going to like Stein.

A tall, spindly man with a drooping moustache and lank brown hair was waiting for me in the ninth-floor hall, just outside the elevator door. His face was pale and horsey, with a sad-eyed look of suffering to it that might have impressed the young girls. He wasn't that old himself. Maybe twenty-eight or -nine. He was dressed even younger than that in torn jeans, cowboy boots, and a faded lumberjack shirt.

"Are you Jay Stein?" I asked.

"Why don't you tell me who you are first?" the man said nervously. He'd been smiling when the elevator door opened, but the smile went away as soon as he saw me.

"My name is Stoner. I work for Phil Pearson, Kirsten Pearson's father."

The man's right hand shot to his shirt pocket as if he'd felt a chest pain. He pulled out a pack of Winstons and shook a cigarette into his palm. His hand was trembling so much that three extra cigarettes fell onto the floor. Making a disgusted face, he reached down and scooped them up.

"I don't think I want to talk to you," he said, stowing the extra cigarettes back in the box.

"You're Jay Stein, aren't you?"

The man lit a cigarette and took a puff.

"C'mon, Jay. You don't have to think about that."

"I'm *Professor* Stein," he said indignantly. "And I've got nothing to say to you—or Phil Pearson. Now get out of here before I call security."

"And what are you going to tell security? That you're screwing one of your students?"

The man's eyes got very large. "That's an outrageous lie!"

There was an open door down the hallway on the left—probably the door to his apartment. Stein started to move in that direction, and I stepped in front of him.

"This is ridiculous," he said, backing up. "I don't know where you're getting your information, but there is nothing between Kirsty Pearson and me." He tapped the cigarette, scattering ashes down his shirt and onto the floor. "We're friends. No more than that."

"You haven't seen your 'friend' in the last couple of days, have you?"

He shook his head, no.

"If you're not seeing her, then I guess you won't mind if I look in your apartment."

"Of course I'd mind. I don't know who you are or why you're asking me these questions. Maybe if you told me what this was about . . ."

"Kirsty's been missing since last Thursday. Her father hired me to find her. I'm told that she's been seeing you."

"Told? By whom, told?"

I didn't say anything.

Stein got an ugly look on his face. "It was that roommate of hers, wasn't it? She put you up to this. Christ, what a joke!" He laughed bitterly.

"I don't think it's funny," I said.

"That's because you don't know what's going on." He laughed again, a smoother laugh, full of confidence. "It's okay. I see what it's about now. I think I can clear this up."

He tried to edge past me, toward his apartment door. But I didn't budge.

"I'm not going to run away," he said calmly. "Let's go down to my apartment, have a beer, and talk this over like civilized people."

Stein's front room was a couple of steps up from Marnee Thompson's Spartan digs. But just a couple. The bookshelves were varnished pine, instead of brick-and-board. The chairs and sofa were cheap Naugahyde copies of top-grain Italian originals. There were a few more ferns, hanging in baskets. Classier artwork on the walls. But it still had the feel of respectable poverty—the assistant professorial kind.

Two archways opened off the living room. One to a lighted matchbox of a kitchen, the other to a dark bedroom. I glanced at the kitchen as I came through the door. The plastic drainer sitting by the sink had one plate in it, one cup, and one saucer. There were no dishes on the counter. No food or drinks, either.

The living room was just as tidy and unpromising. An open book, *Snap* by Abby Frucht, sat on an ottoman in front of an armchair, a stack of papers on the floor beside it. The rest of the furniture looked unlived in, as if it had just been delivered the day before. The only item in the room that smacked of Kirsten Pearson was the overflowing ashtray on the windowsill. And that was just as much Stein as it was Kirsten. He'd already lit another by the time he shut the door.

"Have a seat," he said, walking into the kitchen. "You want a beer?"

"No, thanks."

"I thought guys like you always drank beer," he called out.

He came back with a can of Bud in his hand and the cigarette drooping from his lip.

"You're a detective, aren't you? A private cop?"

"Let's talk about you, instead."

Stein laughed—a real laugh this time. Popping the tab on the beer can, he plopped down on the couch and slung his leg over the armrest. He was obviously feeling a lot safer inside his own apartment, and whatever edge I'd had in the hall was just as obviously gone.

"Tell me the truth," he said. "It was Kirsty's roommate who gave you my name, wasn't it?"

"No."

He grinned. "It had to be her."

"And why is that?"

"Because she's insanely jealous of anyone who comes near Kirsty. The whole world knows Marnee's gay. Except Kirsty, maybe." He took a sip of beer. "Kirsty doesn't think like that. She sees people in terms of her own needs. But she doesn't see *their* needs." He took another sip of beer and scattered cigarette ashes on the couch. "I wouldn't get seriously involved with a kid like her. I couldn't if I wanted to. Sex scares the hell out of her. Men scare the hell out of her."

"You're telling me you two didn't have an affair."

"That's what I'm telling you."

"Then why'd she have a breakdown last spring?"

He shrugged. "Kirsty's crazy, Stoner."

"Crazy enough to fake a relationship with you?"

"Crazier than that. Look, I did take her out a few times,

after class. But there was no great romance between us. That was just her fantasy—or her roommate's. Kirsty didn't really want romance."

"What did she want?"

"A daddy. Someone to look after her, someone with a little more spine than her old man. I mean that kid's need for affection is tremendous."

I said, "Empathy doesn't seem to be one of your strong points either, Stein."

His face flushed angrily. "Kirsty has a long history of emotional trouble dating back to her childhood. There was nothing I could do about her past except encourage her to write about it. And that's exactly what I did."

"What about her childhood?"

"Her father didn't tell you?" he said, looking surprised. "Kirsty's mother was schizophrenic. In and out of mental wards all her life. When Kirsty was six, the mother killed herself. Violently." The man ducked his head as if he was embarrassed by his own avid gossip. "When you're carrying around that kind of genetic baggage, there isn't a whole lot anyone can do to help. I've tried to be a friend to her, but that's not always an easy thing. Kids can . . . misinterpret."

"Try somebody other than a kid."

He didn't say anything.

"When's the last time you saw Kirsten?" I asked.

"Last week. Thursday morning. She came over here to talk." He gave me a pointed look. "*Just* to talk."

"About what?"

Stein sat back in the sofa, clasping his hands behind his head. He was tired of me and the conversation. "Her brother, Ethan, came to town. He wanted to see Kirsty, but she wasn't sure she should go."

"Why would she have a problem seeing her brother?"

"Because he's crazier than she is. He drags her back to the past, and that's a place Kirsty doesn't need to visit, especially now."

"You've talked to the brother?"

"Once. When he came through Chicago last year. I don't think I've ever met anyone that intense. But then writers aren't exactly a relaxed bunch."

"Ethan's a writer, too?"

"Journalist. At least that's what he calls himself. He looks like he's a step above homelessness to me. I think his wife is the only thing that keeps him grounded. That and his weird obsession with his mother. That's really all he and Kirsty share—the mother. Neither one of them has been able to come to terms with her suicide. If you ask me, they never will."

There was a knock at the door. Looking relieved, Stein stood up.

"If you don't mind, I've got some company."

I stood up, too. "What did you tell Kirsty to do about Ethan?"

"I told her not to see him. To go home to Cincinnati. Apparently she didn't take my advice."

"Did she tell you where her brother was staying?"

"Somewhere in town, I guess."

"Can't you do better than that?"

"I've answered enough questions," he said sharply.

Stein went over to the door and opened it. A pretty girl was standing outside with a bottle of Chianti in her hand. She couldn't have been more than nineteen or twenty.

"C'mon in, Lucy. Mr. Stoner's just leaving."

The girl smiled at me winningly as she came into the room.

I walked over to the door. "Stein, if you're lying to me

about Kirsty Pearson, I'm going to get your ass fired. That's a promise."

The girl gasped, as if she couldn't believe anyone would speak to a professor like that.

"Don't threaten me," Stein said, reddening furiously. "If you come here again, I'll call the police."

He slammed the door in my face.

5

The trouble with a dramatic exit is that you can't go back and ask to use the phone.

I had to walk two blocks south on Kenwood to find a booth. By then I was so cold that I figured it would be worse to wait for a cab than to keep walking. So I pushed down the icy, gaslit sidewalks, head ducked against the wind, until I got to 56th Street.

Arthur Heldman's house was on the corner of 56th and Blackstone—a Prairie-style bungalow, L-shaped, parasol-roofed, with dark, glistening curls of frozen ivy climbing its board-and-stone walls. The front door was off to the side, down a driveway. The windows were lighted on that side of the house, as was the lamp above the door.

I knocked hard on the door and could barely feel my fist through the glove, I was that cold.

A tall, heavyset man of about fifty with ruddy cheeks and silvery hair and beard answered my knock. He was wearing wire-rim glasses, a black turtleneck sweater, and checked wool slacks that made him look, rather winningly, like a spiffy St. Nick.

"Can I help you?" he said in a friendly voice.

"You can if you're Professor Heldman."

"I'm Art Heldman. And you are . . . ?"

"My name is Stoner, Professor Heldman. I'm searching for a student of yours, Kirsten Pearson."

"She's lost?" the man said with alarm.

"She's been missing for four days. I've been hired by her father to find her."

"Poor kid," he said, shaking his head. "Please come in."

Heldman ushered me down a hall to an oak-paneled study. The room was furnished with Georgian pieces—a stately armoire, a desk like a three-tiered ship of the line, two mahogany armchairs with embroidered backs, and several bookshelves with mullioned fronts and leaded glass panes. A facsimile of Dr. Johnson's dictionary sat on a stand in one corner, spotlit like a shrine.

Heldman was clearly proud of the room. On his salary, a lot of scrimping and saving must have gone into fitting it out. He let the knickknacks work on me for a moment, then went over to the armoire, took out a bottle of Dewar's, and poured two fingers of Scotch into a tumbler.

"Here." He handed the drink to me. "You look frozen."

"Close to superconductivity."

Heldman laughed hoarsely.

I swallowed half of the drink, and my eyes clouded up. Another couple of swallows, and I started to feel my body again, as if I were putting it on piece by piece like a suit of clothes.

Heldman seated himself on a chair beside a small cherry wood table. There was a second chair across from him. I sat down on it.

"You say Kirsty's missing?" he said.

"For four days."

"You've tried her apartment, of course?" he said, leaning forward with the air of a friendly neighbor.

"That was the first place I looked. She wasn't there. Her roommate suggested that she might be with a man named Stein."

"Jay?" Heldman drew back slightly, as if the neighborhood had changed.

"I was told that Kirsty had been seeing him on a regular basis. He claims that she hasn't been."

The man nodded slowly. He'd started to look less like St.

Nick and more like St. Sebastian, as if the mere mention of
Stein caused him physical pain. I figured it was because I
was talking about a colleague, but it was also possible that
he knew the truth about Stein and Kirsten and wasn't
happy about it.

"You've spoken to Jay?"

"About twenty minutes ago. He hasn't seen Kirsty since
Thursday morning. Apparently she stopped at his apartment before leaving town. Stein says to discuss her
brother."

"She stopped here too. The same morning. And she *did*
mention her brother."

He said it like he was trying to back Stein up. But it was
clear from his tone that Ethan Pearson hadn't been the only
topic of conversation.

"She was thinking about going to see Ethan while he was
in town," Heldman went on.

"Did she say where he was staying?"

"No, just that he was eager to talk to her."

"Do you know what about?"

He shook his head. "Kirsty's always been a little vague
when it comes to Ethan. At least, she has with me. I don't
think he's a healthy influence on her—if that's what you
want to know. At least, he doesn't seem to be from what
I've read of her novel."

"Which novel is that?"

Heldman spread his hands as if he were opening a book in
front of me. "Kirsty's been working on an autobiographical
piece for the past couple of months. A kind of therapeutic
exercise to help her put her life in order after this past
summer. She calls it *Second Chance*."

"Why *Second Chance*?"

I thought of the sign on Kirsty's door.

"Because she doesn't believe in them," he said wryly. "At least, not for her."

"Is Stein in this book?"

Heldman sighed. "Yes. She hasn't finished the last chapter yet, but he'll be a large part of it—and so will her father and her brother, Ethan. You see, Kirsty believes in living out what she writes—or writing what she lives. Sometimes it's hard to tell which."

"Did she mention Stein when you talked on Thursday?"

"Yes." The man stood up, walked over to the armoire, and poured himself a stiff drink. "You already know that she became involved with Jay last year."

"He had an affair with her?"

"I don't know," he said, turning back to me with the bottle in his hand. He splashed a little more Scotch in my glass. "She was pretty damn attached to him—I know that. I'm afraid she still is. She told me on Thursday that she was seeing him again."

"Seeing him meaning sleeping with him?"

"I think so."

The man pursed his lips as if he'd bitten into something rotten. Or maybe he just caught a whiff of what I was thinking about Stein.

"Look, I care for that girl deeply," he said. "And I'll do anything I can to help you find her. But Jay isn't the reason she's disappeared. There isn't one reason."

"Stein blamed it on genes."

Heldman blushed. "I realize he can be an obnoxious ass. But you've got to understand that he stepped into a situation he wasn't equipped to deal with—a situation very few people could deal with. Kirsty's life has a pattern to it that predates Jay—a pattern that has slowly solidified into something like a fate. Events have conspired to make her believe that no matter what she does, she is bound to end as her mother did—crazy or a suicide. Her brother has apparently done a lot to reinforce that belief by constantly obsessing about the mother's death. And of course, so has her father, whose overprotectiveness kept Kirsty a child in many ways. But the point is—so has Kirsty herself.

"For years now, consciously or unconsciously, she has been making choices that will lead her in the direction of suicide. The Stein thing is just one more instance. The fact that she's infatuated with Jay is beside the point. In a way, Kirsty understands that herself. Deep down she's chosen Jay Stein precisely because she knows he will reject her."

"It's a theory," I said.

The man gave me a rueful look. "You don't believe me?"

"I believe the girl is deeply troubled, but I think it's a bit too damn enlightened to blame Kirsten for Jay Stein's callousness. Or to dismiss a need for affection as a death wish."

Heldman blushed. For a second I thought he was going to get pissy, but he surprised me. "I didn't mean for it to sound that way. All I meant to say is that Kirsty honestly believes we are trapped by our pasts. Our childhood pasts. And *no one* gets a second chance at childhood."

He wanted it to sound profoundly sad. It only sounded sadly adolescent to me. But most literature professors I'd known developed that same lump in their throats when they spoke of life's inequities—kind of like narrators in PBS documentaries.

"Was she depressed when you saw her on Thursday morning?" I asked him.

"Not depressed so much as agitated, excited."

"About Stein?"

"Yes, and about seeing her brother, Ethan. It was almost as if she felt she had to choose between the two of them, if for no other reason than to find an ending for her book."

"What does the book have to do with seeing Stein or Ethan?" I asked.

"As I told you, she is living out what she writes. Stein and Ethan represent different paths to her—present and past, roughly. Frankly I'm afraid they lead in the same direction."

"Suicide?"

He nodded. "She thinks it's her destiny."

"I don't believe in destinies," I said, getting to my feet. "Could I use your phone? I need to make a couple of calls."

The man pointed to a phone on the desk. "I'll leave you alone," he said, standing up and walking to the door. "If there's anything I can do . . ."

"I'll let you know," I told him.

I had only one contact in the Chicago area—an ex-FBI agent named Brandt Scheuster, who had opened his own P.I. agency in Skokie. I found his number in my address book and phoned him. All I got that late on a Sunday night was an answering machine. I left my name, Kirsten's number, and told him I'd be back in touch. I tried calling Marnee Thompson at the apartment, but there was no answer there either. Marnee obviously hadn't been forthcoming with me about Kirsten and her brother. But then, I was working for Papa Phil, and Kirsty was her friend.

I thought about phoning Pearson himself, and decided to wait. Judging by how much of his children's pasts—and his own—he'd already concealed, I didn't think I'd get him to talk openly without some leverage. Or a body.

After a time Heldman came back into the room. He had a beautiful little girl of about ten with him.

"This is my daughter, Katie. Katie, Mr. Stoner."

Katie curtsied as if I were royalty.

"Go on, toots," he said, giving her a smack on the rear.

She gave her father an indignant look and marched off up the hall.

"She thinks she's too old to be given a potch on the tuckus."

"She's very pretty."

Heldman smiled proudly. "I think so. Did you finish your calls?"

"All except for a cab to take me back to Kirsty's apartment."

"I could drive you."

"That's all right, Professor. I need you to run another errand."

"Anything," he said.

"How close are you to Jay Stein?"

"He's a colleague," the professor said with a stilted air of professional courtesy. "He came here this past year as an instructor, fresh out of the Iowa workshops. I very much doubt he will be renewed this coming year—if that's what you're getting at."

It wasn't what I was getting at, but I was glad to hear it anyway. Glad to know that forbearance had its limits, even among professors of literature.

"I'm sure that Stein has told me a few self-protective lies," I said. "But there is probably a certain amount of truth mixed in with them. It's important for me to know what Kirsty and he actually talked about on Thursday morning—if she did in fact tell him she was going to see her brother or someone else. Do you think you could . . . ?"

"What?" Heldman said uneasily. "Pump him?"

"I was thinking of something a little more hardball than that. It wouldn't be a lie if you said that you'd just talked to me and that I'd raised some disturbing questions about his conduct, would it?"

"You want me to threaten him?" Heldman said with horror.

"I want you to find out where Kirsten went. Otherwise, she may well be destined for calamity."

Heldman thought it over for a moment. "I'll do what I can" was all he said.

6

I called for a cab and, before leaving, told Heldman to phone me at Kirsten's apartment after he'd talked to Stein. He wasn't comfortable with the idea of blackmailing the man—that was obvious. But I had the gut feeling that he'd get the information I wanted, because he really did care for Kirsten, as I myself was beginning to care for her in spite of my initial misgivings about the case.

On the cab ride back to the apartment I wondered why Phil Pearson had waited for the girl to go missing before calling for help. He had talked vaguely about "disturbing signs" in Kirsten's behavior—he'd talked vaguely about everything having to do with his daughter, as if her past was a personal embarrassment to him. But the signs of Kirsten's disintegration were quite clear to everyone who knew her. They had to be just as clear to her father, who was a trained psychiatrist. Perhaps Pearson couldn't bring himself to intervene in his daughter's life again after his disastrous rescue attempt of the previous summer. Perhaps he thought that another such intervention would drive her over the edge. I didn't know. But there was an inconsistency about his behavior, about everyone's behavior toward Kirsty, that almost amounted to ambivalence. It was as if her friends had decided to let her life run its course, even if it meant her death.

I'm sure they felt they were respecting her wishes, showing her the courtesy of treating her as an adult. But it seemed heartless to me when she was so obviously *not* fully an adult. Even Professor Heldman seemed irresponsible, knowing as he did that Kirsten was close to suicide and still letting her walk off to her self-pronounced doom. Maybe that was the way enlightened people treated each other in academia.

It was past nine when the cabbie dropped me off at the brownstone on 54th. No light was on in the second-floor apartment windows, and no one answered the entry buzzer. I fished through my pocket, found the keys that Pearson had given me, and let myself into the front hall. The hallway was dark, and the cat piss smell was overwhelming. I fumbled up the staircase to the apartment, unlocked the door, and went in.

A sliver of moonlit sky hung in the darkness like a hallucination. It took me a second to realize that it was being reflected off the mirror in Marnee Thompson's bedroom. I found the desk light and clicked it on.

The boxed manuscript was the first thing I saw. The box had been opened and the manuscript removed. At first I thought that Marnee Thompson must have taken it out to read. But on further thought I couldn't see Marnee tampering with Kirsten's things—not with her fierce sense of propriety. Which meant one of two things. Either someone else had broken in and stolen the manuscript. Or Kirsty Pearson herself had come back for it. I liked the idea of Kirsty taking it, for several reasons.

One, the apartment lock hadn't been tampered with, so whoever had removed it had had a key to the room. Two, Kirsty hadn't finished the book yet. According to Art Heldman she was waiting for real life to supply her with an ending. Maybe she'd found that ending over the past four days.

There was a third reason why I liked the idea. If Kirsty had taken the manuscript, it meant she was still alive. And I wanted her to stay alive until I could find her.

I went down the hall to Kirsty's bedroom, flipped on the

light, and went through the trashy room again—carefully this time—looking for any other sign that Kirsty might have returned to the apartment. But nothing else had been moved or taken—the clothes were still disarrayed, the books made their tipsy towers, the birth control pills were hidden in the underwear drawer, the picture of Phil Pearson lay facedown in the panties.

I hadn't examined the loose papers scattered on her desk the first time I'd searched the room. This time I read each one through. They were fragments of prose, mostly. Journal entries that made little sense to me and one that made too much sense, a scrap cut from *The New York Times Magazine* and pasted to a blank page:

> Suicide was a crime—ironically, a capital crime—in most Western nations well into the nineteenth century. In England, failed suicides were frequently nursed back to health in order to be hanged.

There was a fragment of a prose poem, copied out several times. Presumably one of her own:

> *Closing windows at dawn*
> *Against the heat of the day,*
> *He is suddenly lost among bulky*
> *Colorless furnishings*
>
> *The windows stick*
> *in swollen tracks,*
> *the blinds will not close*
>
> *under thin sheets*
> *his feet search out her legs*
> *his hands . . .*

And that was all, as if she'd stopped those hands with her own. I put the paper down and thought about Jay Stein—about paying him another visit—when the phone in the living room rang. I went back down the hall and picked it up. It was Brandt Scheuster, returning my call.

"I've got a missing person, Brandt," I told him. "A Cincinnati girl, going to school up here, who dropped out of sight about four days ago. She's unstable, possibly suicidal. I need you to check with the cops—see if she's been picked up or if they've got her in a morgue. You could canvass hospital emergency rooms and psych wards, too."

I gave him Kirsty's name and physical description.

"I'll see what I can do," Brandt said. "Does she have a car?"

"A yellow VW Bug. I don't know the plates yet, but if you could run her name through Illinois BMV, I'd appreciate it. I'll check in Ohio myself to see if she registered the car down there."

"You want this to go out as an APB, Harry? You want to make it official police business?"

I didn't even have to think about it. "Yeah. I want the kid found."

"If we do locate her . . . ?"

"Call me. I'll be checking into a hotel later tonight. When I have a new number I'll let you know. Until then you can get me here at the girl's apartment."

After finishing with Brandt I called Al Foster at the Cincinnati Police Department and asked him to run Kirsten's name through the Ohio BMV computer. I told him it was urgent.

I'd just hung up when the phone rang again. This time it was Art Heldman.

"I've talked to Jay," he said in a guilty-sounding voice.

"What did he have to say?"

"He repeated the story that he told you—about Ethan, Kirsty's brother." He cleared his throat dramatically. "However, when I . . . pressured him, he admitted that Ethan hadn't been the only focus of the conversation. He and Kirsty did talk about their own relationship as well. Apparently Kirsty wanted to start seeing Jay again—romantically."

"What did Stein say to that?"

"He claims he didn't commit himself either way. He told her that he cared for her and that they would talk again after the holidays. He's fully aware that Kirsten is still in love with him, and he's determined to ease her out of the infatuation slowly and gently."

"Like he did last year?" I said acidly.

"Jays knows he behaved badly last spring. He simply panicked. Kirsten can be demanding. Her needs are so great."

"That's the way it is with nineteen-year-old women, Professor, especially when you abandon them."

Heldman didn't say anything.

"Did Stein give you any sense of how Kirsten reacted to his spiel?"

"He thought he'd talked her into putting everything on hold—the renewed romance *and* the visit to Ethan. He thought she was going back to Cincinnati, as she originally planned to do. I thought she was, too, Stoner. That was definitely the impression I got."

I sighed. "Well, something must have changed her mind."

"I did learn one more thing that may be of interest. Jay didn't tell you because he didn't trust you—possibly because you're working for Kirsten's father, and Kirsty has made it clear to any number of people that her dad *isn't* to be told anything about her life here in Chicago. Dr. Pearson may be a well-meaning man, but he can also be an overbearing one. At times of crisis he seems to overreact. It's almost as if he's afraid that Kirsty's emotional problems will reflect badly on him."

"I have that feeling too," I admitted.

"That's why Jay left out part of the conversation."

"Which part?"

"The part about where Kirsty's brother, Ethan, is staying."

"Stein had an address?"

"Not an address—a name. Kirsty mentioned a motel in Evanston. The University Inn. I looked up the address myself. It's on Lake Shore, south of the campus. According to the desk clerk, Ethan Pearson is still registered there."

"Good work. I'll get a cab immediately."

"I'd like to come along," Heldman said. "I mean I have a car. And I know Kirsty. If she is in a bad way, perhaps I can help."

"All right," I said. "Let's do it."

7

Heldman picked me up outside the brownstone a little before ten.

It took us about thirty minutes to drive up to Evanston, and another fifteen to find The University Inn on the south side of town—a run-down, fifties-style motor court with a small office building in front and Quonset-like motel rooms stretching in parallel rows behind it. The ice-shagged neon sign on the highway berm said "Vacancies." And always would.

Heldman pulled up by the office. Through the steamy picture window I could see a night clerk, resting his elbows on a countertop.

"You want to go in?" Heldman asked. "Or should I?"

"I'll handle it, Professor."

"We're not going to do anything rash, are we? I mean we're not going to use force, right?"

He laughed nervously, but his eyes were dead serious. He was beginning to have second thoughts about intervening in Kirsten's life—second thoughts about me.

I said, "Let's see if Kirsten is here before we decide what we're going to do."

Heldman didn't look reassured. "I don't know. I don't know about this."

I got out of the car and walked into the motel office. A middle-aged clerk in a striped shirt and black gaberdine pants was reading a comic book spread out on the counter. He looked up at me balefully, as if his instincts told me I wasn't a paying customer.

"Can I do for you?" he said, flapping the comic book shut.

He had a slight cast in his left eye that gave him a queasy, distracting stare.

I tried to smile at him pleasantly. "You can tell me what room Ethan Pearson is in. I'm supposed to meet him here around eleven, but I forgot the damn room number."

"That'd be fourteen. Down there on your right."

"Great." I turned toward the door, then looked back at him. "You don't know if Kirsten's here yet, do you? Dark-haired girl, blue eyes, about nineteen?"

"Ain't seen nobody but his wife and kid," he said, flipping the comic book open and bending over it again.

I went back outside and got into Heldman's Audi.

"Room fourteen," I said to him. "On the right."

The professor wheeled the car slowly around the office and down a driveway that ran between the two rows of motel buildings. There were numbered parking slots on either side of the drive—most of them filled with frozen slush. But the one in front of room 14 had a car in it, a yellow VW Bug.

"Christ, I think that's Kirsty's car," Heldman said excitedly.

"It *is* her car. Pull over on the other side of the drive."

Heldman parked the Audi on the right hand berm, flipped off the lights, and turned in his seat to look back through the rear window at number 14. For a moment we both sat there, looking over our shoulders at the lighted motel room window.

"What do we do now?" Heldman asked.

"Talk to her, if she's willing."

"And if she isn't?"

I didn't answer him. What I had to say wasn't what he wanted to hear.

As I started to get out of the car, Heldman grabbed my

coat sleeve. Without thinking, I jerked away—hard. The professor looked shocked, then frightened.

"I won't be a party to coercion," he said, trying to make his voice resolute.

"I'm going to do my job," I said, feeling sorry that he'd come along. "If that bothers you, stay in the car."

"No, I'm coming with you," he said, as if I'd challenged him.

I got out of the car and Heldman got out too. Side by side we walked across the icy driveway to number 14. I stopped by the VW for a moment—to take a quick look. The doors were locked and the windows were solid ice. There was thick ice on the hood and roof, as well. Clearly the car hadn't been used all day—perhaps not for several days.

A short cement walk led from the parking area up to the motel door. I automatically slowed my pace as I neared the door, and Heldman almost ran up my back.

"Sorry," he whispered, and dropped a step behind me.

The curtain in the window was too thick to see through, but I could hear a television going inside the room.

I gave Heldman a glance—to make sure he was out of the way—raised my fist, and knocked.

The television went off abruptly, as if a hand had been clapped to its mouth. There was a moment of dead silence, in which I had the sure feeling that someone inside the room was straining to listen. Then the door opened slowly, and a stocky young woman with a badly bruised face peered out the crack.

Even in the dim porch light I could tell that the bruises had come from a recent beating. She'd tried to hide the black eyes with makeup, but there was nothing she could do about the swollen nose or the fat, twisted bottom lip. She touched at the lip involuntarily, when she saw that my eyes were drawn to it. Then she covered her whole mouth with her right hand, as if that would divert me.

"Yes?" she said behind her hand. Her voice sounded hoarse and weak, as if she'd used it up earlier that day—screaming. "What is it?"

"My name is Stoner. I'm looking for Kirsten Pearson."

"She's not here," the woman said. "She's gone. They're both gone."

The woman dropped her head like a prisoner being sentenced. "They've gone and left us here alone."

A young boy with the solemn, big-eyed face of a refugee was sitting on one of the double beds inside the motel room. He couldn't have been more than three or four, dressed in pajamas and furry slippers. He hopped up and ran over to the woman as we came through the door, hiding his face in her robe. She hugged him to her and sank down on the bed.

"Maybe we should call an ambulance?" Heldman said, staring aghast at the woman's battered face.

She looked up quickly. "No. There's no need. I'm all right." Her voice was queerly placid.

"You don't look all right," Heldman said.

"Nevertheless, I am." She wiped her eyes with the back of her hands. "Who did you say you were?"

"My name is Harry Stoner. This is Professor Arthur Heldman. We're looking for Kirsten Pearson. She's been missing for several days."

The woman nodded as if she already knew that Kirsten was missing. "She's been here with Ethan. Since Thursday, I think. They left this afternoon. Left me here with David."

"You're Ethan's wife?"

The woman nodded again. "Hedda Pearson." She laughed suddenly. "I guess I'm still his wife."

"He did this to you?" I asked.

Hedda Pearson didn't answer me. She sat on the edge of the bed and stared at her frightened son. "Are you police?"

"No. I'm a private investigator. I was hired by Kirsten's father—Ethan's father—to find Kirsty."

"I've never met Ethan's father," the woman said matter-of-factly. "Ethan's told me about him, but we've never met."

The woman stopped talking for a moment. I took that moment to look quickly around the room. There was a lamp table to the right of the door, with a manila folder on it. The folder was open, and I could see a pile of newspaper clippings inside. There were more loose clippings on a bureau across from the beds. And a handful of bloody Kleenex.

"What am I going to do?" Hedda Pearson asked, calmly stroking the boy's head. "Ethan took all our money, the credit cards, the car."

"I can get you money," I told her.

The woman reacted angrily. "I couldn't leave here if I wanted to. I can't go anywhere. Where would I go?"

"Don't you have relatives? Parents?"

"We don't talk since I married."

From where I was sitting I could see why. But the woman obviously didn't.

"I'll simply wait here until he comes back."

"From where?"

"From where he went of course. From the searching . . . from the hunting." The woman shook her head suddenly, violently. Her voice rose to a near-hysterical pitch: "Madness!"

The little boy began to moan softly, as if he'd been infected by his mother's hysteria. The woman glanced down at him guiltily, and her face slowly resumed its queer look of resignation.

I glanced at Heldman, who was standing just inside the door. "Maybe you could get some coffee?"

He nodded. "Of course."

"Do you want some coffee, something to eat?" I said to the woman.

"Some milk for David, please," she said softly. "He hasn't had anything since this morning."

I had the feeling that neither one of them had eaten in hours.

"I'll get the food," Heldman said, and turned to the door eagerly, as if he were only too glad to escape the scene in the bedroom.

He went out, leaving me alone with the woman and her son. The boy, David, stopped crying and crawled up on the bed beside his mother. Frightened or not, he was sleepy and his eyelids kept drooping down over his solemn brown eyes. He didn't look as if he'd been hurt, but I couldn't be sure.

"Is the boy all right?"

"Of course he's all right!" the woman said with outrage. "Ethan would never hurt David."

"What caused the fight?"

"The same thing that always causes our fights," Hedda Pearson said wearily. "He'll read something in the paper. See some anonymous two-inch column, and it starts up again."

"What starts up?"

But Hedda Pearson didn't hear me. "I didn't know about it when I first met him. If I had, I'm not sure what I would have done. Probably the same things. Just like he does." She stared sadly at the sleeping boy. "Only this time . . . I'm frightened for him. I'm frightened he won't come back."

"Why are you afraid for him, Mrs. Pearson? Where have Ethan and Kirsty gone?"

"To look for him—the man in the newspaper." Her eyes got very large, as if she'd suddenly remembered something terrifying. "You've got to find them!"

"Why?"

"Because they're dangerous. They make each other dangerous. And Ethan . . ." Her head dropped to her chest and she began to cry. "Ethan has a gun!"

8

Ten minutes passed before Heldman returned with food and coffee. By then the woman had stopped crying and settled back into her strange waiting state. She woke the boy and fed him a hamburger and some milk. She didn't eat anything herself at first, but after a while she began to eat, just chewing and swallowing automatically.

Heldman hovered over her, trying to help with the boy—trying to help. While he busied himself with Hedda Pearson and her son, I scanned the newspaper clippings on the bureau, looking for the one that had apparently set Ethan Pearson off. As far as I could see, it might have been any of them, for they were all the same. Two-inch columns cut from the back pages of newspapers, the pages with the court news—each column detailing the arraignment, conviction, or release of a murderer. The name of the paper and the date of the article was written in pen at the bottom of each clipping.

> Willie Johnson, 42, is to be released this afternoon from Joliet penitentiary, after serving seven years of a 10–20 year term for homicide in the death of his common-law wife . . .
> *Chicago Sun-Times 8/26/83*

> Arthur Braddock, 35, of 4609 Winton Terrace has been arraigned on the

charge of felony homicide in the
death of Leona Smith . . .
            Cincinnati Enquirer 11/18/76

Stanford Isaiah Lewis, 45, convicted
slayer of Moira Hamill, has been
granted probation after serving ten
years of a life sentence in Lima State
Penitentiary . . .
            Dayton Daily News 3/7/86

Calvin "Beebee" Jackson, 34, of 8567
Prospect has been convicted of ag-
gravated homicide in the death of
LaQuicha Morgan, also of 8567 Prospect . . .
            Cleveland Plain-Dealer 12/2/76

There were twenty of them on the bureau. Twenty homi-
cides, twenty murderers. I couldn't be certain on the basis
of their names alone, but I had the feeling that they were all
black men. They were all about forty-seven or forty-eight
years old, all from the Midwest, and all of them had killed a
woman.

It took me a while longer to spot it, but the criminals had
something else in common. Judging by their dates of release and dates of conviction, it appeared that each of them
had committed a murder in the latter part of 1976. I didn't
know what that meant, but it clearly had some significance
for Ethan Pearson.

As I was sorting through the last of the clippings I noticed
that Hedda Pearson had begun to watch me. I could see her
face in the bureau mirror. She looked more curious than

concerned, as if she wanted to compare notes about her husband's odd collection of killers.

"He started cutting them out after his mother died," Hedda Pearson said into the mirror.

I turned to face her. "Would that have been in 1976?"

"Yes. You're sharp, Mr. Stoner. Estelle died in September of 1976." The woman pointed to the manila folder on the lamp table by the door. "It's all in there, all the details. At least the ones that the reporters could dig up. They missed the real story, though."

"And what is the real story?" I asked.

"What happened afterward. How it changed the family. Ethan most of all. Kirsty was deeply affected by Estelle's death, too. But she was closer to her father. And, of course, Phil was there to look after her. Ethan wasn't close to Phil. He blamed his father for Estelle's breakdowns. He still does. He had no one to lean on once Estelle was gone. No one to console him, to help him channel the anger and frustration from such an enormous tragedy. His mind couldn't handle it. Gradually he went . . . a little crazy. You saw for yourself. All those men in the newspapers. All those men."

"What does he do with the clippings?" I asked the woman.

"He keeps track," she said. "Keeps looking, hunting, searching for the reason Estelle died, for a reason that makes sense to him. His logic is simplicity itself: my mother couldn't have committed suicide and still have loved me, therefore she didn't commit suicide, she was murdered. By one of them—one of the faceless men in the newspaper clippings."

"Was he this . . . obsessed when you married him?" Heldman asked.

The woman smiled. "You mean, *why* did I marry him if he was so crazy?"

She was a smart woman, when she had her wits about her.

"Yes," Heldman said with a blush. "I guess that's what I did mean."

"I didn't care that he was crazy," Hedda Pearson said simply. "I didn't see him that way. He was only nineteen—a sophomore at Oberlin. And I was just eighteen."

Hedda Pearson lightly touched her bruised lip, her swollen eye, down her cheek, as if the bruises didn't matter, as if they weren't there. Then her face changed.

"If I hadn't gotten pregnant, it might have worked. But I did get pregnant. Ethan wasn't ready for fatherhood, for a job and a family. That's when this craziness started in earnest—at least, that's when it started to have an effect, that's when we started to move from city to city."

"Has he ever gone after one of these men before?" I asked.

Hedda Pearson smiled. "No. He never wanted to confront any of them—he wanted to get away from them. He said it was because none of them was the right man—that he had to keep moving until fate delivered the right one to him. But I always told myself that that wasn't the real reason. The real reason was that he didn't ever want it to end. He wanted to keep looking forever, to keep Estelle alive forever. At least that's what I thought until last week."

The woman shuddered, slopping a little coffee on her robe.

"What happened last week?" I asked.

"We were in Ft. Thomas, Kentucky. I'd been working there at NKSU for a couple of months. Ethan was writing an article on the campus. But he started having trouble with the piece. Then he got a rejection on one of his poems. I knew the signs by then, so I could see what was coming. And sure enough on Wednesday morning he marched into the department office and pulled me away from the desk. In front of everyone, he pulled me away.

"He took me out to the car. David was already in the backseat. Our bags in the backseat. He took off, driving straight through to Chicago. To this godforsaken place."

"He came to see Kirsten?"

She nodded. "He had this clipping from a Kentucky paper. A small photograph. He thought she would look at it and remember."

"Did she recognize the man in the photo?"

The woman laughed derisively. "Of course not. There's nothing to remember. There never has been. That isn't the point. Kirsten didn't have to recognize the man. All she had to do was come here and talk to Ethan. Just talk." Hedda Pearson got an ugly look on her face. "She does weird things to him. She always makes him worse, and he makes her worse. It's horrible to see. Like they're having some kind of vicious sex."

"Kirsten came here on Thursday morning?"

"I think it was Thursday. I know they spent the weekend here. The two of them in this room with David and me . . . telling tales about the past, talking baby talk, crying about Estelle as if she'd just died a day or two ago. They just kept getting crazier and crazier, until they were ready to . . ." The woman dropped her head.

"When did they leave?" I asked.

"Late this afternoon." She touched her bruised face.

"You tried to stop him?"

"He had a gun," she said with horror. "They went and bought one yesterday. When I tried to take it away from Ethan, he . . ."

"He beat you up." I said it for her.

She nodded.

"Where was the boy?" Heldman said, looking sick. "Where was David when this happened?"

The woman waved her hand around the tiny room. "Where do you think?"

"He saw?"

"Kirsty held her hands over David's eyes."

"She didn't try to stop it?" Heldman asked.

"She watched," Hedda Pearson said coldly.

9

I tried to get the woman to describe the man in the Kentucky newspaper—the man that Ethan claimed had killed his mother. But Hedda said she'd never actually seen the newspaper photo—Ethan had only told her about it. If the picture was something more than Ethan's fantasy, he'd taken it with him when he and Kirsten had left that afternoon in the grey Plymouth Volare, heading south to finish their lives in an act of murder.

"There is another picture," the woman said, almost as an afterthought.

"Of this man?"

"Of the man Ethan says killed his mother. He drew it right after Estelle's death. He even tried to show it to the police, but of course no one believed him. Not even Ethan's father. It's one of the things that Ethan has always held against Phil." She pointed to the lamp table by the door. "The drawing's over there, in the manila folder on the table. The folder with the clippings about Estelle."

I went over to the table and picked up the folder. Heldman crowded beside me, eager to take a look.

I didn't bother with the clippings. The picture was in the back. It was a surprisingly skillful pencil drawing of a black man in his mid-to-late thirties with lumpy skin, peppery hair, and a thin, mean, frightening-looking face—all sharp bony points from brow to cheekbone to chin. The boy had drawn what I took to be a pointed goatee at the V of the chin, which only added to the man's devilish appearance.

I had the feeling that the drawing was more metaphor than anything else—the portrait of the bogeyman who had robbed a ten-year-old child of his mother. And yet, metaphor or not, the search for the bogeyman had become quite real. Ethan and Kirsten were out there looking for him—looking to kill him. And they had a seven-hour head start on me.

The woman wouldn't take charity, so I ended making a trade. Two hundred dollars for the manila envelope with the clippings and Ethan's drawing of Estelle Pearson's murderer. And another fifty for four chapbooks of Ethan Pearson's poetry.

The woman had a suitcase full of the damn things, like a brush salesman.

As I walked across the deserted motel lot to Heldman's car, holding that pile of yellowed clippings and Ethan's chapbooks in my hands, I had the disturbing feeling that none of what had occurred was real.

Art Heldman had the same feeling. "It's so damn weird," he said in a bewildered voice. "What are we going to do?"

I told him the truth. "I don't know."

Snow began to fall again on the way back to Hyde Park—a needle spray of snow, fierce and fine as icy rain. Through the driver side window I could see it falling on the lake, windblown above the dark water. The only sound in the car was the whisper of the snow beneath the tires.

"I owe you an apology, Stoner," Heldman said after a time. He thought I was still angry from the scene in the parking lot. I wasn't—I wasn't thinking about him.

"You were right. Something has to be done. I guess it should have been done long before this." Heldman glanced over at me quickly. "If you still need my help . . ."

"Thanks. I'll let you know."

"Will you go back to Cincinnati?"

"It seems like the place to start."

"Perhaps the police should be . . . informed."

"They already have been—in Chicago. I'll take care of the rest of them tonight."

"You have somewhere to stay?"

"Just drop me at Kirsty's apartment. I'll see if I can get an early flight in the morning."

"I am sorry," the man said again. "Sorriest of all for Kirsty."

"Her life isn't over yet, Professor. We still have a shot to change things."

I said it, but I wasn't sure I believed it. And neither was he.

Heldman dropped me at Kirsten's apartment at half past twelve. The freshly fallen snow along 54th caught the streetlight, turning the dismal brownstones the pale, low-wattage yellow of gaslamps. I watched Heldman's car disappear down Blackstone, then looked up through the falling snow at Kirsten's second-floor apartment. There was a light in the front room, which might have meant that Marnee Thompson was back. That is, if I hadn't left the light on myself when I'd stopped there earlier that night. I went into the foyer and pressed the intercom on the side wall, thinking I'd use the keys if no one answered. But Marnee Thompson buzzed me through.

As I climbed the stairs to the second-floor landing, the apartment door opened and the girl came out. Although she was wearing a terry robe over men's-cut pajamas, she didn't look as if she'd been sleeping. On the contrary, her face was wide-awake and frightened-looking. For a second I was afraid she was going to tell me that Kirsten Pearson was dead.

"What happened?" I asked.

"An hour or two after you left, Kirsty came to the apartment," the girl said breathlessly. "Mr. Stoner, she was . . . crazy."

Marnee Thompson wrung her hands, as if she'd been infected with some of the same craziness. "I didn't know what to do. After she left I just waited here. I didn't know what else to do."

I put a hand on her shoulder. "Calm down. This could be important."

Marnee Thompson shrugged my hand off. "I know it's important! Don't you think I know that? I wanted to tell you, but I didn't know where you were. Couldn't you have called?"

"I did call. You weren't here."

"I was with Kirsty," she cried. "That's why I wasn't here. I was with Kirsty!"

The girl was almost shouting and very close to tears.

I edged her out of the hall and into the apartment, closing the door behind us. "Easy, Marnee. I'm a friend, remember?"

She gave me a wet-eyed look of frustration. "It's just that I spent a couple of hours, driving around with her in this beat-up car, trying to talk her into staying with me. But she wouldn't listen! I'm so afraid . . . I'm afraid she's going to die."

Marnee Thompson stamped her foot and started to cry. She ran into the living room, curled up in the armchair, and cried—with her hand over her eyes and her knees tucked against her chest.

I went into the tiny kitchen, found a kettle in the cabinet, and started boiling water for coffee. It wasn't just for the girl. I was afraid that if I didn't wake myself up, I'd miss something important—or lose my concentration completely. And then I was pissed off at my bad luck. If I'd stuck around the apartment, I would have found Kirsty in time to stop her and Ethan. Instead, she'd slipped away. For a moment I felt as if fate really was conspiring toward her death, just as Kirsten herself believed.

There was a can of instant on top of the refrigerator. When the kettle started to shriek, I mixed two cups and took them back into the living room.

The girl was still sitting in the chair, stiffly now, her feet planted on the floor as if they were weighted with chains. I handed her a cup and sat down across from her on the desk stool.

"Let's start again," I said. "Kirsty came back here around . . . ?"

"Eight, I think," Marnee said in a dull, cried-out voice. "Maybe a little after."

"She wanted the manuscript?"

"Not just the manuscript. She wanted to say good-bye to me. To tell me . . ." Her voice started to tremble again, but she caught herself before she broke down, crossing her arms and squeezing tightly as if she were physically holding herself together. "To tell me she loved me and to say good-bye."

"Did she tell you where she was going?"

"All she said was that she was going away. That she'd made a decision. The right decision, she called it."

"What was this decision?"

"To kill herself, I think," the girl said with a hopeless look.

I didn't want to give her the chance to brood about it, so I raised my voice a little, startling her. "Was Ethan with Kirsty?"

"Yes. He didn't come into the apartment. But when I went out to the car with Kirsty, he was sitting in the backseat. Kirsty dropped him off at The Eagle while we drove around and talked. I guess she must have picked him up later."

"What did she talk about in the car?"

"Jay, her dad, her mom, her breakdown—everything. She said she'd been confused for so long about her past and that she was just now beginning to see what it meant her to do. She talked like that—like her past was this guiding light. She said she thought, at first, that Jay was her destiny. But now she knew that was wrong. Her destiny was with her family. The way she talked about her mom . . . it scared me."

"What did she say about Estelle?"

"She said she was just like her."

"You mean, suicidal?"

"More than that, I think. She said that for years she'd hated her mother and never understood why. She used to feel terribly guilty about it, as if she had driven her mother crazy. She'd punished herself for that. She talked as if Jay and the breakdown were somehow part of the punishment. But this summer, when she was in therapy, her shrink gave her Pentothal and she remembered something about her mom. She wouldn't tell me what it was, just that it had terrified her at first. But now she said it didn't scare her anymore. Now she understood that she'd been punishing the wrong person."

"Who was the right person?"

Marnee Thompson shook her head. "I don't know."

We sat in the living room for a while, drinking coffee. Marnee slowly calmed down, and once she got her bearings back she started asking *me* questions.

"How did you know that Ethan was with Kirsty?"

"Stein said Kirsty planned to see him this weekend." I gave Marnee a monitory look. "You knew that, didn't you?"

She ducked her head. "I knew a lot of things," she said in

a whisper. "I just couldn't . . . I was afraid to tell you. Except for Jay, I mean."

The girl looked up guiltily. "Did you talk to him? To Jay?"

"We had some words."

"What did he say about me? Something ugly?"

She flushed as if she already knew what Stein had said, as if he'd said it before and it had come back to her.

"Don't worry about him, Marnee. Guys like Stein aren't worth the time."

"I'd like to believe that." She stared at me for a long moment. "Are you going to stay here tonight?"

"I'll probably get a motel room by the airport. I have to fly back to Cincinnati tomorrow, early."

"You could stay," the girl said shyly. "I want you to stay. I could use the company."

"I can't, Marnee. I'd like to, but I can't."

She ducked her head. "Okay," she whispered. "I understand."

But she didn't understand. She thought I was rejecting her because of what Stein told me, and there was no way short of spending the night to prove that I wasn't.

It was a sad way to end it. But she had the resources to survive. Her friend didn't.

As I went out the door I told her that I'd call her, when I had some news about Kirsty.

10

I caught a cab to O'Hare and checked in at the airport Hilton. If the bars had been open, I might not have bothered with the room. But the lounges were shut, and I needed a place to sit and think. I also needed a phone.

The room was clean and featureless, with a view of the snowy runways, still busy with mail and parcel traffic even at that hour of the night. I took a hot shower, ordered some coffee up from room service, then phoned Delta reservations and booked a seat on their first flight to Cincinnati at seven in the morning. After the busboy arrived with the coffee, I called Phil Pearson.

Pearson must have been used to late-night calls. Either that or he was expecting trouble, because he sounded fully alert when he answered the phone. There was no easy way to break the news, so I just told him outright—at least as much of it as I understood. He didn't say a word as I went through his kids' bizarre history—his own history. When I finished, the silence at the other end was so profound that I thought he'd gone off the line.

"Pearson?" I said. "Are you still there?"

"I'm here," the man said in an awful voice.

"Look, I know this is a terrible shock. But there are some things that have to be done immediately if we're going to prevent a tragedy."

"I'm listening."

"Ethan and Kirsten were still in Chicago as of early last night. I'm not completely sure where they've headed, but it's possible that they're going to Cincinnati."

"To find this man, this convict?"

I said, "Yes. They've had at least four or five hours on the road, which would put them south of Indianapolis, almost to the Ohio line. If we alert the Ohio State Patrol and the Cincinnati police, we might be able to stop them before they get in trouble."

"Stop them, how?" the man said in the same deadened voice. "With guns?"

"Of course not. We could arrange to have them detained as missing persons."

"You said my son had a pistol, didn't you? What makes you think he'll stop for anyone?"

He had a point, but he'd also made one. "Someone will have to stop him," I said.

"I don't want the police!" Pearson said, his voice rising. "My children aren't criminals. *I'm* not a criminal."

It was an odd thing to say under the circumstances. But he was badly upset, and it was already clear that he felt personally responsible for his children's problems. And more than a little embarrassed by them.

"I don't want Kirsten or Ethan hurt," he said in a cooler voice. "I don't want anyone hurt."

"Then let me notify the police."

"What exactly would you say?"

"Standard missing persons reports. I don't have to go into detail."

It was precisely what he wanted to hear.

"Do it, then," he said resignedly. "But don't volunteer anything more than necessary. If Kirsty and Ethan are going to survive this—if the family is going to survive this—it's essential that they know I still love them."

He said it with great feeling. But he was saying it to the wrong person. At least that's the way it sounded to me—like a plea for approval.

* * *

After finishing with Pearson, I made the necessary calls to a friend I knew with the State Police and to Al Foster at the CPD. I phoned Brandt Scheuster, too, leaving a message on his machine. By then, it was almost three.

I lay down on the bed and tried to sleep, but the coffee had kicked in. Anyway I knew I was going to have to get up again in a few hours. Clicking on the reading light above the bed I picked Ethan Pearson's manila folder up from the nightstand. The clippings fell out on the bedclothes. A dozen of them, yellowed with age.

I gathered them together, sorted them by date, and read through them one by one. The first clipping was from the September 5, 1976, edition of the *Enquirer*. It was a short article, two paragraphs long, detailing Estelle Pearson's disappearance.

INDIAN HILL WOMAN REPORTED
MISSING

Estelle Pearson, of 3 Woodbine Lane, Indian Hill, has been reported missing by her husband, Dr. Philip Pearson. Mrs. Pearson disappeared on the afternoon of September 3, after failing to show up for a doctor's appointment in Clifton.

Mrs. Pearson has been ill for some time, and it is feared that she may have overmedicated herself or is in some way incapacitated by her illness . . .

A brief description of the woman followed, along with a number to call if Estelle Pearson was found.

The next article appeared two days later. It was considerably more detailed and its tone was grim.

INDIAN HILL WOMAN FEARED
DEAD

> Indian Hill police have launched an extensive search for Estelle Pearson, wife of Dr. Philip Pearson. Mrs. Pearson, 34, was reported missing by her husband on September 3, when she failed to return home after missing an appointment with Dr. Sheldon Sacks, a Clifton psychiatrist.

> Mrs. Pearson has a long history of emotional problems and has been recently hospitalized for depression. It is feared that she may have taken her own life . . .

There was a small photo of the woman with the article. It was difficult to tell much from the newspaper halftone, but she looked like a pretty woman with bee-stung lips and a thin, angular, careworn face.

There were several more paragraphs over the next week, reporting the lack of progress in the Pearson case. And then the big one—the front-page story—on September 14.

INDIAN HILL WOMAN FOUND DEAD
ESTELLE PEARSON, APPARENT SUICIDE

The body of Estelle Pearson, of 3 Woodbine Lane, Indian Hill, was discovered late last night in the Great Miami River by two fishermen, Claude Carter of Delhi and Sam Livingston of Terrace Park. Mrs. Pearson, wife of Indian Hill psychiatrist Dr. Philip Pearson, has been missing since September 3.

The fishermen found Mrs. Pearson's body floating in an estuary of the Miami River, east of Miamitown. She had been in the water for at least ten days, according to Hamilton County Assistant Coroner Dr. Jeffrey Hillman. Pending an inquest, the Cincinnati Police Department is reserving comment on the cause of death. Foul play is not suspected.

Mrs. Pearson was first reported missing on September 3, after she failed to show up for an appointment with her psychiatrist, Dr. Sheldon Sacks of Clifton. There was concern at the time that she might have taken her own life. Dr. Sacks has indicated that Mrs. Pearson was hospitalized for de-

pression in June and on several other
occasions over the past ten years.

Mrs. Pearson, née Estelle Frieberg,
was 34 years old, a Cincinnati native,
and a graduate of Miami University
and the University of Cincinnati
Medical School. She is survived by
her husband, Dr. Philip Pearson, a
psychiatrist, and her two children,
Ethan, 10, and Kirsten, 6.

There was a death notice the following day, an obit with a
large picture of Estelle, taken when she was younger and
less troubled. And about a week later one final paragraph
detailing the findings of the coroner's inquest. Not surprisingly the coroner had ruled Estelle Pearson's death a suicide by drowning. There was no hint that she might have
been murdered.

Ethan's drawing was the last item in the folder. After I'd
read the brief history of his mother's life and death, the line
sketch looked less like an anonymous bogeyman to me and
more like a picture of how the kid himself must have felt
following the suicide—jagged, frightened, full of rage.

Skimming through his chapbooks only confirmed that
feeling. I didn't read all four of them—the poems were
mostly of a piece, anyway. Sentimental elegies for his
mother and his lost childhood. Angry jeremiads about social
ills, full of violent adolescent gripes and not so veiled references to his father and other father figures—men who said
they knew best but constantly let Ethan down. There was a
love poem dedicated to his wife, and one very odd poem
called "The Anniversary."

When we meet again, as we will
We'll talk about that last fall day
And the smell of burning leaves
The sunlight on the lawn
The sound of the wind in the trees
Where I met you.

Seeing is a meeting, after all
Even from a high window
Myself a child of ten taking leave
Of her in the smell of burning leaves
The sunlight on the lawn
The sound of the wind in the dark trees
Where you waited

We'll meet again where you waited
In the trees, in the burning,
in the darkness, in the sound of the wind
And the child will be there too
In the darkness where you waited
A knife blade in the darkness where he's waited
To commemorate this anniversary.

I wouldn't have bet money on it, but I had the feeling that the poem was addressed to Estelle Pearson's murderer. Even if it wasn't, it had a nightmarish resonance to it. Just the thing to drowse over.

11

I didn't get much sleep, maybe three hours. Enough to leave me logy on the flight back to Cincinnati. In a way it was a blessing to be that tired. I didn't have enough energy to get scared about the plane ride.

We landed at Cincinnati International around nine, having lost an hour on the way back. After a cup of coffee at the airport cafeteria I picked up the car in short-term parking and drove to town.

It was a mild, blue December morning. A bit of snow from the previous day's storm still laced the hillsides along the expressway, in the crannies that the sun hadn't yet touched. It would melt within the hour. The day was that warm, like false spring.

I stopped at the office first—to phone the State Patrol and Al Foster at CPD. The grey Volare hadn't been spotted, although Al had managed to get a Kentucky plate number and registration. The car was registered to Hedda Pearson. The address she'd given was 1245 Hidden Fork Road, in Ft. Thomas, Kentucky. There was a phone number on the registration.

I dialed the number and got the manager at The Bluegrass Motel and Motor Court. The name Bluegrass Motel rang a bell, but it wasn't until after we'd begun talking that I remembered that the last of Ethan's postcards was addressed from the place.

The manager, a man named Wilson, was officiously polite in the bow-and-scrape tradition of southern hospitality. I asked him if Ethan Pearson had checked in or out, and he said neither. The Pearsons had left town, but their room was paid up through the end of the month and he expected them back soon. I told him who I was, gave him my phone number, and asked him to call immediately if Ethan did come back. I made it sound important, so Wilson would feel important. He said he would surely call.

I called the Pearsons next—to see if they'd heard from their wandering children. Louise Pearson answered the phone.

"We haven't heard a word, Mr. Stoner." She sounded exhausted, but then she and her husband had had a rough night. "Phil's worked himself into quite a state. This business about the police . . . it would help if you could come out and talk to him. Give him a sense that he's participating in the process and not just sitting back and letting it happen around him. It's the feeling of helplessness that's getting to him—getting to all of us. It . . . well, it stirs up bad memories."

I'd read about those memories the night before. Up to that moment it hadn't hit me that Pearson had been down this road before—waiting for the police to discover what had happened to someone he loved, someone self-destructively crazy. The woman didn't make the connection explicit, but the change in her tone of voice—the change from the backbiting bitterness of the previous day to genuine concern for her husband—was itself telling.

"All right," I told her. "I can make it out there in about an hour."

"Bless you," she said.

There were several Mercedeses parked in the Pearson driveway, when I pulled up around ten-thirty. Two of them had physician's plates. The other one had a bag from Saks in the backseat. I walked around to the front of the house and knocked on the door.

A smart-looking woman with snow-white hair answered. She was in her sixties, immaculately dressed in a Chanel suit and pearls.

"Yes? What can I do for you?" she said coolly.

"My name is Stoner. I'm here to see Dr. Pearson."

Her blue eyes lost their "No Vendors" look. "You're the detective, aren't you?"

"Yes."

"I'm Cora Pearson," she said, holding out her hand and withdrawing it before I could shake with her. "I'm Philip's mother. Please come in."

I followed her down the hall to the grey sitting room. The woman walked as if she were balancing a book on her head, which was probably the way she'd been taught.

Louise Pearson was sitting in one of the red armchairs by the fireplace. She smiled familiarly when she saw me come in.

"It was so good of you to do this, Mr. Stoner," she said, smiling gratefully.

"I wish I had something good to report."

She made a gesture with her hands, as if she were shushing a heckler. "Believe me, just talking to Phil will help."

She glanced at the mother, who was standing by the sideboard, taking the conversation in over her shoulder. The older woman nodded as if she agreed with Louise.

"You've met my mother-in-law, Cora Pearson?"

"Yes."

Louise Pearson stood up a little shakily and started across the room to the door. The mother-in-law touched Louise's left hand sympathetically as she passed, and Louise smiled at her.

"It'll be all right," Cora Pearson whispered.

"I'm going to go see about Phil," Louise said. "He's in with Shelley right now. They should be done soon."

"Shelley?" I asked.

"Sheldon Sacks. He's Phil's best friend. Sort of a family counselor. He's been seeing Kirsty, too. I mean—he saw her over the summer."

She didn't say it, but he'd also been Estelle Pearson's psychiatrist. I'd seen his name in the newspaper clippings.

"It might help if I could talk to Sacks about Kirsten," I said.

The woman bit her lip. "They don't usually talk about their cases. It would breach their code of ethics."

There was a hint of sarcasm in the way she said "code of ethics." But it was slight compared to the way she'd spoken about her husband's profession the day before. Everything about her had changed slightly from the day before, even her looks. She hadn't made up her eyes or mouth, and she was dressed down in jeans and a white blouse. The sunlight pouring through the undraped window washed her complexion out even further, making her seem younger and more vulnerable. In any light she was strikingly good-looking.

Louise left the room. The elder Mrs. Pearson stared after her with concern.

"She doesn't deserve this," she said in a bitter voice. "She's been such a rock." The woman looked down at the silver tea service as if it were all that remained of the family fortune. "None of us deserve this."

I wasn't sure she was talking to me, so I didn't reply.

Mrs. Pearson poured coffee and, as an afterthought, asked me if I'd like a cup.

"Yes," I said. "I've been living on the stuff for the last thirty hours."

She didn't look impressed.

"There is something you should know," she said, handing me the cup.

"Yes?"

"My son has a heart condition. He doesn't like to dwell on it. He resents illness of any kind, as most doctors do. But the fact is he was hospitalized once already, this past summer when Kirsten acted up. If this current tumult doesn't end soon, the children may succeed in killing him."

She said it as if that was their intention.

"I'm doing what I can to end this, Mrs. Pearson," I said. "But unless we can find them . . ."

She threw a hand at me. "They'll be found. They want to be found. And if no one comes to look for them, they'll make their presences known. Attention is all they want. It's all they've ever wanted. I know whereof I speak. After Estelle's death I had the two of them on my hands for almost a year, until Louise relieved me of the burden. They were spoiled then, and they're spoiled now. No one's life goes smoothly. Do you think my life has gone smoothly? No one made that promise. One picks up and continues."

She sounded like she was reading from that book she was carrying on her head. I could imagine what life had been like at Grandma's.

"Self-indulgence is a sin. Harboring resentment against your father is a sin. My son has sacrificed his life for other people. First when his own father died. And then when Estelle killed herself. He's owed a little peace, a little simple gratitude."

Her face flushed and she turned away. I thought she was overcome with anger until I realized that someone else had entered the room. A paunchy, balding man in a rumpled business suit was standing in the doorway, looking vaguely embarrassed.

"Are you Stoner?" he asked.

I nodded.

"I'm Shelley Sacks." He came in and shook with me.

"Louise'll be along in a minute. She's still talking to Phil."
He glanced at Cora Pearson. "Are you all right, Cora?"

"Fine," the woman said without turning toward him.

The man arched an eyebrow skeptically. He had a round
face, round mouth, snub nose, round blue eyes, a round
bald spot on the back of his head—like a kid's drawing of
Dad. His roly-poly paunchiness made him look younger
than he probably was, judging by the grey in his hair.

"Has there been any news?" he asked me.

"None."

"I guess I don't have to tell you that this isn't a good
situation," he said grimly.

"Do you have any suggestions?"

"I'm not a detective. But from what I've been told I think
it would be a good idea to find this man Ethan has fixated on
—as quickly as possible."

"That's what I intended to do."

"I think you might keep a watch on this house. Perhaps
on Stelle's grave. On places Ethan associates with her."

"Like your office?"

The man looked surprised—unpleasantly so, as if he
didn't like surprises.

"What do you mean?"

"You were Estelle's psychiatrist, weren't you?"

He nodded slowly. "How did you know that?"

I told him about Ethan's clippings.

"That's very sad," he said thoughtfully, as if he found it
more interesting than sad. "Obsessions are always sad. They
trail the past endlessly, like beggar children."

"Obsessions aren't always this dangerous, are they?"

"No. Usually they only damage the one who has them.
Ethan's case is special."

"This may be a stupid question, but is it possible he really
did see someone on the day his mother died?"

"Quite possible. Someone on the street. In a car, in a newspaper photo. It isn't the seeing that's at issue. It's the connection he made to his mother's suicide."

"No question it was suicide?"

He shook his head, no. "Estelle was a deeply disturbed woman. I believe she was fated to end her own life."

I winced at the words—at the echo of Kirsten's words—wondering if Sacks was where she first heard them. It was certainly a convenient way to rationalize your failures.

"I didn't mean to sound cynical," he said, as if he had read my mind. "But there *is* a fatality to mental life, to certain disorders in particular. We can ameliorate schizophrenia, palliate. But we can't cure. In all too many cases, we can't even help."

"In Kirsten's case . . . ?" I asked.

"I don't know," he said. "Obviously it depends on the next few days. She has a fresh insight into her problems. She's regressed at the moment. But if she can channel what she's learned . . ."

The man was being vague, and he knew it.

"It's difficult for me to talk about this," he said apologetically. "You do know that Kirsten is my patient?"

I nodded.

"Let me just say that I'm not without hope."

"That's swell, Doctor, but hope's not going to help me find her."

He smiled. "It may help her find herself."

Louise Pearson came back into the room. All three of us turned toward her, and she flushed prettily, as if she was embarrassed by the attention.

"Phil would like to speak with you now, Mr. Stoner," she said.

"All right."

"We'll talk again," Sacks said, as if my hour was up.

I walked out into the hall. Louise led me to a closed door at the end of the corridor. She paused outside.

"Phil's suffering from certain health problems," she said. "Your mother-in-law told me."

"She shouldn't have," Louise said. But I had the feeling that she was relieved that I knew.

She knocked at the door, and Pearson said, "Come in."

The woman patted me on the shoulder. "I'd like to speak with you again before you leave."

I nodded and went into the room.

It was a study lined with bookshelves and mullioned windows. Pearson was sitting on a leather wingback chair in the center of the room, behind a glass desk with brass-sawhorse legs. Even at a distance I could tell that he was in bad shape. His face was drained of color, except for the dark circles beneath his eyes. His hand trembled when he waved me toward a chair in front of him.

"I'm glad you're here," he said.

"I'm afraid I don't have anything to report yet."

He nodded stupidly. His blue eyes had lost their piercing intensity. His speech was dulled too, as if he were heavily tranquilized.

"The police . . . ?"

"I reported Ethan and Kirsten as missing persons. That's all the police know."

I thought that would please him, but it didn't.

"I've given you the wrong impression," he said, looking pained. "I do that sometimes."

He tried to draw himself up in his chair, grimaced, and slumped back again.

"I want you to find my children. I don't care what it costs or what it takes. I was wrong to react the way I did last night. I was thinking of myself, of my own feelings. You know now that my first wife, Estelle, committed suicide.

The thought of having that tragedy dredged up again and publicized . . . it unnerved me."

"You don't have to apologize."

"I feel that I do. I feel that I owe you an explanation of why I withheld certain facts about Kirsten and Ethan. It was not because I don't love them. On the contrary, I'm afraid that I've loved them too much." The man blushed furiously, as if his love for his children was shameful. "When you lose someone you hold dear, when you lose that person to irrational violence, you hold even more tightly to those who are left behind. I have done that to my children. In trying to protect them I have smothered them. Now I'm afraid that it's my fate to lose them too—to lose all that I love."

Pearson's lips trembled violently.

"It is my failure as a father that I was trying to conceal from you," he said with effort. "It was my failure as a husband that made me a coward."

I shouldn't have said anything at all. But I did. "I think you may be shouldering too much blame."

He shook his head. "You don't know. The children do."

This time I didn't answer him.

"You have a plan of some kind?" Pearson asked.

"To try to find the man from the newspaper before Ethan and Kirsty do. The police will be looking for their car. We'll notify local hotels, hospices, and hospitals. Someone should spot them soon."

"Good. I've canceled my appointments for the week. I'll be here if they decide to come home."

"Do they have any special friends in town?"

"I don't think so," Pearson said. "At least I don't think Kirsty does—she's always been so shy. I haven't seen Ethan in some years."

Pearson stared forlornly at his desk, as if he was struck by the pathos of what he'd just said.

"Find them, Mr. Stoner," he said heavily. "Bring them back. Give me the chance to make amends."

"I'll do all I can," I told him.

After finishing with Pearson I went back down the hall to the living room. Sacks and Cora Pearson had left, and Louise Pearson was sitting alone by the fire. She stood up as I came through the door.

"Thank you again, Mr. Stoner," she said warmly. "For everything."

"I'm working for you. No thanks are necessary."

"Thanks anyway for sticking with us, especially after the mixed signals I gave you yesterday. I was very wrong about Kirsty. I thought she was recovering. Maybe she would have if Ethan hadn't shown up. He's always had a powerful effect on her, although he's never managed to talk her into doing anything this stupid before."

From the disgust in her voice, it was obvious that she had had her fill of her stepson long before Sunday night.

"Ethan's given you trouble in the past?"

"He's been nothing but trouble," Louise Pearson said wearily. "He's never forgiven Phil for Estelle's death. And he never will, in spite of Phil's efforts to bribe him back into the family."

"Your husband gives Ethan money?"

"Since he was a kid. It's all that's left between them—the blood money that Phil gives him every month."

"Why do you call it blood money?" I asked.

She smiled. "I meant the term loosely, though in some way I suppose Phil is compensating Ethan for Estelle's death. And keeping this stupid obsession alive."

"Has Ethan ever been in trouble with the police before now?"

"He hasn't the guts for that," Louise Pearson said with crude satisfaction. "Ethan's not much of a doer, but he's a ferocious, bullying talker. Witness how he twisted Kirsty around his finger."

"I don't think it was Ethan alone that led Kirsten to this," I said. "She's had a rotten year. And last week an important relationship went awry."

"What kind of relationship?"

"A romantic one."

The woman looked surprised. "She was having an affair?"

"She was trying to. There's some question about whether she succeeded. The man . . . he's an older man. A teacher at the university."

"You didn't tell Phil that, did you?" Louise Pearson said with alarm.

"No. I didn't tell him much of anything. He didn't look as if he could take it."

"He can't," Louise Pearson said flatly. "Especially that."

The woman took a step closer to me and I caught her sweet, powerful scent again.

"Mr. Stoner, if things should go wrong, please call me. I mean, before you talk to Phil. He'll need careful handling if Kirsten and Ethan land in real trouble."

She handed me a piece of stationery with a phone number on it.

"That's my private number here at the house. I've got a fairly busy social schedule. If I should be out, an answering service will know where to find me."

I told her I'd call when I had some news.

Leaning forward hesitantly the woman kissed me lightly on the cheek. It wasn't meant to be provocative, but it had

that effect on me. It must not have felt right to Louise
Pearson either, for she pulled away at once.

"I'm sorry," she said, reddening. "I'm feeling a little frail
at the moment. And then I'm a physical sort of person,
anyway."

"It's all right," I said. "I liked it."

She laughed feebly.

"Go," she said, waving her hand down the hall to the
front door. "Before I make a fool out of myself."

12

From the Pearson house I drove downtown to the main branch of the Public Library on Vine Street.

The first-floor periodical room was relatively empty that early on a Monday morning—a couple of earnest-looking college students, a few old-age pensioners, and two or three bums, who'd come in out of the cold and fallen asleep on scattered benches, their shopping bags of belongings rolled up for pillows. I skirted the snoozing bums and got a brief workout running down a fleet-footed librarian, who kept turning corners in front of me as I tracked her through the stacks. Once I ran the woman to ground I asked her for advice on where to begin looking for Ethan Pearson's photograph.

"If the article you're interested in was from a paper purchased in the Ft. Thomas area, you should begin with the *Kentucky Post*," she said. "It has the largest circulation in that part of northern Kentucky. You should also try the *Louisville Courier-Journal* and the *Cincinnati Enquirer*, of course. Many northern Kentuckians read the *Enquirer*."

"Do you keep back issues in circulation?" I asked.

"For seven days, then they're recorded on microfiche." She pointed me to the newspaper stacks and told me to come back if I needed to use a microfiche machine.

I found the Wednesday, December 16, edition of the *Kentucky Post* and read through it slowly. The court news was in the local section, but there were no photos or paragraphs on released felons. I tried the *Courier-Journal* next, without any luck. Then the *Enquirer*. Ethan's mystery man wasn't there—or if he was I wasn't seeing him.

I was very tired, and concentrating on the newsprint was maddeningly difficult. I was worried that the fatigue would cause me to overlook something—and even more worried that Ethan's photo didn't exist. If that was the case I'd have nothing to go on, save the chance that the Volare would be spotted by the cops. That is, if the Pearson kids had come back to Cincinnati, which was no ironclad cinch.

I sat, brooding, at the library table for a full minute, before it dawned on me that the photo didn't have to be in Wednesday's papers. Ethan could have spotted the picture in an older newspaper—a paper from the day before or the day before that. Or it could have been that he'd gone down to the library like I had, and combed through months of back issues. Years of them.

That way lay madness.

I dragged myself to my feet and returned to the stacks. The Tuesday the 15th and Monday the 14th editions of the *Post* were the last two papers on the shelves. Anything before them meant sitting in front of a microfiche machine for hours.

I tried the Tuesday paper first and found nothing.

Then I tried the Monday paper—and got lucky. On the fourth page of the Monday the 14th *Post*, the court news page, there was a tiny mugshot of a middle-aged black man. According to the paragraph beneath the photo his name was Herbert Talmadge, and he'd been released from Lexington the week before on parole, after serving thirteen years of a twenty-to-life sentence for the rape and murder of a Kentucky nurse. The killing had occurred in Newport in December, 1976, and it must have been particularly brutal or they wouldn't have printed Talmadge's picture.

Talmadge was clearly a bad character, and that bothered me. But the newspaper picture itself, the tiny mugshot, was just as unsettling. I sat there and stared at it dumbly for a full minute, wondering whether my lack of sleep and the general weirdness of the Pearson case were combining to unhinge me. Simply put, Herbert Talmadge had the same face as the man in Ethan Pearson's drawing—the same V-shaped goatee, the same pointed chin, the same peppery hair and slanted, menacing eyes.

Even allowing for the crudity of a ten-year-old's drawing skills, the resemblance was close enough to give *me* a feeling of déjà vu. It must have scared hell out of Ethan Pearson. What I couldn't imagine was where a ten-year-old kid had run across the likes of Herbert Talmadge. He *had* to have seen him somewhere, because the likeness he'd drawn was just too damn close to be coincidental.

I made a dozen copies of the article on a Xerox machine. Then I found a phone in the lobby and called Al Foster at CPD.

"I need another favor, Al," I said. "Get me a last known address on an ex-con named Herbert Talmadge. He just did thirteen years in Lexington for rape and murder."

"This have something to do with your missing persons?" he asked.

"It might."

"I'll see what I can turn up."

"One more thing?"

"We're here to serve and protect you, Harry."

"Can you dig up a file on Estelle Pearson?" I spelled the name for him. "She committed suicide in September, 1976. I'd like to see the examining officer's notes and the coroner's report."

"What's this one for?"

I didn't tell him, but I was curious to see if Talmadge's name popped up anywhere in the case as a witness or a bystander. He had to be connected to the woman or to Ethan in some way, even if it was only by chance.

* * *

I went back to my office in the Riorley Building and managed to sneak in a couple of hours of sleep on the couch before the phone woke me around one p.m. At least my eyes felt better. I couldn't speak for the rest of my body—it wasn't speaking to me.

The phone call was from Sid McMasters of the CPD. "Al Foster told me to give you a buzz," Sid said. "We got a previous address for Herbert Talmadge."

I picked up a pencil and said, "Go ahead."

"Sixty-seven fifty-five West McMicken. Al said to tell you that Talmadge was a mental case. In and out of Rollman's before he got busted."

Rollman's was a state psychiatric hospital in East Walnut Hills.

"This McMicken address is from '76?"

"Yeah. Al tried to get in touch with the Newport cops to get a current address. But the P.O. in Newport said Talmadge hadn't reported since his release."

"So he's in violation?"

"He will be if he doesn't come in before this Friday. Al also said for you to pick up a report he dug up for you. I'll leave it at the front desk."

"Be right over."

Before I left I called Louise Pearson at the number she'd given me.

"I need you to ask your husband a couple of questions."

"You've made some progress, then?" she said hopefully.

"A little. I've got a name, at least."

"What name?"

"Herbert Talmadge. I think he's the guy that Ethan and Kirsty are looking for."

The woman went off the line briefly. When she came

back on she said, "Could you repeat that? I want to write this down."

"Herbert Talmadge," I said again. "Ask your husband if he recognizes the name. You might also ask him if he worked at Rollman's hospital in the mid-seventies. I'll drop Talmadge's picture off to you later this evening."

"I'm afraid I'm going to the club this evening," the woman said apologetically. "Goddamn cocktail party. I was planning to cancel, but Phil insisted I attend. Perhaps you could meet me in the bar for a drink afterward. Say, around nine?"

"All right."

She gave me the address of the country club and promised to ask Pearson about Talmadge.

After hanging up on Louise I went down to the Fifth Street garage, found my car, and drove over to CPD headquarters on Ezzard Charles. I double-parked in front of a police cruiser, ran in, and picked up the sealed envelope that Sid McMasters had left for me at the front desk. I didn't open the envelope until I got back in the car.

A photo of Estelle Pearson's body, taken at the scene of her death, was the first thing I pulled out. I was sorry I'd looked. If Ethan or Kirsten had seen what was pictured on that riverbank, it was no wonder they'd been severely traumatized. I stuffed the grisly snapshot back in the envelope and tossed it on the front seat. The police and coroner's reports would have to wait—I just didn't have the stomach to go through them at that moment.

Herbert Talmadge's last known address on West McMicken was only about five minutes north of the police station, off Central Parkway in the slum neighborhood called Over-the-Rhine. As far as I knew Over-the-Rhine had always been a slum—crabbed, dismal, little streets

ined with brick tenements and abandoned warehouses. A
place for German and Irish Catholic immigrants to live at
the turn-of-the-last-century. A place for poor blacks and
Appalachians to live until the turn-of-the-next.

An elderly black man and a young black woman were
sitting on folding chairs in front of 6755. A couple of children were playing in a patch of snow on a nearby stoop.
From the way the kids kept glancing at the man and
woman, I figured they were more or less tethered there,
waiting for the big folks to call them in. I parked across the
street from the brownstone, got out into the sun, and
crossed over to the shaded side of McMicken.

The man and woman watched me closely. The kids
dropped their snowballs and stared.

"I'm looking for somebody who used to live here," I said
to the old man.

The woman snorted disgustedly and turned her chair
away from me, as if she was blocking me from her mind.

The man said, "You with the Welfare?"

" 'Course he with the Welfare, foo," the young woman
said over her shoulder. She looked rather pretty in profile,
in spite of the huff she was in. Pretty and tough and proud.

The man had a porkpie hat tilted back on his head and a
checked overcoat wrapped around his body. His skin was
very black, and his yellowed eyes had the rheumy, un-
focused look of old age. His voice was deep and deliberate,
while the woman's was all speed and contempt.

"I'm not with the Welfare, and I'm not a cop. I'm just a
guy looking for somebody."

"Who'd that be?" the old man said.

"Don' you talk to him, Uncle. Don't you say nothin'," the
young woman snapped.

"His name is Herbert Talmadge. He used to live here
back in the seventies."

"Sho," the man said. "I remember Herbie." He looked at the girl. "You 'member Herbie, Lorraine."

Lorraine continued to stare indignantly off into space.

"Ain't seen Herbie in ten, twelve years," the man said.

"Ain't none of my business," Lorraine said in a singsong voice. "Ain't none of yours neither."

"Don' know where he went to," he said, ignoring her. "Herbie had him a temper, though. I can tell you that."

"He was crazy," the girl said suddenly and decisively, as if that was her only word on the subject.

"She's right," the man said. "Herbie *was* crazy. Think he might have had him some trouble with the law."

"He was in jail," I said. "He was released last week."

"That so? And you huntin' for him, huh?"

I nodded.

"Tell you what. You go look up some of his old girlfriends, 'cause that's where Herbie gone to. He liked the ladies."

"Anybody in particular?"

"Woman who used to own this house, Miz Thelma Jackson. He liked her pretty good. You go on and talk to her."

"Know where I can find her?"

"She moved out to Carthage, I think. Don' come by here no more."

I reached in my pocket for my wallet and started to take a ten out. The old man looked offended.

"Ain't no call for that," he said. "We just talkin' like folks. Don' pay folks for talkin', do you?"

"Thanks," I said.

As I walked back across the street to my car I heard the girl say to him, "You *is* a foo," in a loud, contemptuous voice.

13

I stopped at a phone booth in Clifton and looked up Thelma Jackson in the phone book. I didn't find a "Thelma" proper, but there were several listings for T. Jackson, and one of them lived on Anthony Wayne in Carthage.

I dialed the number and a woman with a deep, friendly voice answered.

"Thelma Jackson?" I asked.

"That's me, sugar. Who's callin'?"

"My name is Stoner, Ms. Jackson. I was wondering if I could talk to you."

"You sellin' something, sugar?" she said cheerfully.

"I'm not selling anything. I'm looking for somebody you used to know."

"Now who'd that be?"

"Herbert Talmadge."

There was a momentary silence on the line.

"You a police officer, ain't you?" she said in a slightly less cheerful voice, as if the mention of Talmadge had knocked some of the fun out of her.

"I'm a private detective."

She laughed. "Like Magnum?"

"Like Magnum. I'm just looking to find Talmadge, Ms. Jackson. I'm not going to arrest him."

"Shoot! It wouldn't bother me any if you did arrest him. Herbie was a mean little son of a gun. But the truth is I ain't seen him in going on fourteen years. Don't want to see him again, neither."

"You think I could come out and talk to you about him? I promise not to take much of your time."

"I guess that'd be all right," she said, "seeing how I ain't never met no detective before."

I could smell Carthage as soon as I got to North Bend Road. The juniper scent of gin, the cooked fruit smell of brandy. The huge brick smokestacks of National Distillers, on the south side of Carthage, left liquor on its breath every afternoon.

Thelma Jackson's house was near the distillery, where the liquor smell was thickest. Perhaps that was what accounted for her good humor. You could see the smokestacks from her front yard. You could also hear the traffic on the expressway, below the retaining wall on the opposite side of Anthony Wayne.

She was sitting on the porch of her bungalow when I pulled up. A plump, sixtyish black woman with short grey hair and a pretty brown face. She was wearing a housedress with a heavy knit sweater over the shoulders.

"You're the detective, ain't you?" she called out as I walked into the small front yard.

"Yep."

"You don't look like Magnum," she said with mock disappointment. "You ain't got no moustache. You big enough though. And good-looking."

She gave me a bold look, for a sixty-year-old woman.

"Come on inside. Too damn cold out here."

Thelma Jackson got up, and I followed her through the front door into a prim living room filled with floral-print furniture. I sat down on an overstuffed couch. A vase full of artificial flowers sat on a coffee table in front of me. The room smelled sweetly of air freshener and the brandy smell of the distillery.

The woman tugged at her girdle before settling on a chair across from me. "Why you all looking for Herbie?"

"Somebody hired me to find him."

"In other words, it ain't none of my business, right?"

I smiled at her. "It isn't a criminal matter—I can tell you that."

"Have to be criminal if it come to that nigger. Either that or he got himself locked up in the crazy house again."

The woman's pretty face turned sober-looking. "Herbie wasn't never right in the head. He'd fool you, though, being so quiet all the time."

"What was his problem?"

"Got no idea. He had brains. Been in the service a couple of years, I think. And he was good-looking, too. Had him plenty of women."

Thelma Jackson glanced at me and laughed.

"You heard somethin' about him and me, didn't you?"

Whether she'd read it in my face or just guessed that that was the gossip which had led me to her house, I didn't know. "I heard you used to be his landlady, yes."

"Heard more than that," she said shrewdly. "But it ain't so. I never did take up with Herbie Talmadge, 'cept once. And that once was enough."

The woman yanked at her girdle again. "Never was no prude. I like men. Always will. But Herbie . . ." She shook her head decisively. "Uhm-uh. Girl could get killed by a man like that. Isn't that what he went to jail for—messing with some woman over in Newport?"

"Yes. Rape and murder."

"Being with Herbie," she said in a dead serious voice, "was always what you call 'rape and murder.' You lucky if you *didn't* die, you spent a night with him. Police had him in and out of Rollman's 'bout every month 'cause he done some woman wrong. Sent him there myself, once. They couldn't do nothing to change him though. He wanted to change. Used to cry about it when he got high. But the

doctors said there just wasn't nothing they could do for
him."

"When was the last time you saw him, Ms. Jackson?"

She squinted her eyes, thinking back. "Seems like that
would be the summer of '76. Right before he moved to
Newport. He got out of Rollman's in the spring and started
taking up with some white girl. Herbie followed that ofay
'round like a dog on a chain. Only time I ever seen him act
that way."

"Do you remember what this woman looked like?"

"Not much. She never come in the house. She was always
waiting on him out in the car. She'd honk and he come
running. She had blond hair, I 'member that. Might be she
was a nurse, 'cause I 'member she wore a white uniform
once. Herbie just crazy about that ofay woman."

"You don't know her name, do you?"

She shook her head. "Didn't want to know. Didn't want
to have nothing to do with Herbie, after that one time."

"Is there anyone who might know? A friend of his from
back then?"

"Herbie didn't have no friends," the woman said with a
dry laugh. "He just have himself."

"Did he have a job?"

"Got him some money from the Vets, I think. Most times
he got hard up, he'd just go on back to the hospital. Rest of
the times he'd lay up in his room, stoned on them painkillers he got from the doctors."

"Finding him is important, Ms. Jackson. Is there anything
else you can remember that would help me?"

"I can poke around," she said gamely. "See what I can dig
up. Meantime, you check with that hospital. They gotta
know something 'bout him, seeing how he was practically a
permanent guest."

* * *

I didn't take Thelma's advice about checking at Rollman's. Not that it wasn't a good idea. I just knew from experience that no one at a hospital was going to talk to a private cop without word from somebody higher up. So I went searching for that word at Sheldon Sacks' office on Burnett, a couple blocks east of the psychiatric hospital and just a few blocks north of where I used to live in the Delores.

Sacks' office was on the second floor of a duplex he shared with another psychiatrist. There was a hall at the top of the stairs, with office doors opening off it to the left and a small, glassed-in receptionist's room to the right. I gave the secretary my name and she told me that she'd buzz Sacks when his four o'clock appointment was up. In the meantime I took a seat in a wainscoted waiting room, beside a couple of middle-aged women who were doing their best to keep from screaming.

Just sitting there made me queasy. When the secretary finally called my name, I jumped. She led me back down the hall to one of the office doors and knocked. Sacks called out, "Come in."

"Sorry to have kept you waiting, Stoner," he said as I came through the door.

He waved me over to a stuffed leather chair then sat down behind a large desk. There was a half-empty box of Kleenex on an end table by the chair. Half-full or half-empty—I could never see the fucking difference.

There were a dozen Kleenex on the floor, as if his last patient had had a real crying jag.

The room was paneled in oak and lined with bookshelves on two walls. There was a psychiatrist's couch on the third wall with a framed steamship floating above it. Sacks' desk was on the far wall, in front of a bank of louvered windows.

Just enough sunlight was filtering through the slats to back-light his head and throw his face into shadow.

"What can I do for you?" he asked.

I told him about Herbert Talmadge. He listened intently, moving forward in his chair so that a bit of his round face came into the desk light.

"When did you say he was treated at Rollman's?"

"1976. Possibly earlier."

"That's odd," he said thoughtfully. "I think Phil did part of his residency at Rollman's, in '75."

"Perhaps he treated Talmadge?"

"It's possible," Sacks said, joining his hands.

I waited for him to say something more, but he didn't. He just sat there with his hands knitted together and a blank look on his face, as if he hadn't drawn any conclusions from what he'd said.

"You and Pearson are close friends?"

He nodded. "Since med school. He and Stelle and I were in the same graduating class."

"She was a psychiatrist, too?"

"She never started her internship. She married Phil in 1966 right after we graduated. She had Ethan at the end of that year."

"She didn't go back to school?"

He shook his head. "She wanted to, but her emotional problems made it impossible."

"She was never hospitalized at Rollman's, was she?"

"No. At Jewish and at Holmes."

He wasn't comfortable talking about the woman, and he wasn't trying to disguise it. Given the circumstances, his reticence irritated me.

"Is there a reason you don't want to talk to me about Estelle Pearson?" I said.

The man sighed. "No one likes to talk about his failures,

Mr. Stoner. Especially when that failure involves people whom you love."

He leaned back in his chair, tenting his fingers in front of his face. "It has been thirteen years since Estelle died, and in all those years I don't think a day has passed that I haven't thought about her. Estelle wasn't just my patient. She was my friend."

I was wrong about Sacks. It wasn't professional reticence, at all.

"I am sorry," I said.

"You have no reason to be. You're just doing your job. But for Philip and Louise and me, this is a very painful thing. A tragic thing."

"Pearson seems to blame himself for what's happened," I said.

"He has his reasons, Mr. Stoner," Sheldon Sacks said without elaborating.

I changed the subject back to Ethan and Kirsten. "The picture that Ethan drew in 1976 looks very much like this man Talmadge."

"Perhaps it was Talmadge," the doctor said. "Ethan may have visited his father at Rollman's. He may have seen Talmadge in the halls or on the grounds."

"Yes, but why would he associate the man with his mother's death?"

"Ethan was very close to Estelle. And she, to him. Right before her death Estelle went through an extended manic period, which lasted almost two months. During that time she appeared to regain a good deal of her energy and focus. To the boy it must have seemed as if she was recovering— that he himself had made a difference in her recovery, as in fact he probably did. The manic stage ended abruptly and the depression returned with a vengeance. Estelle's death following so hard upon that brief period of apparent recov-

ery made Ethan feel as if he had somehow failed his
mother. It was my feeling then, and it is my feeling now,
that his obsession is his way of making amends for letting his
mother down. He has sublimated his own guilt and pro-
jected it onto this man, Herbert Talmadge."

"But why Talmadge?"

"Why not?" Sacks said. "His face may have frightened
Ethan. It stuck in his memory. In his confusion over the loss
of his mother he made it the face of his own guilt."

It was neat and logical. But I wasn't sure I believed it. In
my experience people didn't generally remember anonymous faces in that kind of detail—not unless there was a
strong emotional spur to prod their imagination. Like a
loaded gun, or the threat of one.

I didn't debate it with him. I didn't feel confident enough
to debate. But I did ask him if he could arrange for me to
talk with the staff at Rollman's about Talmadge. And he said
that he would call them immediately.

Before leaving I asked one last question. It had bothered
me since Marnee Thompson had mentioned it, and although Kirsten was still his patient I asked him anyway.

"Kirsten told a friend of hers that you gave her some
Pentothal this summer while she was in therapy. Apparently the drug made her remember something about Estelle—something that really shook her up."

"But her memory wasn't about Estelle," the man said
with an open look of fascination. "It was about Philip."

"I don't suppose you'd like to tell me what it was?"

The open look vanished like a dent closing in dough.

"I guess not," I said.

"She's my patient, Mr. Stoner," Sacks said.

I nodded. "She may not be anyone's patient much longer,
Dr. Sacks."

But he didn't say anything.

14

I gave Sacks about half an hour to make his calls to Rollman's. At five-forty I walked across Burnett to the Rollman
grounds. Up in one of the barred third-story windows I
could see a bald man in a white hospital gown watching me
cross the lawn. His queer, drugged-looking face was lit
strangely by the last of the sunset. Even at that distance I
could see his dead eyes following me as I walked into the
shadows at the front of the building.

I wondered if I could remember that face in detail, a few
weeks or months from that moment. Maybe if I was an
impressionable ten-year-old kid, I could have. Maybe I
could have anyway.

From the front Rollman's looked like a high school—red-
brick facade, oblong windows with white trim and glass
double-doors. But the windows were barred and meshed,
and the doors had buzzers on them. I pressed one of the
buzzers and an orderly peered out.

"Visiting hours over, mister," he said.

"My name's Harry Stoner," I said. "Your director should
know who I am."

The orderly gave me a suspicious look, as if he thought I
might be an escapee. He closed the door and walked down
the hall. When he reappeared, the suspicion was gone from
his face.

"Come on," he said, holding the door open. "Dr. McCall
says you can go up."

I followed him down the tile hall. There were tall barred
windows at the end of it. The last daylight pouring through

them was so bright that both of us had to shield our eyes against the glare.

"You take this elevator up to three," he said, pointing to a grey elevator beside the windows. "Nurse upstairs, show you where to go."

I got in the elevator and pressed three. I hadn't noticed it in the lobby hall, but the elevator smelled ripely of disinfectant and stale, recirculated air.

The third floor was an administrative area, judging from the empty typing carrels off the elevator. I followed an arrow sign around a bend in the hallway to the Director's Office. An elderly nurse with grey hair and a stern, wrinkled face was sitting at a desk in front of the office door. A Norfolk pine decorated with tinsel and greeting cards sat on the floor beside her.

"You're Mr. Stoner?" she said, looking up at me.

I nodded.

"Dr. McCall will see you. Just go through there."

I went into the office. It was a large room, mostly taken up with file cabinets and bookshelves. A red-haired man with a horsey face, horn-rim glasses, and buck teeth was sitting behind a desk at the far wall. He was wearing a doctor's smock with a stethoscope hanging from one of the side pockets. His pale skin was lumpy with ancient acne scars. He fingered one of the lumps idly as I walked up to him.

"You're Stoner?" the man said in a businesslike voice.

"Yes."

"Sam McCall."

McCall motioned me to a wooden chair.

There was a manila folder on his desktop. He put two fingers on top of it as if he was taking its pulse.

"This is what you came for, I think," he said, jabbing the folder. "You know we're not supposed to let you see this.

We're not supposed to show it to anyone other than a physician."

"I guess Dr. Sacks told you it's an unusual case."

McCall nodded. "I'm a friend of Phil Pearson's, too. That's why I'm going to let you read through this. But if the matter should somehow end up in court, nothing that you see in here is admissible evidence. Nothing."

He jabbed the folder hard to emphasize his point.

He came out from behind the desk. "I'm going to make nightly rounds. That usually takes a couple of hours. When I come back, the folder goes in the file cabinet. Agreed?"

"Agreed," I said.

"If you need anything else, ask my receptionist, Nurse Rostow."

He went out of the room, leaving the manila folder on his desk.

It took me about an hour and a half to go through Herbert Talmadge's file. Parts of it I couldn't decipher—pages of notes written like a prescription in a doctor's crabbed hand. But a good deal of it had been transcribed by a typist, and those parts made chilling reading.

Talmadge had first been admitted to Rollman's in December 1974, after beating and sodomizing a teenage girlfriend. The examining doctor's diagnosis was acute schizophrenia.

Subject is an intelligent black man, 28 years old, a high school graduate with three years military service. Subject released from military in 1974, after suffering anxiety attacks and hallucinatory episodes. Subject referred to Veterans Administration Hospital, November 1974, diagnosed as schizophrenic, and allowed disability pension.

Subject was remanded to RPI by court order, 3 December, 1974, after attacking a woman friend with a handsaw. Subject has no memory of the attack. Subject maintains the woman is lying, that he has never harmed a woman . . .

Subject fantasizes himself a ladies' man and claims he only does what women want him to do. Subject refuses to speak in detail about hallucinatory episodes.

Talmadge was committed to Rollman's four more times over the next year—each time following a sadistic attack on a woman friend. He was invariably released after a week of observation—perhaps because the girlfriends had dropped the charges against him, perhaps because they had no room for him at Rollman's or no real interest in his care and cure.

In August of 1975, he was committed to Rollman's for a fifth time by Thelma Jackson, his landlady. The interesting part of the '75 episode was the fact that the attending psychiatrist was Phil Pearson, then a senior resident at Rollman's.

Pearson's notes weren't any different from any of the other examining psychiatrists'. He referred to Talmadge's intelligence, his denial of guilt, his refusal to speak in detail about psychotic episodes. There was some speculation about Talmadge's childhood, with the strong suggestion that incest with his mother may have precipitated his psychosis.

I had hoped to find that Pearson was still the attending psychiatrist during Talmadge's last stay at Rollman's, in the spring of 1976. But he wasn't. A Dr. Isaac Goldman had taken over the case.

Either Goldman was more persistent than Pearson or just plain smarter, because for the first time in three years of being shuffled in and out of psychiatric wards Herbert Talmadge spoke freely about himself. Most of his confession seemed to have been dictated to Goldman and another doctor with the initials R.S.

HT: I ain't got nothing against woman in general. But some women just ain't right.

IG: How do you know when they're "not right"?

HT: You shouldn't try to trick me into talking about her.

RS: We're not trying to trick you, Herbert. You told me you wanted to talk about her.

HT: She won't like it.

RS: I would though.

HT: All right. It's my mama that tells me these things. She knows.

IG: Why does she know?

HT: 'Cause of her own wickedness.

IG: Your mother was wicked?

HT: What you call it? Making me do that stuff to her?

IG: What stuff?

HT: You damn well know what stuff. You read my mind, anyway. You see it yourself. I see it in you.

IG: What do you see in me?

HT: Same wickedness in me. I see some bitch wanta spend my money, take my manhood. Party! Well, all right, then. Let's party. I put that fist in her ass, she don't party so good. When it start to hurt, I get . . .

IG: What?

HT: I just want to . . . go all the way, man. Rip it up. All the way.

There were six or seven more pages like that, some of it a lot worse.

After plowing through thirty or forty pages of denials and silence I was astonished that Talmadge had opened up as he had. Perhaps Goldman or the other doctor, R.S., had given him Pentothal. I didn't know. But once he started talking Talmadge didn't want to stop. And what he had to say should have been enough to have him committed for life— sent to Longview or some state hospital for the criminally insane.

And yet he hadn't been committed. Instead he'd been released by Goldman a month later. I stared at the release form, signed by Goldman, initialed by R.S., and couldn't quite believe my eyes.

Six or seven months after that Talmadge had brutally murdered a woman in Newport, and this time he didn't get sent to Rollman's. This time he'd gone to a Kentucky prison for thirteen years. Thirteen years in a cell, with all that craziness cooking inside him.

I was no longer bothered by why Ethan Pearson had happened to pick Herbert Talmadge's face out of the crowd. A child would have had no trouble sensing what was going on behind that face, even if he'd only seen it staring at him, dead-eyed and numb, from behind a barred window. What bothered me a lot was that he *had* chanced to pick that face—that he and his sister were now looking for the man with that face. I could only hope they didn't find him or that the cops or I found him first.

15

When I finished I took Talmadge's folder out to the reception desk and handed it to McCall's grey-haired secretary, Ms. Rostow.

"Thank your boss for me."

"I will," she said.

She spun around in her chair and socked the folder away in a drawer, slamming it shut as if she was filing her resignation.

"How long have you worked here, Ms. Rostow?"

"Since 1965," she said, swiveling back around to face me.

"Do you know Dr. Isaac Goldman?"

"Certainly."

"Is he still on staff here?"

"He never was," she said. "Dr. Goldman and several of his colleagues rotated through here in the mid-seventies, as part of an intern-exchange program with Washington University in St. Louis."

"Do you happen to remember if either of his colleagues had the initials R.S.?"

"No, they did not. The other two interns from St. Louis were Stanley Lee and Calvin Minard."

"Can you think of another staffer from around that time with those initials?"

The woman laughed fecklessly. "We've had a lot of staff changes in thirteen years, Mr. Stoner. You can't expect me to remember all of them. Is it important?"

"Probably not. Did Goldman go back to St. Louis after interning here?"

"Yes. He has a practice in Creve Coeur. We get a card from him each year at the holidays."

The woman pointed to the tinseled dwarf pine decorated with Christmas cards.

"All of our doctors remember us at Christmas," she said with a pleasant smile.

It was almost eight o'clock when I left Rollman's. I headed east to I-71 and Indian Hill. It was a thirty-minute drive to Louise Pearson's country club on Camargo, which meant I was going to be a bit early for our meeting. But I didn't feel like sitting in a chili parlor for an extra half hour, brooding about Herbert Talmadge. I needed to move around, I also needed a drink.

The club was in a woods off Camargo Pike. I had probably passed it a couple of hundred times the day before, when I was looking for Woodbine Lane. The guy manning the gate had my name—and my number, judging from the way he eyed me and the beat-up Pinto. He made me show ID before waving the car through.

The clubhouse was about a half-mile past the gate, down a tar road that cut between the ninth and tenth holes of a moonlit golf course. I heard music before I saw the building —a jazz combo playing "Sentimental Journey." The horn echoed across the golf course, cutting through the cold clear night like taps in a drill yard.

I parked the Pinto in a crowded lot, squeezing in between a Mercedes and a Bentley. As I walked up to the clubhouse I passed a couple making out in a dark car. He was wearing a tux and she was wearing a chiffon evening gown, pearls, and a fur wrap. Aside from that they were doing it pretty much like the rest of us do. Though when I went by the woman winked invitingly—so I might have been wrong.

The club was large and preposterous-looking, half field-stone Romanesque and half redwood A-frame, like a dowager with a fade haircut. The stone and masonry part abutted the golf course. It had been around for a long while, probably since the twenties. The A-frame part, where all the music was coming from, fronted the road and was obviously a new addition. Two silver spruces, twinkling with colored Christmas lights, flanked the tall A-frame door.

I stepped through that door into a Christmas party. The vaulted atrium was decorated with streamers and filled with men and women in evening dress. They didn't exactly stare as one when I came in. But I got enough funny looks to send me scurrying to the far end of the room, where the glow of a lighted bar caught my eye.

The bar was actually in a separate room, through smoked-glass doors that shut out most of the buzz of conversation and too much of the music. It was dark and cozy and empty in the bar. I sat down on a leather stool and asked the red-vested bartender for The Glenlivet, straight up. Up the rail from me a tall, stocky, red-faced man in a tux, the only other person in the place, toyed with a bowl of Spanish peanuts and stared at me openly.

I'd been in enough bars in my life to know when a guy was looking for trouble. The one in the tux was.

"You're not a member here, are you?" he said after a time. His voice was loud and officious-sounding.

I turned in his direction. "You taking a poll?"

He pretended to laugh. "I'm just wondering what you're doing here, that's all."

He was probably having trouble with a woman. And if he wasn't he deserved to be. But it was his bar, so I kept it polite.

"I'm waiting for someone."

The man parked his elbows on the bar behind him and stared at me across his left shoulder. "Who?"

"Who, what?"

"Who are you waiting for?"

I glanced at the bartender but he looked away quickly, as if he didn't want any part of trouble with the guy in the tux.

"I'm waiting for Louise Pearson. Dr. Phil Pearson's wife."

The man threw his head back slightly and opened his mouth as if he was going to laugh. But no sound came out. He stood like that for half a second, gape-mouthed, staring at the ceiling. Then he closed his mouth and looked back across his shoulder at me.

"Are you her new one?"

I started to get angry. "What's that supposed to mean?"

"Her new stud. Mister December."

"What's the matter, fella? She didn't like you hitting on her?"

He swung around on his left elbow, so he was facing me. "Louise likes to be hit on, *fella*. Don't you know that?"

I stared at him.

The bartender slapped his towel on the bar. He was an older man with a grey moustache and a heavily lined face.

"Take it outside, mister," he said to me. "Take it outside or I call the cops."

The guy in the tux laughed. "Forget about it, Pete. He's not going to try anything."

But the bartender knew better. "Take it outside," he said again.

I swallowed the rest of my drink and left.

I was working my way through the crowd, looking for Louise Pearson, when she found me. I heard a woman call my name, turned around, and saw her standing a few feet away, smiling.

"Hi," I said, smiling back.

"Hi, yourself."

She was wearing a midnight-blue evening gown with a modest slit in the leg and a modest plunge at the breast. She looked terrific.

"I thought I saw you go into the bar. In fact I was going to go in after you."

"I think we better steer clear of the bar."

She gave me a confused look. "Why?"

"Not important. I don't have anything new to report anyway. Go back to your party."

"I don't feel like partying." She stared at me for a second curiously, trying to make out what it was that was bothering me about the bar. Then she shrugged. "If you're going to leave I'll come with you. You can drive me home."

"You're not going to like my car."

"I'll take that chance."

Louise picked up a mink wrap in a cloakroom by the door. Together we walked out to the lot. As we made our way through the parked cars she passed her arm through mine.

"What's the matter?" she asked. "Did somebody say something to you in the bar?"

"Nope. It's just been a long day, and I didn't feel like a party."

"Neither did I," she said with a dismal laugh. "I shouldn't have come. I wouldn't have come if Phil hadn't insisted."

She got a peevish look on her face. "Phil always knows what's best for other people. That's why he's in such good shape right now."

Her mood had obviously changed since the morning, back to the tensions of the previous day.

"How's he holding up?"

"About the same," she said indifferently.

Louise eased her arm away from mine as if talking about her husband had made her feel self-conscious. She didn't say anything for a while.

"You must already know that we're not the perfect couple. I mean you must have sensed that."

I didn't say anything.

When she saw the car she started to laugh. "God, you weren't kidding about this thing."

"It's old, but it's game."

I opened the passenger side door and she slipped in. I got in on my side, started the engine, and headed up the access road to Madeira. Neither of us said a word as we drove back to Woodbine Lane.

I pulled up in the driveway behind her husband's Mercedes. Louise turned in the seat to face me.

"Come in," she said in her peremptory way. "We'll have that drink."

"All right."

None of the downstairs lights was lit, but there was a lamp on upstairs in a front room. Louise glanced at it.

"He should be asleep," she said irritably. "He promised me he'd try to sleep."

"He's worried," I said.

"He's panicking," she said with a trace of disgust.

Louise unlocked the door and flipped on a hall light. "I'll go up and put him to bed. You might as well make us some drinks. The lights in the living room are on the left and the liquor is in a red Chinese cabinet by the sideboard. Fix yourself whatever you want, and fix me a martini."

She didn't wait for an answer. She went up the stairs to tend her husband.

I walked down to the living room, found the lights and the liquor, and made a couple of drinks. I took them over to the red leather chairs by the fireplace, putting the martini down on an oval end table. The fire had almost burned out. I stirred it with a poker and got it going again, like the man of the house.

Ten minutes passed before Louise came into the room. She had changed back to the outfit she'd been wearing that afternoon—white blouse and jeans. She looked just as good as she had in the evening gown. Maybe a little better because the denim suited her ripe body.

"I think I've calmed him down," she said, sitting across from me. She picked up the martini and took a sip, staring at me over the rim of the glass. "He won't get much sleep, though. I don't think he'll really sleep until this is over."

I said, "You do know that there's a strong chance it won't work out."

"I've known that for years."

"I meant finding Ethan and Kirsty."

"I know what you meant," Louise said drily. "By the way, Phil did remember that man, Talmadge. He was a patient at Rollman's when Phil did his residency there in '75. Phil couldn't remember anything specific about the case though."

"I looked into it this afternoon. Talmadge is dangerous."

She looked alarmed. "You mean dangerous to Phil?"

"To the children."

"Christ, I pray it doesn't come to that," she said. "I'm half hoping that they're just doing this to make Phil and me sweat."

"Why would they do that to you?"

"Because they don't like me very much," she said with an unhappy smile. "Neither one has ever really forgiven me for trying to play Mom after Estelle died. I don't really blame them, given the circumstances."

But her voice sounded resentful. She heard it herself and

made a contrite face. "You didn't bargain on a family like this one, did you, Stoner? We must look like lunatics to you."

"You have problems," I said.

"It's worse than that, and you know it. We've screwed it all up, Phil and I." Her beautiful face filled with disgust, and she took a quick drink to cover her revulsion. "This thing has sent us back thirteen years. Back to a place where I didn't want to go. Back to feelings I don't want to relive."

"You want to talk about it?"

"You mean you want to hear more Pearson craziness?"

"I want to hear about you."

She lowered the martini glass down and ran a finger around the edge, making it sing.

"All right," she said after a time. "I feel like talking. Just don't analyze, okay? I've had my fill of that for one lifetime."

Louise set the glass down at her feet. "I wasn't what you would call inexperienced when I met Philip. I'd been married before—to the wrong man. Frank was a beauty but he didn't believe in work. At least, he didn't believe that *he* should have to work. He wasn't so fussy when it came to my time. After the divorce I started looking for someone else. Someone with a different set of priorities. Someone I could build a new life with. This kind of life."

She glanced approvingly around the handsome, genteel room.

"Philip seemed like the one. He came from a wealthy family. He had a promising career. He could be sweet and smart and sensitive, even if he did sometimes act as if he owned the keys to everyone else's psyche. And he was terribly unhappy with his marriage and talking divorce. He'd already gone through several affairs when we met. On the surface he looked like the perfect catch."

She sat back in the chair with a sigh. "But Phil wasn't the

strong, competent, sensitive guru he pretended to be. That part of his personality was designed to impress his clients for one hour a week. The rest of him, the part I had to learn to live with, was still stuck in childhood like everybody else."

Her face bunched up, as if she didn't like the carping sound of her voice. "Oh, hell, that's not fair. It's not Phil's fault that he's built the way he is. The past's not anyone's fault. It's just there, like the moon and the stars. Phil's good, rich family wasn't a very happy one, that's all. You've met Cora. She's a prissy, spoiled woman, but she can be dealt with. At least, I can deal with her. It was her husband, Phil's father, Arthur, who was the real joker."

"He's dead?"

"For years. Art was a weak, wifty drunk. He keeled over when Phil was just a teenager. But not before leaving his mark on Phil."

"His mark?"

Louise looked over at the fire. "I'm not a hundred percent positive of this. I mean nobody's ever said it outright, but I'm reasonably sure that Phil was abused by his father."

She shuddered down her spine. "Pretty awful, huh?"

"It happens," I said. "Even in good families."

"I'm sure it does. But when you marry someone who's hiding that sort of thing in his past . . . it has an effect. Living with a man like Phil—a man with an overwhelming need to dominate in small matters and to be constantly reassured about the important ones—can wear you down, especially if you're not well equipped to handle your own needs. I guess I'm strong enough to take it. At least, everyone has automatically made that assumption about me. But his first wife, Estelle, wasn't."

"Did you know her?"

"I feel like I did through talking to Phil and the kids,

through living the same kind of life. Poor Estelle, she tried to accommodate Phil—dropping out of school, abandoning her career before it even got started, having children she probably didn't want, nurturing Phil when he needed nurturing, eating his all-knowing psychiatrist's crap when he didn't. After ten years of that she finally broke apart."

She made it sound as if Pearson had caused the woman's breakdown. "Estelle had emotional troubles all her life, didn't she?"

"That's what Dr. Shelley Sacks would have us believe. But Phil was his friend, too, you know."

"Meaning?"

"Meaning maybe there was a little ex post facto rationalization there, to spare Phil some guilt. I don't know. I know it hasn't spared me any. You see Phil and I had just started our affair when . . ."

Her face reddened, and she looked away from me.

"When Estelle died." I said it for her.

She nodded, her face still turned. "She didn't know, of course. She was too far gone by then to care, anyway. About me, or any of the others that had preceded me. The nurses and secretaries. But *I* knew. I was actually with Phil when he heard that her body had been found."

She shuddered again. "For a year or so after that we really did need each after. Then it was all guilt. We married to assuage the guilt. We've stayed together to hide it."

Louise turned back to me. "And now you know another one of our little secrets. I've tried to be a good wife, a good stepmother. I got what I wanted, didn't I? All this." She waved her hand around the room, then dropped it in her lap. "I have affairs. He has his work. You know the funny thing is he's extremely good at his job—he has an instinct about other people's weaknesses. It gives him the chance to be strong, to dominate." She made a muscle and laughed ironically. "It isn't like that upstairs."

She hadn't mentioned the children. So I did. "His concern for Ethan and Kirsty seems genuine."

She nodded. "It is. Ethan wasn't his fault. He lost him to Estelle when she died. It was her revenge on him, I think. But Kirsty . . . God, how he's tried to make amends to her."

"Amends for what?"

She shook her head. "Enough family history."

Leaning forward she kissed me softly on the mouth. I started to draw her to me, but she pulled away. She put a finger to my lips and ran it slowly down to my chin.

"I like you," she whispered. "After this is over we'll have to do something about that. Until then . . ."

She came close again. "Keep this in mind."

She kissed me again passionately. Then she got up and walked out of the room, leaving me and the fire slowly burning down.

16

It was a long drive back to the apartment on Ohio Avenue. I tried not to think about Louise. But it was hopeless. For better or worse she was part of it for me now—part of the strange legacy of the Pearson case. The case I wasn't going to make personal.

It was past twelve when I got to Ohio Avenue. As I was getting out of the car I remembered the envelope Sid had left for me, Estelle Pearson's last remains. I picked it up off the backseat and took it inside, tossing it on the couch in the living room.

The light on my answering machine was lit, but I didn't play the messages back. I was too tired for business. I was too tired to think about anything. I sat on the couch, with poor Estelle sitting there beside me, and dreamed about the other Mrs. Pearson—the one who'd never quite been able to take her place.

Sometime during the night I must have wandered into the bedroom, because that's where I found myself when the telephone woke me. It was still dark outside, and it had turned very cold. Shivering, I fumbled for the receiver on the nightstand.

"Stoner?" a half-familiar voice said. "It's Al Foster."

"Yeah, Al," I said groggily.

"We've got something for you."

I struggled to sit up. I was still wearing my clothes—or trapped in them. My shirttail was wrapped in the bedding and I had to wrench it loose to straighten up. I glanced at the clock, which was showing 6:15.

"You listening, Harry?" Al said.

"I'm here, for chrissake. What?"

"We found the car—the grey Volare. The Miamitown police came across it about fifteen minutes ago. It was parked on an embankment of the Miami River."

It took me a second to remember that Estelle Pearson's body had been found in the Miami River. It took me another second to realize that Al hadn't mentioned Kirsty and Ethan, that he'd only mentioned the car.

"What about the Pearson children?" I asked.

Al fetched a sigh that sent a chill down my back.

"There's some indication they may have run into trouble."

"What indication?"

"Harry, I'm just relaying what I was told when this was called in a few minutes ago. If you want details you're going to have to go out there yourself and talk to the examining officers."

He gave me an address on Miamitown Road and the name of a cop—Sergeant Larry Parker. Before hanging up I asked whether the Pearsons had been notified.

"I don't know what the Miamitown cops have done," Al said. "But you're the only person we've contacted."

"Keep it that way," I told him. "At least until after I've had a chance to talk to Parker."

"It's your case," he said.

It took me about thirty minutes to drive to Miamitown on the western side of Hamilton County near the Indiana line. It really wasn't much of a town—just a flat stretch of road dotted with Quonset bars, brick storefronts, and one squat diamond-shaped municipal building with a flagpole and a plugged howitzer arranged in front of it like a place setting. There was enough light growing in the sky to backlight the pines on top of the tall forested ridge east of town. I knew that the Great Miami ran beneath the ridge, in a steep, overgrown embankment that was still sunk in darkness. The flashing squad car lights led me to the right spot, a cluster of them blinking like tiny blue Christmas ornaments netted in the pines. I had to turn onto a gravel access road to get to where the cops were parked, past a tin-roofed bait shop, down a short bumpy slope to a dirt clearing above the river.

The Volare was at the back of the clearing—its front wheel resting on some rocks beyond the dirt, where the hill began its slide to the embankment. The car canted down slightly as if someone had parked it there in a rush. Two Miamitown police cruisers were parked on either side of it, and a third cop cruiser was parked behind. I pulled in next to the third cruiser and got out.

Even in the darkness I could see pale foot trails leading away from the clearing, down the hillside to the river. The packed dirt glistened in the half light like a length of bone. A couple of officers with flashlights were making their ways along the trails. The dirt must have been slippery, because the flashlight beams bounced and whirled crazily in the dark—lighting tree trunks, bits of scrap iron, the red staring eyes of a possum. I could hear the river beneath the clearing, coursing over rocks and fallen limbs, running fast and deep with winter snow.

A third cop, a tall stocky man wearing a billed cap and gold patches on his down coat, was standing at the lip of the hill, directing the other two down the trails. He'd stopped to watch me when I got out of the car. After a time he walked over to where I was standing.

"Unless you've got a reason to be here," he said, "you'd best leave."

He had a deep voice—a tough voice. But some of its effect

was lost to the bitter cold. He shivered as he stood there, shifting from foot to foot like a man holding his water.

"My name's Stoner," I said to him. "I'm a P.I. Al Foster of the CPD just called about the Volare. The car is part of a missing persons case I'm working on."

"I thought the name was Pearson," the man said suspiciously. "That's the name we got on the APB."

"That's the name of the family I'm working for. You can get in touch with Mrs. Pearson if you want to check me out."

"Already talked to her," the man said, shifting feet.

"Christ," I said to myself. To the cop, I said, "Exactly what did you tell her?"

He thought about it for a moment. "Better see some ID first." He glanced over at the squad car, as if it were a photo of home. "Maybe we should do it inside, where it's light."

And warm, I said to myself.

I followed him to the cruiser and got in on the passenger side. The man started the engine and flipped on the heater and the overhead light. I could see his name tag for the first time. It read "L. Parker."

I gave Parker my ID. He studied it for a moment then handed it back, flipping off the courtesy light with his other hand.

"We found the car about an hour ago," he said, nodding at the Plymouth. "One of the men was making a routine run down Miamitown when he saw headlights here in the hollow."

"The headlights were left on?"

"A pretty good time, too," the cop said. " 'Cause when he tried to start the car up she wouldn't turn over."

"I take it the keys were in the car."

He nodded. "And these."

He reached into the backseat and pulled out a clear

plastic evidence bag with a pair of stained panties in it. I couldn't tell in the darkness, but the stains looked like blood.

My heart sank. "These were in the Plymouth?"

"On the floor in the back. The panties got a tag in them from a Chicago store—Milady's."

"The missing girl went to school in Chicago."

"That's what the wife said." He ducked his head guiltily. "She seemed like a nice woman. I hated like hell to break this news to her."

I hated it like hell, too. I could scarcely imagine how Phil Pearson had reacted to the news.

"Have you dusted the car for prints?" I asked Parker.

"We're waiting for the State Patrol to send down a criminalistics team. Called it in a goddamn hour ago." He shrugged. "But that's State for you."

He reached into his jacket and pulled out a pack of cigarettes, shaking one out and sticking it in his mouth in a single motion. He offered the pack to me and I said no.

"I guess I should quit," he said, flipping open a silver Zippo and lighting up.

I stared through the windshield at the twisting flashlight beams, shooting up from below the lip of the hill. In the distance the dawn was starting to break above the ridge, purpling the horizon like a fresh, spreading bruise.

"There was nothing else in the car?" I said. "Nothing that a *man* might have carried or worn?"

Parker shook his head, breathing out a thick cloud of grey tobacco smoke. "Just the panties." He gestured toward the windshield. "We're looking down there now for anything else we can turn up. I doubt we'll find much in the dark." He squinted into the dawn light. "When the sun comes up we'll call in some help."

17

I drove straight from Miamitown to Indian Hill. By the time I got to Camargo Pike, it was full morning, grey and turbulent, with a sting of snow already in the air. As I neared Woodbine Lane, an ambulance blew past me, turning west on Camargo, blinkers flashing. I couldn't see inside the ambulance, but I had the awful feeling it was racing Phil Pearson to the hospital.

I knew I was right when I got closer to the Pearson house. Another ambulance—a red emergency vehicle—was parked in the driveway behind a green Porsche 935 and a tan Merc. The tan car belonged to Cora Pearson. I didn't know who belonged to the Porsche.

I parked on the street to keep from blocking the driveway, and walked slowly up to the front door. A tall, handsome man with tan skin and thick grey hair answered my knock. Behind him, down the hall, I could hear Cora Pearson crying.

"I'm Harry Stoner," I said to the grey-haired man. "I work for the Pearsons."

The man smiled as if he recognized my name, flashing a set of teeth so large and white and perfect-looking that I thought, at once, they must be caps. "I'm Saul Lasker," he said in a deep, genial voice. "A friend of Louise and Phil's. Friend and neighbor."

He nodded up the street to another estate house. All I could see of it was the red tile of its roof, billowing like a circus tent behind a protective screen of spruce.

I'd heard of Lasker—at least, I'd seen his name on the financial pages. He was very big in real estate and investment banking. Very big, very rich, very Reagan-Republican. I didn't like him on principle. His kind of money was always tainted with someone else's pain.

"What happened here, Lasker?"

The man tried to stop smiling. But his face wasn't used to bad news. "Phil had an attack about ten minutes ago." He touched the place on his chest where his heart was supposed to be and fought with the smile some more. "I heard the ambulances and came over. He was in the living room when it happened."

"Do you have any idea how bad the attack was?"

"Not good. Louise went with him to the hospital. I'm going to drive Cora over there in a few minutes and try to lend some support, although I guess there's nothing we can do now but pray."

He said it as if it was something he'd heard in a movie.

"What hospital did they take him to?"

"Bethesda North, I think."

"You're not sure?"

"Bethesda North," he said, sounding a little more like twenty million bucks.

I caught the expressway to Reed-Hartman. The hospital was on the east side of the highway—a big glass-and-steel tower, rising out of an ocean of blacktop. I parked as close as I could to the emergency room, but it was still a good walk across the lot to the automatic doors.

I didn't see Louise inside. I figured she was in one of the examination rooms with her husband. I double-checked with a nurse to make sure that Pearson had been admitted, then went over to a waiting area and sat down with three anxious-looking strangers.

Half an hour must have passed before Louise came out. I

could tell from her ashen look that Pearson was in bad shape.

"Oh, God, Harry," she said, slumping beside me in a chair. She covered her face with her hands.

"It's my fault," she said hoarsely. "It's my fault."

"No, it's not," I said.

"You don't understand. They found Ethan's car. I had to tell him they found Ethan's car."

"I know. I talked to the cops."

"You know?" Louise said with surprise. "Then why didn't *you* call me? Why did you let me hear that from a stranger?"

"I got there too late, Louise," I said, feeling bad. "They'd already made the call."

She dropped her hands from her cheeks and stared queerly into space. "I didn't want to tell him, but he knew it was the police. He heard me talking to them." She turned to me with a guilty look. "What was I supposed to do?"

"You had to tell him."

"He went crazy," she said with a trace of horror in her voice. "I've never seen him get that upset, even when . . . even after Estelle. He said things to me. Dreadful things. We fought."

Her head fell to her chest and she sobbed. "They say he may die."

I sat there with Louise for about ten minutes, holding her hand tightly in mine. Lasker finally arrived with Cora Pearson. The woman looked awful, her face blasted, her gait doddering, as if she'd aged twenty years since the day before. Louise got up immediately, walked over to her mother-in-law, and took her in her arms.

Cora Pearson sobbed. "He's not going to die?"

"It's not in our hands anymore," Lasker said.

Louise flashed an angry look at him over Cora's shoulder, and the man's face reddened as if he'd been slapped.

"No, he's not going to die," Louise said to her mother-in-law. She pushed Cora Pearson back and straightened her white hair as if she were grooming a child.

The older woman smiled at her weakly. "You're so good to me, Louise," she said with deep feeling. "Always so good."

Cora walked unsteadily over to the waiting area and sat down on one of the plastic chairs.

I couldn't hear him, but Lasker apparently said something else to Louise, something well-intentioned and inept. She frowned dismissively, and he backed out of the emergency room like he was leaving royalty.

After Lasker left Louise came over to us. "Did you call Shelley?" she asked Cora.

The older woman nodded. "He's on his way."

Louise sat down beside Cora and put an arm around her shoulder. The woman leaned against her heavily. "Don't worry, Mother," Louise whispered. "I'm here with you."

It had come to me when I'd first met Pearson that Louise anchored his life. I was beginning to realize that she anchored the whole family—probably the children too, insofar as they could be reached. It was what she had meant the night before when she'd complained about people automatically relying upon her strength. But that strength was no illusion—it was real and impressive, especially at that moment.

A nurse came into the hall and called Louise's name.

She patted her mother-in-law's shoulder and stood up. "I've got to go," she said to Cora.

"Will I be able to see him?" the woman asked plaintively.

"In a little while," Louise said.

She went over to where the nurse was standing and together they walked off down the hall to the emergency rooms.

I didn't want to leave Cora Pearson alone, so I waited for Shelley Sacks to arrive. The woman didn't say much to me. Her shock was too deep, and there wasn't anything to say.

When Sacks came in, I got to my feet.

The woman looked up at me suddenly. Her face was already red from crying, but the color that rose in her cheeks was more than despair or grief. "*They* did this to him!" she said in a strangled voice. "I hope they die for this—for what they've done."

She didn't mean what she'd said. She might not have realized she was saying it. But the truth was that her curse could already have come true.

18

▮▮▮

Before leaving the hospital I called Sergeant Larry Parker from a pay phone in the lobby to see if the State Patrol forensic team had turned up anything new.

"We haven't found a body in the river," he said grimly. "But State confirmed that the stains on the panties were blood. Type O negative. You might want to check with the Pearsons about the girl's blood type. We've also got some positive lifts off the Plymouth's steering wheel."

"Do you have a make on the prints?"

Parker sighed. "Yeah, but you're not going to like it. The prints belong to a convicted felon named Herbert Talmadge."

"Jesus," I said aloud. The very fact that Ethan and Kirsty had ended up in that clearing with Talmadge—in the same spot where Estelle Pearson had taken her own life—defied logic.

"You know the guy?" Parker said, responding to the pained sound of my voice.

I thought about going into Pearson family history with Parker, then decided against it. It wasn't going to help him find Talmadge. "No, I don't know him."

"Well, he's an honest-to-God bad man, Stoner. If your MPs ran into him, I'm afraid they chanced into serious trouble. State's already put an APB out on him. So has Kentucky. The son of a bitch was released from Lexington the week before last. Ten days and he's already . . ."

He didn't finish the sentence, but I knew what he was thinking. Ten days and he'd already committed murder— or attempted to.

"You don't have any leads yet, do you?"

"None. How 'bout you—did you check on that Chicago store?"

"Not yet."

"Well, I'd appreciate you finding out. And find out about the blood type, too. I'll get in touch if anything else turns up."

I was in a bad mood when I hung up on Parker. And the mood kept deepening on the drive downtown to the office.

Herbert Talmadge wasn't the kind of guy who would take hostages or halfway measures. If the Pearson kids had found him as they apparently had, he'd brought their revenge fantasies to a quick, pitiless end—at best. I didn't want to think about what he might have done at worst.

The very fact that Kirsty and Ethan *had* found Talmadge galled me. They'd found him, and I hadn't. All they'd had to go on was the newspaper article in the *Post*, and yet they'd found him in less than a day, while I was chasing blind leads and making time with Louise Pearson.

I didn't understand how it had happened, how the last chapter of Kirsten's life might have ended up being written by a man with no connection to her own past, a man with no real connection to Ethan's past—save for the brief moment that the boy might have seen him in the hospital ward where his father had once worked. And yet they'd all wound up in that clearing above the river like they were holding communion for the dead mother. For the second time in two days I had the weird feeling that there really was a sinister fatality at work in the Pearsons' lives, leading them on to violent death.

When I got to the office I picked up the phone and started making calls. I went back through the people I'd talked to in Chicago one by one. Art Heldman at the university. Jay

Stein. Marnee Thompson at the girls' apartment. And
Hedda Pearson at her end-of-the-road motel. Not one of
them had ever heard of Herbert Talmadge. Not one of
them could explain how Kirsten or Ethan had known
where to find him. The only thing I managed to learn was
that Kirsty had in fact bought underclothes from Milady's
Shop in the Kenwood Plaza in Hyde Park.

"Why is that important?" Marnee asked uneasily.
"What's happened to Kirsty?"

I didn't tell her what I knew. I didn't tell any of them
about the abandoned car and the bloody underwear. Not
even Hedda Pearson, who had a right to know. I just didn't
have it in me to speak the truth.

After finishing the Chicago calls I ran through my local
connections again. Al Foster at CPD. The Kentucky cops.
The State Patrol.

By eleven-thirty I'd run out of people to call. I felt like I'd
run out of luck too, like poor Kirsty and her brother. Then
Lee Wilson, the manager at Ethan's Ft. Thomas motel,
phoned me. And things began to change.

The Blue Grass Motel and Motor Court was on Hidden
Fork Road, about fifteen miles south of the city off I-471. It
was a well-tended place in spite of its out-of-the-way loca-
tion. The stucco-and-glass office building looked newly
painted. The dozen stucco cottages arrayed in a semicircle
behind were just as fresh-faced and neat. A heart-shaped
swimming pool sat to the side, covered with a tarp for the
winter.

I parked in a space by the pool and caught a whiff of stale
chlorine as I walked over to the office building. Wilson was
waiting for me inside—a dapper, balding man in his mid-
forties with the pink, prissy face of a toady.

"You must be Mr. Stoner," Wilson said as I came up to the counter. "I'm Lee Wilson, the proprietor here."

He held out his hand and I shook with him.

"I woulda called you sooner about this, Mr. Stoner, if I'd been on duty last night. I left your message with Roy, my clerk, but he didn't bother telling me until today. That's the trouble with hired help—you can't trust them to follow up on things."

Wilson laughed mechanically. And when I didn't laugh he stopped laughing too, as if he didn't think it was funny either.

"If I hadn't been going through the receipts, I doubt as I would have seen it. Right there in black and white in the registration book."

I had the feeling that this one went through the receipts every hour on the hour. But I pretended it was the blessing he wanted me to think it was and asked to see the book.

Wilson glanced down at the open register on the counter-top, scanning it critically as if he were totaling figures. His eyes stopped on a line midway down the page, and he pinned a finger to it like he was poking Roy the clerk in the eye.

"Here it is."

He swiveled the book around to me, using his finger as a fulcrum.

I glanced at the book, at the line above Wilson's finger. "Ethan Pearson" was written on it in longhand, along with a check-in time of four p.m. Monday.

"Why did Ethan bother to sign in?" I asked, looking up at Wilson. "I mean he lives here, doesn't he?"

"We like to keep track of our guests," the man said stiffly. "We always ask our semipermanent residents to sign in fresh if they been away for more than a day or two. Saves us some problems and them some potential embarrassment. I mean lights come on in somebody's cottage when they're supposed to be out of town . . . well, you can see my point."

I glanced at the polished wood letterboxes behind the counter. Most of the cubbyholes had room keys dangling from them. But a few had notes and letters in them.

"Did Ethan pick up any messages when he checked in?"

"I asked myself the same thing this morning," Wilson said with a self-congratulatory smile—the amateur detective. "But Roy says there weren't no letters. Ethan did get a phone call, though. And I believe he made one himself."

There was a PBX to the right of the letterboxes, an old-fashioned switchboard with a dial receiver at the base and a headset and plug-in lines. Like everything else in the place it was shiny and neat.

"No way to know who was calling in, is there?" I asked Wilson.

He shook his head, no. "Roy said it was a woman, and the call came around eleven-thirty. That's all I can tell you."

"Do you know who Ethan phoned?"

The man smiled triumphantly, as if he'd caught me in a little trap of his own devising. "Got the number right here," he said, pulling a piece of neatly folded paper out of his shirt pocket. "Don't know who it is, but I got the number."

"When did the call go out?"

The look of triumph faded a bit. "Ain't exactly sure of that. Sometime before he left, I reckon."

"He left again around midnight?"

Wilson nodded. "Like I told you on the phone. Right around midnight. 'Least that's what Roy told me."

The man gave me a conspiratorial look. "He had a woman with him," he whispered. "And it wasn't his wife."

"Did Roy tell you what she looked like?"

"A young girl. Brown hair, glasses. She stayed in the car, Roy said, when the boy signed in."

It sounded like Kirsten, but it didn't have to be her.

I studied the man for a moment—his prissy face. "Think I could take a look in their room?"

Wilson pretended to be shocked. Or maybe he wasn't pretending. He took himself fairly seriously.

"It would save me calling the cops," I said. "Getting a warrant."

The man's shocked look deepened momentarily.

"I guess I could show you the room."

I took out my wallet, pulled two twenties out, and laid them on the counter. "For your trouble."

That swayed him. "We'll go on down there right now. Just let me put the 'Closed' sign in the window."

He picked up the twenties and started to turn away. I caught him by the shirt sleeve and he burped with fright, as if he thought I was about to arrest him for taking a bribe.

"The phone number?" I said, rubbing my fingers together.

Lee Wilson smiled with relief. " 'Course," he said, handing me the square of paper. "Don't want to forget that."

19

Wilson walked me down to the Pearsons' cottage, unlocked the door with a passkey, then backed away discreetly, as if he was leaving me alone with the casket. I pushed the door open and looked inside.

The motel room was dark, except for the arc of sunlight coming through the door. The sun lit up a slice of carpet, the top halves of two unmade beds, and a corner of blank white wall. What looked like fast-food wrappers were scattered on the sheets of the nearest bed. A tin ashtray glittered on the pillows of the far bed. The room stank of cigarette smoke and stale grease—like the smell of Kirsten Pearson's bedroom in Chicago. I flipped on a table light and went inside, closing the door behind me.

It was a tiny room. Just the two twin beds. A nightstand between them. The lamp table by the door. A wooden bureau-desk on the far wall across from the bed. A door to a bathroom beyond the bureau.

I'd been expecting a few personal items. Photographs. Mementos. Books. But the only artifact in the room was the cheap oil painting of a farmhouse that Lee Wilson had hung above the beds. How Ethan and his wife could have called that spare, denuded place home, I couldn't imagine.

I went through the room carefully, starting with the bureau-desk. There was a phone on top and a pad for messages. One of the sheets from the pad lay crumpled up at the foot of the desk chair. I picked it up and smoothed it out. Someone had written the word "Small" on it with a capital S, followed by a slash mark and the number 5. A phone number was printed underneath:

Small/5

555-1543

I wasn't sure what "Small/5" meant. It could have been a dress or blouse size. If so, maybe the number was for a clothing store. It wasn't the same phone number that Ethan had dialed the night before—that was certain. The one that Wilson had written down for me was 555-8200.

I pocketed the sheet of notepaper with the cryptic message on it and turned to the bureau drawers. There were still a few items of clothing in them. Some men's underwear, a couple of tank-top T-shirts, several loose unmatched socks. A pair of boy's pajamas for David. One of Hedda Pearson's blouses, neatly pressed and wrapped in a Brockhaus Dry Cleaner's paper band. I checked the size of the blouse, but it wasn't a small and it wasn't a 5.

I wondered if Kirsten Pearson wore a size 5.

I went through the nightstand drawer next and found a Gideon Bible, a passbook from First National here in the city, and a Greater Cincinnati phone directory with a pencil stuck in the Yellow Pages. The passbook was in the name of E. Pearson—a savings account with deposits made to it every three months for over ten years, from the time Ethan was about fourteen to less than a few weeks before he disappeared. The deposits were always the same—a thousand dollars—and the entire amount was always withdrawn a month or so after it had been put in the account. It was undoubtedly a record of the "blood money" that Louise had told me about—Phil Pearson's pathetic attempt to buy his son's affection and to assuage his own guilt. It was the only item in the room that connected Ethan with his family, a bankbook that the boy hadn't even thought to take with him.

I put the book back in the drawer and opened the phone directory to the page marked by the pencil. It was a page full of RNs' ads and listings. One of the ads had been circled —The Medical Pool with an address on Oak Street near the city hospitals in Clifton. Very near Rollman's, too.

I started to jot The Medical Pool listing down when I realized that it was the same number that Wilson had given me. The same number that Ethan had called the night before. 555-8200. For some reason Ethan had phoned a nursing agency.

I went through the bedclothes and looked under the beds, but aside from a few wilted french fries I didn't find anything. The cigarette butts in the ashtray were Winstons, Kirsty's brand.

The bathroom was next. There was no medicine cabinet, just a flat mirror over the vanitory, a towel rack across from that, and a shower stall on the right. Someone had used the shower fairly recently, because there were fresh waterspots on the tile and long brown hairs in the drain. The plastic trash can by the vanitory had several Kleenex in it. I wouldn't have noticed the tissues if a few of them hadn't been stained with blood. There was also a small smear of blood in the porcelain washbasin, as if Ethan had knicked himself shaving.

I stopped at the motel office on the way out. Wilson was back at work, going through the books again with a vigilant look on his face. I pitied poor Roy the night clerk. His mistakes were Wilson's meat.

"Thanks," I said to the man, handing him the passkey.

"*Por nada,* as our friends south of the border say."

I forced a smile.

"When does your clerk, Roy, come back on?"

"Tomorrow afternoon," Wilson said despairingly. "I just can't be here all the time."

"Ask him to give me a call, will you? And, of course, phone me if Ethan comes back."

"Will do," the man said with a grin and a Boy Scout salute.

He held the salute a moment too long. When I didn't return it he dropped his hand quickly and wiped it on his pants leg, as if his fingers were wet with embarrassment.

As soon as I got back to the office I took out the crumpled piece of notepaper and called the number on it, 555-1543. I was half expecting to get the women's wear department at K mart—some clerk who could explain the "Small/5" notation. But if it was a K mart they were damn busy, because no one answered the phone.

I put that call on hold and dialed the other number, the one that Ethan had called from the motel room, the one for The Medical Pool.

A woman answered as sweetly as if she were already sitting there by the rented bed, mopping my brow.

"You have reached The Medical Pool. How may we help you?"

"Hi," I said to her. "My name's Ethan Pearson. I called you last night, remember?"

"Of course, I remember, Mr. Pearson," the woman said reassuringly. "Was Rita available?"

"I beg your pardon?"

"Rita Scarne. The nurse you requested for emergency service. We paged her at home and transferred your call, don't you remember?"

It appeared that Ethan had made two calls for the price of one.

"Yes, I did talk to her," I said, jotting down the name "Rita Scarne" on a yellow pad. "But I seem to have misplaced her home number."

"Not to worry. I can find it for you." She went off the line for a second. "Are you ready?"

"All set," I said.

"555-1543. Remember, if she's not home, try at Holmes Hospital."

"Thanks again," I said, hanging up.

I'd just tried the number, thinking it was K mart. But it wasn't K mart. It was a nurse named Rita Scarne. Since she obviously wasn't at home I called Holmes Hospital. The patient information service told me that Rita Scarne wasn't on duty that afternoon. They suggested I try Rollman's, where Nurse Scarne also worked part-time.

Rather than phoning Rollman's I drove over to the hospital on Burnett. The attendant at the door recognized me from the day before.

"If you come back to see Dr. McCall, he ain't here. Had a meeting to go to."

"Nurse Rostow will do," I told him.

He checked to make sure Nurse Rostow was at her station, then passed me through. I took the elevator up to the third floor and followed the arrows around the typing carrels to Sam McCall's office. Ms. Rostow smiled at me as I walked up to her desk.

"I hadn't expected to see you again so soon, Mr. Stoner."

"I hadn't expected to be back."

The woman nodded at McCall's door. "He's gone to a board of directors meeting and won't return today."

"This may be something *you* can help me with."

Ms. Rostow's face lit up pleasantly. "I'll certainly try. Have a seat."

I sat down across the desk from her. "Do you know a nurse named Rita Scarne?"

"Of course," she said smartly, as if it was the first round of a quiz show. "Miss Scarne has worked here since late 1974. On and off."

"You mean she's part-time?"

"I meant precisely what I said," the woman said. "Miss Scarne was a full-time nurse here. In fact, she was chief of the nursing staff for a short while.

"A very short while," she added.

"Something happened?"

Nurse Rostow hesitated this time before hitting the buzzer. I had the distinct impression that she didn't care for Rita Scarne and would have told me why if her professional ethics hadn't blocked the way.

"There was some trouble," she said, feeling her way around the block.

"With a doctor?" I asked curiously.

"No," she said. "Miss Scarne had . . . she didn't behave professionally on the wards."

Judging from the blush in old Ms. Rostow's cheeks I had the feeling that the trouble had been sexual.

"I shouldn't have told you that," she said, looking embarrassed. "Rita's an excellent nurse, who has been quite successful in private practice. She is very much in demand. The problem I referred to is old business. Very old."

I changed the subject to spare her any more embarrassment. "When was Rita Scarne head nurse here?"

"In late 1975 and '76."

"So she might have had contact with Herbert Talmadge?"

"I couldn't say for sure. She *was* head nurse, so it's quite possible."

I was thinking of the transcript I'd read—the interview from 1976 in which Talmadge had made his awful confession. Isaac Goldman, the intern from St. Louis, had been Talmadge's psychiatrist at the time. But throughout the interview Goldman had been assisted by someone else, someone with the initials R. S. I'd assumed R. S. was another psychiatrist, now it occurred to me that it might have been head nurse Rita Scarne. She had to have some connection with Talmadge—some connection that was obvious to Ethan Pearson—or I couldn't see why Ethan would have phoned for her.

"Is Miss Scarne on duty today?" I asked.

"I'm not sure. I can check, if you'd like."

"Please."

She picked up a phone, pressed a couple of buttons, and asked, "Is Nurse Scarne on duty?"

After a moment she hung the phone up daintily and said, "No, Miss Scarne is not here today."

I sighed. "It's important that I get hold of her."

"Have you tried Holmes Hospital? Or her house?"

"She's not at Holmes, and I don't have her address."

"I can help you with that," Ms. Rostow said. She flipped through a Rolodex and scribbled an address down on a notepad. "Here."

Rita Scarne must have made a good living, because her home was on Ridge Road in Amberley Village. That's where I decided to go next.

20

Rita Scarne's house was in a wooded dell on the east side of Ridge Road—a two-story Colonial with rounded doors, Dutch windows, and a steep cross gable in front. A black-topped driveway led down to it through a small stand of oak trees. It was just a little past three when I got there, but the sun was already beginning to set. The slanting light caught in the bare limbs of the oaks, turning them gold. Heavy shadows enveloped the trunks, stretching across the yard and up the brick walls of the house.

The driveway terminated in front of a built-in garage. The garage door was open and a green Audi was parked inside. There was a sticker on the rear bumper—"Nurses Are the Best Medicine."

It was a very expensive place—a little too expensive for an unmarried nurse, I thought. But for all I knew she had other sources of income.

I got out of the Pinto and followed a cement walkway to the front door. It was cold in the shady dale and so quiet I could hear the wind creaking in the maples like house noises in the night.

I peered through the small leaded-glass window in the front door before ringing the bell. All I could see was sunlight pouring through French windows at the end of a tiled hallway. When I pressed the buzzer, a woman appeared in the hall. I backed away from the window as she came up to the door and opened it.

"Yes?" she said in a husky, sensuous voice.

Rita Scarne, if that was who the woman was, was a tall, hefty blonde in her mid-forties, with an attractive sun-beaten face and slanting, plum-colored eyes. She was wearing a white mu-mu without much on underneath it, judging from the way the fabric clung to her large breasts and heavy hips. She'd made an early start on the evening, because her breath smelled of bourbon. Her sexy blue eyes looked a little clabbered with it.

"Rita Scarne?"

"That's me. Who are you?"

"My name is Stoner, Ms. Scarne. I wonder if I could talk to you for a minute."

"About what?" the woman said with half a smile. She ran one hand up the jamb of the door, rested the other on her hip and stared at me afresh, as if she liked my looks and didn't care if I knew it.

"It's a personal matter. I promise not to take up much of your time."

"You're not selling something, are you? Like encyclopedias?"

I smiled. "No. I just want to ask you a few questions."

"All right. Go ahead."

"Maybe we could talk inside? It's pretty cold out here."

She closed her eyes thoughtfully then said, "Why not?" And waved me through the door.

"If you're selling insurance, Mr. Stoner, I'm going to be very disappointed," she said as we walked down the hallway to the back of the house. She turned right at a doorway, and I followed her into an enclosed patio, full of cane furniture. The back wall was all glass, and the sun pouring through it filled the room with light.

The woman sat down on a fan-back chair. I sat on a small pillowed sofa across from her. There was a bottle of Old Grand-dad on a small table to her right. Just the bottle—no glasses.

"So what is it you *are* selling, Mr. Stoner?" she said wryly.

"Nothing. I'm a private detective."

"You're kidding," the woman said, looking aghast. She almost reached for the bottle but caught herself.

I took out my wallet and showed her the photostat of my license.

"I'm working for a man named Phil Pearson. A psychiatrist—"

"I know who he is," the woman said sharply.

Rita Scarne gave me a cold, suspicious look—a far cry from the bedroom eyes she'd been making at the front door. "Why would Phil send you to me?"

"He didn't send me. I came because of his kids, Ethan and Kirsty. They've been missing since last Thursday. Pearson hired me to find them."

"I still don't understand why you came to me."

"There's a strong possibility that Ethan Pearson tried to call you last night, Ms. Scarne. At least, he called your agency, The Medical Pool, and they transferred his call to your number. He also received a return phone call from a woman."

"Why would he call me? I haven't seen Ethan or his sister or Phil in years."

"He didn't call?"

"I wasn't even here last night. My sister was house-sitting for me."

"She left no messages?"

"No."

"And you didn't call Ethan?"

She just stared at me.

"Do you have any idea why he would have called The Medical Pool for your number?"

She thought about it for a second. "I did work for Phil once. But that was a long time ago."

"Doing what?"

Rita Scarne gave me an irritated look, as if she were offended by the question—by the idea of being questioned at all. "He hired me to look after his wife, Estelle, if it's any of your business. The experience left a very bad taste."

The woman pursed her lips as if she could still taste it.

"Was Estelle Pearson in your care in 1976?"

Rita Scarne hesitated a moment then nodded, yes.

"That would have been right before she died?"

"Yes," she said bitterly, as if I'd pulled the admission out of her like a tooth. "I was her nurse when she died."

"So Ethan would have remembered you from that time?"

"Oh, yes," the woman said with a dull laugh. "He would have remembered me."

"You had problems with him?"

"You could safely say that. Ethan was a very disturbed kid. It was difficult for me to do my job with him around. He was always spying on me, bossing me about, trying to catch me up. And when he wasn't snooping he was getting in the way. He scarcely left me or his mother alone for a minute. It was exhausting—that kind of attention. And counter-productive."

"You mean he kept you from doing your job."

"I mean he kept driving his mother crazy," she said, losing patience. "Look, the little bastard didn't want Estelle to recover. If she recovered he wouldn't have had her all to himself. When she was depressed she used to dote on his attentions. As she got better she had less time for him. And that really pissed him off. You could see it in his face—a cold, venomous rage."

After thirteen years Rita Scarne's revulsion for Ethan Pearson was still as intense as if he'd just insulted her the day before. I figured that that kind of hatred had to be mutually felt, which made Ethan's apparent desire to get in touch with the woman inexplicable. Unless he and Kirsty felt that they had no choice—that Rita Scarne knew something that no one else could tell them.

I said, "Do you remember another patient of yours from the mid-seventies. A man named Herbert Talmadge?"

Rita Scarne's blue eyes went dead. "Herbert Talmadge?"

"He was a patient at Rollman's when you were head nurse there. Ethan has been looking for him for years now. It could be that was why he contacted you. He may have thought you knew how to find Talmadge."

"That's ridiculous!" The woman's face filled with high spots of color. "I don't even remember this man. Why would I know where he is? What do I have to do with it?"

She brushed her cheeks with the palms of her hands as if she was trying to wipe the blush away. "I think you better leave," she said angrily. "I don't care to talk about this. I don't care to be reassociated with that family's problems. I'm not guilty of anything."

But she certainly didn't act that way. She acted as if she were guilty as sin—and Herbert Talmadge was part of it.

I got up from the chair. "I may want to talk to you again, Ms. Scarne."

"Souls in hell want ice water, too." This time she did pick up the bottle and took a swig. "Get out of my house before I call the cops."

I walked up the hall and out the front door.

As I got in the car I thought about the blond nurse that Talmadge had been seen with—the one that Thelma Jackson had mentioned. On the surface of it I couldn't see why a woman like Rita Scarne would have toyed with a brutal, dangerous man like Talmadge. But if she had it would certainly bring a blush to her cheeks, even after thirteen years. It was something worth looking into.

* * *

I drove away from the house but I didn't go far—just a few blocks north on Ridge to a convenience store with a phone booth on its side wall. I parked by the booth, got out, and started to make calls, looking for someone who could confirm a connection between Rita Scarne and Herbert Talmadge.

I dialed Thelma Jackson first—to see if Rita's name rang a bell. But it didn't.

"Wish I could tell you she was the right one," Thelma said apologetically. "But I don't remember nothing 'bout that nurse, 'cept her blond hair. Can't find nobody else who does, neither. I been asking though."

I told her to keep trying, hung up, and dialed Rollman's.

Nurse Rostow was still on duty. "Could you do me one more favor?" I asked her.

"Again, Mr. Stoner?" she said in a long-suffering voice.

"Do you still have Rita Scarne's employment record from back in the mid-seventies?"

"Mr. Stoner," the woman said. "That's not something I can show you, and you know it."

"I don't want you to show it to me. I just want to find out where Rita was living in 1976."

"I guess the address would be all right," she said after thinking about it. "I mean an address from that long ago would hardly be restricted information."

She went off the line for a second. "Two thirty-four Terrace Avenue. There's also an address for her family in Dayton, Ohio—516 Minton. I believe she was from Dayton originally."

I jotted both addresses down.

"The Terrace residence is in Clifton?"

The woman said, yes.

I had to call long-distance information to make my last call—to Creve Coeur, Missouri. Luckily, Dr. Isaac Goldman had a published number for his psychiatric clinic on Westmoreland Boulevard. I got a secretary who wasn't about to put me through until I told her I was a cop, working on a life-and-death matter.

Goldman came on the line huffily, as if life-and-death matters didn't much impress him unless someone was paying for his time.

"I'm with a patient so please make this brief."

"You were an intern at Rollman's Hospital, here in Cincinnati in 1976. One of your patients was a black man named Herbert Talmadge."

"Yes," he said after a long moment. "I vaguely remember Talmadge. I think I recommended that he be sent to Longview for further treatment."

"As a matter of fact you authorized his release."

"You must be wrong about that. Talmadge had a severe psychosis."

I let that much pass and asked him about Nurse Rita Scarne. "Did she work with Talmadge while you were treating him?"

"Yes. She worked with all the patients on the ward."

"Would she have participated in interviews or tests?"

"Probably. I really don't recall."

"She had no special relationship with Talmadge?"

"Not that I knew of. Anything else?"

"No," I said, letting the disappointment sour my voice.

The man hung up as if he couldn't care less about my disappointments.

I'd accomplished next to nothing with the phone calls, except for worming Rita's old addresses out of Nurse Rostow. And that was a long shot. But it was the best shot I had at the moment. So I got back in the car and headed for 234

Terrace Avenue—looking to find somebody who'd lived there a long while, someone who was a bit of a gossip and a bit of a snoop. Someone who might have seen young, round-heels Rita with a solemn, ferret-faced black man with a terrible kink in his psyche.

21

Terrace Avenue was a short, narrow side street off Clifton Avenue, full of old yellow-brick apartment houses and red-brick duplexes. Like most of the side streets in that neighborhood it was sedate, proper, and a little decrepit-looking —a home for students who could afford high rents and for older couples who couldn't. Two thirty-four was the first duplex on the south side of the street, a two-story bungalow with a bricked-in front porch and a cracked driveway on its side. A fat old man with a square-jawed face and short iron-grey hair was sitting in a rusty lawnchair in the partial shade of the porch overhang. He was wearing a lumberjack shirt, chinos, and a Reds baseball cap. The setting sun lit his face from below like a monument.

"Howdy," I said as I came up the walk. "You know the owner of this place?"

The man nodded. "Sure do. *I'm* the owner. Owned it for the last twenty-three years. Why? You looking to rent?"

"No, I'm trying to find an old friend of mine who used to live here."

"Now who would that be?"

"A nurse named Rita Scarne."

The man laughed hoarsely, falling forward over his gut and grasping his legs as if that was a real knee-slapper. I laughed, too, to make him feel at home.

"Christ, son, where've you been?" he said, still laughing. "That girl, Rita, hasn't lived here since . . . oh, hell, must've been '76 or '77."

"I moved out of town," I told him. "This was the last place she lived before I went away. I sure would like to find her."

"Rita was a hot ticket, all right. She and her roommate. You know them nurses—had men coming and going."

He waved his right hand as if he'd burned it on Rita Scarne's ass. It wouldn't have surprised me if he had. Up close he was a bit disreputable-looking. Shirt misbuttoned, salt-and-pepper beard on his chin, a nose that was a little too red even for that kind of weather.

"Couldn't begin to count the visitors Rita had," he said, rubbing it in.

"Guess I was just one of a crowd."

"You were, son."

"Come to think of it, I do remember one other guy that Rita ran with. I think his name was Talmadge, Herb Talmadge. Feisty little black fella with a goatee?"

The man shook his head decisively. "Nope. No niggers. Not in this house."

"Maybe I got it confused."

"Most like."

He stared at me suspiciously, as if I was that odd breed of animal—a white man who palled with blacks. Or maybe he was wondering whether Rita had actually pirated a black man into the house, like a puppy or a hot plate.

"Well, I don't know where the girl's gone to," he said, still eyeing me. "Christ, we must have rented that upstairs apartment ten or fifteen times since then. Me and the missus."

The man nodded at the stout, iron-bound door to the house as if it were a portrait of the wife. He raised up and sat down again like an automatic pin-setter. I assumed that was my cue to leave.

"You know I'd completely forgotten Rita had a roommate," I said, trying a new tack.

"How could you forget that one?" He pursed his thin lips

and made a silent whistle. "Man, she was pretty. Only lived here a few months, back in '75. But I never forgot her."

"You don't remember her name do you?"

"Carla Chaney," he said nostalgically. "She wasn't real fast or flashy like Rita. But she was a beauty. She and Rita were both beauties."

"You don't know where Carla went, do you? Maybe I could get in touch with Rita through her."

The man lifted his cap and raked his hair with the tips of his fingers. "I think she moved back to Albuquerque," he said, pulling the hat back down over his forehead smartly. "Leastways that's where she was from. Albuquerque, New Mexico."

I thanked the man and started back to the street. About halfway down the walk I looked back at him and said, "You know I think I remember Carla after all. She was a blond girl, wasn't she?"

"Blond and blue-eyed," the man called out. "Just like Rita."

I drove half a block to a Steak N' Egg on Clifton and phoned Albuquerque information from a booth in the corner. They had no listing for a Carla Chaney. But there was a listing for a Nola Chaney on Mesa Drive. I dialed it and had to wait ten rings before a woman answered. It was hard to tell over the phone, but she sounded drunk. Her voice was slurred and brassy, like a muted horn.

"Yes? What is it?" she said irritably.

"Mrs. Chaney?"

"Yeah. This is Nola Chaney."

"I'm an old friend of Carla's, Mrs. Chaney, calling from Cincinnati, Ohio. I've been trying to get in touch with Carla, but I don't know where she's living now. I was hoping you could tell me."

The woman laughed bitterly. "That's a rich one." She laughed again, stretching it out for effect. "Mister, I haven't seen Carla in sixteen years."

"You haven't seen her since 1973?"

"How about that?" Nola Chaney said as if it was even more preposterous when I said it. "Hasn't even called me on the phone. Her own mother. Her own flesh and blood."

"She was doing some nursing the last time I saw her."

"Well, I wouldn't know about that," the woman said. "Carla was a smart girl—maybe she did become a nurse. I always thought she'd end up in L.A. Become a model or something. Had her take tap lessons and elocution and everything."

The woman sighed heavily.

"But she pissed it away getting married so young. Just like me. I fell for a no-good one when I was no more than seventeen. Carla saw what happened. Lord knows, she saw what happened when a girl makes that kind of mistake. So what does she go and do when she's just barely out of high school? Runs off with another pissant son of a bitch no better than her dad Paul was. Not a dime in his pocket. Mean as a snake. But Bobby had the looks all right—and I guess that's all that counts when you're young."

"I didn't realize Carla was married."

"Might not be anymore, if I know my own blood."

"Her husband's name was Bobby?"

"Bobby Tallwood. Airman at the air force base out here." The woman's brassy voice mellowed slightly, as if she was reliving the distant past. "She and Bobby lived in a nice little house out near the base for a couple, three years. Had a kid named Joey. Cute little kid. Bobby didn't treat him right though, and I told him so. Hell, when he got drunk Bob was just as mean as Paul—always used his fists, you know? Don't know how many times Carla come running on home with the baby after Bobby gone on a rampage. But she always went back to him after a day or two. When you're getting it that good, I guess you go back no matter what. Anyway Bobby got transferred to Wright-Patterson in Dayton in '73. Moved down there to Ohio. And that's the last goddamn thing I heard from either one of them."

"Maybe I'll try up in Dayton," I said. "Could be she's still living there?"

"If you find her let me know, huh?"

But she'd hung before I could say that I would.

I called Dayton information, asked for listings for Bobby Tallwood or Carla Chaney, and drew a blank. I tried Cincinnati information on the same two names and didn't do any better. Wherever Carla Chaney was, it didn't look as if I was going to find her easily.

It was close to six when I got off the phone. I hadn't touched base with Louise Pearson in several hours, so I decided to drive to the hospital before going home. In the back of my mind I was thinking that Shelley Sacks might still be in the Bethesda emergency room. Since the Scarne woman had admitted to looking after Estelle Pearson in 1976, Sacks would certainly have known her at that time. And there was an off chance that Louise knew something about her too.

I knew it was a terrible day for the Pearsons—family and friends—and I hated to pester them with questions. But until I was certain that Kirsty was dead I was going to continue to track her. Even if she was dead in the river I knew I'd stay with it. I owed the girl that chance.

22

It was almost six when I pulled into the Bethesda North lot. By then the sun was setting in earnest in high bands of color across the western sky. It made me think of the sunrise that morning, hours earlier. Of the cold desolate clearing with the river running beneath it. They'd been dragging that river all day—Parker and his men—looking to catch something paler than fish belly, puffed up like risen dough.

I went down to the emergency room and was told that Phil Pearson had been transferred to ECU on the top floor. I took the elevator back up.

Shelley Sacks was sitting with Cora Pearson in a white shoebox of a waiting room, just outside the ECU door. Through the picture window on the far wall you could see the parking lot, dotted with mercury lamps that had begun to burn like little torches in the sunset. High on the right wall a television set flashed pictures of a game show.

The woman didn't see me as I came into the room, but Sacks did. He stood up with effort and walked over to where I was standing.

"Hello, Stoner," he said. His round face was grey with fatigue. His voice spiritless.

"How is he?" I asked.

Sacks shook his head. "Not good. He's in a coma, just barely clinging to life."

"I'm sorry."

He nodded sadly. "So am I. Terribly sorry for all of this." He glanced at the mother, sitting glassy-eyed and still in a far corner of the room. "Cora is going to need a great deal of support before this is through."

"How's Louise doing?"

"A rock," he said admiringly. "As always. She's in with Phil. Did you want to see her?"

He gave me a funny look that almost made me blush.

"No," I said, feeling guilty because I *did* want to see the woman—and a little paranoid because I thought Sacks knew why. Louise was fairly open about her love affairs, and I felt as if he'd somehow guessed that I was standing next in line. "I don't need to disturb them right now. You could relay a couple of messages for me, if you would."

"Certainly."

"The police need to know Kirsty's blood type." I thought of the cryptic message on the crumpled notepaper and added: "They need to know her blouse and dress size, too."

Sacks grimaced. "Louise told me about the car and the clothing. The police think that Ethan and Kirsty may be . . . ?"

"Nobody's sure, yet."

He sighed heavily. "I don't suppose there's any good news?"

"I'm afraid not. I have learned that Kirsty and Ethan stopped at Ethan's motel room yesterday. Apparently Ethan tried to get in touch with a psychiatric nurse named Rita Scarne."

"Rita Scarne?" Sacks said with mild surprise. "She was the nurse who took care of Estelle."

"So I understand. I talked to her this afternoon. She seemed to feel a lot of bitterness toward the Pearsons—especially Ethan."

"That's not entirely surprising. Part of Rita's job was to keep Ethan apart from his mother for a few hours every day. In fact *I* suggested that she do that."

"Why?"

"Because he was smothering his mother with attention—

and making Rita's life miserable. Estelle was simply too
weak to say no to Ethan, so I instructed Rita to say no for
her. Ethan became quite upset with Rita because of that—
and with me, too, I think. When Stelle died he blamed both
of us."

"*Was* she in any way to blame for the woman's suicide?"

"Of course not. In fact, she wasn't even at the house on
the day it happened. She'd called in sick with flu early that
morning."

Sacks' round blue eyes clouded up, and his voice caught
in his throat. I knew the excess of emotion wasn't just because of the past—it was partly because his friend was dying
a few feet away from us. But it was also because of the
woman, Estelle Pearson. He must have cared a great deal
for her.

"I thought Stelle would be all right without supervision
for one day, especially since she was scheduled to see me
that afternoon. I phoned her twice that morning, once right
before she was getting ready to leave for the appointment."
He raised an arm as if he were reaching out to guide the
dead woman through his office door, then dropped his hand
heavily against his side. "As you know, she never made it to
the office. She drove to the river instead."

He took a deep breath and brushed at his wet eyes. "Her
VW was found very near the place where Ethan's car was
found. They didn't find her body until several days later."

The fact that Ethan's Volare had ended up near the same
spot as his mother's VW, thirteen years after her death, was
a damn strange coincidence, if it *was* coincidence and not
something else. It had bothered me since Parker had tied
Talmadge to the car. I could see Ethan driving to the river
with Kirsty. What I couldn't see was Herbert Talmadge
going along for that ride. Not unless he'd been tricked or
forced into coming along—or had followed the kids there

on his own. But if he'd followed Kirsty and Ethan to the clearing, then my whole line of speculation went out the window. If he'd followed them, then it was conceivable they hadn't found Herbie—Herbie had somehow found them.

There was a third possibility—one that I'd been trying to shoot down since I first saw Ethan's collection of clippings. But it kept popping back up like a duck in a gallery. Whether they'd found him or he'd found them, it was conceivable that Herbert Talmadge had ended up in that clearing because he'd been there before. Appearances to the contrary, suicides could be faked, although that raised a helluva lot more questions than it answered.

"How soon after his mother's disappearance did Ethan start talking about a murderer?" I asked Sacks.

"Immediately, as far as I know. In fact, Phil called me on the day Stelle dropped out of sight to tell me that Ethan was throwing a violent tantrum. We both agreed it was a hysterical reaction."

"Did Pearson tell you what Ethan was *actually* saying about his mother's disappearance?"

Sacks drew back a little, as if he'd been offended by my question. "Ethan said he'd been watching Stelle from an upstairs window. He saw a man come out of the trees and get in the car with her."

"Talmadge?"

"He had no name for this bogeyman."

"He didn't associate Rita Scarne with the killer, did he?"

The man sighed. "Frankly, Stoner, I never heard the boy talk about any of this. He didn't like me, remember. He blamed me for not taking better care of his mother. I blamed me too. It was a terribly confusing time for all of us."

"Did the cops follow up on the kid's story?"

"I'm not sure."

It was easy enough to check. All I had to do was read through the police reports on Estelle Pearson's suicide when I got back to the apartment.

Sacks was beginning to look a little worn down by the conversation—by the terrible memories it invoked. He had too much else to cope with, so I decided to drop the subject of Estelle Pearson's death.

Before leaving I did ask him how it happened that Rita Scarne had been hired as Estelle Pearson's nurse. Given the woman's spotty employment record it was something that had bothered me.

"Phil liked her," he said simply. "So did Stelle. Rita has a no-nonsense manner that appeals to many people. And then Stelle worked with her once."

"I thought Estelle never practiced medicine."

"She didn't. But for a couple of years she worked as a nurse. Phil was interning, and they needed the money desperately."

"She didn't work at Rollman's, did she?" I said, taking a wild shot. "Say in the mid-seventies?"

"No. Stelle was a surgical nurse at General. In '68 and '69, I believe."

I sighed. For all I knew Talmadge was still in the army in '68 and '69.

"Were you aware that Rita Scarne had some trouble at Rollman's Hospital—trouble that got her fired in 1976?"

"No, I wasn't," Sacks said, looking surprised. "Phil did part of his residence at Rollman's. If there was trouble, it couldn't have been the kind that reflected on Rita's professional competence or he would certainly have known about it."

"I guess that's it then," I said, starting for the door. "Tell Louise I'll be in touch."

Cold night had fallen by the time I got to my car in the hospital lot. Beyond the haze of the mercury lamps and the fluorescent glare of the fast-food joints on Reed-Hartman, a full moon, red as October, climbed the eastern sky. Shivering in the wind I stared at it for a moment—a harvest moon in a winter sky.

I thought about paying Rita Scarne another visit. But until I could confront her with solid evidence connecting her to Talmadge she wasn't about to talk to me. I headed back to my apartment instead—to see if I couldn't find some of that evidence buried in the police reports of Estelle Pearson's suicide, buried in the past.

The manila envelope containing the photos of Estelle Pearson's last remains was sitting on the living room couch —just where I'd left it the night before. Throwing off my topcoat I scooped the folder up, sat down at the trestle table in the bay window, and began to go through its contents, starting with the investigating officer's first report. I was looking specifically for Ethan Pearson's testimony—anything he might have said tying Rita Scarne to the man who'd kidnapped his mother.

I didn't expect to find much—maybe a sentence or two that would look different in light of what had happened over the past few days. But the cold fact was I didn't find anything at all. Nothing about a black man hiding in the trees. Nothing about Estelle being kidnapped. Nothing about Rita Scarne. Nothing about Ethan himself.

The cops had obviously taken their cues from Phil Pearson and Shelley Sacks and ignored the boy. I couldn't blame them. The boy *was* hysterical, and there was real tragedy going on all around them. And yet cops were creatures of habit. Crazy or not, Ethan's accusations should have been routinely logged if only to be dismissed. Which meant that someone had specifically requested that the boy's testimony be omitted from the record—someone with a powerful interest in the case. Given the circumstances I figured that someone had to be Papa Phil Pearson.

I could see it happening. If Ethan had been making a violent scene, Phil might have been small enough to feel it personally, as he had when Kirsty had her breakdown thirteen years later, as he had when he'd hired me. Moreover, he had reasons of his own for not wanting his kid to shoot his mouth off around the police. If the cops had been led too far afield, the investigation could have spilled over into the rest of Pearson's life—exposing his affair with Louise, exposing any number of ugly family secrets. Louise had hinted that Phil had played a larger part in driving his wife crazy than anyone realized. Even if she'd been exaggerating, it would have been one more reason for Phil to hold the line, to limit the investigation to a suicide watch.

Of course, it was just as possible that Phil Pearson had been trying to protect his son on that terrible September afternoon, doing the best that a man with his heightened sense of shame could do to keep Ethan out of the public eye. The truth was probably somewhere in between—where it usually was.

I took a look at the coroner's report after I finished with the police folder. A couple of grisly pictures of Estelle Pearson's body were clipped to the front—one taken at the river, one at the morgue. After ten days in the Miami River the woman's nude body was badly decomposed. The coroner found deep cuts on the face and neck and what he termed "severe accidents" to buttocks, anus, pubes, and pelvis. The injuries might have raised suspicions of rape—especially when coupled with the fact that her body had been found nude—had the woman not jumped into a flooding river. The Miami's current was particularly strong that September, following a week of stormy weather. According to the coroner, driftwood and rock had done the damage to Estelle Pearson's body and the strong current had torn away her clothes. Shreds of her skirt and blouse were later found downstream in a backwater.

The coroner's autopsy revealed traces of Thorazine and alcohol in Estelle Pearson's blood. The Thorazine had been prescribed by Sacks. The booze was her own idea. After the autopsy the cops ran a cursory check of the bars in the Miamitown area on the off chance that someone had spotted Estelle tanking up. But she'd apparently done her drinking alone—perhaps as she sat in her car in the deserted field above the river. According to the coroner, the combination of Thorazine and liquor was probably potent enough to kill her. However, there was water in her lungs, so she was alive when she jumped—even if she'd been close to unconsciousness.

The only question raised at the coroner's inquest was why Estelle had killed herself on that particular afternoon. Shelley Sacks testified that the woman had been making progress since her breakdown in June. But he went on to say that violent mood swings were typical of her manic-depressive illness, and that the combination of alcohol and Thorazine had probably precipitated a psychotic reaction.

He was begging the question of why she'd taken all those drugs in the first place, but the coroner didn't pursue it. It was pretty clear from the rest of his testimony that Sacks didn't really know what had prompted Estelle Pearson to get high and throw herself in the river. As he'd once said to

me and said to the coroner, she was simply "doomed" to
take her own life.

I didn't know what to think when I finished the folder. By
definition suicides always leave unanswered questions behind them, and Estelle Pearson was no exception. If you
were convinced from the start that she'd killed herself,
then you accepted the fact that those questions would
never be satisfactorily answered. Which was precisely what
the cops and the coroner had done. If like Ethan Pearson
you were convinced that the woman had been kidnapped
and murdered, the least you could say, on reading through
the reports, was that the evidence didn't rule out the possibility.

The coroner hadn't been thinking rape and assault when
he examined the corpse, so some of the tests that would
have normally been administered in a criminal investigation—tests for semen, tests for blood type, tests that would
have been consistent with the woman's injuries—simply
weren't performed. The cops hadn't been thinking homicide either, which is why they hadn't bothered to record
Ethan's testimony or come up with anything other than a
spotty timetable of Estelle Pearson's last few hours on
earth. Perhaps self-protectively Shelley Sacks had convinced himself that his friend was hopelessly psychotic, so
he didn't really have to face the question of why, after
several months of progress, the woman had suddenly decided to end her life.

There was room for doubt, all right. And yet, even playing devil's advocate, I couldn't honestly say I believed Estelle Pearson had been murdered by Herbert Talmadge.
The woman's mental balance *was* very fragile. And even if
the evidence of her suicide had a few holes in it, it was still
persuasive. While Talmadge would help to explain the un-

expected suddenness and violence of her death, his pattern of assaults didn't really fit the case. He'd always picked on girlfriends—women he knew. If he'd attacked Estelle Pearson he'd stepped out of character and assaulted a virtual stranger. On the basis of the evidence I couldn't see any reason why.

I'd just finished with the transcripts when the phone rang. I was glad of the interruption—glad to get away from the pictures and the autopsy report. I dropped the folder on the table and walked over to the wallphone in the kitchen. It was Louise Pearson at the other end.

"How's Phil?" I asked after saying hello.

"He gets a bypass tomorrow morning."

"And the chances . . . ?"

"Not good," she said.

"I'm sorry to hear it."

"So am I," Louise said sadly. "We haven't had a happy marriage, Phil and I. Not a . . . happy marriage. But we're tied to one another, nevertheless."

She cleared her throat. "Shelley said you needed to talk to me?"

"A couple of questions about the kids."

"Why bother? It's pretty clear that Kirsty and Ethan aren't coming home, isn't it?"

"It looks that way," I admitted.

"Then why bother? Why bother about any of this hopeless mess?"

I didn't say anything.

"I'm sorry," Louise said after a moment. "It's been awful being in this goddamn hospital for ten hours. Dead time—time to think about all the mistakes. Phil and the kids. Frank."

"Your first husband."

"I was trying to remember why I married him."

"What did you come up with?"

"I loved him, I guess," she said with mild astonishment, as if it surprised her to admit it, as if the love itself surprised her. "At least I don't have to cope with that anymore. It was pure business with Phil. He got what he wanted—me. And I got the life of the country club. It was a fair trade, I suppose. The country club set for Frank."

She cleared her throat again. "What is it you wanted to ask me?"

Rita Scarne was on my mind—because of the police report—so I asked about her.

"How in the world did you come up with that woman's name?" Louise said with a laugh.

"I didn't. Ethan did. He tried to call her last night. At least, I think he did—sometime before he and Kirsty ended up with Talmadge in that clearing above the river. The Scarne woman claims he didn't call."

"You've talked to her?"

"Several hours ago."

"Rita was a hot ticket back in the old days," Louise said.

"You knew her?"

"Phil and I would occasionally run into her at parties after we were married. She was always with someone new —and young. Rita had a bit of a reputation with the hospital personnel."

"For what?"

"For being wild. You know, sexually uninhibited. It was rumored that she liked her sex rough."

"Rough enough to interest a man like Talmadge?"

"I wouldn't know. I shouldn't have been repeating thirteen-year-old gossip in the first place."

"Phil hired her to look after Estelle, didn't he?"

"Yes. He'd worked with Rita at Rollman's and thought

she was a competent nurse. I guess she was—I never heard anyone say different. I can't see why Ethan and Kirsty went looking for her unless they associate her with Estelle."

"Or with Talmadge," I said. "Herbie had a white girl-friend who was a nurse."

"It's possible, I guess. What do you think?"

"I think I'm going to have to talk to her again. Soon."

Before hanging up I told Louise that the cops wanted to know Kirsty's blood type. "I know," she said. "I've already spoken with them."

"When?"

"Lieutenant Parker called here at the hospital about an hour ago. He also wanted to talk to you."

"Did he say what about?"

"That man, Talmadge, I think."

24

▮▮

After finishing with Louise I phoned Parker at the Miamitown PD—and got one of his deputies.

"This is Stoner. I hear your boss is looking for me."

"Yeah, he is," the cop said. "You got a pencil?"

I took out my notebook.

"Six forty-four Reading Road, Apartment five. Park's there, and so are the Cincinnati police."

"What happened?" I said, writing the address down.

"This guy you're looking for—Talmadge. They found him about an hour ago."

Six forty-four Reading Road was right in the heart of the Avondale ghetto—a grimy four-story apartment house with a thirties Moderne facade of black marble window bands and smooth grey block. Small spotlights lit the walkway and the door. The building itself was dark, save for scattered lights in the apartments.

It was past nine when I got there—full dark and cold. But in spite of the bitter weather a small crowd of onlookers had gathered in front of the building—men and women, all black, peering curiously at the cops in the foyer. There were cops everywhere, and patrol cars up and down the street.

I made my way through the crowd into the apartment house lobby. A cop I knew—a patrolman named Klein—pointed me toward Sergeant Larry Parker.

"He's up on the second floor. Apartment five. That's where most of them are."

I went up the staircase to the second floor. The stairwell

smelled of the dry rot that was eating into the banisters; the stairposts shifted in their sockets like loose teeth. From the landing I spotted Parker and Al Foster of the CPD, leaning against the wall outside number 5. There were several other cops in the hall—forensic specialists with evidence kits. A dozen neighbors crowded in doorways and stared wide-eyed at the activity.

Inside apartment 5 a photographic strobe went off with a brilliant flash, spilling harsh white light through the open door. For a split second everyone in the hall was frozen in the glare. The detectives, the wide-eyed bystanders. Like one of Weegee's midnight crime-scene specials. I didn't want to think about what the cops inside the apartment might be photographing.

I walked up to Parker and Foster.

"I been trying to get you for an hour," Parker said when he spotted me.

"You've been here that long?"

He glanced at a wristwatch. "Since a quarter of eight." He looked at Al. "Isn't that when the call first came in?"

Al nodded. "Around then."

I said, "What have you got?"

"What we got," Al said, pushing away from the wall with his elbows and turning to the door, "is Herbert Talmadge's apartment."

"What about Talmadge himself?"

"Take a look," he said, waving me in like an impresario.

I walked through the door into a foursquare room, empty except for a single folding chair and a new-looking portable TV. The pine floors were swollen in ridges where the hot water pipes ran underneath them, giving the place a wavy, seasick feel. There was a stench, too. Not the dry rot smell of the stairs but a fecal smell of decay, like a dead animal in a wall. I didn't know where the stink was coming from until I glanced to my left through a portal leading to a small kitchen.

I couldn't see him clearly because of the criminalistics men surrounding him like mourners at a visitation. But when one of the cops moved, I caught a glimpse of his legs, sprawled at angles as if he'd been struggling to get up. Then I saw his face—that devilish, V-shaped face—grotesquely purpled and swollen in rigor. Herbert Talmadge. Streaks of blood, turned thick brown like molasses, flowed from his body, from a wound I couldn't see.

I looked away, at the seasick room. There were no decorations on the peeling yellow walls. No pictures or papers. A bare mantel to the right with a small dusty mirror above it and a dead fireplace below, charred like a burnt pot. Blinded windows on the far wall, with a stertorous hot water radiator rattling beneath them. Like Ethan Pearson's barren motel room it was the end of the road for Herbert Talmadge.

When the smell began to get to me, I went back into the hall. Al was standing just outside the door.

"You saw?"

I nodded. "How long has he been dead?"

"We won't know for sure until the coroner gets him. But forensic is guessing about twelve hours—maybe a little less."

"So he died around six this morning?"

Foster nodded. "Give or take an hour."

The Pearson kids had left the motel room at midnight Monday. Their abandoned car had been found at six that morning—and it had been in the clearing for an hour or two more than that, judging by the dead battery. That meant that Talmadge could have left his prints in the Volare anytime between midnight and four or five a.m. After that he'd apparently come home to be murdered himself.

I stared uneasily through the door at the circle of cops standing around Herbert Talmadge's corpse. "How did he die?"

"Again, we're not sure," Foster said. "Drug overdose, we think. At least we found an empty bottle of Demerol on the floor—and enough drugs in the bathroom to have put him to sleep forever. But there's a wound, too."

"What kind of wound?"

"Somebody stabbed him in the heart. What we don't know is whether the stabbing occurred before or after Talmadge was dead. Whoever stabbed him didn't like him—that's for sure. They twisted the blade back and forth several dozen times, like a drill bit."

In spite of myself I thought of Ethan and Kirsty Pearson. They had motive, God knew. And Talmadge had died as Ethan foretold in his poem—*a knife blade in the darkness.* "Did you find any evidence connecting Talmadge to the Pearson kids?"

"We found a woman's shoe in the fireplace," Parker said. "Size eight. There was some blood on it. Right now we're not sure whose blood it is. There was some other stuff in the fireplace, some paper—apparently he tried to burn it."

"Any idea what it was?"

"Forensic's got it. We'll know in a day or so." Parker took a breath. "There's something else."

From the look on his face I knew I wasn't going to like it. "What?"

"The back room. There's a mattress and . . . well, it looks like someone was tied down to it and pretty badly used. We found blood, hair, ropes, and a gag. Harry, the blood is type O negative. Same as on the panties."

"Kirsty," I said.

Parker nodded. "They must've found him in the apartment. He overpowered them and. . . . When he was done he drove them out to the Miami and tossed them in like a sack of kittens. It almost looks like Talmadge was waiting for them. I mean, the ropes and gags."

I said, "Didn't anyone in the building hear anything, for chrissake?"

Parker shook his head. "No. At least no one's saying they did."

"Who called the thing in?"

"A neighbor-woman up the hall," Al said. He pulled a notebook from his coat, flipped it open, and glanced at his notes. "When she got home from work today, she smelled that stink in Small's room and phoned us."

"Small?" I said.

"I mean Talmadge," Al said, flipping the note pad shut. "Small's the name she and the neighbors knew him by—the name he rented the apartment under. Herbert Small."

I glanced at the door to the apartment where a pitted brass number dangled from a nail. Number 5. *Small/5.*

"How the hell did they find him?" Parker said with exasperation. "Why did he kill them? Why did he drive them to the river?"

The only question I could answer was the first one— they'd found him because someone had phoned them at the motel and told them where to look. I didn't let Parker know that. I didn't want to.

"The woman who called this in," I said to Al. "You think I could talk to her?"

He nodded. "Across the hall. Number seven."

Her name was Moira Richardson, and she worked as a cleaning woman in Roselawn. She claimed to have no particular interest in Herbert Talmadge, but after I started talking to her I got the feeling that she took an interest in everything that went on in the building—or on the block.

She was a buxom woman with a shrewd, mobile, care-worn face. She spoke very slowly as people do when they want to be taken seriously, when they take themselves seriously. A younger woman, her daughter I thought, sat in a rocking chair in a far corner of the room.

I asked Moira Richardson when Talmadge/Small had moved in.

"Monday a week," she said. "Didn't have no belongings. No furniture."

"Do you know if he had a job?"

"That kind don't never work," the woman said, scowling. "In fact, I couldn't figure out where he got money for rent. Bought him a TV, too. And a car. Now where's a jailbird like that gonna get a TV, less he's pushing drugs or got some woman on the street."

It was an interesting question.

"Did he have any friends in the building?"

"He didn't ever say no more than two or three words to no one. Just come and go—mostly late at night. Girl down the hall said he asked to use her phone once. But she wouldn't let him in. She was scared of him." The woman threw her hand at me dismissively. "I ain't scared of no woolly-headed monkey like that."

"Did you let him use your phone?"

"He never asked me. Knew better than to ask me anything."

"Did you ever see him with anyone outside the building?"

The woman shook her head. "No sir, I didn't."

"I did," the one in the rocking chair chirruped.

She was a plump, pretty girl with soft brown eyes and a tiny, sparrow voice.

"Wha'chu mean 'you did'?" her mother said with massive suspicion.

The girl squirmed in the rocker. At first I thought she was frightened, then I realized she was simply excited at being the center of attention—mine and her mother's.

"I did too see, Mama," she said, twisting her head around and pouting at the far wall with her lower lip. "Saw him in the park with a white lady, last night."

The older woman fell back in her chair, stunned. "Well, I'll be."

"What time last night?" I asked.

"Time I'm coming home on the bus," the girl said. " 'Bout six o'clock. They was in Prospect Park. Way back in the shadows, toward the apartment house."

"You're sure it was Tal . . . Small?"

"Purty sure."

As if someone had snapped his fingers, the mother came rocketing out of her trance, lunging forward in her chair and fixing her daughter with a savage look.

"You didn't see nobody in no park."

"Did too," the girl said, shrinking beneath her mother's doubt.

"You wasting this man's time with your foolishness."

The girl's big brown eyes began to water. "I saw him," she said with trembly lips. "With a white lady."

"What that lady look like?" the mother said, as if she had her now.

The girl's head sank to her breast. "Couldn't see her face. It was too dark."

"You see," the mother said to me triumphantly. "She didn't see nothing. That's why she didn't tell them cops. She knew they'd catch her up on her lies."

"I ain't lying," the girl said, in tears now. "She was a white lady in a long brown coat. And she had on a white dress and white stockings and white shoes."

"Like a nurse?" I said, feeling a chill.

"Yes, sir," the girl said plaintively and looked up at me like I was her savior. "That's what I said to myself. He gone and got him a nurse from the hospital. You believe me, don't you? Tell Mama you believe me."

"Yes," I said. "I do."

25

I didn't tell Parker or Al Foster where I was going when I left the apartment house. I wasn't ready to tell them anything, yet. Not until I'd had the chance to talk to Rita Scarne without the law looking over my shoulder. I could always contact Parker—or threaten to contact him—if Rita wouldn't cooperate. But in the mood I was in I didn't think that was going to be necessary.

It was almost ten-thirty when I turned into the driveway leading to Rita Scarne's handsome house. I flipped off the headlights and coasted slowly down the hill, through the oak grove where the dark trees rustled in the wind. There was enough windowlight coming from the front of the house to guide me toward the garage. I parked the car at an angle in front of it, blocking off any exit. Getting out I walked up to the door, pressed the bell, stepped back into the shadows, and waited. After a time I heard someone fiddling with a bolt lock. The bolt slid free and the door opened a crack. I stepped forward immediately, leaning against the door with my shoulder and forcing it all the way open.

Rita Scarne was standing just inside the hall. She was wearing a brown topcoat over a nurse's uniform—the same outfit she'd worn for her meeting with Talmadge in Prospect Park. A small black leather satchel, like a doctor's bag, sat on the hall floor where she'd dropped it.

"What the hell is this?" she said, looking startled. "You're not welcome here. I thought I made that clear."

"We're going to talk, Rita," I said, grabbing her by the arm.

She tried to jerk away from me, but I pulled her back hard. "Don't," I said, waving a warning finger in her face.

"You can't do this!" she shouted.

"Watch me."

Dragging the woman behind me I walked quickly down the hall to the glassed-in terrace. I yanked Rita Scarne through the door, spun her around and sat her down on the fan-back chair. She stared up at me savagely.

"Now we're going to talk Rita," I said, bending over her. "No bullshit. The truth this time."

"The truth about what?"

"About last night. You remember yesterday evening, don't you? When Ethan called?"

"He didn't call."

"Don't say that! I don't want to hear that! Or about your sister who was house-sitting."

The woman's face reddened furiously. "Well, what the hell do you want to hear? Tell me so we can get this melodrama over with."

"You called the motel and sent those kids to that fucking maniac's apartment, Rita. You may even have told the son of a bitch they were coming. I want to know why. I want to know what those kids knew about you and Herbert Talmadge that made you send them to their deaths."

"Nothing!" she shouted. "There was nothing between me and Herbert Talmadge. I've already told you that."

"You were lying then. And you're lying now. You were seen with Talmadge on McMicken Street before Estelle Pearson died and again Monday night in Prospect Park."

"That's preposterous. Where are you getting your information—from that screwball Pearson kid?"

"I'll make this easy for you. You were fucking Talmadge back in '76, and Ethan found out. A snoopy kid who hated your guts, he saw you and Herbie doing it in the backyard, or the patio, on your lunchbreak, while Estelle was zonked out on Thorazine. Anyway he saw you."

Rita Scarne sneered at me. "Why would I screw a man like that?"

"Because you like men like that, Rita. You always have. Big, brutal, dangerous men. Men who can make it hurt the way you like it. Men like Herbie."

Rita Scarne sat back in the chair and laughed contemptuously. "You've got me confused with somebody else, Stoner."

"Like who?"

"Like you figure it out. Only you're not talking about me."

She reached over to the table where the fifth of Old Grand-dad was still sitting. There was a scant shot left inside, and she swallowed it straight. The whiskey made her face flush again, all the way to the roots of her loose blond hair.

"I don't know anything about Talmadge or the Pearson kids." She settled back in the chair, hugging the bottle to her breasts like a stuffed toy. "You can keep this up all night, and it won't change that."

"You don't understand, Rita. The cops have a witness who'll swear she saw you in Prospect Park with Herbert Talmadge. They've got a record of the call Ethan Pearson made from his motel room to your agency—the call the agency forwarded to your house. They've got drugs that can probably be traced to that bag of yours. A TV your money paid for. And they've got a dead man in an Avondale apartment with a big hole in his chest that you made with your own little hands."

"A dead man?" Rita Scarne said. The fight drained out of her face, leaving the naked fear. "Who's dead?"

"Talmadge, Rita. Herb Talmadge. And Ethan and Kirsty

Pearson. You killed them all this morning, don't you remember? Herb did two for you, and you did Herb." I bent down so my face was only a few inches from hers. "You killed them all and you're going to die for it."

"Bastard!" Raising both hands, she tried to claw my face. I grabbed her wrists and pinned them to the arms of the chair.

"He came after you, didn't he, Rita? Thirteen years and he came after you the day he got out of Lex. What did he want? Drugs? Money? Some of that good, old-fashioned, hardball sex you specialize in? You couldn't say no, could you? Not to Herb. What did he have on you? Something from your days at Rollman's? Something about Estelle?"

The woman looked away.

I stared at her for a moment—at her red, averted face. "It *was* Estelle, wasn't it? What did Talmadge do to Estelle?"

And, suddenly, I didn't have to ask anymore. "Good Christ."

I started to laugh.

I let go of the woman's hands—she wasn't going anywhere—and sat down across from her on the couch, still laughing. It was such a grand joke. "Ethan was telling the truth. Your crazy, drugged-out boyfriend *did* show up at the house, looking for you. Only you weren't there. You were sick. That's it, isn't it? What happened then, Rita? Did Herbie grab Estelle instead? Grab her, pour liquor into her, and rape her. Is that why she killed herself? Or did Herb do that, too?"

Rita Scarne's head sank slowly to her chest.

I sat back in the chair, letting the last of my laughter die away. "And you were afraid to say anything—afraid you'd catch the blame. After all you'd just been fired from Rollman's, so your credibility wasn't so hot. Or maybe Herbie was the reason you got fired in the first place. A little hanky-panky on the psych ward. It's easy enough to check out."

The woman raised her head weakly. "Getting fired had nothing to do with sex," she said in a whisper. "I was fired because of . . . I did a favor for someone."

"What favor?"

She looked at me squarely for the first time since I'd mentioned Estelle Pearson's death. "I got the bastard released. Okay? They were going to send him away for good, and I got him released." She looked down again—at the bottle in her arms. "I stole some drugs from the dispensary, too."

When I'd talked to him on the phone, Dr. Isaac Goldman had claimed he hadn't authorized Talmadge's release—that he'd recommended confinement at Longview. I thought he'd simply forgotten the facts. Now it seemed he'd never known them.

"You forged Goldman's signature?"

"I waited until he left town, so they never knew about the release. It was the drugs that cost me the job. The old biddy, Rostow, found out I'd been taking them from the dispensary. The hospital board agreed not to press charges if I resigned my post."

"What kind of drugs did you steal?"

"Painkillers. Demerol. Talmadge loved the shit. And . . . it made him manageable."

"Manageable? Manageable by whom?"

Rita Scarne sighed heavily. "A friend. She was . . . involved with him. She wanted him out of the hospital."

"Your friend was a nurse?"

"Yes."

"Carla Chaney?" It was the only name that made sense.

The woman jerked as if she'd been prodded. "You know about Carla?"

"Just her name and the fact that she was your room-mate."

Rita Scarne stared at me searchingly, then shook her head as if she hadn't found what she'd been looking for. "You don't know anything. You couldn't."

She said it, but she didn't sound convinced.

"What is it I don't know?" I asked. "Why did Carla want Talmadge out of the hospital? What did it have to do with last night?"

"Last night?" She wasn't paying attention to me any-more. She sat in the chair and stared fearfully out the win-dow at the cold December dark.

"What really happened thirteen years ago?"

Rita Scarne blinked stupidly and stood up. The whiskey bottle slid off her lap, clattering to the floor. "I've got to get out of here," she said in a desperate voice.

"Not until we're finished."

The woman clasped her hands together as if she was praying. "You don't understand. It's falling apart. All of it. I should have known when you first showed up." She glanced through the window again at the dark woods behind the house. "I'm next. It won't stop until no one's left to tell."

"To tell what? For chrissake, make sense."

"I can't," she said. "Not now. Not until I'm sure it's safe. Not until I've made it safe."

"How will you do that?"

But she didn't answer me. "Give me a few hours. Please, Stoner? A few hours to make it safe. Then I'll talk to you about Carla . . . about all of it."

"What's to keep you from running away?"

"Where to?" she said. "I've got no place to run." She sat back down on the chair and raised her clasped hands. "Please, Stoner. Just a few hours."

I glanced at my watch which was showing ten-thirty. "I'll

give you until two-thirty this morning. Then we talk about
you, Herb, Carla, Estelle, this whole damn thing."

She nodded, yes.

I started for the hall.

"Stoner," the woman called out. I looked back at her.
"You were right—Ethan must have seen me with Talmadge."

"I thought you said you had nothing to do with Herb."

"He picked me up at work a couple of times in Carla's
car." The woman laughed dully. "Who knows? Maybe it
was planned that way."

26

I left the house but I didn't go far. Up Ridge to a gravel turnaround about fifty yards from the head of Rita Scarne's driveway. I sat there among the maple trees and the roadside hackberry bushes, listening to the tail end of a basketball game on the car radio, and waiting.

Around eleven-thirty I saw headlights coming up the driveway. A moment later Rita's car—the green Audi—cleared the crest of the hill and nosed out onto Ridge. Turning left the woman blew past me, heading west toward Roselawn. I waited until the taillights disappeared over a small rise, then put the Pinto in gear and started after her.

The night was clear and there wasn't any traffic on the road, so I had no trouble following even at a distance. And then Rita Scarne wasn't making any tricky maneuvers—a left on Section, a right at the Paddock entrance ramp to the interstate. She got on I-75, and I did too, settling back a couple hundred yards behind her as she sped north toward Dayton.

It began to flurry about a half hour after we got on the interstate—big flakes that fluttered lazily in the beams of the headlights and blew back against the windshield in sudden, undulant gusts. Through the side window I watched the dark, featureless hills along the expressway take shape beneath the snow—the stands of trees grow crooked limbs, white and fantastic-looking. Straight in front of me the twin red dots of Rita Scarne's taillights marked the miles.

About forty minutes outside of Cincinnati we hit the Dayton corporation limit. According to Nurse Rostow, Rita

Scarne was from Dayton, Ohio, and I had the feeling that she was headed home.

But she didn't take the first Dayton exit. In fact she went all the way through the city before slowing down and pulling off the interstate on the north side of town. The exit ramp emptied into a working-class suburb of two-story brick houses and foursquare lawns. Red and green Christmas lights were strung on most of the porches. Here and there nativity scenes burned like lighted billboards in the slanting snow.

Rita worked her way through a maze of side streets before finally pulling over in front of a staid red-brick St. Louis with no strings of Christmas lights on its porch, no nativity scene on its narrow lawn. I pulled over across from her and watched through the windshield as she got out of the Audi and walked up to the house. She was carrying the black leather satchel I'd seen in the hall.

The St. Louis had front stoops on either side. Rita walked over to the right-hand stoop and up the stairs to the door. Someone opened the door immediately, as if she was expected.

The door led to a living room with a picture window in front. The window was lighted and the blinds were up. After a time Rita came into view in the window, with a second woman trailing behind her. I couldn't make out the second woman's face because of the falling snow, but she was wearing a nurse's uniform, just like Rita's. The two women embraced for a moment, then walked off into another part of the house, disappearing from sight.

At precisely one a.m., Rita Talmadge came back out onto the stoop at the side of the house. The snowstorm had blown over by then, leaving the night sky spangled with cold, distant stars. I heard Rita say, "Good-bye," to someone inside the doorway, and watched as she walked down to the street and over to the Audi. She wasn't carrying the satchel anymore.

I waited until she drove away, then got out of the Pinto and walked up to the brick St. Louis. The front window was still lit. Through it I could see the second woman standing in the living room, staring queerly off into space. She was a tall buxom blonde like Rita. Only younger than Rita by five or so years and less weathered-looking. I went around to the right side of the house and climbed the stoop. There was a mailbox by the door with a name and number. I'd expected to find "Carla Chaney" written on it, but the placard read "Charlotte Scarne, 516 Minton." I assumed Charlotte was Rita's sister. It was unquestionably Rita's old address. I knocked on the door.

Charlotte Scarne must have thought Rita had come back a second time, for she was smiling when she opened the door. Her smile wilted when she saw me.

"Yes?"

"My name's Stoner, Ms. Scarne. I'd like to talk to you about Rita."

The woman didn't look surprised. She didn't invite me in, either.

"You know who I am?" I asked.

She nodded. "I know. Rita told me."

"Did she tell you what kind of trouble she's in?"

She nodded again.

"If you want to help her, you'll talk to me."

"You're not trying to help her," the woman said scornfully. "You're trying to put her in jail."

"I'm trying to find out what happened to two lost kids, Ms. Scarne. And I don't want to send anyone to jail—especially the wrong person. But if you and Rita don't cooperate, you're not going to leave me a choice."

"I don't know anything," the woman said. But she was a poor, inexperienced liar, and the words caught in her throat.

Charlotte Scarne was definitely not the hard character that her sister was. Everything about her was softer, less coarsened by experience—her voice, her face, her manner. I knew I'd have no trouble working on her—whatever her sister had left behind was visibly weighing her down.

I said, "Ms. Scarne, help me put this thing together before someone else ends up dead."

The woman started as if I'd touched the right nerve. "Rita's afraid of that."

"Can you tell me why?"

"Something from the past—something she shouldn't have done."

Charlotte Scarne stepped back from the door. It was as much of an invitation as I was going to get and I took it, stepping quickly into the room.

It was an old-fashioned parlor full of dusty knickknacks and dark mahogany furniture. Framed photographs of Mom, Pop, and the girls lined the mantel. Other pieces of ancient memorabilia were scattered on end tables and sideboards—china plates from a postwar exposition, a Steuben trout blowing crystal bubbles in a crystal cube, one lorn tin trophy that Dad had won at a company picnic, a wedding picture of the folks fading to yellow in its glass frame.

The room had the feel of arrested development—of life gone sad and sour and still. The whole house was probably the same. A woman like Rita Scarne could never live in a place like that. I had the feeling that her sister, Charlotte, was trapped in it.

"I haven't cleaned yet," the woman said guiltily, as if that explained the dismal room. "I was on duty tonight, and I didn't have a chance to clean."

"It's fine," I said to her.

She laughed dully. "No, it's not." And that was all she said.

I sat down on a dusty tuxedo couch, and the woman wandered over to a chair. "What can you tell me, Charlotte? What's got your sister so frightened?"

Charlotte Scarne looked down at the floor. "All she said was that it had to do with Carla—something she'd done for Carla a long time ago. She wouldn't say any more than that. She told me it was better if I didn't know."

"Carla, meaning Carla Chaney?"

The woman nodded.

"They were like sisters," she said, then flushed a little at the irony in her words. "Carla rented the upstairs rooms for a few months in the winter of '74 and spring of '75, while she was working as a nurse. Rita was a nurse, too. So they just naturally got along."

From the sound of her voice I had the feeling that she hadn't shared her sister's feeling for Nurse Chaney. "You didn't like Carla?"

"I liked her okay," Charlotte said without conviction. "It was just that she was always so . . . ambitious. Carla wanted things, and she didn't seem to care what it took to get them. She kind of infected Rita with her thinking. At least, I felt she did. It was a fact that Rita stopped coming to see us once the two of them moved to Cincinnati. She didn't visit us for almost two years after they left town."

Charlotte Scarne frowned bitterly, as if those two years alone with the folks had cost her something she'd never been paid for. "Rita finally came back in '77 when Dad died. By then she had everything she wanted—car, clothes, money. She paid for Dad's funeral out of her own pocket— several thousand dollars. She paid the last of the mortgage off, too. It was a humbling experience. Especially for Mom. I mean she thought Rita was going straight to hell when she left with Carla. I guess Rita showed her—and me, too."

"How did Rita make so much money in two years, Charlotte?"

"She had a good job. She said she'd saved it. Now I'm not sure."

The woman got up and went over to a mahogany breakfront. Opening a drawer, she lifted out the black leather satchel. "This is what Rita came for. She wanted me to have it, in case . . ." She stared blankly at the satchel, as if it wasn't the legacy she'd expected from her sister.

"What's inside?"

"Money. Ten thousand dollars." She handed the bag to me. "There are some bankbooks, too."

"Did Rita say where she got the money?"

"Some of it was left over from a long time ago. Blood money, she called it. Some of it she said she'd saved on her own. She told me I was to use it to buy myself a new chance at life—I mean if something happened to her." Charlotte Scarne shuddered violently. "I don't want it. I don't want any part of it. Someone died because of it."

"Did Rita say who?"

Charlotte took a deep breath. "Carla, I think."

I stared at the woman for a long moment. "What makes you say that?"

"Because we never saw Carla again after she and Rita left town. Rita never even spoke about her. I mean the two of them were inseparable friends. And then it was as if Carla never existed."

"Maybe she moved away from Cincinnati?"

"I don't think so," Charlotte said. "Whenever I'd ask Rita about Carla, she'd act like it was something she couldn't talk about. Something bad, you know? Carla could be pretty bad. I used to think that something must have happened to

her when she was a kid—something really dreadful—to
make her that way."

"What way is that?" I asked.

"Just . . . brutal," she said, flushing again. "Except for
Rita she didn't really seem to care about anything or anyone—like what was inside her, the caring part, had curled
up and died. I sneaked up to her room once while she was
living here and found this stuff—leather-and-metal stuff. I
didn't know what it meant then, just that it was bad. Later I
realized that Carla liked to be hurt and to hurt other people."

I thought of Herbert Talmadge—a man after Carla's own
heart.

"Your sister said she did a favor for Carla that she'd been
paid money for. Did she give you any hint what that favor
was—if it might have involved a man named Talmadge?"

"All she said was that someone had died as a result. And
that she was afraid she might die, too."

"Why?"

"I don't know," the woman said helplessly.

"Did she mention Kirsty and Ethan Pearson?"

"Who are they?"

"The children of a woman Rita once worked for. A phone
call from them last night might have triggered this whole
thing. You don't know anything about that, do you?"

"Why would I know anything?" the woman said, looking
confused.

"Your sister claimed you were house-sitting for her last
night. And the agency Rita works for forwarded the Pearson kid's call to Rita's house."

"I don't know anything about any call," she said flatly.

"And Rita never mentioned the Pearsons to you?"

"She didn't mention them." Charlotte Scarne shuddered
from head to foot. "Mr. Stoner, Rita acted as if she deserved

to die. Whatever she did, it must have been a pretty terrible thing to make her feel that way."

Although the woman was talking about something in Rita's past, I couldn't help thinking of Herbert Talmadge, lying on that kitchen floor with his heart cut out. Of the deserted, blood-spattered Plymouth, sitting above the river where Estelle Pearson had died. Terrible things indeed.

27

Charlotte was still staring dully at Rita Scarne's satchel when I left the house on Minton Street. To her the money was tainted by death. Tainted also by her own ambivalence toward Rita—the prodigal who had run away from home, leaving Charlotte to live a life of dismal rectitude in that dismal house. No matter that it was probably the life that suited her best. It was less painful to blame Rita. And perhaps Rita had felt some of that blame was deserved. Ten thousand tax-free dollars certainly would have given Charlotte a fresh chance.

It took me forty minutes to get back to Cincinnati and another ten to wend my way up the snowy Amberley Village side streets to Ridge Road and Rita Scarne's house. It was after three in the morning by then, past the time I had set for my meeting with the woman. No matter the time I intended to talk to her.

Because of the snowfall I had trouble finding the entrance to the driveway. I might not have found it at all if it weren't for a pair of fresh tire tracks veering off Ridge and leading down the hill to the house. The treadmarks were a doubly good sign—they meant Rita Scarne had come home. After she'd run to her sister's house in Dayton, I was a little worried that she might keep going—out of the city, out of the state. But she'd decided to come back. With all those bad memories in her head, maybe she didn't have it in her to go anywhere else.

I followed the tire tracks through the oak grove into the snowy dell, and found the green Audi parked in front of the garage. At least I thought it was parked there. But as I got

closer I saw grey smoke trailing from the tailpipe. The
engine had been left running. The parking lights were on
too, throwing a faint yellow wash up the side of the dark
house. The fact that there weren't any lights on in the house
itself bothered me. Even if the woman had dashed inside,
intending to come right back out, there should have been
lights on somewhere.

I pulled up behind the Audi and realized with a start that
Rita Scarne was still sitting in the car. I could see her head
and shoulders in the beam of my headlights. I could see
something else too. The passenger-side window of the Audi
had a spiderweb fracture—the kind that comes from a gun
shot.

"Christ," I said aloud.

Leaving my headlights on I got out into the cold and
walked slowly up to the woman's car. The Audi's radio had
been left on. I could hear it singing softly over the idling
engine. There was a sharp smell of cordite in the air, and
something else. Something that wasn't gunpowder or ex-
haust fumes. Taking a breath I bent down and looked inside
the car.

The driver-side window was open, and a bit of snow had
blown through it, dusting the shoulder of Rita Scarne's coat
and what was left of her face.

She'd been shot in the temple—at very close range because the powder burns had singed her blond hair above
the left ear. The bullet had apparently gone through her
skull, exiting the right side of her head and breaking the
passenger-side window. There was no question Rita Scarne
was dead. Half her brain was lying beside her in the passenger seat.

There was enough light coming from my headlights and
the Audi's dashboard instruments for me to make out a gun

—a snub-nosed .38—lying in the woman's lap next to her outstretched hand. There was a sealed envelope on her lap too, spotted with blood.

I stood up and looked around the car. Two sets of footprints, a woman's shoe, stretched from the driver-side door to the front door of the house and back again—as if Rita had gone inside for a moment. There were no other footprints, man's or woman's, in the front yard snow and no other tire tracks in the driveway, save for those from the Audi and my Pinto.

I glanced back at the woman—at the blood-spattered envelope in her lap. She'd been deeply depressed that night. Talmadge was dead, probably at her hands. The Pearson kids were also dead with her connivance. An ugly thirteen-year-old secret—a secret full of blood and money —was coming back to haunt her. With me and the cops breathing down her neck, she could easily have decided to end it. In fact she'd told her sister she'd deserved to die no more than an hour before, after giving away all she had left to give.

It was probably a suicide, all right. And yet I couldn't quite buy it. Maybe because I hadn't been prepared to find her dead. Maybe because she'd left me with too many unanswered questions. Maybe because I'd half believed her earlier that night when she'd begged me to give her time to make things right. She'd been afraid of someone. Not me or the cops but someone from her past, someone who had paid her the "blood money," someone who had marked her— and Estelle, Talmadge, and the two Pearson kids—for death.

Suicides could be faked—it was like a theme running through the case. The open car window could have meant that she'd been approached in the driveway by someone

who had carefully covered his tracks. It could also have
meant that she'd wanted a breath of air before pulling the
trigger—a breath of air and some elbow room to hold the
gun to her head. Finding the truth of it was a job for a
forensic team and a coroner.

Reaching through the window I flipped off the engine
and pulled the keys out of the ignition. The sudden silence
in the dell was dramatic enough to send a chill down my
back. I looked around the yard again at the dark house and
darker woods beyond it. If there was someone out there
looking back at me, I couldn't see him. But I wanted to get
inside the house anyway—away from that car and my own
paranoia.

The house key was on the ring with the car keys. I found
it, unlocked the front door, and went inside.

There was a phone on a stand in the hallway. I picked the
receiver up and dialed Al Foster at the CPD. While I waited
for him to come on the line I thought about going back
outside and getting the envelope from the car. But I knew
the forensic cops wouldn't like me tampering with evidence. I had enough to answer for already.

We were in the kitchen on the south side of the house—
Parker, Foster, and I. Through the icy windows we could
see the forensic men packing up their gear. It was almost
six-thirty, and grey morning light had just begun to spill
down the hillside, wrapping itself around the oak trunks
and turning the pitted snow in the yard to lead.

The coroner had taken Rita Scarne's body away about ten
minutes before. And now it was just the routine work of
cleaning up after a suicide. That was what the coroner
called it when he'd finished the preliminary exam. The
woman's prints were on the gun butt. A paraffin test had

turned up gunpowder on her fingers. The angle of the bullet was such that only she—or someone bending down beside her and holding the gun right to her skull through the open window—could have pulled the trigger. And there were no other footprints by the car. The ones leading to and from the door were definitely Rita's. And if that wasn't enough there was the note, sealed in the envelope.

I got to see it myself after Parker and Foster had read it— a typed confession on a page of Rita's stationery. It sat between us on the kitchen table, like a dividing line. I picked it up and read it again while we waited for the forensic team to finish—Rita Scarne's last testament.

I am responsible for the deaths of Herbert Talmadge and Estelle, Ethan and Kirsty Pearson. May God forgive me for what I've done and what I'm about to do.

There was no signature. She'd signed it in that car with the gun.

I laid the thing back down on the table. I didn't feel any different than I had the first time I'd read it. Which was to say I didn't know what to think. She hadn't explained anything. And I said so out loud.

Larry Parker eyed me balefully across the kitchen table. "What is your problem, Stoner? This wasn't her life story. It was a suicide note. She'd been caught red-handed committing murder, for chrissake. Or she would have been caught if you'd obeyed the law."

It wasn't the first time we'd gone over that ground in the past few hours, and I was getting a little tired of it and of Parker, who'd started to act very much like a small-town cop.

"There was someone else involved," I said to him. "Someone who'd paid Rita off thirteen years ago. Someone she was afraid of."

"Like who?" Parker said irritably. "And what difference would it make? You heard the coroner. The Scarne woman wasn't murdered—she killed herself."

"It makes a difference if you're interested in why she did it."

"I'm interested in solving three murders. Period. And we've got the evidence to do that."

He held up his right hand and started ticking things off on his fingers. "The shoe we found in Talmadge's apartment is the same size that the Scarne woman wears. There are a couple of bottles of Demerol in her medicine cabinet upstairs just like the ones we found in Herbie's apartment. We got a witness who saw her talking to Talmadge on Monday night. We got a phone call from Ethan to her agency, as well as a note from the motel room, with a name and address that could only come from her. And, lest we forget, we have a fucking confession, typed on her typewriter, on her stationery." Parker dropped his hand to the table. "We got it all."

"Except for the reasons why."

Parker got a pained look on his face. "She'd been making time with this guy, Talmadge, thirteen years ago. The Pearson kid saw them together and remembered Herbie's face. Thirteen years later Talmadge gets out of jail and looks old friend Rita up. She can't say no to him because he's dangerous. Plus he's got something on her—something connected to Estelle Pearson's suicide or to that other woman you mentioned, the Chaney girl."

"Like what?" I asked.

"How do I know what?" he snapped. "Christ, it was your idea. You tell me what. Whatever the reason Rita's scared to death of Talmadge but doesn't know how to get rid of him until the Pearson kids blunder onto the scene. The boy calls her up, and she sics them on Herbie. And when that back-fires she gets Talmadge stoned and does the job herself. Case closed."

"What about the ten thousand bucks? Who paid her that kind of money, Parker? And why? She said someone died because of it."

"She said a lot of things," Parker said uneasily. "Christ Almighty, she was headed for death row. She got fired for stealing drugs, didn't she? Maybe the money came from drugs—or from some other deal she cooked up. Who the hell knows?"

"Or ever will," I said, "if you don't ask a few more questions."

He glared at me. "Well, we can't ask Rita now, can we? Thanks to you."

"We can try to find Carla Chaney," I said. "At least we can try to find out what happened to her."

"*You* try to find her." Parker got up and lumbered over to the door. "I'm going home to get some sleep." He glanced back over his shoulder at me and Foster. "It'll come to-gether. Over the next few days, it'll all fit. Even the money thing. We'll keep dredging the river, but I already know what we're going to find."

"We don't know they're dead," I said.

"I do," Parker said. "The blood on the panties we found in the Plymouth and the blood on the bed in the apartment was Kirsten's. We've confirmed it."

"How?"

"The stepmother gave me the girl's blood type last night when I called the hospital looking for you. Type O nega-tive."

He opened the door then looked back over his shoulder. "You know those papers in the fireplace? Forensic says they could be pages from a diary. Some kind of manuscript, anyway. Does that ring any bells for you?"

"The Pearson girl was writing a book about her life. She was looking for an ending."

"Well, she found one," he said as he went out the door.

28

I spent a few more minutes talking to Foster before going home. He knew the case wasn't as cut-and-dry as Parker wanted it to be. But he also knew that most of the questions I'd raised would never be answered. There was no one left to answer them.

"Thirteen years is a long time, Harry," he said. "There are bound to be loose ends when a thing stretches back that far. Parker's got to make a case for the coroner's jury. And there's enough circumstantial evidence to do that."

"It isn't right, Al," I said, shaking my head.

"Maybe not. But unless you come up with something more than hearsay or a hunch, I'm going to have to stick with Park."

"Do me one favor, will you? Just run the Chaney girl through CID. Okay? Carla Chaney." I gave him her old addresses on Minton Street in Dayton and on Terrace in Cincinnati. "See if you come up with anything."

Al sighed. "Like what?"

"I'd settle for a current address."

He wrote down the girl's name, then got up and went to the door. "You better start resigning yourself to the fact that the Pearson case is history. Or you're going to end up wasting a lot of your time—and mine."

I should have phoned Louise Pearson as soon as I got back to the apartment. But I was too depressed to make the call. Larry Parker had been right about one thing. If I'd told the cops about Rita Scarne, she'd have been in custody at that moment. Instead I'd played it as if it was my case—mine alone. And now Rita was dead. And whatever she had known had died with her.

I lay down on the bed and eventually fell asleep. But it was troubled sleep—full of my own guilt and other people's deaths. The woman in the car with her head split apart. The grey Plymouth with the dark river below it, making a roar like traffic. Kirsten's book, turning fat and black in the fireplace. Talmadge, leaking blood on a battered kitchen floor. A world without second chances.

The alarm woke me around eleven that Wednesday morning. There was sun outside and cold blue sky. I sat in bed for a while, letting the dreams clear out of my head. Dragging myself into the kitchen I fixed coffee, pouring a little Scotch in the cup to brace myself for what lay ahead.

Officially the Pearson case was almost over for everyone but me and the Pearsons. However many of them were left alive on that winter morning.

I took a hot shower, shaved, dressed, and managed to make it out of the apartment and into the car by noon. Phil Pearson would be coming out of surgery about the time I got to Bethesda North, if he'd survived the bypass. With what I had to say it might have been better for him if he didn't survive.

I got to the hospital at twelve-thirty. The woman at the reception desk on the first floor told me that Pearson, P. was in ICU recovery. His condition was critical.

I took the elevator up to the top floor and followed arrows to ICU. The Pearsons, wife and mother, were sitting in a waiting room outside the recovery room door. Pale sunlight coming through the plate-glass window cut across their feet and climbed the far wall, turning it brilliant white. The air was still and cool and full of that quiet that isn't really quiet, just a holding of breath. I felt like holding my breath, too.

The mother saw me first. She had been crying, and powder had run down her cheeks like salt tears.

"Louise," she said in a deadened voice.

Louise leaned forward in the chair, and her face came into the sun. Like the mother, she looked haggard and sick with waiting.

"Hello, Harry," she said.

"Hello, Louise."

Louise glanced at Cora Pearson then stood up slowly, as if she didn't want to alarm the older woman with sudden movements. She came over to me and took my hands in hers.

"I'm very glad you're here," she said with feeling.

"How is he?"

She shook her head. "We don't know. He just came out of surgery twenty minutes ago. Five hours. That's how long it's been."

"Wasn't anyone else here with you?"

"Shelley. He had an emergency a few hours ago. He said he'd be back as soon as he could." She forced a smile. "Now you're here."

I ducked my head. "I have something to tell you."

"Is it about the kids?"

I nodded.

Louise looked back over her shoulder at Cora. "Mother, I'm going to go talk with Mr. Stoner. I'll be right back."

The older woman didn't move—she didn't hear Louise. All her energies were concentrated on the door to ICU Recovery.

We went down the hall to another empty waiting room. Louise closed the door behind us. Taking my hands in hers she drew me close and laid her head wearily on my shoulder. Outside in the corridor an elevator bell went off melodiously, like a shipboard gong.

"Are you going to be okay?" I asked her.

"I guess I am," Louise said, almost as if it surprised her. "Yes, I am. At least, for now. What is it you want to tell me?"

"It isn't good, Louise. Are you up to it?"

Her face went white. "They found the children's bodies," she said, pulling away from me.

"Not yet. But you better brace yourself for it eventually. Rita Scarne committed suicide last night and left a note implying that Kirsty and Ethan were dead. Murdered by Talmadge."

Louise's eyes filled with tears. "I expected it," she said, fighting to control her voice. "I guess we all did. That's why Phil's lying in there now."

She went over to a chair and sat down heavily. For a while she simply stared at the stippled wall.

"How did Rita know they were dead?" she asked after a time.

I explained the whole thing—at least as much of it as I could explain. I saved the part about Rita, Talmadge, and Estelle's death for last. When I told her what I suspected, her face filled with shocked surprise.

"You mean Ethan was right? Stelle really *was* murdered?"

"I don't know for sure. But there is that possibility. There's something else, too. The cops don't seem to care about it but I do."

"Go on."

"Thirteen years ago Rita Scarne was paid a good deal of money. The cops think it was for a drug sale. But I don't. I think it was connected to someone's death, quite possibly Estelle's."

"Why do you say that?" Louise asked. "Why would someone pay Rita off for what Herbert Talmadge did in a drugged fit?"

"Someone may have wanted to keep the whole thing quiet. To keep what had really happened a secret."

"You're not serious?"

"I'm very serious."

She laughed nervously. "But that's crazy. I mean you sound like Ethan—that's how crazy it is."

When I didn't laugh, she stared at me incredulously. "Even if this was true, who would want to do such a thing? I mean who would profit by it?"

It was something I hadn't wanted to think about, especially that morning. But there was one obvious candidate—a man who had already showed me how readily ashamed he was of his children and his past.

Louise caught what I was thinking, and her eyes went dead. "You're not suggesting that Phil . . . ?"

"It's possible," I said uneasily. "I have a hunch he kept Ethan's testimony about Talmadge out of the police report. It's possible that he paid Rita to shut up, too."

"To cover up murder?" Louise shook her head, no. "It's true that he wanted Estelle out of his life. After all those years of hell he wanted to be done with her and start fresh. But he didn't connive at her death, if that's what you're saying. My God, all he had to do was divorce Stelle to be rid of her. In fact, that's precisely what he intended to do at the end of the year."

I sighed. "Well, someone died because of that money. At least that's what Rita told her sister. And I'll tell you something else—Rita acted as if there was another person involved, somebody who was capable of killing." I stared at Louise for a moment. "The name Carla Chaney has popped up a couple of times. Does it ring any bells for you?"

"I've never heard of her. Who is she?"

"A nurse, a friend of Rita Scarne and Herbert Talmadge.

She might be dead, too, as a result of this thing. If not, she's
probably the one person left who can unravel it."

Louise stared at me thoughtfully. "The police are going
to try to find her?"

"*I'm* going to find her," I said. "The police think the case
is closed."

"Perhaps it should be closed. So much death." She
glanced toward the door. "Even Phil. He's going to die—I
know it in my gut."

"He may survive."

"No," she said, shaking her head. "I know he won't. I've
simply got to prepare myself for it. For all of this."

Someone knocked on the door. Louise straightened up
quickly. I straightened up, too. It was Saul Lasker, he of the
Porsche and the mansion house and the fixed, paltry smile.
He was still smiling when I opened the door, although his
grin wavered for a second when he saw me and Louise, as if
the current that ran it had momentarily failed.

"I'm not interrupting anything, am I," he said with a
smooth sort of nastiness.

"No, Saul," Louise said flatly. "When did you get here?"

"A few minutes ago. I was talking with Cora when the
nurse came out of ICU. There's news about Phil." He put
the smile away and put on the deeply earnest number.
"The surgeon wants to talk to you."

Louise looked at me. For just a second her face trembled
with fear.

"Do you want me to come with you?" I said to her.

She shook her head, no. "I've come this far alone. I'll see
it through."

She put her hands to her face as if she was gathering her
strength, then dropped them to her sides.

"I'll be there in a second," she said to Lasker.

He nodded and walked off down the hall.

Louise came over to me and put a hand to my cheek. "You'll call me tonight?"

I didn't have to think about it. "Yes."

She started for the door, then looked back over her shoulder. "Let the police handle this from now on, Harry. There's been too much death. Stirring things up won't bring Kirsty back to life. Or Ethan. It won't change any of it. From what you've told me, it was too late to change anything, anyway. Too late by thirteen years."

I went back to the office and just sat behind the desk for a while, staring out the frosty window at the sunlit city and the cold blue December sky. There were things I could have done—calls I could have made to jog the cops. Instead I sat there waiting, as if I were still sitting in that muffled hospital room. Around one-thirty Lasker phoned to tell me that Phil Pearson had died in recovery.

"Louise asked me to call," he said.

"How's she taking it?"

"She's fine. It's Cora we're worried about . . . she collapsed when she heard about Phil. They have her in ECU right now."

"Christ," I said.

"They're doing everything they can," he said lamely. "I'll call again if there's any further news."

I hung up the phone and stared stupidly at the desktop. The whole Pearson family was dying or dead. Something out of the past had risen up and killed them, and I hadn't been able to do a thing to stop it. All I'd done was make mistakes.

It was the girl that bothered me most. I'd had a chance with Kirsty—if I'd stayed in Marnee's apartment for a few minutes longer, or come back a few minutes earlier, or found that Evanston motel sooner in the day. But she and her brother had managed to keep a few ticks ahead of me, as if they were operating on a different kind of time than I was—a ruthless, malevolent kind of time. A time with murder in its heart. And now there weren't going to be any second chances for her.

Something was very wrong. I knew it in my gut. Taking Parker's case against Rita as gospel it had all been accident, coincidence, mad, vengeful error. Kirsten Pearson had died because Talmadge had impulsively murdered her mother, because Rita Scarne had hidden a guilty secret rather than go to the cops, because Ethan had seen something that no one believed, because thirteen years later all four of them had collided again like a car wreck, with Kirsten riding in the backseat.

Shelley Sacks would have called it "fate," because it was messy the way fates always are. But it wasn't random enough for me. Not with the whole family lying dead. I had no proof, just a guilty feeling that I'd missed it somehow—that we all had. And I couldn't live with that feeling—even if Louise and Parker could.

29

After Lasker's call, I started making phone calls of my own —to anyone who could possibly help me locate Carla Chaney. I tried the nursing agencies first—to see if she was still working locally—and drew a blank. I tried the hospitals and hospices in both Dayton and Cincinnati, without any luck. I tried Nola Chaney again in New Mexico—and got no answer.

Around two I tried Al at the CPD. All he'd come up with was a driver's license application from 1974. It wasn't much, but it was better than nothing.

The address on the application was 678 Aviation Road in Dayton. It sounded like a Wright-Pat address. According to Carla's mother Nola, '73 was the year Carla had moved to Ohio from New Mexico—the year her husband, Bobby Tallwood, had been assigned to Wright-Patterson AFB. Carla applied for the license in November 1974 under her maiden name, Chaney. Perhaps she'd been divorced by then—that was what Nola Chaney had expected. Charlotte Scarne hadn't mentioned Carla's husband or kid either. I decided to find out what had happened to them.

It took me forty-five minutes to drive to Wright-Pat. I used my old D.A.'s deputy badge to get onto the base, and followed the signs to the headquarters building. One of the streets I passed was Aviation Road. I stopped at the corner, just to take a look.

It was a barracks street lined with neat frame Quonsets, row upon row of them like painted lunchboxes on a shelf. A tall wire fence spackled with ice ran behind the houses, separating them off from the huge cantilevered hangars and long tar airstrips. The roar of jet engines was constant. The ground trembled with it like a low-grade earthquake. I supposed you got used to that after a time. Or maybe you didn't. Maybe all you wanted to do was serve your time and get away from it—and the life inside those nondescript huts.

The yellow-brick headquarters building was a few streets north of Aviation Road. There was a flagpole out front and a stone guardhouse. I showed the MPs the pass I'd been issued at the gate, and they waved me through.

There were more guardposts inside the building—a whole series of them. By the time I got to the adjutant's office, three or four different tags hung like battle ribbons from my coat.

I told the adjutant I was looking for an airman named Tallwood, and he referred me to Personnel. It took a couple of more tags to get into the Personnel Office, and that was where I finally found someone to talk to.

His name was Olkiewcz, and he was a top sergeant with a square-jawed, implacable face straight out of Steve Canyon. He'd been stationed at Wright-Pat since the early seventies, and he knew most of the men who had served there by name.

He remembered Airman Tallwood, all right. But he refused to talk about him until I'd stated my business. Since Olkiewcz thought I was from the Cincinnati D.A.'s office, I figured Tallwood had a reputation for off-the-base trouble. But I was wrong.

"He's not wanted for anything," I told Olkiewcz. "I need to speak to him in connection with a missing persons case."

The sergeant allowed himself a tight little smile the size of a baby's fist. "That's funny," he said without sounding amused. " 'Cause you could say that Bob's a missing person, too."

"He's AWOL?"

"Permanently. He's dead, mister."

"When?"

Olkiewcz ran the fingers of his right hand through his hair like a four-pronged comb. "October 9, 1974."

"What makes you remember the date?"

"It wasn't something you were likely to forget—the way it happened, I mean."

I stared at him curiously. "You want to tell me about it?"

"I don't see no reason why I should," Olkiewcz said. "You got your answer—he's dead."

"Look, Sergeant. His wife, Carla, is in some trouble. I'm trying to locate her, and any information I can get about her past could be crucial."

This time he gave *me* a curious look. "What'd she do? Kill somebody?"

"Possibly." I said it because I had the feeling that was what he wanted to hear. His eyes had filled with hate when I'd mentioned Carla's name.

Olkiewcz leaned back in his chair and stared at me coolly. "I shouldn't tell you this, but I'm going to do it anyway. 'Cause I wouldn't want that two-timing bitch to get away with it again."

"Meaning what?"

"Meaning she killed her husband and her kid."

Olkiewcz smiled his tight smile again, then wiped it off his face with his right hand as if it was something that had dribbled out of the corner of his mouth. "Oh, she didn't actually pull a trigger. But she sure as hell drove that boy over the brink. Made him so crazy he killed that little kid of theirs, then turned a shotgun on himself."

"Tallwood killed his son and himself?" I said.

"That's was the way it looked—and nobody could prove different."

"Did anybody try?"

"Sure. The adjutant tried. We all did. Everybody knew the bitch was running around with a nigger. That it was driving Bobby nuts, the way she and the nigger carried on —right there in front of the kid. Crazy little coon. Just as sick as she was. Got four-effed right after it happened."

"This guy was a soldier on the base?"

Olkiewcz nodded. "A psycho. P.T.'d a half-dozen times for attacking nurses. That's how the bitch met him—on the psych ward at the base hospital."

"Carla worked there as a nurse?"

He nodded. "I don't know what she saw in the nigger— he sure as hell didn't have rank or dough. Everybody told Bobby to kick her ass back to New Mexico. But he wouldn't do it. He just kept looking the other way till the day he snapped. The joke is the bitch ended up with his insurance. Ten thousand dollars' worth." Olkiewcz hawked up an oyster of phlegm and spat it into a trash can beside the desk. "No woman's worth that. I don't care how good the pussy."

"The black soldier Carla was screwing, do you remember his name?"

I just wanted to hear him say it. And he did.

"Talmadge. Airman Third Class Herbert Talmadge."

Olkiewcz's story was so obviously tainted with prejudice that I decided to stop at the base hospital where Carla Chaney had worked to double-check it. One of the doctors on the surgical ward, a major named Carson, remembered Carla Chaney fairly well. Carson was a tall, heavyset man in his mid-forties, with the patchy, red-eyed face of a heavy drinker. He wore a pair of extremely thick, government issue glasses. His bleary eyes swam behind them like huge, bewildered fish.

Carson confirmed the bare bones of Olkiewcz's story. Tallwood had killed himself and his son, in October 1974. But he had a different recollection of the wife.

"Carla," he said nostalgically. "Christ, she was a dish. Half the doctors on the ward followed her around with their tongues hanging out. She could have had any one of them—any of us—in a minute. But she stayed married to Bob Tallwood—why I don't know. The son of a bitch used to beat her up every other day. He beat his son up, too."

"Olkiewcz left that part out," I said.

"Olkiewcz is a racist thug. Just like Bob Tallwood was. And then Carla never gave Olkiewcz a tumble, and that probably stuck in his craw."

"You seemed to have gotten along with her."

Carson smiled. "She didn't give *me* a tumble either, if that's what you mean. But yeah, I wanted her. I guess she liked me well enough. We'd talk occasionally on the ward, and I treated her on the QT a couple of times after Bob beat her up. I even tried to talk her into leaving the son of a bitch. But she said Bob would kill her before he gave her a divorce. And if she left him he'd just come after her—and make things that much worse."

"It was lucky for her that he killed himself then, wasn't it?"

"Some people looked at it that way. I didn't."

I asked Carson about Herb Talmadge, but he couldn't place the name.

"For all the attention paid Carla, I never saw her get halfway serious about anybody except Sy Chase. She spent a lot of time with him on the ward and off."

"Chase was a doctor?"

He nodded. "An intern who served here in '73 and '74.

He was politically connected somehow, or his wife's family was. That's why he ended up at Wright instead of in 'Nam. I thought he was an asshole, but Carla went for him."

"How serious was it on Chase's part?"

"I think he would have divorced his wife and married Carla in a minute if she'd been free. But he never got the chance. His hitch was up in June of '74. He left the base a few months before Tallwood shot himself. Never saw him again after that."

"When Tallwood died, was there any hint that Carla might have had a hand in it?"

"There are always rumors after a suicide," Carson said dismissively. "No one ever uncovered any evidence to support them. Bob Tallwood was a vicious man with a violent temper. He'd beaten Carla and his son up plenty of times before. He just went too far on that particular night and killed the kid. Afterward he started drinking and ended up eating a shotgun. I think the rumors about Carla started because she'd been out that night—because she hadn't been killed too. And then she didn't show much emotion when she was told what had happened. Not even about the little boy." The man shook his head. "I don't think Carla had much feeling left after living with Bob. I think he'd killed that part of her for good."

"Meaning she was a sociopath?"

"Meaning like most people who live with constant abuse she was deeply scarred."

"You said she was out on the night of the suicide. Do you know where?"

"She'd gone to stay at a house of a friend, as I recall. A civilian nurse who occasionally worked here on the base."

"Do you remember this nurse's name?"

Carson scratched his head thoughtfully. "I'm sorry. It's just been too many years."

"It wouldn't have been Rita Scarne, would it?"

His big, bleary eyes lit up with recognition. "I think it was Rita Scarne. At least the name rings a bell. How did you know that?"

"Just a lucky guess," I said grimly.

30

Carson didn't know what had become of Carla Chaney after she left Wright-Pat in late '74. Neither did the Records Department at the base hospital, although they confirmed the facts that she and Rita Scarne had been employed as psychiatric nurses at Wright-Pat and that Airman Herbert Talmadge had been one of their patients. They also managed to dig up an office address for Dr. Sy Chase, the man Carson had linked to Carla Chaney. The address on Gallatin Avenue in Cedar Falls, Ohio, was fourteen years old. But Cedar Falls wasn't far out of my way, and I was willing to make a side trip to find out just how serious Carla had been about Sy Chase—whether she'd been serious enough to commit murder. And a terrible murder, at that.

The possibility was there, undeniably. Another suspicious suicide with the same cast of characters who'd popped up in the Pearson woman's case. Only Tallwood's death had been no accident—not with a ten thousand dollar payoff at the end of it, the very amount that Rita Scarne had collected in blood money. If Tallwood hadn't committed suicide, there was a chance he'd been deliberately murdered by Talmadge at Carla's behest, with Rita providing the alibi. And that chance made me rethink what had happened to Estelle Pearson.

I'd assumed that Herb Talmadge had mistaken Stelle for Rita on that September afternoon in 1976—that whatever he'd done to her had been unplanned mayhem, later covered up by Phil Pearson. But the circumstances surrounding Bob Tallwood's death suggested a more sinister scenario. It now seemed possible that Estelle Pearson had been deliberately murdered, too. It would explain why Carla had gone to such lengths to get her hitman Talmadge out of the hospital in June of '76, why Rita had stolen drugs to keep him "manageable" throughout the summer, why Herb had shown up at the Pearson house on the one day of the year that Rita called in sick.

It was possible, all right. And if it was true there had to be another payoff—for Rita and Carla and Herb. The original ten thousand would hardly cover a second homicide. There had to be a payoff and a man to pay it. The only person I could think of with that kind of money and a connection to Stelle was Phil Pearson. I didn't know why he'd want his wife dead or how he'd come to pick Rita, Carla, and Herb to do the job. But if Estelle *had* been murdered Phil was behind it—no matter what Louise said.

There wasn't much to Cedar Falls, Ohio. Just a numbered exit off 74-West, emptying into a short commercial drag lined with two-story brick storefronts—half of them built in the thirties by the WPA. A frayed red-and-white banner of Santa Claus and his reindeer was strung between telephone poles at the head of Main Street. There were no other decorations in store windows or on the sidewalks. Even the banner didn't look festive. The winter wind had dogged it to tatters.

I drove under the torn-up Santa, around a small, deserted park at the end of Main, into the meager fringe of suburbs outlying the town. A raw-faced boy at a Clark service station directed me to Gallatin Street.

Dr. Sy Chase's office was the very last house on Gallatin, a tired frame bungalow with a converted first floor. Beyond Chase's office building the town simply died off into flat, snowy farmland and distant pines glittering in the sun. I parked in a lot beside the building, got out, and walked up to the porch. A sign with a physician's caduceus on it was hanging above the door. I went in.

There was a small glassed-in office immediately to the right of the door and a waiting area to the left. The waiting area was empty, although someone had left an overcoat and purse on one of the chairs. A red-haired nurse with a freckled, sharply featured face was sitting on a stool inside the office. She watched me intently, as if she was half afraid I planned to snatch the purse.

"I'd like to see Dr. Chase," I said, smiling to soothe her nerves.

The alert look on the woman's face turned to confusion. Wrinkling her nose she said, "Why, don't you know that Dr. Chase doesn't work here anymore?"

"He moved?"

"He died. Thirteen, no, fourteen years ago. He had a car accident and died."

"I see," I said with disappointment.

"You were a friend of his?"

"A friend of a friend's."

"I guess you could talk to Dr. Steele. He used to be Dr. Chase's partner." She glanced down at an appointment book on the ledge in front of her. "Doctor doesn't have any patients for the rest of the afternoon. It's always slow like this around Christmas."

"Dr. Steele would be fine."

"Your name?"

"Harry Stoner."

The nurse showed me down a short hall to a white-walled examination room. After a moment Steele came into the room—a short, bony man in his early fifties, with thin grey hair and a lean, fleshless face, grooved like nutmeat at either cheek. He was wearing a white doctor's smock and carrying a styrofoam cup of coffee in his right hand.

Steele took a sip of coffee and eyed me speculatively.

"So you were a friend of Sy's?"

He had a flat, nasal voice with a trace of caution in it—a good voice for a small-town doctor.

"I never met the man," I told him.

Steele looked taken aback. "I thought Sylvie said—"

"I'm searching for someone Dr. Chase used to know. A woman named Carla Chaney."

Steele gave me a long look. "Are you a policeman?"

"Does her name make you think of cops?"

"Frankly, *you* make me think of cops," Steele said.

I grinned at him. "I'm a P.I. working on a missing persons case. Two kids from Cincinnati."

"And you think Carla is involved?"

I nodded.

He stared at me again. "After fourteen years it's hard to imagine how you would end up in Cedar Falls, looking for Carla Chaney. But I guess that doesn't matter. The short and sweet of it is I have no idea where she is. I haven't seen her since the spring of 1975."

"Then she used to live in Cedar Falls?"

"No. She lived in Dayton and commuted to work for a couple of months back at the end of '74 and the beginning of '75."

I assumed those were the months that Carla had spent at the Minton Street house with Rita and Charlotte Scarne, the months before she'd moved to Terrace Avenue.

"What kind of work did she do here?"

"Officially she was Sydney's nurse."

"And unofficially?"

Steele flushed.

Taking another sip of coffee he sat down on a leather stool beside the mirrored cabinet. "I guess it won't matter if I talk about it now. They're all gone anyway. Dead or gone. Even Jeanne."

"Jeanne?"

"Sy's wife," he said. "She left town about a year after Sy was killed in the accident. And no one seems to know what became of her. It's quite a mystery, really. Her parents even hired a detective like you to look into it but . . . no luck."

He said it with deep regret. He had obviously liked the woman. In fact talking about her disappearance made him eye me anew, as if he was considering asking me to look into Jeanne Chase's disappearance.

I said, "You were going to tell me about Carla," to head him off.

"I guess I was," Steele said. "Not to put too fine a point on it Sy was boffing the hell out of her. I mean they were having a four-star affair. At one stage Sy even hinted that he was going to divorce Jeanne and marry Carla."

"But he didn't get the divorce?"

Steele shook his head. "He talked himself out of the idea —or Jeanne did. The truth was Sy was just a bad little boy, who liked to peek up women's skirts. Jeanne knew that about him. When it came down to it, she also knew that Sy would never leave her."

"Why?"

"Jeanne's family had money. If he divorced her he'd lose his meal ticket. And Sy loved the good life too much to throw it away, even for a beauty like Carla. Jeanne knew that about him, too. We all did, except for Carla."

"So Chase broke the affair off?"

Steele shook his head. "He didn't have the guts to tell Carla it was over, so Jeanne did it for him. There was a scene—right here in the office. An ugly tiff. The next day the girl quit and Jeanne went to work in her place. She was trained as a nurse, but what she really wanted to do was keep Sy away from further temptation."

"Did it work?"

Steele laughed dully. "Eventually. Sy kept seeing Carla for a short time after that. I know he gave the girl money out of the office account—to help her relocate in Cincy. It was the kind of thing Sy was always doing, instead of the right thing."

"You didn't like Chase much, did you?" I said.

"No, I didn't," the man said without reflection. "I took him into the practice as a favor to Jeanne's father. But it was clear from the start that Sy was never interested in the life of a country physician in a town like Cedar Falls. He'd done his internship in psychiatry and fancied himself too well educated for general practice. Hell, he was too well educated to work. He was a weak man. A spoiled, self-indulgent man who thought only of his own needs. Frankly I could never figure out what Jeanne or Carla saw in him."

"Perhaps someone who could be easily manipulated," I said, thinking of the "toys" in Carla's apartment. Toys to punish bad little boys.

"That's not a good enough reason," Steele said. "At least it wouldn't have been for a woman like Jeanne. God, I wonder what really happened to her."

But I was thinking of what had happened to the other one —the one who had gone to Cincinnati.

31

Before leaving the office I asked Steele about the accident that had killed Sy Chase—whether there had been any doubt that it *was* an accident. Suspicious deaths seem to follow Carla Chaney around, whether she'd had a hand in them or not.

But Steele said there'd been nothing suspicious about Sy Chase's death. One December night in 1975, on his way home from Cincinnati, he'd driven his car off an icy road and died instantly in the crash. The only possible connection Carla might have had to the accident was incidental—Steele thought he'd might have gone looking for the girl on the night he died.

"At least Jeanne suspected that was what he was up to. She was pretty damn bitter about it, too. Sy swore to her that he'd given Carla up."

"Carla was still living in Cincinnati at the time of the accident?"

"Yes. Like I said, Sy supported her for a while down there—until Jeanne found out about it. Then the money stopped. Carla took a job and that was the end of their affair." He smiled. "Sy was damn bitter about it. You see, it didn't take Carla long to find someone new. After she got the job she dropped Sy like a hot rock."

"When was this?"

"In the fall of '75, I think."

That meant that Carla had probably been living on Sy Chase's money throughout the summer when she'd roomed with Rita Scarne on Terrace Avenue. In the fall she'd found a different way to support herself—and a different boyfriend.

It occurred to me that it would be damn convenient from my angle if Phil Pearson turned out to be Carla's new employer—and lover. Louise said that Phil had had several lovers before her. Nurses and secretaries. Without question he would have looked like a real catch to Carla. A successful, unhappily married man who was talking divorce—that was how Louise had described him in late '76. He probably wasn't much different in the fall of '75. Another Sy Chase, without a wife to rein him in.

A short, passionate affair with a treacherous girl who loved money and had lethally dangerous friends—it could have led to murder. Although what Phil would have gained from killing off Stelle I didn't know. What Carla had stood to gain was easier to figure: a rich husband. As for Rita, she would have settled for some of Phil's cash.

"Do you happen to know who Carla went to work for in Cincinnati?" I asked Steele.

He rubbed the side of his nose. "Some doctor, I think. Sy probably mentioned his name. But after fourteen years . . ."

"It wasn't a psychiatrist named Pearson, was it? Phil Pearson?"

"Frankly I don't remember. Could be I've got the name written down at home in one of my old date books or calendars."

I took out my card and handed it to him. "If you find it, give me a call."

It was past five when I got back to the office. The first thing I did was phone Nurse Rostow to see if Carla Chaney had gone to work at Rollman's Hospital in late 1975—while Phil Pearson had been finishing his residency.

"The name doesn't ring a bell," Nurse Rostow said. "I could consult our records if you wish."

"That would be fine."

While I was waiting for her call back I went through the messages on my answering machine. There was one from Larry Parker, telling me that the State Patrol hadn't found the children's bodies yet. And one from a man named Elroy Stenger. I dialed him up.

"Elroy Stenger," the man said, as if I should have placed his name immediately. "You know? Roy Stenger, out at The Bluegrass Motel?"

"I thought a guy named Wilson ran the motel."

"He does," Stenger said. "I'm the clerk. Wilson said I should call you."

"That was two days ago."

"I been sick. Ain't gonna come in here sick, you know. No matter what that sumbitch Wilson says. He don't pay me enough that I should come in here running no fever. Hell, I don't feel a hunnert percent yet."

Roy Stenger had the whiney, sullen voice of a born loser, a man whose sole tactic was complaint. I could almost see him standing in front of me—thin as a rail, with an anchor tatooed on his arm, his back teeth pulled, a mean blue eye, and an attitude that never quit. I could understand why Wilson had felt like poking him in the nose.

"All right, Roy," I said wearily. "What's up?"

"Ain't nothing *up*," he said, as if I'd thrown him a curve. "Thought you had some questions you wanted to ask me."

"Not anymore."

"You don't want to know about them phone calls?" He didn't wait for me to answer. "There were two. One going out and one coming in. That kid made that first one a little after he and that girlfriend of his drove in on Monday afternoon, maybe 'bout five or six o'clock. I got the number if you want."

"I already have it," I said.

"It was to some nursing agency, I think."

"How did you know that?"

"I listened in on the line. Got nothing better to do 'round here most evenings."

"Did you listen to the second call, too?" I asked curiously. "The one coming in?"

"Nope. The goddamn ice machine went on the fritz again 'round eleven-thirty, so I missed most all of it." He said it like it was a TV show he'd been planning to watch. "It was a woman, though. And she asked for Ethan Pearson by name." He paused to clear his throat. "Maybe it was the woman who come by that night. She was wearing a nurse's outfit. So likely it was."

I sat up in my chair. "What are you talking about?"

"A woman come by the office, 'bout ten o'clock Monday night. She was wearing a nurse's outfit."

"Wilson didn't mention that."

"I didn't tell him is why. Don't tell him everything that goes on 'round here. No reason to."

"What did this woman look like?"

"Didn't see her face. She had on dark glasses and a scarf 'round her head. But she was a good-size woman with blond hair."

It sounded like Rita Scarne.

"What did she want?"

"She left a package for the kid. Just an envelope with some papers or something in it. I rung his room and he come picked it up a few minutes later, after the nurse done left."

"What was she driving, this nurse?"

"An old-make Pontiac. Real beat up."

"You're sure of that?" I said, thinking of Rita's Audi.

"Hell, yes I'm sure. Saw her again last night. 'Bout three a.m."

I didn't say anything for a second. "You saw this same car last night? Wednesday morning?"

"Same car, same woman," he said. "That boy must have given her his key, 'cause she went in his room and come out and drove off. Out the back way, 'round past the pool."

"Did you see her face this time?"

"Nope. Is the boy sick or something? Got him the flu, maybe? Man could catch his death in this kind of cold."

I didn't say it out loud, but that was what Ethan had caught all right, and Kirsty too.

It took me thirty minutes to drive to The Bluegrass Motel.

Stenger was waiting at the desk in the office. Tall and lean, with lax black hair combed straight down across his forehead and a scraggly moustache like a pencil scribble above his sullen mouth. He wore an open-collared white shirt with a plastic name tag pinned to the pocket. Elroy.

It cost me forty dollars to get Wilson to give me the passkey to Ethan's bungalow. Stenger came a good deal cheaper. Ten bucks and he slid the key across the counter with his forefinger.

"Figured you'd be interested in that nurse," he said, congratulating himself on his big score.

"You figured right. This package of papers the woman dropped off on Monday—you didn't happen to look inside, did you?"

" 'Course not," Stenger said, feigning outrage. "I don't pry into nobody else's business and I expect no man to pry into mine. She left that package for the Pearson boy and said to tell him it was from Rita. And that's exactly what I done."

"You didn't happen to catch the license number of Rita's car, did you?"

"Nope."

"Not this morning, either?"

Stenger drew back as if I was asking for the world. "You're damn lucky I saw her at all—way she come sneaking 'round the back entrance that early in the morning."

"You're sure it was three?"

"Sure I'm sure. *Love Boat* just come on Nineteen." He nodded behind him at the grey, fulgent eye of a portable TV, sitting on the manager's desk. "Saw her reflection in the tube. That white uniform."

"She the only one who paid Ethan's room a visit this week?"

"Just her and you, far as I know."

"No cops?" I said skeptically.

Elroy Stenger drew back a step farther. "What'd cops want 'round here?"

From the way he said it, I figured he was in a better position to know than I was. Talking about cops killed off the little hospitality the ten dollars had bought me. Pocketing the bill Elroy turned his back on me and flipped on the TV.

"Just drop that key on the counter when you're through," he called out as I left.

I walked down the tar driveway that led from the office to the cottages. The drive ran past the heart-shaped swimming pool and behind the cottages to the highway. There were no overhead lights along the way, so it was just good luck—or Elroy Stenger's persistent nosiness—that had led him to discover his early morning visitor.

Whoever she was, she wasn't Rita Scarne, who had been sitting dead in her car at three a.m.

* * *

There was no police seal posted on Ethan Pearson's motel room door—Stenger had been right about that. For Parker, Foster, and the Ohio State Patrol the case had apparently ended at first light with the discovery of Rita's body. No one had even bothered to make a routine check of Ethan's room.

I fit the key in the lock and pushed the door open.

At first glance the place looked the same as it had on Tuesday afternoon. The fast-food wrappers on the bed. The tin ashtray on the pillow. The phonebook sitting where I'd left it on the dresser. Hell, there wasn't that much that could have changed. And yet Carla Chaney, or someone else, had taken a huge risk to revisit that room. I wanted to know why.

I went through the place again. The bed, the bath, the nightstand, the bureau. And that's when I found it.

Ethan's bankbook, the one listing his father's regular thousand-dollar deposits to the savings account at First National, was missing from the bureau drawer. As far as I could tell it was the only thing missing.

I sat down on the corner of the bed and stared stupidly at the bureau. There was no sense to it—to someone risking her life to steal a dead boy's bankbook. There had been no money in the savings account—I'd checked. The last thousand-dollar deposit had been removed two weeks before Ethan disappeared—the money had always been removed several weeks after it was deposited.

I reached over, picked up the phone, and dialed the desk. Elroy answered.

"You gotta pay for any calls you make," he said immediately, as if he could see the money coming out of his ten-dollar bonus.

"I'll pay," I said. I took my notebook out of my jacket and

flipped through it until I found the number for The University Inn in Evanston.

"Long-distance gonna cost you extra," Elroy said after I gave him the number.

"Just dial the fucking thing."

I got The University Inn's version of Elroy Stenger after a couple of rings. He put me though to Hedda Pearson.

I hadn't been sure that the woman was still at the motel. But she was there all right, still holding vigil in that little room, still waiting, as she told me she would wait, for Ethan to return home.

"Is there news?" she asked nervously. "Have they found him?"

"Not yet."

Hedda Pearson laughed a terrible laugh. "They think he's dead, don't they? And for what? For some neurotic, oedipal fantasy."

"Ethan's story about his mother may not have been as fantastic as we thought."

Hedda Pearson sucked in her breath as if I'd slapped her. "Is that what you called for? To tell me that I don't know my husband? That I couldn't tell truth from fantasy?"

"I called because I need to know about Ethan's savings account at First National—the one his dad deposited money to every three months."

The woman laughed wretchedly. "Are you insane? First you say this absurd story of Ethan's is true. Then you ask me about imaginary bankbooks."

I stared down at the bureau, at the empty drawer. "You're telling me that you don't know anything about a savings account or a passbook?"

"Yes. That's what I'm telling you. There was no savings account. No money from Ethan's father. He wouldn't have accepted money from his father if it *had* been offered. Don't *you* know that?"

I told the woman I would call her when I had word about her husband. But from the sound of her voice when she hung up, I knew that she would just as soon never hear from me again—or anyone else who took Ethan's fantasies seriously. She'd been more upset by the possibility that she'd been wrong about them than by the possibility that he was dead. But then his obsession had given form to her life for the past four years—it had shaped her relationship to Ethan. Without it she lost her identity as his victim.

After hanging up on Hedda Pearson I phoned Al Foster at the CPD and asked him to do me another favor.

"I need a check run on a savings account at First National Bank, under the name of E. Pearson. I'd like to know who actually owns the account, who deposits to it, and who withdraws from it."

After that morning's scene with Parker I'd expected him to say no—especially to the bank inquiry, which would require a court order. But he didn't.

"I'll see what I can do."

"Why so cooperative?" I asked curiously.

"Let's just say that things aren't working out exactly as expected at this end."

"You want to explain that?"

"When the time is right," Al said.

32

After Al hung up I sat in the motel room for a little while
longer, thinking about the missing bankbook that hadn't
belonged to Ethan Pearson. Someone must have given it to
him on Monday night—probably the nurse who had come
to the motel. The nurse who wasn't Rita Scarne. Presumably the same woman had returned on Wednesday morning, after the boy and his sister were dead, to take the book
back. Roy Stenger claimed the nurse had her own key to
the motel room, but I didn't know whether to believe him
or not. He was pretty damn corruptible when it came to
passkeys—that was how I'd gotten in. The only other way
Carla—or whoever the nurse was—could have gotten a key
was to take it off Ethan Pearson's dead body in Talmadge's
apartment. Or off Talmadge's body on Tuesday morning.

Whether Carla had done all that or not, it figured that the
account book had something to do with Stelle Pearson's
death. Finding and punishing their mother's murderer was
all that Ethan and Kirsty had been interested in.

I picked up the phone again and told Roy to dial Dayton
information. Rita Scarne's sister, Charlotte, had mentioned
bankbooks with money in them—part of the grim inheritance that Rita had left her on Wednesday morning. I
wanted to know whether they connected to Ethan's missing account book.

I got Charlotte's number from information and had Roy
dial it.

"This is Stoner, Charlotte."

"Yes," she said stiffly. "I recognize your voice."

"I need to talk to you about Rita."

It took her a while to speak. Given my part in the tragedy of her sister's death, I understood why. "What about Rita?"

"You mentioned some bankbooks that she gave you. I'd like to have a look at them."

Charlotte Scarne took a deep breath and let it out slowly. "I think maybe you should," she said, sounding relieved.

"Why do you say that?"

"There was an article in the *Daily News* today—about Rita and those children you were looking for. The Pearson children. It said they were presumed dead and that Rita might have played a part in their murders."

"No one's completely sure."

"It's horrible," the woman said, shaken. "So horrible."

At first I thought she meant the accusation itself, but she didn't. "Mr. Stoner, I think Rita did kill them."

"Why?"

"The bankbooks. The ones that you're talking about. Some of them have Ethan' and Kirsten Pearson's names on them."

I didn't put it together until I got inside the woman's house, past the frozen ice on her stairs—ice that still bore my footprints and Rita's—past the frozen, accusatory stare on Charlotte Scarne's face when she answered the door. The black bag was already sitting on the dusty table in the center of the dusty sitting room. I went straight over to it while Charlotte hovered nervously in the hall. There were four bankbooks inside the bag, two in Ethan's name, one in Kirsty's, one in Rita's. I looked at the ones with Ethan's and Kirsty's names on them first—passbooks for three savings accounts at three different Cincinnati S & L's. City Bank, Constellation, and First National. The one from First National bothered me—it looked like the same book I'd found in Ethan's motel room.

"When did Rita give you this book?" I said to Charlotte.

"Last night. You were here, don't you remember?"

I let that pass and took a look inside the other two books. Like the one I'd found in Ethan's drawer they'd been deposited to at three-month intervals for almost a decade—thousand-dollar deposits, circulated among the three accounts so that one of them always had money in it every month of the year. The cash was regularly withdrawn a week or two after the deposits were made. I only had to glance at the single passbook with Rita's name on it to see where that money had gone. The books balanced perfectly. Every penny from the three Ethan and Kirsten Pearson accounts had ended up in Rita's name. One hundred and twenty thousand dollars, paid out over ten years in one thousand dollar monthly increments.

It helped explain Rita's fancy house and car. It helped explain a lot of things.

"She was stealing from that boy and his sister," Charlotte Scarne said in a feverish whisper.

I shook my head, no. "She wasn't stealing from them."

The woman looked confused. "Then why did Rita have their passbooks—and all that cash!"

I sat down on the tuxedo sofa and stared at the black bag full of money. Blood money. "They weren't Ethan's and Kirsty's passbooks, Charlotte. Ethan and Kirsty didn't know a thing about them—at least, they didn't until a few days ago. Those accounts were established by someone who was using their names to launder money."

"Launder?" the woman said.

"To make the deposits look legitimate. To make it seem as if the money was going to Ethan or Kirsty, when it was really being paid to Rita."

"Over a hundred thousand dollars!" Charlotte cried. "Who would do such a thing?"

I could only think of one person with the means. One person who could plausibly use Ethan's and Kirsty's names to hide illegal transactions. He'd died that afternoon. "Phil Pearson."

Charlotte stopped her pacing and sank into a chair beside an octagonal table full of knickknacks. "I don't understand this at all. Wasn't he the one you were working for? Why would he secretly pay Rita money?"

"For something she did for him thirteen years ago," I said, thinking aloud. "Something she and Carla and Herb Talmadge did."

"What?" the woman said with appetite.

"They planned and covered up a murder. Estelle Pearson's murder."

Charlotte Scarne fell back in the chair with a groan. "Oh, God, I knew it! I just knew Rita killed someone!" She threw her hands to her face and sobbed melodramatically, although I detected a bit of triumph mixed with the tears.

Looking around the room, at the dusty furnishings that hadn't changed in three decades, I could see why. Fourteen years before, Rita had run off with a woman she had loved better than her own sister, leaving Charlotte to lead a drab life with her drab parents in that drab house. The woman was owed a little vindication. Perhaps she had felt she was owed more than that.

"Why didn't you show me these passbooks on Wednesday morning, Charlotte?"

The woman stopped sobbing and pulled her hands slowly away from her eyes, drawing down the pink flesh beneath them.

"I didn't look at them myself until after Rita had died."

I shook my head. "That isn't true. It can't be."

She laughed nervously, dropping her hands from her cheeks to her lap. "Are you accusing me of lying?" she said as if the very notion was preposterous—as if I had the wrong sister.

I got up and walked over to the doctor's bag. Reaching inside I took out the First National passbook. "I found this in the Pearson boy's motel room on Tuesday afternoon. Someone gave it to him on Monday night and picked it up again early this morning. Someone dressed as a nurse. Now it's here in your house. How'd that happen?"

The woman blanched. "I . . . I don't know. There must have been another book."

I shook my head again. "If there were more than three of these account books, the deposits to them would have been staggered differently. The books wouldn't balance to the penny. There would be missing months, missing deposits made to the fourth book. No, I think there were just three accounts in Ethan's and Kirsty's names. But I can always check with First National—if you force me to."

"Of course, you could," she said dully, as if that was something that hadn't occurred to her. "You could check the bank."

I asked her again, "When did you get this book, Charlotte?"

The woman's face slowly changed. Age and bitterness came over it, greying the pink, girlish flesh, turning the weak smile into something that looked like it might fall out of her mouth and shatter. Raising her right arm woodenly Charlotte Scarne swept the top of the octagonal table beside her, knocking the mementos—the yellowing picture of Mom and Pop, the crystal trout blowing bubbles in its crystal cube—onto the floor. The picture frame cracked in two. The crystal cube exploded with a loud pop, splashing glass shards against the far wall.

Charlotte Scarne brought her arm back across the table, laid it in her lap and stared at it curiously as if it was something not quite under her control. After a time she looked up at me.

"I took the bankbook to the boy's motel on Monday night," she said in a deadened voice. "I was at Rita's house when his call came in. I knew about the accounts with their names on them. I . . . I wanted to help them."

"You knew about Stelle's murder?"

"I knew about the accounts," she said sharply. "I'd known about them for years. I thought Rita was stealing money from that boy and his sister. I mean why else would she have books with his name on it? Why would she have a house like that? And a car? And so much cash to spend? She'd done something terrible to that boy and his sister. She and that dreadful bitch, Carla. For years Rita had gotten away with it. Why should she keep getting away with it? Lording it over me when Dad died. Making me look small with her dirty money. Even Mother . . ."

Choking with anger Charlotte fixed me with a savage stare. "The boy and his sister deserved to know what Rita had done."

But what she really meant was that her sister deserved to be punished. She still felt that way even though Rita was dead.

"So you told Ethan that Rita had been stealing from him."

"I thought he and his sister would take the book to the police. I didn't know that they would end up dead. I swear to Jesus I didn't."

She dropped her head heavily to her chest. "After you came here I got panicky. I was afraid the police would find the passbook and trace it to me. I already had all the money that she'd given me. I thought they might think, that *you* might think I was . . . that I had something to do with the blackmail. So I went back to the motel after you left and got the book."

"How did you get into Ethan's room?"

"The man at the desk," she said miserably. "I gave him money—and he gave me a key."

She looked too damn guilty to be lying. But then she'd lied to me before about the bankbooks and, more importantly, about what she'd suspected Rita and Carla had been up to—thirteen years past.

"I never knew what the money was for, Mr. Stoner," Charlotte Scarne said as if she was reading my mind. "I just knew Rita was getting it for something bad. Rita was bad."

She started to sob. "Bad," she cried again, like a tattling child.

As I watched her weeping bitter tears that weren't for Rita, I wondered just how large a part Charlotte herself had played in her sister's suicide and, maybe, in the Pearson kids' deaths. I couldn't be sure about what she'd said to Rita or to Ethan on Monday night. I did know that someone had told those kids where to find Talmadge—someone who'd known where to find them *and* Herb. And Rita had had that black bag of blood money packed *before* I showed up on Wednesday morning—ready to take to her sister in Dayton. At the very least there was an ugly possibility that Charlotte had done a little blackmailing of her own. But then the Pearson case was full of ugliness and simmering vengeance. And murder.

"Did you tell your sister that the Pearson boy had called her, Charlotte?" I said, when she'd calmed down.

She shook her head. "No. I didn't tell anyone."

"And you didn't call Ethan back on Monday night?"

She said no, again.

"Somebody called them," I said uneasily.

"It wasn't me," Charlotte said, coming out of the chair

with a horrified look on her face. "I didn't know about that man, Talmadge."

"He never showed up at the house, when Carla was living here in '74 and '75?"

"Never. The men she saw—they were always . . . respectable-looking."

"Do you remember any of their names?"

"One of them was a doctor," the woman said. "I think Carla worked for him."

"Sydney Chase?"

"Yes, he came here. A lot."

"Anyone else?"

"There were other men," Charlotte Scarne said vaguely. "It's been so many years."

"Was one of them Phil Pearson?"

"I don't recall the names."

"Tall, dark hair, blue eyes."

The woman stared at me blankly. "I just don't remember."

33

I took the bankbooks with me when I left the house on Minton Street. I didn't give Charlotte a choice, but the truth was that she didn't really care about the money. Just about Rita—evening things up with Rita. Revenge was almost as much of a theme in her life as it had been in Kirsty's and Ethan's. And it had almost poisoned her life to the same extent.

Before driving off I checked the garage beside the St. Louis. An old brown Pontiac, the car described by Roy Stenger, the motel clerk, was parked inside.

I stopped at a Stuckey's on my way back to Cincinnati and had a cup of coffee and a sandwich. It was past ten and the papery sandwich was the first food I'd eaten all day. I sat there for about fifteen minutes, drinking coffee and thinking about Ethan and Kirsty Pearson.

Getting that bankbook from Charlotte would have confirmed what the kids already suspected—that Rita Scarne was heavily involved in their mother's murder. If they'd used their heads the account book would have told them something else—something they didn't know. That their father had been involved in it, too.

I wasn't sure if Al Foster had looked into the ownership of the savings account yet—I'd check that out when I got back to town. But I would have been very surprised if it didn't belong to Phil Pearson—or jointly to Pearson and Rita. Who else would have used Ethan's and Kirsty's names to cover up a payoff? The names of his kids. It was what Shelley

Sacks would have called "sublimation." It was what I called
smart thinking.

Louise had already told me that Phil regularly sent Ethan
money—"blood money," she called it ironically. Blood
money it was. But not paid for Ethan's imaginary com-
plaints or to assuage Phil's guilt, as Louise had thought. Paid
to cover the cost of a very real murder. And the money
would have been untraceable, if Charlotte Scarne hadn't
taken a hand.

But she had. And the two kids had discovered that Papa
Phil was involved in Mama's murder. They might have
acted on that discovery if someone hadn't called them at
the motel and told them where to find Talmadge. I'd
thought that someone had been Rita Scarne. But after talking to Charlotte I was no longer sure. If Charlotte was
telling me the truth, Rita really *hadn't* known that the kids
had called her on Monday night. She hadn't known that
Ethan and Kirsty were at The Bluegrass Motel, plotting
revenge.

But someone else had known they were there on Monday
—the same person who had known where to find Herb.
What I couldn't figure out was how that someone—Carla or
whoever she was—had come by that knowledge, if it wasn't
through Charlotte or the kids themselves.

It was ten-thirty when I got back to the Riorley Building.
The answering machine on my desk was blinking in the
twilight, its one yellow eye. I played back the messages
while I put Rita Scarne's bagful of money in the office safe.
The first one was from Louise, asking me to come to the
house later that night.

"I've never felt so alone," she said. "Please come here,
after eleven, after the others have left. I need you."

Her voice was weighted down with a desperate loneli-

ness. A burden I was bound to add to if the path I was
following led to Phil. I didn't know how I was going to
handle telling her that I was still working on the case, still
trying to prove her dead husband was a murderer. I didn't
know how I was going to handle Louise herself. She wasn't
inviting me home to talk. I knew that. I also knew that I
wanted her badly enough to go, even on that night.

I played back the other messages and tried not to think
about Louise. But it was no good—the sound of her voice
had started something inside me. I was reaching for the
phone to call her when it rang.

It was Thelma Jackson. Who'd thought I was like Magnum—good, decent, and pure. The sort of man who would
never fuck a dead man's wife on the day he died.

"That ofay nurse you asked me about?" She paused dramatically. "I found somebody who remembers her real
well. Her and Herbie, both."

"Who is that?" I said.

"Old friend of mine from back on McMicken, used to
work in the coffee shop over at Jewish Hospital. She seen
this girl with Herbie a couple of times."

"I already know who the girl is," I said wearily. "What I
need to know is how to find her."

"Sarah don't know where she is now," the woman said.
"She ain't seen her since '76."

I sighed.

"Ain't you gonna come over and chat?" Thelma Jackson
said disappointedly, as if she was looking forward to the
company.

"I'm pretty tired, Thelma."

Thelma put her hand over the receiver and I heard her
say, "He ain't coming," to someone else in the room.

"Tell your friend I'll call her tomorrow about Carla."

"Carla?" Thelma said. "Who's that?"

"Herbie's girlfriend."

"Her name wasn't Carla," the woman said. "Was it, Sarah?"

She went off the line again and I heard her say something to her friend. When she came back on she was full of confidence. "She wasn't no Carla. She was a Jeanne. Jeanne Chase."

It was past eleven by the time I got to Thelma Jackson's bungalow on Anthony Wayne. The air near the distillery smelled of peaches that cold December evening. I took a big whiff of it as I crossed over to the house, and caught a hint of gasoline drifting up from the expressway.

Thelma was standing in the front door as I came onto the porch. Another black woman in her sixties, with a small, gnarled face and a slightly humped back, stood a few feet behind her in the shadows of the living room. The second woman watched shyly while Thelma ushered me in.

"This here's Sarah Washington," Thelma said, turning to the other woman.

"Pleased," Sarah Washington said in a squeaky little voice.

Thelma grinned at her shy friend. "You wouldn't believe it to look at her, but Sarah was wilder than me in her day."

"You hush," Sarah Washington said, looking embarrassed.

I went over to the floral-print couch. The women sat down on chairs opposite me. Both of them were wearing floral-print dresses. Thelma filled hers out impressively, while Sarah's hung from her skinny shoulders like a coat from a hook.

"Ain't he good-looking?" Thelma said to her friend. "Too good-looking for an old woman like me."

She snapped her girdle, and the other one clucked her tongue mournfully. I had the feeling that Thelma Jackson was going to keep snapping and her friend was going to keep clucking all night long—that that was the way they related to each other.

"You remember the nurse that Herbie Talmadge was seeing, Ms. Washington?" I said, trying to steer the conversation toward business.

"Yes, uhm-hm," Sarah Washington said, nodding until I thought her neck might break. "She worked in the Jewish Hospital Doctors' Building back in '75 and '76. I believe her name was Chase. Jeanne Chase."

"You're not sure?"

The woman ducked her tiny head. "Not for absolute sure."

"It couldn't have been Chaney, could it? Carla Chaney?"

"I'm purty sure her last name was Chase. Somebody told me she come down from a Dayton hospital, but I never did know that for a fact."

"She was an RN?"

"No, no." The woman shook her head in the opposite plane. "A receptionist."

"Y'all got to quit that shaking," Thelma said irritably. "Make the rest of us dizzy."

The woman gave her an ugly look.

"Who'd she work for?" I asked.

"I ain't for sure. One of the doctors in the Jewish Hospital Building."

"You tell him what you saw," Thelma prompted.

"I saw her and Herbie Talmadge together," Sarah Washington said, drawing herself up in the chair. "Saw them a couple of times—out in the parking lot."

I said, "By together, you mean . . . ?"

"I mean what I said. They weren't doing more than talking, far as I could see."

She gave Thelma Jackson a quick, sharp look.

"Are you sure this is the same woman that you saw on McMicken Street?" I said to Thelma.

She nodded. "Has to be. Big blond white girl. 'Bout twenty-four, twenty-five years old."

"Is that what she looked like?" I said to Sarah Washington.

The woman bobbed her head like a fighter ducking a bag. "Yes, sir."

Jeanne Chase sounded an awful lot like Carla Chaney, with a new name. Sy Chase's wife's name. It struck me as a kind of grim joke—Carla taking the name of the woman who'd spoiled her chance to become the real Mrs. Chase.

"Did you ever talk to this woman?" I asked Sarah Washington.

"Never did talk to her but once," the woman admitted. "She was in the coffee shop and I waited her table. She acted kind of high-strung, I remember that. Kind of uppity. I figured her for one of those college girls who come and go. You see them all the time. Only reason they work is to snare them some young doctor. And when that don't happen, they just drift on to something else. Stopped seeing her in the spring. And never did see her again after that. Never saw Herbie but one time after that, either. In the fall of that year."

"Where did you see him?"

"Out front of the hospital."

The woman shook her head with what I thought was a dismal accent. It depressed me that I was beginning to understand the code of her gestures. In fact I'd started to bob my head a little, too.

"I thought the boy was waiting on a bus," Sarah Washington said, "but this fancy car come along and picked him up. Big, black car. Doctor's car."

"Did you see who was driving it?"

"Just the license. Had MD on it. I remember that."

34

As soon as I finished with Thelma I went looking for a phone. I found a neon-lit convenience store on North Bend Road, blazing in the dark as if it had been doused with cognac, and called Dr. Steele's office from a booth on the wall. I half expected to get an answering machine, but he answered the phone himself like a good country physician used to night calls.

"Sorry to bother you again," I said, "but I've got a funny situation here. Jeanne Chase, Sy Chase's wife . . . can you describe her for me?"

"Why?" the man said, perking up. "You haven't found her, have you?"

"I've run across her name."

"She was a green-eyed redhead, about five-four, one-twenty. A tough little Irish girl. Real pretty and real smart."

She certainly didn't sound like the woman that Sarah Washington had seen with Talmadge. The woman Sarah Washington had seen still sounded like Carla Chaney.

"Christ," Steele went on eagerly, "if you do find anything about Jeanne you've got to call her folks. When she disappeared their lives virtually ended."

"When did she disappear?"

"In October '76. She'd gone to Cincinnati to interview for a nursing job. She just couldn't stand to work up here anymore without Sy. And she was the type who needed to work. I remember that the detective her folks hired traced her as far as the hospital where the interview took place."

"Do you know which hospital that was?"

"No. It would be in the report the detective made—I'm

sure. I do remember that she called her folks that afternoon
and told them that she wouldn't be coming home right
away. That she'd run into an old friend and would be staying in town a few more days."

"Did she identify the friend?"

"Not that I recall."

"You think you could get me the name of the detective
who worked on the case? I mean without working anybody
up."

"Of course. A doctor gets used to watching what he says."

I dug another quarter from my pocket and phoned Al
Foster at CPD.

"No," he said. "I don't have any news on the Pearson kid's
bank account."

"Well, I do," I told him. "Rita Scarne was drawing money
out of it to the tune of a hundred and twenty grand. Someone was paying her off and using the Pearson kid's account
to launder the cash."

"Got any idea who?"

I did but I wasn't ready to tell the cops yet—not until I
had Pearson's motive for murder pinned down. "It would
help if you could find out who was depositing to the account."

"I've done enough work for the day," Al said wearily.
"Your friend, Carla, I've dug up something on her. You're
not going to like it, though."

"What?"

"You sitting down or standing up?"

"Just tell me."

"She's dead, Harry."

Behind me an ice machine made a thump, like a sack
down a laundry chute.

"That can't be true," I said, wishing I was sitting down.

"I don't want it to be true, either. Parker would be pissed

as hell if I told you this but we've got a couple of slots that your Carla was tailor-made to fit. It turned out that the nurse in Prospect Park, the one that black kid saw with Talmadge, definitely *wasn't* Rita Scarne. We did some checking and the Scarne woman was on private duty until eleven p.m. Monday night. Plus criminalistics lifted a pair of prints off the damn shoe we found in Herb's apartment that don't match Talmadge or Rita. Parker doesn't think it's enough to queer the case for a grand jury, but it's making him sweat."

"You're sure the Chaney woman's dead?"

"For thirteen years. Talmadge killed her. It's why he went to jail. For raping and murdering Nurse Carla Chaney."

It was all there in black and white, in a folder that had been sitting on a parole officer's desk for better than a week. Al had found out about it early that evening after running Carla Chaney's name past Newport CID.

"Hall Scott, Talmadge's parole officer, called to follow up on Herb's murder," Foster said as we sat across his desk from each other in the homicide office of the CPD Building. "We got to talking about the son of a bitch. And the Chaney girl's name popped up. Talmadge must have hated her guts, because he really did a number on her. Beat her up so badly they had to rely on a piece of physical evidence to identify the corpse—a wedding ring on the woman's hand. And then she'd been in the Ohio River for three weeks, which didn't help."

"He dropped her body in the river?"

"Helluva coincidence, huh?" He pushed the manila folder across his desk to me. "Take a look at who made the ID."

I flipped open the folder and scanned the report. The

woman's nude body was found on November 10, 1976—
about two months after Estelle Pearson was pulled from the
Miami. The body—what was left of it after three weeks in
the water—was identified by one Rita Scarne, a nurse and
friend of the deceased. According to the report Scarne
claimed Carla Chaney had been Talmadge's lover and that
she'd been missing since mid-October. There were no relatives listed for Carla. Husband and child, mother and father, were said to be deceased. Without Rita and the ring
Carla would have been just another Jane Doe.

"Did Rita testify against Talmadge at the trial?"

"There wasn't any trial," Foster said. "Herb copped a
plea—second-degree murder. That's why he was released
ten days ago instead of spending another ten years in jail.
The Scarne woman must have been scared to death when
she read he was going to be paroled. Scared enough to use
those kids to try to kill him, scared enough to do it herself
when the scheme backfired."

Only Rita Scarne hadn't known about the kids. I was
beginning to wonder whether she'd known about
Talmadge's release. The person she'd been afraid of—the
person who phoned the kids at that motel—was a lot more
dangerous than Herb. And a lot harder to pin down.

"See what you can dig up on an MP named Jeanne
Chase," I said to Al. "She disappeared close to the same
time that Carla went in the water."

"How close?" he said, perking up.

"I'll find out."

I went back to my office and phoned Dr. Steele again. He
had the name of the detective for me by then—Jim Sanchez
out of Dayton. And something else—something I hadn't
expected.

"I came across the name of that doctor that Carla went to
work for in Cincinnati. I'd written it down on an old calen-

dar." Steele laughed. "I keep stuff like that around. My wife says forever. Anyway the name wasn't Pearson. It was Sacks —Sheldon Sacks."

"No shit!" I said with surprise.

Steele laughed. "That's what it says here. Sheldon Sacks, Jewish Hospital Doctors' Building."

That helped to explain how Carla/Jeanne had come in contact with Phil Pearson, Sacks' closest friend. And as receptionist to Shelley Sacks, Carla would have had access to Sacks' files—to all that useful information about Stelle and Phil's rotten marriage. Information that it was high time I had a look at, too.

I phoned Dayton information and got Jim Sanchez's number. I didn't figure he'd be in his office at ten-thirty on a Friday night. But I was wrong. Like me he was working on a case that troubled him—a missing child. Talking about Jeanne Chase didn't improve his mood.

"I tried like hell on that one," Sanchez said unhappily. "I mean I liked the family, the folks. I wanted to deliver for them. But once Jeanne left that hospital she simply dropped off the face of the earth."

"What hospital was that?"

"Holmes. She'd gone there for an interview with a doctor who'd advertised in one of the nursing journals. You know Jeanne was trained as a nurse."

"Do you remember the doctor's name?"

"I've got it in my files. Hold on a minute." He went off the line for a couple of minutes then came back on, with a sound of papers rustling. "The doctor's name was . . . Morse. Carl Morse. He was a psychiatrist, looking for a nurse who could also act as a receptionist and keep the books. He'd had a girl who did those things for him, but she'd retired the month before."

"Dr. Steele told me that Jeanne called her folks after the

interview to tell them she was going to stay in Cincinnati
for a few days. She said she'd run into an old friend at the
hospital."

"Not a friend. I mean she didn't use the word 'friend.'
What she said was . . ." I heard him rustle through the
papers again. "She saw somebody at the hospital—someone
she knew. Her parents had the impression that seeing this
person upset Jeanne. At least, they thought something had
upset her."

"Jeanne didn't say who this person was, did she?" I asked.

"No," Sanchez said. "But I tried like hell to find out. The
interview was held in the afternoon. And you know how
busy hospitals get. There were scores of people around. It
could have been any of them."

"Morse didn't have any idea who Jeanne might have
seen, did he?"

"No. He claimed no one else came into his office during
the interview. I went up and down the hall to every office
on the floor and no one recalled seeing her. Christ I got a list
of names a mile long. Flaigler, Thomas, Galaty, Pearson—"

"Hold up," I said. "Phil Pearson?"

"Yeah, as a matter of fact. Dr. Philip Pearson. He was
down the hall from Stein. Is that material?"

It could have been, if Phil Pearson had been meeting
with Sacks' secretary.

"What day did Jeanne disappear?"

"Wednesday, October 19, 1976."

I jotted the date down on my desk blotter. Almost three
weeks to the day before "Carla Chaney's" body was found
in the Ohio River.

"I may have something for you on this," I said.

"Christ, that would be terrific. The thing has eaten at me
for thirteen years."

"What I need is a photograph of the Chase woman, he

dental records, and a description of any distinguishing scars or marks."

"You've found her body?" he asked.

"The cops found *a* body," I said carefully. "Thirteen years ago, three weeks after Jeanne disappeared. At the time the body was identified as someone else, but I've got reason to think that it may have been misidentified. Deliberately."

"Why?" Sanchez said eagerly.

But I didn't know why—not for sure. What I *thought* was that someone had been impersonating Jeanne Chase for almost a year—someone who looked very much like Carla Chaney. If Carla had been visiting Phil Pearson that October afternoon, the Chase woman could have seen her, could have found out that she had a double. A woman masquerading as the late Dr. Chase's tony wife. A woman whom the real Jeanne Chase had a terrific grudge against. If Jeanne had confronted Carla with what she knew, it could have cost her her life.

Stelle was only one month dead at that point, and Carla wouldn't have wanted anyone prying into her affairs—especially someone with a score to settle. Plus eliminating the real Jeanne Chase had some extra benefits: Carla would no longer have to worry about exposure, or about crazy Herb Talmadge, who had obviously been set up to take the rap for Jeanne Chase's murder.

It was beginning to look like Carla Chaney had left a whole string of corpses behind her in her metamorphosis from Nola's squalid daughter to the snooty girl that Sarah Washington had seen in Jewish Hospital to whatever she'd become after Phil dumped her for Louise. All it had taken to turn the tide of the past was a half-dozen murders and two accomplices who were willing, for drugs or sex or money, to go along with the mayhem. And Phil Pearson, of course, to finance the deal.

For thirteen years she'd probably lived comfortably i
her new identity—off Phil Pearson's money. Just as Ri
had. In fact it wouldn't have surprised me to learn th
there were three more phony accounts in the kids' name
at three more Cincinnati banks, with regular monthly de
posits to and withdrawals from them. It would have stayed
nice life if Herb had not gotten out of prison, bringing th
past back with a vengeance. But he had gotten out, dra
ging the Pearson kids in his wake.

Somehow Carla had found out about Ethan and Kirst
and tracked them down to the motel. Talmadge had a
ready made himself known to her—Carla had even boug
him a TV to keep him quiet. Looking for a way out she'
callously pitted Kirsty and Ethan against Herb, and whe
that didn't work she'd done the job herself with a handful
pills and a butcher knife.

If Carla Chaney hadn't changed her name again I mig
be able to find her through Shelley Sacks, who'd hired h
in the fall of '75 under the name Jeanne Chase. It was tin
to talk to Sacks, anyway. There was too much that he'd bee
concealing for too long. Motives and memories that cou
help me explain why Phil wanted Stelle dead—and wh
thirteen years later Kirsten Pearson had joined her broth
on their strange ride toward death.

t was almost one when I finished with Jim Sanchez. I knew
hat Shelley Sacks wouldn't be in his office. If he was any-
-here other than at his own home he'd be with Louise. I
vent ahead and phoned the Pearson house, knowing full
ell that she'd expected me to come to her—that she was
:ill expecting it.

Louise answered on the second ring. As soon as I heard
er voice I knew why I'd resisted making the call.

"Hello, Louise."

"Hello, Harry," she said stiffly. "It was nice of you to
heck in."

"I'm sorry, Louise."

She laughed. "Of course you are."

"What do you want me to say?" I said, feeling the same
eadly mix of lust and guilt I'd felt about three hours be-
ore. Knowing deep down that the lust would win out.

"What I want clearly doesn't make any difference to
ou."

"That isn't true."

Her voice dropped to a wounded whisper—so full of pain
at it hurt me. "I needed you, damn you. And you didn't
ome. You left me alone."

I didn't answer her. I didn't know how to answer.

After a moment's silence she found her voice again.
What is it you wanted?"

"Shelley Sacks," I said guiltily. "Is he there with you?"

Louise laughed again. "He went home about two hours
;o. They've all gone home hours ago."

"Where does he live?"

"Two twenty-five Camargo Pike. Is that it?"
She hung up the phone before I could answer her.

I got in the car and started for Sacks' house. Out I-71 in
that rich preserve of mazey woods and hidden drives. B
somewhere along the way I got lost in the dark, and it w
Pearson's house I found myself parked in front of. The
were no lights on. No other cars in the driveway. I sat the
for a long time, listening to the December wind rattling t!
icy branches of the ginko trees, without the guts to go i
without the guts to leave. I don't know how much tin
passed before a light came on above the front door—fier
and white as a spot.

The door opened and I saw her look out. She w
wrapped in a silk robe that seemed to have no color at all
the fierce white light. Louise herself didn't look quite re
in the blazing light. She stared out at me for a long momer
Then the light went out. All I could see in the sudd
darkness was the glimmer of her white wrap, trailing acr
the moonlit lawn like an afterimage.

I got out of the car and went after her. She was shiveri
when I caught up to her. She looked at me wild-eyed, as
she didn't recognize my face. All around us the wi
chimed in the trees.

"It's me," I said over the wind. "It's Harry."

"I thought it was someone else," she said, still looki
wild-eyed. "I thought it was . . . someone."

I pulled her close, wrapped my coat around her sho
ders, and started her back to the house. She leaned heav
against me.

As soon as we got in the door I flipped on the hall lig!
The wind had disheveled her hair, leaving it tangled abc
her face. Shivering all over Louise ducked her head
embarrassment.

"I took some pills," she said weakly. "I was asleep. I heard the car outside. I thought . . ."

Raising her head she reached for me. I pulled her against my chest.

"I had a bad dream," she whispered. "And I was alone."

"I'm here now," I said.

Holding her tight I guided her down the hall and upstairs. There was an open door next to the landing. The room inside was lit faintly by the moon. A canopied bed with lace valances. A smoothly sculpted Italian bureau. A skeletal chair by the window, casting long barred shadows on the rug.

I guided her over to the bed and laid her down on it. She wouldn't let go of my hand.

"Please don't leave me alone," she whispered. "I don't want to be alone tonight."

"I won't leave you alone."

Working loose from her grasp, I went over to the window, picked up the chair and brought it back to the side of the bed. Sitting down I reached out and took her hand again.

"Are you all right?" I said to her.

"Better," she whispered. "You won't go?"

"No."

She lay back on the pillows and stared up at the canopy above her. "I never liked being alone in the dark. There's something in it, something that always terrifies me. Phil says . . ." Her voice caught in her throat. "He said that someday it would swallow me up."

"Why would he say that?"

"To frighten me." She giggled like a child. It sounded strange coming from her—huddled and sad.

She squeezed my hand, then dropped it and rolled onto her side.

"You don't have to sleep in that chair, you know," she said, sounding more like the woman I knew.

I watched her for a time, then got up and lay down on the bed beside her. She put an arm around me.

"Thanks," she whispered.

When I was sure she was asleep I got up and went downstairs. The flickering red-and-blue Christmas tree lights guided me down the hall to Phil Pearson's study. I opened the door and went inside. Enough moonlight was coming through the French windows for me to make my way over to the glass desk. A small lamp sat on one corner. I flipped it on.

Papers were scattered on the desktop where Pearson had left them. I went through several of them—notes on patients, bills. I was hoping to find something to lead me to Carla. But nothing connected to the woman.

I did find something connected to Kirsten, however. Or disconnected. Facedown in the drawer of the desk I found half of a picture that had been torn in two. It was a picture of Kirsten when she was a little girl, standing on a lawn looking up lovingly at someone in the missing half of the photo. I could have been wrong, but I thought it might be the missing half of the photo I'd found in the girl's room in Chicago—the photo of Pearson.

I was staring at it when Louise came in the room.

She startled me so much that I jumped.

"Sorry," she said. "I woke up and thought you'd gone."

"I told you I wouldn't leave."

"People don't always do what they say." She stared at the torn photo in my hand. "What's that?"

"A picture of Kirsten when she was a little girl."

A dark look passed over Louise's face. "He would keep such a thing. His hair shirt."

"What does that mean?"

Louise shook her head sleepily. "What difference does it make anymore? Come back to bed."

"It makes a difference," I said sharply.

Louise stared at me with new interest. "I thought this thing was over."

"It's not over."

"I told you I didn't want you to keep investigating it."

"I know what you said. I'm not working for you now."

Louise went over to a chair and sat down heavily. "Is there something I should know?"

"I think your late husband murdered his first wife."

"Harry, I've already told you that he had no reason to want Stelle dead."

"There was a reason—one you don't know about."

She shook her head. "It's impossible."

"I've got proof."

"There is no proof," she said dismissively.

"It's in my office safe right now. Bankbooks for accounts that Phil established in Ethan's name. Accounts that were used to pay off Rita Scarne."

"Pay her off for what?"

"For helping to arrange Estelle's murder with the help of a woman named Chaney or Chase."

"Chase?" Louise said, looking surprised.

"You know her?"

"Phil had a secretary named Chase. At least I think that was her name." She ducked her head. "Actually the one I'm thinking of was more than Phil's secretary. She was . . . involved with him right before we met."

"This could be important, Louise."

She stared at me for a long moment. "All right, I'll find out tomorrow. I'll go through his old files. Okay?"

I nodded.

She held out her hand. "Now will you come back to bed?"

I got up from the chair and flipped off the light, dropping the torn photo of Kirsten back in the drawer.

Upstairs we made love, although there wasn't much love in it. I wanted her. And she didn't want to be alone in the dark. That was how it started, and how it finished. Just a one-night stand with the beautiful widow.

"Don't brood," she said, running a hand down my chest. "You helped me tonight."

I shook my head. "Did I?"

"Yes," she said, touching my cheek. "Sometimes it's the only thing that does help."

I stared at her voluptuous body, pale white in the moonlight. "You're very beautiful."

She smiled. "No, I'm not."

But she was. Very beautiful.

We lay there for a while without speaking. Outside the cold December wind rattled the casements.

"Once this is over, I'm going to go away," Louise said. "I'm a wealthy woman now that Phil is dead, so I'm going to go away. And when I come back I'm going to marry Saul Lasker."

"Why?" I said with surprise.

"Because he's very rich, my darling. And he'll do anything I want."

"You just said you had money of your own."

"Not enough. There isn't enough of that, ever." She reached down and stroked me gently. "I won't stop seeing you, darling, even after I've married Saul. You're good at this, you know."

I stared at her for a moment, unhappily. I had no claim on her. I doubted if any man ever really had.

"What if I'd said no tonight?" I asked.

She sighed peacefully. "I knew you wouldn't."

36

Dawn broke around seven, filling Louise's bedroom with pale filtered light—the color of the lace on her windows, the pattern of the embroidery in the lace. The light woke me up—I'd scarcely been sleeping. I turned on the mattress and looked at Louise. We'd made love a second time early that morning. It was what she'd needed all along to calm her down, to chase away the ghosts, to put her to sleep. It wasn't what I'd needed.

She'd wanted someone to hold her in the dark. In the day I knew it would be different. Her need would lessen, while mine would remain. What hurt me was that she'd known that—she'd counted on it.

The thought depressed me so much that I got out of bed and started to dress. The moment she felt my weight shift off the mattress Louise opened her eyes, as if her sleep depended on the presence of a body beside her. I didn't flatter myself that it depended on me.

Her face was drawn with fatigue, her eyes puffy with it. She sat up in bed, and the blankets slipped beneath her breasts. Even across the room she smelled of sex—and sleep and the sweet, floral fragrance that she wore.

"You're going?" she said groggily.

"Yes."

Arching her back she breathed out a sigh. Her long nipples hardened in the cold air. "You don't have to go, you know."

"I have things to do," I said.

Louise glanced around the room uncertainly, as if she

didn't remember how we'd gotten there. "I was fairly . . . crazy last night, wasn't I?"

"You got upset. It happens to all of us."

"It doesn't happen to me. If I said anything stupid . . ."

"Don't worry, Louise. I won't tell."

She brushed the hair back from her forehead. "You're pissed off, aren't you?"

"No," I said.

"Yes, you are."

Pushing herself up on the pillows she leaned against the headboard and stared at me sadly. "Harry, I truly like you. You're a good man—good in bed, good for me. But don't try to change me. Okay? I can't be that person. I tried to be someone else when I married Phil. It doesn't work." Her face turned hard and remote. "Sooner or later you run up against your past. And *it* doesn't change. It doesn't want *you* to change, either."

When I didn't say anything, Louise lay back on the pillows and closed her eyes. "I'll try to find that file you wanted. What was her name?"

"Chase. Jeanne Chase."

"Chase," she said dully. "Do the police think she's involved?"

"Parker thinks the case is closed. And since it's his jurisdiction it *will* be closed, unless I can come up with something fast."

"About Phil and this woman?"

"Yes."

"You're wrong, Harry. But I'll find her file for you if I can, and call you later today. I owe you that." She rolled on her side, away from me, so I couldn't see her face.

I drove back slowly to the apartment on Ohio. I'd only had a few hours sleep and I felt very tired. And very old.

Too old to being play love-games with a pro like Louise Pearson.

I would be pushing forty-five come fall. The bachelor-hood I'd half courted was already on me. I'd seen too many years to kid myself about a woman who gave me a hard-on. I wasn't what she wanted. And what she wanted wasn't enough for me.

I took a hot shower when I got home, trying to steam Louise out of my body and brain. But she stayed inside me like a dull ache. She'd stay in there for a while.

After the shower I wandered into the bedroom and sat down heavily on the bed. Through the blinds I could see the day dawning in earnest in a blaze of light. Sleepily I picked up the phone off the nightstand and called Shelley Sacks at his office. He didn't sound particularly happy to hear from me. But then he was still keeping secrets that he knew I wanted to share.

I made an appointment to see him in the afternoon. I didn't mention Jeanne Chase to him. I wanted to see him face-to-face when I did that. It wasn't only Jeanne Chase I wanted to talk to him about.

Lying down on the bed I shut my eyes, thinking I'd rest for a few minutes.

I didn't open them again until the telephone rang around noon.

I'd been dreaming about Louise—about the way she'd looked on the porch, bathed in white light. It turned out to be Louise on the phone. For a few moments I didn't know whether I was awake or asleep.

"Harry," I heard her say in a heavy voice. "The State Patrol just called. They found the kids."

I shook myself. "They found the kids?"

"They're bringing them out of the Miami River right now. They need me to make the identification."

"I'll come get you," I heard myself say.

She hung up. I sat there on the bed for another minute waiting for time to catch up to me—real time not dream time. But I was in it already. As I got dressed I couldn't shake the feeling that I was in them both.

It took me fifteen minutes to drive from Clifton to Indian Hill. Louise was waiting for me outside the door of the estate house. Lasker, her intended, was there too.

"I don't know if I can do this," Louise whispered as I came up beside her.

"Perhaps you shouldn't," Lasker said.

"I can go," I told her. "I know what Kirsty looks like. You can come to the morgue later, if necessary, for Ethan."

"Good," Lasker said, clapping me on the shoulder.

I shrugged his hand off. Hard. For the first time since I'd met him I saw his smile completely vanish. Grinning I squared around to face him.

Louise stepped between us. "I'm going with you," she said to me. To Lasker she said, "Go home."

She went over to the Pinto and got in. Lasker and I eyed each other for a moment, before he drifted over to his Porsche.

I got in the Pinto and drove off.

Louise didn't say anything as we headed up I-71 to 275. The scene with Lasker hadn't registered with her. It woke me up, though.

I gunned the motor as we tore through the rolling farm-land on the western edge of Hamilton county. The day was clear and bright and everything around us sparkled with ice, even the dark, turned earth.

I-275 deposited us on Harrison Pike, heading west past tin bait shops and loaf-shaped diners. The highway jogged southwest at Taylors Creek, and the scattered roadside businesses gave way to undeveloped lots, trashy fields dotted with scrub pine and river maples. To the east I could see the forested ridge that rose above the far bank of the Miami River. I couldn't see the river itself yet, just the ground clutter on its western bank and a few rusted pedestrian bridges—bare steel hoops—rising above the treetops.

A mile farther on the river came into view, thick with plate-ice that flashed in the sun. A mile after that I saw the cop cars—a nest of them in a gravel clearing above the Miami's western bank.

Louise saw them too. Reaching over she grabbed my hand and squeezed it tightly. I glanced at her face. She looked scared to death.

I slowed up and pulled off the highway, turning left onto a slick, gravel lane. Down we went, half sliding toward the police cars and ambulances in the clearing below us.

"Oh, Christ," I heard Louise whisper.

I pulled to a stop and parked the car on flat ground. Glancing at Louise I opened the door and got out into the brilliant sunlight. She got out, too. Together we weaved through the tangle of cars to the riverbank.

The area above the river was teeming with men. Cops and ambulance drivers and newsmen. The air was filled with the smoke of their breath, and the steamy exhalation of the river itself—like a fire in the midst of the deep, frozen cold. A cop stopped us as we started down a dirt trail to the river's edge.

"Officials only," he said, barring the way.

"This is the kids' mother," I said, gesturing to Louise. "Mrs. Pearson."

"Christ, I'm sorry," the cop said heavily. He was just a kid himself, and he looked genuinely hurt. I knew at once that whatever was waiting for us at the end of that trail had to be pretty goddamn awful.

Louise didn't understand that. She looked overwhelmed by the activity going on around us.

I caught sight of Larry Parker standing hands on his hips on an outcropping above the river. I called out to him and he turned his head. His face was grim.

"Wait here," I said to Louise.

She nodded once, quickly.

I let go of her arm and walked over to where Parker was standing.

"They shouldn't have called her here," he said angrily.

"It's bad?"

He pointed down. Immediately below us the bank fell away in a tangle of frozen vines and crusty shale to the water's edge. The Miami was frozen solid all the way across. Two men in wet suits were kneeling on the ice, about ten feet out. They were looking down at something between them. All around them the ice smoked in the sun like doused embers.

Fighting the glare I ducked and squinted to make out what the two divers were looking at. Then I saw it.

It was a human face—or what had been a human face—half submerged in the frozen river. A foot or so to its right a human hand dangled like a wilted lily above the ice. The hand was as white as snow, except for the nails, which had turned jet black with stagnant blood.

"Jesus Christ," I said, turning away. After a moment I asked him if he was sure it was the Pearson children.

Parker nodded. "It's them. We're going to have to use chain saws to cut the bodies out." He glanced over his shoulder at Louise. "They shouldn't have called her down here."

"I'll take her home."

I turned to go and Parker grabbed my arm. "This is terrible thing, Stoner. More terrible than you know. Yo

an see through the ice in places around the girl's body—
ee what the bastard did to her." His mouth filled with bile
nd he spat it out on the dark frozen ground. "If there's
omebody left to punish for this," he said bitterly, "I want to
now."

"I thought you said this case was closed."

"Don't be cute. You've been talking to Foster. You know
ow things stand. If you've got new information I want it. I
vant who's responsible for that."

He pointed to the river.

But I wanted her, too. As badly as Parker did. At that
moment finding Carla Chaney was all I could think of.

37

Louise didn't say a word until we'd gotten in the car and started back to Indian Hill.

"Are they sure it's Ethan and Kirsty?" she said.

"Yes," I said bitterly. "It's them."

Louise's head sank to her breast. "Oh, God. Kirsty."

She put her hands to her ears as if the thing was a noise she could block out of her head.

"I want this to stop." Grabbing my arm she said, "I want *you* to stop."

But I wouldn't have stopped at that moment for anyone

She knew it, too. Dropping her hand to her side, she stared miserably through the window. "You're not going to stop." She said it hollowly, like I'd passed a judgment on her —or her powers of persuasion.

Louise laughed bitterly. "What are you going to find at the end of this, Harry?"

"Carla Chaney."

"I thought you said her name was Chase."

"They're one and the same."

Louise looked surprised. "All right, say you do find her— Chase or Chaney. You think she's just going to let you cart her off to prison for the rest of her life? What are you going to do—shoot her?"

"If necessary."

"Bravo!" she said with heavy sarcasm. "You'll kill the killer and then everyone comes back to life. Phil and Stella and Ethan and Kirsty. Our big happy family."

"There were others."

"And you're going to avenge them all." She laughed
gain. "You're a fool, Harry. A dangerous fool."

"Why dangerous?"

"Because you're trying to change things that can't be
hanged—histories that were built up like limestone over
ears. You blame Carla Chaney-Chase for all this trouble.
ut you're wrong. Each one of us Pearsons is equally to
lame for what happened here. The whole damn family."

She stared at me a moment and then sighed defeatedly.
Oh, hell, go find your woman. Be a hero. Who knows—
aybe she's ready to die, too."

It was almost three when I got to Shelley Sacks' office in
lifton. I pulled up in the lot, parked beside his silver Merc,
alked around a hedge to the front of the duplex, then
pstairs to the second-floor waiting room. There was no one
se in the waiting room. Even the nurse was gone from her
abicle. I wondered if Sacks had gone out, too. But I found
im in his office, sitting behind the desk.

He looked up as I came in. The desk lamp reflecting off
he lenses of his glasses hid his round blue eyes, but the rest
' his face looked drawn.

"Hello, Stoner," he said wearily.

"Where is everyone?"

"I closed the office today. I didn't feel up to other people's
oblems." Tenting his fingers in front of his face, he said,
This has been the worst week I can remember since . . ."

"Estelle died?"

He nodded.

I sat down on a chair across from him. "Why don't we
art there, then. With Stelle and Phil."

Sacks shifted uncomfortably in his chair. "Stoner, I'm not
ing to discuss certain things. I've told you that. I promise
y patients confidentiality."

"Even when they murder each other?"

"What do you mean by that?"

"I mean Phil Pearson killed your friend, Estelle—an then covered up her murder."

"That is a dreadful accusation," Sacks said, unfolding h tented fingers. "A terrible accusation. The man just die for chrissake."

"I have proof. Records of money paid to Rita Scarne b Phil Pearson—a thousand dollars a month for over a de cade, paid out to cover up the murder of his wife. A murde that Phil planned with the help of Rita and two of he friends."

Sacks leaned back in the chair and the reflections in h glasses went out like snuffed candles. I saw his eyes for th first time, troubled, rimmed with red.

"He was paying Rita a thousand dollars a month?"

"To conceal murder."

Sacks shook his head, no. "You're wrong. There was r murder. If Phil was paying the woman money it was fe something else."

"Like what?" I said.

He was going to balk. I could see it in his face. I pounde the desktop with my fist, making him jump.

"I don't want to hear about your ethics again, Sack Those two kids are dead. The State Patrol found their bo ies today in the Miami River."

"Oh, my God," Sacks said, going pale. "Kirsty?"

"Dead," I said harshly. "Ethan is dead. The Scarr woman is dead. Talmadge is dead. Because of somethir that was covered up thirteen years ago. Something *you'* been helping to cover up with your silence ever sinc Ethan told you what he saw that September day. I've rea the transcript of the coroner's inquest. You didn't mention

vord about Ethan, Doctor. You blamed what happened on
ad luck—you're still blaming it on bad luck."

"To an extent that's what it was," the man said defen-
ively.

"Why? Because Phil Pearson wanted it to look that way?"

"Christ, no."

Sacks took off his glasses and pitched them on the desk.
inching the bridge of his nose he shut his eyes and rocked
ack against the window, crumpling up the blind. Sunlight
ltered through the gap, powdering his shoulder and neck
ith pale, golden light. Sacks touched at his neck as if he
ould feel it like a chill.

"Phil didn't try to conceal anything from the police,
toner. I was the one who told the officers to ignore Ethan's
tory."

"Why?"

"Why?" He laughed lamely. "What earthly good would it
ave served to raise suspicions of murder on the basis of a
hild's hysteria? *I* knew Estelle had killed herself. I even
new why. But the police might have seen the situation
ifferently. At the very least, Phil's career would have been
uined. I saw no reason to take that chance."

"How would letting Ethan tell his story have jeopardized
earson?"

"The police are dogmatists," Sacks said. "Once they
arted thinking in terms of a murder they look for motives.
 this case . . . they might have concluded that Phil had a
ason to get rid of Estelle."

I leaned forward eagerly in the chair. Phil Pearson's move for murder was at the heart of the case. It was the one
f two large blanks left in the story—his motive and Carla.
What reason did he have to murder Estelle?"

"You're not listening to me," Sacks said sharply. "I said he
idn't have a motive to be rid of her. It was she who wanted

to be rid of him. If things had worked out differently, E
telle would have divorced Phil that winter."

"*She* would have divorced him?" I said confusedly. "
thought Pearson intended to divorce *Stelle*. That's wh
Louise told me."

Sacks shook his head. "That was wishful thinking—prob
bly fostered by Phil himself. Believe me, he would neve
have divorced Stelle *or* married Louise if fate hadn't take
a hand. Phil simply depended on Stelle too deeply and i
too many ways. Emotionally, physically, financially."

"Financially?"

"All the money was Stelle's. Phil didn't start making
decent living until a couple of years after she died. In fa
he was very poor for those years, because her estate w
tied up in probate."

I didn't say it to Sacks, but that would explain why th
payoffs to Rita had begun three years after Stelle's deat

"Money wasn't the real issue, anyway," Sacks went o
"Phil would never have divorced Stelle if for no other re
son than he needed her forgiveness so badly."

"Forgiveness for what?"

Sacks took a deep breath. "Do you know anything at a
about Phil's family history, about his father in particular

"Louise told me that his father was a drunk. She also sa
that she thought Phil might have been abused by hir
sexually."

Sacks nodded. "Abuse is such a dreadful thing, and at th
same time so commonplace. More often than not it go
undiscovered. And even when it is discovered, it is usual
hushed up by the family or ignored. Unless the children ca
work through the trauma therapeutically, they invariab
have serious emotional problems for the rest of their live
They simply can't love anymore, not as adults. They c
only love dependently—or cruelly. As victims or persec

tors. Tragically that means that many of them end up as abusers themselves."

Suddenly I knew Phil Pearson's ugly secret. Knew why he'd been so afraid of exposure, so evasive about his past and his children's pasts, so terribly afraid of what his son and his daughter might accidentally reveal about him—and themselves.

Hearing Sacks say it aloud only underlined the horror of it.

"In the spring of 1976, Stelle discovered that Phil was . . . that he'd been sexually abusing Kirsten."

"He abused his daughter," I said, feeling it fully.

"It broke Stelle down. Broke both of them down, really. Phil just managed the break differently."

"You mean Louise?"

"And his work. Stelle didn't have his support system. She was quite fragile anyway, with long-standing emotional problems. Problems of self-worth, problems of sexual identity. This thing hit her precisely where she was most vulnerable. She worshiped Phil when they first married. But she had always feared that Phil didn't love her back—that he'd married her for money and social connections. Discovering that he'd been abusing Kirsty simply destroyed the little ego she had left."

Sacks' lips trembled violently, and he put a hand to his mouth to cover them. "I tried so hard to make her well. But as the depression waned, the manic stage began. Her anger welled up, and all she could think about was hurting Phil as he had hurt her. She wanted to expose him, to divorce him, to take his money and his name. Above all she wanted to take Kirsty and Ethan away from Phil forever."

"You don't think that's a motive for murder?"

"You're missing the point," Sacks said irritably. "He was

so racked with guilt himself he thought *he* deserved to be murdered. I think he would have welcomed it."

"I suppose that's why he threw himself into an affair."

"Phil was constantly having affairs. Louise was hardly the first. They were never particularly romantic things, anyway. He just wanted someone to talk to—to ease his loneliness, to assert his manhood. But none of his women, not even Louise, could absolve him for what he'd done to Kirsty. Only Stelle could do that. *Phil knew that, Stoner.* Stelle knew it, too. She knew Phil would do anything to make amends."

"Did that make a difference to her?"

"It might have—over time. If she'd had the chance to work it through. She never got that chance."

For a time neither one of us said anything.

"The abuse," I said. "That was what Kirsty had been repressing?"

"Yes. The affair Kirsten had with her teacher last spring, you know about that, don't you?"

I nodded.

"And you know about the lesbian roommate?"

"I know about Marnee," I said, although frankly I hadn't thought of her as part of Kirsten's psychodrama.

"Kirsten was reenacting this childhood trauma with both of them—symbolically reenacting it. An older man who used her sexually and then rejected her. A woman whose love Kirsty couldn't accept because it was tinged with jealousy and possessiveness. Even her search for this imaginary killer was part of the reenactment—a displacement of her guilt about her father and her rage against her mother onto a convenient stranger."

I thought of the girl's face, floating in the frozen river like a stone flower.

She hadn't gone on that journey with Ethan to kill an

imaginary stranger. In her own mad way she'd made an effort to face the reality of her past. To face the violence inflicted upon her and the violence that had been done to her mother. She hadn't been looking for a scapegoat. She'd been looking for the truth—and for a measure of justice that was long overdue.

"Talmadge wasn't imaginary, Doctor," I said heavily. "Phil used him to kill his wife and then paid Rita to cover it up."

"Use your head, Stoner," Sacks said. "If Rita Scarne *was* blackmailing Phil, it was over his abuse of Kirsty—not Stelle's death. Rita was there, after all, almost every day. Part of the family. She could easily have picked up on this. Stelle didn't hold much back, except around the children."

But I wasn't convinced. Money, prestige, career—not to mention his children. Those were damn good reasons for homicide. Sacks was simply blind to the possibility that Stelle hadn't killed herself. And I thought I understood why. He needed Stelle's suicide the way Ethan Pearson had needed her murder. Because he'd loved the woman and felt he'd failed her. Clinging to the idea of her suicide was a way of both punishing and excusing himself, by injecting an element of fatality into a situation that he couldn't control.

There was no point in debating it with him. Besides there was something else I wanted to know. "Blackmail or murder, two other people were involved in this thing besides Phil and Rita. Two people who had killed once before and disguised it as suicide. You know about Talmadge. You don't know about a nurse named Carla Chaney. Do you remember her?"

The man stared at me blankly. "Why should I?"

"She worked for you in 1975 and '76. In the Jewish Hospital Doctors' Building."

"For me?" Sacks shook his head decisively. "I never hired anyone named Chaney in 1975 or any year."

"You're sure of that?"

"Quite sure."

"How about a woman named Chase?"

Sacks looked startled. "Chase? What would she have to do with it?"

"She and Carla are the same person."

"You're imagining this," he said nervously. "You must be imagining it."

"Why?"

"Because it's impossible, that's why. The woman you're talking about is a friend."

"She was a friend of Phil's, too, wasn't she? In fact I'd be willing to bet that they had a torrid little affair back in late '75 or early '76. Maybe he kept seeing her after he and Louise began their 'platonic' relationship. Because, believe me, Doc, Carla was not a platonic lover. She was an ice-cold bitch who had killed to get ahead—and who probably put the idea of killing in Phil's addled head.

"The woman you know as Jeanne Chase *is* Carla Chaney, Doctor. And Carla Chaney is a borderline psychotic—a woman who arranged to murder her own family and to murder the real Jeanne Chase and to murder Stelle Pearson."

"I don't believe you!" he shouted. "There was no murder!"

But he no longer looked or sounded convinced of that. Jeanne Chase had changed his mind.

38

Although I pressed him hard, Sacks refused to answer any more questions about Jeanne Chase. I had the feeling he was no longer holding back out of principle, but because he wanted to confront the woman himself. And that was a bad idea. He was angry and he was upset—so much so that his voice had begun to shake with emotion and his brow to pop sweat. He looked, for all the world, like a man betrayed by a lover. It was that kind of deep, personal hurt.

"Doc," I warned him, "don't try anything stupid. Carla is very dangerous."

Sacks stared at me for a long moment. "I have been a very great fool," he said in a voice that was just barely under control. "And I will handle this."

I started for the door.

"Stoner?" he said.

I looked back at him.

"She worked here when Stelle had her breakdown. She had access to the files." He took a deep breath and added: "To Phil's file, too."

The thought had already occurred to me. But I didn't like the way he put it. It was almost as if he was telling me what to do, if something should happen to him.

I sat in Sacks' parking lot for a full fifteen minutes before starting the car and driving back to the Riorley Building. Even then I didn't feel right about leaving him alone. He'd had a doomed look on his face when I left the office. And he was a man who believed in fate.

I phoned Al Foster as soon as I got to the office—to see if

he had a lead on Jeanne Chase or the bankbooks. But a desk sergeant told me that he was out. I couldn't just sit there, waiting for Al to get back. And I had no way to find Jeanne Chase, save through Shelley Sacks. What I did have was the bankbooks. I decided to do something about them.

There was a First National branch office right across the street from the Riorley. I walked back down to the lobby, crossed over Vine, and went into the bank. The managers' desks were at the back in a mahogany-paneled alcove set off from the barred cages of the tellers by a short mahogany fence. I sat down on a bench outside the fence until one of the assistant managers came out to collect me.

The tag on his desk said "Steven Moran." And it was clear that Steven Moran was relatively new to the bank and not yet hardened in the ways of commerce. An ordinary, un-businesslike grin kept flirting across his face, and he kept fighting it back like a drunk playing sober. There'd come a time when he wouldn't have to work so hard at looking like a banker.

Getting Steven Moran was a break for me. He *wanted* to help—he thought that was what they'd hired him for.

I took out Ethan's bankbook and told him my story: "A customer left this damn thing in my manager's office last week. Now my manager's gone on vacation and the rest of us can't quite figure out who it belongs to. Nobody remembers an 'E. Pearson' coming in, and we don't have him on file. One of the secretaries suggested that I pop over here and see if you could help with a phone number or an address."

"I can try," Steve Moran said earnestly. "Let me take a look."

I handed him the book and he examined it. Biting his lip he turned to a computer on his desk. The screen was facing away from me so I couldn't see what he was up to. But I heard him punching the keyboard.

"That's odd," he said to himself.

"You have something?"

"Yeah, but it doesn't say E. Pearson." For just a second I could see him wondering whether I was on the level. I smiled affably, and that grin of his came back on. He should have been playing softball instead of sitting behind a desk.

"According to the computer the account is owned by a woman. Jeanne L. Chase."

"No E. Pearson?" I said, trying not to look too confused—although the fact that Phil Pearson wasn't the owner of the account did, in fact, throw me.

"The account's in the name E. Pearson," the kid said, looking a little confused himself. "But Jeanne L. Chase owns it." His grin came back on, as if he'd had a brainstorm. "Maybe she's a relative of the kid's—or a friend of the family. People do that sometimes when a kid is underage."

"Do they?" I said uneasily.

"I've got an address if you want to get in touch with her."

"That would be fine," I said.

"Eighty-nine fifty Kenwood Road. There's no phone listed."

I went from the bank to the underground garage where the car was parked. It was past five when I got onto 71 North. The rush-hour traffic was heavy, and it was close to six when I got off the expressway at the Kenwood exit.

I'd tried not to think about that damn bank account on the way out—about what it meant. Some of it was obvious. Phil Pearson hadn't been paying Rita Scarne off—at least not directly. Jeanne L. Chase had. Which meant that Jeanne L. Chase had access to a lot of money—her own or someone else's. The fact that the account had been established in Ethan's name suggested that Phil was still the likely source.

That's as far as I let myself take it. But I sure as hell didn't like the direction it was going.

The development that Jeanne L. lived in on Kenwood Road only made me more nervous. Eighty-nine fifty was a luxe little complex, a couple miles from the Kenwood shopping district, a couple more miles from Indian Hill. The condos were single units shingled in cedar shakes that had weathered to a seaside grey. They had tall smoked-glass windows and fenced grounds and built-in garages, and each one was twisted like a different letter of the alphabet—or the same letter drawn in a slightly different hand. Stylish hideaways for those who could afford them. Like Phil Pearson.

The sun was down by the time I got to the complex. I flipped on the lights and coasted down a tar drive, past those big block letters. The ground floors were fenced off in front, so all you could see were the second story windows with their dark glass panes reflecting the twilight.

Eighty-nine fifty was the last lot on the street. I knew which one it was without having to hunt for the number. Shelley Sacks' grey Merc was parked in front.

I pulled up behind the Merc and got out. The wind was blowing hard, and I ducked my head against it as I walked toward Jeanne L. Chase's condo. As I got closer to the fence I heard a creaking noise. The fence gate had been left ajar and was swinging in the wind. I looked around—at the other condos on that part of the block. The nearest one was a good thirty yards away—across the drive. There were no lights coming from it. No lights at all on that part of the street. Looking back at the fence I opened the gate fully and went in.

There was a stone walkway inside, cutting across a small

yard to the front door of the condo. I walked up to the door
and knocked. When no one answered I tried the doorknob.
It wasn't locked.

The house was completely dark. Without the twilight to
guide me I had to stand in the doorway for several moments
while my eyes dark-adapted. Eventually I found a dimmer
switch on the wall and pressed it. A row of recessed lights
came on overhead, lighting a carpeted hallway with a large
lacquered mirror on the right-hand wall and several
framed Japanese and Indian prints on the left. The place
looked just as posh as could be, until I glanced at one of the
prints. They were artily framed but what they pictured
were perverse sexual acts—some of them involving children.

I began to notice a stale smell in the hall. A smell like dirt
and old sex mixed together with something else—something fresh and terrible.

I walked quickly to the end of the hall. It forked to the
right and left—right into a large living room, decorated
with Italian leather furniture, left into a stairwell, leading to
the second floor. The living room was dark, so I couldn't see
the framed pictures on the walls. But I could guess what
their subject matter was. Something on an end table
gleamed in the hall light—a water pipe, I thought.

I looked up the dark stairway to my left. The bad smell
seemed stronger there. There was a switch on the wall. I
flipped it on and immediately flipped it off again.

It was a gut reaction—a twitch. There was blood on the
stairs. A good deal of it.

I turned the light back on and started up, stepping over
the dark, glistening spots of blood. The smell of sex and
death grew much stronger as I neared the landing. Sex and
death and flowers. Her scent.

The top floor looked to be one large room, with a tall,

A-frame ceiling. A ceiling fan dangling from the center beam had been left on. It slowly revolved above the brass bed on the floor beneath it. The bed was the only piece of furniture in the room. It gleamed in the semidarkness—the brass fittings, the stained silk sheets. A body lay on the bed —Sheldon Sacks' body. He was naked, bloody from the waist down, and very, very dead.

I didn't examine the body. I didn't want to look at what she'd done to him. He had come there to confront her— perhaps he had summoned her there on the phone after I left the office. Who knows what he had in mind. But he'd been no match for Carla.

Neither had I.

drove back to Sacks' office. I didn't even bother to call the cops. There would be time for the cops later.

I'd found the key to his building in his trousers and a key to the alarm box. I used one to get in and the other to give me some time with his files. It took a few hours. I'd guessed most of it anyway. I was a damn good guesser by then.

I took her employment file with me when I left.

It was almost midnight when I got to Indian Hill—to the unmarked street in the midst of the woods. I pulled up in the driveway and sat there for a while, wondering if she'd come out again, wrapped in silk, to play in the moonlight.

But she didn't come out.

I opened the car door and walked across the lawn.

The front door was open. I went in. Down the hall to the sitting room, where she was waiting by the fire. Behind her the stale Christmas tree winked red and blue.

I sat down across from her on the leather captain's chair.

For a while she looked at the fire—her hand to her cheek, her face sleepy-looking in the firelight, her eyes heavy with sleep. She'd had a long day.

"Shelley told me you'd be coming," she said.

"I just saw him."

She laughed—her teeth red in the firelight. "Did you?"

"What do you have planned for me?"

"For you?" she said. "Oh, I see. You made a joke."

"It's no joke, Louise, Carla, Jeanne. Which do you prefer?"

"Carla is right," she said, letting her head loll against the chair. "Carla is first."

"So I've seen."

"Don't be mean, Harry," Carla Chaney said. "I've seen enough cruelty in my life. Now I want it to stop. I want it all to stop. I'm through."

She showed me her hands—both sides, as if she'd cleaned them real good, cleaned them for me. "See."

But I didn't see.

"I guess I understand about Tallwood and Talmadge. But your own son?"

"That was Talmadge," she said bitterly. "I didn't want that."

"And Jeanne Louise Chase? What did you want him to do with her?"

"She was a vindictive bitch, who would have destroyed me if she could. I didn't let her."

"Which brings us to Stelle—poor Stelle. Without her money and her house and her friends—Phil was just a weak man with no future. And she was going to take it all away from him. Either that or he was going to go back to her and beg her forgiveness. Either way you were screwed. So you got Talmadge out of the hospital, and Rita . . . well, she was already on hand. Or did you recommend her for the nursing job, too? Whisper her name in Phil's ear? Tell her to call in sick on the day you scheduled the job?"

"Something like that," Carla Chaney said.

"Why Shelley? Why the stepkids?"

She smiled sleepily. "Why not you, last night?"

I shuddered where I sat. "That's no answer."

"Shel had been fucking me off and on since I met him—whenever he could get it up, whenever he felt like it, whenever he wanted a dirty thrill. That was what the condo was for—a love nest. What Shel didn't know was that I too

very guy I slept with there. He was fucking Stelle, too,
efore she died—the good doctor. Phil's close friend." She
aughed, baring her teeth. "Tonight he wanted to fuck me
ne more time before he turned me in. I let him do me—in
he ass. Then I gave him what he deserved."

She said it as if that was what every man who had ever
aid a hand on her in violence had deserved—the long line
f abusing men, from Tallwood to Sacks.

"Why Ethan and Kirsty? What did they deserve?"

"Herb was going to kill me," she said simply. "I'd set him
p for Jeanne's murder. Rita and I did. I had to do some-
hing after he got out of prison. When Kirsty called Shelley
n the way to town on Sunday night, I saw a chance."

"She called Sacks?"

"From a phone booth outside Indianapolis. He wanted to
eep it a secret—to let Kirsty work the thing out therapeu-
cally. That was his vanity." Carla Chaney smiled. "He
uldn't keep a secret from me."

"Then it was you who made the call to the motel on
londay and told them where to find Talmadge?"

She noddod. "I didn't think Kirsty was still with Ethan. I
ally didn't. She told Shel on Sunday night that she was
ing to go back to Chicago. I guess it was just bad luck that
he didn't."

I stared at her and she turned away.

"Don't look at me like that," she whispered. "I'm no
onster."

"You told Talmadge they were coming, for chrissake! In
rospect Park on Monday night."

"No, I gave him drugs. So he'd be asleep when they came.
ut he didn't take them until later, until after . . ." Her
outh trembled. "I didn't want Kirsty to die. She was a
tle . . . like me."

For a split second I saw a look on her face that I'd never

seen before, save on the faces of desperate men. "I kille
him *for her,* too."

"C'mon," I said heavily. "We're going to the cops."

Carla shook her head. "I'm not going anywhere. I too
some pills about fifteen minutes ago. Fifteen minutes fro
now . . . I'll be asleep."

"For chrissake, Louise!"

She stared at me almost pityingly. "Don't do anythin
. . . okay? Just stay here until I fall asleep. That's all I ask.
don't like to be alone in the dark. You know that."

"Louise . . ."

"I won't try any tricks. I could have done you last night.
could do you right now. I could make it look like an acc
dent. Believe me."

"I believe you."

"But I've given up. I tried to explain it in the car today
She got to her feet. "Just stay here until I'm asleep. The
you can call the police."

Louise unbuttoned her blouse as she walked over to th
door. I saw her body again—beautiful in the firelight.

"Why are you doing this?" I asked her.

"Because I'm tired." She smiled sadly. "I've lived to
many lives."

I didn't say it but, in truth, it had only been the one.

"I'm going upstairs to the bedroom," she said as sl
walked from the room. "In ten minutes or so, come up a
. . . kiss me good night."

"The toughest, funniest, wisest
private-eye in the field."*

JOHN MILTON

Paradise Lost and Paradise Regained

With a New Introduction by
Susanne Woods

Edited and with Notes by
Christopher Ricks

The Signet Classic Poetry Series
GENERAL EDITOR: JOHN HOLLANDER

A SIGNET CLASSIC

SIGNET CLASSIC
Published by New American Library, a division of
Penguin Putnam Inc., 375 Hudson Street,
New York, New York 10014, U.S.A.
Penguin Books Ltd, 80 Strand,
London WC2R 0RL, England
Penguin Books Australia Ltd, Ringwood,
Victoria, Australia
Penguin Books Canada Ltd, 10 Alcorn Avenue,
Toronto, Ontario, Canada M4V 3B2
Penguin Books (N.Z.) Ltd, 182–190 Wairau Road,
Auckland 10, New Zealand

Penguin Books Ltd, Registered Offices:
Harmondsworth, Middlesex, England

Published by Signet Classic, an imprint of New American Library,
a division of Penguin Putnam Inc.

First Signet Classic Printing, February 1968
First Signet Classic Printing (Woods Introduction), November 2001
10 9 8 7 6 5 4 3

Ⓒ REGISTERED TRADEMARK—MARCA REGISTRADA

Library of Congress Catalog Card Number: 2001041132

Printed in the United States of America

BOOKS ARE AVAILABLE AT QUANTITY DISCOUNTS WHEN USED TO PROMOTE
PRODUCTS OR SERVICES. FOR INFORMATION PLEASE WRITE TO PREMIUM
MARKETING DIVISION, PENGUIN PUTNAM INC., 375 HUDSON STREET, NEW
YORK, NEW YORK 10014.

Contents

Introduction

In 1667 a blind man published a long poem that became an immediate sensation. *Paradise Lost,* followed seven years later by the shorter, more subdued *Paradise Regained,* has thrilled, challenged, and sometimes dismayed readers from the seventeenth to the twenty-first century. Centered around the biblical story of the fall of Adam and Eve, *Paradise Lost* is an epic poem that ranges from heaven to hell and offers an image of the universe and the human condition that reflects the turmoil of Milton's own time, and is still subject to heated debate. *Paradise Regained,* the story of Satan's threefold temptation of Jesus in the wilderness, complements the longer poem.

When Milton was born on December 9, 1608, Shakespeare was still writing plays for his all-male theatrical company, King James I was arguing with Parliament about taxation and religion, and Ben Jonson was producing extravagant court entertainments, called masques, for the separate courts of James and Queen Anne. When Milton died in 1674, the Restoration was in full swing. Charles II numbered one of the first actresses, Nell Gwynn, among his many mistresses, while the first successful woman writer, Aphra Behn, was publishing novels and having her plays produced on the London stage. John Dryden was perfecting the rhyming couplets and civilized satire that were to characterize poetry for the next one hundred years.

From the distance of three hundred years, little on the surface might seem to have changed except the somewhat greater visibility of women in the arts. Yet change characterized seventeenth-century England, with deep and continuing effects. In the sixty-six years of Milton's lifetime the English world, in a phrase from the time, "turned upside down"—a king executed, theaters closed for a generation, religious controversy rampant, Puritans leaving for North America, experimental science born. Milton lived, worked, argued, and wrote in the heat of controversies that swirled around him.

Milton's Life

John Milton Senior, a successful businessman and a musician, had migrated to London in large part because his Protestant views differed from his Catholic yeoman father's.° Young John Milton was the second of three surviving children and the first son. Milton's father recognized and encouraged his son's talents as an intellectual and poet, assuring him an excellent education destined to prepare him for a career in the church. The Scotch Presbyterian Thomas Young, Milton's tutor from the ages of about nine to twelve, introduced young John to classical learning and to radical Protestant theology. From twelve to sixteen Milton attended St. Paul's School, where the headmaster, Alexander Gil, and his son (and Milton's friend), Alexander Gil the younger, continued to nourish Milton's love of learning and encourage his development as a poet. From an early age, Milton combined what would become lifelong interests in religion, the classics, and poetry.

Milton was a student at Christ's College, Cambridge University, from ages eighteen to twenty-three. Despite the reputation of Cambridge, and Christ's, for fostering classical learning and training freethinking ministers, Milton often found the education that led to his bachelor's and master's degrees rigid and stifling. These years (1625–32) coincided with the early years of the reign of King Charles I, notable for heightening religious differences between those who favored the hierarchical rule of bishops and ceremonial worship associated with the new Archbishop of Canterbury, William Laud, and those who preferred a Presbyterian governance and Calvinist theology. Milton had at least one run-in with authority early in his university career, an argument with his tutor that sent him home ("rusticated" him) for a few weeks in 1626. His return to Cambridge, and to a new tutor, did not halt his developing sense of autonomy, nor his increasing belief

---

° Biographical information in this introduction relies on Barbara K. Lewalski, *The Life of John Milton: A Critical Biography* (Oxford: Blackwell, 2000).

in liberty of conscience over obedience to the rules of the English church. Although he proceeded to take the degrees requisite for ordination, he recognized that his unorthodox views would not allow him to serve in the church, and he focused his attention increasingly on a career as a poet. His father must have been disappointed; sometime during the decade after college Milton wrote a Latin elegy, "Ad Patrem," to thank him for his long support and to invite him to accept the younger Milton's calling to be a poet. Disappointed or not, Milton Senior continued to support his son, allowing him to live at home from ages twenty-three to twenty-nine (1632–38) and devote himself almost entirely to studies.

Milton began to publish as a poet during this time at his father's home. His commendatory couplets appeared anonymously in the second folio of Shakespeare's plays (1632), a curious debut for an unknown young poet, which probably owed something to his father's connections in the world of music and drama. In the early 1630s he wrote two masques for the Egerton family, the first, *Arcades,* a praise of the dowager countess of Derby, and the second, *A Mask,* presented in 1634 at Ludlow Castle to celebrate the Earl of Bridgewater's appointment as Lord President of Wales. This entertainment, popularly known as *Comus* after the evil enchanter who drives the plot, summarizes many of Milton's early ideas about the power of virtue, themes in stark contrast to the heroic sensuousness of the court masque as it had evolved under King Charles I and his Catholic wife, Henrietta Maria. In 1637 Milton's pastoral elegy *Lycidas,* on the death of a Cambridge friend, appeared as the last poem in a volume of poetic tributes. Its images of rising and falling, light and dark, and its concern with ideas of fame and virtue prefigure some of Milton's imagery and themes in *Paradise Lost* and *Paradise Regained*. In 1645 Milton gathered *Comus, Lycidas,* and several other works from his youth into a volume titled simply *Poems*.

Milton's vocation as a poet was reinforced during a trip to Italy in 1638–39. There he met and charmed the last remnants of the high Renaissance, the artists and intellectuals of the private academies in Florence who praised his poetry and befriended him. He also met the aged Galileo and, in Naples, Giovanni Battista Manso, a patron of the great sixteenth-century Italian poet Torquato Tasso. News of political trouble in England kept Milton from continuing to Greece, and instead he returned home somewhat before he had planned. Poetry then took a secondary place for twenty years, as Milton engaged in the intricately interwoven political and religious controversies of the English Civil War period, gained influence in Cromwell's government, lost his sight, and with the return of the monarchy in 1660, found himself in some danger of losing his life.

The English Civil War pitted king and bishops against Parliament and the Presbyterian and Congregationalist systems of church government. There were dozens of issues that separated the two groups, from the power of taxation to the doctrine of predestination, with political and theological issues intertwined. Milton's interest was in the free exercise of an informed conscience, and he saw tyranny and superstition as twin evils that must be uprooted and replaced by republican government and free and open debate. Among his first pamphlets, *Of Reformation* (1641) and *The Reason of Church Government* (1642) argue for a church without bishops, answerable to a free people, but do not attack the idea of kingship. His most famous pamphlet, *Areopagitica* (1644), is a speech to Parliament, the new seat of power, arguing against press censorship. Milton also wrote in favor of divorce (what he called "domestic liberty") during an unhappy first marriage, later reconciled. After King Charles was executed in January 1649, Milton wrote in elegant and thoughtful Latin to the horrified intelligentsia of Europe in support of what he called tyrannicide.

During the 1650s Milton served as Latin Secretary to Oliver Cromwell, which meant he composed in Latin the formal state papers and correspondence the government needed to continue its role as a European nation. After Cromwell's death in 1658, it became increasingly clear that the English people would welcome the Stuart monarchy back from exile in France and that Charles I's son would become Charles II. As Milton's colleagues began to accommodate reality, Milton stepped up his writing, urging to the last that England embrace a special godly destiny by rejecting monarchy and a state church in favor of a republican form of government and congregational autonomy.

Milton was briefly imprisoned at the start of the Restoration, spent time in the country to avoid the further attention of monarchists and the plague, and completed his greatest works, *Paradise Lost* (first published in ten books in 1667) and *Paradise Regained* (published in 1671, along with the magnificent biblical drama *Samson Agonistes*). Before his death in 1674, he also completed a revised and expanded version of his collected *Poems* (1673) and the revised, twelve-book version of *Paradise Lost*. Blind and living with the failure of his political and religious causes, he nevertheless spent the final years of his life in great productivity, surrounded by friends and family (including his three "undutiful daughters" and his third evidently more dutiful wife).

Paradise Lost

Milton intended to write an epic poem for the English people in the great tradition of Homer celebrating the Greeks, and Virgil the Romans. In language strongly reminiscent of *The Iliad* and *The Aeneid*, Milton announces his great topic ("Man's first disobedience, and the fruit / Of that forbidden tree") and invokes a "heavenly Muse" to help him tell of "things unattempted yet in prose or rhyme" (PL I, 1–2, 16). In the images of light and darkness, low and high, that pervade the work, he prays:

> . . . *What in me is dark*
> *Illumine, what is low raise and support;*
> *That to the heighth of this great Argument*
> *I may assert Eternal Providence,*
> *And justify the ways of God to men.*
> (PL I, 22–26)

Whether the poem adequately explains "the ways of God to men" is a subject of continuing dispute, but Milton unquestionably offers an imaginative vision of great magnitude and power. In the course of the poem's twelve books we see Satan falling from heaven, rousing his rebel angels, building their city, Pandemonium, and leading a plot to destroy mankind in revenge for the loss of heaven.

We see God, the Son, and the loyal angels observe the Satanic plotting, and Son volunteer to sacrifice himself in order to overturn what God's foreknowledge sees will be a successful subversion of mankind. We see Adam and Eve in joyous possession of Eden, and each other, and a jealous Satan whispering dangerous thoughts into Eve's ear as she dreams. We see the Archangel Raphaël come down to Eden for lunch with Adam and Eve in order to tell the story of the war in heaven, followed by Adam's own account, including his rich new world, the creation of Eve, and God's one test of obedience: that they not eat the fruit of the tree of knowledge of good and evil.

In Book IX, Milton "now must change / [his] Notes to Tragic" (PL IX, 5–6), as Satan again enters the garden, contemplates his own alienation and anger, and admits to himself: "Revenge, at first though sweet / Bitter erelong back on itself recoils" (PL IX, 171–72). He nonetheless descends into the form of a serpent to attempt that revenge against God by tempting mankind into disobedience. We see Adam and Eve separate to tend the garden alone, despite Raphaël's warnings of danger. We see Eve, cleverly manipulated by Satan, whom she believes is a talking serpent, eat the fruit and give it to Adam, who, though not deceived, eats it as well. We see their loss, repentance, God's judgment, and Satan's triumph as he creates a bridge for Sin and Death to enter the world. We see the Archangel Michael giving Adam and Eve a vision of earthly history and the tragic consequences of "Man's First Disobedience," along with the promise of redemption through the sacrifice of the Son. Finally, we see Adam's wonder, joy, frequent misunderstandings, and Michael's corrections as this panorama of the future unfolds.

The poem has epic proportions and language. It is a long narrative, ranging across vast areas of time and space. It begins, like classical epics, in medias res, in the middle of things, with the fall of Satan after the war in heaven. As in classical epic, the earlier part of the story is told over a meal in the middle of the poem, in this case by Raphaël as he enjoys what Eve has prepared. Raphaël

describes the war in heaven by using the physical world
that humankind, locked in time, can understand,

> *By lik'ning spiritual to corporal forms,*
> *As may express them best, but what if Earth*
> *Be but the shadow of Heav'n, and things therein*
> *Each to other like, more than on earth is thought?*
> (PL V, 573–76)

Milton's angels are sensuous creatures, who eat, make
love, and at least once in heaven, fight violently. What if,
indeed, the author seems to suggest, earth and heaven are
more alike than we think?

Although, like Raphaël, Milton seeks to convey an
enormous universe in terms human beings can understand, Milton's "high style" can be initially confusing to
a modern reader. He tends to write in long, periodic sen-
tences, with the principal verb toward the end (as in Latin,
or modern German). He uses epic similes—extended
comparisons that can cover vast distances of time or
space. He makes frequent reference to classical or biblical
stories, common to educated readers of his own time, but
much less so today. Yet he almost always explains those
references within the text, and once a modern reader becomes used to the movement of his blank verse lines and
the somewhat unfamiliar syntax, Milton's magnificent language serves his epic vision very well.

Milton does expect us to know something of the Bible,
however, and designs his rhetorical strategy with that in
mind. At the beginning of *Paradise Lost* we, who have
presumably read the biblical account, know more than
Adam and Eve. We know, as God does, that they will not
remain obedient, despite the happiness they have been
given: "When the woman saw that the tree was good for
food, and that it was pleasant to the eyes, and a tree to
be desired to make one wise, she took of the fruit thereof,
and did eat, and gave also unto her husband with her;
and he did eat" (Genesis 3:6, King James Version). After
Adam and Eve fall, we who have read the biblical stories
of the New Testament know that the story is not over. The
suffering and death which is the "fruit" of this original

disobedience is to be transformed by the obedience of the Son (the topic of *Paradise Regained*). At the end of *Paradise Lost,* however, after the Archangel Michael has revealed the biblical future, we know no more than Adam and Eve; their situation—to work and suffer, not without hope—has become our situation. As they leave the garden, they must make choices no longer easy, though God is still watching out for them, and their comfort is in being together, though never again perfectly:

> *Some natural tears they dropp'd, but wip'd them soon;*
> *The World was all before them, where to choose*
> *Their place of rest, and Providence their guide:*
> *They hand in hand with wand'ring steps and slow,*
> *Through Eden took their solitary way.*
> (PL XII, 645–49)

Critical Issues in *Paradise Lost*

Critics have generally agreed about the basic story *Paradise Lost* seeks to tell, the ambition of Milton's effort, and the magnificence of his language. Beyond that there is much disagreement, even on whether the magnificent language is a good thing. (T. S. Eliot thought not.)° Although "readers' reception of *Paradise Lost* has been, ever since its publication in 1667, largely determined by the prevailing political and religious attitudes" (Stocker, 10), certain controversies about the work recur. The central debate is over what the poem is really saying about God, mankind, and the human condition, and whether it matters to a changing cultural view of the universe. Another is the role of Satan, or its variation: if *Paradise Lost* is an epic, and epics are supposed to have central heroes, who is the hero of the poem?

Unlike the great majority of dissenting Christians with whom Milton aligned himself, Milton believed in free will and the continuing responsibility of Christians to exercise

---

° References to critics refer to works listed in the bibliography; for a good summary of Milton's critical history, see Margarita Stocker, *An Introduction to the Variety of Criticism: Paradise Lost* (London: Macmillan, 1988), and for many of the chief issues in current debate, see Dennis Danielson, ed., *The Cambridge Companion to Milton,* 2d ed. (Cambridge: Cambridge University Press, 1999).

their freedom by making knowledgeable choices. A key question for most readers of *Paradise Lost,* however, is whether Adam and Eve are truly free, and what their freedom says about the goodness of their Creator. In Book III, God, who is outside of time, sees everything that happens in time, including in what we could think of as the future; God therefore sees that Adam and Eve will disobey. God also insists that His foreknowledge does not cause the disobedience (PL III, 93–128). Since the Victorian period, when elite readers began less and less to believe in the picture Milton creates of heaven, hell, and what it means to be human, critics and readers have put a skeptical and sometimes horrified eye on Milton's God, judging Him evil for creating an Adam and Eve who could fall (Empson). Milton's God, however, insists that creating an Adam and Eve who must obey God would deny the foundation of their dignity, and deny the principal way in which they are made in the image of God: their ability to choose and therefore to participate in their own becoming.

The debate over Milton's God and the issue of free will spills over into the debate about the hero of *Paradise Lost.* How could a rebel such as Milton not admire the rebel angel Satan? Readers who know the outline of Milton's own history, or who are moved by Satan's powerful rhetoric in the first two books of *Paradise Lost,* may well see Satan as the hero of *Paradise Lost,* as Romantic poets such as Blake and Shelley did. As the poem progresses, however, Satan's motives and even his language become increasingly less attractive, so that most readers over the centuries have had little trouble seeing him, finally, as the quintessential, unrepentant evil that he knows himself to be. Readers as different as C. S. Lewis and Stanley Fish have made the point that Satan must be an attractive figure in order for the reader to understand the distorting power of evil; we have to be taught that he is the father of lies (*Preface to Paradise Lost; Surprised by Sin*). Barbara Lewalski reminds us that Satan, not God, is most like an earthly monarch, and that Milton objected to human hierarchy as a sinful parody of the true divine hierarchy (*The Life,* 468–69).

In Milton's theology, God is the omnipotent and omni-

scient Creator, whose creatures, including the rebel
angels, cannot possibly overpower Him. In Milton's
scheme, God gives angels and mankind free will in order
to glorify them and Himself. If they rebel, their separation
from God as the source of all power and happiness necessarily diminishes their own. Nonetheless, God, as Adam
understands toward the end of Book XII, will always find
ways to overcome evil by turning it into good. Since the
Son is God's agent in this effort—he wins the war in
heaven and volunteers to save mankind—he, not Satan,
is presumably the hero of *Paradise Lost.*

While critics continue to debate heroism and the fine
points of Milton's theology in *Paradise Lost* (is Milton
antitrinitarian? is it a "fortunate fall"?), a larger question
is the continuing relevance of the work to contemporary
society. In fact, *Paradise Lost* has often been vigorously
ejected from the literary canon that it once helped to con-
struct. The Victorians thought it a "monument to dead
ideas." The New Critics—literary critics who dominated
British and American letters from the 1930s through the
1950s—pronounced Milton bombastic and irrelevant.
Feminist critics in the 1970s saw him as the worst example
of patriarchal canonizing because Eve, though magnificent, is second to Adam, and Milton in his own life sometimes had vexed relationships with women. Critics during
the 1980s who would deconstruct a text into a social docu-
ment absent any true "author" would prefer to ignore
Milton, who may be the first English poet to insist absolutely on his personal identity as author.

Still, cultural critics have found *Paradise Lost* a docu-
ment of continuing interest, and those interested in my-
thology and psychology find rich material in Milton's
imaginative vision (Hill, Frye). Even feminists have noted
that Milton was both of his time, and in some ways in
advance of it (essays in Walker; Wittreich). Milton and
Paradise Lost are not easily pushed out of the canon so
long as we insist on having a canon—a set of works that
most of us agree should be made available and taught
from generation to generation. Every attempt to devalue
Milton's work so far has failed. But the history of both
the man and the work continues to raise issues about
how we see our universe, and what we value in it.

Whether we read it for its magnificent poetry, its imaginative vision, or its complex and passionate view of human suffering, *Paradise Lost* will continue to compel the attention of readers who care about the idea of human freedom.

Paradise Regained

Milton's "brief epic," in four books, is a much simpler and more contained work than *Paradise Lost*. In *Paradise Regained,* Milton tells the story of the Son of God's temptation by Satan in the wilderness, based principally on the account in Luke 4:1–13 (a slightly different version is in Matthew 3:13–4:11). Most Christian writers telling the story of the Son's redemptive acts focus on his suffering, crucifixion, and resurrection. Milton's choice of the temptation in the wilderness is at first surprising, but fits perfectly with Milton's own belief that inner strength, knowledge, and moral choice produce "deeds / Above Heroic, though in secret done" (PR I, 14–15). If Adam's disobedience lost Paradise, the Son's obedience reunites God and mankind.

The story is principally a series of debates between Satan and the Son, or rather of Satan offering temptations and the Son steadfastly rejecting them. As in *Paradise Lost,* Satan hopes to get this man, Jesus, to fall, but unlike Adam and Eve, Jesus stands. Critics have complained about the static nature of the story, but there is a rather remarkable tension. We know, of course, that Jesus will stand, and the Jesus in *Paradise Regained* never seems in danger of falling, but in Milton's story he needs to learn who he is, and what he should be doing on behalf of God. In *Paradise Lost* the Son, from the vantage of timeless heaven, knows about the fall of mankind and volunteers to be the agent of salvation, knowing, as well, it will mean becoming human and dying on behalf of humankind (PL III, 227–65). In *Paradise Regained* the Son is incarnate as Jesus. Although he has help—inner promptings, the dramatic voice from the sky at his baptism by John, "thou art my beloved son; in thee I am well pleased" (Luke 3:22, PR I 29–32)—he is inside time, and must make choices without the absolute vision of the future available to those in heaven.

A central tension of the story lies in Satan's effort to determine who this particular son of God might be, unable to comprehend that he is the same one who conquered Satan and his rebel angels in heaven. In the last of his temptations, Satan takes Jesus to the tower of the temple, setting him on the "highest Pinnacle," telling Him to "stand, if thou wilt stand; to stand upright / Will ask thee skill" (PR IV, 549, 551–52). Or, Satan says, Jesus could cast himself off the tower, and if he is the true Son of God, then God will surely keep him safe from harm. Jesus' response is the simplest in the poem, and taken directly from Luke 4:12:

> *"Also it is written*
> *'Tempt not the Lord thy God,' "* he said and stood,
> But Satan smitten with amazement fell
>   (PR IV, 560–62)

As Adam and Eve gave into temptation, disobeyed, and lost Paradise, this is the moment for Milton when the Son resists temptation, obeys the word of God, and positions himself to regain Paradise. The reader understands that there is a sacrifice to come, but that painful outward symbol of obedience would not be possible without the inner fortitude that this story represents.

To a degree stronger and more visible than his predecessors or contemporaries, Milton valued and praised individual integrity. There was nothing new in his insistence that outward virtue was a product of inward virtue; Plato made the point as early as the fifth century B.C.E. What was new was Milton's insistence on the value of individual conscience and individual choice over every other authority. The most radical Protestants of his own time, such as the Anabaptists or the antiauthoritarian Levellers, set the Bible above all else, or believed, as the Quakers did, that God came to mankind directly through an "inner light." Milton went a step farther, and yet remains a paradox. He allowed biblical interpretation based on an inward light that came as much from study as it did from direct divine inspiration, and tended to see study and divine knowledge as related. Nonetheless, Adam and Eve fall because they desire knowledge of both good and evil, to be "like gods." Jesus, in *Paradise Regained,* resists all temptations, including the temptation of worldly knowledge.

Milton, seeing himself as God's poet, offers these texts of enormous linguistic power and thematic complexity. Rather than telling the reader how to think, he presents portraits of a universe created by a divine power, and invites his reader to engage in exploring the complexities of that universe. Since the fall, as Adam discovers at the end of *Paradise Lost,* each of us must "have [our] fill / Of knowledge, what this vessel can contain" (PL XII, 558–59), but not aspire to be gods. The model of Jesus in *Paradise Regained* fits precisely Adam's recognition that it is not by heroic bombast, such as Satan offers at the beginning of *Paradise Lost,* but by relying on Providence and

> *by small*
> *Accomplishing great things, by things deem'd weak*
> *Subverting worldly strong, and worldly wise*
> *By simply meek*
>
> (PL XII, 566–69)

And just in case this seems a little too passive from a man who lost his eyesight in public service, the Archangel Michael concludes the lesson of Book XII with the admonition that Adam

> *only add*
> *Deeds to thy knowledge answerable, add Faith,*
> *Add Virtue, Patience, Temperance, add Love,*
> *By name to come call'd Charity, the soul*
> *Of all the rest: then will thou not be loath*
> *To leave this Paradise, but shalt possess*
> *A Paradise within thee, happier far.*
>
> (PL XII, 581–87)

Milton invites each reader to test his or her idea of what it means to be human against the stories he tells of "the ways of God to men." The pleasure most readers find in this blind man's rich vision—his storytelling, imagery, powerful language—is likely to keep *Paradise Lost* and *Paradise Regained* part of our cultural conversation for a very long time.

—Susanne Woods

A General Note on the Text

The overall textual policy for the Signet Classic Poetry Series attempts to strike a balance between the convenience and dependability of total modernization, on the one hand, and the authenticity of an established text, on the other. Starting with the Restoration and Augustan poets, the General Editor has set up the following guidelines for the individual editors:

Modern American spelling will be used, although punctuation may be adjusted by the editor of each volume when he finds it advisable. In any case, syllabic final "ed" will be rendered with grave accent to distinguish it from the silent one, which is written out without apostrophe (e.g., "to gild refinèd gold," but "asked" rather than "ask'd"). Archaic words and forms are to be kept, naturally, whenever the meter or the sense may require it.

In the case of poets from earlier periods, the text is more clearly a matter of the individual editor's choice, and the type and degree of modernization has been left to his decision. But in any event, archaic typographical conventions ("i," "j," "u," "v," etc.) have all been normalized in the modern way.

JOHN HOLLANDER

A Note on This Edition

The texts are partially modernized. That of *Paradise Lost* is based on the first edition, 1667, although it follows the twelve-book structure of the second edition, 1674; most of the changes in wording made in 1674 are incorporated, and the rest are recorded in the footnotes. The text of *Paradise Regained* is based on the first edition, 1671. The capitalization and punctuation—with a very few exceptions—have been preserved. Milton's capitalization is not likely to impede a modern reader, and it serves as a reminder that this is a seventeenth-century poem. His punctuation is a trickier matter, but the impulse to tidy it up has been resisted. Although it sometimes may be momentarily puzzling, it has great advantages. It is light and flexible, so that the verse keeps momentum even while it holds open many possibilities as to suggestive relationships among the words and phrases—relationships which a more rigorous punctuation would have sealed up and prevented.

Milton's spelling has been partially modernized. The gain in convenience of reading far outweighs any loss. But the more important of Milton's spellings (*Ammiral, sovran,* etc.) have been retained, together with his emphatic forms *mee, hee, shee,* and his various forms for the past participle (such as *abasht, seduc'd*). An editor is bound to have twinges of regret about any such changes, especially as Milton's spelling may sometimes indicate his pronunciation; but his use of language does already present problems to a modern reader, and the awkwardly unfamiliar spelling must on occasion have proved to be the last straw. Moreover, a partially modernized text is of most help metrically and rhythmically—a good text of Milton will make his words sound in your head or out loud.

The notes have concentrated especially on Milton's words and phrases. It is true that he is a profoundly allusive poet—the Bible and classical literature are continually called upon, and since Milton is a great poet the more we know of his allusions the richer and subtler his writing is seen to be. But it is also characteristic of him to build his allusions in, so that they become self-explanatory:

> hee who to be deem'd
> A God, leap'd fondly into Etna flames,
> Empedocles, and hee . . .   (III 469–71)

Which means that the first priority ought to be, not his allusions, but his words—those which no longer survive, those which have lost part of their seventeenth-century meaning, and those which survive but with a different meaning. The footnotes provide instances (instances only, since the language of *Paradise Lost* is unceasingly active) of his verbal nuances and puns. Nuances and puns are, of course, matters of critical opinion, not of fact—even though there is evidence within the *Oxford English Dictionary* to substantiate such puns.

Chronology

1645   March. *Tetrachordon and Colasterion* (last of
         the divorce pamphlets).
1646   January (new style). *Poems* published.
1649   January 30. Execution of Charles I.
         February. *The Tenure of Kings and Magistrates.*
         March. Appointed Secretary for Foreign
         Tongues to the Council of State.
         October. *Eikonoklastes* (with *Tenure*, a defense
         of the regicides).
1651   February. *Defensio pro Populo Anglicano.*
1652   February or March. Milton became totally blind.
         May. Death of Mary Powell Milton.
1654   May. *Defensio Secunda.*
1655   August. *Pro Se Defensio.*
1656   November. Married Katherine Woodcock.
1658   February. Death of second wife.
         September 3. Death of Oliver Cromwell.
1659   Pamphlets defending religious freedom:
         February. *A Treatise of Civil Power in
         Ecclesiastical Causes.*
         August. *Likeliest Means to Remove Hirelings
         out of the Church.*
1660   February. *The Ready and Easy Way to Establish
         a Free Commonwealth.*
         May. Restoration of Charles II.
         Milton arrested, then released.
1663   February. Married Elizabeth Minshull.
1665   Living in country at Chalfont St. Giles during
         the plague.
1667   February. *Paradise Lost* published in ten books.
1670   *History of Britain* published.
1671   *Paradise Regained* and *Samson Agonistes*
         published.
1673   *Minor Poems* (expanded version of 1645
         edition).
         Of True Religion, Heresy, Schism, Toleration
         (last prose pamphlet).
1674   *Paradise Lost* (second edition) published in
         twelve books.
         Letters and academic exercises published.
         November 8. Milton's death, in London.

Paradise Lost

THE VERSE

The Measure is English Heroic Verse without Rhyme, as that of Homer in Greek, and of Virgil in Latin; Rhyme being no necessary Adjunct or true Ornament of Poem or good Verse, in longer Works especially, but the Invention of a barbarous Age, to set off wretched matter and lame Meter; grac't indeed since by the use of some famous modern Poets, carried away by Custom, but much to their own vexation, hindrance, and constraint to express many things otherwise, and for the most part worse than else they would have exprest them. Not without cause therefore some both Italian and Spanish Poets of prime note have rejected Rhyme both in longer and shorter Works, as have also long since our best English Tragedies, as a thing of itself, to all judicious ears, trivial and of no true musical delight; which consists only in apt Numbers, fit quantity of Syllables, and the sense variously drawn out from one Verse into another, not in the jingling sound of like endings, a fault avoided by the learned Ancients both in Poetry and all good Oratory. This neglect then of Rhyme so little is to be taken for a defect, though it may seem so perhaps to vulgar Readers, that it rather is to be esteem'd an example set, the first in English, of ancient liberty recover'd to Heroic Poem from the troublesome and modern bondage of Rhyming.   [added 1668]

BOOK I

THE ARGUMENT

This first Book proposes first in brief the whole Subject, Man's disobedience, and the loss thereupon of Paradise wherein he was plac't: Then touches the prime cause of his fall, the Serpent, or rather Satan in the Serpent; who revolting from God, and drawing to his side many Legions of Angels, was by the command of God driven out of Heaven with all his Crew into the great Deep. Which action past over, the Poem hastes into the midst of things, presenting Satan with his Angels now fallen into Hell, describ'd here, not in the Center (for Heaven and Earth may be suppos'd as yet not made, certainly not yet accurst) but in a place of utter darkness, fitliest call'd Chaos: Here Satan with his Angels lying on the burning Lake, thunderstruck and astonisht, after a certain space recovers, as from confusion, calls up him who next in Order and Dignity lay by him; they confer of their miserable fall. Satan awakens all his Legions, who lay till then in the same manner confounded; They rise, their Numbers, array of Battle, their chief Leaders nam'd, according to the Idols known afterwards in Canaan and the Countries adjoining. To these Satan directs his Speech, comforts them with hope yet of regaining Heaven, but tells them lastly of a new World and new kind of Creature to be created, according to an ancient Prophecy or report in Heaven; for that Angels were long before this visible Creation, was the opinion of many ancient Fathers. To find out the truth of this Prophecy, and what to determine thereon he refers to a full Council. What his Associates thence attempt. Pandemonium the Palace of Satan rises, suddenly built out of the Deep: The infernal Peers there sit in Council.

[added 1668]

4

Of Man's First disobedience, and the Fruit°
Of that Forbidden Tree, whose mortal° taste
Brought Death into the World, and all our woe,
With loss of Eden, till one greater Man
Restore us, and regain the blissful Seat,   5
Sing Heav'nly Muse, that on the secret top
Of Oreb, or of Sinai, didst inspire
That Shepherd, who first taught the chosen Seed,°
In the Beginning how the Heav'ns and Earth
Rose out of Chaos: Or if Sion Hill   10
Delight thee more, and Siloa's Brook that flow'd
Fast by the Oracle of God;° I thence
Invoke thy aid to my advent'rous Song,
That with no middle flight intends to soar
Above th'Aonian Mount,° while it pursues   15
Things unattempted yet in Prose or Rhyme.
And chiefly Thou O Spirit, that dost prefer
Before all Temples th'upright heart and pure,
Instruct° me, for Thou know'st; Thou from the first
Wast present, and with mighty wings outspread   20
Dove-like sat'st brooding on the vast Abyss
And mad'st it pregnant: What in me is dark
Illumine, what is low raise and support;
That to the heighth of this great Argument°
I may assert° Eternal Providence,   25
And justify° the ways of God to men.
        Say first, for Heav'n hides nothing from thy
            view
Nor the deep Tract of Hell, say first what cause
Mov'd our Grand° Parents in that happy State,
Favour'd of Heav'n so highly, to fall off   30
From their Creator, and transgress his Will

1 **Fruit** including consequences, fruits. 2 **mortal** human and deadly.
7–8 **Of . . . Seed** Moses, who set down GENESIS, was visited by God on
Mount Horeb and Sinai. 11–12 **Siloa's . . . God** near the Temple in
Jerusalem; the brook is to parallel the one haunted by the classical
Muses. 15 **Mount** Helicon, sacred to the Muses. 19 **Instruct** Latin
instruere, to build, perfectly linking "Temples" and "heart." 24 **Argument** subject-matter and process of reasoning. 25 **assert** affirm. 26
justify bear witness to the justice of; both "justify to men" and "ways
of God to men." 29 **Grand** original and pre-eminent.

For° one restraint, Lords of the World besides?
Who first seduc'd them to that foul revolt?
Th'infernal Serpent; he it was, whose guile
35 Stirr'd up with Envy and Revenge, deceiv'd
The Mother of Mankind, what time his Pride
Had cast him out from Heav'n, with all his Host
Of Rebel Angels, by whose aid aspiring
To set himself in Glory above his Peers,
40 He trusted to have equall'd the most High,
If he oppos'd; and with ambitious aim
Against° the Throne and Monarchy of God
Rais'd impious War in Heav'n and Battle proud
With vain attempt. Him the Almighty Power
45 Hurl'd headlong flaming from th'Ethereal Sky
With hideous ruin° and combustion down
To bottomless perdition, there to dwell
In Adamantine° Chains and penal Fire,
Who durst defy th'Omnipotent to Arms.
50 Nine times the Space that measures Day and Night
To mortal men, he with his horrid crew
Lay vanquisht, rolling in the fiery Gulf
Confounded° though immortal: But his doom
Reserv'd him to more wrath; for now the thought
55 Both of lost happiness and lasting pain
Torments him; round he throws his baleful° eyes
That witness'd° huge affliction and dismay
Mixt with obdúrate pride and steadfast hate:
At once as far as Angel's ken° he views
60 The dismal Situation° waste and wild,
A Dungeon° horrible, on all sides round
As one great Furnace flam'd, yet from those flames
No light, but rather darkness visible
Serv'd only to discover sights of woe,
65 Regions of sorrow, doleful shades, where peace
And rest can never dwell, hope never comes

32 **For** both "transgress because of one restraint," and "Lords. . . . except
for one restraint." 42 **Against** both "aim against" and "war
against." 46 **ruin** falling, Latin *ruina*. 48 **Adamantine** of the hardest
rocks or minerals. 53 **Confounded** overthrown 56 **baleful** full both of
woe and of evil. 57 **witness'd** showed his. 59 **Angel's ken** Milton's
spelling "Angels kenn" leaves "kenn" as possibly noun or verb. 60 **Situation** site and predicament. 61 **Dungeon** from *domnionem*, "lord's
tower," from Latin *dominus*, lord. See X 466.

That comes to all; but torture without end
Still urges, and a fiery Deluge, fed
With ever-burning Sulphur unconsum'd:
Such place Eternal Justice had prepar'd   70
For those rebellious, here their Prison ordain'd
In utter° darkness, and their portion set
As far remov'd from God and light of Heav'n
As from the Center° thrice to th'utmost Pole.°
O how unlike the place from whence they fell!   75
There the companions of his fall, o'erwhelm'd
With Floods and Whirlwinds of tempestuous fire,
He soon discerns, and welt'ring by his side
One next himself in power, and next in crime,
Long after known in Palestine, and nam'd   80
Beëlzebub. To whom th'Arch-Enemy,°
And thence in Heav'n call'd Satan, with bold words
Breaking the horrid silence thus began.
      "If thou beest he; but O how fall'n! how
        chang'd
From him, who in the happy Realms of Light   85
Cloth'd with transcendent brightness didst outshine
Myriads though bright: If he whom mutual league,
United thoughts and counsels, equal hope,
And hazard in the Glorious Enterprise,
Join'd with me once, now misery hath join'd   90
In equal ruin: into what Pit thou seest
From what heighth fall'n, so much the stronger prov'd
He with his Thunder: and till then who knew
The force of those dire Arms? yet not for those
Nor what the Potent Victor in his rage   95
Can else inflict do I repent or change,
Though chang'd in outward lustre, that fixt mind
And high disdain, from sense of injur'd merit,
That with the mightiest rais'd me to contend,
And to the fierce contention brought along   100
Innumerable force of Spirits arm'd
That durst dislike his reign, and me preferring,
His utmost power with adverse° power oppos'd

---

72 **utter** outer and total. 74 **the Center** the earth. 74 **utmost Pole** outermost point of the universe. 81 **Arch-Enemy** Hebrew ṣāṭān, adversary. 103 **adverse** hostile, as in "adversary."

In dubious° Battle on the Plains of Heav'n,
105 And shook his throne. What though the field be lost?
All is not lost; the unconquerable Will,
And study of° revenge, immortal hate,
And courage never to submit or yield:
And what is else not to be overcome?°
110 That Glory never shall his wrath or might
Extort from me. To bow and sue for grace
With suppliant knee, and deify his power
Who from the terror of this Arm so late
Doubted° his Empire, that were low indeed,
115 That were an ignominy and shame beneath
This downfall; since by Fate the strength of Gods°
And this Empyreal substance° cannot fail,
Since through experience of this great event
In Arms not worse, in foresight much advanc't,
120 We may with more successful hope° resolve
To wage by force or guile eternal War
Irreconcilable, to our grand Foe,
Who now triúmphs, and in th'excess of joy
Sole reigning holds the Tyranny of Heav'n."
125   So spake th'Apostate Angel, though in pain,
Vaunting aloud, but rackt with deep despair:
And him thus answer'd soon his bold Compeer.
    "O Prince, O Chief of many Throned Powers,
That led th'imbattled Seraphim° to War
130 Under thy conduct, and in dreadful deeds
Fearless, endanger'd Heav'n's perpetual King;
And put to proof his high Supremacy,
Whether upheld by strength, or Chance, or Fate,
Too well I see and rue the dire event,
135 That with sad overthrow and foul defeat
Hath lost us Heav'n, and all this mighty Host
In horrible destruction laid thus low,
As far as Gods and Heav'nly Essences

---

104 **dubious** of which the outcome was doubtful.   107 **study of** zeal
for.   109 **And . . . overcome** "In what else does 'not being overcome'
consist?"   114 **Doubted** feared for.   116 **Gods** Both Satan and God
apply the word to angels.   117 **Empyreal substance** fiery and heavenly
essence (see line 138).   120 **successful hope** hope of success.   128–29
Powers . . . Seraphim two of the nine orders of angels, the others being
Cherubim, Thrones, Dominations, Virtues, Principalities, Archangels,
Angels.

Can Perish: for the mind and spirit remains
Invincible, and vigour soon returns,   *140*
Though all our Glory extinct,° and happy state
Here swallow'd up in endless misery.
But what if he our Conqueror, (whom I now
Of force° believe Almighty, since no less
Than such could have o'erpow'r'd such force as ours) *145*
Have left us this our spirit and strength entire
Strongly to suffer and support our pains,
That we may so suffice his vengeful ire,
Or do him mightier service as his thralls
By right of War, whate'er his business be,   *150*
Here in the heart of Hell to work in Fire,
Or do his Errands in the gloomy Deep;
What can it then avail though yet we feel
Strength undiminisht, or eternal being
To undergo eternal punishment?"   *155*
Whereto with speedy words th'Arch-fiend repli'd.
    "Fall'n Cherub, to be weak is miserable
Doing or Suffering: but of this be sure,
To do aught good never will be our task,
But ever to do ill our sole delight,   *160*
As being the contrary to his high will
Whom we resist. If then his Providence
Out of our evil seek to bring forth good,
Our labour must be to pervert that end,
And out of good still to find means of evil;   *165*
Which oft-times may succeed, so as perhaps
Shall grieve him, if I fail not, and disturb
His inmost counsels from their destin'd° aim.
But see the angry Victor hath recall'd
His Ministers of vengeance and pursuit   *170*
Back to the Gates of Heav'n: The Sulphurous Hail
Shot after us in storm, o'erblown hath laid
The fiery Surge, that from the Precipice
Of Heav'n receiv'd us falling, and the Thunder,
Wing'd with red Lightning and impetuous rage,   *175*
Perhaps hath spent his shafts, and ceases now
To bellow through the vast and boundless Deep.

141 **extinct** extinguished, "Glory" being both splendor and halo.   144
Of force both "necessarily" and "because of this force."   168 **destin'd**
intended (but the sense of "destiny" undercuts Satan's words).

Let us not slip° th'occasion, whether scorn,
Or satiate fury yield it from our Foe.
180 Seest thou yon dreary Plain, forlorn and wild,
The seat of desolation, void of light,
Save what the glimmering of these livid flames
Casts pale and dreadful? Thither let us tend
From off the tossing of these fiery waves,
185 There rest, if any rest can harbour there,
And reassembling our afflicted° Powers,°
Consult how we may henceforth most offend°
Our Enemy, our own loss how repair,
How overcome this dire Calamity,
190 What reinforcement we may gain from Hope,
If not what resolution from despair."
          Thus Satan talking to his nearest Mate
With Head uplift above the wave, and Eyes
That sparkling blaz'd, his other Parts besides
195 Prone on the Flood, extended long and large
Lay floating many a rood,° in bulk as huge
As whom the Fables name of monstrous size,
Titanian, or Earth-born, that warr'd on Jove,
Briareos or Typhon,° whom the Den
200 By ancient Tarsus held, or that Sea-beast
Leviathan,° which God of all his works
Created hugest that swim th'Ocëan stream:
Him haply° slumb'ring on the Norway° foam
The Pilot of some small night-founder'd° Skiff,
205 Deeming some Island, oft, as Sea-men tell,
With fixed Anchor in his scaly rind
Moors by his side under the Lee, while Night
Invests° the Sea, and wished Morn delays:
So stretcht out huge in length the Arch-fiend lay
210 Chain'd on the burning Lake, nor ever thence

---

178 **slip** let slip.   186 **afflicted** struck down   186 **Powers** armies, with a
suggestion of "faculties."   187 **offend** take the offensive against.   196
rood a land-measure, 40 square poles.   198–99 Classical counterparts to
Satan's rebellion, **Briareos** among the Titans, **Typhon** among the "Earth-
born" Giants.   201 **Leviathan** Biblical sea-monster, here the whale. The
tales of its being mistaken for an island were used in the bestiaries as a
type of Satan's deception of man.   203 **haply** perchance.   203 **Norway**
Satan traditionally associated with the north (I 293, V 689).   204 **night-
founder'd** sunk in night, *not yet* literally sunk; see the ominous line
208.   208 **Invests** enwraps.

Had ris'n or heav'd his head, but that the will
And high permission of all-ruling Heaven
Left him at large to his own dark designs,
That with reiterated crimes he might
Heap on himself damnation, while he sought   215
Evil to others, and enrag'd might see
How all his malice serv'd but to bring forth
Infinite goodness, grace and mercy shown
On Man by him seduc't, but on himself
Treble confusion, wrath and vengeance pour'd.   220
Forthwith upright he rears from off the Pool
His mighty Stature; on each hand the flames
Driv'n backward slope their pointing spires, and roll'd
In billows, leave i' th'midst a horrid Vale.°
Then with expanded wings he steers his flight   225
Aloft, incumbent on° the dusky Air
That felt unusual weight, till on dry Land
He 'lights, if it were Land that ever burn'd
With solid, as the Lake with liquid fire;
And such appear'd in hue, as when the force   230
Of subterranean wind transports a Hill
Torn from Pelorus,° or the shatter'd side
Of thund'ring Etna, whose combustible
And fuell'd entrails thence conceiving Fire,
Sublim'd with Mineral fury, aid the Winds,   235
And leave a singed bottom all involv'd°
With stench° and smoke: Such resting found the sole
Of unblest feet. Him follow'd his next Mate,
Both glorying to have 'scap't the Stygian° flood
As Gods, and by their own recover'd strength,   240
Not by the sufferance of supernal° Power.
       "Is this the Region, this the Soil, the Clime,"°
Said then the lost Arch Angel, "this the seat
That we must change for Heav'n, this mournful gloom

222–24 Douglas Bush points out that this suggests the Israelites' miraculous passage through the Red Sea (I 306–10); Satan's doings in the poem
are often a grim parody of God's. 226 **Incumbent on** weighing upon
(contrast I 20–21). 232 **Pelorus** near Etna. 236 **involv'd** rolled
around. 234–37 **entrails . . . stench** the volcanic landscape of Hell, seen
as a disgusting body; so "Sublim'd" here has a sardonic tone (*not* sublime
in any other sense). See III 494. 239 **Stygian** Styx, river of Hell; here the
lake. 241 **supernal** in the heavens above. 242 **Clime** zone and
temperature.

245 For that celestial light? Be it so, since hee
Who now is Sovran° can dispose and bid
What shall be right: farthest from him is best
Whom reason hath equall'd, force hath made supreme
Above his equals. Farewell happy Fields
250 Where Joy for ever dwells: Hail horrors, hail
Infernal world, and thou profoundest Hell
Receive thy new Possessor: One who brings
A mind not to be chang'd by Place or Time.
The mind is its own place, and in itself
255 Can make a Heav'n of Hell, a Hell of Heav'n.
What matter where, if I be still the same,
And what I should be, all but less than hee
Whom Thunder hath made greater? Here at least
We shall be free: th'Almighty hath not built
260 Here for his envy, will not drive us hence:
Here we may reign secure, and in my choice
To reign is worth ambition though in Hell:
Better to reign in Hell, than serve in Heav'n.
But wherefore let we then our faithful friends,
265 Th'associates and co-partners of our loss
Lie thus astonisht° on th'oblivious° Pool,
And call them not to share with us their part
In this unhappy Mansion, or once more
With rallied Arms to try what may be yet
270 Regain'd in Heav'n, or what more lost in Hell?"
         So Satan spake, and him Beëlzebub
Thus answer'd. "Leader of those Armies bright,
Which but th'Omnipotent none could have foil'd,
If once they hear that voice, their liveliest pledge
275 Of hope in fears and dangers, heard so oft
In worst extremes, and on the perilous edge°
Of battle when it rag'd, in all assaults
Their surest signal, they will soon resume
New courage and revive, though now they lie
280 Grovelling and prostrate on yon Lake of Fire,
As we erewhile, astounded and amaz'd,°
No wonder, fall'n such a pernicious° heighth."

---

246 **Sovran** Milton's spelling follows the Italian *sovrano*.   266 **astonisht**
literally thunderstruck, connected with Latin *extonare*, as is "astounded,"
line 281.   266 **oblivious** causing oblivion, like the river Lethe.   276 **edge**
front-line.   281 **amaz'd** overwhelmed.   282 **pernicious** destructive.

He scarce had ceas't when the superior Fiend
Was moving toward the shore; his ponderous shield°
Ethereal temper,° massy, large and round   285
Behind him cast; the broad circumference
Hung on his shoulders like the Moon, whose Orb
Through Optic Glass the Tuscan Artist views
At Ev'ning from the top of Fesole,
Or in Valdarno, to descry new Lands,°   290
Rivers or Mountains in her spotty Globe.
His Spear, to equal which the tallest Pine
Hewn on Norwegian hills, to be the Mast
Of some great Ammiral,° were but a wand,
He walkt with to support uneasy steps   295
Over the burning Marl,° not like those steps
On Heaven's Azure, and the torrid Clime
Smote on him sore besides, vaulted with Fire;
Nathless he so endur'd, till on the Beach
Of that inflamed Sea, he stood and call'd   300
His Legions, Angel Forms, who lay intranc't
Thick as Autumnal Leaves that strow the Brooks
In Vallombrosa,° where th'Etrurian shades
High overarch't embow'r;° or scatter'd sedge°
Afloat, when with fierce Winds Orion arm'd°   305
Hath vext the Red-Sea Coast, whose waves o'erthrew
Busiris and his Memphian Chivalry,°
While with perfidious hatred they pursu'd
The Sojourners of Goshen, who beheld
From the safe shore their floating Carcasses   310

---

284 **shield** Contrast the shield of Achilles; Satan is Milton's "hero," but
such heroism is suspect.   285 **Ethereal temper** tempered in Heaven.
288–90 **Through . . . Lands** The telescope of the skilled Galileo, who lived
at Fiesole above the river Arno; Milton visited him in 1638–39.   294 **Ammiral** admiral's flagship; Milton uses the spelling which gives the true etymology, from *emir* (associating Satan, as elsewhere, with eastern tyrants),
not from *admire*.   296 **Marl** soil.   303 **Vallombrosa** near Florence,
"shady valley"—as in some ways is Hell itself (the whole of the simile
reverberates with correspondences).   304 **embow'r** form a bower, the
pastoral word contrasting with the horrors of Hell.   304 **sedge** the Red
Sea is "sea of sedge" in Hebrew.   305 **Orion arm'd** The constellation
Orion (some of whose stars represent his weapons) ushers in the storms
which "vex" (buffet) the sea.   307 **Busiris . . . Chivalry** Milton takes Busiris as the "perfidious" Pharaoh who hunted down the Israelites, "the
Sojourners of Goshen" in Egypt, with his Egyptian cavalry. "Chivalry"
is etymologically identical with "cavalry"; Milton chooses it as part of his
questioning of chivalric values; see IX 28–41.

And broken Chariot Wheels, so thick bestrown
Abject° and lost lay these, covering the Flood,
Under amazement of their hideous change.
He call'd so loud, that all the hollow Deep
315 Of Hell resounded. "Princes, Potentates,
Warriors, the Flow'r of Heav'n, once yours, now lost,
If such astonishment as this can seize
Eternal spirits; or have ye chos'n this place
After the toil of Battle to repose
320 Your wearied virtue, for the ease you find
To slumber here, as in the Vales of Heav'n?
Or in this abject posture have ye sworn
To adore the Conqueror? who now beholds
Cherub and Seraph rolling in the Flood
325 With scatter'd Arms and Ensigns, till anon
His swift pursuers from Heav'n Gates discern
Th'advantage, and descending tread us down
Thus drooping, or with linked Thunderbolts
Transfix us to the bottom of this Gulf.
330 Awake, arise, or be for ever fall'n."
            They heard, and were abasht, and up they
                sprung
Upon the wing, as when men wont to watch
On duty, sleeping found by whom they dread,
Rouse and bestir themselves ere well awake.
335 Nor did they not perceive the evil plight
In which they were, or the fierce pains not feel;
Yet to their General's Voice they soon obey'd
Innumerable. As when the potent Rod
Of Amram's Son in Egypt's evil day
340 Wav'd round the Coast, upcall'd a pitchy cloud°
Of Locusts, warping° on the Eastern Wind,
That o'er the Realm of impious Pharaoh hung
Like Night, and darken'd all the land of Nile:
So numberless were those bad Angels seen
345 Hovering on wing under the Cope of Hell
'Twixt upper, nether, and surrounding Fires;
Till, as a signal giv'n, th'uplifted Spear
Of their great Sultan waving to direct

312 **Abject** cast down, literal and metaphorical.   338–40 **As ... cloud** Contrasting Moses' rod (working God's will) with Satan's spear.   341 **warping** twisting, writhing themselves forward.

Their course, in even balance down they 'light
On the firm brimstone, and fill all the Plain;   350
A multitude, like which the populous North
Pour'd never from her frozen loins,° to pass
Rhene or the Danaw,° when her barbarous Sons
Came like a Deluge on the South, and spread
Beneath Gibraltar to the Libyan sands.   355
Forthwith from every Squadron and each Band
The Heads and Leaders thither haste where stood
Their great Commander; Godlike shapes and forms
Excelling human, Princely Dignities,
And Powers that erst in Heaven sat on Thrones;   360
Though of their Names in heav'nly Records now
Be no memorial, blotted out and raz'd
By their Rebellion, from the Books of Life.
Nor had they yet among the sons of Eve
Got them new Names, till wand'ring o'er the Earth,   365
Through God's high sufferance for the trial of man,
By falsities and lies the greatest part
Of Mankind they corrupted to forsake
God their Creator, and th'invisible
Glory of him, that made them, to transform   370
Oft to the Image of a Brute, adorn'd
With gay Religions full of Pomp and Gold,
And Devils to adore for Deities:
Then were they known to men by various Names,
And various Idols through the Heathen World.   375
Say, Muse, their Names then known, who first, who
    last,
Rous'd from the slumber, on that fiery Couch,
At their great Emperor's call, as next in worth
Came singly where he stood on the bare strand,
While the promiscuous° crowd stood yet aloof?   380
The chief were those who from the Pit of Hell
Roaming to seek their prey on earth, durst fix
Their Seats long after next the Seat of God,
Their Altars by his Altar, Gods ador'd
Among the Nations round, and durst abide   385

351–52 **A multitude . . . loins** The invasions of the Goths, Huns and Van-
dals, pouring forth—by an evil paradox—from "frozen loins" (contrasted
with "brimstone," burn-stone). 353 **Rhene, Danaw** Rhine, Dan-
ube. 380 **promiscuous** mixed.

Jehovah thund'ring out of Sion, thron'd
Between the Cherubim; yea, often plac'd
Within his Sanctuary itself their Shrines,
Abominations; and with cursed things°
390 His holy Rites, and solemn Feasts profan'd,
And with their darkness durst affront° his light.
First Moloch, horrid King besmear'd with blood
Of human sacrifice, and parents' tears,
Though for the noise of Drums and Timbrels loud
395 Their children's cries unheard, that past through fire
To his grim Idol. Him the Ammonite
Worshipt in Rabba and her wat'ry Plain,
In Argob and in Basan, to the stream
Of utmost Arnon.° Nor content with such
400 Audacious neighbourhood,° the wisest heart
Of Solomon he led by fraud to build
His Temple right against the Temple of God
On that opprobrious Hill,° and made his Grove
The pleasant Valley of Hinnom, Tophet thence
405 And black Gehenna call'd, the Type of Hell.°
Next Chemos,° th'óbscene° dread of Moab's Sons,
From Aroer to Nebo, and the wild
Of Southmost Abarim; in Hesebon
And Horonaim, Seon's° Realm, beyond
410 The flow'ry Dale of Sibma clad with Vines,
And Elealé to th'Asphaltic Pool.°
Peor his other Name, when he entic'd
Israel in Sittim on their march from Nile
To do him wanton rites, which cost them woe.°
415 Yet thence his lustful Orgies he enlarg'd
Even to that Hill of scandal,° by the Grove
Of Moloch homicide, lust hard by hate;
Till good Josiah drove them thence to Hell.

384–89 **things** Altars to heathen gods inside the Temple itself, where were the
golden Cherubim.   391 **affront** confront and insult.   397–99 East of Jordan.
400 **Audacious neighbourhood** daring to live so near.   400–03 Solomon,
seduced by his wives, built temples to Moloch and others on the (shameful)
Mount of Olives (I 416, 443).   404–05 The valley of Hinnom provided
two of the names for Hell: Tophet and Gehenna.   406 **Chemos** heathen
deity.   406 **obscene** abominable, originally a term of augury (ill-omened),
so here applicable to an idol.   409 **Seon** King Sihon.   411 **Asphaltic Pool**
the Dead Sea, suggesting the landscape of Hell.   414 **woe** the plague
spoken of in NUMBERS 25:1–9.   416 **scandal** Biblical term, cause of of-
fense, stumbling-block.

With these came they, who from the bord'ring flood
Of old Euphrates to the Brook that parts   420
Egypt from Syrian ground,° had general Names
Of Baälim and Ashtaroth,° those male,
These Feminine. For Spirits when they please
Can either Sex assume, or both; so soft
And uncompounded is their Essence pure,   425
Not ti'd or manacl'd with joint or limb,
Nor founded on the brittle strength of bones,
Like cumbrous flesh; but in what shape they choose
Dilated or condens't, bright or obscure,
Can execute their airy purposes,   430
And works of love or enmity fulfill.
For those the Race of Israel oft forsook
Their living strength, and unfrequented left
His righteous Altar, bowing lowly down
To bestial° Gods; for which their heads as low   435
Bow'd down in Battle, sunk before the Spear
Of despicable foes. With these in troop
Came Astoreth, whom the Phoenicians call'd
Astarte, Queen of Heav'n, with crescent Horns;
To whose bright Image nightly by the Moon   440
Sidonian° Virgins paid their Vows and Songs,
In Sion also not unsung, where stood
Her Temple on th'offensive Mountain, built
By that uxorious King,° whose heart though large,
Beguil'd by fair Idolatresses, fell   445
To Idols foul. Thammuz came next behind,
Whose annual wound in Lebanon allur'd
The Syrian Damsels to lament his fate
In amorous ditties all a Summer's day,
While smooth Adonis from his native Rock   450
Ran purple to the Sea, suppos'd with blood
Of Thammuz yearly wounded:° the Love-tale
Infected Sion's daughters with like heat,
Whose wanton passions in the sacred Porch

420–21 Besor, the boundary between Palestine and Egypt.   422 (Baälim), Ashtaroth plural of the gods prefixed by Baal-, and of the forms of
the goddess Ashtoreth.   435 bestial (literal and moral).   441 Sidonian
Sidon in Phoenicia.   444 uxorious King Solomon, excessively devoted to
his wives.   446–52 Milton's "Nativity Ode" line 204: "In vain the Tyrian
maids their wounded Thammuz mourn." Thammuz is a counterpart of
Adonis in his death and revival; the river Adonis ran red at times.

455 Ezekiel saw, when by the Vision led
His eye survey'd the dark Idolatries
Of alienated Judah. Next came one
Who mourn'd in earnest, when the Captive Ark
Maim'd his brute Image, head and hands lopt off
460 In his own Temple, on the grunsel°-edge,
Where he fell flat, and sham'd his Worshippers:
Dagon his Name, Sea Monster, upward Man
And downward Fish: yet had his Temple high
Rear'd in Azotus, dreaded through the Coast
465 Of Palestine, in Gath and Ascalon,
And Accaron and Gaza's frontier bounds.
Him follow'd Rimmon,° whose delightful Seat
Was fair Damascus, on the fertile Banks
Of Ábbana and Pharphar, lucid streams.
470 He also against the house of God was bold:
A Leper once he lost and gain'd a King,°
Ahaz his sottish Conqueror, whom he drew
God's Altar to disparage and displace
For one of Syrian mode, whereon to burn
475 His odious off'rings, and adore the Gods
Whom he had vanquisht. After these appear'd
A crew who under Names of old Renown,
Osiris, Isis, Orus and their Train
With monstrous shapes and sorceries abus'd°
480 Fanatic° Egypt and her Priests, to seek
Their wand'ring Gods disguis'd in brutish forms
Rather than human. Nor did Israel 'scape
Th'infection when their borrow'd Gold compos'd
The Calf in Oreb: and the Rebel King
485 Doubled that sin in Bethel and in Dan,°
Lik'ning his Maker to the Grazed Ox,
Jehovah, who in one Night when he pass'd
From Egypt marching, equall'd with one stroke
Both her first-born, and all her bleating Gods.°
490 Belial came last, than whom a Spirit more lewd
Fell not from Heaven, or more gross to love

460 **grunsel** threshold.   467 **Rimmon** Syrian god.   471 The Syrian, Naa-
man, came to God after being cured of leprosy; but King Ahaz of Judah
adopted the Syrian religion.   479 **abus'd** deceived.   480 **Fanatic** inspired
with demonic frenzy, from Latin *fanum*, fane or temple.   484–85 The
golden calf made by Aaron; Jeroboam made two calves of gold.   489
The 10th plague of Egypt.

Vice for itself: To him no Temple stood
Or Altar smok'd; yet who more oft than hee
In Temples and at Altars, when the Priest
Turns Atheist, as did Eli's Sons, who fill'd   495
With lust and violence the house of God.
In Courts and Palaces he also Reigns
And in luxurious° Cities, where the noise
Of riot° ascends above their loftiest Tow'rs,
And injury and outrage: And when Night   500
Darkens the Streets, then wander forth the Sons
Of Belial, flown° with insolence and wine.
Witness the streets of Sodom, and that night
In Gibeah, when the hospitable door
Expos'd a Matron, to avoid worse rape.°   505
These were the prime in order and in might;
The rest were long to tell, though far renown'd,
Th'Ionian Gods, of Javan's° Issue held
Gods, yet confest later than Heav'n and Earth°
Their boasted Parents; Titan° Heav'n's first-born   510
With his enormous brood, and birthright seiz'd
By younger Saturn, he from mightier Jove,
His own and Rhea's Son like measure found;
So Jove usurping reign'd: these first in Crete
And Ida° known, thence on the Snowy top   515
Of cold Olympus rul'd the middle Air
Their highest Heav'n; or on the Delphian Cliff,
Or in Dodona,° and through all the bounds
Of Doric Land;° or who with Saturn old
Fled over Adria to th'Hesperian Fields,   520
And o'er the Celtic roam'd the utmost Isles.°
All these and more came flocking; but with looks
Downcast and damp,° yet such wherein appear'd
Obscure some glimpse of joy, to have found their chief

---

498 luxurious lustful. **499 riot** debauchery, as in riotous living. **502 flown** flushed and welling. **504–05 when . . . rape** *1674*; hospitable Doors/Yielded their Matrons to prevent *1667*. The story of a threatened sodomitical rape, in JUDGES 19:12–30. **508 Javan** ancestor of the Ionians, Greeks. **509 Heav'n and Earth** the deities Uranus and Gaia. **510 Titan** eldest son of Uranus (whom he deposed), and brother of Saturn; Saturn was in turn deposed by Jove. **515 Ida** mountain in Crete where Jove was born. **517–18** Apollo's oracle at Delphi, Jove's at Dodona. **519 Doric Land** southern Greece. **520–21** The fields of Italy and France, and the isles of Britain. **523 damp** as if smothered in smoke.

525 Not in despair, to have found themselves not lost
In loss itself; which on his count'nance cast
Like doubtful° hue: but he his wonted pride
Soon recollecting,° with high words, that bore
Semblance of worth, not substance, gently rais'd
530 Their fainting° courage, and dispell'd their fears.
Then straight commands that at the warlike sound
Of Trumpets loud and Clarions be uprear'd
His mighty Standard; that proud honour claim'd
Azazel as his right, a Cherub tall:
535 Who forthwith from the glittering Staff unfurl'd
Th'Imperial Ensign, which full high advanc't
Shone like a Meteor streaming to the Wind
With Gems and Golden lustre rich imblaz'd,
Seraphic arms and Trophies: all the while
540 Sonórous metal blowing Martial sounds:
At which the universal Host upsent
A shout that tore Hell's Concave, and beyond
Frighted the Reign of Chaos and old Night.
All in a moment through the gloom were seen
545 Ten thousand Banners rise into the Air
With Orient° Colours waving: with them rose
A Forest huge of Spears: and thronging Helms
Appear'd, and serried Shields in thick array
Of depth immeasurable: Anon they move
550 In perfect Phalanx° to the Dorian mood°
Of Flutes and soft Recorders; such as rais'd
To heighth of noblest temper Heroes old
Arming to Battle, and instead of rage
Deliberate valour breath'd, firm and unmov'd
555 With dread of death to light or foul retreat,
Nor wanting power to mitigate and 'suage°
With solemn touches, troubl'd thoughts, and chase
Anguish and doubt and fear and sorrow and pain
From mortal or immortal minds. Thus they
560 Breathing united force with fixed thought
Mov'd on in silence to soft Pipes that charm'd

527 **doubtful** full of doubt.   528 **recollecting** remembering and pulling
together (re-collecting).   530 **fainting** *1674*; fainted *1667*.   546 **Orient**
bright as from the east, from Latin *oriens*, rising (notice "rise" and "rose"
here).   550 **Phalanx** line of battle.   550 **Dorian mood** a musical "mode"
expressive of courage, Dorian being Spartan.   556 **'suage** assuage,
sweeten.

Their painful steps o'er the burnt soil; and now
Advanc't in view they stand, a horrid° Front
Of dreadful length and dazzling Arms, in guise
Of Warriors old with order'd Spear and Shield,   565
Awaiting what command their mighty Chief
Had to impose: He through the armed Files
Darts his experienc't eye, and soon traverse°
The whole Battalion views; their order due,
Their visages and stature as of Gods,   570
Their number last he sums.° And now his heart
Distends with pride, and hard'ning in his strength
Glories: For never since created° man,
Met such imbodied force,° as nam'd with these
Could merit more than that small infantry   575
Warr'd on by Cranes:° though all the Giant brood
Of Phlegra° with th'Heroic Race were join'd
That fought at Thebes and Ilium,° on each side
Mixt with auxiliar° Gods; and what resounds
In Fable or Romance of Uther's Son°   580
Begirt with British and Armoric° Knights;
And all who since, Baptiz'd or Infidel
Jousted in Aspramont or Montalban,°
Damasco, or Morocco, or Trebisond,°
Or whom Biserta° sent from Afric shore   585
When Charlemagne with all his Peerage fell
By Fontarabbia. Thus far these beyond
Compare of mortal prowess,° yet observ'd°
Their dread Commander: he above the rest
In shape and gesture proudly eminent   590
Stood like a Tow'r; his form had yet not lost

---

563 **horrid** including bristling, Latin *horridus.* 568 **traverse** across. 571
sums reckons up. 573 **created** the creation of. 574 **imbodied force** both
power and form (in a body of men). 574–76 In comparison, no army
would come to more than the pigmy army, who fought against the cranes;
"infantry" suggests sardonically an army of babies (infant and infantry
have the same derivation). 577 **Phlegra** where the Giants fought the
Gods. 578 **Thebes and Ilium** scenes of Greek heroism. 579 **auxiliar** the
classical gods intervening helpfully in battle (but "auxiliar Gods" has a
belittling ring). 580 **Uther's Son** King Arthur. 581 **Armoric** from Brit-
tany. 583 **Aspramont or Montalban** in Italy and France, associated with
Charlemagne. 584 **Trebisond** on the Black Sea. 585 **Biserta** port in
Tunisia. 588 **prowess** valor, but the word is cognate with "proud"; the
angels show a more than human pride (I 572, 590, 603). 588 **observ'd**
watched and obeyed.

All her Original° brightness, nor appear'd
Less than Arch Angel ruin'd and th'excess
Of Glory° obscured: As when the Sun new-ris'n
595 Looks through the Horizontal° misty Air
Shorn of his Beams, or from behind the Moon
In dim Eclipse disastrous° twilight sheds
On half the Nations, and with fear of change
Perplexes Monarchs. Darken'd so, yet shone
600 Above them all th'Arch Angel: but his face
Deep scars of Thunder had intrencht, and care
Sat on his faded cheek, but under Brows
Of dauntless courage, and considerate° Pride
Waiting revenge: cruel his eye, but cast
605 Signs of remorse and passion to behold
The fellows of his crime, the followers rather
(Far other once beheld in bliss) condemn'd
For ever now to have their lot in pain,
Millions of Spirits for his fault amerc't°
610 Of Heav'n, and from Eternal Splendors flung
For his revolt, yet faithful how they stood,
Their Glory wither'd. As when Heaven's Fire
Hath scath'd the Forest Oaks, or Mountain Pines,
With singed top their stately growth though bare
615 Stands on the blasted Heath. He now prepar'd
To speak; whereat their doubl'd Ranks they bend
From Wing° to Wing, and half enclose him round
With all his Peers: attention held them mute.
Thrice he assay'd, and thrice in spite of scorn,
620 Tears such as Angels weep, burst forth: at last
Words interwove with sighs found out their way.

        "O Myriads of immortal Spirits, O Powers
Matchless, but with th'Almighty, and that strife
Was not inglorious, though th'event° was dire,
625 As this place testifies, and this dire change
Hateful to utter: but what power of mind
Foreseeing or presaging, from the Depth
Of knowledge past or present, could have fear'd,

---

592 **Original** including "pertaining to its origin," i.e. God.   594 **Glory** including halo.   595 **Horizontal** of the horizon   597 **disastrous** ill-starred, from Latin *astrum*, star.   603 **considerate** conscious.   609 **am-erc't** paying the fine (but notice the derivation *amercié*, being at the mercy of).   617 **Wing** formation.   624 **event** outcome, eventuality.

How such united force of Gods, how such
As stood like these, could ever know repulse?   630
For who can yet believe, though after loss,
That all these puissant° Legions, whose exíle
Hath emptied Heav'n, shall fail to re-ascend
Self-rais'd, and repossess their native seat.
For me, be witness all the Host of Heav'n,   635
If counsels different, or danger shunn'd
By me, have lost our hopes. But he who reigns
Monarch in Heav'n, till then as one secure
Sat on his Throne, upheld by old repute,
Consent or custom, and his Regal State   640
Put forth at full, but still his strength conceal'd,
Which tempted our attempt, and wrought our fall.
Henceforth his might we know, and know our own
So as not either to provoke, or dread
New war, provok't; our better part° remains   645
To work in close design, by fraud or guile
What force effected not: that he no less
At length from us may find, who overcomes
By force, hath overcome but half his foe.
Space may produce new Worlds; whereof so rife   650
There went a fame° in Heav'n that he ere long
Intended to create, and therein plant
A generation, whom his choice regard
Should favour equal to the Sons of Heaven:
Thither, if but to pry, shall be perhaps   655
Our first eruption,° thither or elsewhere:
For this Infernal Pit shall never hold
Celestial Spirits in Bondage, nor th'Abyss
Long under darkness cover. But these thoughts
Full Counsel must mature: Peace is despair'd,   660
For who can think Submission? War then, War
Open or understood must be resolv'd."
            He spake: and to confirm his words, out-flew
Millions of flaming swords, drawn from the thighs
Of mighty Cherubim; the sudden blaze   665
Far round illumin'd hell: highly they rag'd
Against the Highest, and fierce with grasped arms

632 **puissant** powerful.   645 **part** to be acted (in both senses).   651 **fame**
rumor.   656 **eruption** breaking out forcibly (suggesting too the volcanoes
of Hell).

Clash'd on their sounding shields the din of war,
Hurling defiance° toward the vault of Heav'n.
670   There stood a Hill not far whose grisly top
Belch'd fire and rolling smoke; the rest entire
Shone with a glossy scurf, undoubted sign
That in his womb° was hid metallic Ore,
The work of Sulphur. Thither wing'd with speed
675 A numerous Brígade hasten'd. As when bands
Of Pioneers° with Spade and Pickaxe arm'd
Forerun the Royal Camp, to trench a Field,
Or cast a Rampart. Mammon led them on,
Mammon, the least erected° Spirit that fell
680 From heav'n, for even in heav'n his looks and thoughts
Were always downward bent, admiring more
The riches of Heav'n's pavement, trodd'n gold,
Than aught divine or holy else enjoy'd
In vision beatific:° by him first
685 Men also, and by his suggestion° taught,
Ransack'd the Center, and with impious hands
Rifled the bowels of their mother Earth
For Treasures better hid. Soon had his crew
Op'n'd into the Hill a spacious wound
690 And digg'd out ribs of Gold. Let none admire°
That riches grow in Hell; that soil may best
Deserve the precious° bane.° And here let those
Who boast in mortal things, and wond'ring tell
Of Babel, and the works of Memphian° Kings,
695 Learn how their greatest Monuments of Fame,
And Strength and Art are easily outdone
By Spirits reprobate,° and in an hour
What in an age they with incessant toil
And hands innumerable scarce perform.
700 Nigh on the Plain in many cells prepar'd,

669 **defiance** including the older sense, "declaration of war," defiance itself
meaning the breaking of faith.   673 **his womb** the perverted body-
landscape of Hell.   676 **Pioneers** soldiers preparing camp.   679 **erected** el-
evated.   684 **vision beatific** the blessed experience of seeing God.   685
suggestion including temptation.   690 **admire** wonder.   692 **precious** including "for which a price is paid."   692 **bane** originally murderer; the
word survives in poisonous plants (rat's-bane)—notice "soil."
694 **Memphian** Egyptian.   697 **reprobate** rejected by God, a Biblical
term.

That underneath had veins of liquid fire
Sluic'd from the Lake, a second multitude
With wondrous Art founded° the massy Ore,
Severing each kind, and scumm'd the Bullion dross:°
A third as soon had form'd within the ground   705
A various mould, and from the boiling cells
By strange conveyance fill'd each hollow nook,
As in an Organ from one blast of wind
To many a row of Pipes the sound-board breathes.
Anon out of the earth a Fabric huge   710
Rose like an Exhalation, with the sound°
Of Dulcet Symphonies and voices sweet,
Built like a Temple, where Pilasters° round
Were set, and Doric pillars overlaid
With Golden Architrave;° nor did there want   715
Cornice or Frieze, with bossy° Sculptures grav'n,
The Roof was fretted Gold. Not Babylon,
Nor great Alcairo° such magnificence
Equall'd in all their glories, to enshrine
Belus or Serapis their Gods, or seat   720
Their Kings, when Egypt with Assyria strove
In wealth and luxury. Th'ascending pile
Stood fixt her stately heighth, and straight the doors
Op'ning their brazen° folds discover° wide
Within, her ample spaces, o'er the smooth   725
And level pavement: from the arched roof
Pendent by subtle Magic many a row
Of Starry Lamps and blazing Cressets° fed
With Naphtha and Asphaltus yielded light
As from a sky. The hasty multitude   730
Admiring enter'd, and the work some praise
And some the Architect: his hand was known
In Heav'n by many a Tow'red structure high,
Where Scepter'd Angels held their residence,
And sat as Princes, whom the súpreme King   735

---

703 **founded** *1667*; found out *1674*.   704 **scumm'd . . . dross** skimmed the
dregs of the metal, "bullion" being from *bouillon*, to boil; see line
706.   711 **sound** The music of Apollo and of Amphion built the walls of
Troy and Thebes.   713 **Pilasters** square columns.   715 **Architrave** main
beam.   716 **bossy** embossed.   718 **Alcairo** Cairo.   724 **brazen** including
the effrontery of mimicking Heaven.   724 **discover** reveal.   728 **Cressets**
torches, made of "Asphaltus," and burning "Naphtha."

Exalted to such power, and gave to rule,
Each in his Hierarchy, the Orders bright.
Nor was his name unheard or unador'd
In ancient Greece; and in Ausonian land°
740 Men call'd him Mulciber;° and how he fell
From Heav'n, they fabl'd, thrown by angry Jove
Sheer o'er the Crystal Battlements: from Morn
To Noon he fell, from Noon to dewy Eve,
A Summer's day; and with the setting Sun
745 Dropt from the Zenith like a falling Star,
On Lemnos th'Aegaean Isle: thus they relate,
Erring; for he with this rebellious rout°
Fell long before; nor aught avail'd him now
To have built in Heav'n high Tow'rs; nor did he 'scape
750 By all his Engines,° but was headlong sent
With his industrious crew to build in Hell.
Meanwhile the winged Heralds by command
Of Sovran power, with awful Ceremony
And Trumpets' sound throughout the Host proclaim
755 A solemn Council forthwith to be held
At Pandemonium,° the high Capital
Of Satan and his Peers: their summons call'd
From every Band and squared Regiment
By place or choice the worthiest; they anon
760 With hundreds and with thousands trooping came
Attended: all access was throng'd, the Gates
And Porches wide, but chief the spacious Hall
(Though like a cover'd field, where Champions bold
Wont° ride in arm'd, and at the Soldan's° chair
765 Defi'd the best of Paynim° chivalry
To mortal combat or career° with Lance)
Thick swarm'd, both on the ground and in the air,
Brusht with the hiss of rustling wings. As Bees
In springtime, when the Sun with Taurus° rides,
770 Pour forth their populous youth about the Hive
In clusters; they among fresh dews and flowers
Fly to and fro, or on the smoothed Plank,

---

739 **Ausonian land** Italy. 740 **Mulciber** "The Softener" (of metal),
known too as Vulcan. 747 **rout** company. 750 **Engines** contrivances.
756 **Pandemonium** "Abode of all devils." 764 **Wont** were wont to.
764 **Soldan** Sultan. 765 **Paynim** pagan. 766 **career** gallop at full
speed. 769 **with Taurus** in the sign of the Bull.

The suburb of their Straw-built Citadel,
New rubb'd with Balm, expatiate° and confer
Their State-affairs. So thick the airy crowd   775
Swarm'd and were strait'n'd; till the Signal giv'n,
Behold a wonder! they but now who seem'd
In bigness to surpass Earth's Giant Sons
Now less than smallest Dwarfs, in narrow room
Throng numberless, like that Pygmean Race   780
Beyond the Indian Mount, or Faery Elves,
Whose midnight Revels, by a Forest side
Or Fountain some belated° Peasant sees,
Or dreams he sees, while overhead the Moon
Sits Arbitress,° and nearer to the Earth   785
Wheels her pale course, they on their mirth and dance
Intent, with jocund Music charm his ear;
At once with joy and fear his heart rebounds.
Thus incorporeal Spirits to smallest forms
Rcduc'd their shapes immense, and were at large,   790
Though without number° still amidst the Hall
Of that infernal Court. But far within
And in their own dimensions like themselves
The great Seraphic Lords and Cherubim
In close recess and secret conclave° sat   795
A thousand Demi-Gods on golden seats,
Frequent° and full. After short silence then
And summons read, the great consult began.

774 **expatiate** walk at large; the more usual sense, "discourse at length,"
leads into "confer" and "the great consult." 783 **belated** out late. 785 **Arbitress** deciding destinies; this superstition is to be contrasted with the
truth, "Heav'n's high Arbitrator," II 359. 791 **without number** numberless. 795 **conclave** The religious suggestion both hits at cardinals in their
meetings, and suggests blasphemous parody by the fallen angels. 797 **Frequent** crowded.

BOOK II

THE ARGUMENT

The Consultation begun, Satan debates whether another
Battle be to be hazarded for the recovery of Heaven:
some advise it, others dissuade: A third proposal is pre-
ferr'd, mention'd before by Satan, to search the truth of
that Prophecy or Tradition in Heaven concerning another
world, and another kind of creature equal or not much
inferior to themselves, about this time to be created: Their
doubt who shall be sent on this difficult search: Satan their
chief undertakes alone the voyage, is honour'd and applauded. The Council thus ended, the rest betake them
several ways and to several employments, as their inclina-
tions lead them, to entertain the time till Satan return. He
passes on his Journey to Hell Gates, finds them shut, and
who sat there to guard them, by whom at length they are
open'd, and discover to him the great Gulf between Hell
and Heaven; with what difficulty he passes through, directed by Chaos, the Power of that place, to the sight of
this new World which he sought.

      High on a Throne of Royal State, which far
Outshone the wealth of Ormus° and of Ind,
Or where the gorgeous East with richest hand
Show'rs on her Kings Barbaric Pearl and Gold,
5 Satan exalted sat, by merit rais'd
To that bad eminence; and from despair
Thus high uplifted beyond hope, aspires
Beyond thus high, insatiate to pursue
Vain War with Heav'n, and by success° untaught
10 His proud imaginations thus display'd.
      "Powers and Dominions, Deities of Heav'n,

---

2 **Ormus** in the Persian gulf. 9 **success** originally "outcome," whether
good or bad; but the modern sense existed and may add a sardonic note.

For since no deep within her gulf can hold
Immortal vigour, though opprest and fall'n,
I give not Heav'n for lost. From this descent
Celestial virtues° rising, will appear   15
More glorious and more dread than from no fall,
And trust themselves to fear no second fate:
Mee though just right,° and the fixt Laws of Heav'n
Did first create your Leader, next, free choice,
With what besides, in Council° or in Fight,   20
Hath been achiev'd of merit, yet this loss
Thus far at least recover'd, hath much more
Establisht in a safe unenvied Throne
Yielded with full consent. The happier state
In Heav'n, which follows dignity, might draw   25
Envy from each inferior; but who here
Will envy whom the highest place exposes
Foremost to stand against the Thunderer's aim
Your bulwark, and condemns to greatest share
Of endless pain? where there is then no good   30
For which to strive, no strife can grow up there
From Faction; for none sure will claim in hell
Precédence, none, whose portion is so small
Of present pain, that with ambitious mind
Will covet more. With this advantage then   35
To union, and firm Faith, and firm accord,
More than can be in Heav'n, we now return
To claim our just inheritance of old,
Surer to prosper than prosperity
Could have assur'd us; and by what best way,   40
Whether of open War or covert guile,
We now debate; who can advise, may speak."
      He ceas'd, and next him Moloch, Scepter'd
        King,
Stood up, the strongest and the fiercest Spirit
That fought in Heav'n; now fiercer by despair: 45
His trust was with th'Eternal to be deem'd
Equal in strength, and rather than be less
Car'd not to be at all; with that care lost
Went all his fear: of God, or Hell, or worse

---

15 **virtues** including this rank of angels.   18 **just right** the rights of justice.   20 **Council** advice and assembly (Milton's spelling "Counsel").

50　　He reck'd not, and these words thereafter spake.
　　　　　　"My sentence is for open War: Of Wiles,
　　　More unexpert,° I boast not: them let those
　　　Contrive who need, or when they need, not now.
　　　For while they sit contriving, shall the rest,
55　　Millions that stand in Arms, and longing wait
　　　The Signal to ascend, sit ling'ring here
　　　Heav'n's fugitives, and for their dwelling place
　　　Accept this dark opprobrious Den of shame,
　　　The Prison of his Tyranny who Reigns
60　　By our delay? No, let us rather choose
　　　Arm'd with Hell flames and fury all at once
　　　O'er Heav'n's high Tow'rs to force resistless° way,
　　　Turning our Tortures into horrid Arms
　　　Against the Torturer; when to meet the noise
65　　Of his Almighty Engine° he shall hear
　　　Infernal Thunder, and for Lightning see
　　　Black fire and horror shot with equal rage
　　　Among his Angels; and his Throne itself
　　　Mixt with Tartarean° Sulphur, and strange fire,
70　　His own invented Torments. But perhaps
　　　The way seems difficult and steep to scale
　　　With upright wing against a higher foe.
　　　Let such bethink them, if the sleepy drench°
　　　Of that forgetful° Lake benumb not still,
75　　That in our proper° motion we ascend
　　　Up to our native seat: descent and fall
　　　To us is adverse. Who but felt of late
　　　When the fierce Foe hung on our brok'n Rear
　　　Insulting,° and pursu'd us through the Deep,
80　　With what compulsion and laborious flight
　　　We sunk thus low? Th'ascent is easy then;
　　　Th'event° is fear'd; should we again provoke
　　　Our stronger, some worse way his wrath may find
　　　To our destruction: if there be in Hell
85　　Fear to be worse destroy'd: what can be worse
　　　Than to dwell here, driv'n out from bliss, condemn'd

---

52 **More unexpert** less experienced　62 **resistless** irresistible.　65 **Engine** machine of war.　69 **Tartarean** Tartarus, the classical Hell.　73 **drench** potion.　74 **forgetful** causing oblivion.　75 **proper** own natural.　79 **Insulting** with a suggestion of the Latin, "leaping upon."　82 **event** outcome.

In this abhorred deep to utter woe;
Where pain of unextinguishable fire
Must exercise° us without hope of end
The Vassals of his anger, when the Scourge   90
Inexorably,° and the torturing hour
Calls us to Penance? More destroy'd than thus
We should be quite abolisht and expire.
What fear we then? what doubt we to incense
His utmost ire? which to the heighth enrag'd,   95
Will either quite consume us, and reduce
To nothing this essential,° happier far
Than miserable to have eternal being:
Or if our substance be indeed Divine,
And cannot cease to be, we are at worst   100
On this side nothing;° and by proof we feel
Our power sufficient to disturb his Heav'n,
And with perpetual inroads to Alarm,
Though inaccessible, his fatal° Throne:
Which if not Victory is yet Revenge."   105
          He ended frowning, and his look denounc'd°
Desperate revenge, and Battle dangerous
To less than Gods. On th'other side up rose
Belial, in act more graceful and humane;
A fairer person lost not Heav'n; he seem'd   110
For dignity compos'd and high exploit:
But all was false and hollow; though his Tongue
Dropt Manna,° and could make the worse appear
The better reason, to perplex and dash
Maturest Counsels: for his thoughts were low;   115
To vice industrious, but to Nobler deeds
Timorous and slothful: yet he pleas'd the ear,
And with persuasive accent thus began.
          "I should be much for open War, O Peers,
As not behind in hate; if what was urg'd   120
Main reason to persuade immediate War,
Did not dissuade me most, and seem to cast
Ominous conjecture on the whole success:

89 **exercise** work on.   91 **Inexorably** not to be moved even by prayer
(Latin *orare*)—notice "Penance."   97 **essential** essence.   100–01 **at
worst . . . nothing** already in the worst plight short of annihilation.   104 **fatal**
upheld by fate.   106 **denounc'd** proclaimed.   113 **Manna** sweetness (but to
be contrasted with the heavenly gift of miraculous food).

When he who most excels in fact° of Arms,
125 In what he counsels and in what excels
Mistrustful, grounds his courage on despair
And utter dissolution, as the scope°
Of all his aim, after some dire revenge.
First, what Revenge? the Tow'rs of Heav'n are fill'd
130 With Armed watch, that render all access
Impregnable; oft on the bordering Deep
Encamp their Legions, or with óbscure wing
Scout far and wide into the Realm of night,
Scorning surprise. Or could we break our way
135 By force, and at our heels all Hell should rise
With blackest Insurrection, to confound
Heav'n's purest Light, yet our great Enemy
All incorruptible would on his Throne
Sit unpolluted, and th'Ethereal mould
140 Incapable of stain would soon expel
Her mischief, and purge off the baser fire
Victorious. Thus repuls'd, our final hope
Is flat despair: we must exasperate
Th'Almighty Victor to spend all his rage,
145 And that must end us, that must be our cure,
To be no more; sad cure; for who would lose,
Though full of pain, this intellectual being,
Those thoughts that wander through Eternity,
To perish rather, swallow'd up and lost
150 In the wide womb of uncreated night,
Devoid of sense and motion? and who knows,
Let this be good, whether our angry Foe
Can give it, or will ever? how he can
Is doubtful; that he never will is sure.
155 Will he, so wise, let loose at once his ire,
Belike° through impotence,° or unaware,
To give his Enemies their wish, and end
Them in his anger, whom his anger saves
To punish endless? 'Wherefore cease we then?'
160 Say they who counsel War, 'we are decreed,
Reserv'd and destin'd to Eternal woe;
Whatever doing, what can we suffer more,

124 **fact** feat.   127 **scope** target.   156 **Belike** no doubt.   156 **impotence**
lack of self-restraint (sardonically contrasted with God's omnipotence).

What can we suffer worse?' Is this then worst,
Thus sitting, thus consulting, thus in Arms?
What when we fled amain,° pursu'd and struck   165
With Heav'n's afflicting Thunder, and besought
The Deep to shelter us? this Hell then seem'd
A refuge from those wounds; or when we lay
Chain'd on the burning Lake? that sure was worse.
What if the breath that kindl'd those grim fires   170
Awak'd should blow them into sevenfold rage
And plunge us in the Flames? or from above
Should intermitted vengeance Arm again
His red right hand to plague us? what if all
Her stores were op'n'd, and this Firmament   175
Of Hell should spout her Cataracts of Fire,
Impendent horrors, threat'ning hideous fall
One day upon our heads; while we perhaps
Designing or exhorting glorious War,
Caught in a fiery Tempest shall be hurl'd   180
Each on his rock transfixt, the sport and prey
Of racking° whirlwinds, or forever sunk
Under yon boiling Ocean, wrapt in Chains;
There to converse° with everlasting groans,
Unrespited, unpitied, unrepriev'd,   185
Ages of hopeless end; this would be worse.
War therefore, open or conceal'd, alike
My voice dissuades; for what can force or guile
With him, or who deceive his mind, whose eye
Views all things at one view? he from heav'n's heighth 190
All these our motions° vain, sees and derides;
Not more Almighty to resist our might
Than wise to frustrate all our plots and wiles.
Shall we then live thus vile, the race of Heav'n
Thus trampl'd, thus expell'd to suffer here   195
Chains and these Torments? better these than worse
By my advice; since fate inevitable
Subdues us, and Omnipotent Decree,
The Victor's will. To suffer, as to do,
Our strength is equal, nor the Law unjust   200
That so ordains: this was at first resolv'd,

165 **amain** with all speed and force.   182 **racking** both "torturing" and
"driving impetuously."   184 **converse** including the older sense
"live."   191 **motions** proposals.

If we were wise, against so great a foe
Contending, and so doubtful what might fall.
I laugh, when those who at the Spear are bold
205 And vent'rous, if that fail them, shrink and fear
What yet they know must follow, to endure
Exile, or ignominy, or bonds, or pain,
The sentence of their Conqueror: This is now
Our doom; which if we can sustain and bear,
210 Our Súpreme Foe in time may much remit
His anger, and perhaps thus far remov'd
Not mind° us not offending, satisfi'd
With what is punish't; whence these raging fires
Will slack'n, if his breath stir not their flames.
215 Our purer essence then will overcome
Their noxious vapour, or inur'd not feel,
Or chang'd at length, and to the place conform'd
In temper and in nature, will receive
Familiar the fierce heat, and void of pain;
220 This horror will grow mild, this darkness light,°
Besides what hope the never-ending flight
Of future days may bring, what chance, what change
Worth waiting, since our present lot appears
For happy° though but ill, for ill not worst,
225 If we procure not to ourselves more woe."
          Thus Belial with words clothed in reason's garb
Counsell'd ignoble ease, and peaceful sloth,
Not peace: and after him thus Mammon spake.
          "Either to disenthrone the King of Heav'n
230 We war, if war be best, or to regain
Our own right lost: him to unthrone we then
May hope, when everlasting Fate shall yield
To fickle Chance, and Chaos judge the strife:
The former vain to hope argues as vain
235 The latter: for what place can be for us
Within Heav'n's bound, unless Heav'n's Lord supreme
We overpower? Suppose he should relent
And publish Grace to all, on promise made
Of new Subjection; with what eyes could we
240 Stand in his presence humble, and receive

212 **mind** call to mind.   220 **light** both "illumination" and "lightly borne"
(parallel with "mild").   224 **For happy** as to happiness.

Strict Laws impos'd, to celebrate his Throne
With warbl'd Hymns, and to his Godhead sing
Forc't° Halleluliahs; while he Lordly° sits
Our envied Sovran, and his Altar breathes
Ambrosial Odours and Ambrosial Flowers,   245
Our servile offerings. This must be our task
In Heav'n, this our delight; how wearisome
Eternity so spent in worship paid
To whom we hate. Let us not then pursue
By force impossible, by leave obtain'd   250
Unácceptáble, though in Heav'n, our state
Of splendid vassalage, but rather seek
Our own good from ourselves, and from our own
Live to ourselves, though in this vast recess,
Free, and to none accountable, preferring   255
Hard liberty before the easy yoke
Of servile Pomp. Our greatness will appear
Then most conspicuous, when great things of small,
Useful of hurtful, prosperous of adverse
We can create, and in what place soe'er   260
Thrive under evil, and work ease out of pain
Through labour and endurance. This deep world
Of darkness do we dread? How oft amidst
Thick clouds and dark doth Heav'n's all-ruling Sire
Choose to reside, his Glory unobscur'd,   265
And with the Majesty of darkness round
Covers his Throne; from whence deep thunders roar
Must'ring their rage, and Heav'n resembles Hell?
As he our Darkness, cannot we his Light
Imitate when we please? This Desert soil   270
Wants° not her hidden lustre, Gems and Gold;
Nor want we skill or art, from whence to raise
Magnificence; and what can Heav'n show more?
Our torments also may in length of time
Become our Elements,° these piercing Fires   275
As soft as now severe, our temper chang'd
Into their temper; which must needs remove

243 **Forc't** both extorted and strained. 243 **Lordly** including
haughty. 271 **Wants** lacks. 275 **Elements** Demons traditionally dwelt
in the elements (fire, etc.).

The sensible° of pain. All things invite
To peaceful Counsels, and the settl'd State
280 Of order, how in safety best we may
Compose° our present evils, with regard
Of what we are and where,° dismissing quite
All thoughts of War: ye have what I advise."
        He scarce had finisht, when such murmur fill'd
285 Th'Assembly, as when hollow Rocks retain
The sound of blust'ring winds, which all night long
Had rous'd the Sea, now with hoarse cadence lull
Sea-faring men o'erwatcht,° whose Bark by chance
Or Pinnace anchors in a craggy Bay
290 After the Tempest: Such applause was heard
As Mammon ended, and his Sentence pleas'd,
Advising peace: for such another Field°
They dreaded worse than Hell: so much the fear
Of Thunder and the Sword of Michaël
295 Wrought still within them; and no less desire
To found this nether Empire, which might rise
By policy,° and long procéss of time,
In emulation opposite° to Heav'n.
Which when Beëlzebub perceiv'd, than whom,
300 Satan except, none higher sat, with grave
Aspéct he rose, and in his rising seem'd
A Pillar of State; deep on his Front engraven
Deliberation sat and public care;
And Princely counsel in his face yet shone,
305 Majestic though in ruin: sage he stood
With Atlantean° shoulders fit to bear
The weight of mightiest Monarchies; his look
Drew audience and attention still as Night
Or Summer's Noon-tide air, while thus he spake.
        "Thrones and imperial Powers, offspring of
310   heav'n,
Ethereal Virtues; or these Titles now
Must we renounce, and changing style be call'd
Princes of Hell? for so the popular vote

278 **The sensible** that which feels sensations.   281 **Compose** calm, gain
composure in the face of.   282 **where** *1667*; were *1674*.   288 **o'erwatcht**
worn out with watching.   292 **Field** battlefield.   297 **policy** including the
bad sense, political cunning.   298 **opposite** both diametrically different
and antagonistic.   306 **Atlantean** Atlas carried the world.

Inclines, here to continue, and build up here
A growing Empire; doubtless; while we dream,   315
And know not that the King of Heav'n hath doom'd
This place our dungeon, not our safe retreat
Beyond his Potent arm, to live exempt
From Heav'n's high jurisdiction, in new League
Banded against his Throne, but to remain   320
In strictest bondage, though thus far remov'd,
Under th'inevitable° curb, reserv'd
His captive multitude: For he, be sure,
In heighth or depth, still first and last will Reign
Sole King, and of his Kingdom lose no part   325
By our revolt, but over Hell extend
His Empire, and with Iron Scepter rule
Us here, as with his Golden those in Heav'n.
What sit we then projecting Peace and War?
War hath determin'd us,° and foil'd with loss   330
Irreparable; terms of peace yet none
Vouchsaf't or sought; for what peace will be giv'n
To us enslav'd, but custody severe,
And stripes,° and arbitrary° punishment
Inflicted? and what peace can we return,   335
But to our power hostility and hate,
Untam'd reluctance,° and revenge though slow,
Yet ever plotting how the Conqueror least
May reap his conquest, and may least rejoice
In doing what we most in suffering feel?   340
Nor will occasion want, nor shall we need
With dangerous expedition to invade
Heav'n, whose high walls fear no assault or Siege,
Or ambush from the Deep. What if we find
Some easier enterprise? There is a place   345
(If ancient and prophetic fame in Heav'n
Err not) another World, the happy seat
Of some new Race call'd Man, about this time
To be created like to us, though less
In power and excellence, but favour'd more   350

322 **inevitable** inescapable.   330 **determin'd us** brought us to this end
(also suggesting "War has chosen us—it is no longer for *us* to choose
war").   334 **stripes** whippings.   334 **arbitrary** at the will of the powerful,
but the older sense—see line 359—undercuts Beëlzebub: "at the discre-
tion of an authorized arbitrator."   337 **reluctance** struggling.

Of him who rules above; so was his will
Pronounc'd among the Gods, and by an Oath,
That shook Heav'n's whole circumference, confirm'd.
Thither let us bend all our thoughts, to learn
355 What creatures there inhabit, of what mould,
Or substance, how endu'd, and what their Power,
And where their weakness, how attempted best,
By force or subtlety: Though Heav'n be shut,
And Heav'n's high Arbitrator sit secure
360 In his own strength, this place may lie expos'd
The utmost border of his Kingdom, left
To their defence who hold it: here perhaps
Some advantageous act may be achiev'd
By sudden onset, either with Hell fire
365 To waste his whole Creation, or possess
All as our own, and drive as we were driven,
The puny° habitants, or if not drive,
Seduce them to our Party, that their God
May prove their foe, and with repenting hand
370 Abolish his own works. This would surpass
Common revenge, and interrupt his joy
In our Confusion, and our Joy upraise
In his disturbance; when his darling Sons
Hurl'd headlong to partake with us, shall curse
375 Their frail Originals,° and faded bliss,
Faded so soon. Advise if this be worth
Attempting, or to sit in darkness here
Hatching vain Empires." Thus Beëlzebub
Pleaded his devilish Counsel, first devis'd
380 By Satan, and in part propos'd: for whence,
But from the Author of all ill could spring
So deep a malice, to confound the race
Of mankind in one root,° and Earth with Hell
To mingle and involve, done all to spite
385 The great Creator? But their spite still serves
His glory to augment. The bold design
Pleas'd highly those infernal States,° and joy
Sparkl'd in all their eyes; with full assent

367 **puny** weak and "born since [us]," *puisné*.   375 **Originals** *1667*; Original *1674*.   383 **one root** Adam, but the word foreshadows the forbidden Tree, "root of all our woe," IX 645.   387 **States** the estates of the realm, comprising the assembly.

They vote: whereat his speech he thus renews.
      "Well have ye judg'd, well ended long debate,   *390*
Synod° of Gods, and like to what ye are,
Great things resolv'd; which from the lowest deep
Will once more lift us up, in spite of Fate,
Nearer our ancient Seat; perhaps in view
Of those bright confines, whence with neighbouring
   Arms   *395*
And opportune° excursion we may chance
Re-enter Heav'n; or else in some mild Zone
Dwell not unvisited of Heav'n's fair Light
Secure, and at the bright'ning Orient beam
Purge off this gloom; the soft delicious Air,   *400*
To heal the scar of these corrosive Fires
Shall breathe her balm. But first whom shall we send
In search of this new world, whom shall we find
Sufficient? who shall tempt° with wand'ring feet
The dark unbottom'd infinite Abyss   *405*
And through the palpable obscure find out
His uncouth° way, or spread his airy flight
Upborne with indefatigable wings
Over the vast abrupt, ere he arrive
The happy Isle; what strength, what art can then   *410*
Suffice, or what evasion bear him safe
Through the strict Senteries and Stations thick
Of Angels watching round? Here he had need
All circumspection, and we now no less
Choice° in our suffrage; for on whom we send,   *415*
The weight of all and our last hope relies."
      This said, he sat; and expectation held
His look suspense,° awaiting who appear'd
To second, or oppose, or undertake
The perilous attempt: but all sat mute,   *420*
Pondering the danger with deep thoughts; and each
In other's countenance read his own dismay
Astonisht: none among the choice and prime
Of those Heav'n-warring Champions could be found

---

391 **Synod** assembly, usually of clergy. 396 **opportune** well-timed, originally of a wind driving to port, *portus;* notice "excursion" and "Re-enter,"
and II 1041–7. 404 **tempt** attempt (though the evil suggestion is relevant). 407 **uncouth** unknown. 415 **Choice** careful choosing. 418 **suspense** suspended.

425 So hardy as to proffer or accept
Alone the dreadful voyage; till at last
Satan, whom now transcendent glory rais'd
Above his fellows, with Monarchal° pride
Conscious of highest worth, unmov'd thus spake.
430   "O Progeny of Heav'n, Empyreal Thrones,
With reason hath deep silence and demur
Seiz'd us, though undismay'd: long is the way
And hard, that out of Hell leads up to Light;
Our prison strong, this huge convéx of Fire,
435 Outrageous to devour, immures us round
Ninefold, and gates of burning Adamant
Barr'd over us prohibit all egress.
These past, if any pass, the void profound
Of unessential° Night receives him next
440 Wide gaping, and with utter loss of being
Threatens him, plung'd in that abortive gulf.
If thence he 'scape into whatever world,
Or unknown Region, what remains him less
Than unknown dangers and as hard escape.
445 But I should ill become this Throne, O Peers,
And this imperial Sov'ranty, adorn'd
With splendour, arm'd with power, if aught propos'd
And judg'd of public moment, in the shape
Of difficulty or danger could deter
450 Me from attempting. Wherefore do I assume
These Royalties, and not refuse to Reign,
Refusing to accept as great a share
Of hazard as of honour, due alike
To him who Reigns, and so much to him due
455 Of hazard more, as he above the rest
High honour'd sits? Go therefore mighty powers,
Terror of Heav'n, though fall'n; intend° at home,
While here shall be our home, what best may ease
The present misery, and render Hell
460 More tolerable; if there be cure or charm
To respite or deceive, or slack the pain
Of this ill Mansion: intermit no watch
Against a wakeful Foe, while I abroad

428 **Monarchal** literally "ruling alone."   439 **unessential** having no being.
457 **intend** put your mind to.

Through all the coasts of dark destruction seek
Deliverance for us all: this enterprise   *465*
None shall partake with me." Thus saying rose
The Monarch, and prevented° all reply,
Prudent, lest from his resolution° rais'd
Others among the chief might offer now
(Certain to be refus'd) what erst they fear'd;   *470*
And so refus'd might in opinion stand
His rivals, winning cheap the high repute
Which he through hazard huge must earn. But they
Dreaded not more th'adventure than his voice
Forbidding; and at once with him they rose;   *475*
Their rising all at once was as the sound
Of Thunder heard remote. Towards him they bend
With awful reverence prone; and as a God
Extol him equal to the highest in Heav'n:
Nor fail'd they to express how much they prais'd,   *480*
That for the general safety he despis'd
His own: for neither do the Spirits damn'd
Lose all their virtue; lest bad men should boast
Their specious deeds on earth, which glory excites,
Or close ambition varnisht o'er with zeal.   *485*
Thus they their doubtful consultations dark
Ended rejoicing in their matchless Chief:
As when from mountain tops the dusky clouds
Ascending, while the North wind sleeps, o'erspread
Heav'n's cheerful face, the louring° Element   *490*
Scowls o'er the dark'n'd landscape Snow, or show'r;
If chance the radiant Sun with farewell sweet
Extend his ev'ning beam, the fields revive,
The birds their notes renew, and bleating herds
Attest their joy, that hill and valley rings.   *495*
O shame to men! Devil with Devil damn'd
Firm concord holds, men only disagree
Of Creatures rational, though under hope
Of heavenly Grace: and God proclaiming peace,
Yet live in hatred, enmity, and strife   *500*
Among themselves, and levy cruel wars,
Wasting the Earth, each other to destroy:

467 **prevented** forestalled. 468 **resolution** resoluteness. 490 **louring**
glowering.

As if (which might induce us to accord)
Man had not hellish foes enow besides,
505 That day and night for his destruction wait.
      The Stygian Council thus dissolv'd; and forth
In order came the grand infernal Peers,
Midst came their mighty Paramount, and seem'd
Alone th'Antagonist of Heav'n, nor less
510 Than Hell's dread Emperor with pomp Supreme,
And God-like imitated State; him round
A Globe of fiery Seraphim enclos'd
With bright imblazonry, and horrent° Arms.
Then of their Session ended they bid cry
515 With Trumpet's regal sound the great result:
Toward the four winds four speedy Cherubim
Put to their mouths the sounding Alchemy°
By Herald's voice explain'd: the hollow Abyss
Heard far and wide, and all the host of Hell
520 With deaf'ning shout, return'd them loud acclaim.
Thence more at ease their minds and somewhat rais'd
By false presumptuous hope, the ranged powers
Disband, and wand'ring, each his several way
Pursues, as inclination or sad choice
525 Leads him perplext, where he may likeliest find
Truce to his restless thoughts, and entertain
The irksome hours, till his° great Chief return.
Part on the Plain, or in the Air sublime°
Upon the wing, or in swift race contend,
530 As at th'Olympian Games or Pythian fields;
Part curb their fiery Steeds, or shun the Goal°
With rapid wheels, or fronted Brígades form.
As when to warn° proud Cities war appears
Wag'd in the troubl'd Sky, and Armies rush
535 To Battle in the Clouds, before each Van°
Prick forth the Airy Knights, and couch their spears
Till thickest Legions close; with feats of Arms
From either end of Heav'n the welkin° burns.
Others with vast Typhoean° rage more fell

---

513 **horrent** bristling. 517 **sounding Alchemy** trumpets of gold-like
metal. 527 **his** 1667; this 1674. 528 **sublime** aloft. 531 **shun the Goal**
swing round the marking posts. 533 **to warn** as an omen. 535 **Van** vanguard. 538 **welkin** sky. 539 **Typhoean** For the monstrous Typhon, see
I 199; his name (as in "typhoon") means whirlwind—see line 541.

Rend up both Rocks and Hills, and ride the Air   *540*
In whirlwind; Hell scarce holds the wild uproar.
As when Alcides from Oechalia Crown'd
With conquest, felt th'envenom'd robe, and tore
Through pain up by the roots Thessalian Pines,
And Lichas from the top of Oeta threw   *545*
Into th'Euboic Sea.° Others more mild,
Retreated in a silent valley, sing
With notes Angelical to many a Harp
Their own Heroic deeds and hapless fall
By doom of Battle; and complain that Fate   *550*
Free Virtue should enthrall to Force or Chance.
Their song was partial,° but the harmony
(What could it less when Spirits immortal sing?)
Suspended° Hell, and took with ravishment
The thronging audience. In discourse more sweet   *555*
(For Eloquence the Soul, Song charms the Sense,)
Others apart sat on a Hill retir'd,
In thoughts more elevate, and reason'd high
Of Providence, Foreknowledge, Will, and Fate,
Fixt Fate, free will, foreknowledge absolute,   *560*
And found no end, in wand'ring mazes lost.
Of good and evil much they argu'd then,
Of happiness and final misery,
Passion and Apathy,° and glory and shame,
Vain wisdom all, and false Philosophy: *565*
Yet with a pleasing sorcery could charm
Pain for a while or anguish, and excite
Fallacious hope, or arm th'obdured breast
With stubborn patience as with triple steel.
Another part in Squadrons and gross° Bands,   *570*
On bold adventure to discover wide
That dismal world, if any Clime perhaps
Might yield them easier habitation, bend
Four ways their flying March, along the Banks
Of four infernal Rivers that disgorge   *575*

542–46 In his pain, Hercules threw into the sea his companion Lichas,
who had brought the poisoned shirt of Nessus which tortured Hercules.   552 **partial** favorable to themselves (suggesting, too, musical
"parts").   554 **Suspended** held rapt ("suspension," again, being a musical term—meanwhile Milton's parenthesis itself suspends the sentence).
564 **Apathy** the Stoic ideal of imperviousness to suffering.   570 **gross**
massed.

Into the burning Lake their baleful streams;
Abhorred Styx the flood of deadly hate,
Sad Acheron of sorrow, black and deep;
Cocytus, nam'd of lamentation loud
580 Heard on the rueful stream; fierce Phlegethon
Whose waves of torrent fire inflame with rage.°
Far off from these a slow and silent stream,
Lethe the River of Oblivion rolls
Her wat'ry Labyrinth, whereof who drinks
585 Forthwith his former state and being forgets,
Forgets both joy and grief, pleasure and pain.
Beyond this flood a frozen Continent
Lies dark and wild, beat with perpetual storms
Of Whirlwind and dire Hail, which on firm land
590 Thaws not, but gathers heap, and ruin seems
Of ancient pile;° all else deep snow and ice,
A gulf profound as that Serbonian Bog
Betwixt Damiata and mount Casius old,°
Where Armies whole have sunk: the parching Air
595 Burns frore,° and cold performs th'effect of Fire.
Thither by harpy-footed Furies hal'd,°
At certain revolutions all the damn'd
Are brought: and feel by turns the bitter change
Of fierce extremes, extremes by change more fierce,
600 From Beds of raging Fire to starve° in Ice
Their soft Ethereal warmth, and there to pine
Immovable, infixt, and frozen round,
Periods of time, thence hurried back to fire.
They ferry over this Lethean Sound°
605 Both to and fro, their sorrow to augment,
And wish and straggle, as they pass, to reach
The tempting stream, with one small drop to lose
In sweet forgetfulness all pain and woe,
All in one moment, and so near the brink;
610 But fate withstands, and to oppose th'attempt
Medusa° with Gorgonian terror guards

577–81 Giving the derivations of the names of Hell's rivers. 591 **pile** building. 593 Near the mouth of the Nile. 595 **frore** frosty. 596 The monstrous Harpies had talons. 600 **starve** originally to die of cold, hunger, etc., to become rigid (notice the contrast with "Beds," "soft," and then "infixt"). 604 **Sound** channel. 611 **Medusa** the Gorgon who turned men to stone.

The Ford, and of itself the water flies
All taste of living wight,° as once it fled
The lip of Tantalus.° Thus roving on
In cónfus'd march forlorn, th'advent'rous Bands   615
With shudd'ring horror pale, and eyes aghast
View'd first their lamentable lot, and found
No rest: through many a dark and dreary Vale
They pass'd, and many a Region dolorous,
O'er many a Frozen, many a Fiery Alp,   620
Rocks, Caves, Lakes, Fens, Bogs, Dens, and shades
    of death,
A Universe of death, which God by curse
Created evil, for evil only good,
Where all life dies, death lives, and nature breeds,
Perverse, all monstrous, all prodigious° things,   625
Abominable, inutterable, and worse
Than Fables yet have feign'd, or fear conceiv'd,
Gorgons° and Hydras,° and Chimeras° dire.
        Meanwhile the Adversary of God and Man,
Satan with thoughts inflam'd of highest design,   630
Puts on swift wings, and toward the Gates of Hell
Explores his solitary flight; sometimes
He scours the right-hand coast, sometimes the left,
Now shaves with level wing the Deep, then soars
Up to the fiery concave tow'ring high.   635
As when far off at Sea a Fleet descri'd
Hangs in the Clouds, by Equinoctial Winds°
Close sailing from Bengala, or the Isles
Of Ternate and Tidore,° whence Merchants bring
Their spicy Drugs: they on the trading Flood   640
Through the wide Ethiopian° to the Cape
Ply stemming° nightly toward the Pole. So seem'd
Far off the flying Fiend: at last appear
Hell-bounds high reaching to the horrid Roof,
And thrice threefold the Gates; three folds were Brass, 645
Three Iron, three of Adamantine Rock,

613 **wight** person.   614 **Tantalus** who was unable to reach the waters,
"tantalized."   625 **prodigious** ominously extraordinary.   628 **Gorgons**
female monsters with snakes for hair.   628 **Hydra** the nine-headed serpent killed by Hercules.   628 **Chimeras** fire-breathing monsters.   637
Equinoctial Winds trade winds at the time of the equinoxes.   639 **Ternate, Tidore** Malayan islands.   641 **Ethiopian** Indian Ocean.   642 **stem-
ming** heading.

Impenetrable, impal'd° with circling fire,
Yet unconsum'd. Before the Gates there sat
On either side a formidable° shape;
650 The one seem'd Woman to the waist, and fair,
But ended foul in many a scaly fold
Voluminous° and vast, a Serpent arm'd
With mortal sting: about her middle round
A cry° of Hell Hounds never ceasing bark'd
655 With wide Cerberean° mouths full loud, and rung
A hideous Peal: yet, when they list, would creep,
If aught disturb'd their noise, into her womb,
And kennel there, yet there still bark'd and howl'd
Within unseen. Far less abhorr'd than these
660 Vex'd Scylla bathing in the Sea that parts
Calabria from the hoarse Trinacrian shore:°
Nor uglier follow the Night-Hag,° when call'd
In secret, riding through the Air she comes
Lur'd with the smell of infant blood, to dance
665 With Lapland° Witches, while the labouring° Moon
Eclipses at their charms. The other shape,
If shape it might be call'd that shape had none
Distinguishable in member, joint, or limb,
Or substance might be call'd that shadow seem'd,
670 For each seem'd either; black it stood as Night,
Fierce as ten Furies, terrible as Hell,
And shook a dreadful Dart; what seem'd his head
The likeness of a Kingly Crown had on.
Satan was now at hand, and from his seat
675 The Monster moving onward came as fast,
With horrid strides, Hell trembled as he strode.
Th'undaunted Fiend what this might be admir'd,°
Admir'd, not fear'd; God and his Son except,
Created thing naught valu'd he nor shunn'd;
680 And with disdainful look thus first began.
          "Whence and what art thou, execrable° shape,

647 **impal'd** fenced in.   649 **formidable** terrifying.   652 **Voluminous** in
coils.   654 **cry** pack.   655 **Cerberean** Cerberus, the many-headed dog
that guarded the classical Hell.   660–61 Scylla, bathing, was changed into
a monster, and haunted a dangerous rock on the Indian coast opposite
Sicily.   662 **Night-Hag** Hecate, goddess of witchcraft.   665 **Lapland** in
northern Europe, and traditionally associated with witches.   665 **labouring** in eclipse (but with a suggestion of "ruling over childbirth," as the
moon did; notice "womb," "infant").   677 **admir'd** wondered at.   681
execrable accursed.

That dar'st, though grim and terrible, advance
Thy miscreated Front athwart my way
To yonder Gates? through them I mean to pass,
That be assur'd, without leave askt of thee: 685
Retire, or taste thy folly, and learn by proof,
Hell-born, not to contend with Spirits of Heav'n."
        To whom the Goblin° full of wrath repli'd,
"Art thou that Traitor Angel, art thou hee,
Who first broke peace in Heav'n and Faith, till then 690
Unbrok'n, and in proud rebellious Arms
Drew after him the third part of Heav'n's Sons
Conjur'd° against the highest, for which both Thou
And they outcast from God, are here condemn'd
To waste Eternal days in woe and pain?   695
And reck'n'st thou thyself with Spirits of Heav'n,
Hell-doom'd, and breath'st defiance here and scorn,
Where I reign King, and to enrage thee more,
Thy King and Lord? Back to thy punishment,
False fugitive, and to thy speed add wings,   700
Lest with a whip of Scorpions I pursue
Thy ling'ring, or with one stroke of this Dart
Strange horror seize thee, and pangs unfelt before."
        So spake the grisly terror, and in shape,
So Speaking and so threat'ning, grew tenfold   705
More dreadful and deform: on th'other side
Incens't° with indignation Satan stood
Unterrifi'd, and like a Comet burn'd,
That fires the length of Ophiuchus° huge
In th'Arctic Sky, and from his horrid hair°   710
Shakes Pestilence and War. Each at the Head
Levell'd his deadly aim; their fatal hands
No second stroke intend, and such a frown
Each cast at th'other, as when two black Clouds
With Heav'n's Artillery fraught, come rattling on   715
Over the Caspian, then stand front to front°
Hov'ring a space, till Winds the signal blow
To join their dark Encounter in mid-air:

688 **Goblin** evil spirit.   693 **Conjur'd** sworn together.   707 **Incens't** inflamed, from Latin *incendere* (notice "burn'd").   709 **Ophiuchus** "Serpent holder," a northern constellation.   710 **hair** "Comet" is from the
Greek for "long-haired," and is an evil omen.   714–16 The clouds re-
semble great ships ("fraught," stored, as in "freight").

So frown'd the mighty Combatants, that Hell
720 Grew darker at their frown, so matcht they stood;
For never but once more was either like
To meet so great a foe: and now great deeds
Had been achiev'd, whereof all Hell had rung,
Had not the Snaky Sorceress that sat
725 Fast by Hell Gate, and kept the fatal Key,
Ris'n, and with hideous outcry rush'd between.
      "O Father, what intends thy hand," she cri'd,
"Against thy only Son? What fury O Son,
Possesses thee to bend that mortal Dart
730 Against thy Father's head? and know'st for whom;
For him who sits above and laughs the while
At thee ordain'd his drudge, to execute°
Whate'er his wrath, which he calls Justice, bids,
His wrath which one day will destroy ye both."
735   She spake, and at her words the hellish Pest°
Forbore, then these to her Satan return'd:
      "So strange thy outcry, and thy words so
        strange
Thou interposest, that my sudden hand
Prevented spares° to tell thee yet by deeds
740 What it intends; till first I know of thee,
What thing thou art, thus double-form'd, and why
In this infernal Vale first met thou call'st
Me Father, and that Phantasm call'st my Son?
I know thee not, nor ever saw till now
745 Sight more detestable than him and thee."
      T'whom thus the Portress of Hell Gate repli'd;
"Hast thou forgot me then, and do I seem
Now in thine eye so foul, once deem'd so fair
In Heav'n, when at th'Assembly, and in sight
750 Of all the Seraphim with thee combin'd
In bold conspiracy against Heav'n's King,
All on a sudden miserable pain
Surpris'd thee, dim thine eyes, and dizzy swum
In darkness, while thy head flames thick and fast

---

732 **execute** carry out (but what Death executes is execution). 735 **Pest** originally a deadly plague. 739 **Prevented spares** forestalled refrains from. 754–58 To be contrasted with the birth of Athene, goddess of wisdom, from Zeus's head; "the left side" because it was ill-omened, literally "sinister."

Threw forth, till on the left side op'ning wide,   755
Likest to thee in shape and count'nance bright,
Then shining heav'nly fair, a Goddess arm'd
Out of thy head I sprung:° amazement seiz'd
All th'Host of Heav'n; back they recoil'd afraid
At first, and call'd me Sin, and for a Sign   760
Portentous° held me; but familiar grown,
I pleas'd, and with attractive graces won
The most averse, thee chiefly, who full oft
Thyself in me thy perfect image viewing
Becam'st enamour'd, and such joy thou took'st   765
With me in secret, that my womb conceiv'd
A growing burden. Meanwhile War arose,
And fields were fought in Heav'n; wherein remain'd
(For what could else) to our Almighty Foe
Clear Victory, to our part loss and rout   770
Through all the Empyrean: down they fell
Driv'n headlong from the Pitch of Heaven, down
Into this Deep, and in the general fall
I also; at which time this powerful Key
Into my hand was giv'n, with charge to keep   775
These Gates for ever shut, which none can pass
Without my op'ning. Pensive here I sat
Alone, but long I sat not, till my womb
Pregnant by thee, and now excessive grown
Prodigious motion felt and rueful throes.   780
At last this odious offspring whom thou seest
Thine own begotten, breaking violent way
Tore through my entrails, that with fear and pain
Distorted, all my nether shape thus grew
Transform'd: but he my inbred enemy   785
Forth issu'd, brandishing his fatal Dart
Made to destroy: I fled, and cri'd out *Death*;
Hell trembl'd at the hideous Name, and sigh'd
From all her Caves, and back resounded *Death*.
I fled, but he pursu'd (though more, it seems,   790
Inflam'd with lust than rage) and swifter far,
Me overtook his mother all dismay'd,
And in embraces forcible and foul
Engend'ring with me, of that rape begot

761 **Portentous** ominous.

795 These yelling Monsters that with ceaseless cry
    Surround me, as thou saw'st, hourly conceiv'd
    And hourly born, with sorrow infinite
    To me, for when they list into the womb
    That bred them they return, and howl and gnaw
800 My Bowels, their repast; then bursting forth
    Afresh with conscious° terrors vex me round,
    That rest or intermission none I find.
    Before mine eyes in opposition sits
    Grim Death my Son and foe, who sets them on,
805 And me his Parent would full soon devour
    For want of other prey, but that he knows
    His end with mine involv'd; and knows that I
    Should prove a bitter Morsel, and his bane,
    Whenever that shall be; so Fate pronounc'd.
810 But thou O Father, I forewarn thee, shun
    His deadly arrow; neither vainly hope
    To be invulnerable in those bright Arms,
    Though temper'd heav'nly, for that mortal dint,
    Save he who reigns above, none can resist."
815   She finish'd, and the subtle Fiend his lore°
    Soon learn'd, now milder, and thus answer'd smooth.
    "Dear Daughter, since thou claim'st me for thy Sire,
    And my fair Son here show'st me, the dear pledge
    Of dalliance had with thee in Heav'n, and joys
820 Then sweet, now sad to mention, through dire change
    Befall'n us unforeseen, unthought-of, know
    I come no enemy, but to set free
    From out this dark and dismal house of pain,
    Both him and thee, and all the heav'nly Host
825 Of Spirits that in our just pretenses° arm'd
    Fell with us from on high: from them I go
    This uncouth errand sole, and one for all
    Myself expose, with lonely steps to tread
    Th'unfounded° deep, and through the void immense
830 To search with wand'ring quest a place foretold
    Should be, and, by concurring signs, ere now
    Created vast and round, a place of bliss
    In the Purlieus° of Heaven, and therein plac't

---

801 **conscious** inwardly guilty. 815 **lore** lesson. 825 **pretenses**
claims. 829 **unfounded** bottomless. 833 **Purlieus** outer districts.

A race of upstart Creatures, to supply
Perhaps our vacant room, though more remov'd,   835
Lest Heav'n surcharg'd° with potent multitude
Might hap to move new broils: Be this or aught
Than this more secret now design'd, I haste
To know, and this once known, shall soon return,
And bring ye to the place where Thou and Death   840
Shall dwell at ease, and up and down unseen
Wing silently the buxom° Air, embalm'd°
With odours; there ye shall be fed and fill'd
Immeasurably, all things shall be your prey."
He ceas'd, for both seemed highly pleas'd, and Death 845
Grinn'd horrible a ghastly smile, to hear
His famine should be fill'd, and blest his maw°
Destin'd to that good hour: no less rejoic'd
His mother bad, and thus bespake her Sire.
         "The key of this infernal Pit by due,   850
And by command of Heav'n's all-powerful King
I keep, by him forbidden to unlock
These Adamantine Gates; against all force
Death ready stands to interpose his dart,
Fearless to be o'ermatcht by living might.   855
But what owe I to his commands above
Who hates me, and hath hither thrust me down
Into this gloom of Tartarus profound,
To sit in hateful Office° here confin'd,
Inhabitant of Heav'n, and heav'nly-born,   860
Here in perpetual agony and pain,
With terrors and with clamours compast round
Of mine own brood, that on my bowels feed:
Thou art my Father, thou my Author, thou
My being gav'st me; whom should I obey   865
But thee, whom follow? thou wilt bring me soon
To that new world of light and bliss, among
The Gods who live at ease, where I shall Reign
At thy right hand voluptuous, as beseems
Thy daughter and thy darling, without end."   870
         Thus saying, from her side the fatal Key,
Sad instrument of all our woe, she took;

836 **surcharg'd** crowded. 842 **buxom** yielding. 842 **embalm'd** balmy,
but with the funeral associations appropriate to Death. 847 **maw** stomach. 859 **Office** duty.

And towards the Gate rolling her bestial train,
Forthwith the huge Portcullis high updrew,
875 Which but herself not all the Stygian powers
Could once have mov'd; then in the key-hole turns
Th'intrícate wards, and every Bolt and Bar
Of massy Iron or solid Rock with ease
Unfast'ns: on a sudden op'n fly
880 With impetuous recoil and jarring sound
Th'infernal doors, and on their hinges grate
Harsh Thunder, that the lowest bottom shook
Of Erebus.° She op'n'd, but to shut
Excell'd her power; the Gates wide op'n stood;
885 That with extended wings° a Banner'd Host
Under spread Ensigns marching might pass through
With Horse and Chariots rankt in loose array;
So wide they stood, and like a Furnace mouth
Cast forth redounding° smoke and ruddy flame.
890 Before their eyes in sudden view appear
The secrets of the hoary deep, a dark
Illimitable Ocean without bound,
Without dimension, where length, breadth, and heighth,
And time and place are lost; where eldest Night
895 And Chaos, Ancestors of Nature, hold
Eternal Anarchy, amidst the noise
Of endless wars, and by confusion stand.
For hot, cold, moist, and dry, four Champions fierce
Strive here for Mast'ry, and to Battle bring
900 Their embryon° Atoms; they around the flag
Of each his faction, in their several Clans,
Light-arm'd or heavy, sharp, smooth, swift or slow,
Swarm populous, unnumber'd as the Sands
Of Barca or Cyrene's torrid soil,°
905 Levied to side with warring Winds, and poise°
Their lighter wings. To whom these most adhere,
He rules a moment; Chaos Umpire sits,
And by decision more embroils the fray
By which he Reigns: next him high Arbiter
910 Chance governs all. Into this wild Abyss,
The Womb of nature and perhaps her Grave,

883 **Erebus** Hell.   885 **wings** flanking formations.   889 **redounding** overflowing.   900 **embryon** as yet unborn.   904 **torrid soil** In North Africa.   905 **poise** lend weight to.

Of neither Sea, nor Shore, nor Air, nor Fire,
But all these in their pregnant causes mixt
Confus'dly, and which thus must ever fight,
Unless th'Almighty Maker them ordain   *915*
His dark materials to create more Worlds,
Into this wild Abyss the wary fiend
Stood on the brink of Hell and look'd a while,
Pondering his Voyage; for no narrow frith°
He had to cross. Nor was his ear less peal'd   *920*
With noises loud and ruinous (to compare
Great things with small) than when Bellona° storms,
With all her battering Engines bent to raze
Some Capital City, or less than if this frame
Of Heav'n were falling, and these Elements   *925*
In mutiny had from her Axle torn
The steadfast Earth. At last his Sail-broad Vans°
He spreads for flight, and in the surging smoke
Uplifted spurns the ground, thence many a League
As in a cloudy Chair ascending rides   *930*
Audacious, but that seat soon failing, meets
A vast vacuity: all unawares
Flutt'ring his pennons vain plumb-down he drops
Ten thousand fathom deep, and to this hour
Down had been falling, had not by ill chance   *935*
The strong rebuff of some tumultuous cloud
Instínct° with Fire and Nitre hurried him
As many miles aloft: that fury stay'd,
Quencht in a Boggy Syrtis,° neither Sea,
Nor good dry Land: nigh founder'd on he fares,   *940*
Treading the crude consistence, half on foot,
Half flying; behooves him now both Oar and Sail.
As when a Gryphon° through the Wilderness
With winged course o'er Hill or moory° Dale,
Pursues the Arimaspian,° who by stealth   *945*
Had from his wakeful custody purloin'd
The guarded Gold: So eagerly the fiend
O'er bog or steep, through strait, rough, dense, or
    rare,

919 **frith** estuary.   922 **Bellona** goddess of war.   927 **Vans** wings.   937
Instínct charged.   939 **Syrtis** North African quicksand.   943 **Gryphon** a
mythical monster.   944 **moory** marshy.   945 **Arimaspian** member of a
European tribe.

With head, hands, wings, or feet pursues his way,
950 And swims or sinks, or wades, or creeps, or flies:
At length a universal hubbub wild
Of stunning sounds and voices all confus'd
Borne through the hollow dark assaults his ear
With loudest vehemence: thither he plies,
955 Undaunted to meet there whatever power
Or Spirit of the nethermost Abyss
Might in that noise reside, of whom to ask
Which way the nearest coast of darkness lies
Bordering on light; when straight behold the Throne
960 Of Chaos, and his dark Pavilion spread
Wide on the wasteful Deep; with him Enthron'd
Sat Sable-vested Night, eldest of things,
The consort of his Reign; and by them stood
Orcus and Ades, and the dreaded name
965 Of Demogorgon;° Rumour next and Chance,
And Tumult and Confusion all embroil'd,
And Discord with a thousand various mouths.
              T'whom Satan turning boldly, thus. "Ye
              Powers
And Spirits of this nethermost Abyss,
970 Chaos and ancient Night, I come no spy,
With purpose to explore or to disturb
The secrets of your Realm, but by constraint
Wand'ring this darksome desert, as my way
Lies through your spacious Empire up to light,
975 Alone, and without guide, half lost, I seek
What readiest path leads where your gloomy bounds
Confine with° Heav'n; or if some other place
From your Dominion won, th'Ethereal King
Possesses lately, thither to arrive
980 I travel this profound, direct my course;
Directed, no mean recompense it brings
To your behoof,° if I that Region lost,
All usurpation thence expell'd, reduce
To her original darkness and your sway
985 (Which is my present journey) and once more
Erect the Standard there of ancient Night;

964–65 Various names for the gods of Hell.   977 **Confine with** meet the
confines of.   982 **behoof** advantage.

Yours be th'advantage all, mine the revenge."
       Thus Satan; and him thus the Anarch° old
With falt'ring speech and visage incompos'd°
Answer'd. "I know thee, stranger, who thou art,   *990*
That mighty leading Angel, who of late
Made head against Heav'n's King, though overthrown.
I saw and heard, for such a numerous host
Fled not in silence through the frighted deep
With ruin upon ruin, rout on rout,   *995*
Confusion worse confounded; and Heav'n Gates
Pour'd out by millions her victorious Bands
Pursuing. I upon my Frontiers here
Keep residence; if all I can will serve,
That little which is left so to defend   *1000*
Encroacht on still through our intestine° broils
Weak'ning the Scepter of old Night: first Hell
Your dungeon stretching far and wide beneath;
Now lately Heaven and Earth, another World
Hung o'er my Realm, link'd in a golden Chain   *1005*
To that side Heav'n from whence your Legions fell:
If that way be your walk, you have not far;
So much the nearer danger; go and speed;°
Havoc and spoil and ruin are my gain."
       He ceas'd; and Satan stayed not to reply,   *1010*
But glad that now his Sea should find a shore,
With fresh alacrity and force renew'd
Springs upward like a Pyramid° of fire
Into the wild expanse, and through the shock
Of fighting Elements, on all sides round   *1015*
Environ'd wins his way; harder beset
And more endanger'd, than when Argo° pass'd
Through Bosporus betwixt the justling Rocks:
Or when Ulysses on the Larboard° shunn'd
Charybdis,° and by th'other whirlpool steer'd.   *1020*
So he with difficulty and labour hard
Mov'd on, with difficulty and labour hee;

---

988 **Anarch** ruler of anarchy—which yet has no ruler. 989 **incompos'd**
in discomposure and here applied to Chaos. 1001 **intestine** internal. 1008 **speed** hurry and succeed. 1013 **Pyramid** The etymology is
uncertain; it was held to be connected with "pyre," from the Greek for
fire. 1017 **Argo** the ship of Jason and the Argonauts, seeking the
Golden Fleece. 1019 **Larboard** left. 1020 **Charybdis** the whirlpool opposite the rock of Scylla in the Sicilian straits.

But hee once past, soon after when man fell,
Strange alteration! Sin and Death amain
1025 Following his track, such was the will of Heav'n,
Pav'd after him a broad and beat'n way
Over the dark Abyss, whose boiling Gulf
Tamely endur'd a Bridge of wondrous length
From Hell continu'd reaching th'utmost Orb
1030 Of this frail World; by which the Spirits perverse
With easy intercourse pass to and fro
To tempt or punish mortals, except whom
God and good Angels guard by special grace.
But now at last the sacred influence
1035 Of light appears, and from the walls of Heav'n
Shoots far into the bosom of dim Night
A glimmering dawn; here Nature first begins
Her farthest verge, and Chaos to retire
As from her Outmost works a brok'n foe
1040 With tumult less and with less hostile din,
That Satan with less toil, and now with ease
Wafts on the calmer wave by dubious light
And like a weather-beaten Vessel holds°
Gladly the Port, though Shrouds and Tackle torn;
1045 Or in the emptier waste, resembling Air,
Weighs his spread wings, at leisure to behold
Far off th'Empyreal Heav'n, extended wide
In circuit, undetermin'd° square or round,
With Opal Tow'rs and Battlements adorn'd
1050 Of living° Sapphire, once his native Seat;
And fast by hanging in a golden Chain
This pendent° world, in bigness as a Star
Of smallest Magnitude close by the Moon.
Thither full fraught with mischievous revenge,
1055 Accurst, and in a cursed hour he hies.

1043 **holds** makes for. 1048 **undetermin'd** (to Satan's eye) not distinctly. 1050 **living** vivid. 1052 **pendent** hanging—but "Chain" suggests that the universe is like a beautiful jewel or "pendent," liable to be stolen.

BOOK III

THE ARGUMENT

God sitting on his Throne sees Satan flying towards this world, then newly created; shows him to the Son who sat at his right hand; foretells the success of Satan in perverting mankind; clears his own Justice and Wisdom from all imputation, having created Man free and able enough to have withstood his Tempter; yet declares his purpose of grace towards him, in regard he fell not of his own malice, as did Satan, but by him seduc't. The Son of God renders praises to his Father for the manifestation of his gracious purpose towards Man; but God again declares, that Grace cannot be extended towards Man without the satisfaction of divine Justice; Man hath offended the majesty of God by aspiring to Godhead, and therefore with all his Progeny devoted to death must die, unless someone can be found sufficient to answer for his offence, and undergo his Punishment. The Son of God freely offers himself a Ransom for Man: the Father accepts him, ordains his incarnation, pronounces his exaltation above all Names in Heaven and Earth; commands all the Angels to adore him; they obey, and hymning to their Harps in full Choir, celebrate the Father and the Son. Meanwhile Satan alights upon the bare convex of this World's outermost Orb; where wand'ring he first finds a place since call'd The Limbo of Vanity; what persons and things fly up thither; thence comes to the Gate of Heaven, describ'd ascending by stairs, and the waters above the Firmament that flow about it: His passage thence to the Orb of the Sun; he finds there Uriel the Regent of that Orb, but first changes himself into the shape of a meaner Angel; and pretending a zealous desire to behold the new Creation and Man whom God had plac't here, inquires of him the place of his habitation, and is directed; alights first on Mount Niphates.

          Hail holy light, offspring of Heav'n first-born,
Or of th'eternal Coeternal beam
May I express thee unblam'd?° since God is light,
And never but in unapproached light
5   Dwelt from Eternity, dwelt then in thee,
Bright effluence of bright essence increate.°
Or hear'st thou rather° pure Ethereal° stream,
Whose Fountain who shall tell? before the Sun,
Before the Heavens thou wert, and at the voice
10   Of God, as with a Mantle didst invest
The rising world of waters dark and deep,
Won from the void and formless infinite.
Thee I re-visit now with bolder wing,
Escap't the Stygian Pool, though long detain'd
15   In that obscure sojourn, while in my flight
Through utter° and through middle darkness° borne
With other notes than to th'Orphean° Lyre
I sung of Chaos and Eternal Night,
Taught by the heav'nly Muse to venture down
20   The dark descent, and up to reascend,
Though hard and rare: thee I revisit safe,
And feel thy sovran° vital Lamp; but thou
Revisit'st not these eyes, that roll in vain
To find thy piercing ray, and find no dawn;
25   So thick a drop serene hath quencht their Orbs,
Or dim suffusion° veil'd. Yet not the more
Cease I to wander where the Muses haunt°
Clear Spring, or shady Grove, or Sunny Hill,°
Smit with the love of sacred song; but chief
30   Thee Sion° and the flow'ry Brooks beneath
That wash thy hallow'd feet, and warbling flow,

2–3 "Or may I, without being censured, describe thee as co-eternal with
God?"   6 **increate** uncreated.   7 **hear'st thou rather** "dost thou prefer
to be called."   7 **Ethereal** airy and celestial.   16 **utter** outer.   16 **middle
darkness** of Chaos.   17 **Orphean** of Orpheus, who had visited Hell and
to whom was attributed a Hymn to Night.   22 **sovran** supreme and (literally) "from above" (from Latin *super*); it is too a medical term (notice
"vital"), e.g. "sovereign in cases where the eyelids are ulcerated,"
[1793].   25–26 **drop . . . suffusion** diseases of the eye.   26–27 "Yet my
passion for classical poetry has by no means been quenched."   28 Parnassus and Helicon.   30 **Sion** evoking the Hebrew poetry of Scripture.

Nightly I visit: nor sometimes° forget
Those other two equall'd with me in Fate,
So° were I equall'd with them in renown,
Blind Thamyris° and blind Maeonides,°   35
And Tiresias° and Phineus° Prophets old.
Then feed on thoughts, that voluntary° move°
Harmonious numbers;° as the wakeful Bird
Sings darkling, and in shadiest Covert hid
Tunes her nocturnal Note. Thus with the Year   40
Seasons return, but not to me returns
Day, or the sweet approach of Ev'n or Morn,
Or sight of vernal bloom, or Summer's Rose,
Or flocks, or herds, or human face divine;
But cloud instead, and ever-during dark   45
Surrounds me, from the cheerful ways of men
Cut off, and for the Book of knowledge fair
Presented with a Universal blank
Of Nature's works to mee expung'd and raz'd,
And wisdom at one entrance quite shut out.   50
So much the rather thou Celestial light
Shine inward, and the mind through all her powers
Irradiate, there plant eyes, all mist from thence
Purge and disperse, that I may see and tell
Of things invisible to mortal sight.   55
        Now had the Almighty Father from above,
From the pure Empyrean where he sits
High Thron'd above all heighth, bent down his eye,
His own works and their works at once to view:
About him all the Sanctities of Heaven   60
Stood thick as Stars, and from his sight° receiv'd
Beatitude past utterance; on his right
The radiant image of his Glory sat,
His only Son; On Earth he first beheld
Our two first Parents, yet the only two   65
Of mankind, in the happy Garden plac't,
Reaping immortal fruits of joy and love,

32 **sometimes** ever. 34 **So** if only. 35 **Thamyris** a Thracian poet.
35 **Maeonides** Homer. 36 **Tiresias** the blind sage of Thebes. 36 **Phineus**
king of Thrace, blinded by the gods. 37 **voluntary** freely, and with the musical suggestions of a "voluntary," chosen by the performer. 37 **move** put
forth, utter (as in VII 207), and instigate. 38 **numbers** verses, musical
measures. 61 **his sight** seeing him, the Beatific Vision.

Uninterrupted joy, unrivall'd love
In blissful solitude; he then survey'd
70 Hell and the Gulf between, and Satan there
Coasting the wall of Heav'n on this side Night
In the dun Air sublime, and ready now
To stoop° with wearied wings, and willing feet
On the bare outside of this World,° that seem'd
75 Firm land imbosom'd without Firmament,
Uncertain which, in Ocean or in Air.
Him God beholding from his prospect high,
Wherein past, present, future he beholds,
Thus to his only Son foreseeing spake.
80   "Only-begotten Son, seest thou what rage
Transports° our adversary, whom no bounds
Prescrib'd, no bars of Hell, nor all the chains
Heapt on him there, nor yet the main Abyss
Wide interrupt° can hold; so bent he seems
85 On desperate revenge, that shall redound
Upon his own rebellious head. And now
Through all restraint broke loose he wings his way
Not far off Heav'n, in the Precincts of light,
Directly towards the new created World,
90 And Man there plac't, with purpose to assay
If him by force he can destroy, or worse,
By some false guile pervert; and shall pervert;
For man will heark'n to his glozing° lies,
And easily transgress the sole Command,
95 Sole pledge of his obedience: So will fall
Hee and his faithless Progeny: whose fault?
Whose but his own? ingrate,° he had of mee
All he could have; I made him just and right,
Sufficient to have stood, though free to fall.
100 Such I created all th'Ethereal Powers
And Spirits, both them who stood and them who
    fail'd;
Freely they stood who stood, and fell who fell.
Not free, what proof could they have giv'n sincere

---

73 **stoop** descend, with "wings" suggesting the application "of a hawk or other bird of prey: to descend swiftly on its prey"; see III 431–41. 74 **World** universe. 81 **Transports** literally and metaphorically. 84 **Wide interrupt** forming a wide gulf. 93 **glozing** flattering. 97 **ingrate** ungrateful.

Of true allegiance, constant Faith or Love,
Where only what they needs must do, appear'd,   *105*
Not what they would? what praise could they receive?
What pleasure I from such obedience paid,
When Will and Reason (Reason also is choice)
Useless and vain, of freedom both despoil'd,
Made passive both, had serv'd necessity,   *110*
Not mee. They therefore as to right belong'd,
So were created, nor can justly accuse
Their maker, or their making, or their Fate;
As if Predestination over-rul'd
Their will, dispos'd by absolute Decree   *115*
Or high foreknowledge; they themselves decreed
Their own revolt, not I: if I foreknew,
Foreknowledge had no influence on their fault,
Which had no less prov'd certain unforeknown.
So without least impúlse° or shadow of Fate,   *120*
Or aught by me immutably foreseen,
They trespass, Authors to themselves in all
Both what they judge and what they choose; for so
I form'd them free, and free they must remain,
Til they enthrall themselves: I else must change   *125*
Their nature, and revoke the high Decree
Unchangeable, Eternal, which ordain'd
Their freedom, they themselves ordain'd their fall.
The first sort° by their own suggestion° fell,
Self-tempted, self-deprav'd: Man falls deceiv'd   *130*
By the other first: Man therefore shall find grace,
The other none: in Mercy and Justice both,
Through Heav'n and Earth, so shall my glory excel,
But Mercy first and last shall brightest shine."
          Thus while God spake, ambrosial fragrance
                    fill'd   *135*
All Heav'n, and in the blessed Spirits elect
Sense of new joy ineffable difus'd:
Beyond compare the Son of God was seen
Most glorious, in him all his Father shone
Substantially° express'd, and in his face   *140*
Divine compassion visibly appear'd,

---

120 **impúlse** impelling. 129 **first sort** fallen angels. 129 **suggestion**
temptation. 140 **Substantially** a theological term, as in "transubstantiation."

Love without end, and without measure Grace,
Which uttering thus he to his Father spake.
      "O Father, gracious was that word which clos'd
145 Thy sovran sentence, that Man should find grace;
For which both Heav'n and Earth shall high extol
Thy praises, with th'innumerable° sound
Of Hymns and sacred Songs, wherewith thy Throne
Encompass'd shall resound thee ever blest.
150 For should Man finally be lost, should Man
Thy creature late so lov'd, thy youngest Son
Fall circumvented° thus by fraud, though join'd
With his own folly? that be from thee far,
That far be from thee, Father, who art Judge
155 Of all things made, and judgest only right.
Or shall the Adversary thus obtain
His end, and frustrate thine, shall he fulfill
His malice, and thy goodness bring to naught,
Or proud return though to his heavier doom,
160 Yet with revenge accomplish't and to Hell
Draw after him the whole Race of mankind,
By him corrupted? or wilt though thyself
Abolish thy Creation, and unmake,
For him, what for thy glory thou hast made?
165 So should thy goodness and thy greatness both
Be question'd and blasphem'd without defence."
      To whom the great Creator thus repli'd.
"O Son, in whom my Soul hath chief delight,
Son of my bosom, Son who art alone
170 My word, my wisdom, and effectual might,°
All hast thou spok'n as my thoughts are, all
As my Eternal purpose hath decreed:
Man shall not quite be lost, but sav'd who will,
Yet not of will in him, but grace in me
175 Freely vouchsaf't; once more I will renew
His lapsed powers, though forfeit and enthrall'd
By sin to foul exorbitant desires;
Upheld by me, yet once more he shall stand

---

147 **innumerable** in 17th century English, commonly used with a singular noun   152 **circumvented** contrasted with "Encompass'd."   170 **effectual might** through whom my might takes effect, "effectual" having many theological applications, e.g. to prayers, grace.

On even ground against his mortal foe,
By me upheld, that he may know how frail   *180*
His fall'n condition is, and to me owe
All his deliv'rance, and to none but me.
Some I have chosen of peculiar grace
Elect above the rest; so is my will:
The rest shall hear me call, and oft be warn'd   *185*
Their sinful state, and to appease betimes
Th'incensed° Deity, while offer'd grace
Invites; for I will clear their senses dark,
What may suffice, and soft'n stony hearts
To pray, repent, and bring obedience due.   *190*
To prayer, repentance, and obedience due,
Though but endeavour'd with sincere intent,
Mine ear shall not be slow, mine eye not shut.
And I will place within them as a guide
My Umpire Conscience, whom if they will hear,   *195*
Light after light well us'd they shall attain,
And to the end persisting, safe arrive.
This my long sufferance and my day of grace
They who neglect and scorn, shall never taste;
But hard be hard'n'd, blind be blinded more,   *200*
That they may stumble on, and deeper fall;
And none but such from mercy I exclude.
But yet all is not done; Man disobeying,
Disloyal breaks his fealty, and sins
Against the high Supremacy of Heav'n,   *205*
Affecting° Godhead, and so losing all,
To expiate his Treason hath naught left,
But to destruction sacred and devote,°
He with his whole posterity must die,
Die hee or Justice must; unless for him   *210*
Some other able, and as willing, pay
The rigid° satisfaction,° death for death.
Say Heav'nly Powers, where shall we find such love,
Which of ye will be mortal to redeem

187 **incensed** burning with wrath; "appease" suggests the need to offer
"incense" before God, as in "the incensed altar," [1611]. The root of the
words is the same, and see XI 17–20. 206 **Affecting** aiming at. 208 **devote** doomed by a vow. 212 **rigid** strict, with deathly suggestions (see
IX 685). 212 **satisfaction** atonement, the theological term for Christ's
sacrifice.

215 Man's mortal crime, and just th'unjust to save,
    Dwells in all Heaven charity so dear?"
          He ask'd, but all the Heav'nly Choir stood
              mute,
    And silence was in Heaven: on man's behalf
    Patron° or Intercessor none appear'd,
220 Much less that durst upon his own head draw
    The deadly forfeiture, and ransom set.
    And now without redemption all mankind
    Must have been lost, adjudg'd to Death and Hell
    By doom severe, had not the Son of God,
225 In whom the fullness dwells of love divine,
    His dearest mediation thus renew'd.
          "Father, thy word is past, man shall find grace;
    And shall grace not find means, that finds her way,
    The speediest of thy winged messengers,
230 To visit all thy creatures, and to all
    Comes unprevented,° unimplor'd, unsought,
    Happy for man, so coming; he her aid
    Can never seek, once dead in sins and lost;
    Atonement for himself or offering meet,
235 Indebted and undone, hath none to bring:
    Behold mee then, mee for him, life for life
    I offer, on mee let thine anger fall;
    Account mee man; I for his sake will leave
    Thy bosom, and this glory next to thee
240 Freely put off, and for him lastly die
    Well pleas'd, on me let Death wreak all his rage;
    Under his gloomy power I shall not long
    Lie vanquisht; thou hast giv'n me to possess
    Life in myself forever, by thee I live,
245 Though now to Death I yield, and am his due
    All that of me can die, yet that debt paid,
    Thou wilt not leave me in the loathsome grave
    His prey, nor suffer my unspotted Soul
    Forever with corruption there to dwell;
250 But I shall rise Victorious, and subdue
    My Vanquisher, spoil'd of his vaunted spoil;
    Death his death's wound shall then receive, and stoop

---

219 **Patron** defender.   231 **unprevented** unforestalled, before being even
asked for.

Inglorious, of his mortal sting disarm'd.
I through the ample Air in Triumph high
Shall lead Hell Captive maugre° Hell, and show   255
The powers of darkness bound. Thou at the sight
Pleas'd, out of Heaven shalt look down and smile,
While by thee rais'd I ruin all my Foes,
Death last, and with his Carcass glut the Grave:
Then with the multitude of my redeem'd   260
Shall enter Heaven long absent, and return,
Father, to see thy face, wherein no cloud
Of anger shall remain, but peace assur'd,
And reconcilement; wrath shall be no more
Thenceforth, but in thy presence Joy entire."   265
          His words here ended, but his meek aspéct
Silent yet spake, and breath'd immortal love
To mortal men, above which only shone
Filial obedience: as a sacrifice
Glad to be offer'd, he attends the will   270
Of his great Father. Admiration seiz'd
All Heav'n, what this might mean, and whither tend
Wond'ring; but soon th'Almighty thus repli'd:
          "O thou in Heav'n and Earth the only peace
Found out for mankind under wrath, O thou   275
My sole complacence!° well thou know'st how dear
To me are all my works, nor Man the least
Though last created, that for him I spare
Thee from my bosom and right hand, to save,
By losing thee a while, the whole Race lost.   280
Thou therefore whom thou only canst redeem,
Their Nature° also to thy Nature join;
And be thyself Man among men on Earth,
Made flesh, when time shall be, of Virgin seed,
By wondrous birth: Be thou in Adam's room   285
The Head of all mankind, though Adam's Son.
As in him perish all men, so in thee
As from a second root shall be restor'd,
As many as are restor'd, without thee none.
His crime makes guilty all his Sons, thy merit   290

---

255 **maugre** despite. 276 **complacence** source of delight. 281–82
whom . . . their Nature "the nature of them whom only thou canst
redeem."

Imputed° shall absolve them who renounce
Their own both righteous and unrighteous deeds,
And live in thee transplanted,° and from thee
Receive new life. So Man, as is most just,
295 Shall satisfy for Man, be judg'd and die,
And dying rise, and rising with him raise
His Brethren, ransom'd with his own dear life.
So Heav'nly love shall outdo Hellish hate,
Giving° to death, and dying to redeem,
300 So dearly to redeem what Hellish hate,
So easily destroy'd, and still destroys
In those who, when they may, accept not grace.
Nor shalt thou by descending to assume
Man's Nature, less'n or degrade thine own.
305 Because thou hast, though Thron'd in highest bliss
Equal to God, and equally enjoying
Godlike fruition,° quitted all to save
A World from utter loss, and hast been found
By Merit more than Birthright Son of God,
310 Found worthiest to be so by being Good,
Far more than Great or High; because in thee
Love hath abounded more than Glory abounds,
Therefore thy Humiliation shall exalt
With thee thy Manhood also to this Throne;
315 Here shalt thou sit incarnate, here shalt Reign
Both God and Man, Son both of God and Man,
Anointed universal King; all Power
I give thee, reign forever, and assume
Thy Merits;° under thee as Head Supreme
320 Thrones, Princedoms, Powers, Dominions I reduce:
All knees to thee shall bow, of them that bide
In Heaven, or Earth, or under Earth in Hell;
When thou attended gloriously from Heav'n
Shalt in the Sky appear, and from thee send
325 The summoning Arch-Angels to proclaim
Thy dread Tribunal: forthwith from all Winds

291 **Imputed** the doctrine of imputed righteousness.   293 **transplanted**
suggesting a new and better kind of growth; see "root" above.   299 **Giving** yielding.   307 **fruition** pleasure is possession.   318–19 **assume Thy
Merits** take up that to which your merits entitle you, "merits" having the
specific theological sense "good works entitled to reward from God."

The living, and forthwith the cited° dead
Of all past Ages to the general Doom
Shall hast'n, such a peal shall rouse their sleep.
Then all thy Saints assembl'd, thou shalt judge   330
Bad men and Angels, they arraign'd° shall sink
Beneath thy Sentence; Hell, her numbers full,
Thenceforth shall be forever shut. Meanwhile
The World shall burn, and from her ashes spring
New Heav'n and Earth, wherein the just shall dwell,   335
And after all their tribulations long
See golden days, fruitful of golden deeds,
With Joy and Love triúmphing, and fair Truth.
Then thou thy regal Scepter shaft lay by,
For regal Scepter then no more shall need,   340
God shall be All in All. But all ye Gods,
Adore him, who to compass all this dies,
Adore the Son, and honour him as mee."
          No sooner had th'Almighty ceas't, but all
The multitude of Angels with a shout   345
Loud as from numbers without number, sweet
As from blest voices, uttering joy, Heav'n rung
With Jubilee,° and loud Hosannas° fill'd
Th'eternal Regions: lowly reverent
Towards either Throne they bow, and to the ground   350
With solemn adoration down they cast
Their Crowns inwove with Amaranth and Gold,
Immortal Amaranth, a Flow'r which once
In Paradise, fast by the Tree of Life
Began to bloom, but soon for man's offence   355
To Heav'n remov'd where first it grew, there grows,
And flow'rs aloft shading the Fount of Life,
And where the river of Bliss through midst of Heav'n
Rolls o'er Elysian Flow'rs her Amber stream;
With these that never fade the Spirits Elect   360
Bind their resplendent locks inwreath'd with beams,
Now in loose Garlands thick thrown off, the bright
Pavement that like a Sea of Jasper shone
Impurpl'd with Celestial Roses smil'd.
Then Crown'd again their gold'n Harps they took,   365

327 **cited** summoned (legal).   331 **arraign'd** accused.   348 **Jubilee** jubila-
tion.   348 **Hosannas** cries of praise, the literal meaning "Save now" or
"Save, pray" being appropriate to Christ's triumph.

Harps ever tun'd, that glittering by their side
Like Quivers hung, and with Preamble sweet
Of charming symphony they introduce
Their sacred Song, and waken raptures high;
370 No voice exempt, no voice but well could join
Melodious part, such concord is in Heav'n.
        Thee Father first they sung Omnipotent,
Immutable, Immortal, Infinite,
Eternal King; thee Author of all being,
375 Fountain of Light, thyself invisible
Amidst the glorious brightness where thou sitt'st
Thron'd inaccessible, but° when thou shad'st
The full blaze of thy beams, and through a cloud
Drawn round about thee like a radiant Shrine,
380 Dark with excessive bright thy skirts° appear,
Yet dazzle Heav'n, that brightest Seraphim
Approach not, but with both wings veil their eyes.
Thee next they sang of all Creation first,
Begotten Son, Divine Similitude,
385 In whose conspicuous count'nance, without cloud
Made visible, th'Almighty Father shines,
Whom else no Creature can behold; on thee
Imprest the effulgence° of his Glory abides,
Transfus'd on thee his ample Spirit rests.
390 Hee Heav'n of Heavens and all the Powers therein
By thee created, and by thee threw down
Th'aspiring Dominations: thou that day
Thy Father's dreadful Thunder didst not spare,
Nor stop thy flaming Chariot-wheels, that shook
395 Heav'n's everlasting Frame, while o'er the necks
Thou drov'st of warring Angels disarray'd.
Back from pursuit thy Powers with loud acclaim
Thee only extoll'd, Son of thy Father's might,
To execute fierce vengeance on his foes,
400 Not so on Man; him through their malice fall'n,
Father of Mercy and Grace, thou didst not doom
So strictly, but much more to pity incline:
No sooner did thy dear and only Son
Perceive thee purpos'd not to doom frail Man
405 So strictly, but much more to pity inclin'd,

377 **but** except.   380 **skirts** robes.   388 **effulgence** gleaming forth.

He to appease thy wrath, and end the strife
Of Mercy and Justice in thy face discern'd,
Regardless of the Bliss wherein hee sat
Second to thee, offer'd himself to die
For man's offence. O unexampl'd love,   410
Love nowhere to be found less than Divine!
Hail Son of God, Saviour of Men, thy Name
Shall be the copious matter of my Song
Henceforth, and never shall my Harp thy praise
Forget, nor from thy Father's praise disjoin.   415
          Thus they in Heav'n, above the starry Sphere,
Their happy hours in joy and hymning spent.
Meanwhile upon the firm opacous° Globe
Of this round World,° whose first convex° divides
The luminous inferior Orbs,° enclos'd   420
From Chaos and th'inroad of Darkness old,
Satan alighted walks: a Globe far off
It seem'd, now seems a boundless Continent
Dark, waste, and wild, under the frown of Night
Starless expos'd, and ever-threat'ning storms   425
Of Chaos blust'ring round, inclement sky;
Save on that side which from the wall of Heav'n
Though distant far some small reflection gains
Of glimmering air less vext with tempest loud:
Here walk'd the Fiend at large in spacious field.   430
As when a Vulture on Imaus° bred,
Whose snowy ridge the roving Tartar bounds,°
Dislodging° from a Region scarce of prey
To gorge the flesh of Lambs or yeanling° Kids
On Hills where Flocks are fed, flies toward the Springs 435
Of Ganges or Hydaspes, Indian streams;
But in his way 'lights on the barren plains
Of Sericana, where Chineses drive
With Sails and Wind their cany Waggons light:
So on this windy Sea of Land, the Fiend   440
Walk'd up and down alone bent on his prey,

---

418 **opacous** dark, opaque.   419 **World** universe.   419 **first convex** outer
shell.   420 **inferior Orbs** the "spheres" within.   431 **Imaus** mountains of
central Asia.   432 **Tartar bounds** "confines the Tartar," the cruel race of
central Asia (also suggesting Hell, Tartarus, where the vulture Satan
began his journey; see II 858 and X 431).   433 **Dislodging** a hunting
term.   434 **yeanling** newborn.

Alone, for other Creature in this place
Living or liveless to be found was none,
None yet, but store° hereafter from the earth
445 Up hither like Aërial vapours flew
Of all things transitory and vain, when Sin
With vanity had fill'd the works of men:
Both all things vain, and all who in vain things
Built their fond hopes of Glory or lasting fame,
450 Or happiness in this or th'other life;
All who have their reward on Earth, the fruits
Of painful° Superstition and blind Zeal,
Naught seeking but the praise of men, here find
Fit retribution, empty as their deeds;
455 All th'unaccomplisht works of Nature's hand,
Abortive,° monstrous, or unkindly° mixt,
Dissolv'd on earth, fleet hither, and in vain,°
Till final dissolution, wander here,
Not in the neighbouring Moon, as some have dream'd;
460 Those argent Fields more likely habitants,
Translated° Saints, or middle Spirits hold
Betwixt th'Angelical and Human kind:
Hither of ill-join'd Sons and Daughters born
First from the ancient World those Giants came
465 With many a vain exploit, though then renown'd:
The builders next of Babel on the Plain
Of Sennaär, and still with vain design°
New Babels, had they wherewithal, would build:
Others came single; hee who to be deem'd
470 A God, leap'd fondly° into Etna flames,
Empedocles, and hee who to enjoy
Plato's Elysium, leap'd into the Sea,
Cleombrotus, and many more too long,
Embryos and Idiots, Eremites° and Friars
475 White, Black and Grey, with all their trumpery.°
Here Pilgrims roam, that stray'd so far to seek
In Golgotha° him dead, who lives in Heav'n;

444 **store** plenty. 452 **painful** including laborious. 456 **Abortive** untimely born. 456 **unkindly** unnaturally. 457 **in vain** idly. 461 **Translated** like Enoch and Elijah, "translated" to Heaven by miracle. 467 **design** sardonically both intention and architectural plan. 470 **fondly** foolishly. 474 **Eremites** hermits. 475 **trumpery** deceitful trash. 477 **Golgotha** where Christ was crucified.

And they who to be sure of Paradise
Dying put on the weeds° of Dominic,
Or in Franciscan think to pass disguis'd;   480
They pass the Planets seven, and pass the fixt,°
And that Crystálline Sphere whose balance weighs
The Trepidation talkt,° and that first mov'd;°
And now Saint Peter at Heav'n's Wicket° seems
To wait them with his Keys, and now at foot   485
Of Heav'n's ascent they lift their Feet, when lo
A violent cross-wind from either Coast
Blows them transverse ten thousand Leagues awry
Into the devious° Air; then might ye see
Cowls, Hoods and Habits with their wearers tost   490
And flutter'd into Rags, then Relics, Beads,°
Indulgences, Dispenses,° Pardons, Bulls,°
The sport of Winds: all these upwhirl'd aloft
Fly o'er the backside° of the World far off
Into a Limbo° large and broad, since call'd   495
The Paradise of Fools, to few unknown
Long after, now unpeopl'd, and untrod;
All this dark Globe the Fiend found as he pass'd,
And long he wander'd, till at last a gleam
Of dawning light turn'd thitherward in haste   500
His travell'd° steps; far distant hee descries
Ascending by degrees magnificent
Up to the wall of Heaven a Structure high,
At top whereof, but far more rich appear'd
The work as of a Kingly Palace Gate   505
With Frontispiece° of Diamond and Gold
Embellisht, thick with sparkling orient Gems
The Portal shone, inimitable on Earth
By Model, or by shading Pencil drawn.
The Stairs were such as whereon Jacob saw   510
Angels ascending and descending, bands
Of Guardians bright, when he from Esau fled

479 **weeds** robes.   481 **the fixt** the sphere of the stars.   482–83 **whose . . . talkt** "which is responsible for the swaying which is spoken of."   483 **first mov'd** the tenth sphere, the Primum Mobile.   484 **Wicket** gate.   489 **devious** both distant and causing to stray.   491 **Beads** of the rosary.   492 **Dispenses** dispensations.   492 **Bulls** papal edicts.   494 **backside** contemptuous after "Winds," recalling the landscape of Hell.   495 **Limbo** region on the border of Hell.   501 **travell'd** including travailed, weary.   506 **Frontispiece** panel or pediment.

To Padan-Aram in the field of Luz,
Dreaming by night under the open Sky,
515 And waking cri'd, "This is the Gate of Heav'n."
Each Stair mysteriously° was meant, nor stood
There always, but drawn up to Heav'n sometimes
Viewless,° and underneath a bright Sea flow'd
Of Jasper, or of liquid Pearl, whereon
520 Who after came from Earth, sailing arriv'd,
Wafted by Angels, or flew o'er the Lake
Rapt in a Chariot drawn by fiery Steeds.
The Stairs were then let down, whether to dare
The Fiend by easy ascent, or aggravate°
525 His sad exclusion from the doors of Bliss.
Direct against which op'n'd from beneath,
Just o'er the blissful seat of Paradise,
A passage down to th'Earth, a passage wide,
Wider by far than that of after-times
530 Over Mount Sion, and, though that were large,
Over the Promis'd Land to God so dear,
By which, to visit oft those happy Tribes,
On high behests his Angels to and fro
Pass'd frequent, and° his eye with choice regard°
535 From Paneas the fount of Jordan's flood
To Beërsaba, where the Holy Land
Borders on Egypt and the Arabian shore;
So wide the op'ning seem'd, where bounds were set
To darkness, such as bound the Ocean wave.
540 Satan from hence now on the lower stair
That scal'd by steps of Gold to Heav'n Gate
Looks down with wonder at the sudden view
Of all this World at once. As when a Scout°
Through dark and desert ways with peril gone
545 All night; at last by break of cheerful dawn
Obtains° the brow of some high-climbing Hill,
Which to his eye discovers° unaware
The goodly prospect of some foreign land

---

516 **mysteriously** allegorically, as in the Book of Revelation. 518 **Viewless** not in sight. 524 **aggravate** make more burdensome. 534 **and** and so did. 534 **choice regard** careful scrutiny, suggesting too God's "regard" (esteem) for his Chosen People (see the same phrase, I 653). 543 **Scout** The mIitary hint is ominous; see VI 529. 546 **Obtains** gains. 547 **discovers** reveals.

First-seen, or some renown'd Metropolis
With glistering Spires and Pinnacles adorn'd,   550
Which now the Rising Sun gilds with his beams.
Such wonder seiz'd, though after Heaven seen,
The Spirit malign, but much more envy seiz'd
At sight of all this World beheld so fair.
Round he surveys, and well might, where he stood   555
So high above the circling Canopy
Of Night's extended shade; from Eastern Point
Of Libra to the fleecy Star° that bears
Andromeda° far off Atlantic Seas
Beyond th'Horizon; then from Pole to Pole   560
He views in breadth, and without longer pause
Down right into the World's first Region° throws
His flight precipitant,° and winds with ease
Through the pure marble° Air his oblique way
Amongst innumerable Stars, that shone   565
Stars distant, but nigh-hand seem'd other Worlds,
Or other Worlds they seem'd, or happy Isles,
Like those Hesperian Gardens° fam'd of old,
Fortunate Fields, and Groves and flow'ry Vales,
Thrice happy Isles, but who dwelt happy there   570
He stay'd not to inquire: above them all
The golden Sun in splendour likest Heaven
Allur'd his eye: Thither his course he bends
Through the calm Firmament; but up or down
By center, or eccentric, hard to tell,   575
Or Longitude, where the great Luminary°
Aloof° the vulgar° Constellations thick,
That from his Lordly eye keep distance due,
Dispenses Light from far; they as they move
Their Starry dance in numbers° that compute   580
Days, months, and years, towards his all-cheering
    Lamp

558 **Libra . . . Star** the Scales and the Ram.   559 **Andromeda** a northern
constellation.   562 **first Region** of the air.   563 **precipitant** headlong and
speedy.   564 **marble** lucid.   568 **Hesperian Gardens** a Paradise, yet its
apples were stolen.   574–76 Not choosing between Copernicus's theory
(sun-centered) and Ptolemy's (earth-centered).   576 **Luminary** source of
light, including the sense of a person (notice "Lordly")—the poet Skelton
called God a luminary.   577 **Aloof** away from.   577 **vulgar** The stars
form constellations just as the common people form a crowd, Latin *vul-
gus*.   580 **numbers** musical measures.

Turn swift their various motions, or are turn'd
By his Magnetic beam, that gently warms
The Universe, and to each inward part
585 With gentle penetration, though unseen,
Shoots invisible virtue even to the deep:
So wondrously was set his Station bright.
There lands the Fiend, a spot like which perhaps
Astronomer in the Sun's lucent Orb
590 Through his glaz'd Optic Tube yet never saw.
The place he found beyond expression bright,
Compar'd with aught on Earth, Metal or Stone;
Not all parts like, but all alike inform'd°
With radiant light, as glowing Iron with fire;
595 If metal, part seem'd Gold, part Silver clear;
If stone, Carbuncle most or Chrysolite,
Ruby or Topaz, to the Twelve that shone
In Aaron's Breastplate, and a stone besides
Imagin'd rather oft than elsewhere seen,
600 That stone,° or like to that which here below
Philosophers in vain so long have sought,
In vain, though by their powerful Art they bind
Volatile Hermes,° and call up unbound
In various shapes old Proteus° from the Sea,
605 Drain'd through a Limbec° to his Native form.
What wonder then if fields and regions here°
Breathe forth Elixir pure, and Rivers run
Potable° Gold, when with one virtuous° touch
Th'Arch-chemic° Sun so far from us remote
610 Produces with Terrestrial Humour mixt°
Here in the dark so many precious things
Of colour glorious and effect so rare?
Here matter new to gaze the Devil met
Undazzl'd, far and wide his eye commands,
615 For sight no obstacle found here, nor shade,

---

593 **inform'd** imbued. 600 **stone** The "philosopher's stone" which would turn base metals to gold. 602–03 **bind . . . Hermes** use mercury in their experiments, it tending to evaporate. 604 **Proteus** sea god who could continually change his shape, much as substances do in experiments. 605 **Limbec** a still, or glass alembic. 606 **here** in the sun. 608 **Potable** drinkable; such a preparation from gold was used as a medicine, and is here assimilated to the magical elixir. 608 **virtuous** powerful, energizing. 609 **Arch-chemic** greatest alchemist of all. 610 **with . . . mixt** even though mixed with the earth's damp.

But all Sunshine, as when his Beams at Noon
Culminate from th'Equator,° as they now
Shot upward still direct, whence no way round
Shadow from body opaque can fall, and the Air,
Nowhere so clear, sharp'n'd his visual ray   620
To objects distant far, whereby he soon
Saw within ken a glorious Angel stand,
The same whom John saw also in the Sun:
His back was turn'd, but not his brightness hid;
Of beaming sunny Rays, a golden tiar°   625
Circl'd his Head, nor less his Locks behind
Illustrious° on his Shoulders fledge° with wings
Lay waving round; on some great charge employ'd
Hee seem'd, or fixt in cogitation deep.
Glad was the Spirit impure as now in hope   630
To find who might direct his wand'ring flight
To Paradise the happy seat of Man,
His journey's end and our beginning woe.
But first he casts° to change his proper shape,
Which else might work him danger or delay: 635
And now a stripling Cherub he appears,
Not of the prime,° yet such as in his face
Youth smil'd Celestial, and to every Limb
Suitable grace diffus'd, so well he feign'd;
Under a Coronet his flowing hair   640
In curls on either cheek play'd, wings he wore
Of many a colour'd plume sprinkl'd with Gold,
His habit fit for speed succinct,° and held
Before his decent° steps a Silver wand.
He drew not nigh unheard, the Angel bright,   645
Ere he drew nigh, his radiant visage turn'd,
Admonisht by his ear, and straight was known
Th'Arch-Angel Uriel, one of the sev'n
Who in God's presence, nearest to his Throne
Stand ready at command, and are his Eyes   650
That run through all the Heav'ns, or down to th'Earth
Bear his swift errands over moist and dry,

616–17 **as . . . Equator** the shadowless counterpart of the sun's "culmination," high noon at the equator.   625 **tiar** crown.   627 **Illustrious** with luster.   627 **fledge** feathered.   634 **casts** both "cunningly contrives," and "throws off (clothes, appearance)."   637 **prime** mature youth (?).   643 **succinct** close-fitting.   644 **decent** seemly.

O'er Sea and Land: him Satan thus accosts.
   "Uriel, for thou of those sev'n Spirits that stand
655 In sight of God's high Throne, gloriously bright,
The first art wont his great authentic° will
Interpreter through highest Heav'n to bring,
Where all his Sons thy Embassy attend;
And here art likeliest by supreme decree
660 Like honour to obtain, and as his Eye
To visit oft this new Creation round;
Unspeakable desire to see, and know
All these his wondrous works, but chiefly Man,
His chief delight and favour, him for whom
665 All these his works so wondrous he ordain'd,
Hath brought me from the Choirs of Cherubim
Alone thus wand'ring. Brightest Seraph tell
In which of all these shining Orbs hath Man
His fixed seat, or fixed seat hath none,
670 But all these shining Orbs his choice to dwell;
That I may find him, and with secret gaze,
Or open admiration him behold
On whom the great Creator hath bestow'd
Worlds, and on whom hath all these graces pour'd;
675 That both in him and all things, as is meet,
The Universal Maker we may praise;
Who justly hath driv'n out his Rebel Foes
To deepest Hell, and to repair that loss
Created this new happy Race of Men
680 To serve him better: wise are all his ways."
      So spake the false dissembler unperceiv'd;
For neither Man nor Angel can discern
Hypocrisy, the only evil that walks
Invisible, except to God alone,
685 By his permissive will, through Heav'n and Earth:
And oft though wisdom wake, suspicion sleeps
At wisdom's Gate, and to simplicity
Resigns her charge, while goodness thinks no ill
Where no ill seems: Which now for once beguil'd
690 Uriel, though Regent of the Sun, and held
The sharpest-sighted Spirit of all in Heav'n;
Who to the fraudulent Impostor foul

656 **authentic** of firsthand authority.

In his uprightness answer thus return'd.
"Fair Angel, thy desire which tends° to know
The works of God, thereby to glorify   695
The great Work-Master, leads to no excess
That reaches blame, but rather merits praise
The more it seems excess, that led thee hither
From thy Empyreal Mansion thus alone,
To witness with thine eyes what some perhaps   700
Contented with report hear only in Heav'n:
For wonderful indeed are all his works,
Pleasant to know, and worthiest to be all
Had in remembrance always with delight;
But what created mind can comprehend   705
Their number, or the wisdom infinite
That brought them forth, but hid their causes deep.
I saw when at his Word the formless Mass,
This world's material mould, came to a heap:
Confusion heard his voice, and wild uproar   710
Stood rul'd, stood vast infinitude confin'd;
Till at his second bidding darkness fled,
Light shone, and order from disorder sprung:
Swift to their several Quarters hasted then
The cumbrous° Elements, Earth, Flood, Air, Fire,   715
And this Ethereal quíntessence of Heav'n
Flew upward, spirited° with various forms,
That roll'd orbicular,° and turn'd to Stars
Numberless, as thou seest, and how they move;
Each had his place appointed, each his course,   720
The rest in circuit walls this Universe.
Look downward on that Globe whose hither side
With light from hence, though but reflected, shines;
That place is Earth the seat of Man, that light
His day, which else as th'other Hemisphere   725
Night would invade, but there the neighbouring Moon
(So call that opposite fair Star) her aid
Timely interposes, and her monthly round
Still ending, still renewing, through mid-Heav'n,

---

694 **tends** is drawn.   715 **cumbrous** in comparison with the heavenly ether
(like light), the "quíntessence," fifth essence, of which the heavenly bodies
were composed.   717 **spirited** animated.   718 **orbicular** with circular
motion.

730 With borrow'd light her countenance triform°
    Hence fills and empties to enlighten the Earth,
    And in her pale dominion checks° the night.
    That spot to which I point is Paradise,
    Adam's abode, those lofty shades his Bow'r.
735 Thy way thou canst not miss, me mine requires."
         Thus said, he turn'd, and Satan bowing low,
    As to superior Spirits is wont in Heav'n,
    Where honour due and reverence none neglects,
    Took leave, and toward the coast of Earth beneath,
740 Down from th'Ecliptic,° sped° with hop'd success,
    Throws his steep flight in many an Airy wheel,
    Nor stay'd, till on Niphates'° top he 'lights.

730 **triform** having three forms, crescent, full, and waning (and suggesting
the three goddesses of the moon).   732 **checks** both "holds in check,
curbs," and "chequers, variegates with its rays" as in Robert Greene:
"checkt the night with the golden rays," (1590, O.E.D.).   740 **Ecliptic**
the apparent orbit of the sun around the earth.   740 **sped** spurred on,
with a suggestion of "prospered" ("hop'd success").   742 **Niphates**
mountain of Armenia.

BOOK IV

THE ARGUMENT

Satan now in prospect of Eden, and nigh the place where he must now attempt the bold enterprise which he undertook alone against God and Man, falls into many doubts with himself, and many passions, fear, envy, and despair; but at length confirms himself in evil, journeys on to Paradise, whose outward prospect and situation is described, overleaps the bounds, sits in the shape of a Cormorant on the Tree of Life, as highest in the Garden to look about him. The Garden describ'd; Satan's first sight of Adam and Eve; his wonder at their excellent form and happy state, but with resolution to work their fall; overhears their discourse, thence gathers that the Tree of Knowledge was forbidden them to eat of, under penalty of death; and thereon intends to found his temptation, by seducing them to transgress: then leaves them a while, to know further of their state by some other means. Meanwhile Uriel descending on a Sunbeam warns Gabriel, who had in charge the Gate of Paradise, that some evil spirit had escap'd the Deep, and past at Noon by his Sphere in the shape of a good Angel down to Paradise, discovered after by his furious gestures in the Mount. Gabriel promises to find him out ere morning. Night coming on, Adam and Eve discourse of going to their rest: their Bower describ'd; their Evening worship. Gabriel drawing forth his Bands of Night-watch to walk the round of Paradise, appoints two strong Angels to Adam's Bower, lest the evil spirit should be there doing some harm to Adam or Eve sleeping; there they find him at the ear of Eve, tempting her in a dream, and bring him, though unwilling, to Gabriel; by whom question'd, he scornfully answers, prepares resistance, but hinder'd by a Sign from Heaven, flies out of Paradise.

      O for that warning voice, which he who saw
Th'Apocalypse, heard cry in Heav'n aloud,°
Then when the Dragon, put to second rout,
Came furious down to be reveng'd on men,
5   *Woe to the inhabitants on Earth!* that now,
While time was, our first Parents had been warn'd
The coming of their secret foe, and 'scap'd
Haply so 'scap'd his mortal snare; for now
Satan, now first inflam'd with rage, came down,
10 The Tempter ere th'Accuser of mankind,
To wreak on innocent frail Man his loss
Of that first Battle, and his flight to Hell:
Yet not rejoicing in his speed, though bold,
Far off and fearless, nor with cause to boast,
15 Begins his dire attempt, which nigh the birth
Now rolling, boils in his tumultuous breast,
And like a devilish Engine back recoils
Upon himself; horror and doubt distract°
His troubl'd thoughts, and from the bottom stir
20 The Hell within him, for within him Hell
He brings, and round about him, nor from Hell
One step no more than from himself can fly
By change of place: Now conscience wakes despair
That slumber'd, wakes the bitter memory
25 Of what he was, what is, and what must be
Worse; of worse deeds worse sufferings must ensue.
Sometimes towards Eden which now in his view
Lay pleasant,° his griev'd look he fixes sad,
Sometimes towards Heav'n and the full-blazing Sun,
30 Which now sat high in his Meridian Tow'r:
Then much revolving, thus in sighs began.
      "O thou that with surpassing Glory crown'd,
Look'st° from thy sole° Dominion like the God
Of this new World; at whose sight all the Stars
35 Hide their diminisht heads; to thee I call,
But with no friendly voice, and add thy name

1–2 **O for . . . aloud** St. John, REVELATION 12:3–12. 18 **distract** draw
apart, as into madness. 28 **pleasant** Eden is from the Hebrew for "delight, pleasure." 33 **Look'st** both "seems to be" and "surveys." 33 **sole**
unique (suggesting *sol*, sun, as in "the Meridian Sol," 1609).

O Sun, to tell thee how I hate thy beams
That bring to my remembrance from what state
I fell, how glorious once above thy Sphere;°
Till Pride and worse Ambition threw me down   40
Warring in Heav'n against Heav'n's matchless King:
Ah wherefore! he deserv'd no such return
From me, whom he created what I was
In that bright eminence, and with his good
Upbraided none; nor was his service hard.   45
What could be less than to afford him praise,
The easiest recompense, and pay him thanks,
How due! yet all his good prov'd ill in me,
And wrought but malice; lifted up so high
I 'sdain'd° subjection, and thought one step higher 50
Would set me highest, and in a moment quit°
The debt immense of endless gratitude,
So burdensome, still° paying, still to owe;
Forgetful what from him I still receiv'd,
And understood not that a grateful mind   55
By owing owes not, but still pays, at once
Indebted and discharg'd; what burden then?
O had his powerful Destiny ordain'd
Me some inferior Angel, I had stood
Then happy; no unbounded hope had rais'd   60
Ambition. Yet why not? some other Power
As great might have aspir'd, and me though mean
Drawn to his part; but other Powers as great
Fell not, but stand unshak'n, from within
Or from without, to all temptations arm'd.   65
Hadst thou the same free Will and Power to stand?
Thou hadst: whom hast thou then or what to accuse,
But Heav'n's free Love dealt equally to all?
Be then his Love accurst, since love or hate,
To me alike, it deals eternal woe.   70
Nay curs'd be thou; since against his thy will
Chose freely what it now so justly rues.
Me miserable! which way shall I fly
Infinite wrath, and infinite despair?
Which way I fly is Hell; myself am Hell;   75

39 **Sphere** astronomical and hierarchical.   50 **'sdain'd** disdained.   51 **quit**
requite.   53 **still** always.

And in the lowest deep a lower deep
Still threat'ning to devour me opens wide,
To which the Hell I suffer seems a Heav'n.
O then at last relent: is there no place
80   Left for Repentance, none for Pardon left?
None left but by submission; and that word°
Disdain forbids me, and my dread of shame
Among the Spirits beneath, whom I seduc'd
With other promises and other vaunts
85   Than to submit, boasting I could subdue
Th'Omnipotent. Ay me, they little know
How dearly I abide that boast so vain,
Under what torments inwardly I groan:
While they adore me on the Throne of Hell,
90   With Diadem and Scepter high advanc't
The lower still I fall, only supreme
In misery; such joy Ambition finds.
But say I could repent and could obtain
By Act of Grace my former state; how soon
95   Would heighth recall high thoughts, how soon unsay
What feign'd submission swore: ease would recant
Vows made in pain, as violent° and void.
For never can true reconcilement grow
Where wounds of deadly hate have pierc'd so deep:
100   Which would but lead me to a worse relapse,
And heavier fall: so should I purchase dear
Short intermission° bought with double smart.
This knows my punisher; therefore as far
From granting hee, as I from begging peace:
105   All hope excluded thus, behold instead
Of us out-cast, exíl'd, his new delight,
Mankind created, and for him this World.
So farewell Hope, and with Hope farewell Fear,
Farewell Remorse: all Good to me is lost;
110   Evil be thou my Good; by thee at least
Divided Empire with Heav'n's King I hold
By thee, and more than half perhaps will reign;
As Man erelong, and this new World shall know."

81 **that word** "submission." 97 **violent** extorted by force. 102 **intermission** contrasted with enduring "submission" (lines 81, 96).

Thus while he spake, each passion dimm'd
   his face
Thrice chang'd with pale,° ire, envy and despair,   *115*
Which marr'd his borrow'd visage, and betray'd
Him counterfeit, if any eye beheld.
For heav'nly minds from such distempers° foul
Are ever clear. Whereof hee soon aware,
Each perturbation smooth'd with outward calm,   *120*
Artificer of fraud; and was the first
That practis'd falsehood under saintly show,
Deep malice to conceal, couch't° with revenge:
Yet not enough had practis'd to deceive
Uriel once warn'd; whose eye pursu'd him down   *125*
The way he went, and on th'Assyrian mount
Saw him disfigur'd, more than could befall
Spirit of happy sort: his gestures fierce
He mark'd and mad demeanor, then alone,
As he suppos'd, all unobserv'd, unseen.   *130*
So on he fares, and to the border comes
Of Eden, where delicious Paradise,
Now nearer, Crowns with her enclosure green,
As with a rural mound the champaign head°
Of a steep wilderness, whose hairy sides   *135*
With thicket overgrown, grotesque° and wild,
Access deni'd; and overhead upgrew
Insuperable heighth of loftiest shade,
Cedar, and Pine, and Fir, and branching Palm,
A Sylvan Scene, and as the ranks ascend   *140*
Shade above shade, a woody Theatre
Of stateliest view.° Yet higher than their tops
The verdurous wall of Paradise up-sprung:
Which to our general Sire gave prospect large
Into his nether Empire neighbouring round.   *145*
And higher than that Wall a circling row
Of goodliest Trees loaden with fairest Fruit,
Blossoms and Fruits at once of golden hue
Appear'd, with gay enamell'd° colours mixt:

---

115 **pale** pallor.   118 **distempers** disorders, diseases.   123 **couch't** lying
hidden.   134 **champaign head** open plateau.   136 **grotesque** pictur-
esquely irregular (ultimately from grotto, cave).   141–42 **Theatre . . .
view** "theatre" from the Greek for "place for viewing."   149 **enamell'd**
brightly varied.

150 On which the Sun more glad impress'd his beams
     Than in fair Evening Cloud, or humid Bow,°
     When God hath show'r'd the earth; so lovely seem'd
     That Landscape: And of° pure now purer air
     Meets his approach, and to the heart inspires
155 Vernal delight and joy, able to drive
     All sadness but despair: now gentle gales
     Fanning their odoriferous° wings dispense
     Native perfumes, and whisper whence they stole
     Those balmy spoils. As when to them who sail
160 Beyond the Cape of Hope,° and now are past
     Mozambique, off at Sea North-East winds blow
     Sabean° Odours from the spicy shore
     Of Araby the blest,° with such delay
     Well, pleas'd they slack their course, and many a
         League
165 Cheer'd with the grateful° smell old Ocean smiles.
     So entertain'd° those odorous sweets the Fiend
     Who came their bane, though with them better-pleas'd
     Than Asmodeus° with the fishy fume,
     That drove him, though enamour'd, from the Spouse
170 Of Tobit's Son, and with a vengeance° sent
     From Media post to Egypt, there fast° bound.
              Now to th'ascent of that steep savage° Hill
     Satan had journey'd on, pensive and slow;
     But further way found none, so thick entwin'd,
175 As one continu'd brake,° the undergrowth
     Of shrubs and tangling bushes had perplext°
     All path of Man or Beast that past that way:
     One Gate there only was, and that look'd East
     On th'other side: which when th'arch-felon saw
180 Due entrance he disdain'd, and in contempt,
     At one slight bound high overleap'd all bound
     Of Hill or highest Wall, and sheer within

151 **humid Bow** rainbow.   153 **of** following on.   157 **odoriferous** scent-bearing.   160 **Hope** Good Hope (contrast Satan's despair, line 156). 162 **Sabean** from Sheba.   163 **Araby the blest** Arabia Felix.   165 **grateful** pleasing.   166 **entertain'd** received as a guest (but "bane" means murderer—Satan violates such a welcome).   168 **Asmodeus** Tobias (Tobit's son) was to marry a maiden who was pestered by the evil spirit Asmodeus; Raphael instructed Tobias to drive away the spirit by burning fish.   170. **with a vengeance** both "with a curse" and "with all force."   171 **fast** speedily and tightly.   172 **savage** wild (from Latin *silva*, a wood).   175 **brake** thicket.   176 **perplext** made intricate.

'Lights on his feet. As when a prowling Wolf,
Whom hunger drives to seek new haunt for prey,
Watching where Shepherds pen their Flocks at eve   *185*
In hurdl'd Cotes° amid the field secure,°
Leaps o'er the fence with ease into the Fold:
Or as a Thief bent to unhoard the cash
Of some rich Burgher,° whose substantial doors,
Cross-barr'd and bolted fast, fear no assault,   *190*
In at the window climbs, or o'er the tiles;
So clomb this first grand Thief into God's Fold:
So since into his Church lewd° Hirelings climb.
Thence up he flew, and on the Tree of Life,
The middle Tree and highest there that grew,   *195*
Sat like a Cormorant; yet not true Life
Thereby regain'd, but sat devising Death
To them who liv'd; nor on the virtue thought
Of that life-giving Plant, but only us'd
For prospect, what well us'd had been the pledge   *200*
Of immortality. So little knows
Any, but God alone, to value right
The good before him, but perverts best things
To worst abuse, or to their meanest use.
Beneath him with new wonder now he views   *205*
To all delight of human sense expos'd
In narrow room Nature's whole wealth, yea more,
A Heaven on Earth: for blissful Paradise
Of God the Garden was, by him in the East
Of Eden planted; Eden stretch'd her Line   *210*
From Auran Eastward to the Royal Tow'rs
Of great Seleucia, built by Grecian Kings,
Or where the Sons of Eden long before
Dwelt in Telassar: in this pleasant soil
His far more pleasant Garden God ordain'd;   *215*
Out of the fertile ground he caus'd to grow
All Trees of noblest kind for sight, smell, taste;
And all amid them stood the Tree of Life,
High eminent, blooming Ambrosial Fruit
Of vegetable° Gold; and next to Life   *220*
Our Death the Tree of Knowledge grew fast by,

186 **hurdl'd Cotes** sheep pens of wattled bars.   186 **secure** overconfident
in safety.   189 **Burgher** citizen.   193 **lewd** unprincipled.   220 **vegetable**
vegetating, plantlike (contrasted with mineral).

Knowledge of Good bought dear by knowing ill.
Southward through Eden went a River large,
Nor chang'd his course, but through the shaggy hill
225 Pass'd underneath ingulft, for God had thrown
That Mountain as his Garden-mould high rais'd
Upon the rapid current, which through veins
Of porous Earth with kindly° thirst updrawn
Rose a fresh Fountain, and with many a rill
230 Water'd the Garden; thence united fell
Down the steep glade, and met the nether Flood,
Which from his darksome passage now appears,
And now divided into four main Streams,
Runs diverse, wand'ring many a famous Realm
235 And Country whereof here needs no account,
But rather to tell how, if Art could tell,
How from that Sapphire° Fount the crisped° Brooks,
Rolling on Orient Pearl and sands of Gold,
With mazy error° under pendent shades
240 Ran Nectar, visiting each plant, and fed
Flow'rs worthy of Paradise which not nice° Art
In Beds and curious° Knots, but Nature boon°
Pour'd forth profuse on Hill and Dale and Plain,
Both where the morning Sun first warmly smote
245 The open field, and where the unpierc't shade
Embrown'd the noontide Bow'rs: Thus was this place,
A happy rural seat of various view;
Groves whose rich Trees wept odorous Gums and
    Balm,
Others whose fruit burnisht with Golden Rind
250 Hung amiable,° Hesperian Fables° true,
If true, here only,° and of delicious taste:
Betwixt them Lawns, or level Downs, and Flocks
Grazing the tender herb, were interpos'd,
Or palmy hillock, or the flow'ry lap
255 Of some irriguous° Valley spread her store,
Flow'rs of all hue, and without Thorn the Rose:

228 **kindly** natural and beneficial. 237 **Sapphire** blue and precious.
237 **crisped** rippled. 239 **error** in the innocent Latin sense, "wandering"—but already anticipating guilty error (see lines 221–2). 241 **nice**
fastidious. 242 **curious** carefully wrought. 242 **boon** bounteous.
250 amiable **lovely**. 250 **Hesperian Fables** see III 568. 251 **If . . . only**
If the fables are true, they are so only in their application to Eden.
255 **irriguous** watered.

Another side, umbrageous° Grots and Caves
Of cool recess, o'er which the mantling° Vine
Lays forth her purple Grape, and gently creeps
Luxuriant; meanwhile murmuring waters fall   260
Down the slope hills, disperst, or in a Lake,
That to the fringed Bank with Myrtle crown'd,
Her crystal mirror holds, unite their streams.
The Birds their choir apply;° airs,° vernal airs,
Breathing the smell of field and grove, attune°   265
The trembling leaves, while Universal Pan°
Knit with the Graces and the Hours° in dance
Led on th'Eternal Spring.° Not that fair field
Of Enna,° where Prosérpine gath'ring flow'rs,
Herself a fairer flow'r by gloomy Dis   270
Was gather'd, which cost Ceres all that pain
To seek her through the world; nor that sweet Grove
Of Daphne by° Orontes, and th'inspir'd
Castalian Spring° might with this Paradise
Of Eden strive; nor that Nyseian Isle   275
Girt with the River Triton, where old Cham,°
Whom Gentiles Ammon call and Libyan Jove,
Hid Amalthea and her Florid Son°
Young Bacchus from his Stepdame Rhea's° eye;
Nor where Abássin° Kings their issue° Guard,   280
Mount Amara, though this by some suppos'd
True Paradise under the Ethiop Line°
By Nilus' head,° enclos'd with shining Rock,
A whole day's journey high, but wide remote
From this Assyrian Garden, where the Fiend   285
Saw undelighted all delight, all kind

257 **unbrageous** shady. 258 **mantling** forming a mantle, covering.
264 **apply** both "join" and "bring to bear to create an effect" as in
Spenser: "Their pleasant tunes they sweetly thus applied." 264 **airs**
breezes, suggesting tunes ("attune"). 265 **attune** bring into harmony. 266 **Universal Pan** god of all nature, his name from the Greek
for "all." 267 **Graces . . . Hours** the goddesses. 268 **Eternal Spring**
only one season in Eden. 269 **Enna** in Sicily, where Dis (Pluto) snatched
Proserpine to the underworld; her mother Ceres sought her. (Anticipating Satan's seduction of Eve.) 273 **Of Daphne by** named Daphne, near
the river. 274 **Castalian Spring** Castalia, the spring on Mount Parnassus,
sacred to Apollo and the Muses. 276 **Cham** son of Noah, held to be
the god Ammon, Jove. 278 **Florid Son** the beautiful and rosy god of
wine. 279 **Rhea** Bacchus' stepmother, Ammon's wife. 280 **Abássin**
Abyssinian. 280 **issue** children. 282 **Ethiop Line** Equator. 283 **Nilus'
head** Nile's source.

Of living Creatures new to sight and strange:
Two of far nobler shape erect and tall,
Godlike erect, with native Honour clad
290 In naked Majesty seem'd Lords of all,
And worthy seem'd, for in their looks Divine
The image of their glorious Maker shone,
Truth, Wisdom, Sanctitude severe and pure,
Severe, but in true filial freedom plac't;
295 Whence true authority in men;° though both
Not equal, as their sex not equal seem'd;
For contemplation hee and valour form'd,
For softness shee and sweet attractive Grace,
Hee for God only, shee for God in him:
300 His fair large Front° and Eye sublime declar'd
Absolute rule; and Hyacinthine° Locks
Round from his parted forelock manly hung
Clust'ring, but not beneath his shoulders broad:
Shee as a veil down to the slender waist
305 Her unadorned golden tresses wore
Dishevell'd, but in wanton° ringlets wav'd
As the Vine curls her tendrils, which impli'd
Subjection, but requir'd with gentle sway,
And by her yielded, by him best receiv'd,
310 Yielded with coy° submission, modest pride,
And sweet reluctant amorous delay.
Nor those mysterious° parts were then conceal'd,
Then was not guilty shame, dishonest° shame
Of nature's works, honour dishonourable,
315 Sin-bred, how have ye troubl'd all mankind
With shows instead, mere shows of seeming pure,
And banisht from man's life his happiest life,
Simplicity and spotless innocence.
So pass'd they naked on, nor shunn'd the sight
320 Of God or Angel, for they thought no ill:
So hand in hand they pass'd, the loveliest pair

295 **Whence . . . men** from the virtues of their Maker or Author (III
374, etc.), the source of authority. 300 **Front** brow. 301 **Hyacinthine**
colored like hyacinth. 306 **wanton** uncontrolled (here still innocent, but
prophetic). 310 **coy** truly shy. 312 **mysterious** secret, sacramental, awe-
inspiring; the paradox of life before the Fall, since a "mystery" (from the
Greek, "to close lips or eyes") after the Fall is by definition "conceal'd." 313 **dishonest** unchaste.

That ever since in love's embraces° met,
Adam the goodliest man of men since born
His Sons, the fairest of her Daughters Eve.°
Under a tuft of shade that on a green   325
Stood whispering soft, by a fresh Fountain-side
They sat them down, and after no more toil
Of their sweet Gard'ning labour than suffic'd
To recommend° cool Zephyr,° and make ease
More easy, wholesome thirst and appetite   330
More grateful, to their Supper Fruits they fell,
Nectarine° Fruits which the compliant° boughs
Yielded them, sidelong as they sat recline
On the soft downy Bank damaskt° with flow'rs:
The savoury pulp they chew, and in the rind   335
Still as they thirsted scoop the brimming stream;
Nor gentle purpose,° nor endearing smiles
Wanted, nor youthful dalliance as beseems
Fair couple, linkt in happy nuptial League,
Alone as they. About them frisking play'd   340
All Beasts of th'Earth, since wild, and of all chase°
In Wood or Wilderness, Forest or Den;
Sporting the Lion ramp'd, and in his paw
Dandl'd the Kid; Bears, Tigers, Ounces, Pards°
Gamboll'd before them, th'unwieldy Elephant   345
To make them mirth us'd all his might, and wreath'd
His Lithe Proboscis;° close the Serpent sly
Insinuating,° wove with Gordian° twine
His braided train, and of his fatal guile
Gave proof unheeded; others on the grass   350
Coucht, and now fill'd with pasture gazing sat,
Or Bedward ruminating:° for the Sun
Declin'd was hasting now with prone career°

322 **love's embraces** embraced both by each other's love, and by love, God's love.   323–24 This apparently illogical form of speech has both classical and English precedents; it works, too, to *include* Adam and Eve in their descendants—see IX 415–16.   329 **recommend** commend.   329 **Zephyr** mild west wind.   332 **Nectarine** peachlike (suggesting its divine source, nectar).   332 **compliant** pliant (innocent enough, but the other sense, "yielding to desire," is ominous—see IX 994: "compliance bad").   334 **damaskt** patterned, damask also being a rose.   337 **purpose** discourse.   341 **chase** unenclosed land.   344 **Ounces, Pards** lynxes, leopards.   347 **Proboscis** trunk.   348 **Insinuating** winding (ominously prophetic too).   348 **Gordian** intricate like the Gordian knot.   352 **ruminating** chewing the cud.   353 **career** gallop, linked with the word "car," chariot; here the horses of the sun, as in V 139–40.

To th'Ocean Isles,° and in th'ascending Scale
355 Of Heav'n the Stars that usher Evening rose:
When Satan still in gaze, as first he stood,
Scarce thus at length fail'd° speech recover'd sad.
          "O Hell! what do mine eyes with grief behold,
Into our room of bliss thus high advanc't
360 Creatures of other mould, earth-born perhaps,
Not Spirits, yet to heav'nly Spirits bright
Little inferior; whom my thoughts pursue
With wonder, and could love, so lively shines
In them Divine resemblance, and such grace
365 The hand that form'd them on their shape hath pour'd.
Ah gentle pair, yee little think how nigh
Your change approaches, when all these delights
Will vanish and deliver ye to woe,
More woe, the more your taste is now of joy;
370 Happy, but for so happy ill secur'd
Long to continue, and this high seat your Heav'n
Ill fenc't for Heav'n to keep out such a foe
As now is enter'd; yet no purpos'd foe
To you whom I could pity thus forlorn°
375 Though I unpitied: League with you I seek,
And mutual amity so strait, so close,
That I with you must dwell, or you with me
Henceforth; my dwelling haply may not please
Like this fair Paradise, your sense, yet such
380 Accept your Maker's work; he gave it me,
Which I as freely give; Hell shall unfold,
To entertain° you two, her widest Gates,
And send forth all her Kings; there will be room,
Not like these narrow limits, to receive
385 Your numerous offspring; if no better place,
Thank him who puts me loath to this revenge
On you who wrong me not for him who wrong'd.
And should I at your harmless innocence
Melt, as I do, yet public reason just,
390 Honour and Empire with revenge enlarg'd,
By conquering this new World, compels me now
To do what else though damn'd I should abhor."

354 **Ocean Isles** in the west.   357 **fail'd** which had failed him.   374 **for-lorn** lost, doomed.   382 **entertain** welcome formally.

    So spake the Fiend, and with necessity,
The Tyrant's plea, excus'd his devilish deeds.
Then from his lofty stand on that high Tree   *395*
Down he alights among the sportful Herd
Of those four-footed kinds, himself now one,
Now other, as their shape serv'd best his end
Nearer to view his prey, and unespi'd
To mark what of their state he more might learn   *400*
By word or action markt: about them round
A Lion now he stalks with fiery glare,
Then as a Tiger, who by chance hath spi'd
In some Purlieu two gentle Fawns at play,
Straight couches close, then rising changes oft   *405*
His couchant watch, as one who chose his ground
Whence rushing he might surest seize them both
Gript in each paw: when Adam first of men
To first of women Eve thus moving speech,
Turn'd him all ear° to hear new utterance flow.   *410*
    "Sole partner and sole part of all these joys,
Dearer thyself than all; needs must the Power
That made us, and for us this ample World
Be infinitely good, and of his good
As liberal and free as infinite,   *415*
That rais'd us from the dust and plac't us here
In all this happiness, who at his hand
Have nothing merited, nor can perform
Aught whereof hee hath need, hee who requires
From us no other service than to keep   *420*
This one, this easy charge, of all the Trees
In Paradise that bear delicious fruit
So various, not to taste that only Tree
Of Knowledge, planted by the Tree of Life,
So near grows Death to Life, whate'er Death is,   *425*
Some dreadful thing no doubt; for well thou know'st
God hath pronounc't it death to taste that Tree,
The only sign of our obedience left
Among so many signs of power and rule
Conferr'd upon us, and Dominion giv'n   *430*
Over all other Creatures that possess

---

410 **all ear** describing Eve.

Earth, Air, and Sea. Then let us not think hard°
One easy prohibition, who enjoy
Free leave so large to all things else, and choice
435 Unlimited of manifold delights:
But let us ever praise him, and extol
His bounty, following our delightful task
To prune these growing Plants, and tend these Flow'rs,
Which were it toilsome, yet with thee were sweet."
440   To whom thus Eve repli'd. "O thou for whom
And from whom I was form'd flesh of thy flesh,
And without whom am to no end, my Guide
And Head, what thou hast said is just and right.
For wee to him indeed all praises owe,
445 And daily thanks, I chiefly who enjoy
So far the happier Lot, enjoying thee
Pre-eminent by so much odds,° while thou
Like consort to thyself canst nowhere find.
That day I oft remember, when from sleep
450 I first awak't and found myself repos'd
Under a shade on flow'rs, much wond'ring where
And what I was, whence thither brought, and how.
Not distant far from thence a murmuring sound
Of waters issu'd from a Cave and spread
455 Into a liquid Plain, then stood unmov'd
Pure as th'expanse of Heav'n; I thither went
With unexperienc't thought, and laid me down
On the green bank, to look into the clear
Smooth Lake, that to me seem'd another Sky.
460 As I bent down to look, just opposite,
A Shape within the wat'ry gleam appear'd
Bending to look on me, I started back,
It started back, but pleas'd I soon return'd,
Pleas'd it return'd as soon with answering looks°
465 Of sympathy and love, there I had fixt
Mine eyes till now, and pin'd with vain° desire,
Had not a voice thus warn'd me, 'What thou seest,
What there thou seest fair Creature is thyself,

432 **hard** harsh, but the sense "difficult to keep"—contrasting with
"easy"—is not auspicious.   447 **odds** inequality, difference.   460–64 **As . . .
looks** Eve's behavior resembles that of Narcissus; she is still innocent, but
in danger.   466 **vain** futile (but ominously suggesting the "vanity" of
Narcissus and the fallen Eve).

With thee it came and goes: but follow me,
And I will bring thee where no shadow stays°   470
Thy coming, and thy soft embraces, hee
Whose image thou art, him thou shalt enjoy
Inseparably thine, to him shalt bear
Multitudes like thyself, and thence be call'd
Mother of human Race.' What could I do,   475
But follow straight, invisibly thus led?
Till I espi'd thee, fair indeed and tall,
Under a Platan,° yet methought less fair,
Less winning soft, less amiably mild,
Than that smooth wat'ry image; back I turn'd,   480
Thou following cried'st aloud, 'Return fair Eve,
Whom fli'st thou? whom thou fli'st, of him thou art,
His flesh, his bone; to give thee being I lent
Out of my side to thee, nearest my heart
Substantial° Life, to have thee by my side   485
Henceforth an individual° solace dear;
Part of my Soul I seek thee, and thee claim
My other half.' With that thy gentle hand
Seiz'd mine, I yielded, and from that time see
How beauty is excell'd by manly grace   490
And wisdom, which alone is truly fair."
        So spake our general Mother, and with eyes
Of conjugal attraction unreprov'd,°
And meek surrender, half-embracing lean'd
On our first Father, half her swelling Breast   495
Naked met his under the flowing Gold
Of her loose tresses hid: he in delight
Both of her Beauty and submissive Charms
Smil'd with superior Love, as Jupiter
On Juno smiles, when he impregns° the Clouds   500
That shed May Flowers; and press'd her Matron lip
With kisses pure: aside the Devil turn'd
For envy, yet with jealous leer malign
Ey'd them askance, and to himself thus 'plain'd.
        "Sight hateful, sight tormenting! thus these two 505
Imparadis't in one another's arms
The happier Eden, shall enjoy their fill

470 **stays** awaits.   478 **Platan** plane tree.   485 **Substantial** in its essence;
for the religious associations, see III 140.   486 **individual** indivisible, inseparable.   493 **unreprov'd** blameless.   500 **impregns** impregnates.

Of bliss on bliss, while I to Hell am thrust,
Where neither joy nor love, but fierce desire,
510 Among our other torments not the least,
Still unfulfill'd with pain of longing pines;°
Yet let me not forget what I have gain'd
From their own mouths;° all is not theirs it seems:
One fatal° Tree there stands of Knowledge call'd,
515 Forbidden them to taste: Knowledge forbidd'n?
Suspicious, reasonless. Why should their Lord
Envy them that? can it be sin to know,
Can it be death? and do they only stand
By Ignorance, is that their happy state,
520 The proof of their obedience and their faith?
O fair foundation laid whereon to build
Their ruin!° Hence I will excite their minds
With more desire to know, and to reject
Envious commands, invented with design
525 To keep them low whom knowledge might exalt
Equal with Gods; aspiring to be such,
They taste and die: what likelier can ensue?
But first with narrow search I must walk round
This Garden, and no corner leave unspi'd;
530 A chance but° chance may lead where I may meet
Some wand'ring Spirit of Heav'n, by Fountain-side,
Or in thick shade retir'd, from him to draw
What further would be learnt. Live while ye may,
Yet happy pair; enjoy, till I return,
535 Short pleasures, for long woes are to suceed."
        So saying, his proud step he scornful turn'd,
But with sly circumspection, and began
Through wood, through waste, o'er hill, o'er dale his
    roam.
Meanwhile in utmost Longitude,° where Heav'n
540 With Earth and Ocean meets, the setting Sun
Slowly descended, and with right aspéct°
Against the eastern Gate of Paradise

---

511 **pines** tortures.   513 **From . . . mouths** a sardonic pun—see line
527.   514 **fatal** deadly, and of fate.   521–22 **O . . . ruin** "A cruel paradox;
one doesn't, or at this date didn't, build ruins. But there is also a pun-
like effect using two senses of *ruin*, not only what is left after the destructive act, but also the fall itself" (Frank Kermode).   530 **A chance but** there
is a faint chance that.   539 **utmost Longitude** the far west.   541 **with right
aspéct** directly opposite.

Levell'd his evening Rays: it was a Rock
Of Alabaster, pil'd up to the Clouds,
Conspicuous far, winding with one ascent   545
Accessible from Earth, one entrance high;
The rest was craggy cliff, that overhung
Still as it rose, impossible to climb.
Betwixt these rocky Pillars Gabriel sat
Chief of th'Angelic Guards, awaiting night;   550
About him exercis'd Heroic Games
Th'unarmed Youth of Heav'n, but nigh at hand
Celestial Armoury, Shields, Helms, and Spears
Hung high with Diamond flaming, and with Gold.
Thither came Uriel, gliding through the Even   555
On a Sunbeam, swift as a shooting Star
In Autumn thwarts° the night, when vapours fir'd
Impress the Air, and shows the Mariner
From what point of his Compass to beware
Impetuous winds: he thus began in haste.   560
    "Gabriel, to thee thy course by Lot hath giv'n
Charge and strict watch that to this happy place
No evil thing approach or enter in;
This day at heighth of Noon came to my Sphere
A Spirit, zealous, as he seem'd, to know   565
More of th'Almighty's work, and chiefly Man
God's latest Image:° I describ'd° his way
Bent all on speed, and markt his Airy Gait;°
But in the Mount that lies from Eden North,
Where he first 'lighted, soon discern'd his looks   570
Alien from Heav'n, with passions foul obscur'd:
Mine eye pursu'd him still, but under shade
Lost sight of him; one of the banisht crew
I fear, hath ventur'd from the deep, to raise
New troubles;° him thy care must be to find."   575
    To whom the winged Warrior thus return'd:
"Uriel, no wonder if thy perfect sight,
Amid the Sun's bright circle where thou sitt'st,
See far and wide: in at this Gate none pass
The vigilance° here plac't, but such as come   580
Well known from Heav'n; and since Meridian hour

557 **thwarts** crosses. 567 **latest Image** the Son being His first image.
567 **describ'd** descried. 568 **Gait** manner (of flying). 575 **troubles** including "wars, disturbances." 580 **vigilance** vigilant guards.

No Creature thence: if Spirit of other sort,
So minded, have o'erleapt these earthy bounds
On purpose, hard thou know'st it to exclude
585 Spiritual substance with corporeal bar.
But if within the circuit of these walks
In whatsoever shape he lurk, of whom
Thou tell'st, by morrow dawning I shall know."
    So promis'd hee, and Uriel to his charge
590 Return'd on that bright beam, whose point now rais'd
Bore him slope downward to the Sun now fall'n
Beneath th'Azores; whither the prime Orb,°
Incredible how swift, had thither roll'd
Diurnal,° or this less volúble° Earth
595 By shorter flight to th'East, had left him there
Arraying with reflected Purple and Gold
The Clouds that on his Western Throne attend:
Now came still Ev'ning on, and Twilight grey
Had in her sober Livery all things clad;
600 Silence accompanied,° for Beast and Bird,
They to their grassy Couch, these to their Nests
Were slunk, all but the wakeful Nightingale;
She all night long her amorous descant° sung;
Silence was pleas'd: now glow'd the Firmament
605 With living Sapphires: Hesperus that led
The starry Host, rode brightest, till the Moon
Rising in clouded Majesty, at length
Apparent° Queen unveil'd her peerless light,
And o'er the dark her Silver Mantle threw.
    When Adam thus to Eve: "Fair Consort,
610   th'hour
Of night, and all things now retir'd to rest
Mind° us of like repose, since God hath set
Labour and rest, as day and night to men
Successive, and the timely dew of sleep
615 Now falling with soft slumb'rous weight inclines
Our eyelids; other Creatures all day long

592 **prime Orb** sun. 594 **Diurnal** in a day. 594 **volúble** swift-rolling
(Milton's spelling here, "volubil"). 600 **accompanied** The musical suggestion of "accompaniment" (which would make "Silence accompanied" a
quiet paradox) leads into lines 602–04. 603 **descant** melodious accompaniment to a simple theme. 608 **Apparent** plainly seen, manifest. 612 **Mind**
remind.

Rove idle unemploy'd, and less need rest;
Man hath his daily work of body or mind
Appointed, which declares his Dignity,
And the regard of Heav'n on all his ways;   620
While other Animals unactive range,
And of their doings God takes no account.
Tomorrow ere fresh Morning streak the East
With first approach of light, we must be ris'n,
And at our pleasant labour, to reform°   625
Yon flow'ry Arbours, yonder Alleys green,
Our walks at noon, with branches overgrown,
That mock our scant manuring,° and require
More hands than ours to lop their wanton growth:
Those Blossoms also, and those dropping Gums,   630
That lie bestrewn unsightly and unsmooth,
Ask riddance,° if we mean to tread with ease;
Meanwhile, as Nature wills, Night bids us rest."
          To whom thus Eve with perfect beauty
          adorn'd.
"My Author° and Disposer, what thou bidd'st   635
Unargu'd I obey; so God ordains,
God is thy Law, thou mine: to know no more
Is woman's happiest knowledge and her praise.
With thee conversing I forget all time,
All seasons° and their change, all please alike.   640
Sweet is the breath of morn, her rising sweet,
With charm° of earliest Birds; pleasant the Sun
When first on this delightful Land he spreads
His orient Beams, on herb, tree, fruit, and flow'r,
Glist'ring with dew; fragrant the fertile earth   645
After soft showers; and sweet the coming-on
Of grateful Ev'ning mild, then silent Night
With this her solemn Bird and this fair Moon,
And these the Gems of Heav'n, her starry train:
But neither breath of Morn when she ascends   650
With charm of earliest Birds, nor rising Sun
On this delightful land, nor herb, fruit, flow'r,

---

625 **reform** trim. 628 **scant manuring** limited cultivation, from Old
French *manouvrer*, to work with the hands—see the next line. 632 **Ask
riddance** require to be cleared. 635 **Author** creator, and having authority. 640 **seasons** times of day. 642 **charm** including specifically the
sense "song."

Glist'ring with dew, nor fragrance after showers,
Nor grateful Evening mild, nor silent Night
655 With this her solemn Bird, nor walk by Moon,
Or glittering Starlight without thee is sweet.
But wherefore all night long shine these, for whom
This glorious sight, when sleep hath shut all eyes?"
    To whom our general Ancestor repli'd.
660 "Daughter of God and Man, accomplisht° Eve,
Those have their course to finish, round the Earth,
By morrow Ev'ning, and from Land to Land
In order, though to Nations yet unborn,
Minist'ring light prepar'd, they set and rise;
665 Lest total darkness should by Night regain
Her old possession, and extinguish life
In Nature and all things, which these soft fires
Not only enlighten, but with kindly heat
Of various influence foment° and warm,
670 Temper or nourish, or in part shed down
Their stellar virtue on all kinds that grow
On Earth, made hereby apter to receive
Perfection from the Sun's more potent Ray.
These then, though unbeheld in deep of night,
675 Shine not in vain, nor think, though men were none,
That Heav'n would want spectators, God want praise;
Millions of spiritual Creatures walk the Earth
Unseen, both when we wake, and when we sleep:
All these with ceaseless praise his works behold
680 Both day and night: how often from the steep
Of echoing Hill or Thicket have we heard
Celestial voices to the midnight air,
Sole, or responsive each to other's note
Singing their great Creator: oft in bands°
685 While they keep watch, or nightly rounding° walk
With Heav'nly touch of instrumental sounds
In full harmonic number join'd, their songs
Divide° the night, and lift our thoughts to Heaven."
    Thus talking hand in hand alone they pass'd
690 On to their blissful Bower; it was a place

660 **accomplisht** complete, perfected (leading into lines 661, 673).   669 **foment** bathe in heat.   684 **bands** armed bands (a faint musical suggestion then
taken up in lines 685–87).   685 **rounding** making their rounds.   688 **Divide**
into watches, like guards.

Chos'n by the sovran Planter, when he fram'd
All things to man's delightful use; the roof
Of thickest covert was inwoven shade
Laurel and Myrtle, and what higher grew
Of firm and fragrant leaf; on either side   695
Acanthus, and each odorous bushy shrub
Fenc'd up the verdant wall; each beauteous flow'r,
Iris all hues, Roses, and Jessamine
Rear'd high their flourisht° heads between, and
    wrought
Mosaic; underfoot the Violet,   700
Crocus, and Hyacinth with rich inlay
Broider'd·the ground, more colour'd than with stone
Of costliest Emblem:° other Creature here
Beast, Bird, Insect, or Worm durst enter none;
Such was their awe of man. In shadier Bower   705
More sacred and sequester'd,° though but feign'd,°
Pan or Sylvanus° never slept, nor Nymph,
Nor Faunus haunted. Here in close recess
With Flowers, Garlands, and sweet-smelling Herbs
Espoused Eve deckt first her Nuptial Bed,   710
And heav'nly Choirs the Hymenean° sung,
What day the genial° Angel to our Sire
Brought her in naked beauty more adorn'd,
More lovely than Pandora,° whom the Gods
Endow'd with all their gifts, and O too like   715
In sad event,° when to the unwiser Son
Of Japhet brought by Hermes, she ensnar'd
Mankind with her fair looks, to be aveng'd
On him who had stole Jove's authentic° fire.
        Thus at their shady Lodge arriv'd, both stood,   720
Both turn'd, and under op'n Sky ador'd
The God that made both Sky, Air, Earth and Heav'n
Which they beheld, the Moon's resplendent Globe

---

699 **flourisht** adorned with flowers, "flourish" from latin *flos*, flower.
703 **Emblem** inlaid work.   706 **sequester'd** set apart.   706 **feign'd** imagined
by pagan poets (unlike the Biblical truth).   707 **Pan or Sylvanus** pastoral
gods.   711 **Hymenean** marriage song.   712 **genial** ruling over nuptials.   714–19 **Pandora** Prometheus ("Forethought") stole Jove's fire to
benefit mankind; Jove, "to be aveng'd," sent Pandora ("All gifts"), by
his messenger Hermes, to the "unwiser" Epimetheus ("Afterthought"),
who married her, and loosed upon the world the evils from her
box.   716 **event** outcome.   719 **authentic** original.

And starry Pole: "Thou also mad'st the Night,
725 Maker Omnipotent, and thou the Day,
Which we in our appointed work employ'd
Have finisht happy in our mutual help
And mutual love, the Crown of all our bliss
Ordain'd by thee, and this delicious place
730 For us too large, where thy abundance wants°
Partakers, and uncropt falls to the ground.
But thou hast promis'd from us two a Race
To fill the Earth, who shall with us extol
Thy goodness infinite, both when we wake,
735 And when we seek, as now, thy gift of sleep."
          This said unanimous,° and other Rites
Observing none, but adoration pure
Which God likes best, into their inmost bower
Handed° they went; and eas'd the putting off°
740 These troublesome disguises which wee wear,
Straight side by side were laid, nor turn'd I ween
Adam from his fair Spouse, nor Eve the Rites
Mysterious° of connubial Love refus'd:
Whatever Hypocrites austerely talk
745 Of purity and place and innocence,
Defaming as impure what God declares
Pure, and commands to some, leaves free to all.
Our Maker bids increase, who bids abstain
But our Destroyer, foe to God and Man?
750 Had wedded Love, mysterious Law, true source
Of human offspring, sole propriety,°
In Paradise of all things common else.
By thee adulterous lust was driv'n from men
Among the bestial herds to range, by thee
755 Founded in Reason, Loyal, Just, and Pure,
Relations° dear, and all the Charities
Of Father, Son, and Brother first were known.
Far be it, that I should write thee sin or blame,
Or think thee unbefitting holiest place,

---

730 **wants** lacks. 736 **unanimous** with one mind. 739 **Handed** hand in hand, suggesting the dignity of the marriage ceremony; "If say two be but once handed in the Church . . . " (Milton, *Doctrine and Discipline of Divorce*). 739 **eas'd the putting off** having no need to remove. 743 **Mysterious** awe-inspiring. 751 **sole propriety** the one exclusive possession. 756 **Relations** relationships.

Perpetual Fountain of Domestic sweets,   760
Whose Bed is undefil'd and chaste pronounc't,
Present, or past, as Saints and Patriarchs us'd.
Here Love° his golden shafts employs, here lights
His constant Lamp, and waves his purple° wings,
Reigns here and revels; not in the bought smile   765
Of Harlots, loveless, joyless, unendear'd,
Casual fruition, nor in Court Amours
Mixt Dance, or wanton Masque, or Midnight Ball,
Or Serenade, which the starv'd° Lover sings
To his proud fair, best quitted with disdain.   770
These lull'd by Nightingales embracing slept,
And on their naked limbs the flow'ry roof
Show'r'd Roses, which the Morn repair'd.° Sleep on,
Blest pair; and O yet happiest if ye seek
No happier state, and know to know no more.   775
        Now had night measur'd with her shadowy
        Cone
Halfway uphill this vast Sublunar° Vault,
And from their Ivory Port° the Cherubim
Forth issuing at th'accustom'd hour stood arm'd
To their night-watches in warlike Parade,   780
When Gabriel to his next in power thus spake.
       "Uzziel, half these draw off, and coast the
       South
With strictest watch; these other wheel the North,
Our circuit meets full West." As flame they part
Half wheeling to the Shield, half to the Spear.°   785
From these, two strong and subtle Spirits he call'd
That near him stood, and gave them thus in charge.
       "Ithuriel and Zephon, with wing'd speed
Search through this Garden, leave unsearcht no nook,
But chiefly where those two fair Creatures Lodge,   790
Now laid perhaps asleep secure of° harm.
This Ev'ning from the Sun's decline arriv'd
Who° tells of some infernal Spirit seen
Hitherward bent (who could have thought?) escap'd
The bars of Hell, on errand bad no doubt: 795

763 **Love** Cupid with his arrows of love.   764 **purple** brilliant.   769 **starv'd**
suffering in the cold.   773 **repair'd** once more made up the sum of.
777 **Sublunar** under the moon.   778 **Port** gate.   785 **Shield . . . Spear**
left, right.   791 **secure of** unsuspecting.   793 **Who** one who.

Such where ye find, seize fast, and hither bring."
          So saying, on he led his radiant Files,
Dazzling the Moon; these to the Bower direct
In search of whom they sought: him there they found
800 Squat like a Toad, close at the ear of Eve;
Assaying by his Devilish art to reach
The Organs of her Fancy, and with them forge
Illusions as he list, Phantasms and Dreams,
Or if, inspiring venom, he might taint
805 Th'animal Spirits that from pure blood arise
Like gentle breaths from Rivers pure, thence raise
At least distemper'd, discontented thoughts,
Vain hopes, vain aims, inordinate desires
Blown up with high conceits engend'ring pride.°
810 Him thus intent Ithuriel with his Spear
Touch'd lightly; for no falsehood can endure
Touch of Celestial temper, but returns
Of force to its own likeness: up he starts
Discover'd° and surpris'd. As when a spark
815 'Lights° on a heap of nitrous Powder,° laid
Fit for the Tun° some Magazine° to store
Against a rumour'd War, the Smutty grain
With sudden blaze diffus'd, inflames the Air:
So started up in his own shape the Fiend.
820 Back stept those two fair Angels half amaz'd
So sudden to behold the grisly King;
Yet thus, unmov'd with fear, accost him soon.
          "Which of those rebel Spirits adjudg'd to Hell
Com'st thou, escap'd thy prison, and transform'd,
825 Why satt'st thou like an enemy in wait
Here watching at the head of these that sleep?"
          "Know ye not then" said Satan, fill'd with
               scorn,
"Know ye not me? ye knew me once no mate
For you, there sitting where ye durst not soar;
830 Not to know mee argues yourselves unknown,

801–09 There are sexual implications throughout these lines (including
"conceits" as "things conceived"); Eve's dream, caused here by Satan
and recounted later, has erotic force, and Satan's final conquest of her is
presented as in many ways a seduction (e.g. IX 526). 814 **Discover'd**
caught and uncovered. 815 **'Lights** alights, but suggesting "kindles." 815 **nitrous Powder** gunpowder. 816 **Tun** barrel. 816 **Magazine**
building for explosives.

The lowest of your throng; or if ye know,
Why ask ye, and superfluous begin
Your message, like to end as much in vain?"
To whom thus Zephon, answering scorn with scorn.
"Think not, revolted Spirit, thy shape the same,   835
Or undiminisht brightness, to be known
As when thou stood'st in Heav'n upright and pure;
That Glory then, when thou no more wast good,
Departed from thee, and thou resembl'st now
Thy sin and place of doom obscure and foul.   840
But come, for thou, be sure, shalt give account
To him who sent us, whose charge is to keep
This place inviolable, and these from harm."
    So spake the Cherub, and his grave rebuke
Severe in youthful beauty, added grace   845
Invincible: abasht the Devil stood,
And felt how awful goodness is, and saw
Virtue in her shape how lovely, saw, and pin'd
His loss; but chiefly to find here obscrv'd
His lustre visibly impair'd; yet seem'd   850
Undaunted. "If I must contend," said he,
"Best with the best, the Sender not the sent,
Or all at once; more glory will bc won,
Or less be lost." "Thy fear," said Zephon bold,
"Will save us trial what the least can do   855
Single° against thee wicked, and thence weak."
    The Fiend repli'd not, overcome with rage;
But like a proud Steed rein'd, went haughty on,
Champing his iron curb: to strive or fly
He held it vain; awe from above had quell'd   860
His heart, not else dismay'd. Now drew they nigh
The western point, where those half-rounding guards
Just met, and closing stood in squadron join'd
Awaiting next command. To whom their Chief
Gabriel from the Front thus call'd aloud.   865
    "O friends, I hear the tread of nimble feet
Hasting this way, and now by glimpse discern
Ithuriel and Zephon through the shade,
And with them comes a third of Regal port,°

---

856 **Single** both "alone" and "honestly upright" as in Shakespeare's "a
single heart."   869 **port** bearing.

870 But faded splendour wan; who by his gait
And fierce demeanour seems the Prince of Hell,
Not likely to part hence without contést;
Stand firm, for in his look defiance lours."
              He scarce had ended, when those two
              approach'd
875 And brief related whom they brought, where found,
How busied, in what form and posture coucht.
              To whom with stern regard thus Gabriel
              spake.
"Why hast thou, Satan, broke the bounds prescrib'd
To thy transgressions,° and disturb'd the charge°
880 Of others, who approve not to transgress
By thy example, but have power and right
To question thy bold entrance on this place;
Employ'd it seems to violate sleep, and those
Whose dwelling God hath planted here in bliss?"
885   To whom thus Satan with contemptuous brow.
"Gabriel, thou hadst in Heav'n th'esteem of° wise,
And such I held thee; but this question askt
Puts me in doubt. Lives there who loves his pain?
Who would not, finding way, break loose from Hell,
Though thither doom'd? Thou wouldst thyself, no
890   doubt,
And boldly venture to whatever place
Farthest from pain, where thou mightst hope to
      change
Torment with ease, and soonest recompense
Dole with delight, which in this place I sought;
895 To thee no reason; who know'st only good,
But evil hast not tri'd: and wilt object°
His will who bound us? let him surer bar
His Iron Gates, if he intends our stay
In that dark durance:° thus much what was askt.
900 The rest is true, they found me where they say;
But that implies not violence or harm."
              Thus hee in scorn. The warlike Angel mov'd,

---

879 **transgressions** a transgression itself being something which breaks
bounds (Latin *transgredi*). 879 **charge** duty. 886 **hadst . . . th'esteem
of** wast esteemed. 896 **object** put forward as an objection. 899 **durance**
imprisonment (a sardonic pun, since durance is by definition *staying*,
from *durer*).

Disdainfully half smiling thus repli'd.
"O loss of one in Heav'n to judge of wise,°
Since Satan fell, whom folly overthrew,   905
And now returns him from his prison 'scap't,
Gravely in doubt whether to hold them wise
Or not, who ask what boldness brought him hither
Unlicens't from his bounds in Hell prescrib'd;
So wise he judges it to fly from pain   910
However,° and to 'scape his punishment.
So judge thou still, presumptuous, till the wrath,
Which thou incurr'st by flying, meet thy flight
Sev'nfold, and scourge that wisdom back to Hell,
Which taught thee yet no better, that no pain   915
Can equal anger infinite provok't.
But wherefore thou alone? wherefore with thee
Came not all Hell broke loose? is pain to them
Less pain, less to be fled, or thou than they
Less hardy to endure? courageous Chief,   920
The first in flight from pain, hadst thou alleg'd
To thy deserted host this cause of flight,
Thou surely hadst not come sole fugitive."
          To which the Fiend thus answer'd frowning
          stern.
"Not that I less endure, or shrink from pain,   925
Insulting Angel, well thou know'st I stood°
Thy fiercest, when in Battle to thy aid
The blasting volley'd Thunder made all speed
And seconded thy else not dreaded Spear.
But still thy words at random,° as before,   930
Argue thy inexperience what behooves
From hard assays and and ill successes past
A faithful Leader, not to hazard all
Through ways of danger by himself untri'd.
I therefore, I alone first undertook   935
To wing the desolate Abyss, and spy
This new-created World, whereof in Hell
Fame° is not silent, here in hope to find

904 "What a loss to Heaven of one who can so judge wisdom."   911 **However** howsoever.   926 **stood** withstood.   930 **at random** both "haphazard" and—a military term—"at a range other than point-blank" (here, not hitting the target).   938 **Fame** report.

Better abode, and my afflicted Powers°
940 To settle here on Earth, or in mid Air;
Though for possession put to try once more
What thou and thy gay Legions dare against;
Whose easier business were to serve their Lord
High up in Heav'n, with songs to hymn his Throne,
945 And practis'd distances° to cringe, not fight."
            To whom the warrior Angel soon repli'd.
"To say and straight unsay, pretending first
Wise to fly pain, professing next the Spy,
Argues no Leader, but a liar trac't,
950 Satan, and couldst thou 'faithful' add? O name,
O sacred name of faithfulness profan'd!
Faithful to whom? to thy rebellious crew?
Army of Fiends, fit body to fit head;
Was this your discipline and faith engag'd,
955 Your military obedience, to dissolve
Allegiance to th'acknowledg'd Power supreme?
And thou sly hypocrite, who now wouldst seem
Patron of liberty, who more than thou
Once fawn'd, and cring'd, and servilely ador'd
960 Heav'ns awful Monarch? wherefore but in hope
To dispossess him, and thyself to reign?
But mark what I aread° thee now, avaunt;°
Fly thither whence thou fledd'st: if from this hour
Within these hallow'd limits thou appear,
965 Back to th'infernal pit I drag thee chain'd,
And Seal thee so, as henceforth not to scorn
The facile° gates of Hell too slightly barr'd."
            So threat'n'd hee, but Satan to no threats
Gave heed, but waxing more in rage repli'd.
970   "Then when I am thy captive talk of chains,
Proud limitary° Cherub, but ere then
Far heavier load thyself expect to feel
From my prevailing arm, though Heaven's King

939 **afflicted Powers** armies struck down.   945 **practis'd distances** accustomed acts of deference—but sardonically against "distance" as the interval between combatants; "He fights as you sing pricksong, keeps time, distance, and proportion" (*Romeo and Juliet*), where there is too the suggestion of "a musical interval."   962 **aread** advise.   962 **avaunt** begone.   967 **facile** easy.   971 **limitary** on guard duty at the boundary (taking up line 964); Satan's sarcasm includes the 17th-century sense "limited in powers."

BOOK IV   *107*

Ride on thy wings, and thou with thy Compeers,
Us'd to the yoke, draw'st his triumphant wheels   *975*
In progress° through the road of Heav'n Star-pav'd.''
        While thus he spake, th'Angelic Squadron
            bright
Turn'd fiery red, sharp'ning in mooned horns
Their Phalanx,° and began to hem him round
With ported° Spears, as thick as when a field   *980*
Of Ceres° ripe for harvest waving bends
Her bearded Grove of ears, which way the wind
Sways them; the careful° Ploughman doubting° stands
Lest on the threshing-floor his hopeful sheaves
Prove chaff. On th'other side Satan alarm'd°   *985*
Collecting all his might dilated stood,
Like Tenerife° or Atlas unremov'd:°
His stature reacht the Sky, and on his Crest
Sat horror° Plum'd; nor wanted in his grasp
What seem'd both Spear and Shield: now dreadful
            deeds   *990*
Might have ensu'd, nor only Paradise
In this commotion, but the Starry Cope
Of Heav'n perhaps, or all the Elements
At least had gone to wrack, disturb'd and torn
With violence of this conflict, had not soon   *995*
Th'Eternal to prevent such horrid fray
Hung forth in Heav'n his golden Scales,° yet seen
Betwixt Astraea° and the Scorpion sign,
Wherein all things created first he weigh'd,
The pendulous round Earth with balanc't Air   *1000*
In counterpoise, now ponders° all events,
Battles and Realms: in these he put two weights
The sequel° each of parting and of fight;
The latter quick up flew, and kickt the beam;
Which Gabriel spying, thus bespake the Fiend.   *1005*
        "Satan, I know thy strength, and thou know'st
            mine,

976 **progress** state procession.   979 **Phalanx** line of battle.   980 **ported** held
slanting ("port arms").   981 **Ceres** goddess of agriculture.   983 **careful** anxious.   983 **doubting** fearing.   985 **alarm'd** called to arms.   987 **Tenerife**
mountain in the Canary Isles.   987 **unremov'd** unremovable.   989 **horror** from Latin *horrere*, to stand on end (of hair).   997 **Scales** the constellation Libra.   998 **Astraea** Virgo.   1001 **ponders** weighs.   1003 **sequel**
consequence (to Satan).

Neither our own but giv'n; what folly then
To boast what Arms can do, since thine no more
Than Heav'n permits, nor mine, though doubl'd now
1010 To trample thee as mire: for proof look up,
And read thy Lot in yon celestial Sign
Where thou art weigh'd, and shown how light, how
    weak,
If thou resist." The Fiend lookt up and knew
His mounted scale aloft: nor more; but fled
1015 Murmuring, and with him fled the shades of night.

BOOK V

THE ARGUMENT

Morning approach't, Eve relates to Adam her troublesome dream; he likes it not, yet comforts her: They come forth to their day labours: Their Morning Hymn at the Door of their Bower. God to render Man inexcusable sends Raphael to admonish him of his obedience, of his free estate, of his enemy near at hand; who he is, and why his enemy, and whatever else may avail Adam to know. Raphael comes down to Paradise, his appearance describ'd, his coming discern'd by Adam afar off sitting at the door of his Bower; he goes out to meet him, brings him to his lodge, entertains him with the choicest fruits of Paradise got together by Eve; their discourse at Table: Raphael performs his message, minds Adam of his state and of his enemy; relates at Adam's request who that enemy is, and how he came to be so, beginning from his first revolt in Heaven, and the occasion thereof; how he drew his Legions after him to the parts of the North, and there incited them to rebel with him, persuading all but only Abdiel a Seraph, who in Argument dissuades and opposes him, then forsakes him.

Now Morn her rosy steps in th'Eastern Clime°
Advancing, sow'd the Earth with Orient Pearl,
When Adam wak't, so custom'd, for his sleep
Was Airy light, from pure digestion bred,
And temperate vapours bland, which° th'only° sound   5
Of leaves and fuming rills, Aurora's° fan,
Lightly dispers'd, and the shrill Matin Song
Of Birds on every bough; so much the more
His wonder was to find unwak'n'd Eve

1 **Clime** region.   5 **which** (sleep).   5 **only** mere.   6 **Aurora** the dawn.

109

10 With Tresses discompos'd, and glowing Cheek,
    As through unquiet rest: he on his side
    Leaning half-rais'd, with looks of cordial Love
    Hung over her enamour'd, and beheld
    Beauty, which whether waking or asleep,
15 Shot forth peculiar° Graces; then with voice
    Mild, as when Zephyrus on Flora° breathes,
    Her hand soft touching, whisper'd thus. "Awake
    My fairest, my espous'd, my latest found,
    Heav'n's last best gift, my ever-new delight,
20 Awake, the morning shines, and the fresh field
    Calls us, we lose the prime,° to mark how spring
    Our tended Plants, how blows° the Citron Grove,
    What drops the Myrrh, and what the balmy Reed,
    How Nature paints her colours, how the Bee
25 Sits on the Bloom extracting liquid sweet."
            Such whispering wak'd her, but with startl'd
            eye
    On Adam, whom embracing, thus she spake.
            "O Sole in whom my thoughts find all repose,
    My Glory, my Perfection, glad I see
30 Thy face, and Morn return'd, for I this Night,
    Such night till this I never pass'd, have dream'd,
    If dream'd, not as I oft am wont, of thee,
    Works of day past, or morrow's next design,
    But of offence and trouble, which my mind
35 Knew never till this irksome night; methought
    Close at mine ear one call'd me forth to walk
    With gentle voice, I thought it thine; it said,
    'Why sleep'st thou Eve? now is the pleasant time,
    The cool, the silent, save where silence yields
40 To the night-warbling Bird, that now awake
    Tunes sweetest his love-labour'd° song; now reigns
    Full-orb'd the Moon, and with more pleasing light
    Shadowy sets off the face of things; in vain,
    If none regard; Heav'n wakes with all his eyes,
45 Whom to behold but thee, Nature's desire,
    In whose sight all things joy, with ravishment

---

15 **peculiar** especial. 16 **Zephyrus on Flora** the west wind over flowers
(of which Flora was goddess). 21 **prime** early morning. 22 **blows**
blooms. 41 **love-labour'd** wrought both by love and with love.

Attracted by thy beauty still° to gaze.'
I rose as at thy call, but found thee not;
To find thee I directed then my walk;
And on, methought, alone I pass'd through ways   *50*
That brought me on a sudden to the Tree
Of interdicted Knowledge: fair it seem'd,
Much fairer to my Fancy than by day:
And as I wond'ring lookt, beside it stood
One shap'd and wing'd like one of those from Heav'n   *55*
By us oft seen; his dewy locks distill'd
Ambrosia; on that Tree he also gaz'd;
And 'O fair Plant,' said he, 'with fruit surcharg'd,
Deigns none to ease thy load and taste thy sweet,
Nor God, nor Man; is Knowledge so despis'd?   *60*
Or envy, or what reserve° forbids to taste?
Forbid who will, none shall from me withhold
Longer thy offer'd good, why else set here?'
This said he paus'd not, but with vent'rous Arm
He pluckt, he tasted; mee damp horror chill'd   *65*
At such bold words voucht with° a deed so bold:
But he thus overjoy'd, 'O Fruit Divine,
Sweet of thyself, but much more sweet thus cropt,
Forbidd'n here, it seems, as only fit
For Gods, yet able to make Gods of Men: *70*
And why not Gods of Men, since good, the more
Communicated,° more abundant grows,
The Author not impair'd, but honour'd more?
Here, happy Creature, fair Angelic Eve,
Partake thou also; happy though thou art,   *75*
Happier thou mayst be, worthier canst not be:
Taste this, and be henceforth among the Gods
Thyself a Goddess, not to Earth confin'd,
But sometimes in the Air, as wee, sometimes
Ascend to Heav'n, by merit thine, and see   *80*
What life the Gods live there, and such live thou.'
So saying, he drew nigh, and to me held,
Even to my mouth of that same fruit held part

---

47 **still** always.   61 **reserve** restriction.   66 **voucht with** backed by.   72
Communicated imparted; but with "tasted," "Divine," Gods," etc., it
suggests the sense "partake of or administer Holy Communion"—e.g.
"He communicated the mysteries of the blessed body of Christ" (1641).
The whole scene is a diabolical parody of Communion; compare IX 755.

Which he had pluckt; the pleasant savoury smell
85 So quick'n'd appetite, that I, methought,
Could not but taste. Forthwith up to the Clouds
With him I flew, and underneath beheld
The Earth outstretcht immense, a prospect wide
And various: wond'ring at my flight and change
90 To this high exaltation; suddenly
My Guide was gone, and I, methought, sunk down,
And fell asleep; but O how glad I wak'd
To find this but a dream!" Thus Eve her Night
Related, and thus Adam answer'd sad.
95   "Best Image of myself and dearer half,
The trouble of thy thoughts this night in sleep
Affects me equally; nor can I like
This uncouth° dream, of evil sprung I fear;
Yet evil whence? in thee can harbour none,
100 Created pure. But know that in the Soul
Are many lesser Faculties that serve
Reason as chief; among these Fancy next
Her office holds; of all external things,
Which the five watchful Senses represent,
105 She forms Imaginations, Airy shapes,
Which Reason joining or disjoining, frames°
All what we affirm or what deny, and call
Our knowledge or opinion; then retires
Into her private Cell when Nature rests.
110 Oft in her absence mimic Fancy wakes
To imitate her; but misjoining shapes,
Wild work produces oft, and most in dreams,
Ill matching words and deeds long past or late.
Some such resemblances methinks I find
115 Of our last Ev'ning's talk, in this thy dream,
But with addition strange; yet be not sad.
Evil into the mind of God or Man
May come and go, so° unapprov'd, and leave
No spot or blame behind: Which gives me hope
120 That what in sleep thou didst abhor to dream,
Waking thou never wilt consent to do.
Be not disheart'n'd, then, nor cloud those looks

___

98 **uncouth** unknown, strange.   106 **frames** shapes into.   118 **so** both "as in your case," and "provided that it be."

That wont° to be more cheerful and serene
Than when fair Morning first smiles on the World,
And let us to our fresh employments rise   *125*
Among the Groves, the Fountains, and the Flow'rs
That open now their choicest bosom'd smells
Reserv'd from night, and kept for thee in store."
        So cheer'd he his fair Spouse, and she was
          cheer'd,
But silently a gentle tear let fall   *130*
From either eye, and wip'd them with her hair;
Two other precious drops that ready stood,
Each in their crystal sluice, hee ere they fell
Kiss'd as the gracious signs of sweet remorse
And pious awe, that fear'd to have offended.   *135*
        So all was clear'd° and to the Field they haste.
But first from under shady arborous roof,
Soon as they forth were come to open sight
Of day-spring, and the Sun, who scarce uprisen
With wheels yet hov'ring o'er the Ocean brim,   *140*
Shot parallel to the earth his dewy ray,
Discovering° in wide Landscape all the East
Of Paradise and Eden's happy Plains,
Lowly they bow'd adoring, and began
Their Orisons,° each Morning duly paid   *145*
In various style, for neither various style
Nor holy rapture wanted° they to praise
Their Maker, in fit strains pronounc't or sung
Unmeditated, such prompt eloquence
Flow'd from their lips, in Prose or numerous° Verse,   *150*
More tuneable than needed Lute or Harp
To add more sweetness, and they thus began.
        "These are thy glorious works, Parent of good,
Almighty thine this universal Frame,
Thus wondrous fair; thyself how wondrous then!   *155*
Unspeakable,° who sitt'st above these Heavens
To us invisible or dimly seen
In these thy lowest works, yet these declare
Thy goodness beyond thought, and Power Divine:
Speak yee who best can tell, ye Sons of light,   *160*

---

123 **wont** are used. 136 **clear'd** made pure. 142 **Discovering** reveal-
ing. 145 **Orisons** prayers. 147 **wanted** lacked. 150 **numerous** melodious. 156 **Unspeakable** ineffable.

Angels, for yee behold him, and with songs
And choral symphonies, Day without Night,
Circle his Throne rejoicing, yee in Heav'n,
On Earth join all yee Creatures to extol
165 Him first, him last, him midst, and without end.
Fairest of Stars, last in the train of Night,
If better thou belong not to the dawn,°
Sure pledge of day, that crown'st the smiling Morn
With thy bright Circlet, praise him in thy Sphere
170 While day arises, that sweet hour of Prime.
Thou Sun, of this great World both Eye and Soul,
Acknowledge him thy Greater, sound his praise
In thy eternal course, both when thou climb'st,
And when high Noon hast gain'd, and when thou
    fall'st.
175 Moon, that now meet'st the orient Sun, now fli'st
With the fixt Stars, fixt in their Orb that flies,
And yee five other wand'ring Fires° that move
In mystic° Dance not without Song,° resound
His praise, who out of Darkness call'd up Light.
180 Air, and ye Elements the eldest birth
Of Nature's Womb, that in quaternion° run
Perpetual Circle, multiform; and mix
And nourish all things, let your ceaseless change
Vary to our great Maker still new praise.
185 Ye Mists and Exhalations that now rise
From Hill or steaming Lake, dusky or grey,
Till the Sun paint your fleecy skirts with Gold,
In honour to the World's great Author rise,
Whether to deck with Clouds the uncolour'd sky,
190 Or wet the thirsty Earth with falling showers,
Rising or falling still advance his praise.
His praise ye Winds, that from four Quarters blow,
Breathe soft or loud; and wave your tops, ye Pines,
With every Plant, in sign of Worship wave.
195 Fountains and yee, that warble, as ye flow,
Melodious murmurs, warbling tune his praise.
Join voices all ye living Souls, ye Birds,

166–67 The evening star, Hesperus, is the same as the morning star,
Venus. 177 **five . . . Fires** the planets Mars, Venus, Mercury, Jupiter,
Saturn. 178 **mystic** allegorical. 178 **Song** the music of the spheres.
181 **quaternion** group of four.

That singing up to Heaven Gate ascend,
Bear on your wings and in your notes his praise;
Yee that in Waters glide, and yee that walk   *200*
The Earth, and stately tread, or lowly creep;
Witness if I be silent, Morn or Even,
To Hill, or Valley, Fountain, or fresh shade
Made vocal by my Song, and taught his praise.
Hail universal Lord, be bounteous still   *205*
To give us only good; and if the night
Have gathered aught of evil or conceal'd,
Disperse it, as now light dispels the dark."
         So pray'd they innocent, and to their thoughts
Firm peace recover'd soon and wonted calm.   *210*
On to their morning's rural work they haste
Among sweet dews and flow'rs; where any row
Of Fruit-trees overwoody reach'd too far
Their pamper'd boughs, and needed hands to check
Fruitless embraces: or they led the Vine   *215*
To wed her Elm; she spous'd about him twines
Her marriageable arms, and with her brings
Her dow'r th'adopted Clusters, to adorn
His barren leaves. Them thus employ'd beheld
With pity Heav'n's high King, and to him call'd   *220*
Raphaël, the sociable Spirit, that deign'd
To travel with Tobias, and secur'd
His marriage with the seven-times-wedded Maid.°
         "Raphaël," said hee, "thou hear'st what stir
            on Earth
Satan from Hell 'scapt through the darksome Gulf   *225*
Hath rais'd in Paradise, and how disturb'd
This night the human pair, how he designs
In them at once to ruin all mankind.
Go therefore, half this day as friend with friend
Converse with Adam, in what Bow'r or shade   *230*
Thou find'st him from the heat of Noon retir'd,
To respite his day-labour with repast,
Or with repose; and such discourse bring on,
As may advise him of his happy state,
Happiness in his power left free to will,   *235*

221–23 See IV 167–71. The previous husbands of Sara had all been murdered by the evil spirit Asmodeus.

Left to his own free Will his Will though free,
Yet mutable; whence warn him to beware
He swerve not too secure:° tell him withal
His danger, and from whom, what enemy
240 Late fall'n himself from Heav'n, is plotting now
The fall of others from like state of bliss;
By violence, no, for that shall be withstood,
But by deceit and lies; this let him know,
Lest wilfully transgressing he pretend°
245 Surprisal, umadmonisht, unforewarn'd."
          So spake th'Etetnal Father, and fulfill'd
All Justice: nor delay'd the winged Saint
After his charge receiv'd; but from among
Thousand Celestial Ardours,° where he stood
250 Veil'd with his gorgeous wings, up-springing light°
Flew through the midst of Heav'n; th'angelic Choirs
On each hand parting, to his speed gave way
Through all th'Empyreal road; till at the Gate
Of Heav'n arriv'd, the gate self-open'd wide
255 On golden Hinges turning, as by work
Divine the sovran Architect had fram'd.
From hence, no cloud, or, to obstruct his sight,
Star interpos'd, however small he sees,
Not unconform to other shining Globes,
260 Earth and the Gard'n of God, with Cedars crown'd
Above all Hills. As when by night the Glass
Of Galileo, less assur'd, observes
Imagin'd Lands and Regions in the Moon:
Or Pilot from amidst the Cyclades°
265 Delos or Samoa first appearing kens
A cloudy spot. Down thither prone in flight
He speeds, and through the vast Ethereal Sky
Sails between worlds and worlds, with steady wing
Now on the polar winds, then with quick Fan
270 Winnows the buxom° Air; till within soar
Of Tow'ring Eagles, to all the Fowls he seems
A Phoenix, gaz'd by all, as that sole Bird
When to enshrine his relics in the Sun's
Bright Temple, to Egyptian Thebes he flies.

238 **secure** overconfident of safety.   244 **pretend** claim.   249 **Ardours**
bright angels.   250 **light** lightly (but notice "Ardours").   264 **Cyclades**
Aegean islands.   270 **buxom** yielding.

At once on th'Eastern cliff of Paradise   275
He 'lights, and to his proper shape returns
A Seraph wing'd; six wings he wore, to shade
His lineaments Divine; the pair that clad
Each shoulder broad, came mantling o'er his breast
With regal Ornament; the middle pair   280
Girt like a Starry Zone° his waist, and round
Skirted his loins and thighs with downy Gold
And colours dipt in Heav'n; the third his feet
Shadow'd from either heel with feather'd mail
Sky-tinctur'd grain.° Like Maia's son° he stood,   285
And shook his Plumes, that Heav'nly fragrance fill'd
The circuit wide. Straight knew him all the Bands
Of Angels under watch; and to his state,°
And to his message high in honour rise;
For on some message high they guess'd him bound.   290
Their glittering Tents he pass'd, and now is come
Into the blissful field, through Groves of Myrrh,
And flow'ring Odours, Cassia, Nard, and Balm;
A Wilderness of sweets; for Nature here
Wanton'd as in her prime, and play'd at will   295
Her Virgin Fancies, pouring forth more sweet,
Wild above rule or Art; enormous° bliss.
Him through the spicy Forest onward come
Adam discern'd, as in the door he sat
Of his cool Bow'r, while now the mounted Sun   300
Shot down direct his fervid Rays to warm
Earth's inmost womb, more warmth than Adam
    needs;
And Eve within, due at her hour prepar'd
For dinner savoury fruits, of taste to please
True appetite, and not disrelish thirst   305
Of nectarous draughts between, from milky stream,
Berry or Grape: to whom thus Adam call'd.
        "Haste hither Eve, and worth thy sight behold
Eastward among those Trees, what glorious shape

281 **Zone** belt. 285 **grain** dye. 285 **Maia's son** Mercury (Hermes), messenger of the gods. 288 **state** stateliness and rank. 297 **enormous** out
of rule (Latin *norma*); the word is, as yet, innocent because Eden has no
need of rules—but it is ominous too, since the ordinary sense was a bad
one (as in "enormity"). There is the same combination of innocence and
portent in lines 294–95, "Wilderness" and "Wanton'd."

310 Comes this way moving; seems another Morn
    Ris'n on mid-noon; some great behest from Heav'n
    To us perhaps he brings, and will vouchsafe
    This day to be our Guest. But go with speed,
    And what thy stores contain, bring forth and pour
315 Abundance, fit to honour and receive
    Our Heav'nly stranger; well we may afford
    Our givers their own gifts, and large bestow
    From large bestow'd, where Nature multiplies
    Her fertile growth, and by disburd'ning grows
320 More fruitful, which instructs us not to spare."
              To whom thus Eve. "Adam,° earth's hallow'd
                   mould,
    Of God inspir'd,° small store will serve, where store,
    All seasons, ripe for use hangs on the stalk;
    Save what by frugal° storing firmness gains
325 To nourish, and superfluous moist consumes:
    But I will haste and from each bough and brake,
    Each Plant and Juiciest Gourd° will pluck such
         choice°
    To entertain our Angel guest, as hee
    Beholding shall confess that here on Earth
330 God hath dispenst his bounties as in Heav'n."
              So saying, with dispatchful looks in haste
    She turns, on hóspitable thoughts intent
    What choice to choose for delicacy best,
    What order, so contriv'd as not to mix
335 Tastes, not well join'd, inelegant,° but bring
    Taste after taste upheld with kindliest° change,
    Bestirs her then, and from each tender stalk
    Whatever Earth all-bearing Mother yields
    In India° East or West, or middle shore°
340 In Pontus° or the Punic° Coast, or where
    Alcinous° reign'd; fruit of all kinds, in coat,
    Rough, or smooth rind, or bearded husk, or shell

---

321 **Adam** the name from "red earth." 322 **inspir'd** given the breath of
life.   324 **frugal** economical (and from Latin *fruges*, fruits).   327 **Gourd**
fruit of the melon family.   327 **choice** excellence, the "pick."   335 **inelegant** such as would not be delicate in taste (the idea of "choosing," from
Latin *eligere*, to select).   336 **kindliest** most natural.   339 **India** Indies.   339 **middle shore** Mediterranean.   340 **Pontus** in Asia
Minor.   340 **Punic** Carthaginian.   341 **Alcinous** king of the Phaeacians,
who entertained Odysseus and had fine gardens.

She gathers, Tribute large, and on the board
Heaps with unsparing hand; for drink the Grape
She crushes, inoffensive must,° and meads   *345*
From many a berry, and from sweet kernels prest
She tempers dulcet creams, nor these to hold
Wants° her fit vessels pure, then strews the ground
With Rose and Odours from the shrub unfum'd.°
Meanwhile our Primitive° great Sire, to meet   *350*
His godlike Guest, walks forth, without more train
Accompani'd than with his own complete
Perfections, in himself was all his state,
More solemn than the tedious pomp that waits
On Princes, when their rich Retínue long   *355*
Of Horses led, and Grooms besmear'd with Gold
Dazzles the crowd, and sets them all agape.
Nearer his presence Adam though not aw'd,
Yet with submiss approach and reverence meek,
As to a superior Nature, bowing low,   *360*
Thus said. "Native of Heav'n, for other place
None can than Heav'n such glorious shape contain;
Since by descending from the Thrones above,
Those happy places then hast deign'd awhile
To want, and honour these, vouchsafe with us   *365*
Two only, who yet by sovran gift possess
This spacious ground, in yonder shady Bow'r
To rest, and what the Garden choicest bears
To sit and taste, till this meridian heat
Be over, and the Sun more cool decline."   *370*
        Whom thus the Angelic Virtue answer'd mild.
"Adam, I therefore came, nor art thou such
Created, or such place host here to dwell,
As may not oft invite, though Spirits of Heav'n
To visit thee; lead on then where thy Bow'r   *375*
O'ershades; for these mid-hours, till Ev'ning rise
I have at will." So to the Sylvan Lodge
They came, that like Pomona's° Arbour smil'd
With flow'rets deckt and fragrant smells; but Eve
Undeckt, save with herself more lovely fair   *380*
Than Wood-Nymph, or the fairest Goddess feign'd

345 **must** unfermented wine. 348 **Wants** lacks. 349 **unfum'd** not
burned for incense, but naturally scented. 350 **Primitive** from the first
age. 378 **Pomona** goddess of fruit.

Of three that in Mount Ida naked strove,°
Stood to entertain° her guest from Heav'n; no veil
Shee needed, Virtue-proof,° no thought infirm
385 Alter'd her cheek. On whom the Angel *Hail*
Bestowed, the holy salutation us'd
Long after to blest Mary, second Eve.

> "Hail Mother of Mankind, whose fruitful Womb
> Shall fill the World more numerous with thy Sons
390 Than with these various fruits the Trees of God
Have heaped this Table." Rais'd of grassy turf
Their Table was, and mossy seats had round,
And on her ample Square from side to side
All Autumn pil'd, though Spring and Autumn here
395 Danc'd hand in hand. Awhile discourse they hold;
No fear lest Dinner cool; when thus began
Our Author. "Heav'nly stranger, please to taste
These bounties which our Nourisher, from whom
All perfect good unmeasur'd out, descends,
400 To us for food and for delight hath caus'd
The Earth to yield; unsavoury food perhaps
To spiritual Natures; only this I know,
That one Celestial Father gives to all."

> To whom the Angel. "Therefore what he gives
405 (Whose praise be ever sung) to man in part
Spiritual, may of purest Spirits be found
No ingrateful food: and food alike those pure
Intelligential° substances require
As doth your Rational; and both contain
410 Within them every lower faculty
Of sense, whereby they hear, see, smell, touch, taste,
Tasting concoct, digest, assimilate,
And corporeal to incorporeal turn.
For know, whatever was created, needs
415 To be sustain'd and fed; of Elements
The grosser feeds the purer, earth the sea,
Earth and the Sea feed Air, the Air those Fires
Ethereal, and as lowest first the Moon;
Whence in her visage round those spots, unpurg'd

382 **Of three . . . strove** The judgment of Paris, who awarded the apple
to Aphrodite.   383 **entertain** formally welcome.   384 **-proof** armored in.
408 **Intelligential** An intelligence is a spirit, angel, as in VIII 181.

Vapours not yet into her substance turn'd.   *420*
Nor doth the Moon no nourishment exhale
From her moist Continent to higher Orbs.
The Sun that light imparts to all, receives
From all his alimental° recompense
In humid exhalations, and at Even   *425*
Sups with the Ocean: though in Heav'n the Trees
Of life ambrosial fruitage bear, and vines
Yield Nectar, though from off the boughs each Morn
We brush mellifluous° Dews, and find the ground
Cover'd with pearly grain: yet God hath here   *430*
Varied his bounty so with new delights,
As may compare with Heaven; and to taste
Think not I shall be nice."° So down they sat,
And to their viands fell, nor seemingly°
The Angel, nor in mist, the common gloss°   *435*
Of Theologians, but with keen dispatch
Of real hunger, and concoctive° heat
To transubstantiate;° what redounds,° transpires
Through Spirits with ease; nor wonder; if by fire
Of sooty coal th'Empiric° Alchemist   *440*
Can turn, or holds it possible to turn
Metals of drossiest° Ore to perfect Gold
As from the Mine. Meanwhile at Table Eve
Minister'd naked, and their flowing cups
With pleasant liquors crown'd: O innocence   *445*
Deserving Paradise! if ever, then,
Then had the Sons of God excuse to have been
Enamour'd at that sight; but in those hearts
Love unlibidinous reign'd, nor jealousy
Was understood, the injur'd Lover's Hell.   *450*
          Thus when with meats and drinks they had
                suffic'd,
Not burd'n'd Nature, sudden mind arose

---

424 **alimental** nourishing.   429 **mellifluous** flowing with honey, as in
Rowland: "The increase of bees is more in regard of . . . the plenty of
mellifluous dews" (1658).   433 **nice** fastidious.   434 **seemingly** only
seemed.   435 **gloss** explanation.   437 **concoctive** digestive.   438 **transubstantiate** change from one substance to another, with a sardonic pun
against the "Theologians" because of the Roman Catholic doctrine of
"Transubstantiation"; "real" too is a theological term from the Holy
Communion.   438 **redounds** is superfluous.   440 **Empiric** quack experi-
menter.   442 **drossiest** most full of dregs.

In Adam, not to let th'occasion pass
Given him by this great Conference to know
455 Of things above his World, and of their being
Who dwell in Heav'n, whose excellence he saw
Transcend his own so far, whose radiant forms
Divine effulgence, whose high Power so far
Exceeded human, and his wary speech
460 Thus to th'Empyreal Minister he fram'd.

    "Inhabitant with God, now know I well
Thy favour, in this honour done to man,
Under whose lowly roof thou hast vouchsaf't
To enter, and these earthly fruits to taste,
465 Food not of Angels, yet accepted so,
As that more willingly thou couldst not seem
At Heav'n's high feasts to have fed: yet what
   compare?"

    To whom the winged Hierarch° repli'd.
"O Adam, one Almighty is, from whom
470 All things proceed, and up to him return,
If not deprav'd from good, created all
Such to perfection, one first matter all,
Indu'd with various forms, various degrees
Of substance, and in things that live, of life;
475 But more refin'd, more spiritous, and pure,
As nearer to him plac't or nearer tending
Each in their several active Spheres assign'd,
Till body up to spirit work, in bounds
Proportion'd to each kind. So from the root
480 Springs lighter the green stalk, from thence the leaves
More airy, last the bright consummate° flow'r
Spirits odórous breathes: flow'rs and their fruit
Man's nourishment, by gradual scale sublim'd°
To vital Spirits° aspire, to animal,
485 To intellectual, give both life and sense,
Fancy and understanding, whence the soul
Reason receives, and reason is her being,
Discursive, or Intuitive;° discourse
Is oftest yours, the latter most is ours,

---

468 **Hierarch** sacred leader.   481 **consummate** perfected.   483 **sublim'd**
refined.   484 **Spirits** "Spirits" (animal, vital, intellectual) were thought to
permeate the body.   488 **Discursive, or Intuitive** Discourse is reasoning
process; intuition, the immediate apprehension of truth.

Differing but in degree, of kind the same.   490
Wonder not then, what God for you saw good
If I refuse not, but convert, as you,
To proper° substance; time may come when men
With Angels may participate, and find
No inconvenient Diet, nor too light Fare: 495
And from these corporal nutriments perhaps
Your bodies may at last turn all to Spirit,
Improv'd by tract of time, and wing'd ascend
Ethereal, as wee, or may at choice   —
Here or in Heav'nly Paradises dwell;   500
If ye be found obedient, and retain
Unalterably firm his love entire°
Whose progeny you are. Meanwhile enjoy
Your fill what happiness this happy state
Can comprehend, incapable of more."   505
      To whom the Patriarch of mankind repli'd.
"O favourable spirit, propitious guest,
Well hast thou taught the way that might direct
Our knowledge, and the scale° of Nature set
From center to circumference, whereon   510
In contemplation° of created things
By steps we may ascend to God. But say,
What meant that caution join'd, *if ye be found*
Obedient? can wee want obedience then
To him, or possibly his love desert   515
Who form'd us from the dust, and plac'd us here
Full to the utmost measure of what bliss
Human desires can seek or apprehend?"
      To whom the Angel. "Son of Heav'n and Earth,
Attend: That thou art happy, owe to God,   520
That thou continu'st such, owe to thyself,
That is, to thy obedience; therein stand.
This was that caution giv'n thee; be advis'd.
God made thee perfect, not immutable;
And good he made thee, but to persevere   525
He left it in thy power, ordain'd thy will
By nature free, not overrul'd by Fate
Inextricable,° or strict necessity;

493 **proper** my own. 502 **entire** unblemished. 509 **scale** ladder. 511 **contemplation** from Latin *com + templum*, consecrated space (temple); notice "steps," "God." 528 **Inextricable** inescapable.

Our voluntary service he requires,
530 Not our necessitated, such with him
Finds no acceptance, nor can find, for how
Can hearts, not free, be tri'd whether they serve
Willing or no, who will but what they must
By Destiny, and can no other choose?
535 Myself and all th'Angelic Host that stand
In sight of God enthron'd, our happy state
Hold, as you yours, while our obedience holds;
On other surety° none; freely we serve,
Because wee freely love, as in our will
540 To love or not; in this we stand or fall:
And some are fall'n, to disobedience fall'n,
And so from Heav'n to deepest Hell; O fall
From what high state of bliss into what woe!"
        To whom our great Progenitor. "Thy words
545 Attentive, and with more delighted ear
Divine instructor, I have heard, than when
Cherubic Songs by night from neighbouring Hills
Aereal Music send: nor knew I not
To be both will and deed created free;
550 Yet that we never shall forget to love
Our maker, and obey him whose command
Single,° is yet so just, my constant thoughts
Assur'd me and still assure: though what thou tell'st
Hath past in Heav'n, some doubt within me move,
555 But more desire to hear, if thou consent,
The full relation, which must needs be strange,
Worthy of Sacred silence to be heard;
And we have yet large day, for scarce the Sun
Hath finisht half his journey, and scarce begins
560 His other half in the great Zone of Heav'n."
        Thus Adam made request, and Raphaël
After short pause assenting, thus began.
        "High matter thou enjoin'st me, O prime of
                men,
Sad task and hard, for how shall I relate
565 To human sense th'invisible exploits

---

538 **surety** ground of certainty (and with a hint at the specific application
to Christ as our "surety"). 552 **Single** sole (command); also absolute,
as in Milton's *Comus* ("single darkness"), and openly upright (Shakespeare: "a single heart").

Of warring Spirits; how without remorse°
The ruin of so many glorious once
And perfect while they stood; how last unfold
The secrets of another world, perhaps
Not lawful to reveal? yet for thy good   *570*
This is dispens't,° and what surmounts the reach
Of human sense, I shall delineate so,
By lik'ning spiritual to corporal forms,
As may express them best, though what if Earth
Be but the shadow of Heav'n, and things therein   *575*
Each to other like, more than on earth is thought?
    As yet this world was not, and Chaos wild
Reign'd where these Heav'ns now roll, where Earth
  now rests
Upon her Center pois'd, when on a day
(For Time, though in Eternity, appli'd   *580*
To motion, measures all things durable
By present, past, and future) on such day
As Heav'n's great Year° brings forth, th'Empyreal
  Host
Of Angels by Imperial summons call'd,
Innumerable before th'Almighty's Throne   *585*
Forthwith from all the ends of Heav'n appear'd
Under their Hierarchs in orders bright
Ten thousand thousand Ensigns high advanc'd,
Standards, and Gonfalons° 'twixt Van and Rear
Stream in the Air, and for distinction serve   *590*
Of hierarchies, of Orders, and Degrees;
Or in their glittering Tissues bear emblaz'd
Holy Memorials,° acts of Zeal and Love
Recorded eminent. Thus when in Orbs
Of circuit inexpressible they stood,   *595*
Orb within Orb, the Father infinite,
By whom in bliss imbosom'd sat the Son,
Amidst as from a flaming Mount, whose top
Brightness had made invisible, thus spake.
    'Hear all ye Angels, Progeny of Light,   *600*
Thrones, Dominations, Princedoms, Virtues, Powers,
Hear my Decree, which unrevok't shall stand.

566 **remorse** pity. 571 **dispens't** permitted (legal and ecclesiastical).
583 **great Year** the cycle of the years, borrowed from Plato.   589 **Gonfalons** banners.   593 **Memorials** commemorations.

This day I have begot whom I declare
My only Son, and on this holy Hill
605 Him have anointed,° whom ye now behold
At my right hand; your Head I him appoint;
And by my Self have sworn to him shall bow
All knees in Heav'n, and shall confess him Lord:
Under his great Vice-gerent° Reign abide
610 United as one individual° Soul
For ever happy; him who disobeys
Mee disobeys, breaks union, and that day
Cast out from God and blessed vision, falls
Into utter darkness, deep engulft, his place
615 Ordained without redemption, without end.'
        So spake th'Omnipotent, and with his words
All seem'd well pleas'd, all seem'd, but were not all.
That day, as other solemn days, they spent
In song and dance about the sacred Hill,
620 Mystical dance, which yonder starry Sphere
Of Planets and of fixt in all her Wheels
Resembles nearest, mazes intricate,
Eccentric,° intervolv'd, yet regular
Then most, when most irregular they seem:
625 And in their motions° harmony Divine
So smoothes her charming tones, that God's own ear
Listens delighted. Ev'ning now approach'd
(For we have also our Ev'ning and our Morn,
We ours for change delectable, not need)
630 Forthwith from dance to sweet repast they turn
Desirous, all in Circles as they stood,
Tables are set, and on a sudden pil'd
With Angels' Food, and rubied Nectar flows:
In Pearl, in Diamond, and massy Gold,
635 Fruit of delicious Vines, the growth of Heav'n.
On flow'rs repos'd, and with fresh flow'rets crown'd,
They eat, they drink, and in communion sweet
Quaff immortality and joy, secure
Of surfeit where full measure only bounds

---

605 **anointed** the Hebrew meaning of "Messiah." 609 **Vice-gerent** exer-
cising deputed power. 610 **individual** indivisible. 623 **Eccentric** in an
orbit not precisely circular. 625 **motions** including a musical suggestion,
as in "movements."

Excess, before th'all-bounteous King, who show'r'd°   640
With copious hand, rejoicing in their joy.
Now when ambrosial Night with Clouds exhal'd
From that high mount of God, whence light and shade
Spring both, the face of brightest Heav'n had chang'd
To grateful Twilight (for Night comes not there   645
In darker veil) and roseate Dews dispos'd
All but th'unsleeping eyes of God to rest,
Wide over all the Plain, and wider far
Then all this globous Earth in Plain outspread,
(Such are the Courts of God) Th'Angelic throng   650
Disperst in Bands and Files their Camp extend
By living Streams among the Trees of Life,
Pavilions numberless, and sudden rear'd,
Celestial Tabernacles, where they slept
Fann'd with cool Winds, save those who in their
    course   655
Melodious Hymns about the sovran Throne
Alternate° all night long: but not so wak'd
Satan, so call him now, his former name
Is heard no more in Heav'n; he of the first,
If not the first Arch-Angel, great in Power,   660
In favour and preeminence, yet fraught
With envy against the Son of God, that day
Honour'd by his great Father, and proclaim'd
Messiah King anointed, could not bear
Through pride that sight, and thought himself impair'd.   665
Deep malice thence conceiving and disdain,
Soon as midnight brought on the dusky hour
Friendliest to sleep and silence, he resolv'd
With all his Legions to dislodge, and leave
Unworshipt, unobey'd the Throne supreme   670
Contemptuous, and his next subordinate
Awak'ning, thus to him in secret spake.
            'Sleep'st thou Companion dear, what sleep
                can close
Thy eye-lids? and rememb'rest what Decree
Of yesterday, so late hath past the lips   675.
Of Heav'n's Almighty. Thou to me thy thoughts

637–40 **They eat . . . show'r'd** *1674*; They eat, they drink, and with refec-
tion sweet/Are fill'd, before th'all-bounteous King, who show'r'd
1667.   657 **Alternate** sing in alternation (specific musical application).

Wast wont, I mine to thee was wont to impart;
Both waking we were one; how then can now
Thy sleep dissent?° new Laws thou seest impos'd;
680 New Laws from him who reigns, new minds may raise
In us who serve, new Councils, to debate
What doubtful may ensue, more in this place
To utter is not safe. Assemble thou
Of all those Myriads which we lead the chief;
685 Tell them that by command, ere yet dim Night
Her shadowy Cloud withdraws, I am to haste,
And all who under me their Banners wave,
Homeward with flying march where we possess
The Quarters of the North° there to prepare
690 Fit entertainment to receive our King
The great Messiah, and his new commands,
Who speedily through all the Hierarchies
Intends to pass triumphant, and give Laws.'
          So spake the false Arch-Angel, and infus'd
695 Bad influence into th'unwary breast
Of his Associate; hee together calls,
Or several° one by one, the Regent Powers,
Under him Regent, tells, as he was taught,
That the most High commanding, now ere Night,
700 Now ere dim Night had disencumber'd Heav'n,
The great Hierarchal Standard was to move;
Tells the suggested° cause, and casts between
Ambiguous° words and jealousies, to sound
Or taint integrity; but all obey'd
705 The wonted signal, and superior voice
Of their great Potentate; for great indeed
His name, and high was his degree in Heav'n;
His count'nance, as the Morning Star° that guides
The starry flock, allur'd them, and with lies
710 Drew after him the third part of Heav'n's Host:
Meanwhile th'Eternal eye, whose sight discerns
Abstrusest° thoughts, from forth his holy Mount
And from within the golden Lamps that burn
Nightly before him, saw without their light

---

679 **dissent** differ.   689 **North** traditionally associated with Satan. (ISAIAH
14:13).   697 **several** separate.   702 **suggested** both "insinuated" and
"falsely imputed."   703 **Ambiguous** equivocal (duplicity contrasting with "integrity").   708 **Morning Star** Lucifer.   712 **Abstrusest** most hidden.

Rebellion rising, saw in whom, how spread   *715*
Among the sons of Morn, what multitudes
Were banded to oppose his high Decree;
And smiling to his only Son thus said.
        'Son, thou in whom my glory I behold
In full resplendence, Heir of all my might,   *720*
Nearly° it now concerns us to be sure
Of our Omnipotence, and with what Arms
We mean to hold what anciently we claim
Of Deity or Empire, such a foe
Is rising, who intends to erect his Throne   *725*
Equal to ours, throughout the spacious North;
Nor so content, hath in his thought to try
In battle, what our Power is, or our right.
Let us advise,° and to this hazard draw
With speed what force is left, and all employ   *730*
In our defence, lest unawares we lose
This our high place, our Sanctuary, our Hill.'
        To whom the Son with calm aspéct and clear
Light'ning Divine, ineffable, serene,
Made answer. 'Mighty Father, thou thy foes   *735*
Justly hast in derision, and secure
Laugh'st at their vain designs and tumults vain,
Matter to mee of Glory, whom their hate
Illústrates,° when they see all Regal Power
Giv'n me to quell their pride, and in event°   *740*
Know whether I be dextrous° to subdue
Thy Rebels, or be found the worst in Heav'n.'
        So spake the Son, but Satan with his Powers
Far was advanc't on winged speed, an Host
Innumerable as the Stars of Night,   *745*
Or Stars of Morning, Dew-drops, which the Sun
Impearls on every leaf and every flow'r.
Regions they pass'd, the mighty Regencies
Of Seraphim and Potentates and Thrones
In their triple Degrees, Regions to which   *750*
All thy Dominion, Adam, is no more

---

721 **Nearly** closely, particularly. 729 **advise** consult. 739 **Illústrates**
makes illustrious, gives luster to (following on "Light'ning" and
"Glory"). 740 **event** outcome. 741 **dextrous** Christ's powers deriving
from his position on the right hand of God ("dextrous" in a common
17th-century sense); see III 62–64.

Than what this Garden is to all the Earth,
And all the Sea, from one entire globose
Stretcht into Longitude; which having pass'd
755 At length into the limits of the North
They came, and Satan to his Royal seat
High on a Hill, far blazing, as a Mount
Rais'd on a Mount, with Pyramids and Tow'rs
From Diamond Quarries hewn, and Rocks of Gold,
760 The Palace of great Lucifer, (so call
That Structure in the Dialect of men
Interpreted) which not long after, hee
Affecting° all equality with God,
In imitation of that Mount whereon
765 Messiah was declar'd in sight of Heav'n,
The Mountain of the Congregation call'd;
For thither he assembl'd all his Train,
Pretending so commanded to consult
About the great reception of their King,
770 Thither to come, and with calumnious Art
Of counterfeited truth thus held their ears.
        "Thrones, Dominations, Princedoms, Virtues,
            Powers,
If these magnific Titles yet remain
Not merely titular, since by Decree
775 "Another now hath to himself engross't°
All Power, and us eclipst under the name
Of King anointed, for whom all this haste
Of midnight march, and hurried meeting here,
This only to consult how we may best
780 With what may be devis'd of honours new
Receive him coming to receive from us
Knee-tribute yet unpaid, prostration vile,
Too much to one, but double how endur'd,
To one and to his image now proclaim'd?
785 But what if better counsels might erect
Our minds and teach us to cast off this Yoke?
Will ye submit your necks, and choose to bend
The supple° knee? ye will not, if I trust
To know ye right, or if ye know yourselves

763 **Affecting** aspiring to.   775 **engross't** monopolized.   788 **supple** as
in "suppliant."

Natives and Sons of Heav'n possest before   790
By none, and if not equal all, yet free,
Equally free; for Orders and Degrees
Jar not with liberty, but well consist.°
Who can in reason then or right assume
Monarchy over such as. live by right   795
His equals, if in power and splendor less,
In freedom equal? or can introduce
Law and Edíct on us, who without law
Err not, much less for this to be our Lord,
And look for adoration to th'abuse   800
Of those Imperial Titles which assert
Our being ordain'd to govern, not to serve?'
     Thus far his bold discourse without control
Had audience, when among the Seraphim
Abdiel, than whom none with more zeal ador'd   805
The Deity, and divine commands obey'd,
Stood up, and in a flame of zeal severe
The current of his fury thus oppos'd.
     'O argument blasphémous, false and proud!
Words which no ear ever to hear in Heav'n   810
Expected, least of all from thee, ingrate
In place thyself so high above thy Peers.
Canst thou with impious obloquy condemn
The just Decree of God, pronounc't and sworn,
That to his only Son by right endu'd   815
With Regal Scepter, every Soul in Heav'n
Shall bend the knee, and in that honour due
Confess him rightful King? unjust thou say'st
Flatly unjust, to bind with Laws the free,
And equal over equals to let Reign,   820
One over all with unsucceeded° power.
Shalt thou give Law to God, shalt thou dispute
With him the points of liberty, who made
Thee what thou art, and form'd the Pow'rs of Heav'n
Such as he pleas'd, and circumscrib'd their being? 825
Yet by experience taught we know how good,
And of our good, and of our dignity
How provident he is, how far from thought
To make us less, bent rather to exalt

793 **consist** go together, harmonize.   821 **unsucceeded** without successor.

830 Our happy state under one Head more near
United. But to grant it thee unjust,
That equal over equals Monarch Reign:
Thyself though great and glorious dost thou count,
Of all Angelic Nature join'd in one,
835 Equal to him begotten Son, by whom
As by his Word the mighty Father made
All things, ev'n thee, and all the Spirits of Heav'n
By him created in their bright degrees,
Crown'd them with Glory, and to their Glory nam'd
840 Thrones, Dominations, Princedoms, Virtues, Powers,
Essential Powers, nor by his Reign obscur'd,
But more illustrious made, since he the Head
One of our number thus reduc't becomes,
His Laws our Laws, all honour to him done
845 Returns our own. Cease then this impious rage,
And tempt not these; but hast'n to appease
Th'incensed Father, and th'incensed Son,
While Pardon may be found in time besought.'
        So spake the fervent Angel, but his zeal
850 None seconded, as out of season judg'd,
Or singular and rash, whereat rejoic'd
Th'Apostate, and more haughty thus repli'd.
'That we were form'd then say'st thou? and the work
Of secondary hands, by task transferr'd
855 From Father to his Son? strange point and new!
Doctrine which we would know whence learnt: who
        saw
When this creation was? remember'st thou
Thy making, while the Maker gave thee being?
We know no time when we were not as now;
860 Know none before us, self-begot, self-rais'd
By our own quick'ning power, when fatal course
Had circl'd his full Orb, the birth mature
Of this our native Heav'n, Ethereal Sons.
Our puissance is our own, our own right hand
865 Shall teach us highest deeds, by proof to try
Who is our equal: then thou shalt behold
Whether by supplication we intend
Address,° and to begirt th'Almighty Throne

---

868 **Address** dutiful approach, as in "pay one's addresses to."

Beseeching or besieging. This report,
These tidings carry to th'anointed King;   870
And fly, ere evil intercept thy flight.'
          He said, and as the sound of waters deep
Hoarse murmur echo'd to his words applause
Through the infinite Host, nor less for that
The flaming Seraph fearless, though alone   875
Encompass'd round with foes, thus answer'd bold.
          'O alienate from God, O spirit accurst,
Forsak'n of all good; I see thy fall
Determin'd, and thy hapless crew involv'd
In this perfidious fraud, contagion spread   880
Both of thy crime and punishment: henceforth
No more be troubl'd how to quit the yoke
Of God's Messiah; those indulgent Laws
Will not be now vouchsaf't, other Decrees
Against thee are gone forth without recall;   885
That Golden Scepter which thou didst reject
Is now an Iron Rod to bruise and break
Thy disobedience. Well thou didst advise,
Yet not for thy advise or threats I fly
These wicked Tents devoted,° lest the wrath   890
Impendent, raging into sudden flame
Distinguish not: for soon expect to feel
His Thunder on thy head, devouring fire.
Then who created thee lamenting learn,
When who can uncreate thee thou shalt know.'   895
          So spake the Seraph Abdiel faithful found,
Among the faithless, faithful only hee;
Among innumerable false, unmov'd,
Unshaken, unseduc'd; unterrifi'd
His Loyalty he kept, his Love, his Zeal;   900
Nor number, nor example with him wrought
To swerve from truth, or change his constant mind
Though single. From amidst them forth he pass'd,
Long way through hostile scorn, which he sustain'd
Superior,° nor of violence fear'd aught;   905
And with retorted° scorn his back he turn'd
On those proud Tow'rs to swift destruction doom'd.

---

890 **devoted** doomed.   905 **Superior** too great to be overcome.   906 **retorted** flung back.

BOOK VI

THE ARGUMENT

Raphael continues to relate how Michael and Gabriel
were sent forth to Battle against Satan and his Angels.
The first Fight describ'd: Satan and his Powers retire
under Night: He calls a Council, invents devilish Engines,
which in the second day's Fight put Michael and his
Angels to some disorder; But they at length pulling up
Mountains overwhelm'd both the force and Machines of
Satan: Yet the Tumult not so ending, God on the third
day sends Messiah his Son, for whom he had reserv'd the
glory of that Victory: Hee in the Power of his Father coming to the place, and causing all his Legions to stand still
on either side, with his Chariot and Thunder driving into
the midst of his Enemies, pursues them unable to resist
towards the wall of Heaven; which opening, they leap
down with horror and confusion into the place of punishment prepar'd for them in the Deep: Messiah returns with
triumph to his Father.

All night the dreadless Angel unpursu'd
Through Heav'n's wide Champaign° held his way,
   till Morn,
Wak't by the circling Hours, with rosy hand
Unbarr'd the gates of Light. There is a Cave
Within the Mount of God, fast by his Throne,
Where light and darkness in perpetual round
Lodge and dislodge by turns, which makes through
   Heav'n
Grateful vicissitude, like Day and Night;
Light issues forth, and at the other door

5

---

2 **Champaign** plain.

Obsequious° darkness enters, till her hour   *10*
To veil the Heav'n, though darkness there might well
Seem twilight here; and now went forth the Morn
Such as in highest Heav'n, array'd in Gold
Empyreal, from before her vanisht Night,
Shot through° with orient Beams: when all the Plain   *15*
Cover'd with thick embattled Squadrons bright,
Chariots and flaming Arms, and fiery Steeds
Reflecting blaze on blaze, first met his view:
War he perceiv'd, war in procinct,° and found
Already known what he for news had thought   *20*
To have reported: gladly then he mixt
Among those friendly Powers who him receiv'd
With joy and acclamations loud, that one
That of so many Myriads fall'n, yet one
Return'd not lost: On to the sacred hill   *25*
They led him high applauded, and present
Before the seat supreme; from whence a voice
From midst a Golden Cloud thus mild was heard.
        'Servant of God, well done, well hast thou
            fought
The better fight, who single hast maintain'd   *30*
Against revolted multitudes the Cause
Of Truth, in word mightier than they in Arms;
And for the testimony of Truth hast borne
Universal reproach, far worse to bear
Than violence: for this was all thy care   *35*
To stand approv'd in sight of God, though Worlds
Judg'd thee perverse: the easier conquest now
Remains thee, aided by this host of friends,
Back on thy foes more glorious to return
Than scorn'd thou didst depart, and to subdue   *40*
By force, who reason for their Law refuse,
Right reason for their Law, and for their King
Messiah, who by right of merit Reigns.
Go Michael of Celestial Armies Prince,
And thou in Military prowess next   *45*
Gabriel, lead forth to Battle these my Sons
Invincible, lead forth my armed Saints

10 **Obsequious** following dutifully.   15 **Shot through** The military setting
(so "pierced") plays against the visual beauty ("variegated in col-
ors").   19 **procinct** readiness.

By Thousands and by Millions rang'd for fight;
Equal in number to that Godless crew
50 Rebellious, them with Fire and hostile Arms
Fearless assault, and to the brow of Heav'n
Pursuing drive them out from God and bliss,
Into their place of punishment, the Gulf
Of Tartarus, which ready opens wide
55 His fiery Chaos to receive their fall.'
          So spake the Sovran voice, and Clouds began
To darken all the Hill, and smoke to roll
In dusky wreaths, reluctant° flames, the sign
Of wrath awak't: nor with less dread the loud
60 Ethereal Trumpet from on high 'gan blow:
At which command the Powers Militant,
That stood for Heav'n, in mighty Quadrate° join'd
Of Union irresistible, mov'd on
In silence their bright Legions, to the sound
65 Of instrumental Harmony that breath'd
Heroic Ardor to advent'rous deeds
Under their God-like Leaders, in the Cause
Of God and his Messiah. On they move
Indíssolúbly firm; nor obvious° Hill,
70 Nor strait'ning° Vale, nor Wood, nor Stream divides
Their perfect ranks; for high above the ground
Their march was, and the passive Air upbore
Their nimble tread; as when the total kind
Of Birds in orderly array on wing
75 Came summon'd over Eden to receive
Their names of thee; so over many a tract
Of Heav'n they march'd, and many a Province wide
Tenfold the length of this terrene:° at last
Far in th'Horizon to the North appear'd
80 From skirt to skirt a fiery Region, stretcht
In battailous aspéct, and nearer view
Bristl'd with upright beams innumerable
Of rigid Spears, and Helmets throng'd, and Shields
Various, with boastful Argument° portray'd,
85 The banded Powers of Satan hasting on
With furious expedition; for they ween'd

58 **reluctant** struggling. 62 **Quadrate** square. 69 **obvious** in the way. 70 **strait'ning** hemming in. 78 **terrene** earth. 84 **Argument** heraldic slogans.

That selfsame day by fight, or by surprise
To win the Mount of God, and on his Throne
To set the envier of his State, the proud
Aspirer, but their thoughts prov'd fond and vain   *90*
In the mid way: though strange to us it seem'd
At first, that Angel should with Angel war,
And in fierce hosting° meet, who wont to meet
So oft in Festivals of joy and love
Unanimous,° as sons of one great Sire   *95*
Hymning th'Eternal Father: but the shout
Of Battle now began, and rushing sound
Of onset ended soon each milder thought.
High in the midst exalted as a God
Th'Apostate in his Sun-bright Chariot sat   *100*
Idol of Majesty Divine, enclos'd
With Flaming Cherubim, and golden Shields;
Then 'lighted from his gorgeous Throne, for now
'Twixt Host and Host but narrow space was left,
A dreadful interval, and Front to Front   *105*
Presented stood in terrible array
Of hideous length: before the cloudy° Van,°
On the rough edge of battle ere it join'd,
Satan with vast and haughty strides advanc't
Came tow'ring, armed in Adamant and Gold;   *110*
Abdiel that sight endur'd not, where he stood
Among the mightiest, bent on highest deeds,
And thus his own undaunted heart explores.
        'O Heav'n! that such resemblance of the
            Highest
Should yet remain, where faith and realty°   *115*
Remain not; wherefore should not strength and might
There fail where Virtue fails, or weakest prove
Where boldest; though to sight° unconquerable?
His puissance, trusting in th'Almighty's aid,
I mean to try, whose Reason I have tri'd   *120*
Unsound and false; nor is it aught but just,
That he who in debate of Truth hath won,
Should win in Arms, in both disputes alike
Victor; though brutish that contést and foul,

---

93 **hosting** encounter. 95 **Unanimous** of one mind. 107 **cloudy** darkly
foreboding. 107 **Van** vanguard. 115 **realty** honesty. 118 **to sight** to
appearances.

125 When Reason hath to deal with force, yet so
Most reason is that Reason overcome.'
                So pondering, and from his armed Peers
Forth stepping opposite,° halfway he met
His daring foe, at this prevention° more
130 Incens't, and thus securely° him defi'd.
                'Proud, art thou met? thy hope was to have
                        reacht
The heighth of thy aspiring unoppos'd,
The Throne of God unguarded, and his side
Abandon'd at the terror of thy Power
135 Or potent tongue; fool, not to think how vain
Against th'Omnipotent to rise in Arms;
Who out of smallest things could without end
Have rais'd incessant Armies to defeat
Thy folly; or with solitary hand
140 Reaching beyond all limit, at one blow
Unaided could have finisht thee, and whelm'd
Thy Legions under darkness; but thou seest
All are not of thy Train; there be who Faith
Prefer, and Piety to God, though then
145 To thee not visible, when I alone
Seem'd in thy World erroneous to dissent
From all: my Sect thou seest, now learn too late
How few sometimes may know, when thousands err.'
                Whom the grand foe with scornful eye askance
150 Thus answer'd. 'Ill for thee, but in wisht hour
Of my revenge, first sought for thou return'st
From flight, seditious Angel, to receive
Thy merited reward, the first assay
Of this right hand provok't, since first that tongue
155 Inspir'd with contradiction durst oppose
A third part of the Gods, in Synod° met
Their Deities to assert, who while they feel
Vigor Divine within them, can allow
Omnipotence to none. But well thou com'st
160 Before thy fellows, ambitious to win
From me some Plume, that thy success° may show
Destruction to the rest: this pause between

128 **opposite** including "in opposition." 129 **prevention** forestalling. 130 **securely** confidently. 156 **Synod** assembly (usually of clergy). 161 **success** here "ill-fortune."

(Unanswer'd lest thou boast) to let thee know;
At first I thought that Liberty and Heav'n
To heav'nly Souls had been all one; but now   *165*
I see that most through sloth had rather serve,
Minist'ring Spirits, train'd up in Feast and Song;
Such halt thou arm'd, the Minstrelsy° of Heav'n,
Servility with freedom to contend,
As both their deeds compar'd this day shall prove.'   *170*
        To whom in brief thus Abdiel stern repli'd.
'Apostate, still thou err'st, nor end wilt find
Of erring; from the path of truth remote:
Unjustly thou deprav'st° it with the name
Of Servitude to serve whom God ordains,   *175*
Or Nature; God and Nature bid the same,
When he who rules is worthiest, and excels
Them whom he governs. This is servitude,
To serve th'unwise, or him who hath rebell'd
Against his worthier, as thine now serve thee,   *180*
Thyself not free, but to thyself enthrall'd;
Yet lewdly° dar'st our minist'ring upbraid.
Reign thou in Hell thy Kingdom, let mee serve
In Heav'n God ever blest, and his Divine
Behests obey, worthiest to be obey'd,   *185*
Yet Chains in Hell, not Realms expect: meanwhile
From mee return'd, as erst thou said'st, from flight,
This greeting on thy impious Crest receive.'
        So saying, a noble stroke he lifted high,
Which hung not, but so swift with tempest fell   *190*
On the proud Crest of Satan, that no sight,
Nor motion of swift thought, less could his Shield
Such rain intercept: ten paces huge
He back recoil'd; the tenth on bended knee
His massy Spear upstay'd; as if on Earth   *195*
Winds under ground or waters forcing way
Sidelong, had push't a Mountain from his seat
Half sunk with all his Pines. Amazement seiz'd
The Rebel Thrones, but greater rage to see
Thus foil'd their mightiest, ours joy fill'd, and shout,   *200*
Presage of Victory and fierce desire

167–68 **Minist'ring . . . Minstrelsy** The contemptuous jingle brings out the
common origin, Latin *ministerialis*, an official. 174 **deprav'st** slanders.
182 **lewdly** vilely.

Of Battle: whereat Michael bid sound
Th'Arch-Angel trumpet; through the vast of Heav'n
It sounded, and the faithful Armies rung
205 Hosanna to the Highest: nor stood at gaze
The adverse° Legions, nor less hideous join'd
The horrid shock: now storming fury rose,
And clamor such as heard in Heav'n till now
Was never, Arms on Armor clashing bray'd
210 Horrible discord, and the madding Wheels
Of brazen Chariots rag'd; dire was the noise
Of conflict; overhead the dismal hiss
Of fiery Darts in flaming volleys flew,
And flying vaulted either Host with fire.
215 So under fiery Cope together rush'd
Both Battles main,° with ruinous assault
And inextinguishable rage; all Heav'n
Resounded, and had Earth been then, all Earth
Had to her Center shook. What wonder? when
220 Millions of fierce encount'ring Angels fought
On either side, the least of whom could wield
These Elements, and arm him with the force
Of all their Regions: how much more of Power
Army against Army numberless to raise
225 Dreadful combustion° warring, and disturb,
Though not destroy, their happy Native seat;
Had not th'Eternal King Omnipotent
From his stronghold of Heav'n high overrul'd
And limited their might; though number'd such
230 As each divided Legion might have seem'd
A numerous Host,° in strength each armed hand
A Legion; led in fight, yet Leader seem'd
Each Warrior single as in Chief, expért
When to advance, or stand, or turn the sway
235 Of Battle, open when, and when to close
The ridges of grim War; no thought of flight,
None of retreat, no unbecoming deed
That argu'd fear; each on himself reli'd,

---

206 **adverse** as in "adversary." 216 **Battles main** mighty armies, a "main battle" also being a pitched battle, contrasted with skirmishing. 225 **combustion** tumult, including the "fiery" sense of lines 213–15. 230–31 **Legion . . . Host** making use of the application "legion" to a vast multitude.

As only in his arm the moment° lay
Of victory; deeds of eternal fame   240
Were done, but infinite: for wide was spread
That War and various; sometimes on firm ground
A standing fight, then soaring on main wing
Tormented° all the Air; all Air seem'd then
Conflicting Fire: long time in even scale   245
The Battle hung; till Satan, who that day
Prodigious power had shown, and met in Arms
No equal, ranging through the dire attack
Of fighting Seraphim confus'd, at length
Saw where the Sword of Michael smote, and fell'd   250
Squadrons at once, with huge two-handed sway
Brandisht aloft the horrid edge came down
Wide wasting; such destruction to withstand
He hasted, and oppos'd the rocky Orb
Of tenfold Adamant, his ample Shield   255
A vast circumference: At his approach
The great Arch-Angel from his warlike toil
Surceas'd,° and glad as hoping here to end
Intestine° War in Heav'n, the arch foe subdu'd
Or Captive dragg'd in Chains, with hostile frown   260
And visage all inflam'd first thus began.
     'Author of evil, unknown till thy revolt,
Unnam'd in Heav'n, now plenteous, as thou seest
These Acts of hateful strife, hateful to all,
Though heaviest by just measure on thyself   265
And thy adherents: how hast thou disturb'd
Heav'n's blessed peace, and into Nature brought
Misery, uncreated till the crime
Of thy Rebellion? how hast thou instill'd
Thy malice into thousands, once upright   270
And faithful, now prov'd false. But think not here
To trouble Holy Rest; Heav'n casts thee out
From all her Confines. Heav'n the seat of bliss
Brooks not the works of violence and War.
Hence then, and evil go with thee along   275
Thy offspring, to the place of evil, Hell,
Thou and thy wicked crew; there mingle broils,

---

239 **moment** determining influence. 244 **Tormented** agitated (and a
"torment" was an engine of war which hurled stones or darts). 258 **Surceas'd** desisted. 259 **Intestine** internal, civil.

Ere this avenging Sword begin thy doom,
Or some more sudden vengeance wing'd from God
280 Precipitate thee with augmented pain.'
          So spake the Prince of Angels; to whom thus
The Adversary. 'Nor think thou with wind
Of airy threats to awe whom yet with deeds
Thou canst not. Hast thou turn'd the least of these
285 To flight, or if to fall, but that they rise
Unvanquisht, easier to transact with mee
That thou shouldst hope, imperious, and with threats
To chase me hence? err not that so shall end
The strife which thou call'st evil, but wee style
290 The strife of Glory: which we mean to win,
Or turn this Heav'n itself into the Hell
Thou fablest, here however to dwell free,
If not to reign: meanwhile thy utmost force,
And join him nam'd Almighty to thy aid,
295 I fly not, but have sought thee far and nigh.'
          They ended parle,° and both addrest for fight
Unspeakable; for who, though with the tongue
Of Angels, can relate, or to what things
Liken on Earth conspicuous, that may lift
300 Human imagination to such heighth
Of Godlike Power: for likest Gods they seem'd,
Stood they or mov'd, in stature, motion, arms
Fit to decide the Empire of great Heav'n.
Now wav'd their fiery Swords, and in the Air
305 Made horrid Circles; two broad Suns their Shields
Blaz'd opposite, while expectation stood
In horror; from each hand with speed retir'd
Where erst was thickest fight, th'Angelic throng,
And left large field, unsafe within the wind
310 Of such commotion, such as to set forth
Great things by small, If Nature's concord broke,
Among the Constellations war were sprung,
Two Planets rushing from aspéct malign°
Of fiercest opposition in mid Sky,
315 Should combat, and their jarring Spheres confound.
Together both with next to Almighty Arm,

296 **parle** parley.   313 **aspéct malign** astrological position, shedding evil influence.

Uplifted imminent° one stroke they aim'd
That might determine, and not need repeat,
As not of power, at once; nor odds appear'd
In might or swift prevention;° but the sword   320
Of Michael from the Armoury of God
Was giv'n him temper'd so, that neither keen
Nor solid might resist that edge: it met
The sword of Satan with steep force to smite
Descending, and in half cut sheer, nor stay'd,   325
But with swift wheel reverse, deep ent'ring shar'd°
All his right side; then Satan first knew pain,
And writh'd him to and fro convolv'd; so sore
The griding° sword with discontinuous° wound
Pass'd through him, but th'Ethereal substance clos'd 330
Not long divisible, and from the gash
A stream of Nectarous humour° issuing flow'd
Sanguine, such as Celestial Spirits may bleed,
And all his Armour stain'd erewhile so bright.
Forthwith on all sides to his aid was run   335
By Angels many and strong, who interpos'd
Defence, while others bore him on their Shields
Back to his Chariot; where it stood retir'd
From off the files of war; there they him laid
Gnashing for anguish and despite and shame   340
To find himself not matchless, and his pride
Humbl'd by such rebuke, so far beneath
His confidence to equal God in power.
Yet soon he heal'd; for Spirits that live throughout
Vital in every part, not as frail man   345
In Entrails, Heart or Head, Liver or Reins,°
Cannot but by annihilating die;
Nor in their liquid texture mortal wound
Receive, no'more than can the fluid Air:
All Heart they live, all Head, all Eye, all Ear,   350
All Intellect, all Sense, and as they please,
They Limb themselves, and colour, shape or size
Assume, as likes them best, condense or rare.
          Meanwhile in other parts like deeds deserv'd
Memorial, where the might of Gabriel fought,   355

317 **imminent** overhanging.   320 **prevention** anticipation.   326 **shar'd** sheared.   329 **griding** keenly cutting.   329 **discontinuous** gaping (originally a medical term).   332 **humour** liquid.   346 **Reins** kidneys.

And with fierce Ensigns pierc'd the deep array
Of Moloch furious King, who him defi'd,
And at his Chariot-wheels to drag him bound
Threat'n'd, nor from the Holy One of Heav'n
360 Refrain'd° his tongue blasphémous; but anon
Down-clov'n to the waist, with shatter'd Arms
And uncouth° pain fled bellowing. On each wing
Uriel and Raphaël his vaunting foe,
Though huge, and in a Rock of Diamond Arm'd,
365 Vanquish'd Adramelec,° and Asmadai,°
Two potent Thrones, that to be less than Gods
Disdain'd, but meaner thoughts learn'd in their flight,
Mangl'd with ghastly wounds through Plate and Mail.
Nor stood unmindful Abdiel to annoy°
370 The Atheist crew, but with redoubl'd blow
Ariel and Arioc, and the violence
Of Ramiel scorcht and blasted overthrew.
I might relate of thousands, and their names
Eternise here on Earth; but those elect
375 Angels contented with their fame in Heav'n
Seek not the praise of men: the other sort
In might though wondrous and in Acts of War,
Nor of Renown less eager, yet by doom
Cancell'd from Heav'n and sacred memory,
380 Nameless in dark oblivion let them dwell.
For strength from Truth divided and from Just,
Illaudable, naught merits but dispraise
And ignominy, yet to glory aspires
Vainglorious, and through infamy seeks fame:
385 Therefore Eternal silence be their doom.
        And now their mightiest quell'd, the battle
            swerv'd,
With many an inroad gor'd; deformed rout
Enter'd, and foul disorder; all the ground
With shiver'd armor strewn, and on a heap
390 Chariot and Charioteer lay overturn'd
And fiery foaming Steeds; what stood, recoil'd
O'er-wearied, through the faint Satanic Host
Defensive scarce, or with pale fear surpris'd,

360 **Refrain'd** curbed, from Latin *frenum*, a bridle, here following line
358.   362 **uncouth** unknown hitherto.   365 **Adramelec** Samarian
god.   365 **Asmadai** see IV 168.   369 **annoy** injure.

Then first with fear surpris'd and sense of pain
Fled ignominious, to such evil brought   *395*
By sin of disobedience, till that hour
Not liable to fear or flight or pain.
Far otherwise in th'inviolable Saints
In Cubic Phalanx firm advanc't entire,°
Invulnerable, impenetrably arm'd: *400*
Such high advantages their innocence
Gave them above their foes, not to have sinn'd,
Not to have disobey'd; in fight they stood
Unwearied, unobnoxious° to be pain'd
By wound, though from their place by violence mov'd. *405*
      Now Night her course began, and over Heav'n
Inducing darkness, grateful truce impos'd,
And silence on the odious din of War:
Under her Cloudy covert both retir'd,
Victor and Vanquisht: on the foughten field   *410*
Michael and his Angels prevalent°
Encamping, plac'd in Guard their Watches round,
Cherubic waving fires: on th'other part
Satan with his rebellious disappear'd,
Far in the dark dislodg'd, and void of rest,   *415*
His Potentates to Council call'd by night;
And in the midst thus undismay'd began.
     'O now in danger tri'd, now known in Arms
Not to be overpower'd, Companions dear,
Found worthy not of Liberty alone,   *420*
Too mean pretense,° but what we more affect,°
Honour, Dominion, Glory, and renown,
Who have sustain'd one day in doubtful° fight,
(And if one day, why not Eternal days?)
What Heaven's Lord had powerfullest to send   *425*
Against us from about his Throne, and judg'd
Sufficient to subdue us to his will,
But proves not so: then fallible, it seems,
Of future we may deem him, though till now
Omniscient thought. True is, less firmly arm'd,   *430*
Some disadvantage we endur'd and pain,
Till now not known, but known as soon contemn'd,

399 **entire** unbroken (military).   404 **unobnoxious** not liable.   411 **prevalent** prevailing.   421 **pretense** a claim.   421 **affect** aim at.   423 **doubtful** undecided.

Since now we find this our Empyreal form
Incapable of mortal injury
435   Imperishable, and though pierc'd with wound,
· Soon closing, and by native vigour heal'd.
Of evil then so small as easy think
The remedy; perhaps more valid° Arms,
Weapons more violent, when next we meet,
440   May serve to better us, and worse our foes,
Or equal what between us made the odds,
In Nature none: if other hidden cause
Left them Superior, while we can preserve
Unhurt our minds, and understanding sound,
445   Due search and consultation will disclose.'
          He sat; and in th'assembly next upstood
Nisroc,° of Principalities the prime;
As one he stood escap't from cruel fight,
Sore toil'd, his riv'n Arms to havoc hewn,
450   And cloudy in aspéct thus answering spake.
'Deliverer from new Lords, leader to free
Enjoyment of our right as Gods; yet hard
For Gods, and too unequal work we find
Against unequal arms to fight in pain,
455   Against unpain'd, impassive; from which evil
Ruin must needs ensue; for what avails
Valour° or strength, though matchless, quell'd with
     pain
Which all subdues, and makes remiss° the hands
Of Mightiest. Sense of pleasure we may well
460   Spare out of life perhaps, and not repine,
But live content, which is the calmest life:
But pain is perfect misery, the worst
Of evils, and excessive, overturns
All patience. He who therefore can invent
465   With what more forcible we may offend°
Our yet unwounded Enemies, or arm
Ourselves with like defence, to mee deserves
No less than for deliverance what we owe.'
          Whereto with look compos'd Satan repli'd.

---

438 **valid** powerful.   447 **Nisroc** Assyrian god.   456–57 **avails Valour**
The two words are from the same root (Latin *valere*, to be strong or
worth), so the question sharply implies that valor ceases to be itself
when . . .   458 **remiss** forceless.   465 **offend** assail, as in "the offensive."

'Not uninvented that, which thou aright   470
Believ'st so main to our success, I bring;
Which of us who beholds the bright surfáce
Of this Ethereous mould whereon we stand,
This continent of spacious Heav'n, adorn'd
With Plant, Fruit, Flow'r Ambrosial, Gems and Gold,   475
Whose Eye so superficially surveys
These things, as not to mind° from whence they grow
Deep under ground, materials dark and crude,
Of spiritous and fiery spume,° till toucht°
With Heav'n's ray, and temper'd they shoot forth   480
So beauteous, op'ning to the ambient light.
These in their dark Nativity° the Deep°
Shall yield us, pregnant with infernal flame,
Which into hollow Engines long and round
Thick-ramm'd, at th'other bore with touch of fire   485
Dilated and infuriate shall send forth
From far with thund'ring noise among our foes
Such implements of mischief as shall dash
To pieces, and o'erwhelm whatever stands
Adverse, that they shall fear we have disarm'd   490
The Thunderer of his only° dreaded bolt.
Nor long shall be our labour, yet ere dawn,
Effect shall end our wish. Meanwhile revive;
Abandon fear; to strength and counsel join'd
Think nothing hard, much less to be despair'd.'   495
He ended, and his words their drooping cheer°
Enlight'n'd, and their languisht hope reviv'd.
Th'invention all admir'd,° and each; how hee
To be th'inventor miss'd, so easy it seem'd
Once found, which yet unfound most would have
    thought   500
Impossible: yet haply of thy Race
In future days, if Malice should abound,
Someone intent on mischief, or inspir'd
With dev'lish machination° might devise

477 **mind** call to mind.   479 **spume** foam (a technical term in metal-
lurgy).   479 **toucht** including the suggestion "kindled"; see lines 485,
520.   482 **Nativity** native state.   482 **Deep** depths of the earth.   491 **only**
unique.   496 **cheer** mood.   498 **admir'd** wondered at.   504 **machination**
plotting, leading into "instrument" since machination had also been de-
fined in 1613 as "warlike weapon."

505 Like instrument to plague the Sons of men
For sin, on war and mutual slaughter bent.
Forthwith from Council to the work they flew,
None arguing stood, innumerable hands
Were ready, in a moment up they turn'd
510 Wide the Celestial soil, and saw beneath
Th'originals° of Nature in their crude
Conception; Sulphurous and Nitrous Foam
They found, they mingl'd, and with subtle Art,
Concocted and adusted° they reduc'd
515 To blackest grain, and into store convey'd:
Part hidd'n veins digg'd up (nor hath this Earth
Entrails unlike) of Mineral and Stone,
Whereof to found their Engines and their Balls
Of missive° ruin; part incentive° reed
520 Provide, pernicious° with one touch to fire.
So all ere day-spring, under conscious° Night
Secret they finish'd, and in order set,
With silent circumspection unespi'd.
Now when fair Morn Orient in Heav'n appear'd
525 Up rose the Victor Angels, and to Arms
The matin Trumpet Sung: in Arms they stood
Of Golden Panoply, refulgent Host,
Soon banded; others from the dawning Hills
Look'd round, and Scouts each Coast light-armed
scour,
530 Each quarter, to descry the distant foe,
Where lodg'd, or whither fled, or if for fight,
In motion or in halt: him soon they met
Under spread Ensigns moving nigh, in slow
But firm Battalion; back with speediest Sail
535 Zophiel, of Cherubim the swiftest wing,
Came flying, and in mid Air aloud thus cri'd.
     'Arm, Warriors, Arm for fight, the foe at hand,
Whom fled we thought, will save us long pursuit
This day, fear not his flight; so thick a Cloud
540 He comes, and settl'd in his face I see

511 **originals** a geological term.   514 **Concocted and adusted** matured
by heat and scorched (geological).   519 **missive** missile.   519 **incentive**
kindling.   520 **pernicious** both "rapid" (Latin *pernix*) and "destructive"
(Latin *perniciosus*).   521 **conscious** witnessing, with suggestions of shar-
ing a guilty secret.

Sad° resolution and secure:° let each
His Adamantine coat gird well, and each
Fit well his Helm, grip fast his orbed Shield,
Borne ev'n or high, for this day will pour down,
If I conjecture aught, no drizzling show'r,   545
But rattling storm of Arrows barb'd with fire.'
So warn'd he them aware themselves, and soon
In order, quit of all impediment;°
Instant without disturb they took Alarm,°
And onward move Embattl'd; when behold   550
Not distant far with heavy pace the Foe
Approaching gross and huge; in hollow Cube
Training° his devilish Enginry, impal'd°
On every side with shadowing° Squadrons Deep,
To hide the fraud. At interview° both stood   555
Awhile, but suddenly at head appear'd
Satan: And thus was heard Commanding loud.
          'Vanguard, to Right and Left the Front un-
          fold;°
That all may see who hate us, how we seek
Peace and composure,° and with open breast   560
Stand ready to receive them, if they like
Our overture,° and turn not back perverse;
But that I doubt,° however witness Heaven,
Heav'n witness thou anon, while we discharge°
Freely our part:° yee who appointed° stand   565
Do as you have in charge,° and briefly touch°
What we propound,° and loud that all may hear.'
          So scoffing in ambiguous words, he scarce
Had ended; when to Right and Left the Front
Divided, and to either Flank retir'd.   570
Which to our eyes discover'd new and strange,

541 **Sad** steadfast. 541 **secure** confident. 548 **impediment** military baggage. 549 **took Alarm** stood to arms. 553 **Training** hauling. 553 **impal'd**
surrounded for defense. 554 **shadowing** screening (military). 555 **At interview** in mutual view. 558 **unfold** military: "unfolding his troops."
560 **composure** composition, truce, and also "compounded mixture"
(gunpowder) as in line 613. 562 **overture** overtures of peace; opening
of the proceedings; and aperture or orifice (line 577), as in Milton: "break
in at this so great an overture." 563 **doubt** fear. 564 **discharge** fulfill and
fire off. 565 **part** share and (a 17th-century sense) "conflict between two
parties." 565 **appointed** agreed and equipped. 566 **in charge** entrusted
and loaded (weapons). 566 **touch** touch upon and ignite. 567 **propound** punning on "put forward."

A triple-mounted row of Pillars laid
On Wheels (for like to Pillars most they seem'd
Or hollow'd bodies made of Oak or Fir
575 With branches lopt, in Wood or Mountain fell'd)
Brass, Iron, Stony mould, had not their mouths
With hideous orifice gap't on us wide,
Portending hollow truce; at each behind
A Seraph stood, and in his hand a Reed
580 Stood waving tipt with fire; while we suspense,
Collected stood within our thoughts amus'd,°
Not long, for sudden all at once their Reeds
Put forth, and to a narrow vent appli'd
With nicest touch. Immediate in a flame,
585 But soon obscur'd with smoke, all Heav'n appear'd,
From those deep-throated Engines belcht, whose roar
Embowel'd with outrageous noise the Air,
And all her entrails tore, disgorging foul
Their devilish glut,° chain'd° Thunderbolts and Hail
590 Of Iron Globes, which on the Victor Host.
Levell'd,° with such impetuous fury smote,
That whom they hit, none on their feet might stand,
Though standing else as Rocks, but down they fell
By thousands, Angel on Arch-Angel roll'd;
595 The sooner for their Arms, unarm'd they might
Have easily as Spirits evaded swift
By quick contraction or remove; but now
Foul dissipation° follow'd and forc't rout;
Nor serv'd it to relax their serried files.
600 What should they do? if on they rusht, repulse
Repeated, and indecent° overthrow
Doubl'd, would render them yet more despis'd,°
And to their foes a laughter; for in view
Stood rankt of Seraphim another row
605 In posture to displode° their second tire°
Of Thunder: back defeated to return
They worse abhorr'd. Satan beheld their plight,

581 **amus'd** bewildered (also military, of tactics which deceive the
enemy).   586–89 **deep-throated . . . glut** Compare the body-landscape of
Hell.   589 **chain'd** chain-shot, cannonballs linked.   591 **Levell'd** military, to lay a gun.   598 **dissipation** dispersal.   601 **indecent** grace-
less.   602 **despis'd** looked down upon (Latin *despicere*); following
"overthrow."   605 **displode** explode.   605 **tire** volley.

And to his Mates thus in derision call'd.
     'O Friends, why come not on these Victors
       proud?
Erewhile they fierce were coming, and when wee,   *610*
To entertain° them fair with open Front°
And Breast, (what could we more?) propounded terms
Of composition, straight they chang'd their minds,
Flew off, and into strange vagaries fell,
As they would dance, yet for a dance they seem'd   *615*
Somewhat extravagant and wild, perhaps
For joy of offer'd peace: but I suppose
If our proposals once again were heard
We should compel them to a quick result.'°
     To whom thus Belial in like gamesome mood.   *620*
'Leader, the terms we sent were terms of weight,
Of hard contents, and full of force urg'd home,
Such as we might perceive amus'd° them all,
And stumbl'd many, who receives them right,
Had need from head to foot well understand;°   *625*
Not understood, this gift they have besides,
They show us when our foes walk not upright.'
     So they among themselves in pleasant vein
Stood scoffing, height'n'd in their thoughts beyond
All doubt of Victory, eternal might   *630*
To match with their inventions they presum'd
So easy, and of his Thunder made a scorn,
And all his Host derided, while they stood
Awhile in trouble; but they stood not long,
Rage prompted them at length, and found them arms   *635*
Against such hellish mischief fit to oppose.
Forthwith (behold the excellence, the power
Which God hath in his mighty Angels plac'd)
Their Arms away they threw, and to the Hills
(For Earth hath this variety from Heav'n   *640*
Of pleasure situate in Hill and Dale)
Light as the Lightning glimpse they ran, they flew,
From their foundations loos'ning to and fro
They pluckt the seated° Hills with all their load,

---

611 **entertain** receive. 611 **Front** brow and front-line. 619 **result** decision or resolution, with a pun on the etymology, Latin *resultare,* to leap back. 623 **amus'd** see line 581. 625 **understand** both "comprehend" and "be supported" (a common 17th-century sense). 644 **seated** firm-set.

645 Rocks, Waters, Woods, and by the shaggy tops
     Uplifting bore them in their hands: Amaze,
     Be sure, and terror seiz'd the rebel Host,
     When coming towards them so dread they saw
     The bottom of the Mountains upward turn'd;
650 Till on those cursed Engines triple-row
     They saw them whelm'd, and all their confidence°
     Under the weight of Mountains buried deep,
     Themselves invaded next, and on their heads
     Main Promontories flung, which in the Air
655 Came shadowing, and opprest whole Legions arm'd,
     Their armour help'd their harm, crush't in and bruis'd
     Into their substance pent, which wrought them pain
     Implacable, and many a dolorous groan,
     Long struggling underneath, ere they could wind
660 Out of such prison, though Spirits of purest light,
     Purest at first, now gross by sinning grown.
     The rest in imitation to like Arms
     Betook them, and the neighbouring Hills uptore;
     So Hills amid the Air encounter'd Hills
665 Hurl'd to and fro with jaculation° dire,
     That under ground they fought in dismal shade;
     Infernal noise; War seem'd a civil° Game
     To this uproar; horrid confusion heapt
     Upon confusion rose: and now all Heav'n
670 Had gone to wrack, with ruin overspread,
     Had not th'Almighty Father where he sits
     Shrin'd in his Sanctuary of Heav'n secure,
     Consulting° on the sum of things, foreseen
     This tumult, and permitted all, advis'd:°
675 That his great purpose he might so fulfill,
     To honour his Anointed Son aveng'd
     Upon his enemies, and to declare°
     All power on him transferr'd: whence to his Son
     Th'Assessor° of his Throne he thus began.
680   'Effulgence of my Glory, Son belov'd,

651 **confidence** "that which gives confidence, boldness, or security" (Johnson), as in PROVERBS 3:26, "For the Lord shall be thy confidence." 665 **jaculation** throwing. 667 **civil** civilized, orderly (contrasting "civil war"). 673 **Consulting** deliberating. 674 **advis'd** having considered, as in "advisedly." 677 **declare** make manifest. 679 **Assessor** one who sits beside.

Son in whose face invisible is beheld
Visibly, what by Deity I am,
And in whose hand what by Decree I do,
Second Omnipotence, two days are past,
Two days, as we compute the days of Heav'n,   685
Since Michael and his Powers went forth to tame
These disobedient; sore hath been their fight,
As likeliest was, when two such Foes met arm'd;
For to themselves I left them, and thou know'st,
Equal in their Creation they were form'd   690
Save what sin hath impair'd, which yet hath wrought
Insensibly,° for I suspend their doom;
Whence in perpetual fight they needs must last
Endless, and no solution° will be found:
War wearied hath perform'd what War can do,   695
And to disorder'd rage let loose the reins,
With Mountains as with Weapons arm'd, which makes
Wild work in Heav'n, and dangerous to the main.°
Two days are therefore past, the third is thine;
For thee I have ordain'd it, and thus far   700
Have suffer'd,° that the Glory may be thine
Of ending this great War, since none but Thou
Can end it. Into thee such Virtue and Grace
Immense I have transfus'd, that all may know
In Heav'n and Hell thy Power above compare,   705
And this perverse Commotion govern'd thus,
To manifest thee worthiest to be Heir
Of all things, to be Heir and to be King
By Sacred Unction,° thy deserved right.
Go then thou Mightiest in thy Father's might,   710
Ascend my Chariot, guide the rapid Wheels
That shake Heav'n's basis, bring forth all my War,
My Bow and Thunder, my Almighty Arms
Gird on, and Sword upon thy puissant Thigh;
Pursue these sons of Darkness, drive them out   715
From all Heav'n's bounds into the utter Deep:
There let them learn, as likes them, to despise
God and Messiah his anointed King.'
　　　　He said, and on his Son with Rays direct

692 **Insensibly** imperceptibly. 694 **solution** termination. 698 **main**
land. 701 **suffer'd** permitted. 709 **Unction** anointing.

720 Shone full, he all his Father full exprest
Ineffably into his face receiv'd,
And thus the filial Godhead answering spake.
      'O Father, O Supreme of heav'nly Thrones,
First, Highest, Holiest, Best, thou always seek'st
725 To glorify thy Son, I always thee,
As is most just; this I my Glory account,
My exaltation, and my whole delight,
That thou in me well-pleas'd, declar'st thy will
Fulfill'd, which to fufill is all my bliss.
730 Scepter and Power, thy giving, I assume,
And gladlier shall resign, when in the end
Thou shalt be All in All, and I in thee
For ever, and in mee all whom thou lov'st:
But whom thou hat'st, I hate, and can put on
735 Thy terrors, as I put thy mildness on,
Image of thee in all things; and shall soon,
Arm'd with thy might, rid Heav'n of these rebell'd,
To their prepar'd ill Mansion driven down
To chains of Darkness, and th'undying Worm,
740 That from thy just obedience could revolt,
Whom to obey is happiness entire.
Then shall thy Saints unmixt, and from th'impure
Far separate, circling thy holy Mount
Unfeigned Halleluiahs to thee sing,
745 Hymns of high praise, and I among them chief.'
So said, he o'er his Scepter bowing, rose
From the right hand of Glory where he sat,
And the third sacred Morn began to shine
Dawning through Heav'n: forth rush'd with whirlwind
    sound
750 The Chariot of Paternal Deity,
Flashing thick flames, Wheel within Wheel undrawn,
Itself instínct with Spirit, but convóy'd
By four Cherubic shapes, four Faces each
Had wondrous, as with Stars their bodies all
755 And Wings were set with Eyes, with Eyes the Wheels
Of Beryl, and careering Fires between;
Over their heads a crystal Firmament;
Whereon a Sapphire Throne, inlaid with pure
Amber, and colours of the show'ry Arch.
760 Hee in Celestial Panoply all arm'd

Of radiant Urim,° work divinely wrought,
Ascended, at his right hand Victory
Sat Eagle-wing'd, beside him hung his Bow
And Quiver with three-bolted Thunder stor'd,
And from about him fierce Effusion° roll'd   765
Of smoke and bickering° flame, and sparkles dire;
Attended with ten thousand thousand Saints,
He onward came, far off his coming shone,
And twenty thousand (I their number heard)
Chariots of God, half on each hand were seen: 770
Hee on the wings of Cherub rode sublime
On the Crystálline Sky, in Sapphire Thron'd.
Illustrious° far and wide, but by his own
First seen, them unexpected joy surpris'd,
When the great Ensign of Messiah blaz'd   775
Aloft by Angels borne, his Sign in Heav'n:
Under whose Conduct Michael soon reduc'd°
His Army, circumfus'd on either Wing,
Under their Head imbodied° all in one.
Before him Power Divine his way prepar'd;   780
At his command the uprooted Hills retir'd
Each to his place, they heard his voice and went
Obsequious,° Heav'n his wonted face renew'd,
And with fresh Flow'rets Hill and Valley smil'd.
This saw his hapless Foes, but stood obdur'd,   785
And to rebellious fight rallied their Powers
Insensate, hope conceiving from despair.
In heav'nly Spirits could such perverseness dwell?
But to convince the proud what Signs avail,
Or Wonders move th'obdúrate to relent?   790
They hard'n'd more by what might most reclaim,
Grieving to see his Glory, at the sight
Took envy, and aspiring to his heighth,
Stood re-embattl'd fierce, by force or fraud
Weening to prosper, and at length prevail   795
Against God and Messiah, or to fall

---

761 **Urim** oraculous gems.   765 **fierce Effusion** to be contrasted with the usual theological application of "Effusion" to Christ and the Holy Ghost, pouring forth grace.   766 **bickering** flashing.   773 **Illustrious** full of luster.   777 **reduc'd** brought back.   779 **imbodied** organized in a military body.   783 **Obsequious** obedient.

In universal ruin last, and now
To final Battle drew, disdaining flight,
Or faint retreat; when the great Son of God
800 To all his Host on either hand thus spake.
        'Stand still in bright array ye Saints, here stand
Ye Angels arm'd, this day from Battle rest;
Faithful hath been your Warfare, and of God
Accepted, fearless in his righteous Cause,
805 And as ye have receiv'd, so have ye done
Invincibly; but of this cursed crew
The punishment to other hand belongs,
Vengeance is his, or whose he sole appoints;
Number to this day's work is not ordain'd
810 Nor multitude, stand only and behold
God's indignation on these Godless pour'd
By mee; not you but mee they have despis'd,
Yet envied; against mee is all their rage,
Because the Father, t'whom in Heav'n supreme
815 Kingdom and Power and Glory appertains,
Hath honour'd me according to his will.
Therefore to mee their doom he hath assign'd;
That they may have their wish, to try with mee
In Battle which the stronger proves, they all,
820 Or I alone against them, since by strength
They measure all, of other excellence
Not emulous, nor care who them excels;
Nor other strife with them do I vouchsafe.'
        So spake the Son, and into terror chang'd
825 His count'nance too severe to be beheld
And full of wrath bent on his Enemies.
At once the Four spread out their Starry wings
With dreadful shade contiguous, and the Orbs
Of his fierce Chariot roll'd, as with the sound
830 Of torrent Floods, or of a numerous Host.
Hee on his impious Foes right onward drove,
Gloomy as Night; under his burning Wheels
The steadfast Empyrean shook throughout,
All but the Throne itself of God. Full soon
835 Among them he arriv'd; in his right hand
Grasping ten thousand Thunders, which he sent
Before him, such as in their Souls infix'd

Plagues;° they astonisht° all resistance lost,
All courage; down their idle weapons dropp'd;
O'er Shields and Helms, and helmed heads he rode   840
Of Thrones and mighty Seraphim prostráte,
That wish'd the Mountains now might be again
Thrown on them as a shelter from his ire.
Nor less on either side tempestuous fell
His arrows, from the fourfold-visag'd Four,   845
Distinct° with eyes, and from the living Wheels,
Distinct alike with multitude of eyes.
One Spirit in them rul'd, and every eye
Glar'd lightning, and shot forth pernicious fire
Among th'accurst, that wither'd all their strength,   850
And of their wonted vigour left them drain'd,
Exhausted, spiritless, afflicted, fall'n.
Yet half his strength he put not forth, but check'd
His Thunder in mid Volley, for he meant
Not to destroy, but root them out of Heav'n: 855
The overthrown he rais'd, and as a Herd
Of Goats or timorous flock together throng'd
Drove them before him Thunder-struck, pursu'd
With terrors and with furies to the bounds
And Crystal wall of Heav'n, which op'ning wide,   860
Roll'd inward, and a spacious Gap disclos'd
Into the wasteful Deep; the monstrous sight
Struck them with horror backward, but far worse
Urg'd them behind; headlong themselves they threw
Down from the verge of Heav'n, Eternal wrath   865
Burnt after them to the bottomless pit.
          Hell heard th'unsufferable noise, Hell saw
Heav'n ruining from Heav'n and would have fled
Affrighted; but strict Fate had cast too deep
Her dark foundations, and too fast had bound.   870
Nine days they fell; confounded Chaos roar'd,
And felt tenfold confusion in their fall
Through his wild Anarchy, so huge a rout
Encumber'd him with ruin: Hell at last
Yawning receiv'd them whole, and on them clos'd,   875
Hell their fit habitation fraught with fire

838 **Plagues** the scourges of God, including the original sense "wound."
838 **astonisht** thunderstruck.   846 **Distinct** adorned.

Unquenchable, the house of woe and pain.
Disburd'n'd Heav'n rejoic'd, and soon repair'd
Her mural breach, returning whence it roll'd.
880 Sole Victor from th'expulsion of his Foes
Messiah his triumphal Chariot turn'd:
To meet him all his Saints, who silent stood
Eye-witnesses of his Almighty Acts,
With Jubilee advanc'd; and as they went,
885 Shaded with branching palm, each order bright,
Sung Triumph, and him sung Victorious King,
Son, Heir, and Lord, to him Dominion giv'n,
Worthiest to Reign: he celebrated rode
Triumphant through mid Heav'n, into the Courts
890 And Temple of his mighty Father Thron'd
On high; who into Glory him receiv'd,
Where now he sits at the right hand of bliss.
          Thus measuring things in Heav'n by things
               on Earth
At thy request, and that thou mayst beware
895 By what is past, to thee I have reveal'd
What might have else to human Race been hid;
The discord which befell, and War in Heav'n
Among th'Angelic Powers, and the deep fall
Of those too high aspiring, who rebell'd
900 With Satan, hee who envies now thy state,
Who now is plotting how he may seduce
Thee also from obedience, that with him
Bereav'd of happiness thou mayst partake
His punishment, Eternal misery;
905 Which would be all his solace and revenge,
As a despite done against the most High,
Thee once to gain Companion of his woe.
But list'n not to his Temptations, warn
Thy weaker; let it profit thee to have heard
910 By terrible Example the reward
Of disobedience; firm they might have stood,
Yet fell; remember, and fear to transgress."

BOOK VII

THE ARGUMENT

Raphaël at the request of Adam relates how and wherefore this world was first created; that God, after the expel-
ling of Satan and his Angels out of Heaven, declar'd his
pleasure to create another World and other Creatures to
dwell therein; sends his Son with Glory and attendance of
Angels to perform the work of Creation in six days: the
Angels celebrate with Hymns the performance thereof,
and his reascension into Heaven.

Descend from Heav'n Urania, by that name
If rightly thou art call'd, whose Voice divine
Following, above th'Olympian Hill° I soar,
Above the flight of Pegasean wing.°
The meaning,° not the Name I call: for thou   5
Nor of the Muses nine, nor on the top
Of old Olympus dwell'st, but Heav'nly born,
Before the Hills appear'd, or Fountain flow'd,
Thou with Eternal wisdom didst converse,°
Wisdom thy Sister, and with her didst play   10
In presence of th'Almighty Father, pleas'd
With thy Celestial Song. Up led by thee
Into the Heav'n of Heav'ns I have presum'd,
An Earthly Guest, and drawn Empyreal Air,
Thy temp'ring;° with like safety guided down   15
Return me to my Native Element:
Lest from this flying Steed unrein'd, (as once
Bellerophon, though from a lower Clime)

---

3 **Olympian Hill** Olympus, resort of the Muses.   4 **Pegasean wing** Pega-
sus, the winged horse associated with the Muses and Bellerophon (line
18).   5 **meaning** Urania, "Heavenly One"; Milton calls on more than
the "Name" of the classical Muse.   9 **converse** keep company.   15 **Thy
temp'ring** the air tempered (made suitable) by thee.

Dismounted, on th'Aleian° Field I fall
20   Erroneous,° there to wander and forlorn.
Half yet remains unsung, but narrower bound
Within the visible Diurnal° Sphere;
Standing on Earth, not rapt above the Pole,
More safe I Sing with mortal voice, unchang'd
25   To hoarse or mute, though fall'n on evil days,
On evil days though fall'n, and evil tongues;
In darkness, and with dangers compast round,
And solitude; yet not alone, while thou
Visit'st my slumbers Nightly, or when Morn
30   Purples the East: still govern thou my Song,
Urania, and fit audience find, though few.
But drive far off the barbarous dissonance
Of Bacchus° and his Revellers, the Race
Of that wild Rout that tore the Thracian Bard°
35   In Rhodope, where Woods and Rocks had Ears
To rapture,° till the savage clamour drown'd
Both Harp and Voice; nor could the Muse defend
Her Son. So fail not thou, who thee implores:
For thou art Heav'nly, shee an empty dream.
40   Say Goddess, what ensu'd when Raphaël,
The affable° Arch-Angel, had forewarn'd
Adam by dire example to beware
Apostasy, by what befell in Heaven
To those Apostates, lest the like befall
45   In Paradise to Adam or his Race,
Charg'd not to touch the interdicted Tree,
If they transgress, and slight that sole command,
So easily obey'd amid the choice
Of all tastes else to please their appetite,
50   Though wand'ring. He with his consorted Eve
The story heard attentive, and was fill'd
With admiration, and deep Muse to hear
Of things so high and strange, things to their thought
So unimaginable as hate in Heav'n,
55   And War so near the Peace of God in bliss

19 **Aleian** meaning "Land of Wandering." 20 **Erroneous** straying. 22
Diurnal daily (in its astronomical movement). 33 **Bacchus** god of wine.
34 **Bard** the poet-seer Orpheus, murdered by the Bacchantes. 36 **rapture** be raptured. 41 **affable** easy to speak with (Raphael's role in the
poem).

With such confusion: but the evil soon
Driv'n back redounded as a flood on those
From whom it sprung, impossible to mix
With Blessedness. Whence Adam soon repeal'd°
The doubts that in his heart arose: and now   60
Led on, yet sinless, with desire to know
What nearer might concern him, how this World
Of Heav'n and Earth conspicuous° first began,
When, and whereof created, for what cause,
What within Eden or without was done   65
Before his memory, as one whose drouth
Yet scarce allay'd still eyes the current stream,
Whose liquid murmur heard new thirst excites,
Proceeded thus to ask his Heav'nly Guest.

        "Great things, and full of wonder in our ears, 70
Far differing from this World, thou hast reveal'd
Divine Interpreter,° by favour sent
Down from the Empyrean to forewarn
Us timely of what might else have been our loss,
Unknown, which human knowledge could not reach: 75
For which to the infinitely Good we owe
Immortal thanks, and his admonishment
Receive with solemn purpose to observe
Immutably his sovran will, the end
Of what we are. But since thou hast vouchsaf't   80
Gently for our instruction to impart
Things above Earthly thought, which yet concern'd
Our knowing, as to highest wisdom seem'd,
Deign to descend now lower, and relate
What may no less perhaps avail us known,   85
How first began this Heav'n which we behold
Distant so high, with moving Fires adorn'd
Innumerable, and this which yields or fills
All space, the ambient Air wide interfus'd
Embracing round this florid° Earth, what cause   90
Mov'd the Creator in his holy Rest
Through all Eternity so late to build
In Chaos, and the work begun, how soon

---

59 **repeal'd** retracted.   63 **conspicuous** visibly present.   72 **Interpreter**
one who makes known the will of another, a title of Mercury as messenger of the gods.   90 **florid** flowery.

Absolv'd,° if unforbid thou may'st unfold
95 What wee, not to explore the secrets ask
Of his Eternal Empire, but the more
To magnify his works, the more we know.
And the great Light of Day yet wants to run
Much of his Race though steep, suspense in Heav'n
100 Held by thy voice, thy potent voice he hears,
And longer will delay to hear thee tell
His Generation,° and the rising Birth
Of Nature from the unapparent° Deep:
Or if the Star of Ev'ning and the Moon
105 Haste to thy audience, Night with her will bring
Silence, and Sleep list'ning to thee will watch,
Or we can bid his absence, till thy Song
End, and dismiss thee ere the Morning shine."
         Thus Adam his illustrious Guest besought:
110 And thus the Godlike Angel answer'd mild.
"This also thy request with caution askt
Obtain: though to recount Almighty works
What words or tongue of Seraph can suffice,
Or heart of man suffice to comprehend?
115 Yet what thou canst attain, which best may serve
To glorify the Maker, and infer°
Thee also happier, shall not be withheld
Thy hearing, such Commission from above
I have receiv'd, to answer thy desire
120 Of knowledge within bounds; beyond abstain
To ask, nor let thine own inventions° hope
Things not reveal'd, which th'invisible King,
Only Omniscient, hath suppret in Night,
To none communicable in Earth or Heaven:
125 Enough is left besides to search and know.
But Knowledge is as food, and needs no less
Her Temperance over Appetite, to know
In measure what the mind may well contain,
Oppresses else with Surfeit, and soon turns
130 Wisdom to Folly, as Nourishment to Wind.
         Know then, that after Lucifer from Heav'n
(So call him, brighter once amidst the Host

94 **Absolv'd** accomplished.   102 **Generation** creation.   103 **unapparent**
invisible.   116 **infer** render.   121 **inventions** devisings.

Of Angels, than that Star the Stars among)
Fell with his flaming Legions through the Deep
Into his place, and the great Son return'd   *135*
Victorious with his Saints, th'Omnipotent
Eternal Father from his Throne beheld
Their multitude, and to his Son thus spake.
        'At least our envious Foe hath fad'd, who
                thought
All like himself rebellious, by whose aid   *140*
This inaccessible high strength, the seat
Of Deity supreme, us dispossest,
He trusted to have seiz'd, and into fraud
Drew many, whom their place knows here no more;
Yet far the greater part have kept, I see,   *145*
Their station, Heav'n yet populous retains
Number sufficient to possess her Realms
Though wide, and this high Temple to frequent
With Ministeries due and solemn Rites:
But lest his heart exalt him in the harm   *150*
Already done, to have dispeopl'd Heav'n,
My damage fondly deem'd, I can repair
That detriment, if such it be to lose
Self-lost, and in a moment will create
Another World, out of one man a Race   *155*
Of men innumerable, there to dwell,
Not here, till by degrees of merit rais'd
They open to themselves at length the way
Up hither, under long obedience tri'd,
And Earth be chang'd to Heav'n, and Heav'n to
    Earth,   *160*
One Kingdom, Joy and Union without end.
Meanwhile inhabit lax,° ye Powers of Heav'n,
And thou my Word, begotten Son, by thee
This I perform, speak thou, and be it done:
My overshadowing Spirit and might with thee   *165*
I send along, ride forth, and bid the Deep
Within appointed bounds be Heav'n and Earth,
Boundless the Deep, because I am who fill
Infinitude, nor vacuous the space.
Though I uncircumscrib'd myself retire,   *170*

162 **inhabit lax** dwell with ample room.

And put not forth my goodness, which is free
To act or not, Necessity and Chance
Approach not mee, and what I will is Fate.'
      So spake th'Almighty, and to what he spake
175 His Word, the Filial Godhead, gave effect.
Immediate are the Acts of God, more swift
Than time or motion, but to human ears
Cannot without procéss of speech be told,
So told as earthly notion° can receive.
180 Great triumph and rejoicing was in Heav'n
When such was heard declar'd the Almighty's will;
Glory they sung to the most High, good will
To future men, and in their dwellings peace:
Glory to him whose just avenging ire
185 Had driven out th'ungodly from his sight
And th'habitations of the just; to him
Glory and praise, whose wisdom had ordain'd
Good out of evil to create, instead
Of Spirits malign a better Race to bring
190 Into their vacant room, and thence diffuse
His good to Worlds and Ages infinite.
So sang the Hierarchies: Meanwhile the Son
On his great Expedition now appear'd,
Girt with Omnipotence, with Radiance crown'd
195 Of Majesty Divine, Sapience and Love
Immense, and all his Father in him shone.
About his Chariot numberless were pour'd
Cherub and Seraph, Potentates and Thrones,
And Virtues, winged Spirits, and Chariots wing'd,
200 From the Armoury of God, where stand of old
Myriads between two brazen Mountains lodg'd
Against a solemn day, harnest at hand,
Celestial Equipage; and now came forth
Spontaneous, for within them Spirit liv'd,
205 Attendant on their Lord: Heav'n op'n'd wide
Her ever-during Gates, Harmonious sound
On golden Hinges moving,° to let forth
The King of Glory in his powerful Word
And Spirit coming to create new Worlds.

179 **notion** intellect.   207 **moving** including "putting forth, uttering (the 'sound')," as in III 37.

On heav'nly ground they stood, and from the shore   210
They view'd the vast immeasurable Abyss
Outrageous as a Sea, dark, wasteful, wild,
Up from the bottom turn'd by furious winds
And surging waves, as Mountains to assault
Heav'n's heighth, and with the Center mix the Pole.   215
          'Silence, ye troubl'd waves, and thou Deep,
               peace,'
Said then th'Omnific° Word, 'your discord end':
          Nor stay'd, but on the Wings of Cherubim
Uplifted, in Paternal Glory rode
Far into Chaos, and the World unborn;   220
For Chaos heard his voice: him all his Train
Follow'd in bright procession to behold
Creation, and the wonders of his might.
Then stay'd the fervid Wheels, and in his hand
He took the golden Compasses, prepar'd   225
In God's Eternal store, to circumscribe
This Universe, and all created things:
One foot he center'd, and the other turn'd
Round through the vast profundity obscure,
And said, 'thus far extend, thus far thy bounds,   230
This be thy just Circumference, O World.'
Thus God the Heav'n created, thus the Earth,
Matter unform'd and void: Darkness profound
Cover'd th'Abyss: but on the wat'ry calm
His brooding wings the Spirit of God outspread,   235
And vital virtue infus'd, and vital warmth
Throughout the fluid Mass, but downward purg'd
The black tartareous° cold infernal dregs
Adverse to life: then founded,° then conglob'd°
Like things to like, the rest to several place   240
Disparted, and between spun out the Air,
And Earth self-ballanc't on her Center hung.
          'Let there be Light,' said God, and forthwith
               Light
Ethereal, first of things, quintessence pure
Sprung from the Deep, and from her Native East   245
To journey through the airy gloom began,

217 **Omnific** all-making.   238 **tartareous** having gritty deposits (geological), and suggesting Tartarus, Hell.   239 **founded** made firm, and cast like metal.   239 **conglob'd** compacted.

Spher'd in a radiant Cloud, for yet the Sun
Was not; shee in a cloudy Tabernacle
Sojourn'd° the while. God saw the Light was good;
250 And light from darkness by the Hemisphere
Divided: Light the Day, and Darkness Night
He nam'd. Thus was the first Day Ev'n and Morn:
Nor past uncelebrated, nor unsung
By the Celestial Choirs, when Orient Light
255 Exhaling first from Darkness they beheld;
Birth-day of Heav'n and Earth; with joy and shout
The hollow Universal Orb they fill'd,
And touch't their Golden Harps, and hymning prais'd
God and his works, Creator him they sung,
260 Both when first Ev'ning was, and when first Morn.
        Again, God said 'let there be Firmament
Amid the Waters, and let it divide
The Waters from the Waters': and God made
The Firmament, expanse of liquid, pure,
265 Transparent, Elemental Air, diffus'd
In circuit to the uttermost convéx
Of this great Round: partition firm and sure,
The Waters underneath from those above
Dividing: for as Earth, so hee the World
270 Built on circumfluous Waters calm, in wide
Crystálline Ocean, and the loud misrule
Of Chaos far remov'd, lest fierce extremes
Contiguous might distemper the whole frame:
And Heav'n he nam'd the Firmament: So Ev'n
275 And Morning Chorus sung the second Day.
        The Earth was form'd, but in the Womb as yet
Of Waters, Embryon immature involv'd,
Appear'd not: over all the face of Earth
Main Ocean flow'd, not idle, but with warm
280 Prolific humour soft'ning all her Globe,
Fermented the great Mother to conceive,
Satiate with genial° moisture, when God said
'Be gather'd now ye Waters under Heav'n
Into one place, and let dry Land appear.'
285 Immediately the Mountains huge appear

249 **Sojourn'd** The following lines possibly recall that etymologically "sojourn" is to spend the day.   282 **genial** generative.

Emergent, and their broad bare backs upheave
Into the Clouds, their tops ascend the Sky:
So high as heav'd the tumid Hills, so low
Down sunk a hollow bottom broad and deep,
Capacious bed of Waters: thither they   *290*
Hasted with glad precipitance, uproll'd
As drops on dust conglobing from the dry;
Part rise in crystal Wall, or ridge direct,
For haste; such flight the great command impress'd
On the swift floods: as Armies at the call   *295*
Of Trumpet (for of Armies thou hast heard)
Troop to their Standard, so the wat'ry throng,
Wave rolling after Wave, where way they found,
If steep, with torrent rapture,° if through Plain,
Soft-ebbing; nor withstood them Rock or Hill   *300*
But they, or under ground, or circuit wide
With Serpent error° wand'ring, found their way,
And on the washy Ooze deep Channels wore;
Easy, ere God had bid the ground be dry,
All but within those banks, where Rivers now   *305*
Stream, and perpetual draw their humid train
The dry Land, Earth, and the great receptacle°
Of congregated° Waters he call'd Seas:
And saw that it was good, and said, 'Let th'Earth
Put forth the verdant Grass, Herb yielding Seed,   *310*
And Fruit Tree yielding Fruit after her kind;
Whose Seed is in herself upon the Earth.'
He scarce had said, when the bare Earth, till then
Desert and bare, unsightly, unadorn'd,
Brought forth the tender Grass, whose verdure clad   *315*
Her Universal Face with pleasant green,
Then Herbs of every leaf, that sudden flow'r'd
Op'ning their various colours, and made gay
Her bosom smelling sweet: and these scarce blown,
Forth flourish't thick the clust'ring Vine, forth crept *320*
The swelling° Gourd, up stood the corny Reed

299 **rapture** momentum, sums delight too (line 291: "glad precipitance"). 302 **error** meandering; this is consciously still innocent, but "Serpent" too is ominous. 307 **receptacle** a dignified word then, as in the 16th-century theologian, Richard Hooker (O.E.D.): "The soul of man is the receptacle of Christ's presence." 308 **congregated** assembled. 321 **swelling** conjecture by the 18th-century editor Richard Bentley; "smelling" in *1667–74*.

Embattl'd in her field: add the humble Shrub,°
And Bush with frizzl'd hair implicit:° last
Rose as in Dance the stately Trees, and spread
325 Their branches hung with copious Fruit; or gemm'd°
Their Blossoms: with high Woods the Hills were
    crown'd,
With tufts the vallies and each fountain-side,
With borders long the Rivers. That Earth now
Seem'd like to Heav'n, a seat where Gods might dwell,
330 Or wander with delight, and love to haunt
Her sacred shades: though God had yet not rain'd
Upon the Earth, and man to till the ground
None was, but from the Earth a dewy Mist
Went up and water'd all the ground, and each
335 Plant of the field, which ere it was in the Earth
God made, and every Herb, before it grew
On the green stem; God saw that it was good:
So Ev'n and Morn recorded the Third Day.
        Again th'Almighty spake: 'Let there be Lights
340 High in th'expanse of Heaven to divide
The Day from Night; and let them be for Signs,
For Seasons, and for Days, and circling Years,
And let them be for Lights as I ordain
Their Office in the Firmament of Heav'n
345 To give Light on the Earth'; and it was so.
And God made two great Lights, great for their use
To Man, the greater to have rule by Day,
The less by Night alterne: and made the Stars,
And set them in the Firmament of Heav'n
350 To illuminate the Earth, and rule the Day
In their vicissitude, and rule the Night,
And Light from Darkness to divide. God saw,
Surveying his great Work, that it was good:
For of Celestial Bodies first the Sun
355 A mighty Sphere he fram'd, unlightsome first,
Though of Ethereal Mould: then form'd the Moon
Globose, and every magnitude of Stars,
And sow'd with Stars the Heav'n thick as a field:

322 **humble Shrub** including the horticultural "low-growing"; "the humble shrub" contrasted with trees.   323 **implicit** entwined.   325 **gemm'd**
budded, an English as well as Latin usage; it suggests a contrast of Nature
and Art (e.g. the arts which built Pandemonium, I 710–17).

Of Light by far the greater part he took,
Transplanted from her cloudy Shrine, and plac'd   *360*
In the Sun's Orb, made porous to receive
And drink the liquid Light, firm to retain
Her gather'd beams, great Palace now of Light.
Hither as to their Fountain other Stars
Repairing, in their gold'n Urns draw Light,   *365*
And hence the Morning Planet gilds her° horns;
By tincture of reflection they augment
Their small peculiar,° though from human sight
So far remote, with diminution seen.
First in his East the glorious Lamp was seen,   *370*
Regent of Day, and all th'Horizon round
Invested with bright Rays, jocund to run
His Longitude through Heav'n's high road: the gray
Dawn, and the Pleiades° before him danc'd
Shedding sweet influence: less bright the Moon,   *375*
But opposite in levell'd° West was set
His mirror, with full face borrowing her Light
From him, for other light she needed none
In that aspéct,° and still that distance keeps
Till night, then in the East her turn she shines,   *380*
Revolv'd on Heav'n's great Axle, and her Reign
With thousand lesser Lights dividual° holds,
With thousand thousand Stars, that then appear'd
Spangling the Hemisphere: then first adorn'd
With their bright Luminaries that Set and Rose,   *385*
Glad Ev'ning and glad Morn crown'd the fourth day.
　　　　And God said 'let the Waters generate
Reptile with Spawn abundant, living Soul:
And let Fowl fly above the Earth, with wings
Display'd on the op'n Firmament of Heav'n.'   *390*
And God created the great Whales, and each
Soul living, each that crept, which plenteously
The waters generated by their kinds,
And every Bird of wing after his kind;
And saw that it was good, and bless'd them, saying,   *395*
Be fruitful, multiply, and in the Seas
And Lakes and running Streams the waters fill;

366 **her** *1674*; his *1667*.   368 **peculiar** own possession.   374 **Pleiades** a
group of stars.   376 **levell'd** directly opposite.   379 **aspéct** astrological
position.   382 **dividual** distributed.

And let the Fowl be multipli'd on the Earth.
Forthwith the Sounds and Seas, each Creek and Bay
400 With Fry innumerable swarm, and Shoals
Of Fish that with their Fins and shining Scales
Glide under the green Wave, in Sculls° that oft
Bank° the mid Sea: part single or with mate
Graze the Sea-weed their pasture, and through Groves
405 Of Coral stray, or sporting with quick glance
Show to the Sun their wav'd coats dropt with Gold,
Or in their Pearly shells at ease, attend°
Moist nutriment, or under Rocks their food
In jointed Armour watch: on smooth the Seal,
410 And bended Dolphins play: part huge of bulk
Wallowing unwieldy, enormous in their Gait
Tempest the Ocean: there Leviathan°
Hugest of living Creatures, on the Deep
Stretcht like a Promontory sleeps or swims,
415 And seems a moving Land, and at his Gills
Draws in, and at his Trunk spouts out a Sea.
Meanwhile the tepid Caves, and Fens and shores
Their Brood as numerous hatch, from the Egg that
    soon
Bursting with kindly° rupture forth disclos'd
420 Their callow young, but feather'd soon and fledge
They summ'd their Pens,° and soaring th'air sublime
With clang despis'd the ground, under a cloud
In prospect;° there the Eagle and the Stork
On Cliffs and Cedar tops their Eyries build:
425 Part loosely wing the Region, part more wise
In common, rang'd in figure wedge° their way,
Intelligent° of seasons, and set forth
Their Airy Caravan high over Seas
Flying, and over Lands with mutual wing
430 Easing their flight; so steers the prudent Crane
Her annual Voyage, borne on Winds; the Air
Floats, as they pass, fann'd with unnumber'd plumes:

402 **Sculls** schools, shoals. 403 **Bank** form a bank (Daniel Defoe, 1719:
"The banks, so they call the place where they catch the fish"). 407 **attend** watch for. 412 **Leviathan** the innocent contrast to the Satanic Leviathan, I 200–09. 419 **kindly** natural. 420–21 **fledge . . . Pens** fledged,
they completed their total of feathers. 423 **In prospect** from their view-
point. 426 **wedge** fly in a tapering formation. 427 **Intelligent** cognizant.

From Branch to Branch the smaller Birds with song
Solac'd the Woods, and spread their painted wings
Till Ev'n, nor then the solemn Nightingale   *435*
Ceas'd warbling, but all night tun'd her soft lays:
Others on Silver Lakes and Rivers Bath'd
Their downy Breast; the Swan with Arched neck
Between her white wings mantling proudly, Rows
Her state with Oary feet: yet oft they quit   *440*
The Dank,° and rising on stiff Pennons, tow'r
The mid Aereal Sky: Others on ground
Walk'd firm; the crested Cock whose clarion sounds
The silent hours, and th'other whose gay Train
Adorns him, colour'd with the Florid hue   *445*
Of Rainbows and Starry Eyes. The Waters thus
With Fish replenisht, and the Air with Fowl,
Ev'ning and Morn solémniz'd the Fifth day.
          The Sixth, and of Creation last arose
With Ev'ning Harps and Matin, when God said,   *450*
'Let th'Earth bring forth Soul° living in her kind,
Castle and Creeping things, and Beast of th'Earth,
Each in their kind.' The Earth obey'd, and straight
Op'ning her fertile Womb teem'd at a Birth
Innumerous living Creatures, perfect forms,   *455*
Limb'd and full grown: out of the ground uprose
As from his Lair the wild Beast where he wons°
In Forest wild, in Thicket, Brake, or Den;
Among the Trees in Pairs they rose, they walk'd:
The Cattle in the Fields and Meadows green: *460*
Those rare and solitary, these in flocks
Pasturing at once, and in broad Herds upsprung.
The grassy Clods now Calv'd, now half appear'd
The Tawny Lion, pawing to get free
His hinder parts, then springs as broke from Bonds,   *465*
And Rampant shakes his Brinded main; the Ounce,°
The Libbard,° and the Tiger, as the Mole
Rising, the crumbl'd Earth above them threw
In Hillocks; the swift Stag from under ground
Bore up his branching head: scarce from his mould   *470*

---

441 **Dank** water (without disagreeable associations). 451 **Soul** Bentley's
conjecture; Fowle *1667*; Foul *1674*. 457 **wons** dwells. 466 **Ounce**
lynx. 467 **Libbard** leopard.

Behemoth° biggest born of Earth upheav'd
His vastness: Fleec't the Flocks and bleating rose,
As Plants: ambiguous° between Sea and Land
The River Horse° and scaly Crocodile.
475 At once came forth whatever creeps the ground,
Insect or Worm; those wav'd their limber fans
For wings, and smallest Lineaments exact
In all the Liveries deckt of Summer's pride
With spots of Gold and Purple, azure and green:
480 These as a line their long dimension drew,
Streaking the ground with sinuous trace; not all
Minims of Nature;° some of Serpent kind
Wondrous in length and corpulence° involv'd
Their Snaky folds, and added wings. First crept
485 The Parsimonious Emmet,° provident
Of future, in small room large heart enclos'd.
Pattern of just equality perhaps
Hereafter, join'd in her popular Tribes
Of Commonalty: swarming next appear'd
490 The Female Bee that feeds her Husband Drone
Deliciously, and builds her waxen Cells
With Honey stor'd: the rest are numberless,
And thou their Natures know'st, and gav'st them
    Names,
Needless to thee repeated; nor unknown
495 The Serpent subtl'st Beast of all the field,
Of huge extent sometimes, with brazen Eyes
And hairy Main terrific, though to thee
Not noxious, but obedient at thy call.
Now Heav'n in all her Glory shone, and roll'd
500 Her motions, as the great first-Mover's hand
First wheel'd their course; Earth in her rich attire
Consummate° lovely smil'd; Air, Water, Earth,
By Fowl, Fish, Beast, was flown, was swum, was
    walkt
Frequent;° and of the Sixth day yet remain'd:
505 There wanted yet the Master work, the end
Of all yet done; a Creature who not prone

471 **Behemoth** huge Biblical beast, here perhaps the elephant.   473 **ambiguous** amphibious.   474 **River Horse** hippopotamus.   482 **Minims of
Nature** smallest forms of animal life.   483 **corpulence** bulk.   485 **Emmet**
ant.   502 **Consummate** perfected.   504 **Frequent** in throngs.

And Brute as other Creatures, but endu'd
With Sanctity of Reason, might erect
His Stature, and upright with Front° serene
Govern the rest, self-knowing, and from thence   *510*
Magnanimous to correspond with° Heav'n,
But grateful to acknowledge whence his good
Descends, thither with heart and voice and eyes
Directed in Devotion, to adore
And worship God Supreme, who made him chief   *515*
Of all his works: therefore the Omnipotent
Eternal Father (For where is not hee
Present) thus to his Son audibly spake.
            'Let us make now Man in our image, Man
In our similitude, and let them rule   *520*
Over the Fish and Fowl of Sea and Air,
Beast of the Field, and over all the Earth,
And every creeping thing that creeps the ground.'
This said, he form'd thee, Adam, thee O Man
Dust of the ground, and in thy nostrils breath'd   *525*
The breath of Life; in his own Image hee
Created thee, in the Image of God
Express,° and thou becam'st a living Soul.
Male he created thee, but thy consort
Female for Race; then bless'd Mankind, and said,   *530*
'Be fruitful, multiply, and fill the Earth,
Subdue it, and throughout Dominion hold
Over Fish of the Sea, and Fowl of the Air,
And every living thing that moves on the Earth.'
Wherever thus created, for no place   *535*
Is yet distinct by name, thence, as thou know'st
He brought thee into this delicious Grove,
This Garden, planted with the Trees of God,
Delectable both to behold and taste;
And freely all their pleasant fruit for food   *540*
Gave thee, all sorts are here that all th'Earth yields,
Variety without end; but of the Tree
Which tasted works knowledge of Good and Evil,
Thou may'st not; in the day thou eat'st, thou di'st;
Death is the penalty impos'd, beware,   *545*

---

509 **Front** brow.   511 **correspond with** "answer to," in all senses.   528 **Express** exact in likeness.

And govern well thy appetite, lest sin
Surprise thee, and her black attendant Death.
Here finish'd hee, and all that he had made
View'd, and behold all was entirely good;
550 So Ev'n and Morn accomplish'd the Sixth day:
Yet not till the Creator from his work
Desisting, though unwearied, up return'd
Up to the Heav'n of Heav'ns his high abode,
Thence to behold this new created World
555 Th'addition of his Empire, how it show'd
In prospect from his Throne, how good, how fair,
Answering his great Idea.° Up he rode
Follow'd with acclamation and the sound
Symphonious of ten thousand Harps that tun'd
560 Angelic harmonies: the Earth, the Air
Resounded, (thou remember'st, for thou heard'st)
The Heav'ns and all the Constellations rung,
The Planets in their station° list'ning stood,
While the bright Pomp ascended jubilant.
565 'Open, ye everlasting Gates,' they sung,
'Open, ye Heav'ns, your living doors; let in
The great Creator from his work return'd
Magnificent, his Six days' work, a World;
Open, and henceforth oft; for God will deign
570 To visit oft the dwellings of just Men
Delighted, and with frequent intercourse
Thither will send his winged Messengers
On errands of supernal Grace.' So sung
The glorious Train ascending: He through Heav'n,
575 That open'd wide her blazing Portals, led
To God's Eternal house direct the way,
A broad and ample road, whose dust is Gold
And pavement Stars, as Stars to thee appear,
Seen in the Galaxy, that Milky way
580 Which nightly as a circling Zone thou seest
Powder'd with Stars. And now on Earth the Seventh
Ev'ning arose in Eden, for the Sun
Was set, and twilight from the East came on,
Forerunning Night; when at the holy mount
585 Of Heav'n's high-seated top, th'Imperial Throne

557 **Idea** ideal conception.   563 **station** *1674*; stations *1667*.

Of Godhead, fixt for ever firm and sure,
The Filial Power arriv'd, and sat him down
With his great Father, for he also went
Invisible, yet stay'd (such privilege
Hath Omnipresence) and the work ordain'd,   590
Author and end of all things, and from work
Now resting, bless'd and hallow'd the Sev'nth day,
As resting on that day from all his work,
But not in silence holy kept; the Harp
Had work and rested not, the solemn Pipe,   595
And Dulcimer, all Organs of sweet stop,
All sounds on Fret° by String or Golden Wire
Temper'd soft Tunings, intermixt with Voice
Choral or Unison: of incense Clouds
Fuming from Golden Censers hid the Mount.   600
Creation and the Six days' acts they sung,
'Great are thy works, Jehovah, infinite
Thy power; what thought can measure thee or tongue
Relate thee; greater now in thy return
Than from the Giant Angels; thee that day   605
Thy Thunders magnifi'd; but to create
Is greater than created to destroy.
Who can impair thee, mighty King, or bound
Thy Empire? easily the proud attempt
Of Spirits apostate and their Counsels vain   610
Thou hast repell'd, while impiously they thought
Thee to diminish, and from thee withdraw
The number of thy worshippers. Who seeks
To lessen thee, against his purpose serves
To manifest the more thy might: his evil   615
Thou usest, and from thence creat'st more good.
Witness this new-made World, another Heav'n
From Heaven Gate not far, founded in view
On the clear Hyaline,° the Glassy Sea;
Of amplitude almost immense,° with Stars   620
Numerous, and every Star perhaps a World
Of destin'd habitation; but thou know'st
Their seasons: among these the seat of men,
Earth with her nether Ocean circumfus'd,

597 **Fret** the bar which regulates the fingering. 619 **Hyaline** the "sea of glass, like unto crystal" in REVELATION 4:6. 620 **immense** immeasurable.

625 Their pleasant dwelling place. Thrice happy men,
     And sons of men, whom God hath thus advanc't,
     Created in his Image, there to dwell
     And worship him, and in reward to rule
     Over his Works, on Earth, in Sea, or Air,
630 And multiply a Race of Worshippers
     Holy and just: thrice happy if they know
     Their happiness, and persevere upright.'
             So sung they, and the Empyrean rung,
     With Halleluiahs: Thus was Sabbath kept.
635 And thy request think now fulfill'd, that ask'd
     How first this World and face of things began,
     And what before thy memory was done
     From the beginning, that posterity
     Inform'd by thee might know; if else thou seek'st
640 Aught, not surpassing human measure, say."

BOOK VIII

THE ARGUMENT

Adam inquires concerning celestial Motions, is doubtfully
answer'd, and exhorted to search rather things more worthy of knowledge: Adam assents, and still desirous to detain Raphaël, relates to him what he remember'd since
his own Creation, his placing in Paradise, his talk with
God concerning solitude and fit society, his first meeting
and Nuptials with Eve, his discourse with the Angel thereupon; who after admonitions repeated departs.

The Angel ended, and in Adam's Ear
So Charming left his voice, that he awhile
Thought him still speaking, still stood fixt to hear;
Then as new wak't thus gratefully repli'd.°
"What thanks sufficient, or what recompense   5
Equal have I to render thee, Divine
Historian, who thus largely hast allay'd
The thirst I had of knowledge, and vouchsaf't
This friendly condescension° to relate
Things else by me unsearchable, now heard   10
With wonder, but delight, and, as is due,
With glory áttribúted to the high
Creator; something yet of doubt remains,
Which only thy solution can resolve.
When I behold this goodly Frame, this World   15
Of Heav'n and Earth consisting, and compute
Their magnitudes, this Earth a spot, a grain,
An Atom, with the Firmament compar'd
And all her number'd Stars, that seem to roll

1–4 Added in *1674*, when Book VII was divided in two at line 640. *1667*
reads: "To whom thus Adam gratefully repli'd."   9 **condescension** cour-
teous disregard of rank.

20   Spaces incomprehensible (for such
      Their distance argues and their swift return
      Diurnal) merely to officiate° light
      Round this opacous Earth, this punctual° spot,
      One day and night; in all their vast survéy
25   Useless besides, reasoning I oft admire,°
      How Nature wise and frugal could commit
      Such disproportions, with superfluous hand
      So many nobler Bodies to create,
      Greater so manifold to this one use,
30   For aught appears, and on their Orbs impose
      Such restless revolution day by day
      Repeated, while the sedentary° Earth,
      That better might with far less compass move,
      Serv'd by more noble than herself, attains
35   Her end without least motion, and receives,
      As Tribute such a sumless° journey brought
      Of incorporeal speed, her warmth and light;
    · Speed, to describe whose swiftness Number fails."
              So spake our Sire, and by his count'nance
                  seem'd
40   Ent'ring on studious thoughts abstruse, which Eve
      Perceiving where she sat retir'd in sight,
      With lowliness Majestic from her seat,
      And Grace that won who saw to wish her stay,
      Rose, and went forth among her Fruits and Flow'rs,
45   To visit how they prosper'd, bud and bloom,
      Her Nursery;° they at her coming sprung
      And toucht° by her fair tendance gladlier grew.
      Yet went she not, as not with such discourse
      Delighted, or not capable her ear
50   Of what was high: such pleasure she reserv'd,°
      Adam relating, she sole Auditress;
      Her Husband the Relater° she preferr'd
      Before the Angel, and of him to ask

22 **officiate** supply, and with a strong religious suggestion, since an original meaning was "perform divine service." 23 **punctual** tiny like a point,
and the suggestion of exact timing is relevant too. 25 **admire** wonder
(at). 32 **sedentary** motionless. 36 **sumless** incalculable. 46 **Nursery**
both the spot (nursery-garden), and the activity (her leading or fostering). 47 **toucht** both literal (her gardening) and metaphorical (moved
to tender feeling, "gladlier grew"). 50 **reserv'd** postponed. 52 **Relater**
narrator, but following "Husband" it suggests, too, "relative"—Eve preferred the man to whom she was related to relate.

Chose rather; hee, she knew would intermix
Grateful digressions, and solve high dispute   55
With conjugal Caresses, from his Lip
Not Words alone pleas'd her. O when meet now
Such pairs, in Love and mutual Honour join'd?
With Goddess-like demeanour forth she went;
Not unattended, for on her as Queen   60
A pomp° of winning Graces waited still,°
And from about her shot Darts of desire
Into all Eyes to wish her still in sight.
And Raphaël now to Adam's doubt propos'd
Benevolent and facile° thus repli'd.   65
        "To ask or search I blame thee not, for Heav'n
Is as the Book of God before thee set,
Wherein to read his wondrous Works, and learn
His Seasons, Hours, or Days, or Months, or Years:
This to attain, whether Heav'n move or Earth,   70
Imports not, if thou reck'n right, the rest
From Man or Angel the great Architect   •
Did wisely to conceal, and not divulge
His secrets to be scann'd by them who ought
Rather admire; or if they list to try   75
Conjecture, he his Fabric of the Heav'ns
Hath left to their disputes, perhaps to move
His laughter at their quaint Opinions wide°
Hereafter, when they come to model Heav'n
And calculate the Stars, how they will wield   80
The mighty frame, how build, unbuild, contrive
To save appearances,° how gird the Sphere
With Centric and Eccentric° scribbl'd o'er,
Cycle and Epicycle,° Orb in Orb:
Already by thy reasoning this I guess,   85
Who art to lead thy offspring, and supposest
That Bodies bright and greater should not serve
The less not bright, nor Heav'n such journeys run,
Earth sitting still, when she alone receives
The benefit: consider first, that Great   90
Or Bright infers not Excellence: the Earth

61 **pomp** pageant.   61 **still** always.   65 **facile** equable.   78 **wide** astray.
82 **save appearances** explain away difficulties (in the Ptolemaic theory).
83 **Centric and Eccentric** with orbits centered or not centered on the
earth.   84 **Epicycle** small cycle (Ptolemaic term).

Though, in comparison of Heav'n, so small,
Nor glistering, may of solid good contain.
More plenty than the Sun that barren shines,
95 Whose virtue on itself works no effect,
But in the fruitful Earth; there first receiv'd
His beams, unactive else, their vigour find.
Yet not to Earth are those bright Luminaries
Officious,° but to thee Earth's habitant.
100 And for the Heav'n's wide Circuit, let it speak
The Maker's high magnificence, who built
So spacious, and his Line stretcht out so far;
That Man may know he dwells not in his own;
An Edifice too large for him to fill,
105 Lodg'd in a small partition, and the rest
Ordain'd for uses to his Lord best known.
The swiftness of those Circles áttribúte,
Though numberless, to his Omnipotence,
That to corporeal substances could add
110 Speed almost Spiritual; mee thou think'st not slow,
Who since the Morning hour set out from Heav'n
Where God resides, and ere mid-day arriv'd
In Eden, distance inexpressible
By Numbers that have name. But this I urge,
115 Admitting Motion in the Heav'ns to show
Invalid that which thee to doubt it mov'd;
Not that I so affirm, though so it seem
To thee who hast thy dwelling here on Earth.
God to remove his ways from human sense,
120 Plac'd Heav'n from Earth so far, that earthly sight,
If it presume, might err in things too high,
And no advantage° gain. What if the Sun
Be Center to the World, and other Stars
By his attractive virtue° and their own
125 Incited, dance about him various rounds?
Their wand'ring course now high, now low, then hid,
Progressive, retrograde, or standing still,
In six thou seest, and what if sev'nth to these
The Planet Earth, so steadfast though she seem,

99 **Officious** dutiful.   122 **advantage** including the common 17th-century
sense, "point of vantage."   124 **attractive virtue** power of attraction.

Insensibly three° different Motions move?   *130*
Which else to several Spheres thou must ascribe,
Mov'd contrary with thwart obliquities,
Or save the Sun his labour, and that swift
Nocturnal and Diurnal rhomb° suppos'd,
Invisible else above all Stars, the Wheel   *135*
Of Day and Night; which needs not thy belief,
If Earth industrious of herself fetch Day
Travelling East, and with her part averse
From the Sun's beam meet Night, her other part
Still luminous by his ray. What if that light   *140*
Sent from her through the wide transpicuous air,
To the terrestrial Moon be as a Star
Enlight'ning her by Day, as she by Night
This Earth? reciprocal, if Land be there,
Fields and Inhabitants: Her spots thou seest   *145*
As Clouds, and Clouds may rain, and Rain produce
Fruits in her soft'n'd Soil, for some to eat
Allotted there; and other Suns perhaps
With their attendant Moons thou wilt descry
Communicating Male and Female Light,   *150*
Which two great Sexes animate the World,
Stor'd in each Orb perhaps with some that live.
For such vast room in Nature unpossest
By living Soul, desért and desolate,
Only to shine, yet scarce to cóntribute   *155*
Each Orb a glimpse of Light, convey'd so far
Down to this habitable, which returns
Light back to them, is obvious° to dispute.
But whether thus these things, or whether not,
Whether the Sun predominant in Heav'n   *160*
Rise on the Earth, or Earth rise on the Sun,
Hee from the East his flaming road begin,
Or Shee from West her silent course advance
With inoffensive° pace that spinning sleeps
On her soft Axle, while she paces Ev'n,   *165*
And bears thee soft with the smooth Air along,

130 **three** daily, yearly, and on its own axis.   134 **rhomb** the supposed
wheel of the Primum Mobile, the first-moved sphere.   158 **obvious** open.
164 **inoffensive** unstumbling.

Solicit° not thy thoughts with matters hid,
Leave them to God above, him serve and fear;
Of other Creatures, as him pleases best,
170 Wherever plac't, let him dispose: joy thou
In what he gives to thee, this Paradise
And thy fair Eve; Heav'n is for thee too high
To know what passes there; be lowly wise:
Think only what concerns thee and thy being;
175 Dream not of other Worlds, what Creatures there
Live, in what state, condition or degree,
Contented that thus far hath been reveal'd
Not of Earth only but of highest Heav'n."
        To whom thus Adam clear'd of doubt, repli'd.
180 "How fully hast thou satisfied mee, pure
Intelligence° of Heav'n, Angel serene,
And freed from intricacies, taught to live,
The easiest way, nor with perplexing thoughts
To interrupt the sweet of Life, from which
185 God hath bid dwell far off all anxious cares,
And not molest us, unless we ourselves
Seek them with wand'ring thoughts, and notions vain.
But apt the Mind or Fancy is to rove
Uncheckt, and of her roving is no end;
190 Till warn'd, or by experience taught, she learn,
That not to know at large of things remote
From use, obscure and subtle, but to know
That which before us lies in daily life,
Is the prime Wisdom, what is more, is fume,
195 Or emptiness, or fond impertinence,°
And renders us in things that most concern
Unpractis'd, unprepar'd, and still to seek.
Therefore from this high pitch let us descend
A lower flight, and speak of things at hand
200 Useful, whence haply mention may arise
Of something not unseasonable to ask
By sufferance, and thy wonted favour deign'd.
Thee I have heard relating what was done
Ere my remembrance: now hear mee relate
205 My Story, which perhaps thou hast not heard;

167 **Solicit** disturb (from the Latin for "to put in motion"; Raphael remembers the context in which he speaks). 181 **Intelligence** divine spirit. 195 **fond impertinence** foolish irrelevance.

And Day is yet not spent; till then thou seest
How subtly to detain thee I devise,
Inviting thee to hear while I relate,
Fond, were it not in hope of thy reply:
For while I sit with thee, I seem in Heav'n,   210
And sweeter thy discourse is to my ear
Than Fruits of Palm-tree pleasantest to thirst
And hunger both, from labour, at the hour
Of sweet repast; they satiate, and soon fill,
Though pleasant, but thy words with Grace Divine   215
Imbu'd, bring to their sweetness no satiety."
          To whom thus Raphaël answer'd heav'nly
          meek.
"Nor are thy lips ungraceful, Sire of men,
Nor tongue ineloquent; for God on thee
Abundantly his gifts hath also pour'd   220
Inward and outward both, his image fair:
Speaking or mute all comeliness and grace
Attends thee, and each word, each motion forms.
Nor less think wee in Heav'n of thee on Earth
Than of our fellow servant, and inquire   225
Gladly into the ways of God with Man:
For God we see hath honour'd thee, and set
On Man his equal Love: say therefore on;
For I that Day was absent, as befell,
Bound on a voyage uncouth and obscure,   230
Far on excursion toward the Gates of Hell;
Squar'd in full Legion (such command we had)
To see that none thence issu'd forth a spy,
Or enemy, while God was in his work,
Lest hee incent at such eruption bold,   235
Destruction with Creation might have mixt.
Not that they durst without his leave attempt,
But us he sends upon his high behests
For state, as Sovran King, and to inure
Our prompt obedience. Fast we found, fast shut   240
The dismal Gates, and barricado'd strong;
But long ere our approaching heard within
Noise, other than the sound of Dance or Song,
Torment, and loud lament, and furious rage.
Glad we return'd up to the coasts of Light   245
Ere Sabbath Ev'ning: so we had in charge.

But thy relation now; for I attend,
Pleas'd with thy words no less than thou with mine."
          So spake the Godlike Power, and thus our
               Sire.
250 "For Man to tell how human Life began
Is hard; for who himself beginning knew?
Desire with thee still longer to converse
Induc'd me. As new wak't from soundest sleep
Soft on the flow'ry herb I found me laid
255 In Balmy Sweat, which with his Beams the Sun
Soon dri'd, and on the reeking° moisture fed.
Straight toward Heav'n my wond'ring Eyes I turn'd,
And gaz'd awhile the ample Sky, till rais'd
By quick instinctive motion up I sprung,
260 As thitherward endeavouring, and upright
Stood on my feet; about me round I saw
Hill, Dale, and shady Woods, and sunny Plains,
And liquid Lapse° of murmuring Streams; by these,
Creatures that liv'd, and mov'd, and walk'd, or flew,
265 Birds on the branches warbling; all things smil'd,
With fragrance and with joy my heart o'erflow'd.
Myself I then perus'd, and Limb by Limb
Survey'd, and sometimes went, and sometimes ran
With supple joints, as lively vigour led:
270 But who I was, or where, or from what cause,
Knew not; to speak I tri'd, and forthwith spake,
My Tongue obey'd and readily could name
Whate'er I saw. 'Thou Sun,' said I, 'fair Light,
And thou enlight'n'd Earth, so fresh and gay,
275 Ye Hills and Dales, ye Rivers, Woods, and Plains,
And ye that live and move, fair Creatures, tell,
Tell, if ye saw, how came I thus, how here?
Not of myself; by some great Maker then,
In goodness and in power preeminent;
280 Tell me, how may I know him, how adore,
From whom I have that thus I move and live,
And feel that I am happier than I know.'
While thus I call'd, and stray'd I knew not whither,
From where I first drew Air, and first beheld

256 **reeking** rising in vapor (without disagreeable associations). 263 **Lapse** fall (consciously literal, since Paradise is as yet innocent; but "the Lapse of Man" was a 17th-century phrase for the Fall).

This happy Light, when answer none return'd,   285
On a green shady Bank profuse of Flow'rs
Pensive I sat me down; there gentle sleep
First found me, and with soft oppression seiz'd
My drowsed sense, untroubl'd, though I thought
I then was passing to my former state   290
Insensible, and forthwith to dissolve:
When suddenly stood at my Head a dream,
Whose inward apparition° gently mov'd
My Fancy to believe I yet had being,
And liv'd: One came, methought, of shape Divine,   295
And said, 'thy Mansion wants thee, Adam, rise,
First Man, of Men innumerable ordain'd
First Father, call'd by thee I come thy Guide
To the Garden of bliss, thy seat prepar'd.'
So saying, by the hand he took me rais'd,   300
And over Fields and Waters, as in Air
Smooth sliding without step, last led me up
A woody Mountain; whose high top was plain,
A Circuit wide, enclos'd, with goodliest Trees
Planted, with Walks, and Bowers, that what I saw   305
Of Earth before scarce pleasant seem'd. Each Tree
Load'n with fairest Fruit, that hung to the Eye
Tempting, stirr'd in me sudden appetite
To pluck and eat; whereat I wak'd, and found
Before mine Eyes all real, as the dream   310
Had lively shadow'd: Here had new begun
My wand'ring, had not hee who was my Guide
Up hither, from among the Trees appear'd,
Presence Divine. Rejoicing, but with awe
In adoration at his feet I fell   315
Submiss: he rear'd me, and 'Whom thou sought'st I
    am,'
Said mildly, 'Author of all this thou seest
Above, or round about thee or beneath.
This Paradise I give thee, count it thine
To Till and keep, and of the Fruit to eat: 320
Of every Tree that in the Garden grows
Eat freely with glad heart; fear here no dearth:
But of the Tree whose operation brings

293 **apparition** appearing.

Knowledge of good and ill, which I have set
325 The Pledge of thy Obedience and thy Faith,
Amid the Garden by the Tree of Life,
Remember what I warn thee, shun to taste,
And shun the bitter consequence: for know,
The day thou eat'st thereof, my sole command
330 Transgrest, inevitably thou shalt die;
From that day mortal, and this happy State
Shalt lose, expell'd from hence into a World
Of woe and sorrow.' Sternly he pronounc'd
The rigid interdiction, which resounds
335 Yet dreadful in mine ear, though in my choice
Not to incur; but soon his clear aspéct
Return'd and gracious purpose° thus renew'd.
'Not only these fair bounds, but all the Earth
To thee and to thy Race I give; as Lords
340 Possess it, and all things that therein live,
Or live in Sea, or Air, Beast, Fish, and Fowl.
In sign whereof each Bird and Beast behold
After their kinds; I bring them to receive
From thee their Names, and pay thee fealty
345 With low subjection; understand the same
Of Fish within their watery residence,
Not hither summon'd, since they cannot change
Their Element to draw the thinner Air.'
As thus he spake, each Bird and Beast behold
350 Approaching two and two, These cow'ring low
With blandishment, each Bird stoop'd on his wing.
I nam'd them, as they pass'd, and understood
Their Nature, with such knowledge God endu'd
My sudden apprehension: but in these
355 I found not what methought I wanted still;
And to the Heav'nly vision thus presum'd.
            'O by what Name, for thou above all these,
Above mankind, or aught than mankind higher,
Surpassest far my naming, how may I
360 Adore thee, Author of this Universe,
And all this good to man, for whose well-being
So amply, and with hands so liberal
Thou hast provided all things: but with mee

337 **purpose** discourse.

I see not who partakes. In solitude
What happiness, who can enjoy alone,   365
Or all enjoying, what contentment find?'
Thus I presumptuous; and the vision bright,
As with a smile more bright'n'd, thus repli'd.
  'What call'st thou solitude, is not the Earth
With various living creatures, and the Air   370
Replenisht, and all these at thy command
To come and play before thee, know'st thou not
Their language and their ways, they also know,
And reason not contemptibly; with these
Find pastime, and bear rule; thy Realm is large.'   375
So spake the Universal Lord, and seem'd
So ordering. I with leave of speech implor'd,
And humble deprecation thus repli'd.
  'Let not my words offend thee, Heav'nly
    Power,
My Maker, be propitious while I speak.   380
Hast thou not made me here thy substitute,°
And these inferior far beneath me set?
Among unequals what society
Can sort, what harmony or true delight?
Which must be mutual, in proportion due   385
Giv'n and receiv'd; but in disparity
The one intense, the other still remiss°
Cannot well suit with either, but soon prove
Tedious alike: Of fellowship I speak
Such as I seek, fit to participate   390
All rational delight, wherein the brute
Cannot be human consort; they rejoice
Each with their kind, Lion with Lioness;
So fitly them in pairs thou hast combin'd;
Much less can Bird with Beast, or Fish with Fowl   395
So well converse,° nor with the Ox the Ape;
Worse then can Man with Beast, and least of all.'
  Whereto th'Almighty answer'd, not displeas'd.
'A nice° and subtle happiness I see
Thou to thyself proposest, in the choice   400
Of thy Associates, Adam, and wilt taste

---

381 **substitute** deputy.   387 **intense . . . remiss** taut and slack, taking up the
metaphor of "harmony."   396 **converse** associate.   399 **nice** fastidious.

No pleasure, thou in pleasure, solitary.
What think'st thou then of mee, and this my State,
Seem I to thee sufficiently possest
405 Of happiness, or not? who am alone
From all Eternity, for none I know
Second to mee or like, equal much less.
How have I then with whom to hold converse
Save with the Creatures which I made, and those
410 To me inferior, infinite descents
Beneath what other Creatures are to thee?'
              He ceas'd, I lowly answer'd. 'To attain
The heighth and depth of thy Eternal ways
All human thoughts come short, Supreme of things;
415 Thou in thyself art perfect, and in thee
Is no deficience found; not so is Man,
But in degree, the cause of his desire
By conversation with his like to help,
Or solace his defects. No need that thou
420 Shouldst propagate, already infinite;
And through all numbers absolute, though One;
But Man by number is to manifest
His single imperfection,° and beget
Like of his like, his Image multipli'd,
425 In unity° defective, which requires
Collateral love, and dearest amity.
Thou in thy secrecy although alone,
Best with thyself accompanied, seek'st not
Social communication, yet so pleas'd,
430 Canst raise thy Creature to what heighth thou wilt
Of Union or Communion, deifi'd;
I by conversing cannot these erect
From prone, nor in their ways complacence° find.'
Thus I embold'n'd spake, and freedom us'd
435 Permissive, and acceptance found, which gain'd
This answer from the gracious voice Divine.
              'Thus far to try thee, Adam, I was pleas'd,
And find thee knowing not of Beasts alone,
Which thou hast rightly nam'd, but of thyself,
440 Expressing well the spirit within thee free,

---

423 **single imperfection** imperfection in being single.   425 **unity** one-
ness.   433 **complacence** satisfaction.

My Image, not imparted to the Brute,
Whose fellowship therefore unmeet for thee
Good reason was thou freely shouldst dislike,
And be so minded still; I, ere thou spak'st,
Knew it not good for Man to be alone,   *445*
And no such company as then thou saw'st
Intended thee, for trial only brought,
To see how thou could'st judge of fit and meet:
What next I bring shall please thee, be assur'd,
Thy likeness, thy fit help, thy other self,   *450*
Thy wish, exactly to thy heart's desire.'
        Hee ended, or I heard no more, for now
My earthly by his Heav'nly overpower'd,
Which it had long stood under, strain'd to the heighth
In that celestial Colloquy sublime,   *455*
As with an object that excels° the sense,
Dazzl'd and spent, sunk down, and sought repair
Of sleep, which instantly fell on me, call'd
By Nature as in aid, and clos'd mine eyes.
Mine eyes he clos'd, but op'n left the Cell   *460*
Of Fancy my internal sight, by which
Abstráct° as in a trance methought I saw,
Though sleeping, where I lay, and saw the shape
Still glorious before whom awake I stood;
Who stooping op'n'd my left side, and took   *465*
From thence a Rib, with cordial spirits° warm,
And Life-blood streaming fresh; wide was the wound,
But suddenly with flesh fill'd up and heal'd:
The Rib he form'd and fashion'd with his hands;
Under his forming hands a Creature grew,   *470*
Manlike, but different sex, so lovely fair,
That what seem'd fair in all the World, seem'd now
Mean, or in her summ'd up, in her contain'd
And in her looks, which from that time infus'd
Sweetness into my heart, unfelt before,   *475*
And into all things from her Air inspir'd
The spirit of love and amorous delight.
She disappear'd, and left me dark, I wak'd
To find her, or for ever to deplore

---

456 **excels** literally, rises above (the context suggests gazing into the sky).   462 **Absráct** withdrawn.   466 **cordial spirits** the hearts vital spirits.

480 Her loss, and other pleasures all abjure:
     When out of hope, behold her, not far off,
     Such as I saw her in my dream, adorn'd
     With what all Earth or Heaven could bestow
     To make her amiable: On she came,
485 Led by her Heav'nly Maker, though unseen,
     And guided by his voice, nor uninform'd
     Of nuptial Sanctity and marriage Rites:
     Grace was in all her steps, Heav'n in her Eye,
     In every gesture dignity and love.
490 I overjoy'd could not forbear aloud.
             'This turn hath made amends; thou hast
                     fulfill'd
     Thy words, Creator bounteous and benign,
     Giver of all things fair, but fairest this
     Of all thy gifts, nor enviest. I now see
495 Bone of my Bone, Flesh of my Flesh, my Self
     Before me; Woman is her Name, of Man
     Extracted; for this cause he shall forgo
     Father and Mother, and to his Wife adhere;
     And they shall be one Flesh, one Heart, one Soul.'
             She heard me thus, and though divinely
500   brought,
     Yet Innocence and Virgin Modesty,
     Her virtue and the conscience° of her worth,
     That would be woo'd, and not unsought be won,
     Not obvious,° not obtrusive, but retir'd,
505 The more desirable, or to say all,
     Nature herself, though pure of sinful thought,
     Wrought in her so, that seeing me, she turn'd;
     I follow'd her, she what was Honour knew,
     And with obsequious° Majesty approv'd
510 My pleaded reason. To the Nuptial Bow'r
     I led her blushing like the Morn: all Heav'n,
     And happy Constellations on that hour
     Shed their selectest influence; the Earth
     Gave sign of gratulation, and each Hill;
515 Joyous the Birds; fresh Gales and gentle Airs
     Whisper'd it to the Woods, and from their wings

---

502 **conscience** consciousness.   504 **obvious** "forward."   509 **obsequious** obedient (gently paradoxical in combination with "Majesty").

Flung Rose, flung Odours from the spicy Shrub,
Disporting, till the amorous Bird of Night
Sung Spousal, and bid haste the Ev'ning Star
On his Hill top, to light the bridal Lamp.   520
Thus I have told thee all my State, and brought
My Story to the sum of earthly bliss
Which I enjoy, and must confess to find
In all things else delight indeed, but such
As us'd or not, works in the mind no change,   525
Nor vehement° desire, these delicacies
I mean of Taste, Sight, Smell, Herbs, Fruits, and
    Flow'rs,
Walks, and the melody of Birds; but here
Far otherwise, transported I behold,
Transported touch; here passion first I felt,   530
Commotion strange, in all enjoyments else
Superior and unmov'd, here only weak
Against the charm of Beauty's powerful glance.
Or Nature fail'd in mee, and left some part
Not proof° enough such Object to sustain,   535
Or from my side subducting, took perhaps
More than enough; at least on her bestow'd
Too much of Ornament, in outward show
Elaborate,° of inward less exact.°
For well I understand in the prime end   540
Of Nature her th'inferior, in the mind
And inward Faculties, which most excel,
In outward also her resembling less
His Image who made both, and less expressing
The character of that Dominion giv'n   545
O'er other Creatures; yet when I approach
Her loveliness, so absolute° she seems
And in herself complete, so well to know
Her own, that what she wills to do or say,
Seems wisest, virtuousest, discreetest,° best;   550
All higher knowledge in her presence falls
Degraded, Wisdom in discourse with her
Loses discount'nanc't, and like folly shows;

---

526 **vehement** from "deprived of the mind" (Latin *mens*), following line
525.   535 **proof** armored.   539 **Elaborate** highly worked.   539 **exact**
brought to perfection.   547 **absolute** perfect, with a suggestion of complete power.   550 **discreetest** most discerning.

Authority and Reason on her wait,
555 As one intended first, not after made
Occasionally;° and to consúmmate all,
Greatness of mind and nobleness their seat
Build in her loveliest, and create an awe
About her, as a guard Angelic plac't."
560 To whom the Angel with contracted brow.
        "Accuse not Nature, she hath done her part;
Do thou but thine, and be not diffident°
Of Wisdom, she deserts thee not, if thou
Dismiss not her, when most thou need'st her nigh,
565 By áttribúting overmuch to things
Less excellent, as thou thyself perceiv'st
For what admir'st thou, what transports thee so,
An outside? fair no doubt, and worthy well
Thy cherishing, thy honouring, and thy love,
570 Not thy subjection: weigh with her thyself;
Then value: Oft times nothing profits more
Than self-esteem, grounded on just and right
Well manag'd; of that skill the more thou know'st,
The more she will acknowledge thee her Head,
575 And to realities yield all her shows;
Made so adorn for thy delight the more,
So awful, that with honour thou may'st love
Thy mate, who sees when thou art seen least wise.
But if the sense of touch whereby mankind
580 Is propagated seem such dear delight
Beyond all other, think the same vouchsaf't
To Cattle and each Beast; which would not be
To them made common and divulg'd, if aught
Therein enjoy'd were worthy to subdue
585 The Soul of Man, or passion in him move.
What higher in her society thou find'st
Attractive, human, rational, love still;
In loving thou dost well, in passion not,
Wherein true Love consists not; love refines
590 The thoughts, and heart enlarges, hath his seat
In Reason, and is judicious, is the scale
By which to heav'nly Love thou may'st ascend,
Not sunk in carnal pleasure, for which cause

556 **Occasionally** for a particular occasion.   562 **diffident** distrustful.

Among the Beasts no Mate for thee was found."
      To whom thus half-abash't Adam repli'd.   595
"Neither her outside form'd so fair, nor aught
In procreation common to all kinds
(Though higher of the genial° Bed by far,
And with mysterious reverence I deem)
So much delights me, as those graceful acts,   600
Those thousand decencies that daily flow
From all her words and actions, mixt with Love
And sweet compliance, which declare unfeign'd
Union of Mind, or in us both one Soul;
Harmony to behold in wedded pair   605
More grateful than harmonious sound to the ear.
Yet these subject not;° I to thee disclose
What inward thence I feel, not therefore foil'd,
Who meet with various objects, from the sense
Variously representing; yet still free   610
Approve the best, and follow what I approve.
To love thou blam'st me not, for love thou say'st
Leads up to Heaven, is both the way and guide;
Bear with me then, if lawful what I ask;
Love not the heav'nly Spirits, and how their Love   615
Express they, by looks only, or do they mix
Irradiance, virtual° or immediate touch?"
      To whom the Angel with a smile that glow'd
Celestial rosy red, Love's proper hue,
Answer'd. "Let it suffice thee that thou know'st   620
Us happy, and without Love no happiness.
Whatever pure thou in the body enjoy'st
(And pure thou wert created) we enjoy
In eminence, and obstacle find none
Of membrane, joint, or limb, exclusive° bars: 625
Easier than Air with Air, if Spirits embrace,
Total they mix, Union of Pure with Pure
Desiring; nor restrain'd conveyance° need
As Flesh to mix with Flesh, or Soul with Soul.
But I can now no more; the parting Sun   630
Beyond the Earth's green Cape° and verdant Isles

---

598 **genial** generative. 607 **subject not** do not bring into subjection.
617 **virtual** in essence. 625 **exclusive** having the power to exclude. 628 **restrain'd conveyance** restricted conveying. 631 **green Cape** Cape Verde islands.

Hesperean sets, my Signal to depart.
Be strong, live happy, and love, but first of all
Him whom to love is to obey, and keep
635 His great command; take heed lest Passion sway
Thy Judgement to do aught, which else free Will
Would not admit; thine and of all thy Sons
The weal or woe in thee is plac't; beware.
I in thy persevering shall rejoice,
640 And all the Blest: stand fast; to stand or fall
Free in thine own Arbitrement it lies.
Perfect within, no outward aid require;
And all temptation to transgress repel."
     So saying, he arose; whom Adam thus
645 Follow'd with benediction. "Since to part,
Go heav'nly Guest, Ethereal Messenger,
Sent from whose sovran goodness I adore.
Gentle to me and affable hath been
Thy condescension, and shall be honour'd ever
650 With grateful Memory: thou to mankind
Be good and friendly still, and oft return."
          So parted they, the Angel up to Heav'n
From the thick shade, and Adam to his Bow'r.

BOOK IX

THE ARGUMENT

Satan having compast the Earth, with meditated guile returns as a mist by Night into Paradise, enters into the Serpent sleeping. Adam and Eve in the Morning go forth to their labours, which Eve proposes to divide in several places, each labouring apart: Adam consents not, alleging the danger, lest that Enemy, of whom they were forewarn'd, should attempt her found alone: Eve loath to be thought not circumspect or firm enough, urges her going apart, the rather desirous to make trial of her strength; Adam at last yields: The Serpent finds her alone; his subtle approach, first gazing, then speaking, with much flattery extolling Eve above all other Creatures. Eve wond'ring to hear the Serpent speak, asks how he attain'd both human speech and such understanding not till now; the Serpent answers, that by tasting of a certain Tree in the Garden he attain'd to Speech and Reason, till then void of both: Eve requires him to bring her to that Tree, and finds it to be the Tree of Knowledge forbidden: The Serpent now grown bolder, with many wiles and arguments induces her at length to eat; she pleas'd with the taste deliberates awhile whether to impart thereof to Adam or not, at last brings him of the Fruit, relates what persuaded her to eat thereof: Adam at first amaz'd, but perceiving her lost, resolves through vehemence of love to perish with her; and extenuating the trespass, eats also of the Fruit: The effects thereof in them both; they seek to cover their nakedness; then fall to variance and accusation of one another.

No more of talk where God or Angel Guest
With Man, as with his Friend, familiar° us'd
To sit indulgent, and with him partake
Rural repast, permitting him the while
5   Venial° discourse unblam'd: I now must change
Those Notes to Tragic; foul distrust, and breach
Disloyal on the part of Man, revolt,
And disobedience: On the part of Heav'n
Now alienated, distance and distaste,
10   Anger and just rebuke, and judgement giv'n,
That brought into this World a world of woe,
Sin and her shadow Death, and Misery
Death's Harbinger: Sad task, yet argument°
Not less but more Heroic than the wrath
15   Of stern Achilles° on his Foe pursu'd
Thrice Fugitive about Troy Wall; or rage
Of Turnus for Lavinia° disespous'd,
Or Neptune's ire or Juno's, that so long
Perplex'd the Greek° and Cytherea's Son;°
20   If answerable° style I can obtain
Of my Celestial Patroness, who deigns
Her nightly visitation° unimplor'd,
And dictates to me slumb'ring, or inspires
Easy my unpremeditated Verse:
25   Since first this Subject for Heroic Song
Pleas'd me long choosing, and beginning late;
Not sedulous by Nature to indite
Wars, hitherto the only Argument
Heroic deem'd, chief mast'ry to dissect°
30   With long and tedious havoc fabl'd Knights
In Battles feign'd; the better fortitude
Of Patience and Heroic Martyrdom
Unsung; or to describe Races and Games,

2 **familiar** affable, habitual, and as if within a famly.   5 **Venial** allow-
able.   13 **argument** story.   15 **Achilles** in the *Iliad*.   17 **Lavinia** whose
betrothal was broken in the *Aeneid*.   19 **Greek** Odysseus, persecuted by
Neptune.   19 **Son** Aeneas, son of Venus, persecuted by Juno.   20 **answerable** fitting.   22 **visitation** with the previous line, the religious gravity
hints at the Visitation of Our Lady, the Virgin Mary.   29 **dissect** cut in
pieces, and analyze.

Or tilting Furniture,° emblazon'd Shields,
Impresses° quaint, Caparisons and Steeds;   35
Bases° and tinsel Trappings, gorgeous Knights
At Joust and Tournament; then marshall'd Feast
Serv'd up in Hall with Sewers,° and Seneshals;°
The skill of Artifice or Office mean,
Not that which justly gives Heroic name   40
To Person or to Poem. Mee of these
Nor skill'd nor studious, higher Argument
Remains, sufficient of itself to raise
That name, unless an age too late, or cold
Climate, or Years damp my intended° wing   45
Deprest,° and much they may, if all be mine,
Not Hers who brings it nightly to my Ear.
        The Sun was sunk, and after him the Star
Of Hesperus, whose Office is to bring
Twilight upon the Earth, short Arbiter   50
'Twixt Day and Night, and now from end to end
Night's Hemisphere had veil'd the Horizon round:
When Satan who late fled before the threats
Of Gabriel out of Eden, now improv'd°
In meditated fraud and malice, bent   55
On man's destruction, maugre° what might hap
Of heavier on himself, fearless return'd.
By Night he fled, and at Midnight return'd
From compassing the Earth, cautious of day,
Since Uriel Regent of the Sun descri'd   60
His entrance, and forewarn'd the Cherubim
That kept their watch; thence full of anguish driv'n,
The space of seven continu'd Nights he rode
With darkness, thrice the Equinoctial Line°
He circl'd, four times cross'd the Car of Night   65
From Pole to Pole, traversing each Colure;°
On the eighth return'd, and on the Coast averse
From entrance or Cherubic Watch, by stealth
Found unsuspected way. There was a place,

---

34 **tilting Furniture** equipment for jousting.   35 **Impresses** heraldic devices.   36 **Bases** accoutrements for horses.   38 **Sewers** stewards.   38 **Seneshals** ceremonial servants.   45 **intended** including the literal "outstretched" (as in "extended").   46 **Deprest** including the literal "pressed down."   54 **improv'd** increased (in evil).   56 **maugre** despite.   64 **Equinoctial Line** path of the sun.   66 **Colure** circle from the poles.

Now not, though Sin, not Time, first wrought the
70   change,
Where Tigris at the foot of Paradise
Into a Gulf shot under ground, till part
Rose up a Fountain by the Tree of Life;
In with the River sunk, and with it rose
75   Satan involv'd in rising Mist, then sought
Where to lie hid; Sea he had searcht and Land
From Eden over Pontus, and the Pool
Mæotis, up beyond the River Ob;°
Downward as far Antarctic; and in length
80   West from Orontes to the Ocean barr'd
At Darien,° thence to the Land where flows
Ganges and Indus: thus the Orb he roam'd
With narrow search; and with inspection deep
Consider'd every Creature, which of all
85   Most opportune might serve his Wiles, and found
The Serpent subtlest Beast of all the Field.
Him after long debate, irresolute
Of thoughts revolv'd, his final sentence chose
Fit Vessel, fittest Imp° of fraud, in whom
90   To enter, and his dark suggestions° hide
From sharpest sight: for in the wily Snake,
Whatever sleights none would suspicious mark,
As from his wit and native subtlety
Proceeding, which in other Beasts observ'd
95   Doubt might beget of Diabolic pow'r
Active within beyond the sense of brute.
Thus he resolv'd, but first from inward grief
His bursting passion into plaints thus pour'd:
        "O Earth, how like to Heav'n, if not preferr'd
100   More justly, Seat worthier of Gods, as built
With second thoughts, reforming what was old!
For what God after better worse would build?
Terrestrial Heav'n, danc't round by other Heav'ns
That shine, yet bear their bright officious Lamps,
105   Light above Light, for thee alone, as seems,
In thee concentring all their precious beams
Of sacred influence: As God in Heav'n

78 **Ob** in Siberia. 81 **Darien** Panama. 89 **Imp** offspring (of the
devil). 90 **suggestions** temptations.

Is Center, yet extends to all, so thou
Cent'ring receiv'st from all those Orbs; in thee,
Not in themselves, all their known virtue appears   110
Productive in Herb, Plant, and nobler birth
Of Creatures animate with gradual° life
Of Growth, Sense, Reason, all summ'd up in Man.
With what delight could I have walkt thee round
If I could joy in aught, sweet interchange   115
Of Hill and Valley, Rivers, Woods and Plains,
Now Land, now Sea, and Shores with Forest crown'd,
Rocks, Dens, and Caves; but I in none of these
Find place or refuge; and the more I see
Pleasures about me, so much more I feel   120
Torment within me, as from the hateful siege
Of contraries; all good to me becomes
Bane, and in Heav'n much worse would be my state.
But neither here seek I, no nor in Heav'n
To dwell, unless by mast'ring Heav'n's Supreme;   125
Nor hope to be myself less miserable
By what I seek, but others to make such
As I, though thereby worse to me redound:
For only in destroying I find ease
To my relentless thoughts; and him destroy'd,   130
Or won to what may work his utter loss,
For whom all this was made, all this will soon
Follow, as to him linkt in weal or woe,
In woe then; that destruction wide may range:
To mee shall be the glory sole among   135
The infernal Powers, in one day to have marr'd
What he *Almighty* styl'd, six Nights and Days
Continu'd making, and who knows how long
Before had been contriving, though perhaps
Not longer than since I in one Night freed   140
From servitude inglorious wellnigh half
Th'Angelic Name, and thinner left the throng
Of his adorers: hee to be aveng'd,
And to repair his numbers thus impair'd,
Whether such virtue spent of old now fail'd   145
More Angels to Create, if they at least
Are his Created or to spite us more,

112 **gradual** in stages.

Determin'd to advance into our room
A Creature form'd of Earth, and him endow,
150 Exalted from so base original,
With Heav'nly spoils, our spoils: What he decreed
He effected; Man he made, and for him built
Magnificent this World, and Earth his seat,
Him Lord pronounc'd, and, O indignity!
155 Subjected to his service Angel wings,
And flaming Ministers to watch and tend
Their earthy Charge: Of these the vigilance
I dread, and to elude, thus wrapt in mist
Of midnight vapour glide obscure, and pry
160 In every Bush and Brake, where hap may find
The Serpent sleeping, in whose mazy folds
To hide me, and the dark intent I bring.
O foul descent! that I who erst contended
With Gods to sit the highest, am now constrain'd
165 Into a Beast, and mixt with bestial slime,
This essence to incarnate° and imbrute,
That to the height of Deity aspir'd;
But what will not Ambition and Revenge
Descend to? who aspires must down as low
170 As high he soar'd, obnoxious° first or last
To basest things. Revenge, at first though sweet,
Bitter erelong back on itself recoils;
Let it; I reck not, so it 'light well aim'd,
Since higher I fall short, on him who next
175 Provokes my envy, this new Favorite
Of Heav'n, this Man of Clay, Son of despite,
Whom us the more to spite his Maker rais'd
From dust: spite then with spite is best repaid."
        So saying, through each Thicket Dank or Dry,
180 Like a black mist low creeping, he held on
His midnight search, where soonest he might find
The Serpent: him fast sleeping soon he found
In Labyrinth° of many a round self-roll'd,
His head the midst, well stor'd with subtle wiles:
185 Not yet in horrid Shade or dismal Den,

166 **incarnate** the Satanic counterpart of the Incarnation.   170 **obnoxious**
exposed.   183 **Labyrinth** with a suggestion of the dangerous monster
(the Minotaur).

Nor° nocent° yet, but on the grassy Herb
Fearless unfear'd he slept: in at his Mouth
The Devil enter'd, and his brutal sense,
In heart or head, possessing soon inspir'd
With act intelligential; but his sleep   *190*
Disturb'd not, waiting close th'approach of Morn.
Now when as sacred Light began to dawn
In Eden on the humid Flow'rs, that breath'd
Their morning Incense, when all things that breathe,
From th'Earth's great Altar send up silent praise   *195*
To the Creator, and his Nostrils fill
With grateful° Smell, forth came the human pair
And join'd their vocal Worship to the Choir
Of Creatures wanting voice, that done, partake
The season, prime for sweetest Scents and Airs: *200*
Then cómmune how that day they best may ply
Their growing work: for much their work outgrew
The hands' dispatch of two Gard'ning so wide.
And Eve first to her Husband thus began.
        "Adam, well may we labour still to dress   *205*
This Garden, still to tend Plant, Herb and Flow'r,
Our pleasant task enjoin'd, but till more hands
Aid us, the work under our labour grows,
Luxurious by restraint; what we by day
Lop overgrown, or prune, or prop, or bind,   *210*
One night or two with wanton growth derides
Tending to wild. Thou therefore now advise
Or hear what to my mind first thoughts present,
Let us divide our labours, thou where choice
Leads thee, or where most needs, whether to wind   *215*
The Woodbine round this Arbour, or direct
The clasping Ivy where to climb, while I
In yonder Spring of Roses intermixt
With Myrtle, find what to redress till Noon:
For while so near each other thus all day   *220*
Our task we choose, what wonder if so near
Looks intervene and smiles, or object new
Casual discourse draw on, which intermits
Our day's work brought to little, though begun

186 **Nor** *1674*; Not *1667*. 186 **nocent** harmful (the opposite of "innocent"). 197 **grateful** pleasing, and expressing gratitude.

225   Early, and th'hour of Supper comes unearn'd."
              To whom mild answer Adam thus return'd.
      "Sole Eve, Associate sole, to me beyond
      Compare above all living Creatures dear,
      Well hast thou motion'd, well thy thoughts employ'd
230   How we might best fulfill the work which here
      God hath assign'd us, nor of me shalt pass
      Unprais'd: for nothing lovelier can be found
      In woman, than to study household good,
      And good works in her Husband to promote.
235   Yet not so strictly hath our Lord impos'd
      Labour, as to debar us when we need
      Refreshment, whether food, or talk between,
      Food of the mind, or this sweet intercourse
      Of looks and smiles, for smiles from Reason flow,
240   To brute deni'd, and are of Love the food,
      Love not the lowest end of human life.
      For not to irksome toil, but to delight
      He made us, and delight to Reason join'd.
      These paths and Bow'rs doubt not but our joint hands
245   Will keep from Wilderness with ease, as wide
      As we need walk, till younger hands erelong
      Assist us: But if much convérse perhaps
      Thee satiate, to short absence I could yield.
      For solitude sometimes is best society,
250   And short retirement urges sweet return.
      But other doubt possesses me, lest harm
      Befall thee sever'd from me; for thou know'st
      What hath been warn'd us, what malicious Foe
      Envying our happiness, and of his own
255   Despairing, seeks to work us woe and shame
      By sly assault; and somewhere nigh at hand
      Watches, no doubt, with greedy hope to find
      His wish and best advantage, us asunder,
      Hopeless to circumvent us join'd, where each
260   To other speedy aid might lend at need;
      Whether his first design be to withdraw
      Our fealty from God, or to disturb
      Conjugal Love, than which perhaps no bliss
      Enjoy'd by us excites his envy more;
265   Or this, or worse, leave not the faithful side
      That gave thee being, still shades thee and protects.

The Wife, where danger or dishonour lurks,
Safest and seemliest by her Husband stays,
Who guards her, or with her the worst endures."
    To whom the Virgin Majesty of Eve,   *270*
As one who loves, and some unkindness meets,
With sweet austere composure thus repli'd.
    "Offspring of Heav'n and Earth, and all
       Earth's Lord,
That such an Enemy we have, who seeks
Our ruin, both by thee inform'd I learn,   *275*
And from the parting Angel overheard
As in a shady nook I stood behind,
Just then return'd at shut of Evening Flow'rs.
But that thou shouldst my firmness therefore doubt
To God or thee, because we have a foe   *280*
May tempt it, I expected not to hear.
His violence thou fear'st not, being such,
As wee, not capable of death or pain,
Can either not receive, or can repel.
His fraud is then thy fear, which plain infers   *285*
Thy equal fear that my firm Faith and Love
Can by his fraud be shak'n or seduc't;
Thoughts, which how found they harbour in thy
    breast,
Adam, misthought of her to thee so dear?"
    To whom with healing words Adam repli'd.   *290*
"Daughter of God and Man, immortal Eve,
For such thou art, from sin and blame entire:
Not diffident° of thee do I dissuade
Thy absence from my sight, but to avoid
Th'attempt itself, intended by our Foe.   *295*
For hee who tempts, though in vain, at least asperses
The tempted with dishonour foul, suppos'd
Not incorruptible of Faith, not proof
Against temptation: thou thyself with scorn
And anger wouldst resent the offer'd wrong,   *300*
Though ineffectual found: misdeem not then,
If such affront I labour to avert
From thee alone, which on us both at once
The Enemy, though bold, will hardly dare,

293 **diffident** distrustful.

305 Or daring, first on mee th'assault shall 'light.
Nor thou his malice and false guile contemn;
Subtle he needs must be, who could seduce
Angels, nor think superfluous others' aid.
I from the influence of thy looks receive
310 Access° in every Virtue, in thy sight
More wise, more watchful, stronger, if need were
Of outward strength; while shame, thou looking on,
Shame to be overcome or over-reacht
Would utmost vigour raise, and rais'd unite.
315 Why shouldst not thou like sense within thee feel
When I am present, and thy trial choose
With me, best witness of thy Virtue tri'd."
        So spake domestic Adam in his care
And Matrimonial Love, but Eve, who thought
320 Less áttribúted to her Faith sincere,
Thus her reply with accent sweet renew'd.
        "If this be our condition, thus to dwell
In narrow circuit strait'n'd by a Foe,
Subtle or violent, we not endu'd
325 Single with like defence, wherever met,
How are we happy, still° in fear of harm?
But harm precedes not sin: only our Foe
Tempting affronts us with his foul esteem
Of our integrity: his foul esteem
330 Sticks no dishonour on our Front, but turns
Foul on himself; then wherefore shunn'd or fear'd
By us? who rather double honour gain
From his surmise prov'd false, find peace within,
Favour from Heav'n, our witness from th'event.°
335 And what is Faith, Love, Virtue unassay'd
Alone, without exterior help sustain'd?
Let us not then suspect our happy State
Left so imperfect by the Maker wise,
As not secure to single or combin'd.
340 Frail is our happiness, if this be so,
And Eden were no Eden thus expos'd."
        To whom thus Adam fervently repli'd.
"O Woman, best are all things as the will
Of God ordain'd them, his creating hand

310 **Access** accession.   326 **still** always.   334 **event** outcome.

Nothing imperfect or deficient left   345
Of all that he Created, much less Man,
Or aught that might his happy State secure,
Secure from outward force; within himself
The danger lies, yet lies within his power:
Against his will he can receive no harm.   350
But God left free the Will, for what obeys
Reason, is free, and Reason he made right,
But bid her well beware, and still erect,°
Lest by some fair appearing good surpris'd
She dictate false, and misinform the Will   355
To do what God expressly hath forbid.
Not then mistrust, but tender love enjoins,
That I should mind° thee oft, and mind thou me.
Firm we subsist, yet possible to swerve,
Since Reason not impossibly may meet   360
Some specious object by the Foe suborn'd,
And fall into deception unaware,
Not keeping strictest watch, as she was warn'd.
Seek not temptation then; which to avoid
Were better, and most likely if from mee   365
Thu sever not: Trial will come unsought.
Wouldst thou approve thy constancy, approve
First thy obedience; th'other who can know,
Not seeing thee attempted, who attest?
But if thou think, trial unsought may find   370
Us both securer° than thus warn'd thou seem'st
Go; for thy stay, not free, absents thee more;
Go in thy native innocence, rely
On what thou hast of virtue, summon all,
For God towards thee hath done his part, do thine."   375
     So spake the Patriarch of Mankind, but Eve
Persisted, yet submiss, though last, repli'd.
     "With thy permission then, and thus fore-
          warn'd
Chiefly by what thy own last reasoning words
Touch'd only, that our trial, when least sought,   380
May find us both perhaps far less prepar'd,
The willinger I go, nor much expect

353 **still erect** always alert (and with "Godlike erect" contrasted with the
Fall).   358 **mind** remind.   371 **securer** too confident.

A Foe so proud will first the weaker seek;
So bent, the more shall shame him his repulse."

385　Thus saying, from her Husband's hand her hand
Soft she withdrew, and like a Wood-Nymph light
Oread or Dryad,° or of Delia's° Train,
Betook her to the Groves, but Delia's self
In gait surpass'd and Goddess-like deport,

390　Though not as shee with Bow and Quiver arm'd,
But with such Gard'ning Tools as Art yet rude,
Guiltless of° fire had form'd, or Angels brought.
To Pales,° or Pomona,° thus adorn'd,
Likest she seem'd, Pomona when she fled

395　Vertumnus,° or to Ceres° in her Prime,
Yet Virgin of Proserpina from Jove.
Her long with ardent look his Eye pursu'd
Delighted, but desiring more her stay.
Oft he to her his charge of quick return

400　Repeated, shee to him as oft engag'd
To be return'd by Noon amid the Bow'r,
And all things in best order to invite
Noontide repast, or Afternoon's repose.
O much deceiv'd, much failing, hapless Eve,

405　Of thy presum'd return! event perverse!
Thou never from that hour in Paradise
Found'st either sweet repast, or sound repose;
Such ambush hid among sweet Flow'rs and Shades
Waited with hellish rancour imminent

410　To intercept thy way, or send thee back
Despoil'd of Innocence, of Faith, of Bliss.
For now, and since first break of dawn the Fiend,
Mere Serpent in appearance, forth was come,
And on his Quest, where likeliest he might find

415　The only two of Mankind, but in them
The whole included Race, his purpos'd prey.
In Bow'r and Field he sought, where any tuft
Of Grove or Garden-Plot more pleasant lay,

---

387 **Oread or Dryad** wood- or moontain-nymph.　387 **Delia** Diana, goddess of hunting.　392 **Guiltless of** without experience of (but fire is associated with guilt in the story of Prometheus—see IV 715–19—and "Guiltless"
is prophetic here).　393 **Pales** goddess of pastures.　393 **Pomona** goddess
of fruit.　395 **Vertumnus** god of the seasons and of gardens.　395 **Ceres**
goddess of agriculture; see IV 268–72.

Their tendance or Plantation for delight,
By Fountain or by shady Rivulet   420
He sought them both, but wish'd his hap might find
Eve separate, he wish'd, but not with hope
Of what so seldom chanc'd, when to his wish,
Beyond his hope, Eve separate he spies,
Veil'd in a Cloud of Fragrance, where she stood,   425
Half spi'd, so thick the Roses bushing round
About her glow'd, oft stooping to support
Each Flow'r of slender stalk, whose head though gay
Carnation, Purple, Azure, or speckt with Gold,
Hung drooping unsustain'd, them she upstays   430
Gently with Myrtle band, mindless the while,
Herself, though fairest unsupported Flow'r,
From her best prop so far, and storm so nigh.
Nearer he drew, and many a walk travers'd
Of stateliest Covert, Cedar, Pine, or Palm,   435
Then voluble° and bold, now hid, now seen
Among thick-wov'n Arborets° and Flow'rs
Imborder'd on each Bank, the hand of Eve:
Spot more delicious than those Gardens feign'd
Or of reviv'd Adonis,° or renown'd   440
Alcinous, host of old Laertes' Son,°
Or that, not Mystic,° where the Sapient King°
Held dalliance with his fair Egyptian Spouse.°
Much hee the Place admir'd, the Person more.
As one who long in populous City pent,   445
Where Houses thick and Sewers annoy° the Air,
Forth issuing on a Summer's Morn to breathe
Among the pleasant Villages and Farms
Adjoin'd, from each thing met conceives delight,
The smell of Grain, or tedded° Grass, or Kine,   450
Or Dairy, each rural sight, each rural sound;
If chance with Nymphlike step fair Virgin pass,
What pleasing seem'd, for her now pleases more,
She most, and in her look sums all Delight.

436 **voluble** rolling; the suggestion of fluent speech darkly anticipates Satan's
skill—contrast the pronunciation (and Milton's spelling "volubil") in IV
594.   437 **Arborets** shrubs.   440 **Adonis** in the myth, restored to life for
half of each year.   441 **Laertes' Son** Odysseus.   442 **Mystic** allegorical; possibly also mythical.   442 **Sapient King** Solomon.   443 **Egyptian Spouse**
Pharaoh's daughter.   446 **annoy** make noisome.   450 **tedded** spread out
to dry.

455 Such Pleasure took the Serpent to behold
     This Flow'ry Plat, the sweet recess of Eve
     Thus early, thus alone; her Heav'nly form
     Angelic, but more soft, and Feminine,
     Her graceful Innocence, her every Air
460 Of gesture or least action overaw'd
     His Malice, and with rapine sweet bereav'd
     His fierceness of the fierce intent it brought:
     That space the Evil one abstracted stood
     From his own evil, and for the time remain'd
465 Stupidly° good, of enmity disarm'd,
     Of guile, of hate, of envy, of revenge;
     But the hot Hell that always in him burns,
     Though in mid Heav'n, soon ended his delight,
     And tortures him now more, the more he sees
470 Of pleasure not for him ordain'd: then soon
     Fierce hate he recollects,° and all his thoughts
     Of mischief, gratulating, thus excites.
          "Thoughts, whither have ye led me, with what
               sweet
     Compulsion thus transported to forget
475 What hither brought us, hate, not love, nor hope
     Of Paradise for Hell, hope here to taste
     Of pleasure, but all pleasure to destroy,
     Save what is in destroying, other joy
     To me is lost. Then let me not let pass
480 Occasion which now smiles, behold alone
     The Woman, opportune to all attempts,
     Her Husband, for I view far round, not nigh,
     Whose higher intellectual more I shun,
     And strength, of courage haughty, and of limb
485 Heroic built, though of terrestrial mould,
     Foe not informidable, exempt from wound,
     I not; so much hath Hell debas'd, and pain
     Enfeebl'd me, to what I was in Heav'n.
     Shee fair, divinely fair, fit Love for Gods,
490 Not terrible, though terror be in Love
     And beauty, not approacht by stronger hate,
     Hate stronger, under show of Love well-feign'd,

465 **Stupidly** in a stupor.   471 **recollects** remembers and recollects.

The way which to her ruin now I tend."
      So spake the Enemy of Mankind, enclos'd
In Serpent, Inmate bad, and towards Eve   495
Address'd his way, not with indented wave,
Prone on the ground, as since, but on his rear,
Circular base of rising folds, that tow'r'd
Fold above fold a surging Maze, his Head
Crested aloft, and Carbuncle° his Eyes;   500
With burnisht Neck of verdant Gold, erect
Amidst his circling Spires,° that on the grass
Floated redundant:° pleasing was his shape,
And lovely, never since of Serpent kind
Lovelier, not those that in Illyria chang'd   505
Hermione and Cadmus, or the God
In Epidaurus; nor to which transform'd
Ammonian Jove, or Capitoline was seen,
Hee with Olympias, this with her who bore
Scipio the heighth of Rome.° With tract oblique   510
At first, as one who sought accéss, but fear'd
To interrupt, side-long he works his way.
As when a Ship by skilful Steersman wrought
Nigh River's mouth or Foreland, where the Wind
Veers oft, as oft so steers, and shifts her Sail;   515
So varied hee, and of his tortuous Train
Curl'd many a wanton wreath in sight of Eve,
To lure her Eye; shee busied heard the sound
Of rustling Leaves, but minded not, as us'd
To such disport before her through the Field,   520
From every Beast, more duteous at her call,
Then at Circean° call the Herd disguis'd.
Hee bolder now, uncall'd before her stood;
But as in gaze admiring: Oft he bow'd
His turret Crest, and sleek enamell'd Neck,   525
Fawning, and lick'd the ground whereon she trod.
His gentle dumb expression turn'd at length
The Eye of Eve to mark his play; he glad

---

500 **Carbuncle** a fiery jewel. 502 **Spires** spirals. 503 **redundant** wave-like. 505–10 Cadmus and Harmonia were changed to serpents; Aescu-lapius, god of medicine, came from his temple at Epidaurus in the form of a serpent; the same form was taken by Jupiter Ammon, who was the father of Alexander the Great (the mother being Olympias), and by Jupi-ter Capitoline, father of Scipio who defeated Hannibal. 522 **Circean** Circe, the sorceress in the *Odyssey* who turned men to beasts.

Of her attention gain'd, with Serpent Tongue
530 Organic,° or impulse of vocal Air,
His fraudulent temptation thus began.
          "Wonder not, sovran Mistress, if perhaps
Thou canst, who art sole Wonder, much less arm
Thy looks, the Heav'n of mildness, with disdain,
535 Displeas'd that I approach thee thus, and gaze
Insatiate, I thus single, nor have fear'd
Thy awful brow, more awful thus retir'd.
Fairest resemblance of thy Maker fair,
Thee all things living gaze on, all things thine
540 By gift, and thy Celestial Beauty adore
With ravishment beheld, there best beheld
Where universally admir'd; but here
In this enclosure wild, these Beasts among,
Beholders rude, and shallow to discern
545 Half what in three is fair, one man except,
Who sees thee? (and what is one?) who shouldst be
      seen
A Goddess among Gods, ador'd and serv'd
By Angels numberless, thy daily Train."
          So gloz'd° the Tempter, and his Proem° tun'd;
550 Into the Heart of Eve his words made way,
Though at the voice much marvelling; at length
Not unamaz'd she thus in answer spake.
"What may this mean? Language of Man pronounc't
By Tongue of Brute, and human sense exprest?
555 The first at least of these I thought deni'd
To Beasts, whom God on their Creation-Day
Created mute to all articulate sound;
The latter I demur,° for in their looks
Much reason, and in their actions oft appears.
560 Thee, Serpent, subtlest beast of all the field
I knew, but not with human voice endu'd;
Redouble then this miracle, and say,
How cam'st thou speakable of mute, and how
To me so friendly grown above the rest
565 Of brutal kind, that daily are in sight?

530 **Organic** as its organ. 549 **gloz'd** flattered. 549 **Proem** pre-
lude. 558 **demur** hesitate about.

Say, for such wonder claims attention due."
     To whom the guileful Tempter thus repli'd.
"Empress of this fair World, resplendent Eve,
Easy to mee it is to tell thee all
What thou command'st, and right thou shouldst be
   obey'd: 570
I was at first as other Beasts that graze
The trodden Herb, of abject thoughts and low,
As was my food, nor aught but food discern'd
Or Sex, and apprehended nothing high:
Till on a day roving the field, I chanc'd   575
A goodly Tree far distant to behold
Loaden with fruit of fairest colours mixt,
Ruddy and Gold: I nearer drew to gaze;
When from the boughs a savoury odour blown,
Grateful to appetite, more pleas'd my sense   580
Than smell of sweetest Fennel, or the Teats
Of Ewe or Goat dropping with Milk at Ev'n,
Unsuckt of Lamb or Kid, that tend their play.
To satisfy the sharp desire I had
Of tasting those fair Apples, I resolv'd   585
Not to defer; hunger and thirst at once,
Powerful persuaders, quick'n'd at the scent
Of that alluring fruit, urg'd me so keen.
About the Mossy Trunk I wound me soon,
For high from ground the branches would require   590
Thy utmost reach or Adam's: Round the Tree
All other Beasts that saw, with like desire
Longing and envying stood, but could not reach.
Amid the Tree now got, where plenty hung
Tempting so nigh, to pluck and eat my fill   595
I spar'd not, for such pleasure till that hour
At Feed or Fountain never had I found.
Sated at length, erelong I might perceive
Strange alteration in me, to degree
Of Reason in my inward Power, and Speech   600
Wanted° not long, though to this shape retain'd.
Thenceforth to Speculations high or deep
I turn'd my thoughts, and with capacious mind
Consider'd all things visible in Heav'n,

601 **Wanted** lacked.

605 Or Earth, or Middle,° all things fair and good;
But all that fair and good in thy Divine
Semblance, and in thy Beauty's heav'nly Ray
United I beheld; no Fair to thine
Equivalent or second, which compell'd
610 Mee thus, though importúne perhaps, to come
And gaze, and worship thee of right declar'd
Sovran of Creatures, universal Dame."°
　　　　So talk'd the spirited° sly Snake; and Eve
Yet more amaz'd unwary thus repli'd.
615 　　　　"Serpent, thy overpraising leaves in doubt
The virtue of that Fruit, in thee first prov'd:
But say, where grows the Tree, from hence how far?
For many are the Trees of God that grow
In Paradise, and various, yet unknown
620 To us, in such abundance lies our choice,
As leaves a greater store of Fruit untoucht,
Still hanging incorruptible, till men
Grow up to their provision,° and more hands
Help to disburden Nature of her Bearth."°
625 　　　　To whom the wily Adder, blithe and glad.
"Empress, the way is ready, and not long,
Beyond a row of Myrtles, on a Flat,
Fast by a Fountain, one small Thicket past
Of blowing° Myrrh and Balm; if thou accept
630 My conduct, I can bring thee thither soon:"
　　　　"Lead then," said Eve. Hee leading swiftly
　　roll'd
In tangles, and made intricate seem straight,
To mischief swift. Hope elevates, and joy
Bright'ns his Crest, as when a wand'ring Fire
635 Compáct° of unctuous vapour, which the Night
Condenses, and the cold environs round,
Kindl'd through agitation to a Flame,
Which oft, they say, some evil Spirit attends,
Hovering and blazing with delusive Light,
640 Misleads th'amaz'd Night-wanderer from his way
To Bogs and Mires, and oft through Pond or Pool,

---

605 **Middle** air.　612 **universal Dame** mistress of the universe.　613 **spir-ited** including "possessed by a spirit."　623 **their provision** what they provide.　624 **her Bearth** what she bears.　629 **blowing** blossoming.　635 **Compáct** compacted; like "unctuous" (oily), a scientific term for vapors.

There swallow'd up and lost, from succour far.
So glister'd the dire Snake, and into fraud
Led Eve our credulous° Mother, to the Tree
Of prohibition, root of all our woe;   645
Which when she saw, thus to her guide she spake.
          "Serpent, we might have spar'd our coming
                    hither,
Fruitless to me, though Fruit be here to excess,
The credit of whose virtue rest with thee,
Wondrous indeed, if cause of such effects.   650
But of this Tree we may not taste nor touch;
God so commanded, and left that Command
Sole Daughter of his voice; the rest, we live
Law to ourselves, our Reason is our Law."
          To whom the Tempter guilefully repli'd.   655
"Indeed? hath God then said that of the Fruit
Of all these Garden Trees ye shall not eat,
Yet Lords declar'd of all in Earth or Air?"
          To whom thus Eve yet sinless. "Of the Fruit
Of each Tree in the Garden we may eat,   660
But of the Fruit of this fair Tree amidst
The Garden, God hath said, Ye shall not eat
Thereof, nor shall ye touch it, lest ye die."
          She scarce had said, though brief, when now
                    more bold
The Tempter, but with show of Zeal and Love   665
To Man, and indignation at his wrong,
New part puts on, and as to passion mov'd,
Fluctuates° disturb'd, yet comely, and in act
Rais'd, as of some great matter to begin.
As when of old some Orator renown'd   670
In Athens or free Rome, where Eloquence
Flourish'd, since mute, to some great cause addrest,
Stood in himself collected, while each part,
Motion, each act won audience ere the tongue,
Sometimes in heighth began, as no delay   675
Of Preface brooking through his Zeal of Right.
So standing, moving, or to heighth upgrown

---

644 **credulous** overready to believe (sadly contrasted with the original
sense of the word, "faithful," as in "a credulous and plain heart is accepted with God," [1605]).   668 **Fluctuates** moves like a wave.

The Tempter all impassion'd thus began.
      "O Sacred, Wise, and Wisdom-giving Plant,
680 Mother of Science,° Now I feel thy Power
Within me clear, not only to discern
Things in their Causes, but to trace the ways
Of highest Agents, deem'd however wise.
Queen of this Universe, do not believe
685 Those rigid threats of Death; ye shall not Die:
How should ye? by the Fruit? it gives you Life
To Knowledge: By the Threat'ner? look on mee,
Mee who have touch'd and tasted, yet both live,
And life more perfect have attain'd than Fate
690 Meant mee, by vent'ring higher than my Lot.
Shall that be shut to Man, which to the Beast
Is open? or will God incense his ire
For such a petty Trespass, and not praise
Rather your dauntless virtue, whom the pain
695 Of Death denounc't,° whatever thing Death be,
Deterr'd not from achieving what might lead
To happier life, knowledge of Good and Evil;
Of good, how just? of evil, if what is evil
Be real, why not known, since easier shunn'd?
700 God therefore cannot hurt ye, and be just;
Not just, not God; not fear'd then, nor obey'd:
Your fear itself of Death removes the fear.
Why then was this forbid? Why but to awe,
Why but to keep ye low and ignorant,
705 His worshippers; he knows that in the day
Ye Eat thereof, your Eyes that seem so clear,
Yet are but dim, shall perfectly be then
Op'n'd and clear'd, and ye shall be as Gods,
Knowing both Good and Evil as they know.
710 That ye should be as Gods, since I as Man,
Internal Man, is but proportion meet,
I of brute human, yee of human Gods.
So ye shall die perhaps, by putting off
Human, to put on Gods, death to be wisht,
715 Though threat'n'd, which no worse than this can bring.
And what are Gods that Man may not become
As they, participating God-like food?

680 **Science** knowledge.   695 **denounc't** threatened.

The Gods are first, and that advantage use
On our belief, that all from them proceeds;
I question it, for this fair Earth I see,   720
Warm'd by the Sun, producing every kind,
Them nothing: If they all things, who enclos'd
Knowledge of Good and Evil in this Tree,
That whoso eats thereof, forthwith attains
Wisdom without their leave? and wherein lies   725
Th'offence, that Man should thus attain to know?
What can your knowledge hurt him, or this Tree
Impart against his will if all be his?
Or is it envy, and can envy dwell
In heav'nly breasts? these, these and many more   730
Causes import your need of this fair Fruit.
Goddess humane,° reach then, and freely taste."
          He ended, and his words replete with guile
Into her heart too easy entrance won:
Fixt on the Fruit she gaz'd, which to behold   735
Might tempt alone, and in her ears the sound
Yet rung of his persuasive words, impregn'd
With Reason, to her seeming, and with Truth;
Meanwhile the hour of Noon drew on, and wak'd
An eager appetite, rais'd by the smell   740
So savoury of that Fruit, which with desire,
Inclinable now grown to touch or taste,
Solicited her longing eye; yet first.
Pausing awhile, thus to herself she mus'd.
     "Great are thy Virtues, doubtless, best of
                         Fruits,   745
Though kept from Man, and worthy to be admir'd,
Whose taste, too long forborne, at first assay
Gave elocution to the mute, and taught
The Tongue not made for Speech to speak thy praise:
Thy praise hee also who forbids thy use,   750
Conceals not from us, naming thee the Tree
Of Knowledge, knowledge both of good and evil;
Forbids us then to taste, but his forbidding
Commends thee more, while it infers the good
By thee communicated, and our want: 755
For good unknown, sure is not had, or had

---

732 **humane** benevolent, with a hint of line 712.

And yet unknown, is as not had at all.
In plain then, what forbids he but to know,
Forbids us good, forbids us to be wise?
760 Such prohibitions bind not. But if Death
Bind us with after-bands, what profits then
Our inward freedom? In the day we eat
Of this fair Fruit, our doom is, we shall die.
How dies the Serpent? hee hath eat'n and lives,
765 And knows, and speaks, and reasons, and discerns,
Irrational till then. For us alone
Was death invented? or to us deni'd
This intellectual food, for beasts reserv'd?
For Beasts it seems: yet that one Beast which first
770 Hath tasted, envies not, but brings with joy
The good befall'n him, Author unsuspect,°
Friendly to man, far from deceit or guile.
What fear I then, rather what know to fear
Under this ignorance of Good and Evil,
775 Of God or Death, of Law or Penalty?
Here grows the Cure° of all, this Fruit Divine,
Fair to the Eye, inviting to the Taste,
Of virtue to make wise: what hinders then
To reach, and feed at once both Body and Mind?"
780   So saying, her rash hand in evil hour
Forth reaching to the Fruit, she pluck'd, she ate:
Earth felt the wound, and Nature from her seat
Sighing through all her Works gave signs of woe,
That all was lost. Back to the Thicket slunk
785 The guilty Serpent, and well might, for Eve
Intent now wholly on her taste, naught else
Regarded, such delight till then, as seem'd,
In Fruit she never tasted, whether true
Or fancied so, through expectation high
790 Of knowledge, nor was Godhead from her thought.
Greedily she ingorg'd without restraint,
And knew not eating Death: Satiate at length,
And height'n'd as with Wine, jocund and boon,
Thus to herself she pleasingly began.
795   "O Sovran, virtuous, precious of all Trees

---

771 **Author unsuspect** an authority not to be suspected.   776 **Cure** with
a grim hint of the earlier sense, "care, trouble," Latin *cura*.

In Paradise, of operation blest
To Sapience,° hitherto obscur'd, infam'd,°
And thy fair Fruit let hang, as to no end
Created; but henceforth my early care,
Not without Song, each Morning, and due praise   800
Shall tend thee, and the fertile burden ease
Of thy full branches offer'd free to all;
Till dieted by thee I grow mature
In knowledge, as the Gods who all things know;
Though others envy what they cannot give;   805
For had the gift been theirs, it had not here
Thus grown. Experience, next to thee I owe,
Best guide; not following thee, I had remain'd
In ignorance, thou op'n'st Wisdom's way,
And giv'st accéss, though secret she retire.   810
And I perhaps am secret; Heav'n is high,
High and remote to see from thence distinct
Each thing on Earth; and other care perhaps
May have diverted from continual watch
Our great Forbidder, safe with all his Spies   815
About him. But to Adam in what sort
Shall I appear? shall I to him make known
As yet my change, and give him to partake
Full happiness with mee, or rather not,
But keep the odds of Knowledge in my power   820
Without Copartner? so to add what wants°
In Female Sex, the more to draw his Love,
And render me more equal, and perhaps,
A thing not undesirable, sometime
Superior; for inferior who is free?   825
This may be well: but what if God have seen,
And Death ensue? then I shall be no more,
And Adam wedded to another Eve,
Shall live with her enjoying, I extinct;
A death to think. Confirm'd then I resolve,   830
Adam shall share with me in bliss or woe:
So dear I love him, that with him all deaths
I could endure, without him live no life."
          So saying, from the Tree her step she turn'd,

---

797 **Sapience** an important word in the poem, because it combines
"knowledge" and "tasting"; see lines 1017–20. 797 **infam'd** slandered.
821 **wants** is lacking.

835 But first low Reverence done, as to the power
    That dwelt within, whose presence had infus'd
    Into the plant scential° sap, deriv'd
    From Nectar, drink of Gods. Adam the while
    Waiting desirous her return, had wove
840 Of choicest Flow'rs a Garland to adorn
    Her Tresses, and her rural labours crown
    As Reapers oft are wont their Harvest Queen.
    Great joy he promis'd to his thoughts, and new
    Solace in her return, so long delayed;
845 Yet oft his heart, divine of° something ill,
    Misgave him; hee the falt'ring measure° felt;
    And forth to meet her went, the way she took
    That Morn when first they parted; by the Tree
    Of Knowledge he must pass, there he her met,
850 Scarce from the Tree returning; in her hand
    A bough of fairest fruit that downy smil'd,
    New-gather'd, and ambrosial smell diffus'd.
    To him she hasted, in her face excuse
    Came Prologue, and Apology to prompt,
855 Which with bland words at will she thus addrest.
         "Hast thou not wonder'd, Adam, at my stay?
    Thee I have misst, and thought it long, depriv'd
    Thy presence, agony of love till now
    Not felt, nor shall be twice, for never more
860 Mean I to try, what rash untri'd I sought,
    The pain of absence from thy sight. But strange
    Hath been the cause, and wonderful to hear:
    This Tree is not as we are told, a Tree
    Of danger tasted, nor to evil unknown
865 Op'ning the way, but of Divine effect
    To open Eyes, and make them Gods who taste;
    And hath been tasted such: the Serpent wise,
    Or not restrain'd as wee, or not obeying,
    Hath eat'n of the fruit, and is become,
870 Not dead, as we are threat'n'd, but thenceforth
    Endu'd with human voice and human sense,
    Reasoning to admiration, and with mee
    Persuasively hath so prevail'd, that I

837 **scential** granting knowledge.   845 **divine of** divining (but "divine" is a pregnant word in the context).   846 **falt'ring measure** his heartbeat (with the hint that Eve's "measure," temperance—as at VII 128—has faltered).

Have also tasted, and have also found
Th'effects to correspond, opener mine Eyes,   *875*
Dim erst,° dilated Spirits, ampler Heart,
And growing up to Godhead; which for thee
Chiefly I sought, without thee can despise.
For bliss, as thou hast part, to me is bliss,
Tedious, unshar'd with thee, and odious soon.   *880*
Thou therefore also taste, that equal Lot
May join us, equal Joy, as equal Love;
Lest thou not tasting, different degree
Disjoin us, and I then too late renounce
Deity for thee, when Fate will not permit."   *885*
          Thus Eve with Count'nance blithe her story
              told;
But in her Cheek distemper° flushing glow'd.
On th'other side, Adam, soon as he heard
The fatal Trespass done by Eve, amaz'd,
Astonied° stood and Blank, while honor chill   *890*
Ran through his veins, and all his joints relax'd;
From his slack hand the Garland wreath'd for Eve
Down dropp'd, and all the faded Roses shed:
Speechless he stood and pale, till thus at length
First to himself he inward silence broke.   *895*
          "O fairest of Creation, last and best
Of all God's Works, Creature in whom excell'd
Whatever can to sight or thought be form'd,
Holy, divine, good, amiable, or sweet!
How art thou lost, how on a sudden lost,   *900*
Defac't, deflow'r'd, and now to Death devote?°
Rather how hast thou yielded to transgress
The strict forbiddance, how to violate
The sacred Fruit forbidd'n! some cursed fraud
Of enemy hath beguil'd thee, yet unknown,   *905*
And mee with thee hath ruin'd, for with thee
Certain my resolution is to Die;
How can I live without thee, how forgo
Thy sweet Converse and Love so dearly join'd,
To live again in these wild Woods forlorn?   *910*
Should God create another Eve, and I

876 **erst** formerly.   887 **distemper** disorder, disease; also the 17th-century
sense, "intoxication"—see lines 793, 1008, 1050.   890 **Astonied** para-
lyzed.   901 **devote** doomed.

Another Rib afford, yet loss of thee
Would never from my heart; no no, I feel
The Link of Nature draw me: Flesh of Flesh,
915 Bone of my Bone thou art, and from thy State
Mine never shall be parted, bliss or woe."
   So having said, as one from sad dismay
Recomforted, and after thoughts disturb'd
Submitting to what seem'd remédiless,
920 Thus in calm mood his Words to Eve he turn'd.
    "Bold deed thou hast presum'd, advent'rous
      Eve,
And peril great provok't, who thus hath dar'd
Had it been only coveting to Eye
That sacred Fruit, sacred to abstinence,
925 Much more to taste it under ban to touch.
But past who can recall, or done undo?
Not God Omnipotent, nor Fate, yet so
Perhaps thou shalt not Die, perhaps the Fact°
Is not so heinous now, foretasted Fruit,
930 Profan'd first by the Serpent, by him first
Made common and unhallow'd ere our taste;
Nor yet on him found deadly, he yet lives,
Lives, as thou said'st, and gains to live as Man
Higher degree of Life, inducement strong
935 To us, as likely tasting to attain
Proportional ascent, which cannot be
But to be Gods, or Angels Demi-gods.
Nor can I think that God, Creator wise,
Though threat'ning, will in earnest so destroy
940 Us his prime Creatures' dignifi'd so high,
Set over all his Works, which in our Fall,
For us created, needs with us must fail,
Dependent made; so God shall uncreate,
Be frustrate, do, undo, and labour lose,
945 Not well conceiv'd of God, who though his Power
Creation could repeat, yet would be loath
Us to abolish, lest the Adversary
Triumph and say; 'Fickle their State whom God
Most Favours, who can please him long? Mee first
950 He ruin'd, now Mankind; whom will he next?'

928 **Fact** deed.

Matter of scorn, not to be given the Foe.
However I with thee have fixt my Lot,
Certain to undergo like doom, if Death
Consort with thee, Death is to mee as Life;
So forcible within my heart I feel   955
The Bond of Nature draw me to my own,
My own in thee, for what thou art is mine;
Our State cannot be sever'd, we are one,
One Flesh; to lose thee were to lose myself."
    So Adam, and thus Eve to him repli'd.   960
"O glorious trial of exceeding Love,
Illustrious evidence, example high!
Engaging me to emulate, but short
Of thy perfection, how shall I attain,
Adam, from whose dear side I boast me sprung,   965
And gladly of our Union hear thee speak,
One Heart, one Soul in both; whereof good proof
This day affords, declaring thee resolv'd,
Rather than Death or aught than Death more dread
Shall separate us, linkt in Love so dear,   970
To undergo with mee one Guilt, one Crime,
If any be, of tasting this fair Fruit,
Whose virtue, for of good still good proceeds,
Direct, or by occasion hath presented
This happy trial of thy Love, which else   975
So eminently never had been known.
Were it I thought Death menac't would ensue
This my attempt, I would sustain alone
The worst, and not persuade thee, rather die
Deserted, than oblige° thee with a fact°   980
Pernicious to thy Peace, chiefly assur'd
Remarkably so late of thy so true,
So faithful Love unequall'd; but I feel
Far otherwise th'event,° not Death, but Life
Augmented, op'n'd Eyes, new Hopes, new Joys,   985
Taste so Divine, that what of sweet before
Hath toucht my sense, flat seems to this, and harsh.
On my experience, Adam, freely taste,
And fear of Death deliver to the Winds."
    So saying, she embrac'd him, and for joy   990

980 **oblige** make liable to penalty.   980 **fact** deed.   984 **event** outcome.

Tenderly wept, much won that he his Love
Had so ennobl'd, as of choice to incur
Divine displeasure for her sake, or Death.
In recompense (for such compliance bad
995 Such recompense best merits) from the bough
She gave him of that fair enticing Fruit
With liberal hand: he scrupl'd not to eat
Against his better knowledge, not deceiv'd,
But fondly overcome with Female charm.
1000 Earth trembl'd from her entrails, as again
In pangs, and Nature gave a second groan,
Sky lour'd and muttering Thunder, some sad drops
Wept at completing of the mortal Sin
Original; while Adam took no thought,
1005 Eating his fill, nor Eve to iterate
Her former trespass fear'd, the more to soothe
Him with her lov'd society, that now
As with new Wine intoxicated both
They swim in mirth, and fancy that they feel
1010 Divinity within them breeding wings
Wherewith to scorn the Earth: but that false Fruit
Far other operation first display'd,
Carnal desire inflaming, hee on Eve
Began to cast lascivious Eyes, she him
1015 As wantonly repaid; in Lust they burn:
Till Adam thus 'gan Eve to dalliance move.
        "Eve, now I see thou art exact of taste,
And elegant, of Sapience no small part,
Since to each meaning° savour we apply,
1020 And Palate call judicious; I the praise
Yield thee, so well this day thou hast purvey'd.°
Much pleasure we have lost, while we abstain'd
From this delightful Fruit, nor known till now
True relish,° tasting; if such pleasure be
1025 In things to us forbidden, it might be wish'd,
For this one Tree had been forbidden ten.
But come, so well refresh't, now let us play,
As meet is, after such delicious Fare;

1019 **each meaning** "tasting" and "knowledge." 1021 **purvey'd** provided
foodstuffs.   1024 **relish** as with "Sapience," punning on the etymology,
here connected with "release" (no real relish till we released ourselves
from the forbidding).

For never did thy Beauty since the day
I saw thee first and wedded thee, adorn'd   *1030*
With all perfections, so inflame my sense
With ardor to enjoy thee, fairer now
Than ever, bounty of this virtuous Tree."
     So said he, and forbore not glance or toy°
Of amorous intent, well understood   *1035*
Of Eve, whose Eye darted contagious Fire.
Her hand he seiz'd, and to a shady bank,
Thick overhead with verdant roof embow'r'd
He led her nothing loath; Flow'rs were the Couch,
Pansies, and Violets, and Asphodel,   *1040*
And Hyacinth, Earth's freshest softest lap.
There they their fill of Love and Love's disport
Took largely, of their mutual guilt the Seal,°
The solace of their sin, till dewy sleep
Oppress'd them, wearied with their amorous play.   *1045*
Soon as the force of that fallacious Fruit,
That with exhilarating vapour bland
About their spirits had play'd, and inmost powers
Made err, was now exhal'd, and grosser sleep
Bred of unkindly° fumes, with conscious° dreams   *1050*
Encumber'd, now had left them, up they rose
As from unrest, and each the other viewing,
Soon found their Eyes how op'n'd, and their minds
How dark'n'd; innocence, that as a veil
Had shadow'd them from knowing ill, was gone,   *1055*
Just confidence, and native righteousness,
And honour from about them, naked left
To guilty shame; hee cover'd, but his Robe
Uncover'd more. So rose the Danite strong
Herculean Samson from the Harlot-lap   *1060*
Of Phílistéan Dálilah, and wak'd
Shorn of his strength, They destitute and bare
Of all their virtue: silent, and in face
Confounded long they sat, as struck'n mute,
Till Adam, though not less than Eve abasht,   *1065*
At length gave utterance to these words constrain'd.
     "O Eve, in evil hour thou didst give ear

1034 **toy** caress.   1043 **Seal** in contrast to true lovemaking, which seals
and consummates the marriage.   1050 **unkindly** unnatural.   1050 **conscious** having guilty knowledge.

To that false Worm, of whomsoever taught
To counterfeit Man's voice, true in our Fall,
1070 False in our promis'd Rising; since our Eyes
Op'n'd we find indeed, and find we know
Both Good and Evil, Good lost, and Evil got,
Bad Fruit of Knowledge, if this be to know,
Which leaves us naked thus, of Honour void,
1075 Of Innocence, of Faith, of Purity,
Our wonted Ornaments now soil'd and stain'd,
And in our Faces evident the signs
Of foul concupiscence; whence evil store;
Even shame, the last of evils; of the first
1080 Be sure then. How shall I behold the face
Henceforth of God or Angel, erst with joy
And rapture so oft beheld? those heav'nly shapes
Will dazzle now this earthly, with their blaze
Insufferably bright. O might I here
1085 In solitude live savage, in some glade
Obscur'd, where highest Woods impenetrable
To Star or Sun-light, spread their umbrage broad,
And brown as Evening: Cover me ye Pines,
Ye Cedars, with innumerable boughs
1090 Hide me, where I may never see them more.
But let us now, as in bad plight,° devise
What best may for the present serve to hide
The Parts of each from other, that seem most
To shame obnoxious, and unseemliest seen,
Some Tree whose broad smooth Leaves together
1095   sew'd,
And girded on our loins, may cover round
Those middle parts, that this newcomer, Shame,
There sit not, and reproach us as unclean."
So counsell'd hee, and both together went
1100 Into the thickest Wood, there soon they chose
The Figtree, not that kind for Fruit renown'd,
But such as at this day to Indians known
In Malabar or Decan spreads her Arms
Branching so broad and long, that in the ground
1105 The bended Twigs take root, and Daughters grow

1091 **plight** with a grimly punning suggestion of the meaning "pleat"
(drapery), the same word as "plight."

About the Mother Tree, a Pillar'd shade
High overarch't, and echoing Walks between;
There oft the Indian Herdsman shunning heat
Shelters in cool, and tends his pasturing Herds
At Loopholes cut through thickest shade: Those
   Leaves   *1110*
They gather'd, broad as Amazonian Targe,°
And with what skill they had, together sew'd,
To gird their waist, vain Covering if to hide
Their guilt and dreaded shame; O how unlike
To that first naked Glory. Such of late   *1115*
Columbus found th'American so girt
With feather'd Cincture, naked else and wild
Among the Trees on Isles and woody Shores.
Thus fenc't, and as they thought, their shame in part
Cover'd, but not at rest or ease of Mind,   *1120*
They sat them down to weep, nor only Tears
Rain'd at their Eyes, but high Winds worse within
Began to rise, high Passions, Anger, Hate,
Mistrust, Suspicion, Discord, and shook sore
Their inward State of Mind, calm Region once   *1125*
And full of Peace, now tost and turbulent:
For Understanding rul'd not, and the Will
Heard not her lore, both in subjection now
To sensual Appetite, who from beneath
Usurping over sovran Reason claim'd   *1130*
Superior sway: From thus distemper'd breast,
Adam, estrang'd in look and alter'd style,
Speech intermitted thus to Eve renew'd.

      "Would thou hadst heark'n'd to my words,
          and stay'd
With me, as I besought thee, when that strange   *1135*
Desire of wand'ring this unhappy Morn,
I know not whence possess'd thee; we had then
Remain'd still happy, not as now, despoil'd
Of all our good, sham'd, naked, miserable.
Let none henceforth seek needless cause to approve *1140*
The Faith they owe;° when earnestly they seek

1111 **Targe** shield.   1141 **owe** own.

Such proof, conclude, they then begin to fail."
　　　　　To whom soon mov'd with touch of blame
　　　　　　thus Eve.
"What words have past thy Lips, Adam severe,
1145 Imput'st thou that to my default, or will
Of wandering, as thou call'st it, which who knows
But might as ill have happ'n'd thou being by,
Or to thyself perhaps: hadst thou been there,
Or here th'attempt, thou couldst not have discern'd
1150 Fraud in the Serpent, speaking as he spake;
No ground of enmity between us known,
Why hee should mean me ill, or seek to harm.
Was I to have never parted from thy side?
As good have grown there still a lifeless Rib.
1155 Being as I am, why didst not thou the Head
Command me absolutely not to go,
Going into such danger as thou said'st?
Too facile then thou didst not much gainsay,
Nay, didst permit, approve, and fair dismiss.
1160 Hadst thou been firm and fixt in thy dissent,
Neither had I transgress'd, nor thou with mee."
　　　　　To whom then first incenst Adam repli'd.
"Is this the Love, is this the recompense
Of mine to thee, ingrateful Eve, exprest
1165 Immutable° when thou wert lost, not I,
Who might have liv'd and joy'd immortal bliss,
Yet willingly chose rather Death with thee:
And am I now upbraided, as the cause
Of thy transgressing? not enough severe,
1170 It seems, in thy restraint: what could I more?
I warn'd thee, I admonish'd thee, foretold
The danger, and the lurking Enemy
That lay in wait; beyond this had been force,
And force upon free Will hath here no place.
1175 But confidence then bore thee on, secure
Either to meet no danger, or to find
Matter of glorious trial; and perhaps
I also err'd in overmuch admiring
What seem'd in thee so perfect, that I thought
1180 No evil durst attempt thee, but I rue

1164–5 **exprest Immutable** which was manifested as unchangeable.

That error now, which is become my crime,
And thou th'accuser. Thus it shall befall
Him who to worth in Women overtrusting
Lets her Will rule; restraint she will not brook,
And left to herself, if evil thence ensue,   *1185*
Shee first his weak indulgence will accuse."
    Thus they in mutual accusation spent
The fruitless hours, but neither self-condemning,
And of their vain contést appear'd no end.

BOOK X

THE ARGUMENT

Man's transgression known, the Guardian Angels forsake Paradise, and return up to Heaven to approve their vigilance, and are approv'd, God declaring that The entrance of Satan could not be by them prevented. He sends his Son to judge the Transgressors, who descends and gives Sentence accordingly; then in pity clothes them both, and reascends. Sin and Death sitting till then at the Gates of Hell, by wondrous sympathy feeling the success of Satan in this new World, and the sin by Man there committed, resolve to sit no longer confin'd in Hell, but to follow Satan their Sire up to the place of Man: To make the way easier from Hell to this World to and fro, they pave a broad Highway or Bridge over Chaos, according to the Track that Satan first made; then preparing for Earth, they meet him proud of his success returning to Hell; their mutual gratulation. Satan arrives at Pandemonium, in full assembly relates with boasting his success against Man; instead of applause is entertained with a general hiss by all his audience, transform'd with himself also suddenly into Serpents, according to his doom giv'n in Paradise; then deluded with a show of the forbidden Tree springing up before them, they greedily reaching to take of the Fruit, chew dust and bitter ashes. The proceedings of Sin and Death; God foretells the final Victory of his Son over them, and the renewing of all things; but for the present commands his Angels to make several alterations in the Heavens and Elements. Adam more and more perceiving his fall'n condition heavily bewails, rejects the condolement of Eve; she persists and at length appeases him: then to evade the Curse likely to fall on their Offspring, proposes to Adam violent ways, which he approves not, but conceiving better hope, puts her in mind of the late Promise made them, that her Seed should be reveng'd on

the Serpent, and exhorts her with him to seek Peace of
the offended Deity, by repentance and supplication.

Meanwhile the heinous and despiteful act
Of Satan done in Paradise, and how
Hee in the Serpent had perverted° Eve,
Her Husband shee, to taste the fatal fruit,
Was known in Heav'n; for what can 'scape the Eye   5
Of God All-seeing or deceive his Heart
Omniscient, who in all things wise and just,
Hinder'd not Satan to attempt the mind
Of Man, with strength entire, and free Will arm'd,
Complete to have discover'd and repulst   10
Whatever wiles of Foe or seeming Friend.
For still° they knew, and ought to have still
    remember'd
The high Injunction not to taste that Fruit,
Whoever tempted; which they not obeying,
Incurr'd, what could they less, the penalty,   15
And manifold in sin, deserv'd to fall.
Up into Heav'n from Paradise in haste
Th'Angelic Guards ascended, mute and sad
For Man, for of his state by this they knew,
Much wond'ring how the subtle Fiend had stol'n   20
Entrance unseen. Soon as th'unwelcome news
From Earth arriv'd at Heaven Gate, displeas'd
All were who heard, dim sadness did not spare
That time Celestial visages, yet mixt
With pity, violated not their bliss.   25
About the new-arriv'd, in multitudes
Th'ethereal People ran, to hear and know
How all befell: they towards the Throne Supreme
Accountable made haste to make appear
With righteous plea, their utmost vigilance,   30
And easily approv'd; when the most High
Eternal Father from his secret Cloud,
Amidst in Thunder utter'd thus his voice.

3 **perverted** including the specific application to turning from a religious
belief.   12 **still** always.

"Assembl'd Angels, and ye Powers return'd
35 From unsuccessful charge, be not dismay'd,
Nor troubl'd at these tidings from the Earth,
Which your sincerest care could not prevent,
Foretold so lately what would come to pass,
When first this Tempter cross'd the Gulf from Hell.
40 I told ye then he should prevail and speed
On his bad Errand, Man should be seduc't
And flatter'd out of all, believing lies
Against his Maker; no Decree of mine
Concurring to necessitate his Fall,
45 Or touch with lightest moment of impulse
His free Will, to her own inclining left
In ev'n scale. But fall'n he is, and now
What rests,° but that the mortal Sentence pass
On his transgression, Death denounc't° that day,
50 Which he presumes already vain and void,
Because not yet inflicted, as he fear'd,
By some immediate stroke; but soon shall find
Forbearance no acquittance ere day end.
Justice shall not return as bounty scorn'd.
55 But whom send I to judge them? whom but thee
Vicegerent Son, to thee I have transferr'd
All Judgement, whether in Heav'n, or Earth, or Hell.
Easy it might be seen that I intend
Mercy colléague with Justice, sending thee
60 Man's Friend, his Mediator, his design'd
Both Ransom and Redeemer voluntary,
And destin'd Man himself to judge Man fall'n."
So spake the Father, and unfolding bright
Towards the right hand his Glory, on the Son
65 Blaz'd forth unclouded Deity; he full
Resplendent all his Father manifest
Express'd, and thus divinely answer'd mild.
"Father Eternal, thine is to decree,
Mine both in Heav'n and Earth to do thy will
70 Supreme, that thou in mee thy Son belov'd
Mayst ever rest well pleas'd. I go to judge
On Earth these thy transgressors, but thou know'st,
Whoever judg'd, the worst on mee must 'light,

---

48 **rests** remains.   49 **denounc't** formally threatened.

When time shall be, for so I undertook
Before thee; and not repenting, this obtain   75
Of right, that I may mitigate their doom
On me deriv'd,° yet I shall temper so
Justice with Mercy, as may illústrate° most
Them° fully satisfied, and thee appease.
Attendance none shall need, nor Train, where none   80
Are to behold the Judgement, but the judg'd,
Those two; the third best absent is condemn'd,
Convict by flight, and Rebel to all Law
Conviction° to the Serpent none belongs."

       Thus saying, from his radiant Seat he rose   85
Of high collateral glory: him Thrones and Powers,
Princedoms, and Dominations ministrant
Accompanied to Heaven Gate, from whence
Eden and all the Coast in prospect lay.
Down he descended straight; the speed of Gods   90
Time counts not, though with swiftest minutes wing'd.
Now was the Sun in Western cadence° low
From Noon, and gentle Airs due at their hour
To fan the Earth now wak'd, and usher in
The Ev'ning cool when he from wrath more cool   95
Came the mild Judge and Intercessor both
To sentence Man: the voice of God they heard
Now walking in the Garden, by soft winds
Brought to their Ears, while day declin'd, they heard,
And from his presence hid themselves among   100
The thickest Trees, both Man and Wife, till God
Approaching, thus to Adam call'd aloud.

      "Where art thou Adam, wont with joy to meet
My coming seen far off? I miss thee here,
Not pleas'd, thus entertain'd with solitude,   105
Where obvious° duty erewhile appear'd unsought:
Or come I less conspicuous, or what change
Absents thee, or what chance detains? Come forth."
He came, and with him Eve, more loath, though first
To offend, discount'nanc't both, and discompos'd;   110
Love was not in their looks, either to God

---

77 **deriv'd** brought down, diverted.   78 **illústrate** set in the best light.
79 **Them** justice and mercy.   84 **Conviction** proof of guilt.   92 **cadence**
falling (and with the musical hint taken up in "Airs due at their hour"
and "usher in").   106 **obvious** coming forward to meet.

Or to each other, but apparent° guilt,
And shame, and perturbation, and despair,
Anger, and obstinacy, and hate, and guile.
115 When Adam falt'ring long, thus answer'd brief.
      "I heard thee in the Garden, and of thy voice
Afraid, being naked, hid myself." To whom
The gracious Judge without revile repli'd.
      "My voice thou oft hast heard, and hast not fear'd,
120 But still rejoic't, how is it now become
So dreadful to thee? that thou art naked, who
Hath told thee? hast thou eaten of the Tree
Whereof I gave thee charge thou shouldst not eat?"
      To whom thus Adam sore beset repli'd.
125 "O Heav'n! in evil strait this day I stand
Before my Judge, either to undergo
Myself the total Crime, or to accuse
My other self, the partner of my life;
Whose failing, while her Faith to me remains,
130 I should conceal, and not expose to blame
By my complaint; but strict necessity
Subdues me, and calamitous constraint,
Lest on my head both sin and punishment,
However insupportable, be all
135 Devolv'd; though should I hold my peace, yet thou
Wouldst easily detect what I conceal.
This Woman whom thou mad'st to be my help,
And gav'st me as thy perfect gift, so good,
So fit, so accéptáble, so Divine,
140 That from her hand I could suspect no ill,
And what she did, whatever in itself,
Her doing seem'd to justify the deed;
Shee gave me of the Tree, and I did eat."
      To whom the sovran Presence thus repli'd.
145 "Was shee thy God, that her thou didst obey
Before his voice, or was shee made thy guide,
Superior, or but equal, that to her
Thou didst resign thy Manhood, and the Place
Wherein God set thee above her made of thee,
150 And for thee, whose perfection far excell'd

112 **apparent** manifest.

Hers in all real dignity: Adorn'd
She was indeed, and lovely to attract
Thy Love, not thy Subjection, and her Gifts
Were such as under Government well seem'd,
Unseemly to bear rule, which was thy part   155
And person, hadst thou known thyself aright."
   So having said, he thus to Eve in few:
"Say Woman, what is this which thou hast done?"
     To whom sad Eve with shame nigh over-
     whelm'd
Confessing soon, yet not before her Judge   160
Bold or loquacious, thus abasht repli'd.
   "The Serpent me beguil'd and I did eat."
    Which when the Lord God heard, without
    delay
To Judgement he proceeded on th'accused
Serpent though brute, unable° to transfer   165
The Guilt on him who made him instrument
Of mischief, and polluted from the end
Of his Creation; justly then accurst,
As vitiated in Nature: more to know
Concern'd not Man (since he no further knew)   170
Nor alter'd his offence; yet God at last
To Satan first in sin his doom appli'd,
Though in mysterious terms, judg'd as then best:
And on the Serpent thus his curse let fall.
   "Because thou hast done this, thou art accurst   175
Above all Cattle, each Beast of the Field;
Upon thy Belly grovelling thou shalt go,
And dust shalt eat all the days of thy Life.
Between Thee and the Woman I will put
Enmity, and between thine and her Seed;   180
Her Seed shall bruise thy head, thou bruise his heel."
   So spoke this Oracle, then verifi'd
When Jesus son of Mary second Eve,
Saw Satan fall like Lightning down from Heav'n,
Prince of the Air; then rising from his Grave   185
Spoil'd Principalities and Powers, triumpht
In open show, and with ascension bright
Captivity led captive through the Air,

165 **unable** the serpent being powerless to . . .

The Realm itself of Satan long usurpt,
190 Whom he shall tread at last under our feet;
Ev'n hee who now foretold his fatal bruise,
And to the Woman thus his Sentence turn'd.
    "Thy sorrow I will greatly multiply
By thy Conception; Children thou shalt bring
195 In sorrow forth, and to thy Husband's will
Thine shall submit, hee over thee shall rule."
        On Adam last thus judgement he pronounc'd.
"Because thou hast heark'n'd to the voice of thy
    Wife,
And eaten of the Tree concerning which
200 I charg'd thee, saying: Thou shalt not eat thereof,
Curs'd is the ground for thy sake, thou in sorrow
Shalt eat thereof all the days of thy Life;
Thorns also and Thistles it shall bring thee forth
Unbid, and thou shalt eat th'Herb of the Field,
205 In the sweat of thy Face shalt thou eat Bread,
Till thou return unto the ground, for thou
Out of the ground wast taken, know thy Birth,
For dust thou art, and shalt to dust return."
        So judg'd he Man, both Judge and Saviour sent,
210 And th'instant stroke of Death denounc't that day
Remov'd far off; then pitying how they stood
Before him naked to the air, that now
Must suffer change, disdain'd not to begin
Thenceforth the form of servant to assume,
215 As when he wash'd his servants' feet, so now
As Father of his Family he clad
Their nakedness with Skins of Beasts, or slain,
Or as the Snake with youthful Coat repaid;°
And thought not much to clothe his Enemies:
220 Nor hee their outward only with the Skins
Of Beasts, but inward nakedness, much more
Opprobrious, with his Robe of righteousness,
Arraying cover'd from his Father's sight.
To him with swift ascent he up return'd,
225 Into his blissful bosom reassum'd
In glory as of old, to him appeas'd
All, though all-knowing, what had past with Man

218 **repaid** recompensed.

Recounted, mixing intercession sweet.
Meanwhile ere thus was sinn'd and judg'd on Earth,
Within the Gates of Hell sat Sin and Death,   230
In counterview within the Gates, that now
Stood open wide, belching outrageous flame
Far into Chaos, since the Fiend pass'd through,
Sin opening, who thus now to Death began.
            "O Son, why sit we here each other viewing   235
Idly, while Satan our great Author thrives
In other Worlds, and happier Seat provides
For us his offspring dear? It cannot be
But that success attends him; if mishap,
Ere this he had return'd, with fury driv'n   240
By his Avengers,° since no place like this
Can fit his punishment, or their revenge.
Methinks I feel new strength within me rise,
Wings growing, and Dominion giv'n me large
Beyond this Deep; whatever draws me on,   245
Or sympathy, or some connatural force
Powerful at greatest distance to unite
With secret amity things of like kind
By secretest conveyance.° Thou my Shade
Inseparable must with mee along: 250
For Death from Sin no power can separate.
But lest the difficulty of passing back
Stay his return perhaps over this Gulf
Impassable, impervious, let us try
Advent'rous work, yet to thy power and mine   255
Not unagreeable, to found a path
Over this Main from Hell to that new World
Where Satan now prevails, a Monument
Of merit high to all th'infernal Host,
Easing their passage hence, for intercourse,   260
Or transmigration, as their lot shall lead.
Nor can I miss the way, so strongly drawn
By this new-felt attraction and instínct."
            Whom thus the meager Shadow answer'd soon.
"Go whither Fate and inclination strong   265
Leads thee, I shall not lag behind, nor err

241 **Avengers** *1674*; Avenger *1667*.   249 **conveyance** with associations of
underhand cunning.

The way, thou leading, such a scent I draw
Of carnage, prey innumerable, and taste
The savour of Death from all things there that live:
270 Nor shall I to the work thou enterprisest
Be wanting, but afford thee equal aid."
          So saying, with delight he snuff'd the smell
Of mortal change on Earth. As when a flock
Of ravenous Fowl, though many a League remote,
275 Against the day of Battle, to a Field,
Where Armies lie encampt, come flying, lur'd
With scent of living Carcasses design'd
For death, the following day, in bloody fight.
So scented the grim Feature, and upturn'd
280 His Nostril wide into the murky Air,
Sagacious° of his Quarry from so far.
Then Both from out Hell Gates into the waste
Wide Anarchy of Chaos damp and dark
Flew diverse, and with Power (their Power was great)
285 Hovering upon the Waters; what they met
Solid or slimy, as in raging Sea
Tost up and down, together crowded drove
From each side shoaling towards the mouth of Hell.
As when two Polar Winds blowing adverse
290 Upon the Cronian° Sea, together drive
Mountains of Ice, that stop th'imagin'd way
Beyond Petsora° Eastward, to the rich
Cathaian° Coast. The aggregated Soil
Death with his Mace petrific,° cold and dry,
295 As with a Trident smote, and fix't as firm
As Delos° floating once; the rest his look
Bound with Gorgonian° rigor not to move,
And with Asphaltic slime; broad as the Gate,
Deep to the Roots of Hell the gather'd beach
300 They fasten'd, and the Mole° immense wrought on
Over the foaming deep high Archt, a Bridge
Of length prodigious joining to the Wall
Immovable of this now fenceless° world

---

281 **Sagacious** quick of scent.   290 **Cronian** Arctic.   292 **Petsora** river in
Siberia.   293 **Cathaian** Chinese.   294 **petrific** turning to stone.   296 **Delos**
an Aegean island, called up by Neptune's trident and fixed firm by
Jove.   297 **Gorgonian** the Gorgons' gaze turning men to stone.   300 **Mole**
massive bridge or pier.   303 **fenceless** defenseless.

Forfeit to Death; from hence a passage broad,
Smooth, easy, inoffensive° down to Hell.   305
So, if great things to small may be compar'd.
Xerxes, the Liberty of Greece to yoke,
From Susa° his Memnonian Palace high
Came to the Sea, and over Hellespont
Bridging his way, Europe with Asia join'd,   310
And scourg'd with many a stroke th'indignant waves.°
Now had they brought the work by wondrous Art
Pontifical,° a ridge of pendent Rock
Over the vext Abyss, following the track
Of Satan, to the selfsame place where hee   315
First 'lighted from his Wing, and landed safe
From out of Chaos to the outside bare
Of this round World: with Pins of Adamant
And Chains they made all fast, too fast they made
And durable; and now in little space   320
The Confines met of Empyrean Heav'n
And of this World, and on the left hand Hell
With long reach interpos'd; three sev'ral ways
In sight, to each of these three places led.
And now their way to Earth they had descri'd,   325
To Paradise first tending, when behold
Satan in likeness of an Angel bright
Betwixt the Centaur and the Scorpion steering
His Zenith, while the Sun in Aries rose:
Disguis'd he came, but those his Children dear   330
Their Parent soon discern'd, though in disguise.
Hee, after Eve seduc't, unminded slunk
Into the Wood fast by, and changing shape
To observe the sequel, saw his guileful act
By Eve, though all unwitting, seconded   335
Upon her Husband, saw their shame that sought
Vain covertures; but when he saw descend
The Son of God to judge them, terrifi'd
Hee fled, not hoping to escape, but shun
The present, fearing guilty what his wrath   340
Might suddenly inflict; that past, return'd
By Night, and list'ning where the hapless Pair

305 **inoffensive** without obstacle. 308 **Susa** in Persia. 311 **And . . .
waves** In his anger after the waters destroyed a bridge. 313 **Pontifical**
bridgemaking.

Sat in their sad discourse, and various plaint,
Thence gather'd his own doom, which understood
345 Not instant, but of future time. With joy
And tidings fraught, to Hell he now return'd,
And at the brink of Chaos, near the foot
Of this new wondrous Pontifice, unhop't
Met who to meet him came, his Offspring dear.
350 Great joy was at their meeting, and at sight
Of that stupendious Bridge his joy increas'd.
Long hee admiring stood, till Sin, his fair
Enchanting Daughter, thus the silence broke.
          "O Parent, these are thy magnific deeds,
355 Thy Trophies, which thou view'st as not thine own,
Thou art their Author and prime Architect:
For I no sooner in my Heart divin'd,
My Heart, which by a secret harmony
Still moves with thine, join'd in connection sweet,
360 That thou on Earth hadst prosper'd, which thy looks
Now also evidence, but straight I felt
Though distant from thee Worlds between, yet felt
That I must after thee with this thy Son;
Such fatal consequence unites us three:
365 Hell could no longer hold us in her bounds,
Nor this unvoyageable Gulf obscure
Detain from following thy illustrious track.
Thou host achiev'd our liberty, confin'd
Within Hell Gates till now, thou us impow'r'd
370 To fortify thus far, and overlay
With this portentous Bridge the dark Abyss.
Thine now is all this World, thy virtue hath won
What thy hands builded not, thy Wisdom gain'd
With odds what War hath lost, and fully aveng'd
375 Our foil in Heav'n; here thou shalt Monarch reign,
There didst not; there let him still Victor sway,
As Battle hath adjudg'd, from this new World
Retiring, by his own doom alienated,
And henceforth Monarchy with thee divide
380 Of all things, parted by th'Empyreal bounds,
His Quadrature,° from thy Orbicular World,
Or try thee now more dang'rous to his Throne."

381 **Quadrature** Heaven as a square.

Whom thus the Prince of Darkness answer'd
    glad.
"Fair Daughter, and thou Son and Grandchild both,
High proof ye now have giv'n to be the Race   385
Of Satan (for I glory in the name,
Antagonist of Heav'n's Almighty King)
Amply have merited of me, of all
Th'Infernal Empire, that so near Heav'n's door
Triumphal with triumphal act have met,   390
Mine with this glorious Work, and made one Realm
Hell, and this World, one Realm, one Continent
Of easy thoroughfare. Therefore while I
Descend through Darkness, on your Road with ease
To my associate Powers, them to acquaint   395
With these successes, and with them rejoice,
You two this way, among these numerous Orbs
All yours, right down to Paradise descend;
There dwell and Reign in bliss, thence on the Earth
Dominion exercise and in the Air,   400
Chiefly on Man, sole Lord of all declar'd,
Him first make sure your thrall, and lastly kill.
My Substitutes I send ye, and Create
Plenipotent on Earth, of matchless might
Issuing from mee: on your joint vigor now   405
My hold of this new Kingdom all depends,
Through Sin to Death expos'd by my explóit.
If your joint power prevail, th'affairs of Hell
No detriment° need fear, go and be strong."
    So saying he dismiss'd them, they with speed 410
Their course through thickest Constellations held
Spreading their bane; the blasted Stars lookt wan,
And Planets, Planet-struck,° real Eclipse
Then suffer'd. Th'other way Satan went down
The Causey° to Hell Gate; on either side   415
Disputed Chaos over-built exclaim'd,
And with rebounding surge the bars assail'd,
That scorn'd his indignation: through the Gate,
Wide open and unguarded, Satan pass'd,

---

409 **detriment** the word's astrological application (including "eclipse")
leading into the following lines.   413 **Planet-struck** plagued by an even
more evil influence than what they themselves shed.   415 **Causey**
causeway.

420 And all about found desolate; for those
    Appointed to sit there, had left their charge,
    Flown to the upper World; the rest were all
    Far to the inland retir'd, about the walls
    Of Pandemonium, City and proud seat
425 Of Lucifer, so by allusion call'd,
    Of that bright Star to Satan paragon'd.
    There kept their Watch the Legions, while the Grand
    In Council sat, solicitous what chance
    Might intercept their Emperor sent, so hee
430 Departing gave command, and they observ'd.
    As when the Tartar from his Russian Foe
    By Astracan over the Snowy Plains
    Retires, or Bactrian Sophi° from the horns
    Of Turkish Crescent, leaves all waste beyond
435 The Realm of Aladule, in his retreat
    To Tauris or Casbeen. So these the late
    Heav'n-banisht Host, left desert utmost Hell
    Many a dark League, reduc't in careful Watch
    Round their Metropolis, and now expecting
440 Each hour their great adventurer from the search
    Of Foreign Worlds: he through the midst unmarkt,
    In show plebeian Angel militant
    Of lowest order, past; and from the door
    Of that Plutonian° Hail, invisible
445 Ascended his high Throne, which under state
    Of richest texture spread, at th'upper end
    Was plac't in regal lustre. Down awhile
    He sat, and round about him saw unseen:
    At last as from a Cloud his fulgent head
450 And shape Star-bright appear'd, or brighter, clad
    With what permissive glory since his fall
    Was left him, or false glitter: All amaz'd
    At that so sudden blaze the Stygian throng
    Bent their aspéct, and whom they wish'd beheld,
455 Their mighty Chief return'd: loud was th'acclaim:
    Forth rushed in haste the great consulting Peers,
    Rais'd from their dark Divan,° and with like joy
    Congratulant approach'd him, who with hand

433 **Bactrian Sophi** Persian king.   444 **Plutonian** Pluto, god of Hell.
457 **Divan** oriental council.

Silence, and with these words attention won.
      "Thrones, Dominations, Princedoms, Virtues,
         Powers,   460
For in possession such, not only of right,
I call ye and declare ye now, return'd
Successful beyond hope, to lead ye forth
Triumphant out of this infernal Pit
Abominable, accurst, the house of woe,   465
And Dungeon of our Tyrant: Now possess,
As Lords, a spacious World, to our native Heaven
Little inferior, by my adventure hard
With peril great achiev'd. Long were to tell
What I have done, what suffer'd, with what pain   470
Voyag'd th'unreal, vast, unbounded deep
Of horrible confusion, over which
By Sin and Death a broad way now is pav'd
To expedite° your glorious march; but I
Toil'd out my uncouth passage, forc't to ride   475
Th'untractable Abyss, plung'd in the womb
Of unoriginal° Night and Chaos wild,
That jealous of their secrets fiercely oppos'd
My journey strange, with clamorous uproar
Protesting Fate supreme; thence how I found   480
The new created World, which fame in Heav'n
Long had foretold, a Fabric wonderful
Of absolute perfection, therein Man
Plac't in a Paradise, by our exíle
Made happy: Him by fraud I have seduc'd   485
From his Creator, and the more to increase
Your wonder, with an Apple; he thereat
Offended, worth your laughter, hath giv'n up
Both his beloved Man and all his World,
To Sin and Death a prey, and so to us,   490
Without our hazard, labour, or alarm,
To range in, and to dwell, and over Man
To rule, as over all he should have rul'd.
True is, mee also he hath judg'd, or rather
Mee not, but the brute Serpent in whose shape   495
Man I deceiv'd: that which to mee belongs,

---

474 **expedite** speed (in origin "free the feet"). 477 **unoriginal** un-originated.

Is enmity, which he will put between
Mee and Mankind; I am to bruise his heel;
His Seed, when is not set, shall bruise my head:
500   A World who would not purchase with a bruise,
Or much more grievous pain? Ye have th'account
Of my performance: What remains, ye Gods,
But up and enter now into full bliss."
        So having said, awhile he stood, expecting
505   Their universal shout and high applause
To fill his ear, when contrary he hears
On all sides, from innumerable tongues
A dismal universal hiss, the sound
Of public scorn; he wonder'd, but not long
510   Had leisure, wond'ring at himself now more;
His Visage drawn he felt to sharp and spare,
His Arms clung to his Ribs, his Legs entwining
Each other, till supplanted° down he fell
A monstrous Serpent on his Belly prone,
515   Reluctant,° but in vain, a greater power
Now rul'd him, punisht in the shape he sinn'd,
According to his doom: he would have spoke,
But hiss for hiss return'd with forked tongue
To forked tongue, for now were all transform'd
520   Alike, to Serpents all as áccessóries
To his bold Riot: dreadful was the din
Of hissing through the Hall, thick swarming now
With complicated° monsters, head and tail,
Scorpion and Asp, and Amphisboena° dire,
525   Cerastes horn'd, Hydrus,° and Ellops° drear,
And Dipsas° (Not so thick swarm'd once the Soil
Bedropt with blood of Gorgon,° or the Isle
Ophiusa°) but still greatest hee the midst,
Now Dragon grown, larger than whom the Sun
530   Engendered in the Pythian Vale on slime,
Huge Python,° and his Power no less he seem'd
Above the rest still to retain; they all

513 **supplanted** overthrown, Satan himself being traditionally the "sup-
planter" of Adam and Eve.   515 **Reluctant** struggling.   523 **complicated**
entwined.   524 **Amphisboena** fabled to have a head at each end.
525 **Hydrus** water snake.   525 **Ellops** a kind of serpent.   526 **Dipsas**
whose bite produced raging thirst.   526–27 **Soil . . . Gorgon** The blood
of Medusa bred snakes in Libya.   528 **Ophiusa** named after its "serpents."   531 **Python** serpent slain by Apollo.

Him follow'd issuing forth to th'open Field,
Where all yet left of that revolted Rout
Heav'n-fall'n, in station stood or just array,   *535*
Sublime with expectation when to see
In Triumph issuing forth their glorious Chief;
They saw, but other sight instead, a crowd
Of ugly Serpents; horror on them fell,
And horrid sympathy; for what they saw,   *540*
They felt themselves now changing; down their arms,
Down fell both Spear and Shield, down they as fast,
And the dire hiss renew'd, and the dire form
Catcht by Contagion, like in punishment,
As in their crime. Thus was th'applause they meant,   *545*
Turn'd to exploding° hiss, triumph to shame
Cast on themselves from their own mouths. There
    stood
A Grove hard by, sprung up with this their change,
His will who reigns above, to aggravate
Their penance, laden with fair Fruit, like that   *550*
Which grew in Paradise, the bait of Eve
Us'd by the Tempter: on that prospect strange
Their earnest eyes they fix'd, imagining
For one forbidden Tree a multitude
Now ris'n, to work them further woe or shame;   *555*
Yet parcht with scalding thirst and hunger fierce,
Though to delude them sent, could not abstain,
But on they roll'd in heaps, and up the Trees
Climbing, sat thicker than the snaky locks
That curl'd Megæra:° greedily they pluck'd   *560*
The Fruitage fair to sight, like that which grew
Near that bituminous Lake where Sodom flam'd;
This more delusive, not the touch, but taste
Deceiv'd; they fondly thinking to allay
Their appetite with gust,° instead of Fruit   *565*
Chew'd bitter Ashes, which th'offended taste
With spattering noise rejected: oft they assay'd,
Hunger and thirst constraining, drugg'd as oft,
With hatefullest disrelish writh'd their jaws
With soot and cinders fill'd; so oft they fell   *570*

---

546 **exploding** hooting (off the stage, Latin *explaudare*, literally the opposite of "th'applause").   560 **Megæra** one of the Furies.   565 **gust** relish.

Into the same illusion, not as Man
Whom they triumph'd once lapst. Thus were they
    plagu'd
And worn with Famine, long and ceaseless hiss,
Till their lost shape, permitted, they resum'd,
575 Yearly enjoin'd, some say, to undergo
This annual humbling certain number'd days,
To dash their pride, and joy for Man seduc't.
However some tradition they dispers'd
Among the Heathen of their purchase° got,
580 And Fabl'd how the Serpent, whom they call'd
Ophion with Eurynome,° the wide-
Encroaching Eve perhaps, had first the rule
Of high Olympus, thence by Saturn driv'n
And Ops,° ere yet Dictæan° Jove was born.
585 Meanwhile in Paradise the hellish pair
Too soon arriv'd, Sin there in power before,
Once actual, now in body, and to dwell
Habitual habitant; behind her Death
Close following pace for pace, not mounted yet
590 On his pale Horse: to whom Sin thus began.
            "Second of Satan sprung, all-conquering
                Death,
What think'st thou of our Empire now, though earn'd
With travail difficult, not better far
Than still at Hell's dark threshold to have sat watch,
595 Unnam'd, undreaded, and thyself half starv'd?"
            Whom thus the Sin-born Monster answer'd
                soon.
"To mee, who with eternal Famine pine,
Alike is Hell, or Paradise, or Heaven,
There best, where most with ravin° I might meet;
600 Which here, though plenteous, all too little seems
To stuff this Maw, this vast unhide-bound° Corpse."
            To whom th'incestuous Mother thus repli'd.
"Thou therefore on these Herbs, and Fruits, and
    Flow'rs
Feed first, on each Beast next, and Fish, and Fowl,

---

579 **purchase** plunder.   581 **Ophion . . . Eurynome** the Titan Ophion,
"Serpent," and his wife Eurynome, "Wide-ruling."   584 **Ops** wife of Saturn.   584 **Dictæan** from Dicte in Crete.   599 **ravin** prey.   601 **unhide-
bound** slack-skinned.

No homely morsels, and whatever thing   *605*
The Scyth of Time mows down, devour unspar'd,
Till I in Man residing through the Race,
His thoughts, his looks, words, actions all infect,
And season him thy last and sweetest prey."
      This said, they both betook them several ways,   *610*
Both to destroy, or unimmortal make
All kinds, and for destruction to mature
Sooner or later; which th'Almighty seeing,
From his transcendent Seat the Saints among,
To those bright Orders utter'd thus his voice.   *615*
      "See with what heat these Dogs of Hell
        advance
To waste and havoc yonder World, which I
So fair and good created, and had still
Kept in that state, had not the folly of Man
Let in these wasteful Furies, who impute   *620*
Folly to mee, so doth the Prince of Hell
And his Adherents, that with so much ease
I suffer them to enter and possess
A place so heav'nly, and conniving° seem
To gratify my scornful Enemies,   *625*
That laugh, as if transported with some fit
Of Passion, I to them had quitted all,
At random yielded up to their misrule;
And know not that I call'd and drew them thither
My Hell-hounds, to lick up the draff and filth   *630*
Which man's polluting Sin with taint hath shed
On what was pure, till cramm'd and gorg'd, nigh burst
With suckt and glutted offal, at one sling
Of thy victorious Arm, well-pleasing Son,
Both Sin, and Death, and yawning Grave at last   *635*
Through Chaos hurl'd, obstruct the mouth of Hell
For ever, and seal up his ravenous Jaws.
Then Heav'n and Earth renew'd shall be made pure
To sanctity that shall receive no stain:
Till then the Curse pronounc't on both precedes."°   *640*
      Hee ended, and the heav'nly Audience loud
Sung Halleluia, as the sound of Seas,
Through multitude that sung: "Just are thy ways,

---

624 **conniving** winking at, overlooking.   640 **precedes** takes precedence.

Righteous are thy Decrees on all thy Works;
645 Who can extenuate° thee? Next, to the Son,
Destin'd restorer of Mankind, by whom
New Heav'n and Earth shall to the Ages rise,
Or down from Heav'n descend." Such was their song,
While the Creator calling forth by name
650 His mighty Angels gave them several charge,
As sorted best with present things. The Sun
Had first his precept so to move, so shine,
As might affect the Earth with cold and heat
Scarce tolerable, and from the North to call
655 Decrepit Winter, from the South to bring
Solstitial summer's heat. To the blanc Moon
Her office they prescrib'd, to th'other five
Their planetary motions and aspécts°
In Sextile, Square, and Trine, and Opposite,
660 Of noxious efficacy, and when to join
In Synod° unbenign, and taught the fixt°
Their influence malignant when to show'r,
Which of them rising with the Sun, or falling,
Should prove tempestuous: To the Winds they set
665 Their comers, when with bluster to confound
Sea, Air, and Shore, the Thunder when to roll
With terror through the dark Aereal Hall.
Some say he bid his Angels turn askance
The Poles of Earth twice ten degrees and more
670 From the Sun's Axle; they with labour push'd
Oblique the Centric Globe:° Some say the Sun
Was bid turn Reins from th'Equinoctial Road
Like distant breadth to Taurus with the Sev'n
Atlantic Sisters, and the Spartan Twins
675 Up to the Tropic Crab; thence down amain
By Leo and the Virgin and the Scales,
As deep as Capricorn, to bring in change
Of Seasons to each Clime; else had the Spring
Perpetual smil'd on Earth with vernant Flow'rs,
680 Equal in Days and Nights, except to those
Beyond the Polar Circles; to them Day
Had unbenighted shone, while the low Sun

645 **extenuate** belittle. 658 **aspécts** astrological positions. 661 **Synod**
astrological conjunction. 661 **fixt** "sphere" of fixed stars. 671 **Globe**
earth.

To recompense his distance, in their sight
Had rounded still th'Horizon, and not known
Or East or West, which had forbid the Snow   685
From cold Estotiland,° and South as far
Beneath Magellan.° At that tasted Fruit
The Sun, as from Thyestean° Banquet, turn'd
His course intended; else how had the World
Inhabited, though sinless, more than now,   690
Avoided pinching cold and scorching heat?
These changes in the Heav'ns, though slow, produc'd
Like change on Sea and Land, sideral blast,°
Vapour, and Mist, and Exhalation hot,
Corrupt and Pestilent: Now from the North   695
Of Norumbega,° and the Samoed° shore
Bursting their brazen Dungeon, arm'd with ice
And snow and hail and stormy gust and flaw,°
Boreas and Cæcias and Argestes loud
And Thrascias rend the Woods and Seas upturn;   700
With adverse blast up-turns them from the South
Notus and Afer black with thund'rous Clouds
From Serraliona;° thwart of these as fierce
Forth rush the Levant and the Ponent Winds
Eurus and Zephyr with their lateral noise,   705
Sirocco, and Libecchio.° Thus began
Outrage from lifeless things; but Discord first
Daughter of Sin, among th'irrational,
Death introduc'd through fierce antipathy:
Beast now with Beast 'gun war, and Fowl with Fowl, 710
And Fish with Fish; to graze the Herb all leaving,
Devour'd each other; nor stood much in awe
Of Man, but fled him, or with count'nance grim
Glar'd on him passing: these were from without
The growing miseries, which Adam saw   715
Already in part, though hid in gloomiest shade,
To sorrow abandon'd, but worse felt within,
And in a troubl'd Sea of passion tost,

---

686 **Estotiland** in North America. 687 **Magellan** at the extremity of
South America. 688 **Thyestean** The flesh of Thyestes' sons was served to
him. 693 **sideral blast** malign influence from the stars. 696 **Norumbega** in
North America. 696 **Samoed** Siberian. 698 **flaw** squall. 703 **Serraliona**
Sierra Leone. 699–706 **Boreas . . . Libecchio** the winds in classical and
Italian terminology.

Thus to disburd'n sought with sad complaint.
720   "O miserable of happy! is this the end
Of this new glorious World, and mee so late
The Glory of that Glory, who now become
Accurst of blessed, hide me from the face
Of God, whom to behold was then my heighth
725 Of happiness: yet well, if here would end
The misery, I deserv'd it, and would bear
My own deservings; but this will not serve;
All that I eat or drink, or shall beget,
Is propagated curse. O voice once heard
730 Delightfully, *Increase and multiply,*
Now death to hear! for what can I increase
Or multiply, but curses on my head?
Who of all Ages to succeed, but feeling
The evil on him brought by me, will curse
735 My Head, 'Ill fare our Ancestor impure,
For this we may thank Adam'; but his thanks
Shall be the execration; so besides
Mine own that bide° upon me, all from mee
Shall with a fierce reflux on mee redound,
740 On mee as on their natural center 'light
Heavy, though in their place.° O fleeting joys
Of Paradise, dear bought with lasting woes!
Did I request thee, Maker, from my Clay
To mould me Man, did I solicit thee
745 From darkness to promote me, or here place
In this delicious Garden? as my Will
Concurr'd not to my being, it were but right
And equal° to reduce me to my dust,
Desirous to resign, and render back
750 All I receiv'd, unable to perform
Thy terms too hard, by which I was to hold
The good I sought not. To the loss of that,
Sufficient penalty, why hast thou added
The sense of endless woes? inexplicable
755 Thy Justice seems; yet to say truth, too late,
I thus contést; then should have been refus'd
Those terms whatever, when they were propos'd:

738 **bide** insistently dwell.   741 **though . . . place** this being unnatural,
since their weight is their tendency to their own center.   748 **equal**
equitable.

Thou didst accept them; wilt thou enjoy the good,
Then cavil the conditions? and though God
Made thee without thy leave, what if thy Son   760
Prove disobedient, and reprov'd, retort,
'Wherefore didst thou beget me? I sought it not':
Wouldst thou admit for his contempt of thee
That proud excuse? yet him not thy election,
But Natural necessity begot.   765
God made thee of choice his own, and of his own
To serve him, thy reward was of his grace,
Thy punishment then justly is at his Will.
Be it so, for I submit, his doom is fair,
That dust I am, and shall to dust return: 770
O welcome hour whenever! why delays
His hand to execute what his Decree
Fix'd on this day? why do I overlive,
Why am I mockt with death, and length'n'd out
To deathless pain? how gladly would I meet   775
Mortality my sentence, and be Earth
Insensible, how glad would lay me down
As in my Mother's lap? there I should rest
And sleep secure; his dreadful voice no more
Would Thunder in my ears, nor fear of worse   780
To mee and to my offspring would torment me
With cruel expectation. Yet one doubt
Pursues me still, lest all I cannot die,
Lest that pure breath of Life, the Spirit of Man
Which God inspir'd, cannot together perish   785
With this corporeal Clod; then in the Grave,
Or in some other dismal place, who knows
But I shall die a living Death? O thought
Horrid, if true! yet why? it was but breath
Of Life that sinn'd; what dies but what had life   790
And sin? the Body properly hath neither.
All of me then shall die: let this appease
The doubt, since human reach no further knows.
For though the Lord of all be infinite,
Is his wrath also? be it, man is not so,   795
But mortal doom'd. How can he exercise
Wrath without end on Man whom Death must end?
Can he make deathless Death? that were to make
Strange contradiction, which to God himself

800 Impossible is held, as Argument
    Of weakness, not of Power. Will he, draw out,
    For anger's sake, finite to infinite
    In punisht man, to satisfy his rigour
    Satisfi'd never; that were to extend
805 His Sentence beyond dust and Nature's Law,
    By which all Causes else according still
    To the reception of their matter° act,
    Not to th'extent of their own Sphere. But say
    That Death be not one stroke, as I suppos'd,
810 Bereaving sense, but endless misery
    From this day onward, which I feel begun
    Both in me, and without me, and so last
    To perpetuity; Ay me, that fear
    Comes thund'ring back with dreadful revolution
815 On my defenceless head; both Death and I
    Am found Eternal, and incorporate° both,
    Nor I on my part single, in mee all
    Posterity stands curst: Fair Patrimony
    That I must leave ye, Sons; O were I able
820 To waste it all myself, and leave ye none!
    So disinherited how would ye bless
    Me now your Curse! Ah, why should all mankind
    For one man's fault thus guiltless be condemn'd,
    If guiltless? But from mee what can proceed,
825 But all corrupt, both Mind and Will deprav'd,
    Not to do only, but to will the same
    With me? how can they then° acquitted stand
    In sight of God? Him after all Disputes
    Forc't I absolve: all my evasions vain
830 And reasonings, though through Mazes, lead me still
    But to my own conviction: first and last
    On mee, mee only, as the source and spring
    Of all corruption, all the blame 'lights due;
    So might the wrath. Fond wish! couldst thou support
835 That burden heavier than the Earth to bear,
    Than all the World much heavier, though divided
    With that bad Woman? Thus what thou desir'st
    And what thou fear'st, alike destroys all hope

807 **reception . . . matter** receptivity of their materials.   816 **incorporate**
united in one body.   827 **they then** *1674*; they *1667*.

Of refuge, and concludes° thee miserable
Beyond all past example and future,   *840*
To Satan only like both crime and doom.
O Conscience, into what Abyss of fears
And horrors hast thou driv'n me; out of which
I find no way, from deep to deeper plung'd!"
     Thus Adam to himself lamented loud   *845*
Through the still Night, not now, as ere man fell,
Wholesome and cool, and mild, but with black Air
Accompanied, with damps and dreadful gloom,
Which to his evil Conscience represented
All things with double terror: On the ground   *850*
Outstretcht he lay, on the cold ground, and oft
Curs'd his Creation, Death as oft accus'd
Of tardy execution, since denounc't°
The day of his offence. "Why comes not Death,"
Said hee, "with one thrice ácceptáble stroke   *855*
To end me? Shall Truth fail to keep her word,
Justice Divine not hast'n to be just?
But Death comes not at call, Justice Divine
Mends not her slowest pace for prayers or cries.
O Woods, O Fountains, Hillocks, Dales and Bow'rs,   *860*
With other echo late I taught your Shades
To answer, and resound far other Song."
Whom thus afflicted when sad Eve beheld,
Desolate where she sat, approaching nigh,
Soft words to his fierce passion she assay'd: *865*
But her with stern regard he thus repell'd.
     "Out of my sight, thou Serpent,° that name
       best
Befits thee with him leagu'd, thyself as false
And hateful; nothing wants, but that thy shape,
Like his, and colour Serpentine may show   *870*
Thy inward fraud, to warn all Creatures from thee
Henceforth; lest that too heav'nly form, pretended°
To hellish falsehood, snare them. But for thee
I had persisted happy, had not thy pride
And wand'ring vanity, when least was safe,   *875*

---

839 **concludes** conclusively proves, and puts an end to, does for ("I will conclude thee, and annihilate thee," [1612]. 853 **denounc't** threatened. 867 **Serpent** The name Eve was thought to be cognate with the Hebrew for serpent. 872 **pretended** extended as a screen.

Rejected my forewarning, and disdain'd
Not to be trusted, longing to be seen
Though by the Devil himself, him overweening
To over-reach, but with the Serpent meeting
880 Fool'd and beguil'd, by him thou, I by thee,
To trust thee from my side, imagin'd wise,
Constant, mature, proof against all assaults,
And understood not all was but a show
Rather than solid virtue, all but a Rib
885 Crooked by nature, bent, as now appears,
More to the part siníster° from me drawn,
Well if thrown out, as supernumerary
To my just number found. O why did God,
Creator wise, that peopl'd highest Heav'n
890 With Spirits Masculine, create at last
This novelty on Earth, this fair defect
Of Nature, and not fill the World at once
With Men as Angels without Feminine,
Or find some other way to generate
895 Mankind? this mischief had not then befall'n,
And more that shall befall, innumerable
Disturbances on Earth through Female snares,
And strait conjunction° with this Sex: for either
He never shall find out fit Mate, but such
900 As some misfortune brings him, or mistake,
Or whom he wishes most shall seldom gain
Through her perverseness, but shall see her gain'd
By a far worse, or if she love, withheld
By Parents, or his happiest choice too late
905 Shall meet, already linkt and Wedlock-bound
To a fell Adversary, his hate or shame:
Which infinite calamity shall cause
To Human life, and household peace confound."
      He added not, and from her turn'd, but Eve
910 Not so repulst, with Tears that ceas'd not flowing,
And tresses all disorder'd, at his feet
Fell humble, and embracing them, besought
His peace, and thus proceeded in her plaint.
      "Forsake me not thus, Adam, witness Heav'n

886 **siníster** left side, with evil associations.   898 **conjunction** including
union in marriage, and sexual union.

What love sincere, and reverence in my heart   915
I bear thee, and unwitting have offended,
Unhappily deceiv'd; thy suppliant
I beg, and clasp thy knees; bereave me not,
Whereon I live, thy gentle looks, thy aid,
Thy counsel in this uttermost distress,   920
My only strength and stay: forlorn of thee,
Whither shall I betake me, where subsist?
While yet we live, scarce one short hour perhaps,
Between us two let there be peace, both joining,
As join'd in injuries, one enmity   925
Against a Foe by doom express assign'd us,
That cruel Serpent: On me exercise not
Thy hatred for this misery befall'n,
On me already lost, mee than thyself
More miserable; both have sinn'd, but thou   930
Against God only, I against God and thee,
And to the place of judgement will return,
There with my cries importune Heaven, that all
The sentence from thy head remov'd may 'light
On me, sole cause to thee of all this woe,   935
Mee mee only just object of his ire."
          She ended weeping, and her lowly plight,
Immovable till peace obtain'd from fault
Acknowledg'd and deplor'd, in Adam wrought
Commiseration; soon his heart relented   940
Towards her, his life so late and sole delight,
Now at his feet submissive in distress,
Creature so fair his reconcilement seeking,
His counsel whom she had dispeas'd, his aid;
As one disarm'd, his anger all he lost,   945
And thus with peaceful words uprais'd her soon.
          "Unwary, and too desirous, as before,
So now of what thou know'st not, who desir'st
The punishment all on thyself; alas,
Bear thine own first, ill able to sustain   950
His full wrath whose thou feel'st as yet least part,
And my displeasure bear'st so ill. If Prayers
Could alter high Decrees, I to that place
Would speed before thee, and be louder heard,
That on my head all might be visited,   955
Thy frailty and infirmer Sex forgiv'n,

To me committed and by me expos'd.
But rise, let us no more contend, nor blame
Each other, blam'd enough elsewhere, but strive
960 In offices of Love, how we may light'n
Each other's burden in our share of woe;
Since this day's Death denounc't, if aught I see,
Will prove no sudden, but a slow pac't evil,
A long day's dying to augment our pain,
965 And to our Seed (O hapless Seed!) deriv'd."
        To whom thus Eve, recovering heart, repli'd.
"Adam, by sad experiment I know
How little weight my words with thee can find,
Found so erroneous, thence by just event
970 Found so unfortunate; nevertheless,
Restor'd by thee, vile as I am, to place
Of new acceptance, hopeful to regain
Thy Love, the sole contentment of my heart,
Living or dying from thee I will not hide
975 What thoughts in my unquiet breast are ris'n,
Tending to some relief° of our extremes,°
Or end, though sharp and sad, yet tolerable,
As in our evils, and of easier choice.
If care of our descent° perplex us most,
980 Which must be born to certain woe, devour'd
By Death at last, and miserable it is
To be to others cause of misery,
Our own begotten, and of our Loins to bring
Into this cursed World a woeful Race,
985 That after wretched Life must be at last
Food for so foul a Monster, in thy power
It lies, yet ere Conception to prevent
The Race unblest, to being yet unbegot.
Childless thou art, Childless remaine: So Death
990 Shall be deceiv'd° his glut, and with us two
Be forc'd° to satisfy his Rav'nous Maw.
But if thou judge it hard and difficult,
Conversing, looking, loving, to abstain
From Love's due Rites, Nuptial embraces sweet,

---

976 **relief** from Latin *relevare*, raise again (following "ris'n"). 976 **extremes** extreme hardships. 979 **descent** descendants. 990 **deceiv'd**
cheated out of. 991 **forc'd** "Glut" and "Maw" suggest a grim pun in
"forc'd," to clash with "stuffed full," as in "forced meats."

And with desire to languish without hope, 995
Before the present° object languishing
With like desire, which would be misery
And torment less than none of what we dread,
Then both ourselves and Seed at once to free
From what we fear for both, let us make short,° 1000
Let us seek Death, or hee not found, supply
With our own hands his Office on ourselves;
Why stand we longer shivering under fears,
That show no end but Death, and have the power,
Of many ways to die the shortest choosing, 1005
Destruction with destruction to destroy."
  She ended here, or vehement despair
Broke off the rest; so much of Death her thoughts
Had entertain'd, as dy'd her Cheeks with pale.
But Adam with such counsel nothing sway'd, 1010
To better hopes his more attentive mind
Labouring had rais'd, and thus to Eve repli'd.
  "Eve, thy contempt of life and pleasure seems
To argue in thee something more sublime
And excellent than what thy mind contemns; 1015
But self-destruction therefore sought, refutes
That excellence thought in thee, and implies,
Not thy contempt, but anguish and regret
For loss of life and pleasure overlov'd.
Or if thou covet death, as utmost end 1020
Of misery, so thinking to evade
The penalty pronounc't, doubt not but God
Hath wiselier arm'd his vengeful ire than so
To be forestall'd; much more I fear lest Death
So snatcht will not exempt us from the pain 1025
We are by doom to pay; rather such acts
Of cóntomácy° will provoke the highest
To make death in us live: Then let us seek
Some safer resolution, which methinks
I have in view, calling to mind with heed 1030
Part of our Sentence, that thy Seed shall bruise
The Serpent's head; piteous amends, unless
Be meant, whom I conjecture, our grand Foe

---

996 **present** in your presence. 1000 **make short** lose no time. 1027 **cón-tumácy** resistance to authority, with a specifically legal application.

Satan, who in the Serpent hath contriv'd
1035 Against us this deceit: to crush his head
Would be revenge indeed; which will be lost
By death brought on ourselves, or childless days
Resolv'd, as thou proposest; so our Foe
Shall 'scape his punishment ordain'd, and wee
1040 Instead shall double ours upon our heads.
No more be mention'd then of violence
Against ourselves, and wilful barrenness,
That cuts us off from hope, and savours only
Rancour and pride, impatience and despite,
1045 Reluctance against God and his just yoke
Laid on our Necks. Remember with what mild
And gracious temper he both heard and judg'd
Without wrath or reviling; wee expected
Immediate dissolution, which we thought
1050 Was meant by Death that day, when lo, to thee
Pains only in Child-bearing were foretold,
And bringing forth, soon recompens't with joy,
Fruit of thy Womb: On mee the Curse aslope
Glanc'd on the ground, with labour I must earn
1055 My bread; what harm? Idleness had been worse;
My labour will sustain me; and lest Cold
Or Heat should injure us, his timely care
Hath unbesought provided, and his hands
Cloth'd us unworthy, pitying while he judg'd;
1060 How much more, if we pray him, will his ear
Be open, and his heart to pity incline,
And teach us further by what means to shun
Th'inclement Seasons, Rain, Ice, Hail and Snow,
Which now the Sky with various Face begins
1065 To show us in this Mountain, while the Winds
Blow moist and keen, shattering the graceful locks
Of these fair spreading Trees; which bids us seek
Some better shroud,° some better warmth to cherish
Our Limbs benumb'd, ere this diurnal Star
1070 Leave cold the Night, how we his gather'd beams
Reflected, may with matter sere° foment,°

1068 **shroud** shelter.   1071 **sere** dry.   1071 **foment** stimulate to heat.

Or by collision of two bodies grind
The Air attrite° to Fire, as late the Clouds
Justling or pusht with Winds rude in their shock
Tine° the slant Lightning, whose thwart flame driv'n
    down   *1075*
Kindles the gummy bark of Fir or Pine,
And sends a comfortable heat from far,
Which might supply the Sun: such Fire to use,
And what may else be remedy or cure
To evils which our own misdeeds have wrought,   *1080*
Hee will instruct us praying, and of Grace
Beseeching him, so as we need not fear
To pass commodiously this life, sustain'd
By him with many comforts, till we end
In dust, our final rest and native home.   *1085*
What better can we do, than to the place
Repairing where he judg'd us, prostrate fall
Before him reverent, and there confess
Humbly our faults, and pardon beg, with tears
Watering the ground, and with our sighs the Air   *1090*
Frequenting,° sent from hearts contrite, in sign
Of sorrow unfeign'd, and humiliation meek.
Undoubtedly he will relent and turn
From has displeasure; in whose look serene,
When angry most he seem'd and most severe.   *1095*
What else but favour, grace, and mercy shone?"
      So spake our Father penitent, nor Eve
Felt less remorse: they forthwith to the place
Repairing where he judg'd them prostrate fell
Before him reverent, and both confess'd   *1100*
Humbly their faults, and pardon begg'd, with tears
Watering the ground, and with their sighs the Air
Frequenting, sent from hearts contrite, in sign
Of sorrow unfeign'd, and humiliation meek.

1073 **attrite** by friction.   1075 **Tine** ignite.   1091 **Frequenting** thronging.

BOOK XI

THE ARGUMENT

The Son of God presents to his Father the Prayers of our
first Parents now repenting, and intercedes for them: God
accepts them, but declares that they must no longer abide
in Paradise; sends Michael with a Band of Cherubim to
dispossess them; but first to reveal to Adam future things:
Michael's coming down. Adam shows to Eve certain
signs; he discerns Michael's approach, goes out to meet
him: the Angel denounces their departure. Eve's Lamentation. Adam pleads, but submits: The Angel leads him
up to a high Hill, sets before him in vision what shall happen till the Flood.

Thus they in lowliest plight repentant stood
Praying, for from the Mercy-seat above
Prevenient° Grace descending had remov'd
The stony from their hearts, and made new flesh
5   Regenerate grow instead, that sighs now breath'd
Unutterable, which the Spirit of prayer
Inspir'd, and wing'd for Heav'n with speedier flight
Than loudest Oratory: yet their port
Not of mean suitors, nor important less
10   Seem'd their Petition, than when th'ancient Pair
In Fables old, less ancient yet than these,
Deucalion and chaste Pyrrha° to restore
The Race of Mankind drown'd, before the Shrine
Of Themis° stood devout. To Heav'n their prayers
15   Flew up, nor miss'd the way, by envious winds
Blown vagabond or frustrate: in they pass'd

---

3 **Prevenient** a theological term for God's grace, preceding repentance
and predisposing the heart. 12 **Deucalion . . . Pyrrha** classical counterparts to Noah and his wife. 14 **Themis** goddess of justice.

Dimensionless° through Heav'nly doors; then clad
With incense, where the Golden Altar fum'd,
By their great Intercessor, came in sight
Before the Father's Throne: Them the glad Son   20
Presenting, thus to intercede began.
          "See Father, what first fruits on Earth are
                sprung
From thy implanted Grace in Man, these Sighs
And Prayers, which in this Golden Censer, mixt
With Incense, I thy Priest before thee bring,   25
Fruits of more pleasing savour from thy seed
Sown with contrition in his heart, than those
Which his own hand manuring° all the Trees
Of Paradise could have produc't, ere fall'n
From innocence. Now therefore bend thine ear   30
To supplication, hear his sighs though mute;
Unskilful with what words to pray, let mee
Interpret for him, mee his Advocate
And propitiation, all his works on mee
Good or not good engraft, my Merit those   35
Shall perfect, and for these my Death shall pay.
Accept me, and in mee from these receive
The smell of peace toward Mankind, let him live
Before thee reconcil'd, at least his days
Number'd, though sad, till Death, his doom (which I   40
To mitigate thus plead, not to reverse)
To better life shall yield him, where with mee
All my redeem'd may dwell in joy and bliss,
Made one with me as I with thee am one."
          To whom the Father, without Cloud, serene.   45
"All thy request for Man, accepted Son,
Obtain, all thy request was my Decree:
But longer in that Paradise to dwell,
The Law I gave to Nature him forbids:
Those pure immortal Elements that know   50
No gross, no unharmonious mixture foul,
Eject him tainted now, and purge him off
As a distemper, gross to air as gross,
And mortal food, as may dispose him best

17 **Dimensionless** immaterial.   28 **manuring** see IV 628.

55 For dissolution° wrought by Sin, that first
Distemper'd all things, and of incorrupt
Corrupted. I at first with two fair gifts
Created him endow'd, with Happiness
And Immortality: that fondly lost,
60 This other serv'd but to eternize woe;
Till I provided Death; so Death becomes
His final remedy, and after Life
Tri'd in sharp tribulation, and refin'd
By Faith and faithful works, to second Life,
65 Wak't in the renovation of the just,
Resigns him up with Heav'n and Earth renew'd.
But let us call to Synod all the Blest
Through Heav'n's wide bounds; from them I will not
        hide
My judgements, how with Mankind I proceed,
70 As how with peccant° Angels late they saw;
And in their state, though firm, stood more confirm'd."
        He ended, and the Son gave signal high
To the bright Minister that watch'd, hee blew
His Trumpet, heard in Oreb since perhaps
75 When God descended, and perhaps once more
To sound at general Doom. Th'Angelic blast
Fill'd all the Regions: from their blissful Bow'rs
Of Amaranthine Shade, Fountain or Spring,
By the waters of Life, where'er they sat
80 In fellowships of joy: the Sons of Light
Hasted, resorting to the Summons high,
And took their Seats; till from his Throne supreme
Th'Almighty thus pronounc'd his sovran Will.
        "O Sons, like one of us Man is become
85 To know both Good and Evil, since his taste
Of that defended° Fruit; but let him boast
His knowledge of Good lost, and Evil got,
Happier, had it suffic'd him to have known
Good by itself, and Evil not at all.
90 He sorrows now, repents, and prays contríte,
My motions° in him, longer than they move,
His heart I know, how variable and vain

55 **dissolution** dissoluteness and eventual death. 70 **peccant** sin-
ning. 86 **defended** forbidden. 91 **motions** workings of God is the soul
(theological).

Self-left. Lest therefore his now bolder hand
Reach also of the Tree of Life, and eat,
And live for ever, dream at least to live   95
For ever, to remove him I decree,
And send him from the Garden forth to Till
The Ground whence he was taken, fitter soil.
      Michael, this my behest have thou in charge,
Take to thee from among the Cherubim   100
Thy choice of flaming Warriors, lest the Fiend
Or in behalf of° Man, or to invade
Vacant possession some new trouble raise:
Haste thee, and from the Paradise of God
Without remorse° drive out the sinful Pair,   105
From hallow'd ground th'unholy, and denounce°
To them and to their Progeny from thence
Perpetual banishment. Yet lest they faint
At the sad Sentence rigorously urg'd,
For I behold them soft'n'd and with tears   110
Bewailing their excess,° all terror hide.
If patiently thy bidding they obey,
Dismiss them not disconsolate; reveal
To Adam what shall came in future days,
As I shall thee enlighten, intermix   115
My Cov'nant in the Woman's seed renew'd;
So send them forth, though sorrowing, yet in peace:
And on the East side of the Garden place,
Where entrance up from Eden easiest climbs,
Cherubic watch, and of a Sword the flame   120
Wide waving, all approach far off to fright,
And guard all passage to the Tree of Life:
Lest Paradise a réceptácle prove
To Spirits foul, and all my Trees their prey,
With whose stol'n Fruit Man once more to delude."   125
      He ceas'd; and th'Archangelic Power prepar'd
For swift descent, with him the Cohort bright
Of watchful Cherubim; four faces each
Had, like a double Janus,° all their shape
Spangl'd with eyes more numerous than those   130

102 **in behalf of** possibly "with regard to," possibly "claiming to act in
the name of" (see line 125).   105 **remorse** compunction.   106 **denounce**
formally announce.   111 **excess** violation.   129 **Janus** Roman god with
two faces.

Or Argus,° and more wakeful than to drowze,
Charm'd with Arcadian Pipe, the Pastoral Reed
Of Hermes, or his opiate Rod.° Meanwhile
To resalute the World with sacred Light
135 Leucothea° wak'd, and with fresh dews imbalm'd
The Earth, when Adam and first Matron Eve
Had ended now their Orisons, and found,
Strength added from above, new hope to spring
Out of despair, joy, but with fear yet linkt;
140 Which thus to Eve his welcome words renew'd.
        "Eve, easily may Faith admit, that all
The good which we enjoy, from Heav'n descends
But that from us aught should ascend to Heav'n
So prevalent° as to concern the mind
145 Of God high-blest, or to incline his will,
Hard to belief may seem; yet this will Prayer,
Or one short sigh of human breath, up-borne
Ev'n to the Seat of God. For since I sought
By Prayer th'offended Deity to appease,
150 Kneel'd and before him humbl'd all my heart,
Methought I saw him placable and mild,
Bending his ear; persuasion in me grew
That I was heard with favour; peace return'd
Home to my breast, and to my memory
155 His promise, that thy Seed shall bruise our Foe;
Which then not minded in dismay, yet now
Assures me that the bitterness of death
Is past, and we shall live. Whence Hail to thee,
Eve rightly call'd,° Mother of all Mankind,
160 Mother of all things living, since by thee
Man is to live, and all things live for Man."
        To whom thus Eve with sad demeanour meek.
"Ill worthy I such title should belong
To me transgressor, who for thee ordain'd
165 A help, became thy snare; to mee reproach
Rather belongs, distrust and all dispraise:
But infinite in pardon was my Judge,
That I who first brought Death on all, am grac't

131 **Argus** with his hundred eyes on guard. 133 **Rod** The wand of
Hermes (Mercury) put Argus to sleep. 135 **Leucothea** goddess of
dawn. 144 **prevalent** strongly prevailing. 159 **rightly call'd** "Eve" was
said to mean "Life."

The source of life; next favourable thou,
Who highly thus to entitle me vouchsaf'st,   170
Far other name deserving. But the Field
To labour calls us now with sweat impos'd,
Though after sleepless Night; for see the Morn,
All unconcern'd will our unrest, begins
Her rosy progress smiling; let us forth,   175
I never from thy side henceforth to stray,
Where'er our day's work lies, though now enjoin'd
Laborious, till day droop; while here we dwell,
What can be toilsome in these pleasant Walks?
Here let us live, though in fall'n state, content."   180
          So spake, so wish'd much-humbl'd Eve, but
                Fate
Subscribed not; Nature first gave Signs, imprest
On Bird, Beast, Air, Air suddenly eclips'd
After short blush of Morn; nigh in her sight
The Bird of Jove,° stoopt° from his airy tow'r,   185
Two Birds of gayest plume before him drove:
Down from a Hill the Beast that reigns° in Woods,
First Hunter then, pursu'd a gentle brace,
Goodliest of all the Forest, Hart and Hind;
Direct to th'Eastern Gate was bent their flight.   190
Adam observ'd, and with his Eye the chase
Pursuing, not unmov'd to Eve thus spake.
          "O Eve, some further change awaits us nigh,
Which Heav'n by these mute signs in Nature shows
Forerunners of his purpose, or to warn   195
Us haply too secure° of our discharge
From penalty, because from death releast
Some days; how long, and what till then our life,
Who knows, or more than this, that we are dust,
And thither must return and be no more.   200
Why else this double object in our sight
Of flight pursu'd in th'Air and o'er the ground
One way the self-same hour? why in the East
Darkness ere Day's mid-course, and Morning light
More orient in yon Western Cloud that draws   205
O'er the blue Firmament a radiant white,

185 **Bird of Jove** eagle. 185 **stoopt** plunged. 187 **Beast that reigns** lion. 196 **secure** confident.

And slow descends, with something heav'nly fraught."
        He err'd not, for by this the heavenly Bands
Down from a Sky of Jasper 'lighted now
210 In Paradise, and on a Hill made halt,
A glorious Apparition, had not doubt
And carnal fear that day dimm'd Adam's eye.
Not that more glorious, when the Angels met
Jacob in Mahanaim, where he saw
215 The field Pavilion'd with his Guardians bright;
Nor that which on the flaming Mount appear'd
In Dothan, cover'd with a Camp of Fire,
Against the Syrian King, who to surprise
One man,° Assassin-like had levied War,
220 War unproclaim'd. The Princely Hierarch
In their bright stand,° there left his Powers to seize
Possession of the Garden; hee alone,
To find where Adam shelter'd, took his way,
Not unperceiv'd of Adam, who to Eve,
225 While the great Visitant approach'd, thus spake.
        "Eve, now expect great tidings, which perhaps
Of us will soon determine, or impose
New Laws to be observ'd; for I descry
From yonder blazing Cloud that veils the Hill
230 One of the heav'nly Host, and by his Gait
None of the meanest, some great Potentate
Or of the Thrones above, such Majesty
Invests him coming; yet not terrible,
That I should fear, nor sociably mild,
235 As Raphaël, that I should much confide,
But solemn and sublime, whom not to offend,
With reverence I must meet, and thou retire."
He ended; and th'Arch-Angel soon drew nigh,
Not in his shape Celestial, but as Man
240 Clad to meet Man; over his lucid° Arms
A military Vest of purple shone'd
Livelier than Meliboean,° or the grain°
Of Sarra,° worn by Kings and Heroes old
In time of Truce; Iris° had dipt the woof;

219 **One man** Elisha, protected against the Syrians by a miracle.
221 **stand** station (military).   240 **lucid** bright.   242 **Meliboean** the purple
dye from Thessaly.   242 **grain** dye.   243 **Sarra** Tyre.   244 **Iris** goddess
of the rainbow.

His starry Helm unbuckl'd show'd him prime   *245*
In Manhood where Youth ended; by his side
As in a glistering Zodiac° hung the Sword,
Satan's dire dread, and in his hand the Spear.
Adam bow'd low, hee Kingly from his State
Inclin'd not, but his coming thus declar'd.   *250*
      "Adam, Heav'n's high behest no Preface needs:
Sufficient that thy Prayers are heard, and Death,
Then due by sentence when thou didst transgress,
Defeated of his seizure many days
Giv'n thee of Grace, wherein thou may'st repent,   *255*
And one bad act with many deeds well done
May'st cover: well may then thy Lord appeas'd
Redeem thee quite from Death's rapacious claim;
But longer in this Paradise to dwell
Permits not; to remove thee I am come,   *260*
And send thee from the Garden forth to till
The ground whence thou wast tak'n, fitter Soil."
      He added not, for Adam at the news
Heart-struck with chilling grip of sorrow stood,
That all his senses bound; Eve, who unseen   *265*
Yet all had heard, with audible lament
Discover'd soon the place of her retire.
      "O unexpected stroke, worse than of Death!
Must I thus leave thee Paradise? thus leave
Thee Native Soil, these happy Walks and Shades,   *270*
Fit haunt of Gods? where I had hope to spend,
Quiet though sad, the respite° of that day
That must be mortal to us both. O flow'rs,
That never will in other Climate grow,
My early visitation, and my last   *275*
At Ev'n, which I bred up with tender hand
From the first op'ning bud, and gave ye Names,
Who now shall rear ye to the Sun, or rank
Your Tribes, and water from th'ambrosial Fount?
Thee lastly nuptial Bow'r, by mee adorn'd   *280*
With what to sight or smell was sweet; from thee
How shall I part, and whither wander down
Into a lower World, to° this obscure

247 **Zodiac** the belt of the constellations.   272 **respite** time granted till
the coming.   283 **to** compared to.

And wild, how shall we breathe in other Air
285 Less pure, accustom'd to immortal Fruits?"
          Whom thus the Angel interrupted mild.
"Lament not Eve, but patiently resign
What justly thou halt lost; nor set thy heart,
Thus over-fond, on that which is not thine;
290 Thy going is not lonely, with thee goes
Thy Husband, him to follow thou art bound;
Where he abides, think there thy native soil."
          Adam by this from the cold sudden damp
Recovering, and his scatter'd spirits return'd,
295 To Michael thus his humble words address'd.
          "Celestial, whether among the Thrones, or
              nam'd
Of them the Highest, for such of shape may seem
Prince above Princes, gently hast thou told
Thy message, which might else in telling wound,
300 And in performing end us; what besides
Of sorrow and dejection and despair
Our frailty can sustain, thy tidings bring,
Departure from this happy place, our sweet
Recess,° and only consolation left
305 Familiar to our eyes, all places else
Inhospitable appear and desolate,
Nor knowing us nor known: and if by prayer
Incessant I could hope to change the will
Of him who all things can, I would not cease
310 To weary him with my assiduous cries:
But prayer against his absolute Decree
No more avails than breath against the wind,
Blown stifling back on him that breathes it forth:
Therefore to his great bidding I submit.
315 This most afflicts me, that departing hence,
As from his face I shall be hid, depriv'd
His blessed count'nance; here I could frequent,
With worship, place by place where he vouchsaf'd
Presence Divine, and to my Sons relate;
320 On this Mount he appear'd, under this Tree
Stood visible, among these Pines his voice
I heard, here with him at this Fountain talk'd:

304 **Recess** place of retirement.

So many grateful° Altars I would rear
Of grassy Turf, and pile up every Stone
Of lustre from the brook, in memory,   325
Or monument to Ages, and thereon
Offer sweet smelling Gums and Fruits and Flow'rs:
In yonder nether World where shall I seek
His bright appearances, or footstep trace?
For though I fled him angry, yet recall'd   330
To life prolong'd and promis'd Race, I now
Gladly behold though but his utmost skirts
Of glory, and far off his steps adore."
      To whom thus Michael with regard benign.
"Adam, though know'st Heav'n his, and all the Earth,   335
Not this Rock only; his Omnipresence fills
Land, Sea, and Air, and every kind that lives,
Fomented by his virtual° power and warm'd:
All th'Earth he gave thee to possess and rule,
No déspicáble gift; surmise not then   340
His presence to these narrow bounds confin'd
Of Paradise or Eden: this had been
Perhaps thy Capital Seat, from whence had spread
All generations, and had hither come
From all the ends of th'Earth, to celebrate   345
And reverence thee their great Progenitor.
But this preeminence thou hast lost, brought down
To dwell on even ground now with thy Sons:
Yet doubt not but in Valley and in Plain
God is as here, and will be found alike   350
Present, and of his presence many a sign
Still following thee, still compassing thee round
With goodness and paternal Love, his Face
Express, and of his steps the track Divine.
Which that thou may'st believe, and be confirm'd,   355
Ere thou from hence depart, know I am sent
To show thee what shall come in future days
To thee and to thy Offspring; good with bad
Expect to hear, supernal Grace contending
With sinfulness of Men; thereby to learn   360
True patience, and to temper joy with fear

---

323 **grateful** pleasing to God and expressing gratitude.   338 **virtual** inherently life-giving.

And pious sorrow, equally inur'd
By moderation either state to bear,
Prosperous or adverse: so shalt thou lead
365 Safest thy life, and best prepar'd endure
Thy mortal passage when it comes. Ascend
This Hill; let Eve (for I have drencht her eyes)
Here sleep below while thou to foresight wak'st,
As once thou slep'st, while Shee to life was form'd."
370   To whom thus Adam gratefully repli'd.
"Ascend, I follow thee, safe Guide, the path
Thou lead'st me, and to the hand of Heav'n submit,
However chast'ning, to the evil turn
My obvious° breast, arming to overcome
375 By suffering, and earn rest from labour won,
If so I may attain." So both ascend
In the Visions of God: It was a Hill
Of Paradise the highest, from whose top
The Hemisphere of Earth in clearest Ken
380 Stretcht out to amplest reach of prospect lay.
Not higher that Hill nor wider looking round,
Whereon for different cause the Tempter set
Our second Adam in the Wilderness,
To show him all Earth's Kingdoms and their Glory.
385 His Eye might there command wherever stood
City of old or modern Fame, the Seat
Of mightiest Empire, from the destin'd Walls
Of Cambalu, seat of Cathaian Khan
And Samarkand by Oxus,° Temir's° Throne,
390 To Paquin° of Sinæan° Kings, and thence
To Agra and Lahor of great Mogúl
Down to the golden Chersonese,° or where
The Persian in Ecbatan sat, or since
In Hispahan, or where the Russian Czar
395 In Moscow, or the Sultan in Bizance,°
Turkéstan-born; nor could his eye not ken
Th'Empire of Negus° to his utmost Port
Ercoco and the less Maritine Kings
Mombaza, and Quiloa, and Melind,°

374 **obvious** exposed.   389 **Oxus** Asian river.   389 **Temir** the Tartar
ruler Timur.   390 **Paquin** Peking.   390 **Sinæan** Chinese.   392 **Chersonese** East Indies.   395 **Bizance** Byzantium.   397 **Negus** title of Abyssinian kings.   399 **Mombaza ... Melind** in East Africa.

And Sofala thought° Ophir, to the Realm   400
Of Congo, and Angola farthest South;
Or thence from Niger Flood to Atlas Mount
The Kingdoms of Almansor,° Fez and Sus,
Morocco and Algiers, and Tremisen;
On Europe thence, and where Rome was to sway   405
The World: in Spirit perhaps he also saw
Rich Mexico the seat of Motezume,°
And Cusco° in Peru, the richer seat
Of Atabalipa,° and yet unspoil'd°
Guiana, whose great City Geryon's Sons°   410
Call El Dorado: but to nobler sights
Michael from Adam's eyes the Film remov'd
Which that false Fruit that promis'd clearer sight
Had bred; then purg'd with Euphrasy and Rue
The visual Nerve, for he had much to see;   415
And from the Well of Life three drops instill'd.
So deep the power of these Ingredients pierc'd,
Ev'n to the inmost seat of mental sight,
That Adam now enforc't to close his eyes,
Sunk down and all his Spirits became intranst: 420
But him the gentle Angel by the hand
Soon rais'd, and his attention thus recall'd.
          "Adam, now ope thine eyes, and first behold
Th'effects which thy original crime hath wrought
In some to spring from thee, who never touch'd   425
Th'excepted Tree,° nor with the Snake conspir'd,
Nor sinn'd thy sin, yet from that sin derive
Corruption to bring forth more violent deeds."
          His eyes he op'n'd, and beheld a field,
Part arable and tilth, whereon were Sheaves   430
New reapt, the other part sheep-walks and folds;
I'th' midst an Altar as the Land-mark stood
Rustic, of grassy sward; thither anon
A sweaty Reaper from his Tillage brought
First-Fruits, the green Ear, and the yellow Sheaf,   435
Uncull'd, as came to hand; a Shepherd next

400 **thought** thought to be the legendary region.   403 **Almansor** Muslim
ruler.   407 **Motezume** Montezuma, Aztec ruler.   408 **Cusco** Inca capital
409 **Atabalipa** Inca ruler.   409 **unspoil'd** unplundered.   410 **Geryon's
Sons** the Spaniards.   426 **Th'excepted Tree** a traditional phrase for the
Tree of Knowledge ("excluded, forbidden").

More meek came with the Firstlings of his Flock
Choicest and best; then sacrificing, laid
The Inwards and their Fat, with Incense strew'd,
440 On the cleft Wood, and all due Rites perform'd.
His Off'ring soon propitious Fire from Heav'n
Consum'd with nimble glance, and grateful steam;
The other's not, for his was not sincere;°
Whereat hee inly rag'd, and as they talk'd,
445 Smote him into the Midriff with a stone
That beat out life; he fell, and deadly pale
Groan'd out his Soul with gushing blood effus'd.
Much at that sight was Adam in his heart
Dismay'd, and thus in haste to th'Angel cri'd.
450   "O Teacher, some great mischief hath befall'n
To that meek man, who well had sacrific'd;
Is Piety thus and pure Devotion paid?"
          T'whom Michael thus, hee also mov'd, repli'd.
"These two are Brethren, Adam, and to come
455 Out of thy loins; th'unjust the just hath slain,
For envy that his Brother's Offering found
From Heav'n acceptance; but the bloody Fact°
Will be aveng'd, and th'other's Faith approv'd
Lose no reward, though here thou see him die,
460 Rolling in dust and gore." To which our Sire.
          "Alas, both for the deed and for the cause!
But have I now seen Death? Is this the way
I must return to native dust? O sight
Of terror, foul and ugly to behold,
465 Horrid to think, how horrible to feel!"
          To whom thus Michael. "Death thou hast seen
In his first shape on man; but many shapes
Of Death, and many are the ways that lead
To his grim Cave, all dismal; yet to sense
470 More terrible at th'entrance than within.
Some, as thou saw'st, by violent stroke shall die,
By Fire, Flood, Famine, by Intemperance more
In Meats and Drinks, which on the Earth shall bring
Diseases dire, of which a monstrous crew
475 Before thee shall appear; that thou may'st know
What misery th'inabstinence of Eve

443 **sincere** including the literal "pure, uncontaminated."   457 **Fact** deed.

Shall bring on men." Immediately a place
Before his eyes appear'd, sad, noisome, dark,
A Lazar-house it seem'd, wherein were laid
Numbers of all diseas'd, all maladies   480
Of ghastly Spasm, or racking torture, qualms°
Of heart-sick Agony, all feverous kinds,
Convulsions, Epilepsies, fierce Catarrhs,
Intestine Stone and Ulcer, Colic pangs,
Demoniac Frenzy, moping Melancholy   485
And Moon-struck madness, pining Atrophy,
Marasmus,° and wide-wasting Pestilence,°
Dropsies, and Asthmas, and Joint-racking Rheums.
Dire was the tossing, deep the groans, despair
Tended the sick busiest from Couch to Couch;   490
And over them triumphant Death his Dart
Shook, but delay'd to strike, though oft invok't
With vows, as their chief good, and final hope.
Sight so deform what heart of Rock could long
Dry-ey'd behold? Adam could not, but wept,   495
Though not of Woman born; compassion quell'd
His best of Man, and gave him up to tears
A space, till firmer thoughts restrain'd excess,
And scarce recovering words his plaint renew'd.
     "O miserable Mankind, to what fall   500
Degraded, to what wretched state reserv'd!
Better end here unborn. Why is life giv'n
To be thus wrested from us? rather why
Obtruded on us thus? who if we knew
What we receive, would either not accept   505
Life offer'd, or soon beg to lay it down,
Glad to be so dismisst in peace. Can thus
Th'Image of God in man created once
So goodly and erect, though faulty since,
To such unsightly sufferings be debas't   510
Under inhuman pains? Why should not Man,
Retaining still Divine similitude
In part, from such deformities be free,
And for his Maker's Image sake exempt?"

481 **qualms** plagues.   487 **Marasmus** consumption.   485–87 **Demoniac . . .
Pestilence** Lines added *1674*.

"Their Maker's Image," answer'd Michael,
515   "then
Forsook them, when themselves they vilifi'd
To serve ungovern'd appetite, and took
His Image whom they serv'd, a brutish vice,
Inductive mainly° to the sin of Eve.
520 Therefore so abject is their punishment,
Disfiguring not God's likeness, but their own,
Or if his likeness, by themselves defac't
While they pervert pure Nature's healthful rules
To loathsome sickness, worthily, since they
525 God's Image did not reverence in themselves."
          "I yield it just," said Adam, "and submit.
But is there yet no other way, besides
These painful passages, how we may came
To Death, and mix with our connatural dust?"
530   "There is," said Michael, "if thou well observe
The rule of not too much, by temperance taught
In what thou eat'st and drink'st, seeking from thence
Due nourishment, not gluttonous delight,
Till many years over thy head return:
535 So may'st thou live, till like ripe Fruit thou drop
Into thy Mother's lap, or be with ease
Gather'd, not harshly pluckt, for death mature:
This is old age; but then thou must outlive
Thy youth, thy strength, thy beauty, which will change
540 To wither'd weak and gray; thy Senses then
Obtuse, of taste of pleasure must forgo,
To what thou hast, and for the Air of youth
Hopeful and cheerful, in thy blood will reign
A melancholy damp of cold and dry
545 To weigh thy spirits down, and last consume
The Balm of Life." To whom our Ancestor.
          "Henceforth I fly not Death, nor would pro-
          long
Life much, bent rather how I may be quit
Fairest and easiest of this cumbrous charge,
550 Which I must keep till my appointed day
Of rend'ring up, and patiently attend

519 **Inductive mainly** powerful as inducement.

My dissolution." Michael repli'd.°
      "Nor love thy Life, nor hate; but what thou
         liv'st
Live well, how long or short permit to Heav'n:
And now prepare thee for another sight."   555
      He look'd and saw a spacious Plain, whereon
Were Tents of various hue; by some were herds
Of Cattle grazing: others, whence the sound
Of Instruments that made melodious chime
Was heard, of Harp and Organ; and who° mov'd   560
Their stops and chords was seen: his volant° touch
Instínct° through all proportions low and high
Fled and pursu'd transverse the resonant fugue.°
In other part stood one° who at the Forge
Labouring, two massy clods of Iron and Brass   565
Had melted (whether found where casual° fire
Had wasted woods on Mountain or in Vale,
Down to the veins of Earth, thence gliding hot
To some Cave's mouth, or whether washt by stream
From underground) the liquid Ore he drain'd   570
Into fit moulds prepar'd; from which he form'd
First his own Tools; then, what might else be wrought
Fusile° or grav'n in metal. After these,
But on the hither side a different sort
From the high neighbouring Hills, which was their
    Seat,   575
Down to the Plain descended: by their guise
Just men they seem'd, and all their study bent
To worship God aright, and know his works
Not hid, nor those things last which might preserve
Freedom and Peace to men: they on the Plain   580
Lang had not walkt, when from the Tents behold
A Bevy of fair Women, richly gay
Gems and wanton dress; to the Harp they sung
Soft amorous Ditties, and in dance came on:
The Men though grave, ey'd them, and let their eyes 585
Rove without rein, till in the amorous Net
Fast caught, they lik'd, and each his liking chose;

551–52 *1674*; "Of rend'ring up." Michael to him replied. *1667*.   560 **who**
Jubal (Genesis 4:21).   561 **volant** flying.   562 **Instínct** skillfully impelled.   563 **fugue** from Latin *fuga*, flight.   564 **one** Tubal Cain.   566 **casual** accidental.   573 **Fusile** by melting or casting.

And now of love they treat till th'Ev'ning Star°
Love's Harbinger appear'd; then all in heat
590 They light the Nuptial Torch, and bid invoke
Hymen, then first to marriage Rites invok't;
With Feast and Music all the Tents resound.
Such happy interview and fair event
Of love and youth not lost, Songs, Garlands, Flow'rs,
595 And charming Symphonies attach'd° the heart
Of Adam, soon inclin'd to admit delight,
The bent of Nature; which he thus express'd.
        "True opener of mine eyes, prime Angel blest,
Much better seems this Vision, and more hope
600 Of peaceful days portends, than those two past;
Those were of hate and death, or pain much worse,
Here Nature seems fulfill'd in all her ends."
        To whom thus Michael. "Judge not what is
        best
By pleasure, though to Nature seeming meet,
605 Created, as thou art, to nobler end
Holy and pure, conformity divine.
Those Tents thou saw'st so pleasant, were the Tents
Of wickedness, wherein shall dwell his Race
Who slew his Brother; studious they appear
610 Of Arts that polish Life, Inventors rare,
Unmindful of their Maker, though his Spirit
Taught them, but they his gifts acknowledg'd none.
Yet they a beauteous offspring shall beget;
For that fair female Troop thou saw'st, that seem'd
615 Of Goddesses, so blithe, so smooth, so gay,
Yet empty of all good wherein consists
Woman's domestic honour and chief praise;
Bred only and completed to the taste
Of lustful appetence, to sing, to dance,
620 To dress, and troll the Tongue, and roll the Eye.
To these that sober Race of Men, whose lives
Religious titl'd them the Sons of God,
Shall yield up all their virtue, all their fame
Ignobly, to the trains and to the smiles
625 Of these fair Atheists, and now swim in joy,
(Erelong to swim at large) and laugh; for which

588 **Ev'ning Star** Venus.   595 **attach'd** laid hold of.

The world erelong a world of tears must weep."
      To whom thus Adam of short joy bereft.
"O pity and shame, that they who to live well
Enter'd so fair, should turn aside to tread   630
Paths indirect, or in the mid-way faint!
But still I see the tenor of Man's woe
Holds on the same, from Woman to begin."
      "From Man's effeminate° slackness it begins,"
Said th'Angel, "who should better hold his place   635
By wisdom, and superior gifts receiv'd.
But now prepare thee for another Scene."
      He look'd and saw wide Territory spread
Before him, Towns, and rural works between,
Cities of Men with lofty Gates and Tow'rs,   640
Concourse in Arms, fierce Faces threat'ning War,
Giants of mighty Bone, and bold emprise;°
Part wield their Arms, part curb the foaming Steed,
Single or in Array of Battle rang'd
Both Horse and Foot, nor idly must'ring stood;   645
One way a Band select from forage drives
A herd of Beeves, fair Oxen and fair Kine
From a fat Meadow ground; or fleecy Flock,
Ewes and their bleating Lambs over the Plain,
Their Booty; scarce with Life the Shepherds fly,   650
But call in aid, which makes° a bloody Fray;
With cruel Tournament the Squadrons join;
Where Cattle pastur'd late, now scatter'd lies
With Carcasses and Arms th'ensanguin'd Field
Deserted: Others to a City strong   655
Lay Siege, encamp; by Battery, Scale, and Mine,
Assaulting; others from the Wall defend
With Dart and Jav'lin, Stones and sulphurous Fire;
On each hand slaughter and gigantic° deeds.
In other part the scepter'd Heralds call   660
To Council in the City Gates: anon
Grey-headed men and grave, with Warriors mixt,
Assemble, and Harangues are heard, but soon
In factious opposition, till at last

634 **effeminate** unmanly, with suggestion of "dominated by women."
642 **emprise** martial enterprise.   651 **makes** *1674*; tacks *1667*.   659 **gigan-tic** giantlike.

665   Of middle Age one° rising, eminent
     In wise deport, spake much of Right and Wrong,
     Of Justice, of Religion, Truth and Peace,
     And Judgement from above: him old and young
     Exploded,° and had seiz'd with violent hands,
670   Had not a Cloud descending snatch'd him thence
     Unseen amid the throng: so violence
     Proceeded, and Oppression, and Sword-Law
     Through all the Plain, and refuge none was found.
     Adam was all in tears, and to his guide
675   Lamenting turn'd full sad; "O what are these,
     Death's Ministers, not Men, who thus deal Death
     Inhumanly to men, and multiply
     Ten-thousand-fold the sin of him who slew
     His Brother; for of whom such massacre
680   Make they but of their Brethren, men of men?
     But who was that Just Man, whom had not Heav'n
     Rescu'd, had in his Righteousness been lost?"
          To whom thus Michael; "These are the
           product
     Of those ill-mated Marriages thou saw'st;
685   Where good with bad were matcht, who of themselves
     Abhor to join; and by imprudence mixt,
     Produce prodigious Births of body or mind.
     Such were these Giants, men of high renown;
     For in those days Might only shall be admir'd,
690   And Valour and Heroic Virtue call'd;
     To overcome in Battle, and subdue
     Nations, and bring home spoils with infinite
     Man-slaughter, shall be held the highest pitch
     Of human Glory, and for Glory done
695   Of triumph, to be styl'd great Conquerors,
     Patrons of Mankind, Gods, and Sons of Gods,
     Destroyers rightlier call'd and Plagues of men.
     Thus Fame shall be achiev'd, renown on Earth,
     And what most merits fame in silence hid.
700   But hee the seventh from thee, whom thou beheld'st
     The only righteous in a World perverse,
     And therefore hated, therefore so beset

---

665 **Of . . . one** Enoch was very aged, but not for a prophet (GENESIS 5:21–4).   669 **Exploded** hooted at.

With Foes for daring single to be just,
And utter odious Truth, that God would come
To judge them with his Saints: Him the most High   *705*
Rapt in a balmy Cloud with winged Steeds
Did, as thou saw'st, receive, to walk with God
High in Salvation and the Climes of bliss,
Exempt from Death; to show thee what reward
Awaits the good, the rest what punishment;   *710*
Which now direct thine eyes and soon behold."
       He look'd, and saw the face of things quite
         chang'd;
The brazen Throat of War had ceast to roar,
All now was turn'd to jollity and game,
To luxury° and riot,° feast and dance,   *715*
Marrying or prostituting, as befell,
Rape or Adultery, where passing fair
Allur'd them; thence from Cups to civil Broils.
At length a Reverend Sire among them came,
And of their doings great dislike declar'd,   *720*
And testifi'd against their ways; hee oft
Frequented their Assemblies, whereso met,
Triumphs or Festivals, and to them preach'd
Conversion and Repentance, as to Souls
In prison under Judgements imminent: *725*
But all in vain: which when he saw, he ceas'd
Contending, and remov'd his Tents far off;
Then from the Mountain hewing Timber tall,
Began to build a Vessel of huge bulk,
Measur'd by Cubit, length, and breadth, and heighth, *730*
Smear'd round with Pitch, and in the side a door
Contriv'd, and of provisions laid in large
For Man and Beast: when lo a wonder strange!
Of every Beast, and Bird, and Insect small
Came sevens, and pairs, and enter'd in, as taught   *735*
Their order: last the Sire, and his three Sons
With their four Wives; and God made fast the door.
Meanwhile the Southwind rose, and with black wings
Wide hovering, all the Clouds together drove
From under Heav'n; the Hills to their supply   *740*
Vapour, and Exhalation dusk and moist,

715 **luxury** lust.   715 **riot** riotousness.

Sent up amain; and now the thick'n'd Sky
Like a dark Ceiling stood; down rush'd the Rain
Impetuous, and continu'd till the Earth
745 No more was seen; the floating Vessel swum
Uplifted; and secure with beaked prow
Rode tilting o'er the Waves, all dwellings else
Flood overwhelm'd, and them with all their pomp
Deep under water roll'd; Sea cover'd Sea,
750 Sea without shore; and in their Palaces
Where luxury late reign'd, Sea-monsters whelp'd
And stabl'd; of Mankind, so numerous late,
All left, in one small bottom swum embark't.
How didst thou grieve then, Adam, to behold
755 The end of all thy Offspring, end so sad,
Depopulation; thee another Flood,
Of tears and sorrow a Flood thee also drown'd,
And sunk thee as thy Sons; till gently rear'd
By th'Angel, on thy feet thou stood'st at last,
760 Though comfortless, as when a Father mourns
His Children, all in view destroy'd at once;
And scarce to th'Angel utter'dst thus thy plaint.
        "O Visions ill foreseen! better had I
Liv'd ignorant of future, so had borne
765 My part of evil only, each day's lot
Enough to bear; those now, that were dispenst
The burd'n of many Ages, on me 'light
At once, by my foreknowledge gaining Birth
Abortive, to torment me ere their being,
770 With thought that they must be. Let no man seek
Henceforth to be foretold what shall befall
Him or his Children, evil he may be sure,
Which neither his foreknowing can prevent,
And hee the future evil shall no less
775 In apprehension than in substance feel
Grievous to bear: but that care now is past,
Man is not whom to warn: those few escap't
Famine and anguish will at last consume
Wand'ring that wat'ry Desert: I had hope
780 When violence was ceas't, and War on Earth,
All would have then gone well, peace would have
    crown'd
With length of happy days the race of man;

But I was far deceiv'd; for now I see
Peace to corrupt no less than War to waste.
How comes it thus? unfold, Celestial Guide,   785
And whether here the Race of man will end."
To whom thus Michael. "Those whom last thou saw'st
In triumph and luxurious wealth, are they
First seen in acts of prowess eminent
And great exploits, but of true virtue void;   790
Who having spilt much blood, and done much waste
Subduing Nations, and achiev'd thereby
Fame in the World, high titles, and rich prey,
Shall change their course to pleasure, ease, and sloth,
Surfeit, and lust, till wantonness and pride   795
Raise out of friendship hostile deeds in Peace.
The conquer'd also, and enslav'd by War
Shall with their freedom lost all virtue lose
And fear of God, from whom their piety feign'd
In sharp contést of Battle found no aid   800
Against invaders; therefore cold in zeal
Thenceforth shall practise how to live secure,
Worldly or dissolute, on what their Lords
Shall leave them to enjoy; for th'Earth shall bear
More than enough, that temperance may be tri'd:°   805
So all shall turn degenerate, all deprav'd,
Justice and Temperance, Truth and Faith forgot;
One Man except, the only Son of light
In a dark Age, against example good,
Against allurement, custom, and a World   810
Offended; fearless of reproach and scorn,
Or violence, hee of their wicked ways
Shall them admonish, and before them set
The paths of righteousness, how much more safe,
And full of peace, denouncing wrath to come   815
On their impenitence; and shall return
Of them derided, but of God observ'd
The one just Man alive; by his command
Shall build a wondrous Ark, as thou beheld'st,
To save himself and household from amidst   820
A World devote° to universal rack.
No sooner hee with them of Man and Beast

805 **tri'd** tested.   821 **devote** doomed.

Select for life shall in the Ark be lodg'd,
And shelter'd round, but all the Cataracts
825 Of Heav'n set open on the Earth shall pour
Rain day and night, all fountains of the Deep
Broke up, shall heave the Ocean to usurp
Beyond all bounds, till inundation rise
Above the highest Hills: then shall this Mount
830 Of paradise by might of waves be mov'd
Out of his place, push'd by the horned° flood,
With all his verdure spoil'd, and Trees adrift
Down the great River to the op'ning Gulf,
And there take root an Island salt and bare,
835 The haunt of Seals and Orcs,° and Sea-mews' clang.
To teach thee that God áttribútes to place
No sanctity, if none be thither brought
By Men who there frequent, or therein dwell.
And now what further shall ensue, behold.''
840   He look'd, and saw the Ark hull° on the flood,
Which now abated, for the Clouds were fled,
Driv'n by a keen North-wind, that blowing dry
Wrinkl'd the face of Deluge, as decay'd;
And the clear Sun on his wide wat'ry Glass
845 Gaz'd hot, and of the fresh Wave largely drew,
As after thirst, which made their flowing shrink
From standing lake to tripping ebb, that stole
With soft foot towards the deep, who now had stopt
His Sluices, as the Heav'n his windows shut.
850 The Ark no more now floats, but seems on ground
Fast on the top of some high mountain fixt.
And now the tops of Hills as Rocks appear;
With clamour thence the rapid Currents drive
Towards the retreating Sea their furious tide.
855 Forthwith from out the Ark a Raven flies,
And after him, the surer messenger,
A Dove sent forth once and again to spy
Green Tree or ground whereon his foot may 'light;
The second time returning, in his Bill
860 An Olive leaf he brings, pacific sign:
Anon dry ground appears, and from his Ark
The ancient Sire descends with all his Train;

831 **horned** branching.   835 **Orcs** whales.   840 **hull** drift.

Then with uplifted hands, and eyes devout,
Grateful to Heav'n, over his head beholds
A dewy Cloud, and in the Cloud a Bow   *865*
Conspicuous with three listed° colours gay,
Betok'ning peace from God, and Cov'nant new.
Whereat the heart of Adam erst so sad
Greatly rejoiced, and thus his joy broke forth.
        "O thou who° future things canst represent   *870*
As present, Heav'nly instructor, I revive
At this last sight, assur'd that Man shall live
With all the Creatures, and their seed preserve.
Far less I now lament for one whole World
Of wicked Sons destroy'd, than I rejoice   *875*
For one Man found so perfect and so just,
That God vouchsafes to raise another World
From him, and all his anger to forget.
But say, what mean those colour'd streaks in Heav'n,
Distended° as the Brow of God appeas'd,   *880*
Or serve they as a flow'ry verge to bind
The fluid skirts of that same wat'ry Cloud,
Lest it again dissolve and show'r the Earth?"
            To whom th'Archangel. "Dextrously thou
    aim'st;
So willingly doth God remit his Ire,   *885*
Though late repenting him of Man deprav'd,
Griev'd at his heart, when looking down he saw
The whole Earth fill'd with violence, and all flesh
Corrupting each their way; yet those remov'd,
Such grace shall one just Man find in his sight,   *890*
That he relents, not to blot out mankind,
And makes a Covenant never to destroy
The Earth again by flood, nor let the Sea
Surpass his bounds, nor Rain to drown the World
With Man therein or Beast; but when he brings   *895*
Over the Earth a Cloud, will therein set
His triple-colour'd Bow, whereon to look
And call to mind his Cov'nant: Day and Night,
Seed time and Harvest, Heat and hoary Frost
Shall hold their course, till fire purge all things new, *900*
Both Heav'n and Earth, wherein the just shall dwell."

866 **listed** striped.   870 **who** *1674*; that *1667*.   880 **Distended** extended.

BOOK XII

THE ARGUMENT

The Angel Michael continues from the Flood to relate
what shall succeed; then, in the mention of Abraham,
comes by degrees to explain, who that Seed of the Woman
shall be, which was promised Adam and Eve in the Fall;
his Incarnation, Death, Resurrection, and Ascension; the
state of the Church till his second Coming. Adam greatly
satisfied and recomforted by these Relations and Promises descends the Hill with Michael; wakens Eve, who all
this while had slept, but with gentle dreams compos'd to
quietness of mind and submission. Michael in either hand
leads them out of Paradise, the fiery Sword waving behind
them, and the Cherubim taking their Situations to guard
the Place.

As one who in his journey bates° at Noon,
Though bent on speed, so here th'Arch-Angel paus'd
Betwixt the world destroy'd and world restor'd,
If Adam aught perhaps might interpose;
Then with transition sweet new Speech resumes.° 5
"Thus thou hast seen one World begin and end;
And Man as from a second stock proceed.
Much thou hast yet to see, but I perceive
Thy mortal sight to fail; objects divine
Must needs impair and weary human sense: 10
Henceforth what is to come I will relate,
Thou therefore give due audience, and attend.
This second source of Men, while yet but few,
And while the dread of judgement past remains
Fresh in their minds, fearing the Deity, 15
With some regard to what is just and right

1 **bates** stops briefly for rest and refreshment.   1–5 Added *1674*, when
the final Book was divided into two Books.

282

Shall lead their lives, and multiply apace,
Labouring the soil, and reaping plenteous crop,
Corn, wine and oil; and from the herd or flock,
Oft sacrificing Bullock, Lamb, or Kid,   20
With large Wine-offerings pour'd, and sacred Feast
Shall spend their days in joy unblam'd, and dwell
Long time in peace by Families and Tribes
Under paternal rule; till one° shall rise
Of proud ambitious heart, who not content   25
With fair equality, fraternal state,
Will arrogate Dominion undeserv'd
Over his brethren, and quite dispossess
Concord and law of Nature from the Earth;
Hunting (and Men not Beasts shall be his game)   30
With War and hostile snare such as refuse
Subjection to his Empire tyrannous:
A mighty Hunter thence he shall be styl'd
Before the Lord, as in despite of Heav'n,
Or from Heav'n claiming second Sovranty;   35
And from Rebellion shall derive his name,°
Though of Rebellion others he accuse.
Hee with a crew, whom like Ambition joins
With him or under him to tyrannize,
Marching from Eden towards the West, shall find   40
The Plain, wherein a black bituminous gurge°
Boils out from under ground, the mouth of Hell;
Of Brick, and of that stuff they cast to build
A City and Tow'r, whose top may reach to Heav'n;
And get themselves a name, lest far disperst   45
In foreign Lands their memory be lost,
Regardless whether good or evil fame.
But God who oft descends to visit men
Unseen, and through their habitations walks
To mark their doings, them beholding soon,   50
Comes down to see their City, ere the Tower
Obstruct Heav'n-Tow'rs, and in derision sets
Upon their Tongues a various° Spirit to raze
Quite out their Native Language, and instead
To sow a jangling noise of words unknown: 55

24 **one** Nimrod (GENESIS 10:8–10).   36 **his** name "Nimrod" was thought
to be from the Hebrew "to rebel."   41 **gurge** whirlpool.   53 **various** calcu-
lated to cause differences.

Forthwith a hideous gabble rises loud
Among the Builders; each to other calls
Not understood, till hoarse, and all in rage,
As mockt they storm; great laughter was in Heav'n
60 And looking down, to see the hubbub strange
And hear the din; thus was the building left
Ridiculous, and the work Confusion° nam'd."
   Whereto thus Adam fatherly displeas'd.
"O execrable Son so to aspire
65 Above his Brethren, to himself assuming
Authority usurpt, from God not giv'n:
He gave us only over Beast, Fish, Fowl
Dominion absolute; that right we hold
By his donation; but Man over men
70 He made not Lord; such title to himself
Reserving, human left from human free.
But this Usurper his encroachment proud
Stays not on Man; to God his Tower intends
Siege and defiance: Wretched man! what food
75 Will he convey up thither to sustain
Himself and his rash Army, where thin Air
Above the Clouds will pine his entrails gross,
And famish him of Breath, if not of Bread?"
   To whom thus Michael. "Justly thou abhorr'st
80 That Son, who on the quiet state of men
Such trouble brought, affecting° to subdue
Rational Liberty; yet know withal,
Since thy original lapse, true Liberty
Is lost, which always with right Reason dwells
85 Twinn'd, and from her hath no dividual° being:
Reason in man obscur'd, or not obey'd,
Immediately inordinate desires
And upstart Passions catch the Government
From Reason, and to servitude reduce
90 Man till then frèe. Therefore since hee permits
Within himself unworthy Powers to reign
Over free Reason, God in Judgement just
Subjects him from without to violent Lords;
Who oft as undeservedly enthrall

62 **Confusion** thought to be the meaning of "Babel." 81 **affecting** aspiring. 85 **dividual** divisible.

His outward freedom: Tyranny must be,   95
Though to the Tyrant thereby no excuse.
Yet sometimes Nations will decline so low
From virtue, which is reason, that no wrong,
But Justice, and some fatal curse annext
Deprives them of their outward liberty,   100
Their inward lost: Witness th'irreverent Son°
Of him who built the Ark, who for the shame
Done to his Father, heard this heavy curse,
Servant of Servants, on his vicious Race.
Thus will this latter, as the former World,   105
Still tend from bad to worse till God at last
Wearied with their iniquities, withdraw
His presence from among them, and avert
His holy Eyes; resolving from thenceforth
To leave them to their own polluted ways;   110
And one peculiar° Nation to select
From all the rest, of whom to be invok'd,
A Nation from one faithful man to spring:
Him° on this side Euphrates yet residing,
Bred up in Idol-worship; O that men   115
(Canst thou believe?) should be so stupid grown,
While yet the Patriarch liv'd, who 'scap'd the Flood,
As to forsake the living God, and fall
To worship their own work in Wood and Stone
For Gods! yet him God the most High vouchsafes   120
To call by Vision from his Father's house,
His kindred and false Gods, into a Land
Which he will show him, and from him will raise
A mighty Nation, and upon him show'r
His benediction so, that in his Seed   125
All Nations shall be blest; hee straight obeys,
Not knowing to what Land, yet firm believes:
I see him, but thou canst not, with what Faith
He leaves his Gods, his Friends, and native Soil
Ur of Chaldea, passing now the Ford   130
To Haran, after him a cumbrous Train
Of Herds and Flocks, and numerous servitude;°
Not wand'ring poor, but trusting all his wealth

101 **Son** Ham, son of Noah. 111 **peculiar** traditionally applied to the
Jews as God's own chosen people. 114 **Him** Abraham. 132 **servitude**
servants.

With God, who call'd him, in a land unknown.
135 Canaan he now attains, I see his Tents
Pitcht about Sechem, and the neighbouring Plain
Of Moreh; there by promise he receives
Gift to his Progeny of all that Land;
From Hamath Northward to the Desert South
140 (Things by their names I call, though yet unnam'd)
From Hermon East to the great Western Sea,
Mount Hermon, yonder Sea, each place behold
In prospect, as I point them; on the shore
Mount Carmel; here the double-founted stream
145 Jordan, true limit Eastward; but his Sons
Shall dwell to Senir, that long ridge of Hills.
This ponder, that all Nations of the Earth
Shall in his Seed be blessed; by that Seed
Is meant thy great deliverer, who shall bruise
150 The Serpent's head; whereof to thee anon
Plainlier shall be reveal'd, This Patriarch blest,
Whom faithful Abraham due time shall call,
A Son, and of his Son a Grandchild° leaves,
Like him in faith, in wisdom, and renown;
155 The Grandchild with twelve Sons increast, departs
From Canaan, to a Land hereafter call'd
Egypt, divided by the River Nile;
See where it flows, disgorging at seven mouths
Into the Sea: to sojourn in that Land
160 He comes invited by a younger Son°
In time of dearth, a Son whose worthy deeds
Raise him to be the second in that Realm
Of Pharaoh: there he dies; and leaves his Race
Growing into a Nation, and now grown
165 Suspected to a sequent King, who seeks
To stop their overgrowth, as inmate guests
Too numerous; whence of guests he makes them slaves
Inhospitably, and kills their infant Males:
Till by two brethren (those two brethren call
170 Moses and Aaron) sent from God to claim
His people from enthralment, they return
With glory and spoil back to their promis'd Land.

153 **Son . . . Grandchild** Isaac and Jacob.   160 **Son** Joseph.

But first the lawless Tyrant, who denies°
To know their God, or message to regard,
Must be compell'd by Signs and Judgements dire;   *175*
To blood unshed the Rivers must be turn'd,
Frogs, Lice and Flies must all his Palace fill
With loath'd intrusion, and fill all the land;
His Cattle must of Rot and Murrain die,
Botches and blains must all his flesh emboss,°   *180*
And all his people; Thunder mixt with Hail,
Hail mixt with fire must rend th'Egyptian Sky
And wheel on th'Earth, devouring where it rolls;
What it devours not, Herb, or Fruit, or Grain,
A darksome Cloud of Locusts swarming down   *185*
Must eat, and on the ground leave nothing green:
Darkness must overshadow all his bounds,
Palpable darkness, and blot out three days;
Last with one midnight stroke all the first-born
Of Egypt must lie dead. Thus with ten wounds   *190*
The° River-dragon tam'd at length submits
To let his sojourners depart, and oft
Humbles his stubborn heart, but still as Ice
More hard'n'd after thaw, till in his rage
Pursuing whom he late dismiss'd, the Sea   *195*
Swallows him with his Host, but them lets pass
As on dry land between two crystal walls,
Aw'd by the rod of Moses so to stand
Divided, till his rescu'd gain their shore:
Such wondrous power God to his Saint will lend,   *200*
Though present in his Angel, who shall go
Before them in a Cloud, and Pillar of Fire,
By day a Cloud, by night a Pillar of Fire,
To guide them in their journey, and remove
Behind them, while th'obdúrate King pursues: *205*
All night he will pursue, but his approach
Darkness defends° between till morning Watch;
Then through the Fiery Pillar and the Cloud
God looking forth will trouble all his Host
And craze° their Chariot-wheels: when by command   *210*
Moses once more his potent Rod extends

---

173 **denies** refuses. 180 **emboss** cover with swellings. 191 **The** *1674*;
This *1667*. 207 **defends** forbids. 210 **craze** crack.

Over the Sea; the Sea his Rod obeys;
On their embattl'd ranks the Waves return,
And overwhelm their War:° the Race elect
215 Safe towards Canaan from the shore advance
Through the wild Desert, not the readiest way,
Lest ent'ring on the Canaanite alarm'd°
War terrify them inexpért, and fear
Return them back to Egypt, choosing rather
220 Inglorious life with servitude; for life
To noble and ignoble is more sweet
Untrain'd in Arms, where rashness leads not on.
This also shall they gain by their delay
In the wide Wilderness, there they shall found
225 Their government, and their great Senate choose
Through the twelve Tribes, to rule by Laws ordain'd:
God from the Mount of Sinai, whose gray top
Shall tremble, he descending, will himself
In Thunder, Lightning and loud Trumpets' sound
230 Ordain them Laws; part such as appertain
To civil Justice, part religious Rites
Of sacrifice, informing them, by types
And shadows, of that destin'd Seed to bruise
The Serpent, by what means he shall achieve
235 Mankind's deliverance. But the voice of God
To mortal ear is dreadful; they beseech
That Moses might report to them his will,
And terror cease; he grants what they besought,°
Instructed that to God is no access
240 Without Mediator, whose high Office now
Moses in figure bears, to introduce
One greater, of whose day he shall foretell,
And all the Prophets in their Age the times
Of great Messiah shall sing. Thus Laws and Rites
245 Establisht, such delight hath God in Men
Obedient to his will, that he vouchsafes
Among them to set up his Tabernacle,
The holy One with mortal Men to dwell:
By his prescript a Sanctuary is fram'd
250 Of Cedar, overlaid with Gold, therein

214 **War** troops.   217 **alarm'd** in arms.   238 **what they besought** *1674*;
them their desire *1667*.

An Ark and in the Ark his Testimony,
The Records of his Cov'nant, over these
A Mercy-seat of Gold between the wings
Of two bright Cherubim, before him burn
Seven Lamps as in a Zodiac representing   255
The Heav'nly fires; over the Tent a Cloud
Shall rest by Day, a fiery gleam by Night,
Save when they journey, and at length they come,
Conducted by his Angel to the Land
Promis'd to Abraham and his Seed: the rest   260
Were long to tell, how many Battles fought,
How many Kings destroy'd, and Kingdoms won,
Or how the Sun shall in mid Heav'n stand still
A day entire, and Night's due course adjourn,
Man's voice commanding, Sun in Gibeon stand,   265
And thou Moon in the vale of Aialon,
Till Israel° overcome; so call the third
From Abraham, Son of Isaac, and from him
His whole descent, who thus shall Canaan win."
          Here Adam interpos'd. "O sent from Heav'n,   270
Enlight'ner of my darkness, gracious things
Thou hast reveal'd, those chiefly which concern
Just Abraham and his Seed: now first I find
Mine eyes true op'ning, and my heart much eas'd,
Erewhile perplext with thoughts what would become   275
Of mee and all Mankind; but now I see
His day, in whom all Nations shall be blest,
Favour unmerited by me, who sought
Forbidd'n knowledge by forbidd'n means.
This yet I apprehend not, why to those   280
Among whom God will deign to dwell on Earth
So many and so various Laws are giv'n;
So many Laws argue so many sins
Among them; how can God with such reside?"
          To whom thus Michael. "Doubt not but that
                sin   285
Will reign among them, as of thee begot;
And therefore was Law given them to evince°
Their natural pravity,° by stirring up

267 **Israel** Jacob.   287 **evince** both indicate and subdue.   288 **natural
pravity** Original Sin.

Sin against Law to fight; that when they see
290 Law can discover sin, but not remove,
Save by those shadowy expiations weak,
The blood of Bulls and Goats, they may conclude
Some blood more precious must be paid for Man,
Just for unjust, that in such righteousness
295 To them by Faith imputed, they may find
Justification towards God, and peace
Of Conscience, which the Law by Ceremonies
Cannot appease, nor Man the moral part
Perform, and not performing cannot live.
300 So Law appears imperfect, and but giv'n
With purpose to resign them in full time
Up to a better Cov'nant disciplin'd
From shadowy Types° to Truth, from Flesh to Spirit,
From imposition of strict Laws, to free
305 Accceptance of large Grace, from servile fear
To filial, works of Law to works of Faith.
And therefore shall not Moses, though of God
Highly belov'd, being but the Minister
Of Law, his people into Canaan lead;
310 But Joshua whom the Gentiles Jesus° call,
His Name and Office bearing, who shall quell
The adversary Serpent, and bring back
Through the world's wilderness long-wander'd man
Safe to eternal Paradise of rest.
315 Meanwhile they in their earthly Canaan plac't
Long time shall dwell and prosper, but when sins
National interrupt their public peace,
Provoking God to raise them enemies:
From whom as oft he saves them penitent
320 By Judges first, then under Kings; of whom
The second, both for piety renown'd
And puissant deeds, a promise shall receive
Irrevocable, that his Regal Throne
For ever shall endure; the like shall sing
325 All Prophecy, That of the Royal Stock
Of David (so I name this King) shall rise
A Son, the Woman's Seed to thee foretold,

303 **shadowy Types** allegorical anticipations in the Old Testament of the
truths of the New Testament.   310 **Joshua . . . Jesus** the same name,
"Saviour."

Foretold to Abraham, as in whom shall trust
All Nations, and to Kings foretold, of Kings
The last, for of his Reign shall be no end.   330
But first a long succession must ensue,
And his next Son° for Wealth and Wisdom fam'd,
The clouded Ark of God till then in Tents
Wand'ring, shall in a glorious Temple enshrine.
Such follow him, as shall be register'd   335
Part good, part bad, of bad the longer scroll,
Whose foul Idolatries, and other faults
Heapt to the popular sum,° will so incense
God, as to leave them, and expose their Land,
Their City, his Temple, and his holy Ark   340
With all his sacred things, a scorn and prey
To that proud City, whose high Walls thou saw'st
Left in confusion, Babylon thence call'd.
There in captivity he lets them dwell
The space of seventy years, then brings them back,   345
Rememb'ring mercy, and his Cov'nant sworn
To David, 'stablisht as the days of Heav'n.
Return'd from Babylon by leave of Kings
Their Lords, whom God dispos'd, the house of God
They first re-edify, and for a while   350
In mean estate live moderate, till grown
In wealth and multitude, factious they grow;
But first among the Priests dissension springs,
Men who attend the Altar, and should most
Endeavour Peace; their strife pollution brings   355
Upon the Temple itself: at last they seize
The Scepter, and regard not David's Sons,
Then lose it to a stranger,° that the true
Anointed King Messiah might be born
Barr'd of his right: yet at his Birth a Star   360
Unseen before in Heav'n proclaims him come,
And guides the Eastern Sages, who inquire
His place, to offer Incense, Myrrh, and Gold;
His place of birth a solemn Angel tells
To simple Shepherds, keeping watch by night;   365
They gladly thither haste, and by a Choir

332 **his next Son** David's son Solomon.   338 **popular sum** people's total
(of sins).   358 **stranger** Antipater (father of Herod), made ruler of Jerusalem by the Romans.

Of squadron'd Angels hear his Carol sung.
A Virgin is his Mother, but his Sire
The Power of the Most High; he shall ascend
370 The Throne hereditary, and bound his Reign
With earth's wide bounds, his glory with the Heav'ns."
          He ceas'd, discerning Adam with such joy
Surcharg'd, as had like grief been dew'd in tears,
Without the vent of words, which these he breath'd.
375   "O Prophet of glad tidings, finisher
Of utmost hope! now clear I understand
What oft my steadiest thoughts have searcht in vain,
Why our great expectation should be call'd
The seed of Woman: Virgin Mother, Hail,
380 High in the love of Heav'n, yet from my Loins
Thou shalt proceed, and from thy Womb the Son
Of God most High; So God with man unites.
Needs must the Serpent now his capital° bruise
Expect with mortal pain: say where and when
385 Their fight, what stroke shall bruise the Victor's heel."
          To whom thus Michael. "Dream not of their
              fight,
As of a Duel, or the local wounds
Of head or heel: not therefore joins the Son
Manhood to God-head, with more strength to foil
390 Thy enemy; nor so is overcome
Satan, whose fall from Heav'n, a deadlier bruise,
Disabl'd not to give thee thy death's-wound:
Which hee, who comes thy Saviour, shall recure,
Not by destroying Satan, but his works
395 In thee and in thy Seed: nor can this be,
But by fulfilling that which thou didst want,°
Obedience to the Law of God, impos'd
On penalty of death, and suffering death,
The penalty to thy transgression due,
400 And due to theirs which out of thine will grow:
So only can high Justice rest appaid.°
The Law of God exact he shall fulfill
Both by obedience and by love, though love
Alone fulfill the Law; thy punishment

383 **capital** to his head, and deadly. 396 **want** lack. 401 **appaid**
satisfied.

He shall endure by coming in the Flesh   405
To a reproachful life and cursed death,
Proclaiming Life to all who shall believe
In his redemption, and that his obedience
Imputed becomes theirs by Faith, his merits
To save them, not their own, though legal works.   410
For this he shall live hated, be blasphem'd,
Seiz'd on by force, judg'd, and to death condemn'd
A shameful and accurst, nail'd to the Cross
By his own Nation, slain for bringing Life;
But to the Cross he nails thy Enemies,   415
The Law that is against thee, and the sins
Of all mankind, with him there crucifi'd,
Never to hurt them more who rightly trust
In this his satisfaction; so he dies,
But soon revives, Death over him no power   420
Shall long usurp; ere the third dawning light
Return, the Stars of Morn shall see him rise
Out of his grave, fresh as the dawning light,
Thy ransom paid, which Man from death redeems,
His death for Man, as many as offer'd Life   425
Neglect not, and the benefit embrace
By faith not void of works: this God-like act
Annuls thy doom, the death thou shouldst have di'd,
In sin for ever lost from life; this act
Shall bruise the head of Satan, crush his strength   430
Defeating Sin and Death, his two main arms,
And fix far deeper in his head their stings
Than temporal death shall bruise the Victor's heel,
Or theirs whom he redeems, a death like sleep,
A gentle wafting to immortal Life.   435
Nor after resurrection shall he stay
Longer on Earth than certain times to appear
To his Disciples, Men who in his Life
Still follow'd him; to them shall leave in charge
To teach all nations what of him they learn'd   440
And his Salvation, them who shall believe
Baptizing in the profluent stream, the sign
Of washing them from guilt of sin to Life
Pure, and in mind prepar'd, if so befall,
For death, like that which the redeemer di'd.   445
All Nations they shall teach; for from that day

Not only to the Sons of Abraham's Loins
Salvation shall be Preacht, but to the Sons
Of Abraham's Faith wherever through the world;
450 So in his seed all Nations shall be blest.
Then to the Heav'n of Heav'ns he shall ascend
With victory, triúmphing through the air
Over his foes and thine; there shall surprise
The Serpent, Prince of air, and drag in Chains
455 Through all his realm, and there confounded leave;
Then enter into glory, and resume
His Seat at God's right hand, exalted high
Above all names in Heav'n; and thence shall come,
When this world's dissolution shall be ripe,
460 With glory and power to judge both quick and dead,
To judge th'unfaithful dead, but to reward
His faithful, and receive them into bliss,
Whether in Heav'n or Earth, for then the Earth
Shall all be Paradise, far happier place
465 Then this of Eden, and far happier days."
        So spake th'Archangel Michael, then paus'd,
As at the World's great period;° and our Sire
Replete with joy and wonder thus repli'd.
        "O goodness infinite, goodness immense!°
470 That all this good of evil shall produce,
And evil turn to good; more wonderful
Than that which by creation first brought forth
Light out of darkness! full of doubt I stand,
Whether I should repent me now of sin
475 By mee done and occasion'd, or rejoice
Much more, that much more good thereof shall spring,
To God more glory, more good-will to Men
From God, and over wrath grace shall abound.
But say, if our deliverer up to Heav'n
480 Must reascend, what will betide the few
His faithful, left among th'unfaithful herd,
The enemies of truth; who then shall guide
His people, who defend? will they not deal
Worse with his followers than with him they dealt?"
        "Be sure they will," said th'Angel; "but from
485   Heav'n

467 **period** ending.   469 **immense** immeasurable.

Hee to his own a Comforter will send,
The promise of the Father, who shall dwell
His Spirit within them, and the Law of Faith
Working through love, upon their hearts shall write,
To guide them in all truth, and also arm   490
With spiritual Armour, able to resist
Satan's assaults, and quench his fiery darts,
What Man can do against them, not afraid,
Though to the death, against such cruelties
With inward consolations recompens't,   495
And oft supported so as shall amaze
Their proudest persecutors: for the Spirit
Pour'd first on his Apostles, whom he sends
To evangelize the Nations, then on all
Baptiz'd, shall them with wondrous gifts endue   500
To speak all Tongues, and do all Miracles,
As did their Lord before them. Thus they win
Great numbers of each Nation to receive
With joy the tidings brought from Heav'n: at length
Their Ministry perform'd, and race well run,   505
Their doctrine and their story written left,
They die; but in their room, as they forewarn,
Wolves shall succeed for teachers, grievous Wolves,
Who all the sacred mysteries of Heav'n
To their own vile advantages shall turn   510
Of lucre and ambition, and the truth
With superstitions and traditions taint,
Left only in those written Records pure,
Though not but by the Spirit understood.
Then shall they seek to avail themselves of names,   515
Places and titles, and with these to join
Secular power, though feigning still to act
By spiritual, to themselves appropriating
The Spirit of God, promis'd alike and giv'n
To all Believers; and from that pretense,   520
Spiritual Laws by carnal power shall force
On every conscience; Laws which none shall find
Left them enroll'd, or what the Spirit within
Shall on the heart engrave. What will they then
But force the Spirit of Grace itself, and bind   525
His consort Liberty; what, but unbuild
His living Temples, built by Faith to stand,

Their own Faith not another's: for on Earth
Who against Faith and Conscience can be heard
530   Infallible? yet many will presume:
Whence heavy persecution shall arise
On all who in the worship persevere
Of Spirit and Truth; the rest, far greater part,
Will deem in outward Rites and specious forms
535   Religion satisfi'd; Truth shall retire
Bestuck with sland'rous darts, and works of Faith
Rarely be found: so shall the World go on,
To good malignant; to bad men benign,
Under her own weight groaning, till the day
540   Appear of respiration° to the just,
And vengeance to the wicked, at return
Of him so lately promis'd to thy aid,
The Woman's seed, obscurely then foretold,
Now amplier known the Saviour and thy Lord
545   Last in the Clouds from Heav'n to be reveal'd
In glory of the Father, to dissolve
Satan with his perverted World, then raise
From the conflagrant mass, purg'd and refin'd,
New Heav'ns, new Earth, Ages of endless date
550   Founded in righteousness and peace and love,
To bring forth fruits Joy and eternal Bliss."
          He ended; and thus Adam last repli'd.
"How soon hath thy prediction, Seer blest,
Measur'd this transient World, the Race of time,
555   Till time stand fixt: beyond is all abyss,
Eternity, whose end no eye can reach.
Greatly instructed I shall hence depart,
Greatly in peace of thought, and have my fill
Of knowledge, what this vessel can contain;
560   Beyond which was my folly to aspire.
Henceforth I learn, that to obey is best,
And love with fear the only God, to walk
As in his presence, ever to observe
His Providence, and on him sole depend,
565   Merciful over all his works, with good
Still overcoming evil, and by small
Accomplishing great things, by things deem'd weak

540 **respiration** freedom, the chance to breathe again.

Subverting worldly strong, and worldly wise
By simply meek; that suffering for Truth's sake
Is fortitude to highest victory,   570
And to the faithful Death and Gate of Life;
Taught this by his example whom I now
Acknowledge my Redeemer ever blest."
      To whom thus also th'Angel last repli'd:
"This having learnt, thou has attain'd the sum   575
Of wisdom; hope no higher, though all the Stars
Thou knew'st by name, and all th'Ethereal Powers,
All secrets of the deep, all Nature's works,
Or works of God in Heav'n, Air, Earth, or Sea,
And all the riches of this World enjoy'dst,   580
And all the rule, one Empire; only add
Deeds to thy knowledge answerable, add Faith,
Add Virtue, Patience, Temperance, add Love,
By name to come call'd Charity, the soul
Of all the rest: then wilt thou not be loath   585
To leave this Paradise, but shalt possess
A Paradise within thee, happier far.
Let us descend now therefore from this top
Of Speculation;° for the hour precise
Exacts our parting hence; and see the Guards,   590
By mee encampt on yonder Hill, expect
Their motion, at whose Front a flaming Sword,
In signal of remove, waves fiercely round;
We may no longer stay: go, waken Eve;
Her also I with gentle Dreams have calm'd   595
Portending good, and all her spirits compos'd
To meek submission: thou at season fit
Let her with thee partake what thou hast heard,
Chiefly what may concern her Faith to know,
The great deliverance by her Seed to come   600
(For by the Woman's Seed) on all Mankind.
That ye may live, which will be many days,
Both in one Faith unanimous though sad,
With cause for evils past, yet much more cheer'd
With meditation on the happy end."   605
      He ended, and they both descend the Hill;
Descended, Adam to the Bow'r where Eve

588–89 **top Of Speculation** hill of extensive view.

Lay sleeping ran before, but found her wak't;
And thus with words not sad she him receiv'd.
      "Whence thou return'st, and whither went'st,
610   I know;
For God is also in sleep, and Dreams advise,
Which he hath sent propitious, some great good
Presaging, since with sorrow and heart's distress
Wearied I fell asleep: but now lead on;
615 In mee is no delay; with thee to go,
Is to stay here; without thee here to stay,
Is to go hence unwilling; thou to mee
Art all things under Heav'n, all places thou,
Who for my wilful crime art banisht hence.
620 This further consolation yet secure
I carry hence; though all by mee is lost,
Such favour I unworthy am vouchsaf't,
By mee the Promis'd Seed shall all restore."
          So spake our Mother Eve, and Adam heard
625 Well pleas'd, but answer'd not; for now too nigh
Th'Archangel stood, and from the other Hill
To their fixt Station, all in bright array
The Cherubim descended; on the ground
Gliding Metéorous,° as Ev'ning Mist
630 Ris'n from a River o'er the Marish glides,
And gathers ground fast at the Labourer's heel
Homeward returning. High in Front advanc't,
The brandisht Sword of God before them blaz'd
Fierce as a Comet; which with torrid heat,
635 And vapour as the Libyan Air adust,
Began to parch that temperate Clime; whereat
In either hand the hast'ning Angel caught
Our ling'ring Parents, and to th'Eastern Gate
Led them direct, and down the Cliff as fast
640 To the subjected° Plain; then disappear'd.
They looking back, all th'Eastern side beheld
Of Paradise, so late their happy seat,
Wav'd over by that flaming Brand, the Gate
With dreadful Faces throng'd and fiery Arms:
645 Some natural tears they dropp'd, but wip'd them soon;

629 **Metéorous** aloft like a meteor.   640 **subjected** lying below.

The World was all before them, where to choose
Their place of rest, and Providence their guide:
They hand in hand with wand'ring steps and slow,
Through Eden took their solitary way.

Paradise Regained

BOOK I

I who erewhile the happy Garden sung,
By one man's disobedience lost, now sing
Recover'd Paradise to all mankind,
By one man's firm obedience fully tri'd
Through all temptation, and the Tempter foil'd   5
In all his wiles, defeated and repuls't,
And Eden rais'd in the waste Wilderness.
       Thou Spirit who ledd'st this glorious Eremite°
Into the Desert, his Victorious Field
Against the Spiritual Foe, and brought'st him thence   10
By proof the undoubted Son of God, inspire,
As thou art wont, my prompted Song else mute,
And bear through heighth or depth of nature's
   bounds
With prosperous wing full-summ'd° to tell of deeds
Above Heroic, though in secret done,   15
And unrecorded° left through many an Age,
Worthy t'have not remain'd so long unsung.
       Now had the great Proclaimer° with a voice
More awful than the sound of Trumpet, cri'd
Repentance, and Heaven's Kingdom nigh at hand   20
To all Baptiz'd: to his great Baptism flock'd
With awe the Regions round, and with them came
From Nazareth the Son of Joseph deem'd
To the flood Jordan, came as then obscure,
Unmarkt, unknown; but him the Baptist soon   25
Descri'd, divinely warn'd, and witness bore
As to his worthier, and would have resign'd
To him his Heavenly Office, nor was long
His witness unconfirm'd: on him baptiz'd
Heaven open'd, and in likeness of a Dove   30
The Spirit descended, while the Father's voice
From Heav'n pronounc'd him his beloved Son.

---

8 **Eremite** hermit. 14 **full-summ'd** with full complement of feathers.   16 **unrecorded** "record," to sing, as in Shakespeare: "Tune my distresses, and record my woes." 18 **Proclaimer** John the Baptist.

That heard the Adversary,° who roving still
About the world, at that assembly fam'd
35 Would not be last, and with the voice divine
Nigh Thunder-struck th'exalted man, to whom
Such high attest° was giv'n, awhile survey'd
With wonder, then with envy fraught and rage
Flies to his place, nor rests, but in mid air°
40 To Council summons all his mighty Peers,
Within thick Clouds and dark ten-fold involv'd,
A gloomy Cónsistory;° and them amidst
With looks aghast and sad he thus bespake.
        "O ancient Powers of Air and this wide world,
45 For much more willingly I mention Air,
This our old Conquest, than remember Hell
Our hated habitation; well ye know
How many Ages, as the years of men,
This Universe we have possest,° and rul'd
50 In manner at our will th'affairs of Earth,
Since Adam and his facile° consort Eve
Lost Paradise deceiv'd by me, though since
With dread attending° when that fatal wound
Shall be inflicted by the Seed of Eve
55 Upon my head, long the decrees of Heav'n
Delay, for longest time to him is short;
And now too soon for us the circling hours
This dreaded time have compast, wherein we
Must bide the stroke of that long-threat'n'd wound,
60 At least if so we can, and by the head
Broken be not intended all our power
To be infring'd,° our freedom and our being
In this fair Empire won of Earth and Air;
For this ill news I bring, the Woman's seed
65 Destin'd to this, is late of woman born,
His birth to our just° fear gave no small cause,
But his growth now to youth's full flow'r, displaying
All virtue, grace and wisdom to achieve
Things highest, greatest, multiplies my fear.
70 Before him a great Prophet, to proclaim

33 **Adversary** see *PL* 1 81.   37 **attest** testimony.   39 **mid air** see lines 45-
46.   42 **Cónsistory** council, as of the classical gods.   49 **possest** including
"of a demon: to occupy or dominate."   51 **facile** easily led.   53 **attending**
awaiting.   62 **infring'd** shattered.   66 **just** well-founded.

His coming, is sent Harbinger, who all
Invites, and in the Consecrated stream
Pretends° to wash off sin, and fit them so
Purified to receive him pure, or rather
To do him honour as their King; all come,   75
And he himself among them was baptiz'd,
Not thence, to be more pure, but to receive
The testimony of Heaven, that who he is
Thenceforth the Nations may not doubt; I saw
The Prophet do him reverence, on him rising   80
Out of the water, Heav'n above the Clouds
Unfold her Crystal Doors, thence on his head
A perfect Dove descend, whate'er it meant,
And out of Heav'n the Sov'reign voice I heard,
'This is my Son belov'd, in him am pleas'd.'   85
His Mother then is mortal, but his Sire,
He who obtains° the Monarchy of Heav'n,
And what will he not do to advance his Son?
His first-begot we know, and sore have felt,
When his fierce thunder drove us to the deep;   90
Who this is we must learn, for man he seems
In all his lineaments, though in his face
The glimpses of his Father's glory shine.
Ye see our danger on the utmost edge
Of hazard, which admits no lone debate,   95
But must with something sudden be oppos'd,
Not force, but well-couch't° fraud, well-woven snares,
Ere in the head of Nations he appear
Their King, their Leader, and Supreme on Earth.
I, when no other durst, sole undertook   100
The dismal expedition to find out
And ruin Adam, and the exploit perform'd
Successfully; a calmer voyage now
Will waft me; and the way found prosperous once
Induces best to hope of like success."   105
          He ended, and his words impression left
Of much amazement to th'infernal Crew,
Distracted and surpris'd with deep dismay
At these sad tidings; but no time was then
For long indulgence to their fears or grief: 110

73 **Pretends** claims.   87 **obtains** holds.   97 **couch't** hidden.

Unanimous they all commit the care
And management of this main° enterprise
To him their great Dictator, whose attempt
At first against mankind so well had thriv'd
115 In Adam's overthrow, and led their march
From Hell's deep-vaulted Den to dwell in light,
Regents and Potentates, and Kings, yea gods
Of many a pleasant Realm and Province wide.
So to the Coast of Jordan he directs
120 His easy° steps; gilded with snaky wiles,
Where he might likeliest find this new-declar'd,
This man of men, attested Son of God,
Temptation and all guile on him to try;
So to subvert whom he suspected rais'd
125 To end his Reign on Earth so long enjoy'd:
But contrary unwitting he fulfill'd
The purpos'd Counsel pre-ordain'd and fixt
Of the most High, who in full frequence° bright
Of Angels, thus to Gabriel smiling spake.
130   "Gabriel this day by proof thou shalt behold,
Thou and all Angels cónversant on Earth
With man or men's affairs, how I begin
To verify that solemn message late,
On which I sent thee to the Virgin pure
135 In Galilee, that she should bear a Son
Great in Renown, and call'd the Son of God;
Then told'st her doubting how these things could be
To her a Virgin, that on her should come
The Holy Ghost, and the power of the highest
140 O'ershadow her: this man born and now up-grown,
To show him worthy of his birth divine
And high prediction, henceforth I expose
To Satan; let him tempt and now assay
His utmost subtlety, because he boasts
145 And vaunts of his great cunning to the throng
Of his Apostasy;° he might have learnt
Less overweening, since he fail'd in Job,
Whose constant perseverance overcame
Whate'er his cruel malice could invent.

112 **main** mighty. 120 **easy** unhurried. 128 **frequence** assembly.
146 **Apostasy** renegades.

He now shall know I can produce a man   *150*
Of female Seed, far abler to resist
All his solicitations, and at length
All his vast force, and drive him back to Hell,
Winning by Conquest what the first man lost
By fallacy surpris'd. But first I mean   *155*
To exercise him in the Wilderness,
There he shall first lay down the rudiments
Of his great warfare, ere I send him forth
To conquer Sin and Death the two grand foes,
By Humiliation and strong Sufferance: *160*
His weakness shall o'ercome Satanic strength
And all the world, and mass of sinful flesh;
That all the Angels and Ethereal Powers,
They now, and men hereafter may discern,
From what consummate virtue I have chose   *165*
This perfect Man, by merit call'd my Son,
To earn Salvation for the Sons of men."
        So spake the Eternal Father, and all Heaven
Admiring° stood a space, then into Hymns
Burst forth, and in Celestial measures mov'd,   *170*
Circling the Throne and Singing, while the hand
Sung with the voice, and this the argument.°
        "Victory and Triumph to the Son of God
Now ent'ring his great duel, not of arms,
But to vanquish by wisdom hellish wiles.   *175*
The Father knows the Son; therefore secure
Ventures his filial Virtue, though untri'd,
Against whate'er may tempt, whate'er seduce,
Allure, or terrify, or undermine.
Be frustrate all ye stratagems of Hell,   *180*
And devilish machinations come to nought."
        So they in Heav'n their Odes and Vigils°
            tun'd:
Meanwhile the Son of God, who yet some days
Lodg'd in Bethabara where John baptis'd,
Musing and much revolving in his breast,   *185*
How best the mighty work he might begin
Of Saviour to mankind, and which way first

169 **Admiring** in wonder.   172 **argument** subject.   182 **Vigils** observances.

Publish° his God-like office now mature,
One day forth walk'd alone, the Spirit leading;
190 And his deep thoughts, the better to converse
With solitude, till far from track of men,
Thought following thought, and step by step led on,
He ent'red now the bordering Desert wild,
And with dark shades and rocks environ'd round,
195 His holy Meditations thus pursu'd.
          "O what a multitude of thoughts at once
Awak'n'd in me swarm, while I consider
What from within I feel myself, and hear
What from without comes often to my ears,
200 Ill-sorting with my present state compar'd.
When I was yet a child, no childish play
To me was pleasing, all my mind was set
Serious to learn and know, and thence to do
What might be public good; myself I thought
205 Born to that end, born to promote all truth,
All righteous things: therefore above my years,
The Law of God I read, and found it sweet,
Made it my whole delight, and in it grew
To such perfection, that ere yet my age
210 Had measur'd twice six years, at our great Feast
I went into the Temple, there to hear
The Teachers of our Law, and to propose
What might improve my knowledge or their own;
And was admir'd by all, yet this not all
215 To which my Spirit aspir'd, victorious deeds
Flam'd in my heart, heroic acts, one while
To rescue Israel from the Roman yoke,
Then to subdue and quell o'er all the earth
Brute violence and proud tyrannic pow'r,
220 Till truth were freed, and equity restor'd:
Yet held it more humane, more heavenly first
By winning words to conquer willing hearts,
And make persuasion do the work of fear;
At least to try, and teach the erring Soul
225 Not wilfully mis-doing, but unware
Misled; the stubborn only to subdue.
These growing thoughts my Mother soon perceiving

188 **Publish** manifest.

By words at times cast forth inly rejoic'd,
And said to me apart, 'High are thy thoughts
O Son, but nourish them and let them soar   230
To what heighth sacred virtue and true worth
Can raise them, though above example high;
By matchless Deeds express thy matchless Sire.
For know, thou art no Son of mortal man,
Though men esteem thee low of Parentage,   235
Thy Father is the Eternal King, who rules
All Heaven and Earth, Angels and Sons of men,
A messenger from God foretold thy birth
Conceiv'd in me a Virgin, he foretold
Thou shouldst be great and sit on David's Throne,   240
And of thy Kingdom there should be no end.
At thy Nativity a glorious Choir
Of Angels in the fields of Bethlehem sung
To Shepherds watching at their folds by night,
And told them the Messiah now was born,   245
Where they might see him, and to thee they came;
Directed to the Manger where thou lay'st,
For in the Inn was left no better room:
A Star, not seen before in Heav'n appearing
Guided the Wise Men thither from the East,   250
To honour thee with Incense, Myrrh, and Gold,
By whose bright course led on they found the place,
Affirming it thy Star new-grav'n in Heaven,
By which they knew thee King of Israel born.
Just Simeon and Prophetic Anna, warn'd   255
By Vision, found thee in the Temple, and spake
Before the Altar and the vested Priest,
Like things of thee to all that present stood.'
This having heard, straight I again revolv'd
The Law and Prophets, searching what was writ   260
Concerning the Messiah, to our Scribes
Known partly, and soon found of whom they spake
I am; this chiefly, that my way must lie
Through many a hard assay even to the death,
Ere I the promis'd Kingdom can attain,   265
Or work Redemption for mankind, whose sins'
Full weight must be transferr'd upon my head.
Yet neither thus disheart'n'd or dismay'd,
The time prefixt I waited, when behold

270 The Baptist, (of whose birth I oft had heard,
     Not knew by sight) now come, who was to come
     Before Messiah and his way prepare.
     I as all others to his Baptism came,
     Which I believ'd was from above; but he
275 Straight knew me, and with loudest voice proclaim'd
     Me him (for it was shown him so from Heaven)
     Me him whose Harbinger he was; and first
     Refus'd on me his Baptism to confer,
     As much his greater, and was hardly° won;
280 But as I rose out of the laving stream,
     Heaven open'd her eternal doors, from whence
     The Spirit descended on me like a Dove,
     And last the sum° of all, my Father's voice,
     Audibly heard from Heav'n, pronounc'd me his,
285 Me his beloved Son, in whom alone
     He was well pleas'd; by which I knew the time
     Now full, that I no more should live obscure,
     But openly begin, as best becomes
     The Authority which I deriv'd from Heaven.
290 And now by some strong motion I am led
     Into this Wilderness, to what intent
     I learn not yet, perhaps I need not know;
     For what concerns my knowledge God reveals."
          So spake our Morning Star then in his rise,
295 And looking round on every side beheld
     A pathless Desert, dusk with horrid shades;
     The way he came not having mark'd, return
     Was difficult, by human steps untrod;
     And he still on was led, but with such thoughts
300 Accompanied of things past and to come
     Lodg'd in his breast, as well might recommend
     Such Solitude before choicest Society.
     Full forty days he pass'd, whether on hill
     Sometimes, anon in shady vale, each night
305 Under the covert of some ancient Oak,
     Or Cedar, to defend him from the dew,
     Or harbour'd in one Cave, is not reveal'd;
     Nor tasted human food, nor hunger felt
     Till those days ended, hunger'd then at last

279 **hardly** only with difficulty.   283 **sum** crowning point.

Among wild Beasts: they at his sight grew mild,   310
Nor sleeping him nor waking harm'd, his walk
The fiery Serpent fled, and noxious Worm,°
The Lion and fierce Tiger glar'd aloof.
But now an aged man in Rural weeds,
Following, as seem'd, the quest of some stray Ewe,   315
Or wither'd sticks to gather; which might serve
Against a Winter's day when winds blow keen,
To warm him wet return'd from field at Eve,
He saw approach, who first with curious eye
Perus'd him, then with words thus utt'red spake.   320
       "Sir, what ill chance hath brought thee to this
         place
So far from path or road of men, who pass
In Troop or Caravan,° for single none
Durst ever, who return'd, and dropt not here
His Carcass, pin'd with hunger and with drouth?   325
I ask the rather, and the more admire,
For that to me thou seem'st the man, whom late
Our new baptising Prophet at the Ford
Of Jordan honour'd so, and call'd thee Son
Of God; I saw and heard, for we sometimes   330
Who dwell this wild, constrain'd by want, come forth
To Town or Village nigh (nighest is far)
Where aught we hear, and curious are to hear,
What happ'ns new; Fame° also finds us out."
       To whom the Son of God. "Who brought me
        hither   335
Will bring me hence, no other Guide I seek."
       "By Miracle he may," repli'd the Swain,
"What other way I see not, for we here
Live on tough roots and stubs, to thirst inur'd
More than the Camel, and to drink go far,   340
Men to much misery and hardship born;
But if thou be the Son of God, Command
That out of these hard stones be made thee bread;
So shalt thou save thyself and us relieve
With Food, whereof we wretched seldom taste."   345
      He ended, and the Son of God repli'd.
"Think'st thou such force in Bread? is it not written

312 **Worm** snake.   323 **Caravan** company of travelers.   334 **Fame** rumor.

(For I discern thee other than thou seem'st)
Man lives not by Bread only, but each Word
350 Proceeding from the mouth of God; who fed
Our Fathers here with Manna; in the Mount
Moses was forty days, nor ate nor drank,
And forty days Elijah without food
Wand'red this barren waste, the same I now:
355 Why dost thou then suggest to me distrust,
Knowing who I am, as I know who thou art?"
              Whom thus answer'd th'Arch Fiend now un-
           disguis'd.
" 'Tis true, I am that Spirit unfortunate,
Who leagu'd with millions more in rash revolt
360 Kept not my happy Station, but was driv'n
With them from bliss to the bottomless deep,
Yet to that hideous place not so confin'd
By rigor unconniving,° but that oft
Leaving my dolorous Prison I enjoy
365 Large liberty to round this Globe of Earth,
Or range in th'Air, nor from the Heav'n of Heav'ns
Hath he excluded my resort sometimes.
I came among the Sons of God, when he
Gave up into my hands Uzzean° Job
370 To prove him, and illústrate° his high worth;
And when to all his Angels he propos'd
To draw the proud King Ahab into fraud
That he might fall in Ramoth, they demurring,
I undertook that office, and the tongues
375 Of all his flattering Prophets glibb'd with lies
To his destruction, as I had in charge.
For what he bids I do; though I have lost
Much lustre of my native brightness, lost
To be belov'd of God, I have not lost
380 To love, at least contémplate and admire
What I see excellent in good, or fair,
Or virtuous, I should so have lost all sense.
What can be then less in me than desire
To see thee and approach thee, whom I know
385 Declar'd the Son of God, to hear attent°

363 **unconniving** unwinking.   369 **Uzzean** from Uz.   370 **illústrate** set in its
true light.   385 **attent** attentively.

Thy wisdom, and behold thy God-like deeds?
Men generally think me much a foe
To all mankind: why should I? they to me
Never did wrong or violence, by them
I lost not what I lost, rather by them   390
I gain'd what I have gain'd, and with them dwell
Copartner in these Regions of the World,
If not disposer;° lend them oft my aid,
Oft my advice by presages and signs,
And answers, oracles, portents and dreams,   395
Whereby they may direct their future life.
Envy they say excites me, thus to gain
Companions of my misery and woe.
At first it may be; but long since with woe
Nearer acquainted, now I feel by proof,   400
That fellowship in pain divides not smart,
Nor lightens aught each man's peculiar° load.
Small consolation then, were Man adjoin'd:
This wounds me most (what can it less) that Man,
Man fall'n shall be restor'd, I never more."   405
          To whom our Saviour sternly thus repli'd.
"Deservedly thou griev'st, compos'd of lies
From the beginning, and in lies wilt end;
Who boast'st release from Hell, and leave to come
Into the Heav'n of Heavens; thou com'st indeed,   410
As a poor miserable captive thrall,
Comes to the place where he before had sat
Among the Prime in Splendor, now depos'd,
Ejected, emptied, gaz'd, unpitied, shunn'd,
A spectacle of ruin or of scorn   415
To all the Host of Heaven; the happy place
Imparts to thee no happiness, no joy,
Rather inflames thy torment, representing
Lost bliss, to thee no more communicable,
So never more in Hell than when in Heaven.   420
But thou art serviceable to Heaven's King.
Wilt thou impute to obedience what thy fear
Extorts, or pleasure to do ill excites?
What but thy malice mov'd thee to misdeem
Of righteous Job, then cruelly to afflict him   425

393 **disposer** contrast *PL* IV 635.   402 **peculiar** own.

With all inflictions, but his patience won?
The other service was thy chosen task,
To be a liar in four hundred mouths;°
For lying is thy sustenance, thy food.
430 Yet thou pretend'st° to truth; all Oracles
By thee are giv'n, and what confest more true
Among the Nations? that hath been thy craft,
By mixing somewhat true to vent more lies.
But what have been thy answers, what but dark
435 Ambiguous and with double sense deluding,
Which they who ask'd have seldom understood,
And not well understood as good not known?
Who ever by consulting at thy shrine
Return'd the wiser, or the more instruct
440 To fly or follow what concern'd him most,
And run not sooner to his fatal snare?
For God hath justly giv'n the Nations up
To thy Delusions; justly, since they fell
Idolatrous, but when his purpose is
445 Among them to declare his Providence
To thee not known, whence hast thou then thy truth,
But from him or his Angels President°
In every Province, who themselves disdaining
To approach thy Temples, give thee in command
450 What to the smallest tittle thou shalt say
To thy Adorers; thou with trembling fear,
Or like a Fawning Parasite obey'st;
Then to thyself ascrib'st the truth foretold.
But this thy glory shall be soon retrench'd;
455 No more shalt thou by oracling abuse
The Gentiles; henceforth Oracles are ceast,
And thou no more with Pomp and Sacrifice
Shalt be inquir'd at Delphos° or elsewhere,
At least in vain, for they shall find thee mute.
460 God hath now sent his living Oracle
Into the World, to teach his final will,
And sends his Spirit of Truth henceforth to dwell
In pious Hearts, an inward Oracle

---

428 four hundred mouths Ahab (lines 372–75) was deceived by 400 lying
prophets.   **430 pretend'st** lay claim.   **447 President** presiding.   **458
Delphos** Apollo's oracle.

To all truth requisite for men to know."
      So spake our Saviour; but the subtle Fiend,   465
Though inly stung with anger and disdain,
Dissembl'd, and this Answer smooth return'd.
     "Sharply thou hast insisted on rebuke,
And urg'd me hard with doings, which not will
But misery hath rested from me; where   470
Easily canst thou find one miserable,
And not enforc'd oft-times to part from truth;
If it may stand him more in stead to lie,
Say and unsay, feign, flatter, or abjure?
But thou art plac't above me, thou art Lord;   475
From thee I can and must submiss° endure
Check or reproof, and glad to 'scape so quit.°
Hard are the ways of truth, and rough to walk,
Smooth on the tongue discourst, pleasing to th'ear,
And tuneable as Sylvan Pipe or Song;   480
What wonder then if I delight to hear
Her dictates from thy mouth? most men admire
Virtue, who follow not her lore: permit me
To hear thee when I come (since no man comes)
And talk at least, though I despair to attain.   485
Thy Father, who is holy, wise and pure,
Suffers the Hypocrite or Atheous Priest
To tread his Sacred Courts, and minister
About his Altar, handling holy things,
Praying or vowing, and vouchsaf'd his voice   490
To Balaam Reprobate, a Prophet yet
Inspir'd; disdain not such access to me."°
      To whom our Saviour with unalter'd brow.
"Thy coming hither, though I know thy scope,°
I bid not or forbid; do as thou find'st   495
Permission from above; thou canst not more."
      He added not; and Satan bowing low
His gray dissimulation, disappear'd
Into thin Air diffus'd: for now began
Night with her sullen wing to double-shade   500
The Desert, Fowls in their clay nests were couch't;
And now wild Beasts came forth the woods to roam.

---

476 **submiss** submissive. 477 **quit** free, clear. 492 **disdain . . . me** "do
not refuse to me such access (to your person)." 494 **scope** aim.

BOOK II

Meanwhile the new-baptis'd, who yet remain'd
At Jordan with the Baptist, and had seen
Him whom they heard so late expressly call'd
Jesus Messiah Son of God declar'd,
5   And on that high Authority had believ'd,
And with him talkt, and with him lodg'd, I mean
Andrew and Simon, famous after known
With others though in Holy Writ not nam'd,
Now missing him their joy so lately found,
10   So lately found, and so abruptly gone,
Began to doubt, and doubted many days,
And as the days increas'd, increas'd their doubt:
Sometimes they thought he might be only shown,
And for a time caught up to God, as once
15   Moses was in the Mount, and missing long;
And the great Thisbite° who on fiery wheels
Rode up to Heaven, yet once again to come.
Therefore as those young Prophets then with care
Sought lost Elijah, so in each place these
20   Nigh to Bethabara; in Jericho
The City of Palms, Aenon, and Salem° Old,
Machærus° and each Town or City wall'd
On this side the broad lake Genezaret,°
Or in Perea,° but return'd in vain.
25   Then on the bank of Jordan, by a Creek:
Where winds with Reeds, and Osiers whisp'ring play
Plain Fishermen; no greater men them call,
Close in a Cottage low together got
Their unexpected loss and plaints out-breath'd.
30   "Alas, from what high hope to what relapse
Unlook'd for are we fall'n, our eyes beheld
Messiah certainly now come, so long
Expected of our Fathers; we have heard

---

16 **Thisbite** Elijah.   21 **Aenon, and Salem** in Samaria.   22 **Machærus** fortress east of the Dead Sea.   23 **Genezaret** Sea of Galilee.   24 **Perea** east of Jordan.

His words, his wisdom full of grace and truth,
Now, now, for sure, deliverance is at hand,   35
The Kingdom shall to Israel be restor'd:
Thus we rejoic'd, but soon our joy is turn'd
Into perplexity and new amaze:
For whither is he gone, what accident
Hath rapt him from us? will he now retire   40
After appearance, and again prolong
Our expectation? God of Israel,
Send thy Messiah forth, the time is come;
Behold the Kings of the Earth how they oppress
Thy chosen, to what heighth their pow'r unjust   45
They have exalted, and behind them cast
All fear of thee, arise and vindicate
Thy Glory, free thy people from their yoke,
But let us wait; thus far hath perform'd,
Sent his Anointed, and to us reveal'd him,   50
By his great Prophet, pointed at and shown,
In public, and with him we have convers'd;
Let us be glad of this, and all our fears
Lay on his Providence; he will not fail
Nor will withdraw him now, nor will recall,   55
Mock us with his blest sight, then snatch him hence,
Soon we shall see our hope, our joy return."
        Thus they out of their plaints new hope resume
To find whom at the first they found unsought:
But to his Mother Mary, when she saw   60
Others return'd from Baptism, not her Son,
Nor left at Jordan, tidings of him none;
Within her breast, though calm; her breast though
    pure,
Motherly cares and fears got head, and rais'd
Some troubl'd thoughts, which she in sighs thus clad.   65
        "O what avails me now that honor high
To have conceiv'd of God, or that salute
'Hail highly favor'd, among women blest';
While I to sorrows am no less advanc't,
And fears as eminent, above the lot   70
Of other women, by the birth I bore,
In such a season born when scarce a Shed
Could be obtain'd to shelter him or me

From the bleak air; a Stable was our warmth,
75 A Manger his, yet soon enforc't to fly
    Thence into Egypt, till the Murd'rous King
    Were dead, who sought his life, and missing fill'd
    With Infant blood the streets of Bethlehem;
    From Egypt home return'd, in Nazareth
80 Hath been our dwelling many years, his life
    Private, unactive, calm, contemplative,
    Little suspicious to any King; but now
    Full grown to Man, acknowledg'd, as I hear,
    By John the Baptist, and in public shown,
85 Son own'd from Heaven by his Father's voice;
    I look't for some great change; to Honour? no,
    But trouble, as old Simeon plain foretold,
    That to the fall and rising he should be
    Of many in Israel, and to a sign
90 Spoken against, that through my very Soul
    A sword shall pierce, this is my favour'd lot,
    My Exaltation to Afflictions high;
    Afflicted I may be, it seems, and blest;
    I will not argue that, nor will repine.
95 But where delays he now? some great intent
    Conceals him: when twelve years he scarce had seen,
    I lost him, but so found, as well I saw
    He could not lose himself; but went about
    His Father's business; what he meant I mus'd,
100 Since understand; much more his absence now
    Thus long to some great purpose he obscures.
    But I to wait with patience am inur'd;
    My heart hath been a store-house long of things
    And sayings laid up, portending strange events."
105   Thus Mary pondering oft, and oft to mind
    Recalling what remarkably had pass'd
    Since first her Salutation heard, with thoughts
    Meekly compos'd awaited the fulfilling:
    The while her Son tracing the Desert wild,
110 Sole but with holiest Meditations fed,
    Into himself descended, and at once
    All his great work to come before him set;
    How to begin, how to accomplish best
    His end of being on Earth, and mission high:

For Satan with sly preface° to return   *115*
Had left him vacant,° and with speed was gone
Up to the middle Region of thick Air,
Where all his Potentates in Council sat;
There without sign of boast, or sign of joy,
Solicitous and blank° he thus began.   *120*
     "Princes, Heaven's ancient Sons, Ethereal
      · Thrones,
Demonian Spirits now, from the Element
Each of his reign allotted, rightlier call'd,
Powers of Fire, Air, Water, and Earth beneath,
So may we hold our place and these mild seats   *125*
Without new trouble; such an Enemy
Is ris'n to invade us, who no less
Threat'ns than our expulsion down to Hell;
I, as I undertook, and with the vote
Consenting in full frequence° was empow'r'd,   *130*
Have found him, view'd him, tasted° him, but find
Far other labour to be undergone
Than when I dealt with Adam first of Men,
Though Adam by his Wife's allurement fell,
However to this Man inferior far,   *135*
If he be Man by Mother's side at least,
With more than human gifts from Heav'n adorn'd,
Perfections absolute, Graces divine,
And amplitude of mind to greatest Deeds.
Therefore I am return'd, lest confidence   *140*
Of my success with Eve in Paradise
Deceive ye to persuasion over-sure
Of like succeeding here; I summon all
Rather to be in readiness with hand
Or counsel to assist; lest I who erst   *145*
Thought none my equal, now be over-match'd."
     So spake the old Serpent doubting, and from
      all
With clamour was assur'd their utmost aid
At his command; when from amidst them rose
Belial the dissolutest Spirit that fell,   *150*
The sensuallest, and after Asmodai°

115 **preface** saying beforehand.   116 **vacant** at leisure.   120 **Solicitous and blank** anxious and nonplussed.   130 **frequence** assembly.   131 **tasted** made trial of.   151 **Asmodai** see *PL* IV 168–71.

The fleshliest Incubus,° and thus advis'd.
  "Set women in his eye and in his walk,
Among daughters of men the fairest found;
155 Many are in each Region passing fair
As the noon Sky; more like to Goddesses
Than Mortal Creatures, graceful and discreet,
Expért in amorous Arts, enchanting tongues
Persuasive, Virgin majesty with mild
160 And sweet allay'd, yet terrible to approach,
Skill'd to retire, and in retiring draw
Hearts after them tangl'd in Amorous Nets.
Such object hath the power to soft'n and tame
Severest temper, smooth the rugged'st brow,
165 Enerve,° and with voluptuous hope dissolve,
Draw out with credulous desire, and lead
At will the manliest, resolutest breast,
As the Magnetic° hardest Iron draws.
Women, when nothing else, beguil'd the heart
170 Of wisest Solomon, and made him build,
And made him bow to the Gods of his Wives."
   To whom quick answer Satan thus return'd.
"Belial, in much uneven scale thou weigh'st
All others by thyself; because of old
175 Thou thyself doat'st on womankind, admiring
Their shape, their colour, and attractive grace,
None are, thou think'st, but taken with such toys.
Before the Flood thou with thy lusty Crew,
False titl'd Sons of God, roaming the Earth
180 Cast wanton eyes on the daughters of men,
And coupl'd with them, and begot a race.
Have we not seen, or by relation heard,
In Courts and Regal Chambers how thou lurk'st,
In Wood or Grove by mossy Fountain-side,
185 In Valley or Green Meadow to waylay
Some beauty rare, Calisto, Clymene,
Daphne, or Semele, Antiopa,
Or Amymóne, Syrinx, many more
Too long, then lay'st thy scapes° on names ador'd,
190 Apollo, Neptune, Jupiter, or Pan,

152 **Incubus** a demon which had intercourse with women in their
sleep.   165 **Enerve** enervate, weaken.   168 **Magnetic** magnet.   189 **scapes**
lustful escapades.

Satyr, or Faun, or Sylvan?° But these haunts
Delight not all; among the Sons of Men,
How many have with a smile made small account
Of beauty and her lures, easily scorn'd
All her assaults, on worthier things intent?   *195*
Remember that Pellean Conqueror,°
A youth, how all the Beauties of the East
He slightly° view'd, and slightly over-pass'd;
How hee° surnam'd of Africa dismiss'd
In his prime youth the fair Iberian maid.   *200*
For Solomon he liv'd at ease, and full
Of honour, wealth, high fare, aim'd not beyond
Higher design than to enjoy his State;°
Thence to the bait of Women lay expos'd;
But he whom we attempt is wiser far   *205*
Than Soloman, of more exalted mind,
Made and set wholly on the accomplishment
Of greatest things; what woman will you find,
Though of this Age the wonder and the fame,
On whom his leisure will vouchsafe an eye   *210*
Of fond° desire? or should she confident,
As sitting Queen ador'd on Beauty's Throne,
Descend with all her winning charms begirt
To enamour, as the Zone° of Venus once
Wrought that effect on Jove, so Fables tell;   *215*
How would one look from his Majestic brow
Seated as on the top of Virtue's hill,
Discount'nance her despis'd, and put to rout
All her array; her female pride deject,
Or turn to reverent awe? for Beauty stands   *220*
In the admiration only of weak minds
Led captive; cease to admire, and all her Plumes
Fall flat and shrink into a trivial toy,
At every sudden slighting quite abasht:
Therefore with manlier objects we must try   *225*
His constancy, with such as have more show
Of worth, of honour, glory, and popular praise;
Rocks whereon greatest men have oftest wreck'd;

191 **Sylvan** Sylvanus, a forest god (*PL* IV 107–8).   196 **that . . . Conqueror** Alexander the Great, from Pella in Macedon.   198 **slightly** slightingly.   199 **hee** Scipio Africanus.   203 **State** high rank.   211 **fond** including "foolish."   214 **Zone** belt.

Or that which only seems to satisfy
230 Lawful desires of Nature, not beyond;
And now I know he hungers where no food
Is to be found, in the wide Wilderness;
The rest commit to me, I shall let pass
No advantage, and his strength as oft assay."
235   He ceas'd and heard their grant in loud
          acclaim;
Then forthwith to him takes a chosen band
Of Spirits likest to himself in guile
To be at hand, and at his beck appear,
If cause were to unfold some active° Scene
240 Of various persons each to know his part;
Then to the Desert takes with these his flight;
Where still from shade to shade the Son of God
After forty days fasting had remain'd,
Now hung'ring first, and to himself thus said.
245   "Where will this end? four times ten days I
          have pass'd
Wand'ring this woody maze, and human food
Nor tasted, nor had appetite; that Fast
To Virtue I impute not, or count part
Of what I suffer here; if Nature need not,
250 Or God support Nature without repast
Though needing, what praise is it to endure?
But now I feel I hunger, which declares,
Nature hath need of what she asks; yet God
Can satisfy that need some other way,
255 Though hunger still remain: so it remain
Without this body's wasting, I content me,
And from the sting of Famine fear no harm,
Nor mind it, fed with better thoughts that feed
Mee hungering more to do my Father's will."
260   It was the hour of night, when thus the Son
Commun'd in silent walk, then laid him down
Under the hospitable covert nigh
Of Trees thick interwoven; there he slept,
And dreamed, as appetite is wont to dream,
265 Of meats and drinks, Nature's refreshment sweet;
Him thought, he by the Brook of Cherith stood

239 **active** lively, with a hint of "acted."

And saw the Ravens with their horny beaks
Food to Elijah bringing Even and Morn,
Though ravenous,° taught to abstain from what they
   brought:
He saw the Prophet also how he fled   270
Into the Desert, and how there he slept
Under a Juniper; then how awak't,
He found his Supper on the coals prepar'd,
And by the Angel was bid rise and eat,
And ate the second time after repose,   275
The strength whereof suffic'd him forty days;
Sometimes that with Elijah he partook,
Or as a guest with Daniel° at his pulse.°
Thus wore out night, and now the Herald Lark
Left his ground-nest, high tow'ring to descry   280
The morn's approach, and greet her with his Song:
As lightly from his grassy Couch up rose
Our Saviour, and found all was but a dream,
Fasting he went to sleep, and fasting wak'd.
Up to a hill anon his steps he rear'd,   285
From whose high top to ken the prospect round,
If Cottage were in view, Sheep-cote or Herd;
But Cottage, Herd or Sheep-cote none he saw,
Only in a bottom° saw a pleasant Grove,
With chant of tuneful Birds resounding loud;   290
Thither he bent his way, determin'd there
To rest at noon, and enter'd soon the shade
High rooft and walks beneath, and alleys brown
That open'd in the midst a woody Scene,
Nature's own work it seem'd (Nature taught Art)   295
And to a Superstitious eye the haunt
Of Wood-Gods and Wood-Nymphs; he view'd it
   round,
When suddenly a man before him stood,
Not rustic as before, but seemlier clad,
As one in City, or Court, or Palace bred,   300

269 **ravenous** not etymologically connected with "Ravens." "If it had
been justified by derivation, as perhaps it claims to be, it would have been
all right; the meaning would be 'though as every one admits, so that their
name itself implies it, this required a serious miracle.'" (William Empson). 278 **Daniel** the prophet. 278 **pulse** peas and beans. 289 **bottom** valley.

And with fair speech these words to him address'd.
    "With granted leave officious° I return,
But much more wonder that the Son of God
In this wild solitude so long should bide
305 Of all things destitute, and well I know,
Not without hunger. Others of some note,
As story tells, have trod this Wilderness;
The Fugitive Bond-woman with her Son
Out cast Nebaioth, yet found he relief
310 By a providing Angel; all the race
Of Israel here had famish'd, had not God
Rain'd from Heaven Manna, and that Prophet bold
Native of Thebès° wand'ring here was fed
Twice by a voice inviting him to eat.
315 Of thee these forty days none hath regard,
Forty and more deserted here indeed."
        To whom thus Jesus; "what conclud'st thou
           hence?
They all had need, I as thou seest have none."
        "How hast thou hunger then?" Satan repli'd,
320 "Tell me if Food were now before thee set,
Would'st thou not eat?" "Thereafter as I like
The giver," answer'd Jesus. "Why should that
Cause thy refusal," said the subtle Fiend,
"Hast thou not right to all Created things,
325 Owe not all Creatures by just right to thee
Duty and Service, nor to stay till bid,
But tender all their power? nor mention I
Meats by the Law unclean, or offer'd first
To Idols, those young Daniel could refuse;
330 Nor proffer'd by an Enemy, though who
Would scruple that, with want opprest? behold
Nature asham'd, or better to express,
Troubl'd that thou shouldst hunger, hath purvey'd
From all the Elements her choicest store
335 To treat thee as beseems, and as her Lord
With honour, only deign to sit and eat."
        He spake no dream, for as his words had end,
Our Saviour lifting up his eyes beheld
In ample space under the broadest shade

302 **officious** dutiful.   313 **Thebès** Thisbe, the city of Elijah.

A Table richly spread, in regal mode,   340
With dishes pil'd, and meats of noblest sort
And savour, Beasts of chase, or Fowl of game,
In pastry built, or from the spit; or boil'd,
Grisamber-steam'd;° all Fish from Sea or Shore,
Freshet,° or purling Brook, of shell or fin,   345
And exquisitest name, for which was drain'd
Pontus° and Lucrine Bay,° and Afric Coast.
Alas how simple, to these Cates° compar'd,
Was that crude° Apple that diverted° Eve!
And at a stately sideboard by the wine   350
That fragrant smell diffus'd, in order stood
Tall stripling youths rich clad, of fairer hue
Then Ganymede° or Hylas,° distant more
Under the Trees now tripp'd, now solemn stood
Nymphs of Diana's° train, and Naiades°   355
With fruits and flowers from Amalthea's horn,°
And Ladies of th'Hesperides, that seem'd
Fairer than feign'd of old, or fabl'd since
Of Fairy Damsels met in Forest wide
By Knights of Logres, or of Lyonnesse,°   360
Lancelot or Pelleas, or Pellenore,°
And all the while Harmonious Airs were heard
Of chiming strings, or charming pipes and winds
Of gentlest gale Arabian odours fann'd
From their soft wings, and Flora's° earliest smells.   365
Such was the Splendour, and the Temper now
His invitation earnestly renew'd.
            "What doubts° the Son of God to sit and eat?
These are not Fruits forbidden, no interdict
Defends° the touching of these viands pure,   370
Their taste no knowledge works, at least of evil,
But life preserves, destroys life's enemy,
Hunger, with sweet restorative delight.
All these are Spirits of Air, and Woods, and Springs,

344 **Grisamber-steam'd** cooked in rich ambergris. 345 **Freshet** stream. 347 **Pontus** Black Sea. 347 **Lucrine Bay** near Naples. 348 **Cates** delicacies. 349 **crude** uncooked and sour. 349 **diverted** turned awry. 353 **Ganymede** Jove's cupbearer. 353 **Hylas** friend of Hercules. 355 **Diana** goddess of hunting. 355 **Naiades** river-nymphs. 356 **horn** the rich cornucopia of the nymph Amalthea. 360 **Logres ... Lyonesse** Arthurian regions. 361 **Lancelot ... Pellenore** Arthurian knights. 365 **Flora** goddess of flowers. 368 **What doubts** why fears. 370 **Defends** forbids.

375 Thy gentle Ministers, who came to pay
     Thee homage, and acknowledge thee their Lord:
     What doubt'st thou Son of God? sit down and eat."
          To whom thus Jesus temperately repli'd:
     "Said'st thou not that to all things I had right?
380 And who withholds my pow'r that right to use?
     Shall I receive by gift what of my own,
     When and where he likes me best, I can command?
     I can at will, doubt not, as soon as thou,
     Command a Table in this Wilderness,
385 And call swift flights of Angels ministrant
     Array'd in Glory on my cup to attend:
     Why shouldst thou then obtrude this diligence,
     In vain, where no acceptance it can find,
     And with my hunger what halt thou to do?
390 Thy pompous° Delicacies I contemn,°
     And count thy specious gifts no gifts but guiles."
          To whom thus answer'd Satan malcontent:
     "That I have also power to give thou seest,
     If of that pow'r I bring thee voluntary
395 What I might have bestow'd on whom I pleas'd,
     And rather opportunely in this place
     Chose to impart to thy apparent° need,
     Why shouldst thou not accept it? but I see
     What I can do or offer is suspéct;
400 Of these things others quickly will dispose
     Whose pains have earn'd the far-fet° spoil." With that
     Both Table and Provision vanish'd quite
     With sound of Harpies'° wings, and Talons heard;
     Only the impórtune Tempter still remain'd,
405 And with these words his temptation pursu'd.
          "By hunger, that each other Creature tames,
     Thou art not to be harm'd, therefore not mov'd;
     Thy temperance invincible besides,
     For no allurement yields to appetite,
410 And all thy heart is set on high designs,
     High actions; but wherewith to be achiev'd?
     Great acts require great means of enterprise,
     Thou art unknown, unfriended, low of birth,

390 **pompous** oversplendid.   390 **contemn** despise.   397 **apparent** manifest.   401 **far-fet** far-fetched.   403 **Harpies** monsters, half-woman and
half-bird.

A Carpenter thy Father known, thyself
Bred up in poverty and straits at home;   *415*
Lost in a Desert here and hunger-bit:
Which way or from what hope dost thou aspire
To greatness? whence Authority deriv'st,
What Followers, what Retínue canst thou gain,
Or at thy heels the dizzy Multitude,   *420*
Longer than thou canst feed them on thy cost?
Money brings Honour, Friends, Conquest, and Realms;
What rais'd Antipater the Edomite,
And his Son Herod plac'd on Judah's Throne;
(Thy throne) but gold that got him puissant friends? *425*
Therefore, if at great things thou wouldst arrive,
Get Riches first, get Wealth, and Treasure heap,
Not difficult, if thou hearken to me,
Riches are mine, Fortune is in my hand;
They whom I favour thrive in wealth amain,   *430*
While Virtue, Valour, Wisdom sit in want."
        To whom thus Jesus patiently repli'd;
"Yet Wealth without these three is impotent,
To gain dominion or to keep it gain'd.
Witness those ancient Empires of the Earth,   *435*
In heighth of all their flowing wealth dissolv'd:
But men endu'd with these° have oft attain'd
In lowest poverty to highest deeds;
Gideon and Jephtha, and the Shepherd lad,°
Whose offspring on the Throne of Judah sat   *440*
So many Ages, and shall yet regain
That seat, and reign in Israel without end.
Among the Heathen, (for throughout the World
To me is not unknown what hath been done
Worthy of Memorial) canst thou not remember   *445*
Quintius, Fabricius, Curius, Regulus?
For I esteem those names of men so poor
Who could do mighty things, and could contemn
Riches though offer'd from the hand of Kings.
And what in me seems wanting, but that I   *450*
May also in this poverty as soon
Accomplish what they did, perhaps and more?

437 **these** the three qualities of line 431.   439 **the . . . lad** David.

Extol not Riches then, the toil° of Fools,
The wise man's cumbrance if not snare, more apt
455   To slacken Virtue, and abate her edge,
Than prompt her to do aught may merit praise.
What if with like aversion I reject
Riches and Realms; yet not for that a Crown,
Golden in show, is but a wreath of thorns,
460   Brings dangers, troubles, cares, and sleepless nights
To him who wears the Regal Diadem,
When on his shoulders each man's burden lies;
For therein stands the office of a King,
His Honour, Virtue, Merit and chief Praise,
465   That for the Public all this weight he bears.
Yet he who reigns within himself, and rules
Passions, Desires, and Fears, is more a King;
Which every wise and virtuous man attains:
And who attains not, ill aspires to rule
470   Cities of men, or headstrong Multitudes,
Subject himself to Anarchy within,
Or lawless passions in him which he serves.
But to guide Nations in the way of truth
By saving° Doctrine, and from error lead
475   To know, and knowing worship God aright,
Is yet more Kingly, this attracts the Soul,
Governs the inner man, the nobler part,
That other o'er the body only reigns,
And oft by force, which to a generous mind
480   So reigning can be no sincere delight.
Besides to give a Kingdom hath been thought
Greater and nobler done, and to lay down
Far more magnanimous, than to assume.
Riches are needless then, both for themselves,
485   And for thy reason why they should be sought,
To gain a Scepter, oftest better miss't."

453 **toil** trap and labor: 474 **saving** which grants salvation.

BOOK III

So spake the son of God, and Satan stood
Awhile as mute confounded what to say,
What to reply, confuted and convinc't
Of his weak arguing, and fallacious drift;
At length collecting all his Serpent wiles,   5
With soothing words renew'd, him thus accosts.
      "I see thou know'st what is of use to know,
What best to say canst say, to do canst do;
Thy actions to thy words accord, thy words
To thy large heart give utterance due, thy heart   10
Contains of good, wise, just, the perfect shape.
Should Kings and Nations from thy mouth consult,
Thy Counsel would be as the Oracle
Urim and Thummim,° those oraculous gems
On Aaron's breast: or tongue of Seers old   15
Infallible; or wert thou sought to° deeds
That might require th'array of war, thy skill
Of conduct would be such, that all the world
Could not sustain thy Prowess, or subsist
In battle, though against thy few in arms.   20
These God-like Virtues wherefore dost thou hide?
Affecting private life, or more obscure
In savage Wilderness, wherefore deprive
All Earth her wonder at thy acts, thyself
The fame and glory, glory the reward   25
That sole excites to high attempts the flame
Of most erected Spirits, most temper'd pure
Ethereal, who all pleasures else despise,
All treasures and all gain esteem as dross,
And dignities and powers all but the highest?   30
Thy years are ripe, and over-ripe, the Son
Of Macedonian Philip° had ere these
Won Asia and the Throne of Cyrus held

14 **Urim and Thummim** sacred stones worn by the priest. 16 **sought to**
"seek," to make it one's aim. 31–32 **Son . . . Philip** Alexander the
Great.

       At his dispose, young Scipio had brought down
35   The Carthaginian pride, young Pompey quell'd
       The Pontic King° and in triúmph had rode.
       Yet years, and to ripe years judgement mature,
       Quench not the thirst of glory, but augment.
       Great Julius,° whom now all the world admires
40   The more he grew in years, the more inflam'd
       With glory, wept that he had liv'd so long
       Inglorious: but thou yet art not too late."
               To whom our Saviour calmly thus repli'd.
       "Thou neither dost persuade me to seek wealth
45   For Empire's sake, nor Empire to affect°
       For glory's sake by all thy argument.
       For what is glory but the blaze of fame,
       The people's praise, if always praise unmixt?
       And what the people but a herd confus'd,
50   A miscellaneous rabble, who extol
       Things vulgar, and well-weigh'd, scarce worth the
           praise
       They praise and they admire they know not what;
       And know not whom, but as one leads the other;
       And what delight to be by such extoll'd,
55   To live upon their tongues and be their talk,
       Of whom to be disprais'd were no small praise?
       His lot who dares be singularly good.
       Th'intelligent among them and the wise
       Are few, and glory scarce of few is rais'd.
60   This is true glory and renown, when God
       Looking on the Earth, with approbation marks
       The just man, and divulges° him through Heaven
       To all his Angels, who with true applause
       Recount his praises; thus he did to Job,
65   When to extend his fame through Heaven and Earth,
       As thou to thy reproach mayst well remember,
       He ask'd thee, 'Hast thou seen my servant Job?'
       Famous he was in Heaven, on Earth less known;
       Where glory is false glory, áttribúted
70   To things not glorious, men not worthy of fame.
       They err who count it glorious to subdue

---

36 **Pontic King** Mithridates. 39 **Julius** Caesar. 45 **affect** aim at.
62 **divulges** publicly proclaims.

By Conquest far and wide, to over-run
Large Countries, and in field great Battles win,
Great Cities by assault: what do these Worthies,
But rob and spoil, burn, slaughter, and enslave   75
Peaceable Nations, neighbouring, or remote,
Made Captive, yet deserving freedom more
Then those their Conquerors, who leave behind
Nothing but ruin wheresoe'er they rove,
And all the flourishing works of peace destroy,   80
Then swell with pride, and must be titl'd Gods,
Great Benefactors of mankind, Deliverers,
Worship't with Temple, Priest and Sacrifice;
One is the Son of Jove, of Mars the other,
Till Conqueror Death discover them scarce men,   85
Rolling in brutish vices, and deform'd,
Violent or shameful death their due reward.
But if there be in glory aught of good,
It may by means far different be attain'd
Without ambition, war, or violence;   90
By deeds of peace, by wisdom eminent,
By patience, temperance; I mention still
Him whom thy wrongs with Saintly patience borne,
Made famous in a Land and times obscure;
Who names not now with honour patient Job?   95
Poor Socrates (who next more memorable?)
By what he taught and suffer'd for so doing,
For truth's sake suffering death unjust, lives now
Equal in fame to proudest Conquerors.
Yet if for fame and glory aught be done,   100
Aught suffer'd; if young African° for fame
His wasted Country freed from Punic rage,
The deed becomes unprais'd, the man at least,
And loses, though but verbal, his reward.
Shall I seek glory then, as vain men seek   105
Oft not deserv'd? I seek not mine, but his
Who sent me, and thereby witness whence I am."
    To whom the Tempter murmuring thus repli'd.
"Think not so slight of glory; therein least
Resembling thy great Father: he seeks glory,   110
And for his glory all things made, all things

---

101 **African** Scipio Africanus.

Orders and governs, nor content in Heaven
By all his Angels glorifi'd, requires
Glory from men, from all men good or bad,
115 Wise or unwise, no difference, no exemption;
Above all Sacrifice, or hallow'd gift
Glory he requires, and glory he receives
Promiscuous from all Nations, Jew, or Greek,
Or Barbarous,° nor exception hath declar'd;
120 From us his foes pronounc't glory he exacts."
       To whom our Saviour fervently repli'd.
"And reason; since his word all things produc'd,
Though chiefly not for glory as prime end,
But to show forth his goodness, and impart
125 His good communicable to every soul
Freely; of whom what could he less expect
Than glory and benediction, that is thanks,
The slightest, easiest, readiest recompense
From them who could return him nothing else,
130 And not returning that would likeliest render
Contempt instead, dishonour, obloquy?
Hard recompense, unsuitable return
For so much good, so much beneficence.
But why should man seek glory? who of his own
135 Hath nothing, and to whom nothing belongs
But condemnation, ignominy, and shame?
Who for so many benefits receiv'd
Turn'd recreant to God, ingrate° and false,
And so of all true good himself despoil'd,
140 Yet, sacrilegious, to himself would take
That which to God alone of right belongs;
Yet so much bounty is in God, such grace,
That who advance his glory, not their own,
Them he himself to glory will advance."
145   So spake the Son of God; and here again
Satan had not to answer, but stood struck
With guilt of his own sin, for he himself
Insatiable of glory had lost all,
Yet of another Plea bethought him soon.
150   "Of glory as thou wilt," said he, "so deem,
Worth or not worth the seeking, let it pass:

119 **Barbarous** non-Greek.   138 **ingrate** ungrateful.

But to a Kingdom thou art born, ordain'd
To sit upon thy Father David's Throne;
By Mother's side thy Father, though thy right
Be now in powerful hands, that will not part   155
Easily from possession won with arms;
Judæa now and all the promis'd land
Reduc't a Province under Roman yoke,
Obeys Tiberius; nor is always rul'd
With temperate sway; oft have they violated   160
The Temple, oft the Law with foul affronts,
Abominations rather, as did once
Antiochus:° and think'st thou to regain
Thy right by sitting still or thus retiring?
So did not Machabeus: he indeed   165
Retir'd unto the Desert, but with arms;
And o'er a mighty King so oft prevail'd,
That by strong hand his Family obtain'd,
Though Priests, the Crown, and David's Throne
    usurp'd,
With Modin and her Suburbs once content.   170
If Kingdom move thee not, let move thee Zeal,
And Duty; Zeal and Duty are not slow;
But on Occasion's forelock watchful wait.
They themselves rather are occasion best,
Zeal of thy Father's house, Duty to free   175
Thy Country from her Heathen servitude;
So shalt thou best fulfill, best verify
The Prophets old, who sung thy endless reign,
The happier reign the sooner it begins,
Reign then; what canst thou better do the while?"   180
    To whom our Saviour answer thus return'd.
"All things are best fulfill'd in their due time,
And time there is for all things, Truth hath said:
If of my reign Prophetic Writ hath told
That it shall never end, so when begin   185
The Father in his purpose hath decreed,
He in whose hand all times and seasons roll.
What if he hath decreed that I shall first
Be tri'd in humble state, and things adverse,

163 **Antiochus** king of Syria against whom Judas Maccabeus (line 165—
he was born in "Modin," line 170) led the Jews.

190 By tribulations, injuries, insults,
    Contempts, and scorns, and snares, and violence,
    Suffering, abstaining, quietly expecting
    Without distrust or doubt, that he may know
    What I can suffer, how obey? who best
195 Can suffer, best can do; best reign, who first
    Well hath obey'd; just trial ere I merit
    My exaltation without change or end.
    But what concerns it thee when I begin
    My everlasting Kingdom, why art thou
200 Solicitous, what moves thy inquisition?
    Know'st thou not that my rising is thy fall,
    And my promotion will be thy destruction?"
        To whom the Tempter inly rackt repli'd.
    "Let that come when it comes; all hope is lost
205 Of my reception into grace; what worse?
    For where no hope is left, is left no fear;
    If there be worse, the expectation more
    Of worse torments me than the feeling can.
    I would be at the worst; worst is my Port,
210 My harbour and my ultimate repose,
    The end I would attain, my final good.
    My error was my error, and my crime
    My crime; whatever for itself condemn'd,
    And will alike be punish'd; whether thou
215 Reign or reign not; though to that gentle brow
    Willingly I could fly, and hope thy reign,
    From that placid aspéct and meek regard,
    Rather than aggravate my evil state,
    Would stand between me and thy Father's ire,
220 (Whose ire I dread more than the fire of Hell)
    A shelter and a kind of shading cool
    Interposition, as a summer's cloud.
    If I then to the worst that can be haste,
    Why move thy feet so slow to what is best,
225 Happiest both to thyself and all the world,
    That thou who worthiest art shouldst be their King?
    Perhaps thou linger'st in deep thoughts detain'd
    Of the enterprise so hazardous and high;
    No wonder, for though in thee be united
230 What of perfection can in man be found,
    Or human nature can receive, consider

Thy life hath yet been private, most part spent
At home, scarce view'd the Galilean Towns,
And once a year Jerusalem, few days'
Short sojourn; and what thence couldst thou observe?   235
The world thou hast not seen, much less her glory,
Empires, and Monarchs, and their radiant Courts,
Best school of best experience, quickest in sight
In all things that to greatest actions lead.
The wisest, unexperienc't, will be ever   240
Timorous and loath, with novice modesty,
(As he° who seeking Asses found a Kingdom)
Irresolute, unhardy, unadvent'rous:
But I will bring thee where thou soon shalt quit
Those rudiments, and see before thine eyes   245
The Monarchies of the Earth, their pomp and state,
Sufficient introduction to inform
Thee, of thyself so apt, in regal Arts,
And regal Mysteries; that thou may'st know
How best their opposition to withstand."   250
        With that (such power was giv'n him then) he
                took
The Son of God up to a Mountain high.
It was a Mountain at whose verdant feet
A spacious plain outstretch't in circuit wide
Lay pleasant; from his side two rivers° flow'd,   255
Th'one winding, the other straight and left between
Fair Champaign° with less° rivers intervein'd,
Then meeting join'd their tribute to the Sea:
Fertile of corn the glebe,° of oil and wine,
With herds the pastures throng'd, with flocks the hills, 260
Huge Cities and high-tow'r'd, that well might seem
The seats of mightiest Monarchs, and so large
The Prospect was, that here and there was room
For barren desert fountainless and dry.
To this high mountain-top the Tempter brought   265
Our Saviour, and new train of words began.
        "Well have we speded, and o'er hill and dale,
Forest and field, and flood, Temples and Towers
Cut shorter many a league; here thou behold'st

242 **he** Saul who, while seeking his father's asses, met the prophet Samuel.   255 **two rivers** Tigris and Euphrates.   257 **Champaign** field.   257 **less** lesser.   259 **glebe** soil.

270 Assyria and her Empire's ancient bounds,
    Araxes° and the Caspian lake, thence on
    As far as Indus East, Euphrates West,
    And oft beyond; to South the Persian Bay,
    And inaccessible° the Arabian drouth:
275 Here Nineveh, of length within her wall
    Several days' journey, built by Ninus old,
    Of that first golden Monarchy the seat,
    And seat of Salmanassar,° whose success
    Israel in long captivity still mourns;
280 There Babylon the wonder of all tongues,
    As ancient, but rebuilt by him° who twice
    Judah and all thy Father David's house
    Led captive, and Jerusalem laid waste,
    Till Cyrus° set them free; Persepolis
285 His City there thou seest, and Bactra there;
    Ecbatana her structure vast there shows,
    And Hecatompylos her hundred gates,
    There Susa by Choaspes, amber stream,
    The drink of none but Kings; of later fame
290 Built by Emathian,° or by Parthian hands,
    The great Seleucia, Nisibis, and there
    Artaxata, Teredon, Tesiphon,
    Turning with easy eye thou may'st behold.
    All these the Parthian, now some Ages past,
295 By great Arsaces led, who founded first
    That Empire, under his dominion holds
    From the luxurious° Kings of Antioch° won.
    And just in time thou com'st to have a view
    Of his great power; for now the Parthian King
300 In Ctesiphon hath gather'd all his Host
    Against the Scythian, whose incursions wild
    Have wasted Sogdiana; to her aid
    He marches now in haste; see, though from far,
    His thousands, in what martial equipage
305 They issue forth, Steel Bows, and Shafts their arms
    Of equal dread in flight, or in pursuit;
    All Horsemen, in which fight they most excel;

271 **Araxes** Armenian river.   274 **inaccessible** impenetrable.   278 **Sal-manassar** king of Assyria.   281 **him** Nebuchadnezzar who conquered Je-rusalem.   284 **Cyrus** ruler of Persia.   290 **Emathian** Macedonian.   297 **luxurious** voluptuous.   297 **Antioch** capital of Syria.

See how in warlike muster they appear,
In Rhombs and wedges,° and half moons, and wings."
    He look't and saw what numbers numberless   *310*
The City-gates out-pour'd, light armed Troops
In coats of Mail and military pride;
In Mail their horses clad, yet fleet and strong,
Prancing their riders bore, the flower and choice
Of many Provinces from bound to bound;   *315*
From Arachosia, from Candaor East,
And Margiana to the Hyrcanian cliffs
Of Caucasus, and dark Iberian dales,
From Atropatia and the neighbouring plains
Of Ádiabéne, Media, and the South   *320*
Of Susiana to Balsara's hav'n.
He saw them in their forms of battle rang'd,
How quick they wheel'd, and flying behind them shot
Sharp sleet of arrowy showers against the face
Of their pursuers, and overcame by flight;   *325*
The field all iron cast a gleaming brown,
Nor wanted clouds of foot,° nor on each horn,
Cuirassiers all in steel for standing fight;
Chariots or Elephants endorst with° Towers
Of Archers, nor of labouring Pioneers,   *330*
A multitude with Spades and Axes arm'd
To lay hills plain, fell woods, or valleys fill,
Or where plain was raise hill, or overlay
With bridges rivers proud, as with a yoke;
Mules after these, Camels and Dromedaries,   *335*
And Waggons fraught with Utensils of war.
Such forces met not, nor so wide a camp,
When Agrican° with all his Northern powers
Besieg'd Albracca, as Romances tell;
The City of Gallaphrone, from thence to win   *340*
The fairest of her Sex Angelica
His daughter, sought by many Prowest° Knights,
Both Paynim,° and the Peers of Charlemagne.
Such and so numerous was their Chivalry;°

309 **Rhombs and wedges** formations, lozenge-shaped and pointed.
327 **clouds of foot** multitudes of foot soldiers. 329 **endorst with** their
backs supporting. 338 **Agrican** king of the Tartars (the romance from
Boiardo's *Orlando Innamorato*). 342 **Prowest** most valiant. 343 **Paynim** pagan. 344 **Chivalry** see *PL* I 307.

345 At sight whereof the Fiend yet more presum'd,
    And to our Saviour thus his words renew'd.
         "That thou may'st know I seek not to engage°
    Thy Virtue, and not every way secure
    On no slight grounds thy safety; hear, and mark
350 To what end I have brought thee hither and shown
    All this fair sight; thy Kingdom though foretold
    By Prophet or by Angel, unless thou
    Endeavour, as thy Father David did,
    Thou never shalt obtain; prediction still
355 In all things, and all men, supposes means,
    Without means us'd, what it predicts revokes.
    But say thou wert possess'd of David's Throne
    By free consent of all, none opposite,°
    Samaritan or Jew; how couldst thou hope
360 Long to enjoy it quiet and secure,
    Between two such enclosing enemies
    Roman and Parthian? therefore one of these
    Thou must make sure thy own, the Parthian first
    By my advice, as nearer and of late
365 Found able by invasion to annoy
    Thy country, and captive lead away her Kings
    Antigonus, and old Hyrcanus bound,
    Maugre° the Roman: it shall be my task
    To render thee the Parthian at dispose;
370 Choose which thou wilt by conquest or by league.
    By him thou shalt regain, without him not,
    That which alone can truly re-install thee
    In David's royal seat, his true Successor,
    Deliverance of thy brethren, those ten Tribes
375 Whose offspring in his Territory yet serve
    In Habor, and among the Medes dispers't,
    Ten° Sons of Jacob, two of Joseph lost
    Thus long from Israel; serving as of old
    Their Fathers in the land of Egypt serv'd,
380 This offer sets before thee to deliver.
    These if from servitude thou shalt restore
    To their inheritance, then, nor till then,
    Thou on the Throne of David in full glory,

347 **engage** ensnare. 358 **opposite** opposing. 368 **Maugre** despite. 377 **Ten** the ten tribes of Israel, two of them "of Joseph."

From Egypt to Euphrates and beyond
Shalt reign, and Rome or Caesar not need fear."   385
　　　To whom our Saviour answer'd thus unmov'd.
"Much ostentation vain of fleshly arm,
And fragile arms, much instrument of war
Long in preparing, soon to nothing brought,
Before mine eyes thou hast set; and in my ear   390
Vented much policy,° and projects deep
Of enemies, of aids, battles and leagues,
Plausible° to the world, to me worth naught.
Means I must use thou say'st, prediction else
Will unpredict and fail me of the Throne: 395
My time I told thee, (and that time for thee
Were better farthest off) is not yet come;
When that comes think not thou to find me slack
On my part aught endeavouring, or to need
Thy politic maxims, or that cumbersome   400
Luggage of war there shown me, argument
Of human weakness rather than of strength.
My brethren, as thou call'st them; those Ten Tribes
I must deliver, if I mean to reign
David's true heir, and his full Scepter sway   405
To just extent over all Israel's Sons;
But whence to thee this zeal, where was it then
For Israel, or for David, or his Throne,
When thou stood'st up his Tempter to the pride
Of numb'ring Israel, which cost the lives   410
Of threescore and ten thousand Israelites
By three days' Pestilence? such was thy zeal
To Israel then, the same that now to me.
As for those captive Tribes, themselves were they
Who wrought their own captivity, fell off   415
From God to worship Calves, the Deities
Of Egypt, Baal next and Ashtaroth,°
And all the Idolatries of Heathen round,
Besides their other worse than heathenish crimes;
Nor in the land of their captivity   420
Humbled themselves, or penitent besought
The God of their forefathers; but so di'd

391 **policy** cunning plans. 393 **Plausible** commendable. 417 **Baal . . . Ashtaroth** see *PL* I 422.

Impenitent, and left a race behind
Like to themselves, distinguishable scarce
425 From Gentiles, but by Circumcision vain,
And God with Idols in their worship join'd.
Should I of these the liberty regard,
Who freed, as to their ancient Patrimony,
Unhumbl'd, unrepentant, unreform'd,
430 Headlong would follow; and to their Gods perhaps
Of Bethel and of Dan? no, let them serve
Their enemies, who serve Idols with God.
Yet he at length, time to himself best known,
Rememb'ring Abraham by some wondrous call
435 May bring them back repentant and sincere,
And at their passing cleave the Assyrian flood,°
While to their native land with joy they haste,
As the Red Sea and Jordan once he cleft,
When to the promis'd land their Fathers pass'd;
440 To his due time and providence I leave them."
        So spake Israel's true King, and to the Fiend
Made answer meet, that made void all his wiles.
So fares it when with truth falsehood contends.

436 **Assyrian flood** Euphrates.

BOOK IV

Perplex'd and troubl'd at his bad success°
The Tempter stood, nor had what to reply,
Discover'd in his fraud, thrown from his hope,
So oft, and the persuasive Rhetoric
That sleek't his tongue, and won so much on Eve,   *5*
So little here, nay lost; but Eve was Eve,
This far his over-match, who self-deceiv'd
And rash, before-hand had no better weigh'd
The strength he was to cope with, or his own:
But as a man who had been matchless held   *10*
In cunning, over-reach't where least he thought,
To salve his credit, and for very spite
Still will be tempting him who foils him still,
And never cease, though to his shame the more;
Or as a swarm of flies in vintage time,   *15*
About the wine-press where sweet must° is pour'd,
Beat off, returns as oft with humming sound;
Or surging waves against a solid rock,
Though all to shivers dash't, the assault renew,
Vain batt'ry, and in froth or bubbles end;   *20*
So Satan, whom repulse upon repulse
Met ever; and to shameful silence brought,
Yet gives not o'er though desperate° of success,
And his vain importunity pursues.
He brought our Saviour to the western side   *25*
Of that high mountain, whence he might behold
Another plain, long but in breadth not wide;
Wash'd by the Southern Sea, and on the North
To equal length back'd with a ridge of hills
That screen'd the fruits of the earth and seats of men   *30*
From cold Septentrion° blasts, thence in the midst
Divided by a river, of whose banks
On each side an Imperial City stood,
With Towers and Temples proudly elevate

---

1 **success** outcome. 16 **must** unfermented wine. 23 **desperate** despairing. 31 **Septentrion** northern.

35 On seven small Hills, with Palaces adorn'd,
    Porches and Theatres, Baths, Aqueducts,
    Statues and Trophies, and Triumphal Arcs,
    Gardens and Groves presented to his eyes,
    Above the heighth of Mountains interpos'd.
40 By what strange Parallax° or Optic skill
    Of vision multiplied through air, or glass
    Of Telescope, were curious to inquire:
    And now the Tempter thus his silence broke.
         "The City which thou seest no other deem
45 Than great and glorious Rome, Queen of the Earth
    So far renown'd, and with the spoils enricht
    Of Nations; there the Capitol thou seest
    Above the rest lifting his stately head
    On the Tarpeian rock, her Citadel
50 Impregnable, and there Mount Palatine
    The Imperial Palace, compass huge, and high
    The Structure, skill of noblest Architects,
    With gilded battlements, conspicuous far,
    Turrets and Terraces, and glittering Spires.
55 Many a fair Edifice besides, more like
    Houses of Gods (so well I have dispos'd
    My Airy Microscope) thou may'st behold
    Outside and inside both, pillars and roofs
    Carv'd work, the hand of fam'd Artificers
60 In Cedar, Marble, Ivory or Gold.
    Thence to the gates cast round thine eye, and see
    What conflux issuing forth, or ent'ring in,
    Praetors,° Proconsuls to their Provinces
    Hasting or on return, in robes of State;
65 Lictors and rods the ensigns of their power,
    Legions and Cohorts, turms of horse° and wings:
    Or Embassies from Regions far remote
    In various habits on the Appian road,°
    Or on the Aemilian,° some from farthest South,
70 Syene, and where the shadow both way falls,

---

40 **Parallax** apparent displacment of an object caused by actual change of
the point of observation. 63 **Praetors** magistrates, and their attendants,
"Lictors" with their rods. 66 **turms of horse** divisions of cavalry. 68 **Ap-
pian road** from Rome to Brindisi. 69 **Aemilian** road northward from
Rome.

Meroë° Nilotic Isle, and more to West,
The Realm of Bocchus° to the Black-moor Sea;
From the Asian Kings and Parthian among these,
From India and the golden Chersoness,°
And utmost Indian Isle Tapróbanè,   75
Dusk faces with white silken Turbans wreath'd:
From Gallia,° Gades,° and the British West,
Germans and Scythians, and Sarmatians North
Beyond Danubius to the Tauric Pool.°
All Nations now to Rome obedience pay,   80
To Rome's great Emperor, whose wide domain
In ample Territory, wealth and power,
Civility of Manners, Arts, and Arms,
And long Renown thou justly may'st prefer
Before the Parthian; these two Thrones except,   85
The rest are barbarous, and scarce worth the sight,
Shar'd among petty Kings too far remov'd;
These having shown thee, I have shown thee all
The Kingdoms of the world, and all their glory.
This Emperor° hath no Son, and now is old,   90
Old and lascivious, and from Rome retir'd
To Capreæ an Island small but strong
On the Campanian shore, with purpose there
His horrid lusts in private to enjoy,
Committing to a wicked Favourite°   95
All public cares, and yet of him suspicious,
Hated of all, and hating; with what ease
Endu'd with Regal Vines as thou art,
Appearing, and beginning noble deeds,
Might'st thou expel this monster from his Throne   100
Now made a sty, and in his place ascending
A victor, people free from servile yoke?
And with my help thou may'st; to me the power
Is given, and by that right I give it thee.
Aim therefore at no less than all the world,   105
Aim at the highest, without the highest attain'd
Will be for thee no sitting, or not long
On David's Throne, be prophesi'd what will."

70–71 **Syene . . . Meroë** in Egypt. 72 **Bocchus** king of Mauretania.
74 **Chersoness** East Indies. 77 **Gallia** France. 77 **Gades** Cadiz. 79 **Tauric
Pool** Sea of Azov. 90 **Emperor** Tiberius, in Capri. 95 **Favourite**
Sejanus.

      To whom the Son of God unmov'd repli'd.
110 "Nor doth this grandeur and majestic show
    Of luxury, though call'd magnificence,
    More than of arms before, allure mine eye,
    Much less my mind; though thou shouldst add to tell
    Their sumptuous gluttonies, and gorgeous feasts
115 On Citron° tables or Atlantic° stone;
    (For I have also heard, perhaps have read)
    Their wines of Setia, Cales, and Falerne,°
    Chios and Crete,° and how they quaff in Gold,
    Crystal and Myrrhine° cups emboss'd with Gems
120 And studs of Pearl, to me should'st tell who thirst
    And hunger still: then Embassies thou show'st
    From Nations far and nigh; what honor that,
    But tedious waste of time to sit and hear
    So many hollow compliments and lies,
125 Outlandish flatteries? then proceed'st to talk
    Of the Emperor, how easily subdu'd,
    How gloriously; I shall, thou say'st, expel
    A brutish monster: what if I withal
    Expel a Devil who first made him such?
130 Let his tormenter Conscience find him out,
    For him I was not sent, nor yet to free
    That people victor once, now vile and base,
    Deservedly made vassal, who once just,
    Frugal, and mild, and temperate, conquer'd well,
135 But govern ill the Nations under yoke,
    Peeling° their Provinces, exhausted all
    By lust and rapine; first ambitious grown
    Of triumph that insulting vanity;
    Then cruel, by their sports to blood inur'd
140 Of fighting beasts, and men to beasts expos'd,
    Luxurious° by their wealth, and greedier still,
    And from the daily Scene° effeminate.
    What wise and valiant man would seek to free
    These thus degenerate, by themselves enslav'd,
145 Or could of inward slaves make outward free?
    Known therefore when my season comes to sit

115 **Citron** citrus wood. 115 **Atlantic** from the Atlas mountains.
117 **Setia . . . Falerne** in Italy. 118 **Chios and Crete** Aegean islands. 119 **Myrrhine** of fine stone. 136 **Peeling** pillaging. 141 **Luxurious** voluptuous. 142 **Scene** theater.

On David's Throne, it shall be like a tree
Spreading and over-shadowing all the Earth,
Or as a stone that shall to pieces dash
All Monarchies besides throughout the world,   150
And of my Kingdom there shall be no end:
Means there shall be to this, but what the means,
Is not for thee to know, nor me to tell."
      To whom the Tempter impudent repli'd.
"I see all offers made by me how slight   155
Thou valu'st, because offer'd, and reject'st:
Nothing will please the difficult and nice,°
Or nothing more than still to contradict:
On the other side know also thou, that I
On what I offer set as high esteem,   160
Nor what I part with mean to give for naught;
All these which in a moment thou behold'st
The Kingdoms of the world to thee I give;
For giv'n to me, I give to whom I please,
No trifle; yet with this reserve, not else,   165
On this condition, if thou wilt fall down,
And worship me as thy superior Lord,
Easily done, and hold them all of me;
For what can less so great a gift deserve?"
      Whom thus our Saviour answer'd with disdain.   170
"I never lik'd thy talk, thy offers less,
Now both abhor, since thou hast dar'd to utter
The abominable terms, impious condition;
But I endure the time, till which expir'd,
Thou hast permission on me. It is written   175
The first of all Commandments, 'Thou shalt worship
The Lord thy God, and only him shalt serve';
And dar'st thou to the Son of God propound
To worship thee accurst, now more accurst
For this attempt bolder than that on Eve,   180
And more blasphémous? which expect to rue.
The Kingdoms of the world to thee were giv'n,
Permitted rather, and by thee usurp't.
Other donation° none thou canst produce:
If given, by whom but by the King of Kings,   185
God over all supreme? if giv'n to thee,

157 **nice** fastidious.   184 **donation** grant.

By thee how fairly is the Giver now
Repaid? But gratitude in thee is lost
Long since. Wert thou so void of fear or shame,
190 As offer them to me the Son of God,
To me my own, on such abhorred pact,
That I fall down and worship thee as God?
Get thee behind me; plain thou now appear'st
That Evil one, Satan for ever damn'd."
195   To whom the Fiend with fear abasht repli'd.
"Be not so sore offended, Son of God;
Though Sons of God both Angels are and Men,
if I to try whether in higher sort
Than these thou bear'st that title, have propos'd
200 What both from Men and Angels I receive,
Tetrarchs° of fire, air, flood, and on the earth
Nations besides from all the quarter'd winds,
God of this world invok't and world beneath;
Who then thou art, whose coming is foretold
205 To me so fatal, me it most concerns.
The trial hath endamag'd thee no way,
Rather more honour left and more esteem;
Me naught advantag'd, missing what I aim'd.
Therefore let pass, as they are transitory,
210 The Kingdoms of this world; I shall no more
Advise thee, gain them as thou canst, or not.
And thou thyself seem'st otherwise inclin'd
Than to a worldly Crown, addicted more
To contemplation and profound dispute,
215 As by that early action may be judg'd,
When slipping from thy Mother's eye thou went'st
Alone into the Temple; there was found
Among the gravest Rabbis disputant
On points and questions fitting Moses' Chair,
220 Teaching not taught; the childhood shows the man,
As morning shows the day. Be famous then
By wisdom; as thy Empire must extend,
So let extend thy mind o'er all the world,
In knowledge, all things in it comprehend,
225 All knowledge is not couch't in Moses' Law,
The Pentateuch° or what the Prophets wrote,

201 **Tetrarchs** regents.   226 **Pentateuch** first five Books of the Bible.

The Gentiles also know, and write, and teach
To admiration, led by Nature's light;
And with the Gentiles much thou must converse,
Ruling them by persuasion as thou mean'st,   230
Without their learning how wilt thou with them,
Or they with thee hold conversation meet?
How wilt thou reason with them, how refute
Their Idolisms, Traditions, Paradoxes?
Error by his own arms is best evinc't.°   235
Look once more ere we leave this specular° Mount
Westward, much nearer by Southwest, behold
Where on the Aegean shore a City stands
Built nobly, pure the air, and light the soil,
Athens the eye of Greece, Mother of Arts   240
And Eloquence, native to famous wits°
Or hóspitáble, in her sweet recess,
City or Suburban, studious walks and shades;
See there the Olive Grove of Academe,
Plato's retirement, where the Attic Bird°   245
Trills her thick-warbl'd notes the summer long,
There flow'ry hill Hymettus with the sound
Of Bees' industrious murmur oft invites
To studious musing; there Ilissus rolls
His whispering stream; within the walls then view   250
The schools of ancient Sages; his° who bred
Great Alexander to subdue the world,
Lyceum there, und painted Stoa° next;
There thou shaft hear and learn the secret power
Of harmony in tones and numbers hit   255
By voice or hand, and various-measur'd verse,
Aeolian charms and Dorian Lyric Odes,°
And his who gave them breath, but higher sung,
Blind Melesigenes thence Homer call'd,
Whose Poem Phœbus challeng'd for his own.   260
Thence what the lofty grave Tragedians taught
In Chorus or Iambic,° teachers best
Of moral prudence, with delight receiv'd

235 **evinc't** conquered. 236 **specular** of observation. 241 **wits** gifted
men. 245 **Attic Bird** nightingale. 251 **his** Aristotle, who taught Alexander. 253 **Lyceum . . . Stoa** the park and the colonnade where the philosophers taught in Athens. 257 **Aeolian . . . Odes** The verse of Sappho and
of Pindar. 262 **Iambic** the meter of tragedy.

In brief sententious precepts, while they treat
265 Of fate, and chance, and change in human life;
High actions, and high passions best describing:
Thence to the famous Orators repair,
Those ancient, whose resistless eloquence
Wielded at will that fierce Democraty,
270 Shook the Arsenal° and fulmin'd° over Greece,
To Macedon, and Artaxerxes'° Throne;
To sage Philosophy next lend thine ear,
From Heaven descended to the low-rooft house
Of Socrates, see there his Tenement,
275 Whom well inspir'd the Oracle pronounc'd
Wisest of men; from whose mouth issu'd forth
Mellifluous streams that water'd all the schools
Of Academics old and new, with those
Surnam'd Peripatetics, and the Sect
280 Epicurean, and the Stoic severe;
These here revolve, or, as thou lik'st, at home,
Till time mature thee to a Kingdom's weight;
These rules will render thee a King complete
Within thyself, much more with Empire join'd."
285   To whom our Saviour sagely thus repli'd.
"Think not but that I know these things, or think
I know them not; not therefore am I short
Of knowing what I ought: he who receives
Light from above, from the fountain of light,
290 No other doctrine needs, though granted true;
But these are false, or little else but dreams,
Conjectures, fancies, built on nothing firm.
The first° and wisest of them all profess'd
To know this only, that he nothing knew;
295 The next° to fabling fell and smooth conceits,
A third sort° doubted all things, though plain sense;
Others in virtue plac'd felicity,
But virtue join'd with riches and long life,
In corporal pleasure he,° and careless ease,
300 The Stoic last in Philosophic pride,
By him call'd virtue; and his virtuous man,
Wise, perfect in himself, and all possessing

270 **Arsenal** Athenian building. 270 **fulmin'd** thundered. 271 **Artax-erxes** of Persia. 293 **The first** Socrates. 295 **The next** Plato. 296 **A third sort** followers of Pyrrho. 299 **he** Epicurus.

Equal to God, oft shames not to prefer,
As fearing God nor man, contemning all
Wealth, pleasure, pain or torment, death and life,   *305*
Which when he lists, he leaves, or boasts he can,
For all his tedious talk is but vain boast,
Or subtle shifts conviction to evade.
Alas what can they teach, and not mislead;
Ignorant of themselves, of God much more,   *310*
And how the world began, and how man fell
Degraded by himself, on grace depending?
Much of the Soul they talk, but all awry,
And in themselves seek virtue, and to themselves
All glory arrogate, to God give none,   *315*
Rather accuse him under usual names,
Fortune and Fate, as one regardless quite
Of mortal things. Who therefore seeks in these
True wisdom, finds her not, or by delusion
Far worse, her false resemblance only meets,   *320*
An empty cloud. However many books
Wise men have said are wearisome; who reads
Incessantly, and to his reading brings not
A spirit and judgement equal or superior,
(And what he brings, what needs he elsewhere seek)   *325*
Uncertain and unsettl'd still remains,
Deep verst in books and shallow in himself,
Crude or intoxicate, collecting toys,
And trifles for choice matters, worth a sponge;
As Children gathering pebbles on the shore.   *330*
Or if I would delight my private hours
With Music or with Poem, where so soon
As in our native Language can I find
That solace? All our Law and Story° strew'd
With Hymns, our Psalms with artful terms° inscrib'd,   *335*
Our Hebrew Songs and Harps in Babylon,
That pleas'd so well our Victors' ear, declare
That rather Greece from us these Arts derived;
Ill imitated, while they loudest sing
The vices of their Deities, and their own   *340*
In Fable, Hymn, or Song, so personating
Their Gods ridiculous, and themselves past shame.

334 **Story** history.   335 **artful terms** artistic figures of speech.

Remove their swelling Epithets thick laid
As varnish on a Harlot's cheek, the rest,
345 Thin sown with aught of profit or delight,
Will far be found unworthy to compare
With Sion's songs, to all true tastes excelling,
Where God is praised aright, and Godlike men,
The Holiest of Holies, and his Saints;
350 Such are from God inspir'd, not such from thee;
Unless where moral virtue is express't
By light of Nature not in all quite lost.
Their Orators thou then extoll'st, as those
The top of Eloquence, Statists° indeed,
355 And lovers of their Country, as may seem;
But herein to our Prophets far beneath,
As men divinely taught, and better teaching
The solid rules of Civil Government
In their majestic unaffected style
360 Than all the Oratory of Greece and Rome.
In them is plainest taught, and easiest learnt,
What makes a Nation happy, and keeps it so,
What ruins Kingdoms, and lays Cities flat;
These only with our Law best form a King."
365   So spake the Son of God; but Satan now
Quite at a loss, for all his darts were spent,
Thus to our Saviour with stern brow repli'd.
        "Since neither wealth, nor honour, arms nor
            arts,
Kingdom nor Empire pleases thee, nor aught
370 By me propos'd in life contemplative,
Or active, tended on by glory, or fame,
What dost thou in this World? the Wilderness
For thee is fittest place, I found thee there,
And thither will return thee, yet remember
375 What I foretell thee, soon thou shalt have cause
To wish thou never hadst rejected thus
Nicely or cautiously my offer'd aid,
Which would have set thee in short time with ease
On David's Throne; or Throne of all the world,
380 Now at full age, fullness of time, thy season,
When Prophecies of thee are best fulfill'd.

354 **Statists** statesmen.

Now contrary, if I read aught in Heaven,
Or Heav'n write aught of Fate, by what the Stars
Voluminous,° or single characters,
In their conjunction met, give me to spell,   385
Sorrows, and labours, opposition, hate,
Attends° thee, scorns, reproaches, injuries,
Violence and stripes, and lastly cruel death,
A Kingdom they portend thee, but what Kingdom,
Real or Allegoric I discern not,   390
Nor when, eternal sure, as without end,
Without beginning; for no date prefixt
Directs me in the Starry Rubric° set.''
    So saying he took (for still he knew his power
Not yet expir'd) and to the Wilderness   395
Brought back the Son of God, and left him there,
Feigning to disappear. Darkness now rose,
As daylight sunk, and brought in louring night
Her shadowy offspring unsubstantial both,
Privation mere of light and absent day.   400
Our Saviour meek and with untroubl'd mind
After his airy jaunt,° though hurried sore,
Hungry and cold betook him to his rest,
Wherever, under some concourse of shades
Whose branching arms thick intertwin'd might shield 405
From dews and damps of night his shelter'd head,
But shelter'd slept in vain, for at his head
The Tempter watch'd, and soon with ugly dreams
Disturb'd his sleep; and either Tropic° now
'Gan thunder, and both ends of Heav'n, the Clouds   410
From many a horrid rift abortive pour'd
Fierce rain with lightning mixt, water with fire
In ruin° reconcil'd: nor slept the winds
Within their stony caves, but rush'd abroad
From the four hinges of the world, and fell   415
On the vext° Wilderness, whose tallest Pines,
Though rooted deep as high, and sturdiest Oaks
Bow'd their Stiff necks, loaden with stormy blasts,
Or torn up sheer: ill wast thou shrouded° then,

383–84 **the Stars Voluminous** the copious book of the stars.   387 **Attends**
awaits.   393 **Rubric** heading of a book.   402 **jaunt** fatiguing journey.
409 **either Tropic** each part of the sky.   413 **ruin** falling.   416 **vext** buf-
feted.   419 **shrouded** sheltered.

420 O patient Son of God, yet only° stood'st
    Unshaken; nor yet stay'd the terror there,
    Infernal Ghosts, and Hellish Furies, round
    Environ'd thee, some howl'd, some yell'd, some
        shriek'd,
    Some bent at thee their fiery darts, while thou
425 Satt'st unappall'd in calm and sinless peace.
    Thus pass'd the night so foul till morning fair
    Came forth with Pilgrim steps in amice° gray;
    Who with her radiant finger still'd the roar
    Of thunder, chas'd the clouds, and laid the winds,
430 And grisly Specters, which the Fiend had rais'd
    To tempt the Son of God with terrors dire.
    And now the Sun with more effectual beams
    Had cheer'd the face of Earth, and dri'd the wet
    From drooping plant, or dropping tree; the birds
435 Who all things now behold more fresh and green,
    After a night of storm so ruinous,
    Clear'd up their choicest notes in bush and spray
    To gratulate the sweet return of morn;
    Nor yet amidst this joy and brightest morn
440 Was absent, after all his mischief done,
    The Prince of darkness, glad would also seem
    Of this fair change, and to our Saviour came,
    Yet with no new device, they all were spent,
    Rather by this his last affront resolv'd,
445 Desperate of better course, to vent his rage,
    And mad despite° to be so oft repell'd.
    Him walking on a Sunny hill he found,
    Back'd on the North and West by a thick wood,
    Out of the wood he starts in wonted shape;
450 And in a careless mood thus to him said.
            "Fair morning yet betides thee Son of God,
    After a dismal night; I heard the rack
    As Earth and Sky would mingle; but myself
    Was distant; and these flaws,° though mortals fear
        them
455 As dangerous to the pillar'd frame of Heaven,
    Or to the Earth's dark basis underneath,

420 **only** uniquely.   427 **amice** hood.   446 **despite** spite.   454 **flaws**
squalls.

Are to the main° as inconsiderable,
And harmless, if not wholesome, as a sneeze
To man's less universe, and soon are gone;
Yet as being oft-times noxious where they 'light   460
On man, beast, plant, wasteful and turbulent,
Like turbulencies in the affairs of men,
Over whose heads they roar, and seem to point,
They oft fore-signify and threaten ill:
This Tempest at this Desert most was bent;   465
Of men at thee, for only thou here dwell'st.
Did I not tell thee, if thou didst reject
The perfect season offer'd with my aid
To win thy destin'd seat, but wilt prolong
All to the push of Fate, pursue thy way   470
Of gaining David's Throne no man knows when,
For both the when and how is nowhere told,
Thou shalt be what thou art ordain'd, no doubt;
For Angels have proclaim'd it, but concealing
The time and means: each act is rightliest done,   475
Not when it must, but when it may be best.
If thou observe not this, be sure to find,
What I foretold thee, many a hard assay
Of dangers, and adversities and pains,
Ere thou of Israel's Scepter get fast hold;   480
Whereof this ominous night that clos'd thee round,
So many terror, voices, prodigies
May warn thee, as a sure fore-going sign."
        So talk'd he, while the Son of God went on
And stay'd not, but in brief him answer'd thus.   485
        "Mee worse than wet thou find'st not; other
            harm
Those terrors which thou speak'st of, did me none;
I never fear'd they could, though noising loud
And threat'ning nigh; what they can do as signs
Betok'ning, or ill boding, I contemn   490
As false portents, not sent from God, but thee;
Who knowing I shall reign past thy preventing,
Obtrud'st thy offer'd aid, that I accepting
At least might seem to hold all power of thee,
Ambitious spirit, and wouldst be thought my God,   495

457 **main** land.

And storm'st refus'd, thinking to terrify
Mee to thy will; desist, thou art discern'd
And toil'st in vain, nor me in vain molest."
      To whom the Fiend now swoll'n with rage
      repli'd:
500 "Then hear, O Son of David, Virgin-born;
For Son of God to me is yet in doubt,
Of the Messiah I have heard foretold
By all the Prophets; of thy birth at length
Announc't by Gabriel with the first I knew,
505 And of the Angelic Song in Bethlehem field,
On thy birth-night, that sung thee Saviour born.
From that time seldom have I ceas'd to eye
Thy infancy, thy childhood, and thy youth,
Thy manhood last, though yet in private bred;
510 Till at the Ford of Jordan whither all
Flock'd to the Baptist, I among the rest,
Though not to be Baptis'd, by voice from Heav'n
Heard thee pronounc'd the Son of God belov'd.
Thenceforth I thought thee worth my nearer view
515 And narrower Scrutiny, that I might learn
In what degree or meaning thou art call'd
The Son of God, which bears no single sense;
The Son of God I also am, or was,
And if I was, I am; relation stands;
520 All men are Sons of God; yet thee I thought
In some respect far higher so declar'd.
Therefore I watch'd thy footsteps from that hour,
And follow'd thee still on to this waste wild;
Where by all best conjectures I collect
525 Thou art to be my fatal enemy.
Good reason then, if I before-hand seek
To understand my Adversary, who
And what he is; his wisdom, power, intent,
By parle,° or composition, trace, or league
530 To win him, or win from him what I can.
And opportunity I here have had
To try thee, sift thee, and confess have found thee
Proof against all temptation as a rock
Of Adamant, and as a Center, firm

529 **parle** parley.

To the utmost of mere man both wise and good,   535
Not more; for Honours, Riches, Kingdoms, Glory
Have been before contemn'd, and may again:
Therefore to know what more thou art than man,
Worth naming Son of God by voice from Heav'n,
Another method I must now begin."   540
          So saying he caught him up, and without wing
Of Hippogrif° bore through the Air sublime
Over the Wilderness and o'er the Plain;
Till underneath them fair Jerusalem,
The holy City lifted high her Towers,   545
And higher yet the glorious Temple rear'd
Her pile, far off appearing like a Mount
Of Alabaster, topp't with Golden Spires:
There on the highest Pinnacle he set
The Son of God; and added thus in scorn: 550
          "There stand, if thou wilt stand; to stand up-
              right
Will ask thee skill; I to thy Father's house
Have brought thee, and highest plac't, highest is best,
Now show thy Progeny;° if not to stand,
Cast thyself down; safely if Son of God: 555
For it is written, 'He will give command
Concerning thee to his Angels, in their hands
They shall uplift thee, lest at any time
Thou chance to dash thy foot against a stone.' "
          To whom thus Jesus: "Also it is written,   560
'Tempt not the Lord thy God,' " he said and stood.
But Satan smitten with amazement fell
As when Earth's Son Antæus (to compare
Small things with greatest) in Irassa strove
With Jove's Alcides,° and oft foil'd still rose,   565
Receiving from his mother Earth new strength,
Fresh from his fall, and fiercer grapple join'd,
Throttl'd at length in the Air, expir'd and fell;
So after many a foil the Tempter proud,
Renewing fresh assaults, amidst his pride   570
Fell whence he stood to see his Victor fall.
And as that Theban Monster° that propos'd

542 **Hippogrif** mythical beast. 554 **Progeny** parentage. 565 **Alcides**
Hercules. 572 **Monster** the Sphinx, her riddle solved by Oedipus.

Her riddle, and him, who solv'd it not, devour'd;
That once found out and solv'd, for grief and spite
575   Cast herself headlong from th'Ismenian steep,
So struck with dread and anguish fell the Fiend,
And to his crew, that sat consulting, brought
Joyless triumphals° of his hop't success,
Ruin, and desperation, and dismay,
580   Who durst so proudly tempt the Son of God.
So Satan fell and straight a fiery Globe°
Of Angels on full sail of wing flew nigh,
Who on their plumy Vans receiv'd him soft
From his uneasy station, and upbore
585   As on a floating couch through the blithe Air,
Then in a flowery valley set him down
On a green bank, and set before him spread
A table of Celestial Food, Divine,
Ambrosial, Fruits fetcht from the tree of life,
590   And from the fount of life Ambrosial drink,
That soon refresh'd him wearied, and repair'd
What hunger, if aught hunger had impair'd,
Or thirst, and as he fed, Angelic Choirs
Sung Heavenly Anthems of his victory
595   Over temptation, and the Tempter proud.
       "True Image of the Father whether thron'd
In the bosom of bliss, and light of light
Conceiving, or remote from Heaven, enshrin'd
In fleshly Tabernacle, and human form,
600   Wand'ring the Wilderness, whatever place,
Habit, or state, or motion, still expressing
The Son of God, with Godlike force endu'd
Against th'Attempter of thy Father's Throne,
And Thief of Paradise; him long of old
605   Thou didst debel,° and down from Heav'n cast
With all his Army, and now thou past aveng'd
Supplanted° Adam, and by vanquishing
Temptation, hast regain'd lost Paradise,
And frústrated the conquest fraudulent:
610   He never more henceforth will dare set foot
In Paradise to tempt; his snares are broke:

578 **triumphals** tokens of triumph.   581 **Globe** squadron.   605 **debel**
vanquish.   607 **Supplanted** overthrown.

For though that seat of earthly bliss be fail'd,
A fairer Paradise is founded now
For Adam and his chosen Sons, whom thou
A Saviour art come down to re-install,   615
Where they shall dwell secure, when time shall be
Of Tempter and Temptation without fear.
But thou, Infernal Serpent, shalt not long
Rule in the Clouds; like an Autumnal Star
Or Lightning thou shalt fall from Heav'n trod down   620
Under his feet: for proof, ere this thou feel'st
Thy wound, yet not thy last and deadliest wound
By this repulse receiv'd, and hold'st in Hell
No triumph; in all her gates Abaddon° rues
Thy bold attempt; hereafter learn with awe   625
To dread the Son of God: he all unarm'd
Shall chase thee with the terror of his voice
From thy Demoniac holds, possession foul,
Thee and thy Legions, yelling they shall fly,
And beg to hide them in a herd of Swine,   630
Lest he command them down into the deep
Bound, and to torment sent before their time.
Hail Son of the most High, heir of both worlds,
Queller of Satan, on thy glorious work
Now enter, and begin to save mankind."   635
        Thus they the Son of God our Saviour meek
Sung Victor, and from Heavenly Feast refresht
Brought on his way with joy; hee unobserv'd
Home to his Mother's house private return'd.

624 **Abbadon** Hell.

SELECTED BIBLIOGRAPHY

EDITIONS

Patterson, F. A. et al., eds. *The Complete Works of John Milton* (18 Vols.). New York: Columbia University Press, 1931–38.

Hughes, M. Y., ed. *John Milton: The Complete Poems and Major Prose.* New York: Odyssey Press, 1957.

Shawcross, John T., ed. *The Complete Poetry of John Milton.* New York: Doubleday, 1971.

BIOGRAPHY

Brown, Cedric C. *John Milton: A Literary Life.* London: Macmillan, 1995.

Bush, Douglas. *John Milton: A Sketch of His Life and Writings.* New York: Macmillan, 1964.

Darbishire, Helen, ed. *The Early Lives of Milton.* London: Constable and Co., 1932.

Hill, Christopher. *Milton and the English Revolution.* London: Faber and Faber, 1977.

Johnson, Samuel. "Milton." In his *Lives of the Poets.* Vol. 1 Ed. George Birkbeck Hill. Oxford: Clarendon, 1905.

Levi, Peter. *Eden Renewed: The Public and Private Life of John Milton.* London: Macmillan, 1996.

Lewalski, Barbara Kiefer. *The Life of John Milton: A Critical Biography.* Blackwell Critical Biographies. Oxford: Blackwell, 2000.

Parker, William Riley. *Milton: A Biography.* 2nd ed. Rev. Gordon Campbell. Oxford: Clarendon, 1996.

Shawcross, John T. *John Milton: The Self and the World.* Lexington: University of Kentucky Press, 1993.

Wilson, A. N. *The Life of John Milton.* New York: Oxford University Press, 1983.

CRITICISM

Barker, Arthur, ed. *Milton: Modern Essays in Criticism*. New York: Oxford University Press, 1965.

Bennett, Joan S. *Reviving Liberty: Radical Christian Humanism in Milton's Great Poems*. Cambridge, MA: Harvard University Press, 1989.

Blamires, Harry. *Milton's Creation: A Guide Through* Paradise Lost. London: Methuen, 1971.

Bloom, Harold, ed. *John Milton's* Paradise Lost. Modern Critical Interpretations. New York: Chelsea House, 1987.

——. *John Milton*. Modern Critical Views. New York: Chelsea House, 1986.

Burnett, Archie. *Milton's Style: The Shorter Poems*, Paradise Regained, *and* Samson Agonistes. London: Longman, 1981.

Danielson, Dennis, ed. *The Cambridge Companion to Milton*. 2nd ed. Cambridge: Cambridge University Press, 1999.

Eliot, T. S. "Milton I and II." In his *On Poets and Poetry*. New York: Farrar, Straus and Giroux, 1957.

Empson, William. *Milton's God*. 2nd ed. London: Chatto and Windus, 1965.

Fish, Stanley Eugene. *How Milton Works*. Cambridge MA: Harvard University Press, 2001.

——. *Surprised by Sin: The Reader in* Paradise Lost. 2nd ed. Cambridge, MA: Harvard University Press, 1998.

Frye, Northrop. *The Return of Eden: Five Essays on Milton's Epic*. Toronto: University of Toronto Press, 1965.

Gardner, Helen. *A Reading of* Paradise Lost. New York and London: Oxford University Press, 1965.

Grose, Christopher. *Milton and the Sense of Tradition*. New Haven, CT: Yale University Press, 1988.

Hanford, James Holly, and James G. Taaffe. *A Milton Handbook*. 5th ed. New York: Appleton-Century-Crofts, 1970.

Hunter, Jr., William B., gen. ed. *A Milton Encyclopedia*. 9 vols. Lewisburg, PA: Bucknell University Press, 1978–83.

Kendrick, Christopher, ed. *Critical Essays on John Milton*. New York: G. K. Hall, 1995.

Lewalski, Barbara Kiefer. *Milton's Brief Epic: The Genre, Meaning, and Art of* Paradise Regained. Providence, RI: Brown University Press, 1966.

——. *Paradise Lost and the Rhetoric of Literary Forms*. Princeton, NJ: Princeton University Press, 1985.

Lewis, C. S. *A Preface to* Paradise Lost. Rev. enl. ed. New York and London: Oxford University Press, 1960.

Martz, Louis L. *Milton: Poet of Exile*. 2nd ed. New Haven, CT: Yale University Press, 1986.

——, ed. *Milton*, Paradise Lost: *A Collection of Critical Essays*. Englewood Cliffs, NJ: Prentice-Hall, 1966.

Pruitt, Kristin A., and Charles W. Durham, eds. *Living Texts: Interpreting Milton*. Selinsgrove, PA: Susquehanna University Press, 2000.

Ricks, Christopher. *Milton's Grand Style*. Oxford: Clarendon, 1963.

Shawcross, John T. Paradise Regain'd: *Worthy T'Have Not Remain'd So Long Unsung*. Pittsburgh, PA: Duquesne University Press, 1988.

——. *With Mortal Voice: The Creation of* Paradise Lost. Lexington: University of Kentucky Press, 1982.

Stocker, Margarita. *An Introduction to the Variety of Criticism: Paradise Lost*. London: Macmillian, 1988.

Summers, Joseph H. *The Muse's Method: An Introduction to* Paradise Lost. London: Chatto and Windus, 1962.

Turner, James Grantham. *One Flesh: Paradisal Marriage and Sexual Relations in the Age of Milton*. Oxford: Clarendon, 1987.

Walker, Julia M. *Milton and the Idea of Woman*. Urbana: University of Illinois Press, 1988.

Weston, Peter. *John Milton*, Paradise Lost. Penguin Critical Studies. London: Penguin, 1990.

Wittreich, Jr., Joseph A. *Feminist Milton*. Ithaca, NY: Cornell University Press, 1987.

——, ed. *Calm of Mind: Tercentenary Essays on* Paradise Regained *and* Samson Agonistes. Cleveland: Case Western Reserve University Press, 1971.